THE

CUBA

READER

History, Culture, Politics

Edited by Aviva Chomsky, Barry Carr, and Pamela Maria Smorkaloff

DUKE UNIVERSITY PRESS   DURHAM AND LONDON 2003

3rd printing, 2006

© 2003 Duke University Press · All rights reserved

Printed in the United States of America on acid-free paper ∞

Designed by Rebecca M. Giménez · Typeset in Monotype Dante

by Tseng Information System · Library of Congress Cataloging-

in-Publication Data appear on the last printed page of the book.

Contents

III   *The Struggle for Independence*

IV   *Neocolonialism*

V   Building a New Society

VI   *Culture and Revolution*

VII   *The Cuban Revolution and the World*

VIII   *The "Período Especial" and the Future of the Revolution*

Acknowledgments

If we really tried to thank everyone whose help and support contributed to the compiling of this book, the acknowledgments would probably be as long as the book itself. Most of all, we are grateful to the authors whose work appears here. Many of them were extraordinarily generous with their time and their work, and we are happy if we can contribute to bringing it to a wider public. We are especially grateful to the wonderfully talented Melbourne-based Tania Jovanovic, whose photographs grace the second half of this volume.

The Salem State College Library (especially the underappreciated Interlibrary Loan Department), the Graduate School, the Bureau of Faculty Research, the Vice President's Faculty/Librarian Research Support Fund, and the Instructional Media Center provided financial and logistical support for this project. We would like to thank Carlos Ortiz, especially, and everyone in the College of Humanities and Social Sciences at Montclair State University for their kindness, and support for this project, over the last three years. We are also grateful to Gene Bell-Villada, Joan Casanovas, Denise Condon, Lance Eaton, Ana Echevarría-Morales, Alfredo Prieto, Yanilsa Núñez, Joel Suárez, and Amanda Warnock for their help with technical, logistical, and translation issues.

Valerie Millholland of Duke University Press has been a true pleasure to work with over the years. Her enthusiasm for this project kept us on track through many difficult times. Miriam Angress, Katie Courtland, Rebecca Giménez, Natalie Hanemann, and Kate Lothman at Duke, and copyeditor Sonya Manes, helped bring the book smoothly to publication. We also thank Juan Antonio Blanco and the anonymous readers from Duke University Press for their very useful comments at different stages of the manuscript.

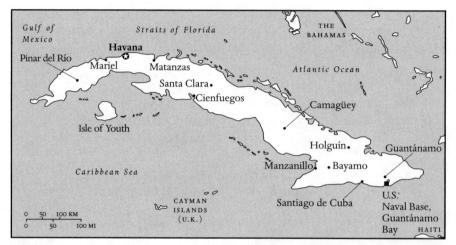

Map of Cuba

Introduction

The following joke, circulating in Cuba at the end of the 1990s, pokes fun at the ways that ideology colors interpretation of events on the island:

> When Pope John Paul visited Havana in 1998, he was personally welcomed by Fidel Castro, who invited him to tour the city. They rode in the Popemobile, and since it was a warm day, they opened the roof. Everything was fine until they reached the Malecón, when suddenly a gust of wind blew up and swept the Pope's *zuchetto* off his head and out into the sea. There it floated, bobbing on the waves.
>
> "Don't worry, Your Holiness," exclaimed Fidel, "I'll get it for you!" He jumped over the side of the Popemobile, leaped over the seawall, and sped out over the water. Yes, he actually walked on top of the water, all the way out to where the zuchetto lay floating on the waves. Then he turned and dashed back, still skimming over the surface, leaped over the seawall, and jumped back into the Popemobile, without getting a drop of water on his clothes. "Here, Your Holiness," he panted.
>
> The next day, newspapers all over the world reported this amazing incident.
>
> In *Granma*, the Cuban Communist Party newspaper, the headline read "Fidel Is God; He Walks on Water."
>
> In *L'Osservatore Romano*, the Vatican newspaper, the headline read "Pope Performs a Miracle: Makes Fidel Castro Walk on Water."
>
> And in the *Miami Herald*, read by the Cuban exile community in Miami, the headline read "Castro Doesn't Know How to Swim."

When someone picks up a book on Cuba, inevitably the first and decisive question is "which side is it on?" A reviewer who praises a book on Cuba as "balanced" probably acknowledges certain successes of the Cuban Revolution (especially in areas such as education, health, sports, and international relations), and critiques U.S. policy toward Cuba as counterproductive, while at the same time criticizing the Cuban government's top-down and repressive policies. Books that support the revolution tend to concentrate on the areas of success; those that oppose it tend to focus on the latter issues.

Is there, then, anything new to say about Cuba and its revolution?

The editors of this reader came together in part because of our shared perspective on a range of social, intellectual, and political issues, which this reader necessarily reflects. All of us share a commitment to social justice, which has shaped our study of the peoples of Latin America and the Caribbean and which gives us considerable sympathy for the social, cultural, and economic goals pursued by successive generations of Cubans who have fought for a fairer, more egalitarian Cuba. We see Cuba as a Latin American and a Caribbean country, structured by a common history of colonialism and resistance, neocolonialism, and poverty.

We also came together as a group of scholars who share a long-term commitment to the study of Cuba. Barry Carr is an Australian historian who has worked on Mexican and Cuban history since the late 1960s. He has authored numerous articles and book chapters dealing with the history of work and workers in the Cuban sugar industry in the twentieth century, as well as several books on Mexican labor history and the history of the Left—including *El movimiento obrero y la política en México*, and *Marxism and Communism in Twentieth-Century Mexico*. Aviva Chomsky is a U.S.-based historian who has studied Central America and the Caribbean for twenty years. Author of *West Indian Workers and the United Fruit Company in Costa Rica* and the editor, with Aldo Lauria-Santiago, of *Identity and Struggle at the Margins of the Nation-State: The Laboring Peoples of Central America and the Hispanic Caribbean*, she has taught Latin American history since 1990. Pamela Maria Smorkaloff is a Cuban American scholar who has been researching Cuban literary history since the 1980s. She has published *Cuban Writers on and off the Island: Contemporary Narrative Fiction* and *Readers and Writers in Cuba: A Social History of Print Culture, 1830s–1990s*, among others.

Do our scholarly credentials mean that we have produced a reader that is "balanced"? We sought to give the book a chronological and thematic balance, rather than a schematic political balance. Thus, our goal was to offer a comprehensive, multifaceted vision of Cuban society, politics, and culture throughout the last five centuries. This is not a reader whose main focus is the Cuban Revolution, though inevitably the revolution occupies an important space. The first four parts, which comprise approximately half the book, focus on topics prior to the 1959 revolution; and the revolution per se is one of several topics we focus on in the post-1959 parts.

Another goal was to interweave scholarly analyses with the voices of Cubans and other actors in, participants in, and firsthand commentators on the events and times. The latter, called primary source documents by historians, make up the bulk of this reader's selections. Outside observers, however, also contribute an important perspective. Many of them are Cubans themselves—historians, anthropologists, sociologists who have devoted their lives to the study of different threads of the Cuban tapestry. Some are scholars from other countries who have done the same.

We have granted equal importance to the three themes of the reader: history, culture, and politics. A chronological narrative structures the first four parts. But history is more than a series of dates and events. Although the part titles reflect a generally agreed-on chronological periodization—the pre-Columbian period, the colonial period, the independence period, and the neo-colonial period—the creative work lies in whose voices, whose interpretations, and whose analyses we choose to reflect these periods. We have been guided by the belief that there is no history without culture and politics. Slave testimonies and excerpts from novels that grapple with the question of race and slavery are interwoven with discussion by intellectuals of the time, poetry, and recent scholarly and historical analyses of Cuba's colonial period. All these documents make up history.

Thus the reader includes many different kinds of voices. Well-known political documents included in the book's first half are José Martí's 1891 "Our America," which became a rallying cry for generations of Latin Americans attempting to define their national and cultural identities; the Platt Amendment, which structured the U.S. relationship with Cuba between 1902 and 1934; Julio Antonio Mella's "Where Is Cuba Headed?" a foundational document for the Revolution of 1933; and Fidel Castro's celebrated "History Will Absolve Me," which played a similar role in the 1959 Revolution. Among the political documents included in the second half of the book is John F. Kennedy's 1962 speech announcing the presence of Soviet missiles in Cuba.

Many of the selections, however, are relatively unknown; some appear here for the first time in English. Included in earlier parts of the book, Renée Méndez Capote's *Memories of a Cuban Girl Who Was Born with the Century* gives a vivid account, from a female perspective, of everyday life during the period of Martí and the Platt Amendment; a waiter (Cipriano Chinea Palero) and a prostitute ("Pilar") describe their lives in the context of the corruption and inequality decried by Mella; in the latter parts of the book author Humberto Arenal evokes the crumbling of the lifestyle of the bourgeoisie after 1959; and Cuban American fiction writers Roberto Fernández and Achy Obejas comment wryly on the humor and the tragedy of the experience of emigration. We have sought to create an ongoing counterpoint between history "from above" —through the voices of the powerful—and history "from below"—through the sometimes harder to uncover voices of the poor, the marginalized, and the excluded.

For the 1959–89 period, we have organized the parts by theme. Part V, "Building a New Society," looks at how the Cuban Revolution tried to break with Cuba's past and construct something fundamentally new. Animated by nationalism, utopianism, and a belief that human nature was fundamentally malleable, revolutionary leaders and tens of thousands of followers set about abolishing the corruption, inequalities, and economic dependence of the past. The documents in part V explore aspects of the social and economic reforms that contributed to the ongoing process of the Cuban Revolution. A broad understanding of Cuban culture during the revolutionary period is the focus of part VI, "Culture and Revolution." Revolutionizing culture itself—both creating a radically original culture, and democratizing access to what had previously resided in the realm of high or elite culture—was another political goal of the revolutionary leadership. This movement created innumerable opportunities for cultural production and participation, an effervescence of cultural experimentation. It also, however, imposed restrictions on what kinds of cultural production were considered appropriately revolutionary, restrictions that frustrated and even destroyed some Cuban artists. Popular religion and culture evolved according to their own rhythm and manner, sometimes in conjunction with official policy, sometimes with stubborn independence.

A key theme throughout this volume is the global nature of Cuban history and society. But globalization goes beyond politics and economics: it involves every aspect of life and culture. In part VII we explore Cuba's global connections and significance in the revolutionary period with this broader view in mind. Literature, religion, music, and art, and Cuban ideas about race, gender, and national identity—as well as more explicitly political ideologies—formed over the centuries in the context of international links and relationships. Cuban internationalism is clearly not limited to the revolutionary period, but it is true that the revolution inspired and worked with social movements around the world. Cuban internationalism also became a foreign policy obsession in the United States for more than forty years. Hundreds of thousands of Cubans came to the United States during that time, transforming Miami and creating their own complex culture while also becoming important players in U.S. politics. Cuba also became a player in the international sphere, as its involvement in Africa and Latin America gave it a significance far outweighing its size.

Because the collapse of the Soviet bloc in 1989 was a watershed in the history of Cuba's revolution, we have included a separate section, part VIII, that focuses on the post-1989 period. The history of this period is still being written, but we try to impart the flavor of the existing contradictions through songs and fiction, as well as through personal accounts and scholarly analyses. Like most of the authors of the selections we include in this part, we reserve final judgment on the direction of events. Instead, we feel ourselves humbled by the dizzying pace of change and by the intensity with which Cubans continue to debate and hope to mold their future.

I

Indigenous Society and Conquest

There are no written accounts of pre-1492 Cuba and no indigenous accounts of the European conquest. Cuba's indigenous population was not organized into the elaborate hierarchies that existed in Mexico and Peru, and the population was virtually wiped out within fifty years of the conquest. Only in the past fifty years have Cuban archeologists excavated the pre-Columbian artifacts that have allowed them to begin to piece together a picture of the original Ciboney inhabitants of the island and of their replacement by the Taíno prior to 1492.

Nevertheless, indigenous peoples and the experience of conquest remain important in today's Cuba for several different reasons. The conquest itself led to a set of institutions, relationships, and ideologies that had a long-lasting effect on Cuba's development. It was also the conquest that set the stage for Cuba's incorporation into the growing Atlantic economy, later characterized by the importation of slaves and the production of sugar. In addition, although the depopulation of indigenous peoples was severe, they nevertheless left important cultural legacies. In some areas of Cuba, as José Barreiro describes, there are communities that still identify ethnically with their indigenous past. And everywhere in Cuba, stories of indigenous resistance to Spanish rule are much a part of commonsense knowledge of their country's history.

Except for Barreiro's contemporary oral histories, we have no written accounts by indigenous sources that describe their own lives and society. The Spanish priest Bartolomé de Las Casas, however, recorded countless indigenous testimonies as part of his crusade to stop the cruelties of the conquest. Although mediated by Las Casas's own agenda, these testimonies still stand as unique historical documents that capture the voices of those who had no other means of entering the historical record.

Christopher Columbus "Discovers" Cuba

Christopher Columbus

When Christopher Columbus arrived in the Caribbean in 1492, he was convinced that he was near the coast of Japan and China. Europeans termed his landfall a "discovery," though in recent years those more critical of Europe's endeavor have pointed out that while it was a discovery for Europe, the terms encounter or even invasion more accurately capture the nature of the event for the inhabitants of the Americas.

The natives Columbus encountered in the Bahamas indicated that a large island lay to the south, and he concluded that it must be Japan (which he called Chipangu) they were talking about. Although there may be some wishful thinking in his comment about Cuba's trade and wealth, it does indicate that the Caribbean natives had a good knowledge of the region's geography and were less isolated than some accounts have suggested. The following excerpts from Columbus's logbook constitute the first written accounts of Cuba and give the first European impressions of the island.

Wednesday, 24 October

Last night at midnight I raised anchor from Cabo del Isleo on the north side of the island of Isabela, where I had lain, and set sail for the island of Colba, which these people tell me is very large and has much trade. They say that it contains gold and spices and large ships and merchandize and have told me by signs that I should steer west-southwest to find it, and I think this is right, for if I am to believe the indications of all these Indians and those I have on board — I do not know their language — this is the island of Chipangu of which such marvelous tales are told, and which in the globes that I have seen and on the painted map of the world appears to lie in this region.

So I steered west-southwest till day, and at dawn the wind dropped and it rained, as it had done almost all night, and I lay there with very little wind until after midday and then it began to blow very gently. I then raised all sail, the mainsail and two bonnets, and the foresail and spritsail, the mizzen, main topsail, and the boat's sail on the poop. I continued on my course till nightfall and then Cabo Verde at the western end of the south coast of Fernandina lay

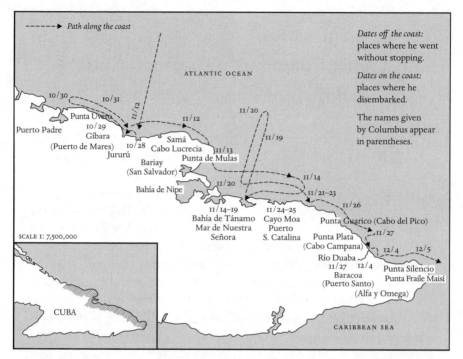

Columbus's exploration of Cuba in 1492. Instituto de Historia, *La colonia: Evolución socioeconómica y formación nacional hasta 1867* (Havana: Editora Política, 1994), 69.

to the northwest seven leagues away. It was now blowing hard and I did not know what course to follow for the island of Colba.

I did not want to go looking for it at night, for these islands lie in very deep water and no soundings can be taken at more than two lombard [an early high-powered cannon] shots from the shore. The bottom is patchy, with rocks in some parts and sand in others, and so it is not possible to anchor safely except where you can see. I therefore decided to lower all sails, except the foresail, and to proceed under it. After a while the wind became much stronger and I made a considerable distance, which disturbed me as the clouds were thick and it was raining. I ordered the foresail to be furled and that night we went less than two leagues. . . .

Sunday, 28 October

They sailed on south-southwest in search of the nearest point in Colba and he entered a very beautiful river, very free from shoals and other dangers. And all along the coast the water was very deep up to the shore. The mouth of the river was twelve fathoms and wide enough for ships to beat about. He anchored as he says a lombard shot upstream. The Admiral says he had never seen a more beautiful country. It was covered with trees right down to the river and these were lovely and green and different from ours, and each bore its own fruit or flowers. There were many birds, large and small, which sung sweetly, and there were a great number of palms of a different kind from those of Guinea and from ours. They were of moderate height with no bark at the foot, and the Indians cover their houses with them. The land is very flat.

The Admiral got into the boat and went ashore, where he found two houses which he believed to belong to fishermen who had fled in terror. In one of these he found a dog that did not bark, and in both houses there were nets of palm fiber and lines and horn fishhooks and bone harpoons and other fishing tackle, and there were many hearths. He believed that many people lived in each house. He gave orders that nothing should be touched in either, and his order was obeyed. The vegetation was as abundant as in April and May in Andalusia. He found much purslane and wild amaranth. He returned to the boat and went some distance up the river. He said that it was such a great joy to see the plants and trees and to hear the birds singing that he could not leave them and return. He says that this island is the most beautiful that eyes have ever seen. It has many good harbors and deep rivers, and it seems that the seas are never rough because the vegetation on the shore grows almost to the sea's edge, which is unusual where the seas are rough. So far, he had not encountered rough seas anywhere in these islands. He says that the island contains very lovely mountains, which do not form long chains but are very high. All the rest of the land is high also, like Sicily. It has plenty of water, as he gathered from the Indians from Guanahani whom he had with him, who told him by signs that it was ten large rivers and that they cannot go round it in their canoes in twenty days.

When he brought the ships close to shores two boats or canoes came out, but on seeing the sailors entering the boat and rowing about to take soundings for an anchorage, they fled. The Indians said that there are gold fields and pearls in the island and the Admiral saw that this was a likely place for pearls, since there were mussels, which are a sign of them. The Admiral understood that the Grand Khan's ships come there and that they are large and that the mainland is a ten days' journey away. The Admiral called this river and harbor San Salvador.[1]

TRANSLATED BY J. M. COHEN

Note

1. This is Bariay Bay in the island of Cuba.

The Devastation of the Indies

Bartolomé de Las Casas

Bartolomé de Las Casas was a Dominican friar who became famous — or notorious — in the 1500s for his denunciations of Spanish atrocities against the indigenous populations of the Americas. In the Spanish court, Las Casas found an audience among those who wished to curb the growing power of local Spanish officials in the colonies and to reassert greater centralized authority. His works were seized upon a century later by northern European colonizers who used them to defend their own, supposedly kinder and gentler, conquests in the Americas, giving rise to the so-called Black Legend of the cruelties of Spanish conquest.

Las Casas (1484–1556) came to America in 1502, and after living in Hispaniola for several years he traveled to Cuba, where he was granted an encomienda, or entrustment, of the indigenous village of Canarreo (near Trinidad). The encomienda was essentially a grant of Indian labor, enforced by the Crown and the new colonial authorities. After several years, Las Casas renounced his encomienda and dedicated the rest of his life to trying to convince the Spanish public and the Spanish Crown to abolish the institution.

The story of Hatuey recounted here remains an important historical myth in Cuba today. It is interesting to note the contrast between this story and the story of Pocahontas, perhaps the best-known mythical Indian in U.S. popular culture. Unlike Pocahontas, who is revered for her collaboration with the Europeans, Hatuey is celebrated for his resistance and martyrdom at the hands of the Spanish.

The Island of Cuba

In the year 1511, the Spaniards passed over to the island of Cuba, which as I have said is at the same distance from Hispaniola as the distance between Valladolid and Rome, and which was a well-populated province. They began and ended in Cuba as they had done elsewhere, but with much greater acts of cruelty.

Among the noteworthy outrages they committed was the one they perpetrated against a cacique, a very important noble, by name Hatuey, who had come to Cuba from Hispaniola with many of his people, to flee the calamities and inhuman acts of the Christians. When he was told by certain Indians that the Christians were now coming to Cuba, he assembled as many of his followers as he could and said this to them: "Now you must know that they are saying the Christians are coming here, and you know by experience how they have put So and So and So and So, and other nobles to an end. And now they are coming from Haiti (which is Hispaniola) to do the same here. Do you know why they do this?" The Indians replied: "We do not know. But it may be that they are by nature wicked and cruel." And he told them: "No, they do not act only because of that, but because they have a God they greatly worship and they want us to worship that God, and that is why they struggle with us and subject us and kill us."

He had a basket full of gold and jewels and he said: "You see their God here, the God of the Christians. If you agree to it, let us dance for this God, who knows, it may please the God of the Christians and then they will do us no harm." And his followers said, all together, "Yes, that is good, that is good!" And they danced round the basket of gold until they fell down exhausted. Then their chief, the cacique Hatuey, said to them: "See here, if we keep this basket of gold they will take it from us and will end up by killing us. So let us cast away the basket into the river." They all agreed to do this, and they flung the basket of gold into the river that was nearby.

This cacique, Hatuey, was constantly fleeing before the Christians from the time they arrived on the island of Cuba, since he knew them and of what they were capable. Now and then they encountered him and he defended himself, but they finally killed him. And they did this for the sole reason that he had fled from those cruel and wicked Christians and had defended himself against them. And when they had captured him and as many of his followers as they could, they burned them all at the stake.

When tied to the stake, the cacique Hatuey was told by a Franciscan friar who was present, an artless rascal, something about the God of the Christians and of the articles of the Faith. And he was told what he could do in the brief time that remained to him, in order to be saved and go to Heaven. The cacique, who had never heard any of this before, and was told he would go to Inferno, where, if he did not adopt the Christian Faith, he would suffer eternal torment, asked the Franciscan friar if Christians all went to Heaven. When told that they did he said he would prefer to go to Hell. Such is the fame and honor that God and our Faith have earned through the Christians who have gone out to the Indies.

On one occasion when we went to claim ten leagues of a big settlement, along with food and maintenance, we were welcomed with a bounteous quantity of fish and bread and cooked victuals. The Indians generously gave us all they could. Then suddenly, without cause and without warning, and in my presence, the Devil inhabited the Christians and spurred them to attack the Indians, men, women, and children, who were sitting there before us. In the massacre that followed, the Spaniards put to the sword more than three thousand souls. I saw such terrible cruelties done there as I had never seen before nor thought to see.

A few days later, knowing that news of this massacre had spread through the land, I sent messengers ahead to the chiefs of the Province of Havana, knowing they had heard good things about me, telling them we were about to visit the town and telling them they should not hide but should come out to meet us, assuring them that no harm would be done to them. I did this with the full knowledge of the captain. And when we arrived in the province, there came out to welcome us twenty-one chiefs and caciques, and our captain, breaking his pledge to me and the pledge I had made to them, took all these chieftains captive, intending to burn them at the stake, telling me this would be a good thing because those chiefs had in the past done him some harm. I had great difficulty in saving those Indians from the fire, but finally succeeded.

Afterward, when all the Indians of this island were subjected to servitude and the same ruin had befallen there as on the island Hispaniola, the survivors began to flee to the mountains or in despair to hang themselves, and there were husbands and wives who hanged themselves together with their children, because the cruelties perpetrated by one very great Spaniard (whom I knew) were so horrifying. More than two hundred Indians hanged themselves. And thus perished a countless number of people on the island of Cuba.

That tyrant Spaniard, representative of the king of Spain, demanded, in the *repartimiento* [a system of draft labor], that he be given three hundred Indians. At the end of three months all but thirty of them had died of the hard labor in the mines, which is to say only a tenth of them had survived. He demanded another allocation of Indians, and they also perished in the same way. He demanded still another large allocation, and those Indians also perished. Then he died, and the devil bore him away.

In three or four months, when I was there, more than seventy thousand children, whose fathers and mothers had been sent to the mines, died of hunger.

And I saw other frightful things. The Spaniards finally decided to track down the Indians who had taken refuge in the mountains. There they created amazing havoc and thus finished ravaging the island. Where had been a flourishing population, it is now a shame and pity to see the island laid waste and turned into a desert.

TRANSLATED BY HERMA BRIFFAULT

Spanish Officials and Indigenous Resistance

Various Spanish Officials

Although Hatuey is the best-known indigenous rebel-hero, indigenous resistance to the Spanish continued after his death, belying the myth that the indigenous population simply disappeared without a fight. The following brief documents were collected from the Cuban archives by Cuban historian Hortensia Pichardo.

[In 1530 the *cabildo* (town council) of Santiago, in eastern Cuba, wrote to the Crown:]

Over the past four years we have continually informed Your Majesty how in this island there are always rebel Indians who have greatly harmed the Christians and the tame Indians. . . . Your Majesty should know that in addition to other Indians that have rebelled in other provinces, in the Province of Baracoa there is one who is called Guamá, who has a following of over fifty Indians and has been in rebellion for a long time, and he has cultivated a good deal of land in the backlands, and even though up till now he has not done us any harm besides the fact that every day he takes in more tame Indians, we believe that much harm might come to the island in the future as more and more join him: we humbly beg Your Majesty to take care of this because it could be that this problem leads to an explosion in the land that would be difficult to calm. We have spoken to [Governor] Gonzalo de Guzmán about this, but it seems to us that he is not giving the problem the serious attention it deserves.

[A report three years later described the ongoing struggle between the town and the unsubdued followers of Guamá.]

There have been many rebel Indians who have carried out many killings and robberies. Five years ago, then-governor Gonzalo de Guzmán raised two squadrons against them, one paid for by [Governor] Rojas, and they were subdued. But one year later other groups of maroons [escaped slaves or Indians living in areas outside of Spanish control] rebelled, and Rojas mobilized three companies of Spaniards, blacks, and Indians, and was thus able to avoid a great deal of damage. For over ten years the Indian chief Guamá has been in rebellion in the province of Cagua, and Governor Gonzalo de Guzmán did not dare raise troops against him, nor did the Visiting Judge Vadillo, and after Rojas became governor, he organized a detachment of Spaniards and Indians and calmed things down; after some time passed, and Guamá's settlement had grown, a company of Spaniards, Indians, and blacks killed him and destroyed most of his people. Based on testimony of those who captured Guamá, Rojas feared that [Indian rebel] Enriquillo, from Hispaniola, had come here, and two months ago he went to Baracoa with a military force that he himself paid for, and now he has just sent another, to find out whether the rumor is true.

[After the defeat, a dispute arose between the soldiers and the former *encomenderos* of the runaways over who had the right to control the labor of —basically, enslave—those captured. Seven Indian prisoners were brought before the judge in chains and questioned. The court scribe recorded their testimonies.]

The aforementioned captain and his comrades testified that they had captured these Indians in the backlands where they were runaways and that they had been in Guamá's settlement for a long time, and so, because they had been runaways for a long time, they ask Your Honor to, using their testimony and their confessions, or any other criteria you deem appropriate, declare those who so deserve to be slaves, and the others, who are less guilty, to be servants [*naborías*].

[The Indians were then questioned. Pichardo points out that the runaway Indian testimonies accusing Guamá and his followers of crimes and atrocities must be read with a certain skepticism, since we are reading a Spanish transcription of testimony taken through a Spanish interpreter, and that there was ample room for the Spaniards to shape the testimony into the form most convenient to their purposes. The captured Indians might also have geared their testimonies to their audience.]

Señor Manuel de Rojas separately called the Indian Perico and an interpreter, and asked him the following.

He asked the interpreter to ask the aforementioned Indian his name; he said Perico and that he is the servant of García de Barreda.

Another was called for by Manuel de Rojas and asked how many years he had been a runaway; he responded through the interpreter that he has been a runaway in the settlement of the aforementioned Guamá for six years.

The interpreter was told to ask this Indian whether he had been a runaway and rebel from the Spanish [*xpianos*] in the mountains and the backlands for the entire six years until now when he and the other runaways were captured by Captain Obregón and his comrades; he responded through the interpreter that for those entire six years until today he had been a runaway in the settlement and in company of said Guamá and in the backlands until now when the Spanish [xpianos] captured him.

The interpreter was told to ask the Indian whether he had seen that Guamá and other Indian runaways from his settlement had killed any Spaniards or peaceful Indians or robbed or done any harm to the Spanish [xpianos] and peaceful Indians or whether he had done so or helped anybody to do so; he responded through the interpreter that he had not killed nor robbed anybody but that he had seen that many Indians were missing from Guamá's settlement and that it was commonly known among the Indians of the settlement that Guamá killed them, taking them secretly away from the settlement and there killing them one by one.

The interpreter was instructed to ask the Indian how many people remained in the backlands from those who were part of Guamá's settlement; he responded through the interpreter that there were ten men with one boy and five women and five young children.

The interpreter was told to ask the Indian where they had planned to go if the Spanish went to hunt them down and where they went after Captain Diego Barva destroyed Guamá's settlement; he responded through the interpreter that the other Indians withdrew some seven or eight leagues from the settlement and that after they came back to the settlement for food and they left the women and children hidden in the backlands and that the people who still remain at large will have to return there for food and do what they did before because of the food that they still have there.

The above is what the afore-mentioned Indian testified and declared to these questions, signed, Francisco Pozuelo. . . .

And then Señor Manuel de Rojas ordered the interpreter under sworn oath to ask another Indian from among those taken from the settlement to appear before him, and to ask him what his name was and whose servant he was and how long he had been a runaway; he responded through the interpreter that his name was Alexo and that he came from Ynagua, which is in the province of Guantanavó, and that he is the servant of the *fator* [commission merchant] Fernando de Castro and that he has been a runaway for five years and that he went with Captain Juan Pérez to Guamá's settlement and that since then he has remained a runaway until now that the Spanish [xpianos] captured him with the other runaways.

The interpreter was told to ask the Indian whether after he ran away any Spaniard or peaceful Indian had been killed, or any huts burned or robbed, or any other damage had been done; he responded "no" through the interpreter.

The interpreter was told to ask the Indian how many people from Guamá's group remained in the backlands; he said ten men with one boy and five women with five children, and that he believes they will return to the settlement for food because they do not have any anywhere else, because that is what they have been doing up until now since Captain Diego Barva destroyed the settlement and they were not planning to make a new settlement elsewhere. Rather they were staying close to the old settlement and they ate from there and he believes that the other Indians who remain runaways will continue doing so and they will not go anywhere else.

The interpreter was told to ask the Indian whether he had seen the aforementioned Juan Pérez or Guamá kill or rob any person; he responded through the interpreter that he had not seen it, but that it was well known in the settlement among the Indians that Guamá killed many of the Indians of the settlement, secretly taking them away from the settlement by tricking them and that said Guamá killed a brother of his, Olguamá, treacherously and with an ax while he was sleeping, and that this was public knowledge among the Indians of the settlement and that Alexo had been with Fernando de Guamá up until now and that he is named Guamayry [Guamayry is amended] who is now captain of the other *cimarrones* and that this is the truth of what the Indian has said, signed, Francisco Pozuelo. . . .

The interpreter was told to ask an Indian woman from among those who had been brought before the captain what her name was and from where and how long she had been a runaway; she responded through the interpreter that her name was Marica and that she was from the province of Guantanavó and servant [naboría] of Rodrigo de Baeza.

The interpreter was told to ask the Indian how long she had been a runaway with Guamá; she said that she had been a runaway with Guamá for seven years, according to what the interpreter reported that this Indian responded, and that she was taken by an Indian man named Alonsyco who was her husband and belonged to Juan de Madroña, and that this husband of hers was killed by Guamá because he loved her, in order to take her for himself, and that after Alonsyco was killed Guamá took her for his woman and had her in his power until he died and this is the truth of what this Indian has said, under oath, signed, Francisco Pozuelo.

And then he ordered the interpreter under oath to ask another Indian woman, who was brought before His Honor from among those whom Obregón brought, what her name was and whose servant [naboría] she was and where she was from and how long she had been a runaway; she responded through the interpreter that her name was Margarida and from Jamayca and she was servant [naboría] of Bartolomé Aserrador of this island and that she had been a runaway in the settlement of Guamá for five years and that she saw how Guamá killed the Indians, and that this is the truth of what this Indian said and declared, under oath, signed, Francisco Pozuelo.

TRANSLATED BY AVIVA CHOMSKY

A World Destroyed

Juan Pérez de la Riva

In Cuba, as in elsewhere in the Americas, indigenous populations declined by 90 to 100 percent in most of the areas where Europeans settled, although in comparison with the dense population of the neighboring island of Hispaniola, Cuba was a relatively underpeopled island. Unlike Las Casas, who blames indigenous deaths on Spanish cruelty, Cuban historian Juan Pérez de la Riva (1913–1976) sees disease and, even more so, cultural collapse and suicide, as the main culprits. He surveys the available archaeological and colonial sources and estimates the preconquest population of Cuba to be between one hundred and two hundred thousand, which was reduced to a mere four thousand just forty years after the first Spanish landing. Note that Pérez de la Riva emphasizes the drastic nature of the demographic collapse, rather than the elements of biological and cultural survival discussed by José Barreiro in a later selection.

Epidemics and other infectious diseases introduced by Europeans and Africans, which we will discuss below, along with the indiscriminate massacres carried out by the conquistadors in the early years, were not the only causes of the dramatic depopulation. Other causes, and perhaps the most important ones, have been left out of the historiography.

The Clash of Two Civilizations

The Spanish invasion induced a psychological trauma among the Taíno and the Ciboney of an intensity that is difficult to imagine. The three hundred expeditionaries who disembarked with Velázquez in the eastern region of Cuba at the beginning of 1511 were aware of the dangers they faced if they could not quickly establish themselves through terror. Gold, and only gold, was what they were looking for, and this was also King Ferdinand's interest, even though on the surface these greedy and predatory expeditions ostensibly aimed at "populating," and controlling, civilizing, and converting the indigenous populations to Catholicism.

In Cuba the gold was all alluvial, and the deposits were almost always a long way from the indigenous towns, for the Indians were not in the least interested in this yellow metal that so attracted the Spanish. Thus the Spaniards' first step was to remove large portions of the population to areas far away from their settlements, with tragic physical and moral consequences.

Fernando Ortiz noted correctly that "to be bound to the mines, to their monotonous, insane, and hard labor, without any tribal meaning, without religious rituals, involved destroying the roots which gave meaning to Indian culture." Their idols destroyed, their religion ridiculed by the fanatical friars who preached a rival system that was incomprehensible to them; their traditional leaders murdered or continually harassed and humiliated, their ancestral society, which had at least guaranteed a certain security in the form of a stable family community, shattered; their wives and daughters abducted by the Spanish; Indians alone and defenseless in the face of a powerful and cruel foreign group, lost all interest in a life that had become devoid of meaning.

While the conquistadors thought that the Indian population was dispersed evenly throughout the island, they killed indiscriminately, stabbing and gleefully using their hunting dogs to tear them apart. They scattered the population of towns that could have been used as centers of production. It did not take long for the results of this bloodbath and the dispersion of huge numbers of Taíno to be felt: the only really populated region of the island, the north and central/western part of Oriente, was rapidly depopulated. . . .

If it had not been for the fantastic multiplication of the pigs that Velázquez brought from Hispaniola, the conquistadors themselves, absolute masters of one hundred thousand kilometers of fertile lands covered with forest and savanna, would have had to abandon their conquest, which was as useless to them as the sands of a desert.

The Pig, Resource and Resistance

The European pig found a suitable environment in the tropical forest, and it multiplied with fantastic speed as long as it found sufficient food among the wild fruits, roots, and vines. In this way a natural resource, the forest, became valuable with very little investment in labor. The Spanish also introduced cattle and horses, but the latter's fertility rate is at least fifteen times less than that of the pig in similar ecological conditions.

But if the pig almost instantaneously resolved the needs of the European population for fats and meat, and after a few years those of the sedentary Indian population as well, after 1520 pigs became a serious problem for the fugitive Indians because they deprived them of the food resources traditionally provided by the forest, and they also disrupted, if not ruined, the food plots that they could carve out the small clearings deep in the most impenetrable parts of the forest.

Later the pig caused problems even for the Europeans, because it forced them to fence in their fields. Solid post fences made of wood or split cedar required huge sums of money. In no country was the old Castilian adage more apt: livestock kill plants. . . .

Main Causes of the Extinction of the Aboriginal Population

In the space of forty years a population of one hundred thousand was reduced to less than five thousand, thanks to Spanish colonization. Similar holocausts occurred in Mexico and Peru, but on the mainland millions rather than tens of thousands of people fell victim to Western "civilization" and the lust for gold and silver that characterized the sixteenth century.

What were the main causes of this disaster, and their relative importance, in Cuba?

The major and most frequently mentioned cause of the population collapse were the massacres and terror employed by the conquistadors to take over the island, and the murders, or assassinations, committed by the colonizers to subordinate, also through terror, the Indian population that had been "given in trust" to them according to the laws passed by the Castilian Crown.

But in spite of the horror that such savage and systematic cruelty evokes, it was only responsible for some 10 percent of the demographic loss suffered by the indigenes.

Part of the loss is attributable to the famine caused by the rapid displacement of the population to new workplaces with limited capacity to produce food. On the one hand, the invaders were in too much of a hurry to find gold, and believed that they would have access to an inexhaustible supply of people; on the other they had no experience with tropical agriculture, and had to depend on the Indo-cuban tradition with its low productivity.

Then came the new diseases brought from Europe and also from Africa: smallpox, measles, yaws, and above all, influenza and other bronchopulmonary diseases, all unknown in the Americas, and against which the Indian did not have the relative immunity of the European. These epidemics, according to contemporaries, produced huge mortality. In 1519, between one-third and one-half of the indigenous population of some districts of eastern Cuba died from epidemics that have not been well identified. . . . In 1528 another epidemic, apparently smallpox, is said to have decimated the already reduced population. Colds and influenza seem to have been even more devastating. They turned rapidly into bronchopneumonia, which was inevitably fatal. According to Herrera Fritot this was one of the most serious continuing causes of the annihilation of the indigenous population. But in any case the role disease played in the disappearance of the Indians seems to have been exaggerated and we do not believe that it can account for more than 20 percent of the deaths.

Without question a much more important factor was undoubtedly the rise in child mortality, due to malnutrition or lack of maternal care, when women were obliged to work in panning gold or in agriculture. The infant mortality rate may have possibly at least doubled in the first two decades. It has been said that for every mestizo, one fewer Indian was born: it's a felicitous phrase, but since the number of Spaniards was tiny, some two thousand in 1519, and then even fewer, it is impossible to assign much importance to this cause.

It is clear that the most important cause of the disappearance of the Indians was the brutal clash of two civilizations. . . . The Indians' mental responses were mortally wounded, and they deliberately sought death, absurdly, to free themselves from another absurdity, which was even worse. For the more self-confident Indians, rebellion was an option: an affirmation of their being; for the others, life lost its meaning, which led them to imagine the impossibility of existing, and death as the only escape route.

Suicide and the Indo-cubans

. . . In analyzing the causes of their disappearance we must give suicide the place it deserves and try to evaluate its social importance. We will never be able to establish the annual rate of suicide among the Indians, but it must have been enormous: several times greater than that of the Chinese coolies in Cuba, which reached five hundred per one hundred thousand inhabitants in the second half of the nineteenth century. . . .

To what extent was suicide responsible for the disappearance of the indigenous population? Perhaps some 30 percent, perhaps more. . . . The chronicles indignantly recount individual and collective suicides by the desperate Indians; strangling themselves, ingesting the poisonous juices of the bitter yucca, or also eating earth, a last remnant of their native religion. . . .

The archives contain innumerable tales of horrendous punishments committed by the *encomenderos* in their haste to contain through terror the uncontainable desire for self-destruction that took hold of the Indians. The judicial testimony of Vasco Parcallo de Figueroa in 1522 is irrefutable proof:

> He was asked if he had ordered the cutting off of testicles and members and other body parts of some Indians and ordered that others be burned, and whether thus cut off [the testicles], he had ordered the victim to eat them;

he said that he had done so. He was asked how many Indians he had inflicted this punishment on. . . . He said three, and a boy, and that the three Indians were already almost dead from eating dirt. . . . He had their penises and testicles cut off. . . . and he made them eat them soaked in dirt, and afterwards he had them burned, and he had others burned also, up to twelve, because they ate dirt. . . . He said that in the Provinces of Camagüey and Guamahaya over half or even three quarters had killed themselves, or had died just from eating dirt, and that to avoid this happening he carried out this punishment, and that first he had many masses said and made them participate in processions to urge them to reject this evil.

This dramatic document needs no comment, but we simply add that after having confessed to all of this and in addition to splashing boiling lard over other Indians who he suspected of eating earth, Vasco Parcallo was never bothered by Spanish justice, even though it is true, according to his deposition, he was always careful to order mass to be said before torturing the Indians.

Conclusion

Summarizing the external factors that contributed to the disappearance of the indigenous population and considering that it took some forty years for the population to be virtually extinguished, we would list, in order of importance: (1) suicide 35 percent; (2) epidemics 25 percent; (3) increases in infant mortality 20 percent; (4) massacres and homicides 12 percent; (5) famines 8 percent. This order of course changed over time. It is likely that between 1512 to 1517 the greatest cause of mortality was famine, followed by genocide, suicide, and child mortality. After this date, when the Indian population was reduced to one-fourth of its initial size, *mestizaje*, which we had so far not considered, came into play. Thus from 1526 to 1540 the order might be as follows: a rise in infant mortality, epidemics, suicides, mestizaje, famine, genocide. After 1550, when the indigenous population had been reduced to some five or six thousand, mestizaje surely became the main cause of the extinction of the indigenous race.

We could restate the above conclusions more simply and accurately by saying that the death rate tripled or quadrupled during the first fifteen years after the Spanish invasion, while the birthrate fell by one third. The period of most rapid population decline is from 1512 to 1524. After this, mortality rates declined progressively, but always maintaining a depopulation rate of over 5 percent a year until 1550. In characterizing the Indian demographic pattern this way in the period of the extinction of the race, we would be taking into account external as well as internal causes. Suicide was not the only way in which the Indians rejected western civilization. Voluntary reduction of the birthrate through deliberately induced abortion and coitus interruptus were also important factors in the rapid extinction of the race, which have not been discussed in our analysis.

Accepting the demographic premises presented above, we can concretize the extinction of the Indo-cuban population in the following figures: 1511, 100,000; 1515, 47,000; 1520, 18,700; 1525, 10,000; 1530, 7,600; 1535, 6,600; 1540, 5,450; 1545, 4,800; 1550, 4,300; 1555, 8,900. After that the pattern of mortality and birthrate must be similar for whites and Indians, but mestizaje rapidly absorbed the Indians into the white population. "The Indians are disappearing," said Bishop Sarmiento in 1556, "and they do not reproduce because the Spaniards and the mestizos marry Indians because of the lack of women, and the Indian [man] is lucky to find an eighty-year-old wife." The Indians who remained had by then lost almost all of their cultural characteristics, as would happen later, in the second generation, to the Africans.

Thus, inescapably, the race which had originally populated the Cuban archipelago was extinguished; the reign of terror that the Spanish practiced as their system of government was futile, as was the Christian resignation preached by the swarm of friars who came with them, promising eternal happiness in exchange for submission here on earth. Nothing could change the fate of the vanquished victor: misery and solitude in a landscape that was difficult to tame. Deprived of a labor force and lacking precious metals, Cuba in the fourth decade of the sixteenth century faced the sad prospect of becoming one of "the useless islands."

TRANSLATED BY AVIVA CHOMSKY

For complete references and notes, consult the work as cited in the acknowledgment of copyrights section.

ıration" and Cuba

ᴌᴇrnando Ortiz

Fernando Ortiz (1881–1969) is probably the best-known early-twentieth-century Cuban intellectual. He is known in particular for his anthropological studies of Afro-Cuban culture and for celebrating the hybrid nature of Cuban ethnicity. His masterpiece, Cuban Counterpoint: Tobacco and Sugar, *which is still in print in both Cuba and the United States, is a fundamental work in the understanding and construction of Cuban political economy and identity. In the selection included here, Ortiz introduces the word* transculturation *to describe the origins and nature of Cuba's population. He examines the characteristics and destruction of Cuba's indigenous populations, and he argues that since the conquest, European, African, and Asian peoples have migrated (under very different circumstances) to the island, leading to the creation of a radically new culture characterized by uprooting and mixing of all the different demographic elements.*

It is worth noting here too how different this interpretation of Cuban history is from traditional interpretations of U.S. history, which have tended to emphasize the essentially Anglo-Saxon origin of "mainstream" U.S. culture and institutions and which assume that "other" immigrants have either acculturated into this mainstream culture ("melting pot") or maintained alternative cultural and ethnic identities ("multiculturalism"). In the Cuban ajiaco—*a traditional Taíno stew of vegetables, roots, and meats, which Ortiz uses as a metaphor for Cuba's cultural and ethnic mixture—the ingredients do not "melt" but rather contribute individually with their distinctiveness.*

I have chosen the word *transculturation* to express the highly varied phenomena that have come about in Cuba as a result of the extremely complex transmutations of culture that have taken place here, and without a knowledge of which it is impossible to understand the evolution of the Cuban folk, either in the economic or in the institutional, legal, ethical, religious, artistic, linguistic, psychological, sexual, or other aspects of its life.

The real history of Cuba is the history of its intermeshed transculturations. First came the transculturation of the Paleolithic Indian to the Neolithic, and the disappearance of the latter because of his inability to adjust himself to the culture brought in by the Spaniards. Then the transculturation of an unbroken stream of white immigrants. They were Spaniards, but representatives of different cultures and themselves torn loose, to use the phrase of the time, from the Iberian Peninsula groups and transplanted to a New World, where everything was new to them, nature and people, and where they had to readjust themselves to a new syncretism of cultures. At the same time there was going on the transculturation of a steady human stream of African Negroes coming from all the coastal regions of Africa along the Atlantic, from Senegal, Guinea, the Congo, and Angola and as far away as Mozambique on the opposite shore of that continent. All of them snatched from their original social groups, their own cultures destroyed and crushed under the weight of the cultures in existence here, like sugarcane ground in the rollers of the mill. And still other immigrant cultures of the most varying origins arrived, either in sporadic waves or a continuous flow, always exerting an influence and being influenced in turn: Indians from the mainland, Jews, Portuguese, Anglo-Saxons, French, North Americans, even yellow Mongoloids from Macao, Canton, and other regions of the sometime Celestial Kingdom. And each of them torn from his native moorings, faced with the problem of disadjustment and readjustment, of deculturation and acculturation—in a word, of transculturation. . . .

These questions of sociological nomenclature are not to be disregarded in the interests of a better understanding of social phenomena, especially in Cuba, whose history, more than that of any other country of America, is an intense, complex, unbroken process of transculturation of human groups, all in a state of transition. The concept of transculturation is fundamental and indispensable for an understanding of the history of Cuba, and, for analogous reasons, of that of America in general.

TRANSLATED BY HARRIET DE ONIS

Survival Stories

José Barreiro

Finally, contemporary anthropologist and Associate Director of the American Indian Program at Cornell University José Barreiro, disputes the widely held notion—accepted by both Pérez de la Riva and Ortiz—that indigenous populations were totally destroyed in Cuba. He has studied isolated populations in eastern Cuba who still identified themselves as "indigenous" in the 1980s and 1990s, and he explores the different markers of indigenous identity in today's Cuba. It is clear from his interviews that the indigenous peoples of Cuba did not simply disappear in the 1500s. Barreiro places Ortiz's work in the political and academic context of his own time but insists that we broaden Ortiz's concept of transculturation to incorporate the indigenous as well as the European, African, and Asian elements in today's Cuba.

The old Indian woman, a descendant of Cuba's Taíno-Arawak people, bent over and touched the leaves of a small tree. Her open-palmed hand lifted the round, green leaves in a light handshake. "These are good for inflammations of the ovaries," she said. "I gave them to all my young women." "She knows a lot," her daughter, Marta, said. "She doesn't need a pharmacy. You have something wrong with your body, she can make you a tea—*un cocimiento*—and fix you up."

The mother and two sisters, part of a large extended family known in this town for its Indian ancestry, continued to show me their patio. Around an old well, where they wash their laundry, they pointed out more than a dozen herbs and other useful plants. The Cobas Hernández clan, from which María and her several daughters, her son Pedro and his brothers spring, counts several living generations of families from here to the town of Baracoa, about thirty km west from Los Arados on the eastern tip of Cuba's north coast. They are not the only such extended family, and they are not the only people of clear Indian ancestry in Cuba still living in their aboriginal areas.

It may surprise many social scientists that nestled in the mountains of the Oriente region (eastern Cuba), from Baracoa and Punta Maisí on the north coast all the way to the Pico Turquino, the highest mountain in Cuba, there are *caseríos* and barrios, within an extended population of at least one to three thousand people who are clearly of indigenous lineage. They were called *cubeños* by Father Bartolomé de Las Casas, who helped some of their communities to survive, and are descendants of the original Taínos who met Columbus.

In March and April 1989, I traveled to Santiago de Cuba to attend a conference, "Seeds of Commerce," mutually sponsored by the Smithsonian Institution and a Cuban research center, the Casa del Caribe. I took the opportunity to extend my visit for two weeks, first in the Baracoa–Punta Maisí region and then west to the savanna country of Camagüey. I wanted to ascertain the veracity of testimonies and stories that I had heard as a child and that have been increasingly confirmed in Cuban academic journals, to the effect that Taíno-Arawak descendants still inhabit the eastern region of Cuba. I wanted to reacquaint myself with the people of *guajiro* background still prevalent in the Camagüey countryside. During that trip and in several subsequent visits from 1995 to 1999, I have conducted interviews with numerous families, and very particularly with the elder and herbalist, don Panchito Ramírez Rojas, from the community of Caridad de los Indios. A growth of interest in Taíno culture and identity throughout the Caribbean, including Cuba, is generating more research and evidence in this context.

I heard about the Indian families of Baracoa while I was growing up in the Camagüey region, some two hundred kilometers west of Baracoa, during the 1950s, before I migrated to the United States at age twelve.

Among my closest elders, Don Joseíto Veloz (born 1891) migrated to Camagüey from the vicinity of the oriental mountain city of Bayamo, from a place called Jiguaní. Don Joseíto told stories about the old communities in and near Baracoa. He was himself what is called in Camagüey a "guajiro," and one who pointed out the Indian origins of many of his customs and lifeways: the thatch-roof *bohío* made out of the royal palm so abundant in Cuba; his yucca field or *conuco*, the use of the lunar phases to plant the Cuban root crops; and his custom of eating the yucca bread, *casabe* with the traditional Taíno soup, called the "*ajiaco*." My father as well, through his guajiro grandfather, don Joaquín Cabrera, had met and told me of the "Indians of Yateras." I heard many times during my childhood how guajiro ways of our *monte* had roots in the Taíno knowledge of the Cuban ancestors. Guajiro identity, customs, and lifestyle are still prevalent throughout the Camagüey and Oriente region.[1]

More recently, after writing for some years on diverse Indian cultures, indigenous development, agriculture, and human rights issues, I noticed several articles in the Cuban press detailing studies carried out among the Indian descendants in the Baracoa region. The studies were carried out by investigators from the University of Havana, in cooperation with scientists from Belgium, Czechoslovakia, and the then Soviet Union.

Rivero de la Calle Study

At the University of Havana, I met the chief investigator of those studies, Manuel Rivero de la Calle, a gentle, soft-spoken scholar who is dean of Cuban anthropology. He started work in the Oriente area in the mid-1960s, leading a team that for several years conducted studies in physical and biological anthropology with an extended "base" population in the Yateras municipality of the new province of Guantánamo, not far from Baracoa.

Rivero's biological study, conducted in two stages—1964 and 1972–1973—focused exclusively on certifying racial composition on a sample of three hundred people of Indian origin in the Yateras municipality. His methodology included anthropometric measurements and somatometric observations (body measurements; following the International Biologic Program), serologic characteristics, and family genealogies.

The methodology of "physical anthropology," which uses anthropometric measurements, is considered antiquated by North American scholars and insulting by many Indians. Nevertheless, it proves fruitful in initially identifying the effusive Cuban indigenous population, even though there was little or no ethnographic work with the local population—as Indians or even as mestizo mountain folk—which in earlier decades might have yielded more indigenous bases.

Nevertheless, Rivero's conclusions challenged official academic and sociological positions in Cuba—positions accepted by the international academy—that the Indian population of Cuba was totally extinguished by 1550. Indeed, the scientists in that particular study found that at least one thousand people conforming to physical characteristics associated with the Arawak branch of Amazonian Indian peoples live in Yateras alone. The studies assert what oral and written historical sources have also attested: the Yateras Indians are a core group in a larger pattern of extended families and communities of similar Indian origin, now increasingly intermarried with other Cubans of Iberian and African ancestry.

Historical References

The existence of an Indian population and identity in Cuba was vehemently denied for most of the twentieth century, primarily by the Cuban scholar Fernando Ortiz. A liberal professor of Hispanic ancestry, Ortiz saw, with considerable evidence, that the question of Indian identity could be used as a ploy by the right wing to obfuscate black issues. Deeply conversant in all the social sciences, Ortiz was limited by a Havana base and by a purist, "bell jar" anthropological perspective of Indianness. This perspective maintains that American Indians cease to be "real" Indians as they adapt Western tools and methods. Indian "cultures" are assumed frozen at the moment of contact with "the West." The continuity and reconstructions of identity we have come to understand were not so visible in Ortiz's time. Although he framed the primordial theme of "transculturation" in Cuban letters, and deeply studied the history and archaeology of the Indo-cuban cultures, Ortiz conceived the contemporary tree of Cuban multiethnicity with a strictly Ibero-African trunk. The assertion became that all Cuban Indians, purportedly a weak and timid people, were exterminated by 1550. It followed that all things Indian were lost from Cuban reality.

Nevertheless, the historic and ethnographic record supports the Indian presence in eastern Cuba—the existence of its actual population of descendants and its cultural extensions throughout a great deal of Cuban culture. Both Rivero and Antonio Núñez Jiménez, a prominent Cuban naturalist—and other historical references—confirm the existence of dozens of Indian family nuclei (caseríos) in the extended region of Oriente, from Baracoa to Punta Maisí, to the Sierra Maestra and the Pico Turquino. In the absence of a proper census, it is hard to hazard a guess as to the total population of Indian descendants in the general Oriente area, but it probably comes to several thousand people. . . .

Oral history of Yateras Indians corroborates court records indicating that the Indian caseríos at Tiguabos and Palenque and Indian settlements in the San Andrés valley were dispossessed, farm by farm, during the nineteenth century. Those Indian populations, many with the family names of Rojas and Ramírez, resettled in the more remote valley of Yateras and formed part of a community called Caridad de los Indios. All along that valley of the Río Toa and down to Baracoa and Yumurí, and along the coast to Los Arados, in Punta Maisí, the families of Rojas and Ramírez, as well as the Romeros, the Cobas, the Riveros, many of the Jiménez, Hernández, Veloz, and Cabrera, retain history, identity, and customs rooted in the Cuban Arawak traditions, the old Taíno homeland.[2]

Among the People

. . . In subsequent trips from 1995 to 1999, I visited Caridad de los Indios, in Yateras, near Guantánamo, where I met elder and cacique of the area, Don Panchito Ramírez Rojas, his wife, Reina, his elder uncle Opublio, and many others of the mountain community. I conducted extended interviews with these elders, which became the basis for the book *Panchito: Mountain Cacique* (Santiago de Cuba: Ediciones Catedral, 1999). These interviews with Panchito elicited many expressions in Panchito's vernacular, as well as cultural, agricultural, and spiritual practices relative to nature and to specific concepts and deities that are clearly Amerindian in origin.

Panchito, his family, and their continuing cultural expressions as Cuban Indian people are as indigenous as they are deeply Cuban in the extended sense. Panchito sometimes lectures on the use of herbal medicines in the "Indigenous Legacies of the Caribbean" conferences, held annually in Baracoa, Cuba. This is not surprising. Cuban planners know that during the special period, Cuban endemic knowledge of herbal and cropping systems provided a bottom-line, grassroots line of defense against the deprivations caused by the loss of Soviet oil.

Motoring and hiking can offer interesting surprises in this part of Cuba. On the way from Baracoa to Punta Maisí, we stopped at a guajiro cemetery near the coast. An indigenous touch: many of the simple graves were covered by small, thatch "houses" and surrounded by large seashells. The shells (*Strombus gigas Linneo*), known in the area by their Taíno name, *guamo*, are believed to protect the deceased from bothersome spirits; guajiro families still use them to call one another across remote valleys.

One evening in Baracoa, I witnessed a communal dance, kept alive by only one Indian caserío at Guirito. The dance, called *quiriba*, has been passed down the generations by several related families. The quiriba certainly has French elements to it (many French people settled in the general region of Oriente after the black revolution in Haiti in the mid-1800s), but is significantly unique in that it has survived within an Indian community.

All the agriculturists confirmed, with great certainty, the practice of planting root crops by the waning moon (*luna menquante*). The assertion is that both yucca and *boniato* (a native sweet potato) will "rot early" (*se pica temprano*) if not planted by the waning moon. In cutting wood, too, local guajiros argue that it will rot faster if cut in the full or ascending moons. One old man near the banks of the Río Toa spoke of fishing by the moon for a fish called the *teti*, which is scarce at other times.

At Los Arados, I also visited an elementary school; the principal asked the Indian children to gather, and about twenty-five students quickly surrounded us. Some were more reticent than others, but all affirmed their Indian background. Many of their names corresponded to the family names identified with Indianness.

Idalis Ramírez (left) and her great-uncle, Opublio Ramírez, Taíno descendants from the Rojas-Ramírez clan of Caridad de los Indios, Guantánamo, Cuba. Idalis is a "dream-healer." Photo by José Barreiro.

From left to right, Reina Ramírez, Reina Rojas, Panchito Ramírez (cacique), and great-uncle Opublio. All four are well-regarded herbalists and healers. Photo by José Barreiro.

My questions concentrated on a person's basis or rationale for claiming an Indian identity. All pointed to family history: "We are an Indian family. It has been always that way." "We do Indian things, like my mother, she drinks from a *jícara*, nothing else, she won't use a glass or a cup." "We know the wilderness [*manigua*]."

Panchito Ramírez: "We know we are Indian because of our grandparents. There are Indians all over these mountains, at Caridad, at Ranchería, at La Escondida. La Escondida was the hideout in the early days. We remember all that. Like we remember Hatuey and ancient cacique of this place, Guamá. My grandfather told me, 'Do not let this beautiful way that we have die.' He gave me my music and he gave me my knowledge of the forest. So I am thankful to the *ancianos* that they kept these things for us."

In a short walk in the forest, Panchito and his wife, Reina, identified more than forty medicinal plants. They use the Four Directions as a deity in their prayers and invoke the powers of many trees and plants in their supplications. Among the sacraments they burn during ceremonies are tobacco and copal. Even though these natural ways are not exclusive to the Indo-cuban folks in the region, many elements certainly appear to have originated in indigenous culture and become diffused in the transculturation of the Cuban people.[3]

Going toward the Punta Maisí lighthouse one day, I asked [Alejandro] Hartmann [a Baracoa historian] about the reluctance of some Cuban academics to accept the Indian identity in this area of Cuba. He responded, "Well, even Rivero, he refuses to say the people here are Indians—he defines them as 'descendants' of Indians. It is common to say that there are no Indians left in Cuba."

"But I am here," Pedro Hernández said from the backseat. "Indians or descendants, it's the same thing. They, the old Taínos, were here. Now, we, my generation, we are here. We don't live exactly like they did, but we are still here."

Not only Hernández, but everyone interviewed expressed interest in a reunion of Indian families or families that hold indigenous knowledge in the region. The idea that people with Indian backgrounds and identity could meet and exchange oral histories and natural knowledge was appealing to everyone I interviewed. Several people from the *etnia* participated in the Columbus Quincentenary activities in 1992, and expressed interest in some kind of ongoing event to observe the occasion and the survival of Cuban indigenous people and lifeways. Since the aboriginal ancestors of this region, the Taíno, were the first American Indians to greet Columbus, the idea seemed pertinent.

The Legend of Yumurí

At Guirito, I talked with Dora Romero Palmero, 78, her son, Pedro Cobas Romero, 53; and her daughter, Mirta, 48. Grandmother Dora, as with María Cobas Hernández in Los Arados, had been a midwife and was still a well-known herbalist. Dora Romero, from an Indian family, had earlier married a Cobas. Her son, Pedro Cobas Romero, was a cousin to Pedro Hernández Cobas from Los Arados—yet the two had never met.

Pedro Cobas said, "Our people have suffered a lot. I myself went to work as a boy of six, picking coffee. That was the time you started work then. The adults in our families recognized each other as Indian, but we children were directed not to talk about it."

He retold a legend about the promontory at the mouth of the Yumurí, a river that flows into the Atlantic not far from Guirito. It is said that during the Spanish conquest the Indian families who could not escape enslavement by the conquistadors climbed the mountain and cursed their pursuers. Entire families committed suicide by jumping. "How horrible that was," Hartmann commented. "But it is understandable, a proper thing," Cobas responded. "The conquistadors treated them so badly in the mines and the fields. After they had lost in combat, this was their only way left to defeat the Spanish, by killing themselves. That way they could not be humiliated. And they died with their dignity."

Cobas also retold the stories of Hatuey and Guamá, two Taíno caciques who led the wars against the early Spanish conquest. "Hatuey was from what is now Haiti, but Guamá was a cacique here. Hatuey crossed over to warn Guamá and other chiefs about the evil of the Spanish, what they had done to the Taínos on that island. They say Hatuey brought a basket of gold in his canoe and told our people this gold was the only god the Spanish adored."

Both Hatuey and Guamá were killed, but not before instigating a ten-year resistance to the conquest. Other uprisings occurred in the area into the late 1500s. "They say a Spanish friar wanted to baptize Hatuey as the soldiers got ready to burn him at the stake," Cobas said. "He informed Hatuey that if baptized as a Christian, he would go to Heaven; but Hatuey, who despised the Christians, refused the baptism. He preferred to go to Hell, he said."

Notes

For complete references and notes, consult the work as cited in the acknowledgment of copyrights section.

1. Camagüey is an agricultural region. Many of the traditions of the guajiro country culture

in Camagüey are quite similar to those found in the Baracoa area. The term *guajiro* is synonymous in Cuba with *campesino*, or countryman-peasant. There are contending schools of thought on the etymology of the word, but everyone agrees it is deeply rooted. Caribbean scholar José Juan Arrom gives it a Taíno etymology, meaning "one of us." It would have been the term applied to the new mestizo generation by the Taíno elders. Some scholars, including Fernando Ortiz, point to a Yucatec, Carib, or Colombian coastal origin for the term, though all concur that *guajiro* describes what is most autochthonous in the increasingly transculturated Cuban identity. Guajiros of Venezuela, the *wayyu* used the word *waxir* for the man of his house.

2. As recently as 18 June 1988 ("Indians of Cuba," *Granma Newspaper*), a Cuban historian, Marta Rey, asserted that the Indian families are limited to two families, the Rojas and the Ramírez. However the Indo-cuban mestizo base is more extended than that. Rivero de la Calle confirmed to this author that "there are more families of Indo-cubans than the two names of Rojas and Ramírez," Video interview, June 1998. Rey proclaims that the Indian families are too racially mixed to be called Indians, and states, perhaps too categorically, "There are no absolutely legitimate Indians left in our country."

3. See the video, "Taino: Indigenous Survival in the Caribbean," produced by José Barreiro and Rich Brotman, RichPaw Productions, New York, 1998.

II

Sugar, Slavery, and Colonialism

By the end of the 1500s the plantation complex, in which Spanish colonists imported African slaves to produce sugar sold in Europe, had been established in the Caribbean. But for two centuries, Cuba's main importance in the international system was strategic, rather than productive: control of the Caribbean sea lanes was key to control of New World silver, and European governments and pirates competed for access to this wealth. In 1608 the population of the island was twenty thousand, with half of those living in the city of Havana (which was established as the capital in 1607); by 1700 the population had grown only to fifty thousand, still with half of these in Havana.[1] By the middle of the 1700s, Cuban colonists took advantage of a shifting international situation (the decline of sugar in Brazil with the expulsion of the Dutch; technological developments in the milling process; the Bourbon reforms in the Spanish empire, which stimulated trade; the U.S. revolution, which cut the colonies' ties to the British Caribbean and led them to seek other Caribbean trading partners) to exponentially increase the production of sugar—and, inevitably, the numbers of slaves imported.

During the nineteenth century the demography of Cuba was transformed. Between 1700 and 1791 Cuba's population grew slowly to 272,300: 153,559 whites, 54,151 free people of color, and 64,590 slaves.[2] The population of African origin doubled by 1810, to 217,000 slaves and 109,000 free people of color, and it increased again by 1847, to 437,000 slaves and 153,000 free people of color. Between 1841 and 1861, whites were a minority.[3] By 1869 the population of Cuba had grown to 1,399,809: 763,176 whites, 238,927 free people of color, 34,420 Asians, and 363,286 slaves.[4]

Despite ups and downs in the export and production of sugar, it has remained a primary feature in Cuba's society and economy through the onset of the twenty-first century. Sugar required investment, the importation of foreign labor, and markets abroad—thus a separation of Cuba's "domestic" affairs from its insertion in a world system of trade and migration is impossible. Sugar shaped the institution of African slavery in Cuba, and Cuba was among the last areas in the Americas to abolish slavery, doing so between 1880 and 1886. (The only later abolition occurred in Brazil, in 1888.) Although not all Cubans were involved directly in the sugar economy, it did fundamentally affect the development of colonial society.

This section examines colonial society in Cuba, from several different angles. We begin with the sugar plantation: the social and economic mainstay of colonial society. We include documents that describe life on the sugar plantation and the slave system that supported it. Not all slaves, however, labored on sugar plantations. We move from the sugar plantation to examine slavery in its different forms and how the institution of slavery affected the people that lived with it—and how the people who lived with it affected the institution. Sugar contributed to a huge population growth on the island, with immigrants arriving (voluntarily or involuntarily) from Europe, Asia, Africa, and Latin America; these immigrants in turn contributed to the social, cultural, and political *ajiaco* (a Taíno stew, used as a metaphor for Cuba's different cultural elements) that was Cuba. Several selections deal with these new Cubans. Finally, we turn to intellectual and cultural aspects of the colonial system, and look at nineteenth-century Cuban writing on what sugar, slavery, and colonial status meant for Cuban development and identity.

Notes

1. Louis A. Pérez Jr., *Cuba: Between Reform and Revolution.* 2d ed. (New York: Oxford University Press, 1995), 38, 46. Pérez also notes that the African slave population grew from one thousand in 1550 to five thousand in 1650.

2. Pérez, *Cuba*, 63, citing United States War Department, *Informe sobre el censo de Cuba, 1899* (Washington, D.C., 1900).

3. Louis A. Pérez Jr., ed., *Slaves, Sugar, and Colonial Society: Travel Accounts of Cuba, 1801–1899* (Wilmington, Del.: Scholarly Resources, 1992), xv.

4. Hortensia Pichardo, *Documentos para la historia de Cuba*, 4 vols. (Havana: Editorial de Ciencias Sociales, 1973), 4:367, cited from Carlos de Sedano y Cruzat, *Cuba desde 1850 a 1873*, 152–53.

A Physician's Notes on Cuba

John G. F. Wurdemann

South Carolina–born physician John G. F. Wurdemann (1810–1849) was one of many European and U.S. travelers who published an account of his experiences in exotic lands in the nineteenth century. He traveled to Cuba in 1843, suffering from tuberculosis and hoping that the climate would prove salutary. He published his impressions anonymously, first in the Magnolia *magazine, then as a book. In this selection, he gives a vivid description of the technical aspects of sugar production. He describes the functioning of a sugar plantation with some admiration, despite his acknowledgment of the suffering of the slaves.*

The sugar estate spreads out its solitary but extensive field of cane, with nothing to vary the prospect but the isolated royal palms scattered irregularly over the whole. While the coffee planter's chief care is to unite in his estate beauty with profit, the only object of the sugar planter is money, often regardless if it be attained at the expense of the welfare of his laborers. In society he holds a higher rank than the other, as with us the sea-island cotton and rice planter arrogate a higher station than one who cultivates the short staple and raises his own provisions. When, however, we recollect that in the palmy days of sugar, the incomes of not a few of them were each more than two hundred thousand dollars, and that even now the crops of many sell for more than one hundred thousand dollars, they might well be considered the natural princes of the land. The capital invested in a sugar estate is also so large, that it alone gives a certain degree of importance to the planter, if he even be, as is often the case, inextricably involved in debt.

A visit to a sugar district will soon dispel from the mind of the traveler all doubts of creole enterprise. It is true that some estates still grind the cane by ox power, and have but rude contrivances for preparing the sugar; but on many of them the most perfect machinery is employed, and steam, laborsaving steam, has taken the place of manual labor. There is considerable rivalry among the planters to produce the best sugar and the greatest quantity and so great was the enterprise of one of my neighbors, that, in the midst of the grinding sea-

Laplante, Acana sugar plantation. Reprinted in Robert Paquette, *Sugar Is Made with Blood: The Conspiracy of La Escalera and the Conflict between Empires over Slavery in Cuba* (Middletown, Conn.: Wesleyan University Press, 1988), following 46. Reprinted with permission of Wesleyan University Press.

son, he removed his steam engine for the erection of another on the plan of those used in France for making beet sugar. The syrup, clarified by animal charcoal, was boiled by steam, and the sugar prepared in a vacuum; the whole cost forty thousand dollars, some said more. As the cutting of the cane ceases when the rains commence, the saccharine matter being greatly diminished by its regrowth, he ran a risk of losing half his crop by the costly experiment. . . .

A sugar plantation, during the manufacture of sugar, presents a picture not only of active industry but of unremitting labor. The oxen are reduced toward the end of the season to mere skeletons, many of them dying from overlabor; the Negroes are allowed but five hours' sleep, but although subjected to this inordinate tasking of their physical powers, in general, preserve their good looks. Before the introduction of the steam engine, and the example of a milder treatment of the Negro by foreign residents in Cuba, the annual loss by death was fully 10 percent., including, however, new slaves, many of whom died from the change of climate. At present the annual loss in Limonar, I was informed by an intelligent English physician, does not exceed 2.5 percent., even including the old. On some plantations, on the south side of the island, the custom still prevails of excluding all female slaves, and even on those where the two sexes are well proportioned in number they do not increase. On a sugar estate employing two hundred slaves, I have seen only three or four children. That this arises from mismanagement is proved by the rapid increase on a few estates where the Negroes are well cared for. The Saratoga sugar estate, which with the Carlotta belongs to a highly intelligent merchant of Havana, is noted for the great number of children born on it; while several coffee estates, where the slaves are deprived of sufficient rest, are also unproductive.

It cannot be denied that the slave's life, while employed in the manufacture of sugar, is a very laborious one; from November until the end of May his physical powers are tasked to the utmost; still his peculiar frame of mind, that dwells only on the present, sustains him under it. The weightiest cares cannot drive sleep from his eyelids, or deprive him of his appetite; and so well do the Negroes appear even at the end of the grinding season, that one would be tempted to doubt the amount of labor they have performed. During the rest of the year their daily tasks are comparatively light, consisting chiefly in removing the weeds from the fields, and cutting fuel for the next winter.

The greater portion, during the grinding season, are employed in cutting the cane. This is done by a short, swordlike cleaver, one stroke sufficing to cut the stalk close to the ground, and another to remove the unripe tops, which with their leaves are thrown in one long heap, while the rest, divided into two or more sticks, are thrown in another. The latter are removed in carts to the mill, and the tops are left for the cattle to feed on. In the best-constructed mills a revolving platform conveys the canes to the rollers, through which they pass, and which express from them all the juice. The crushed stalks fall on another revolving [platform] and are carried off to a spot where a number of Negroes are waiting with baskets to convey them into the yard. They are there exposed to the sun until quite dry, when they are packed under large sheds, and used as fuel for boiling the cane juice.

The juice flows from the rollers through a gutter into a large reservoir, in which it is gently heated, and where it deposits the dirt and portions of cane that have escaped with it from the rollers. From this it is drawn off into a large cauldron, where it undergoes a rapid boiling, and has its acidity corrected by the admixture of more less lime. When reduced to a certain degree, it is dipped out by ladles into another cauldron, where it is suffered to boil until it reaches the granular point. It is now removed by large ladles into a long wooden trough, and stirred by long paddles until cold.

The mass now consists of the granulated sugar and its molasses, and when it is intended simply to remove the latter and make the quality called *muscovado*, it is conveyed into wooden cisterns twelve feet square and two deep, and thence into the hogsheads, where it undergoes its final draining, the molasses escaping through a hole into gutters, which carry it to a general reservoir.

To make the white Havana quality, it is removed from the trough into earthen or tin conical pans, each capable of holding about eighty pounds of the mass, having at their apices openings closed with a few dried cane leaves, through which the molasses percolates, and falls into gutters below. Clay, made into a soft paste by being well mixed with water, is next spread over the sugar about three inches thick. The water, separating slowly from it, passes through the brown sugar below, and washes off the molasses from each grain, converting it into the quality known by the name of Havana white. After a certain time the mass becomes consolidated, and the loaf is removed from the pan, and carried to the dryers, large wooden frames fixed on railways, on which they can be readily rolled under cover of the shed when it rains. The base of the conical loaf is the whitest, while the apex is of a dirty-brown hue, and the intervening portion of a light brown. It is divided into these three kinds by the Negroes, who with their cleavers walk over the sugar with their bare feet, cutting the masses into small lumps. To a stranger the sight of two or three dozen half-naked Negroes thus employed under a broiling sun, and sweating over their task, is far from being pleasant; and I have known more than one who have been afterward very sparing in the use of clayed sugar. A machine has, however, been lately invented for crushing the loaves, and the present unclean method will probably be generally abandoned.

In well-constructed furnaces the dried cane stalks, called *bagassa*, are found sufficient for boiling the juice, but wood is required to produce steam for the engine. This is brought to the mill at the expense of great labor; and in consequence of its great consumption, large tracts of land are now bare of forests, and the difficulty of procuring fuel increases every year. Much labor is also expended in raising water from the deep wells to supply the engine boiler, the amount of which may be imagined by the reader, when he learns that they are from one to four hundred feet deep, and that the water is generally drawn up by single buckets. During the dry season the sugar planter is also in constant dread of his fields being fired by some malicious neighbor, when in a few hours his whole crop and perhaps all his buildings might be destroyed. The canes are so thickly planted, and their numerous dead leaves form such a closely interwoven mass, that when ignited while the wind is fresh, the flames spread with inconceivable rapidity over the whole field. Although the prince of agriculturists, the sugar planter is now at the mercy of any of the canaille he may have offended, and an opportunity is not infrequently taken at this season to revenge some past slight or injury.

As soon as the fire is discovered the large bell of the estate, which can be heard several miles, is rapidly tolled, and the neighboring estates at the summons disgorge their troops of slaves, who hasten to the spot. Alleys are cut through the field to the leeward of the burning portion and counter fires ignited, and a large quantity of cane is often thus saved. In some cases the alley is cut too close to the fire, which sweeping across it surrounds the workers, some of whom are not infrequently suffocated by the dense clouds of smoke. I was present on one occasion, and the scene was most exciting. The roaring of the flames, the sharp cracking of the burning cane, the volumes of smoke that now and then swept along the ground, enveloping everything in its dark cloud, the gang of half-naked Negroes, numbering more than five hundred, with their swordlike machetes, hewing down the canes, while others with torches were setting fire to the windward edge of the road, the mounted *mayorales* with long swords and holsters galloping about, and shouting out orders and counter-orders, and a certain vague sense of danger, combined to render the whole a most animating sight.

The Death of the Forest

Manuel Moreno Fraginals

The eastward expansion of sugar cultivation in the nineteenth century brought about the destruction of huge areas of forestland. The scale of this ecological disaster is conveyed in the following extract from the study The Sugar Mill, *written by the doyen of Cuban sugar studies, Manuel Moreno Fraginals (1920–2001).*

Up until the end of the eighteenth century, Cubans took pride in their forests. The whole island was a stand of precious wood—mahogany, cedar, ebony, dagame [a tree of the *Rubiaceae* family native to Cuba], quebracho—among which soared giant palms. Early chroniclers could not suppress their amazement at our trees in whose shade, they insisted, one could walk from one end of the island to the other. The Laws of the Indies guarded this wealth jealously, taking the socially responsible position that the forests were not the landowner's property since they also belonged to future generations. Before sugar, before tobacco, before cattle, it was precious wood that symbolized the Far Antilles. From Cuban wood was carved the gorgeous ceilings of the Escorial, its still-intact doors and windows, and the incredible mahogany table, the world's largest made from a single piece. Boards from giant Cuban trees made the doors of San Francisco El Grande in Madrid, and Cuban wood abounded in the Royal Palace. Documents tell us that a typical form of English and French piracy was to plunder the forests of the semi-populated island: how much Cuban wood went into English and French palaces we do not know. . . .

Large-scale manufacture rang the forest's death knell. The best sugar master of the early nineteenth century left us this crisp sentence: "The sugar mill's need for firewood is alarming—and where are the forests that can meet it?" He was José Ignacio Echegoyen, Arango's technician at La Ninfa, later proprietor of the giant La Asunción mill. Firewood consumption depended on the kettle system. The unit by which it was calculated was the "task," a cubic volume of three × two × one yards. A *caballería* [33.6 acres] of forest was estimated to yield about one thousand tasks. The "Spanish train" consumed one task of firewood for each five or six arrobas of clayed sugar. Use of the Jamaica train more than doubled the yield, to thirteen arrobas per task. We can easily calculate that at the end of the eighteenth century about five hundred caballerías of forest were being felled each year to be burned in making sugar, plus many more for building new mills.

With sugar's advance, tree clearing became a well-paid activity for the small Havana peasantry of the late eighteenth and early nineteenth centuries. They received between three hundred and five hundred pesos for "cleaning" one caballería. As prices rose over the years, the work became the specialty of teams employed on a piecework basis. Although slaves were often used for wood cutting, it became more and more a free worker's job as the institution of slavery became bloated. Masters found that their blacks constantly disappeared into the woods and it was hard to catch them.

We must make a clear distinction between ground that was cleared for planting cane and building mills, and forests cut down for firewood. In the first case the method was simple. A machete gang first tackled the reeds and vines, leaving clear spaces around the big trunks. This "chopping" of the undergrowth was followed by the "toppling" of ancient trees. After thirty or forty days came the "burning" of the chopped, now-dry vegetation. If it was a "slash and leave" job, the trunks not consumed by the fire stayed where they had fallen and sugar mill slaves stacked them for use as fuel. If it was a "slash and burn" job, the fires were repeated and the trunks cut small so they would burn completely. When some of the timber remained unburned, it was piled into small bonfires (*fogatas*), a process known as *foguerear*. The most precious woods— ebony, mahogany, quebracho—were generally of great size and took two or three fires to burn.

No one can calculate the extent of sugar's forest depredation. We have suggested that it ran to five hundred caballerías a year in the late eighteenth century; by 1809 it was twice as much, and in 1830 sugar men Andrés de Zayas and José María Dau estimated it at two thousand caballerías—half for fuel and half burned up to make room for new mills. The figure rose to four thousand in 1844, at which point the junta charged with protecting the trees announced that the forest laws had given "happy and satisfactory results."

The right to destroy the forests was one of the sugar men's great legal victories. . . .

The death of the forest was also, in part, the long-term death of the island's fabled fertility. This was an old Antillean process with which our sugarocrats were already acquainted. Slave labor involved the use of crude techniques with a low yield. To compensate for manufacturing deficiencies, the highest agri-

Casa de Caldera (Boiler House) del Ingenio Flor de Cuba. C. Naranjo and T. Mallo, eds., *Cuba: La perla de las antillas. Actas de las 1 jornadas de historia* (Madrid: Ediciones Doce Calles), 74.

cultural yield was sought, but this was in no way the result of rational soil utilization, only of the exceptional richness of recently cleared virgin land. First plantings of a dead forest commonly produced well over 120,000 arrobas of cane per caballería. Annual cane cutting and neglect of the hilling and strawing of shoots lowered the crop of a field which was neither irrigated nor fertilized. When a critical point was reached it was abandoned, another forest was cut, and the fabulous cane production statistics were again repeated.

The Cuban hacendado did not invent this barbaric system: it was born with Antillean sugar, a typical product of the plantation. Technicians called it "extensive cultivation," while Liebig and Sagra gave it the more precise name of "plunder culture." The English used the same system in the small islands and were soon left without trees; by 1749 they were calling their once-fertile lands "poor and worn out." French producers, one up on them at the time, were working land that was "fresh and fertile," but a century later a traveler noted that "the inhabitants can't even find roots to feed themselves." It was an exaggerated version of what had happened in Europe, attributed by Marx to the insuperable limitations with which private property always confronts the most rational agriculture. On top of all the agricultural and economic motivations for destroying forests came the wars of independence. In the campaign plans drawn up by generals Concha, Valmaseda, Caballero de Rodas, Ceballo, and

Azcárraga, it was estimated that fifty-five million trees would be felled for the various military arteries and roads.

A fantastic footnote on the contradictions of Cuban sugar production is that in the same years that the island was burning its own timber wealth, it was the top buyer of United States lumber. From the end of the eighteenth century, pine and cypress boards for making sugar boxes were arriving at Havana ports. The lumber trade was one of the United States' best-paying businesses. Imports, without counting contraband, ran between six hundred thousand and one million pesos a year in the first two decades of the nineteenth century. José de Arango called this trade "shameful." He complained about the fate of our forests, "given to the flames or remaining in useless abundance while we empty our pockets for the foreigner's benefit.". . .

Sugar exterminated the forests. Deaf and blind to history, focusing on the present, the sugarocracy destroyed in years what only centuries could replace and at the same time destroyed much of the island's fertility by soil erosion and the drying-up of thousands of streams. An extra debit item on the ledger of an irrational system of exploitation based solely on calculations of immediate profit was the resulting Cuban contempt for trees. Yet the poet Pobeda sang in praise of trees, and among other voices heralding the future was that of Sagra, who wrote: "At this stage of maturity, when man is enriched by the conquests of science and illuminated in his endeavors by moral sentiments, he faces the great enterprise of exploiting his planet not merely for his own generation but for those to come. This cannot be done unless individual, ephemeral, and transitory interests are subordinated to the general and eternal interests of all humanity."[1]

Of Cuba's forests, its legendary mahogany, almost nothing remains today. In 1962 one could still see the *palanqueros* at work on the Río Sagua, whose waters flow gently between treeless banks. They drive a long iron-pointed pole into the riverbed until they feel they have struck timber; they dive, secure it, and drag it to the bank. A hard, slow, monotonous job, like the throes of death. Day by day they bring up from the river bottom bits of the trees that sugar cut down. They live off the corpses of the forest. All that remains to them of the ancient wealth is the echo of an old folksong:

Tomorrow I go to Sagua
To cut me some boughs
To make me a house
On the slopes of Jumagua.[2]

TRANSLATED BY CEDRIC BELFRAGE

Notes

For complete references and notes, consult the work as cited in the acknowledgment of copyrights section.

1. These are the final words in Sagra's chapter on forests in *Cuba in 1860*.

2. This is a traditional folksong, transmitted orally, collected by Professor José Sainz Triana of the Universidad Central de Las Villas.

Autobiography of a Slave

Juan Francisco Manzano

On the sugar plantation, slaves had few opportunities to record their stories. Thus the accounts that we do have from the perspective of the slave are more likely to reflect the experiences of those who were successful at resisting or escaping slavery. We have included an excerpt from the only known autobiography written by a slave in Cuba, that of the poet Juan Francisco Manzano (1797?–1854?). Unlike the majority of slaves, who labored in the fields, Manzano was a house slave. His vivid testimony depicts the harsh and arbitrary nature of life under slavery despite his supposed position of relative privilege inside slave society.

From the time when I could first do anything, my destiny was to be a page. In Havana as in Matanzas, from my most tender years, I stayed up more than half the night. In Havana, if not on a night at the theater, at a gathering in the home of the Marquis de Monte Hermoso, or in the home of the pious mistresses Cárdenas, from which we would leave at ten after having dined, the outing would begin and last until eleven or twelve at night. In Matanzas, whether on specified days or others, we ate at the Count of Jibacoa's or at Don Juan Manuel O'Farrell's home. Wherever it might be, we spent the afternoon and evening in the home of the Señoras Gómez, where all the most prominent and honorable people in the town met to play card games — *tresillo, matillo,* or *burro*. I could not budge from the back of my mistress's stool until it was time to depart, which was usually at about twelve midnight, when we left for El Molino. If I fell asleep during the gathering, or if by some chance my lantern went out when I was sitting behind the coachman (even if it was because the deep ruts left by the carts filled with water, which splashed up when the wheels hit them and penetrated the slots in my tin-plate lantern), upon arrival the overseer or the administrator was awakened and I was sent to sleep in the stocks. At dawn, the latter or the former would do a job on me and not as if I were a child.[1]

But sleep holds such sway over the human spirit that four or five nights did not go by before it happened again. Nobody, absolutely nobody could help me, not even my poor mother. More than twice, daybreak found my mother

Slaves serving whites and working in the boiling house, Cuban sugar plantation. Reprinted in Paquette, *Sugar Is Made with Blood*, following 46. Reprinted by permission of Wesleyan University Press.

and brother waiting up for me while I, locked up, awaited a painful dawn. My mother already lived in such apprehension that, when I did not arrive more or less on time, she came down from her shack and approached the door of what used to be the men's infirmary, where the stocks were located to the left. To see if I was there she would call me, "Juan." Sobbing, I would answer her and she would say from outside, "Oh, my son!" Then she would call to her husband from the grave, because by then my father had already died. Three times in less than two months, I remember having seen this scene repeated, as well as others in which I found myself as time went by. Among the most memorable for me, however, was the following one.

We were leaving town and it was already very late. Seated as always, hanging onto a bar with one hand and a lantern in the other, and with the coach moving rather more slowly than usual, I fell asleep in such a way that I let go of the lantern but so well that it landed upright. After about twenty paces I suddenly opened my eyes, found the lantern missing, saw the light where it lay, jumped down, and ran to grab it. Before I got to it I fell twice on the rough road, and stumbling, finally reached it, then wanted to fly after the coach, which was already at a considerable distance from me. But how surprised I was to see the carriage accelerate its pace, so that I was exerting myself in vain to catch up to it, and it disappeared from my sight.

I already knew what was to befall me. I walked along, crying. When I drew near the house, I found myself grabbed by Señor Silvestre, the young overseer. As he led me to the stocks, he ran into my mother, who, following her heart, ended up increasing my misfortunes.

Upon seeing me, she tried to ask me what I had done, when the overseer, who demanded silence, endeavored to stop her, refusing to hear of pleas, entreaties, or gifts; irritated because they had made him get up at that hour, he raised his hand and struck my mother with his whip. I felt this blow in my heart. All at once I screamed and was transformed from a gentle lamb into a lion. I wrenched myself loose from his grip with a strong yank of my arm, and I attacked him with teeth and fists.

You can imagine how many kicks, punches, and other blows I sustained. My mother and I were led to the same place and locked up. There we moaned in unison. Meanwhile my two brothers, Florencio and Fernando, were crying alone at home. They must have been about twelve and five years old. Today, the latter is in the service of the physician Don Pintado.

It was barely sunrise when the overseer and two of his assistants removed us; each of the mulattoes leading his prey to the sacrificial site. For being bold, I suffered more than was ordered, but the sacred laws of nature worked again with marvelous results.

My mother's mistake was that she assaulted the overseer when she saw he was about to kill me and, while he was dealing with her, I was able to stand up. When the watchmen arrived from the yard where the coffee beans are dried,[2] they led us away and I saw my mother put in the sacrificial place for the first time in her life. Even though she lived on the plantation, as the wife of a slave who knew how to conduct himself and command respect from everyone, she was exempt from work.

Bewildered, seeing my mother in this position, I could neither cry nor think nor flee. I was trembling as the four blacks shamelessly overpowered her and threw her on the ground to whip her. I prayed to God. For her sake I endured everything. But when I heard the first crack of the whip I became a lion, a tiger, the fiercest beast, and I was about to lose my life at the hands of the aforementioned Silvestre. But let us pass over the rest of this painful scene in silence. . . .

In 1810, if I am not mistaken, I was my mistress's lapdog. One can say this because it was my duty to always follow her, except into her rooms, and then I was to remain at the door, keeping everyone out or calling whomever she requested, or demanding silence if I thought she was sleeping.

One afternoon we went out to the garden for quite a while. I was helping my mistress pick flowers or transplant little bushes as a kind of entertainment.

Black postilion drawing a
quitrín (gig), a Cuban chaise
with women of planter or
merchant class. Reprinted in
Paquette, *Sugar Is Made with
Blood*, following 46. Reprinted
by permission of Wesleyan
University Press.

Meanwhile the gardener was walking all around the garden fulfilling his responsibilities. As we were leaving, without knowing exactly what I was doing, I
picked a leaf, nothing more than a small leaf from a geranium. Unaware of what
I was doing, I held that extremely fragrant plant in my hand. Distracted by
the verses consigned to my memory, I was walking two or three steps behind
my mistress. Unconscious of what I was doing, I tore the leaf to shreds, which
produced an even stronger aroma. As she entered one of the anterooms, my
mistress drew back, for what reason I do not know. I stepped aside, but upon
coming face to face with me she noticed the fragrance. Suddenly angered, she
asked me in a sharp, upset tone of voice, "What do you have in your hands?"
My body immediately froze; barely able to stand up because both my legs were
trembling, I dropped the handful of shredded leaves on the floor.

She grabbed my hands, smelled them, and picked up the pieces, which became a pile, a bush, an outstanding audacity. My nose was shattered, and I was
handed over to the administrator who immediately showed up, Don Lucas
Rodríguez, an emigrant from Santo Domingo.

It must have been about six in the afternoon, and it was the worst part of
the winter. The coach was set to leave for town. I was to follow them. But
how fragile is the fate of he who is subject to continuous mishaps. My life was
never predictable, and this time, like many others, would confirm this, as we
shall see.

I was sent to the stocks. If it still exists, in that place, which was once an infirmary for men, about fifty beds would fit on each side. Here is where the sick on
the plantation were received, along with those from the San Miguel sugar mill.
At that time it was empty and not functioning as an infirmary. That is where
the stocks were, and only some cadavers were stored there until it was time to
carry them to town to be buried. There, forced to remain standing, frozen by
the cold and with nothing to cover me, I was locked up. I was scarcely alone in
that place when it seemed that all the dead were rising and wandering up and

down the length of that room. A broken-down shutter banged incessantly out over the river or ditch, near a noisy torrent of water falling from a cliff. And each blow seemed to be a dead person who was entering through the window from the afterlife. Imagine what kind of night I must have spent.

No sooner had the first light of day appeared when I heard the lock turn. An assistant overseer entered, followed by the administrator. They took out a board, propped up against a beam that supports a bunch of hoop-poles for tobacco, about fifty of them, hanging from the roof. At the foot of the board I saw the administrator wrapped in his cloak. From under the handkerchief that covered his mouth, in a husky voice, he ordered my hands to be tied. They were tied like Jesus Christ's. They lifted me and placed my feet into two openings in the board. My feet were also tied. Dear God! Let us draw a curtain over this scene. My blood was shed. I lost consciousness, and when I came to I found myself in the doorway of the oratory chapel in the arms of my mother, overwhelmed with tears.

On Father Don Jaime Florit's counsel, she left, forsaking the plan she had to intercede for I do not know what purpose. At nine or a little after, my mistress awoke, her first concern was to verify if I had been treated well. The administrator, who was expecting her, called me and presented me to her. She asked me if I wanted to take some leaves from her geranium again. As I refused to respond, I came very near being punished again, so I finally had to answer "no."

It must have been about eleven when I began to swell. I was put in a room. For three days, without respite, I was in that state. They bathed me and applied ointments. My mother did not visit me there except at night, when she thought the others were in town. On the sixth day, when I was no longer in a life-threatening state, I walked about a bit. It was about noon when I came upon my mother, who was crossing the drying yard. She found me and said, "Juan, I have here the money for your freedom. You see, your father has died and you are now going to be the father of your brothers. They will no longer punish you. Juan, be careful, I have . . ." A stream of tears was my only response, and she cried, too. I went about my work. But the result of all this was that my mother ended up with no money and I was left to await some uncertain time that has yet to come.

After this episode, the following event occurred. When I was at El Molino, some birds—capons and chickens—were brought from the sugar mill. As I was the one who always looked out for visitors, it unfortunately fell to me to receive them. I took the delivery receipt inside, leaving the birds in the dining room or corridor, under the little bower located at the entrance. They read the receipt and ordered me to take it to the other side of the plantation to deliver it to Don Juan Mato, who was the steward or watchman over there. I took every-

Monteros, a class of rural, poor whites, with slave or servant in the background. Reprinted in Paquette, *Sugar Is Made with Blood*, 46. Reprinted by permission of Wesleyan University Press.

thing from the muleteer, dismissing him, and was content, since in the interim I took a breather. I handed over what I had been given, and I remember that they were three capons and two chickens.

Some two weeks or more had passed when I was called to give an account of a missing capon. Right away I said that there had been three plus two chickens and that had been what I had delivered. This was all there was to it. But the next morning I saw the overseer from the sugar mill approaching. He spoke a long while with my mistress and then left. We served lunch, and when I was going to take the first bite, savoring the moment . . . my mistress called me. She told me to go the overseer's house and tell him I do not remember what. That gave me a bad feeling. My heart raced and I went, trembling. Since normally I was accustomed to turning myself in, so it was that I went with great misgivings.

I arrived at the door, and both of them were there, the plantation overseer and the aforementioned person. I gave him the message, and, ignoring it, he told me, "Come in, boy." As I was in the habit of getting on well with these people, since I fell into their hands so often, I obeyed him. I was going to repeat the message when Señor Domínguez, that was the name of the overseer from the sugar mill, grabbed me by the arm, saying, "He is looking for me." He took out a rope made of flimsy hemp, tied me up like a criminal, mounted his horse, and, pushing me ahead, ordered me to run.

We quickly distanced ourselves from that neighborhood so that neither my mother, nor my second brother, nor the other boys or girls would see me, because they would all immediately cry, the house would become a sorrowful place, and they would protect me. We had gone about a fourth of a league when, tired of running in front of the horse, I tripped and fell. No sooner had I hit the ground than two dogs or two beasts, which were following him, attacked me. One of them, holding my entire left cheek in his mouth, sank his fang all the way through to my molar. The other one perforated my thigh and my left calf, with the utmost voracity and speed. These scars persist in spite of the twenty-four years that have transpired since then. The overseer leaped from the horse onto the dogs and separated them. I was bleeding profusely, especially from my left leg, which fell numb. He grabbed me with one hand by the rope that bound me, hurling a stream of obscenities at me. This yank dislocated my right arm, which has not yet healed. In bad weather I suffer certain pains like those of gout.

Walking as well as I was able, we arrived at the sugar mill. I was tied with two ropes fastened around two rocks. My bite wounds were cured with some kind of ointment, and I was placed in the stocks. The fatal night arrived. All the people formed a line; an assistant overseer, the overseer, and five blacks pulled me out into the middle. Around me they shouted, "Drop."[3] They mercilessly threw me on the ground, as one throws a sack that has no feelings, one holding down each hand and foot and another seated on my back. They asked me about the chicken or capon. I did not know what to say because I knew nothing about it. I suffered twenty-five lashes. I said a thousand different things because they were demanding I tell the truth and I did not know which truth they wanted. I thought that saying I had taken it would suffice and the whipping would stop, but then I would have to say what became of the money, so I found myself in another dilemma. I said that I had bought a hat. "Where is the hat?" It was a lie. I said I had bought shoes; there were none. I said so many things, over and over again, trying to see how to free myself from so much torture.

I suffered these torments for nine nights; I said nine thousand different things as they shouted at me, "Tell the truth!" and whipped me. I no longer had anything left to say, anything that it seemed might end their punishing me. But not because I knew such things.

When this business was finished, I would go to drive oxen at night or in

Servant trying to kiss a statue. Victor Patricio de Landaluze, *Sirviente tratando de besar un busto*. Museo Nacional de Bellas Artes, Havana. Reproduced in Adelaida de Juan, *Pintura cubana: Temas y variaciones* (Mexico City: Universidad Nacional Autónoma de México, 1980).

the morning, depending on which shift fell to me. Every morning a note was sent about what I had said the night before.[4] After ten days, on Monday, the news spread through the entire sugar mill, and finally the reason for such punishment was known. Then the muleteer, Dionisio Covadonga (who was the muleteer), appeared before the overseer and told him not to punish me any further because the capon or chicken in question had been eaten by the steward, Don Manuel Pipa. The day he gave the birds to Dionisio so he could take them with the message that afternoon to El Molino, unbeknownst to Don Dionisio, one capon chicken remained behind in the kitchen. At eleven that night, when he returned from town with the rations for the next day, he saw it. The next morning he told the steward, believing only that someone had stolen it and hidden it in his hut, which was the kitchen. The steward told him that it was one of the ones that were to have been taken to El Molino, but in spite of this, he took it and left it in his room. The next day, his cook prepared it for him.

The mulatta, Simona, was called and questioned. She declared everything to be true. The overseer asked why they had not said anything before. Dionisio said that nobody knew because all that one heard was talk about some capon or other, but nobody knew which capon, and if I had not told Simona and Dionisio which was the capon in question, nobody would have understood.

I do not know if this matter was reported, but the fact is that from that day on the punishment stopped. I was assigned to loosen up the dry bagasse with a hook and to pile it up for transport in baskets to the ovens.[5]

TRANSLATED BY EVELYN PICON GARFIELD

Notes

For complete references and notes, consult the work as cited in the acknowledgment of copyrights section.

1. The job of administering lashes.

2. A certain square expanse of land, leveled and covered with concrete, with borders or low walls, where coffee beans are dried in the sun (*Pichardo*).

3. In *Los Negros esclavos*, Ortiz tells us that *tumbadero* was the place habitually destined for punishment by flogging; the slaves threw themselves on the ground (*tumbar*) so that the whip would mark the harsh stamp of slavery's oppression on their backs (246).

4. To the mistress.

5. The crushed, juiceless remains of sugarcane as it comes from the mill, often used as fuel in the mill.

Biography of a Runaway Slave

Miguel Barnet

Cuban anthropologist and novelist Miguel Barnet (b. 1940) recorded an extraordinary oral history of Esteban Montejo (1860–1973), a slave who escaped the plantation and survived alone in the mountains for many years near the end of the century. Miguel Barnet's Biography of a Runaway Slave *launched a new genre of Latin American writing—the testimonio—and the book, first published in Cuba in 1964, quickly gained itself a reputation as a "window from below" on slavery and the experience of the* cimarrón *(runaway).*

All the slaves lived in barracoons. Those living quarters are gone now so nobody can see them. But I seen them, and I never had a good thought about them. The masters sure did say that barracoons were little boxes of gold. The slaves didn't like living in those conditions because being closed-in suffocated them. The barracoons were big although there were some mills that had small ones. It depended on the number of slaves in the workforce. About two hundred slaves of all different colors lived at Flor de Sagua. The barracoon was in the form of two rows that faced each other, with a big door in the middle and a thick padlock that locked the slaves in at night. There were barracoons made of wood and others made of cement with tiled roofs. Both kinds had a dirt floor and were filthy as hell. There certainly was no modern kind of ventilation inside. A little hole in the wall of the room or a little tiny window with bars was all there was. So the place swarmed with fleas and ticks that gave the entire workforce infections and sickness. Those ticks were witches. And so the only thing to get rid of them was hot lard, and sometimes even that didn't work. The masters wanted the barracoons to look clean outside so they painted them with whitewash. The blacks themselves were given that task. The master would say to them, "Get some whitewash and spread it evenly." The whitewash was prepared in big buckets in the barracoons, in the central patio.

Horses and goats didn't go into the barracoons, but there was always some fool dog sniffing around looking for food. People had to stay in the rooms of the barracoons, which were small and hot. Rooms! In reality they were furnaces. They had doors with latchkeys so nobody would get robbed. But watch out for the little criollos who were born rascally, with a thieving instinct. They would get out from under the covers at night to go around stealing like the dickens.

In the center of the barracoons, the women washed their husband's clothes, their children's, and their own. They washed in washtubs. Washtubs during slavery weren't like the ones today. Those then were more rustic. And you had to take them to the river so they would swell up to hold water because they were made of codfish boxes, the big ones.

Outside the barracoon there weren't any trees, nor inside either. The barracoon was bare dirt, empty, and lonely. A black man couldn't get used to that. Blacks like trees, woods. Maybe the Chinese could! Africa was full of trees, ceibas, cedars, banyan trees. Not China. Over there they had plants that grew along the ground, creepers, purslane, morning glories. . . . Since the rooms were tiny, the slaves did their business in a latrine, as they called it. It was in a corner of the barracoon. That's a place everybody went to. And to dry your *fotingo*, afterward, you had to use plants like feverfew and corncobs.

The mill's bell was at the gateway. It was struck by the assistant overseer. At four-thirty in the morning they rang the Ave María. I think there were nine strokes. You had to get up right away. At six in the morning they struck another bell which was the line-up bell, and you had to form up on the dirt in front of the barracoon. The men on one side and the women on the other. Then into the fields until eleven in the morning, when we ate beef jerky, 'taters, and bread. Then, at sunset, came the prayer bell. At eight-thirty they rang the last bell for bed. It was called silence. . . .

But it was the small gardens that saved many slaves. They provided them real nourishment. Almost all the slaves had their *conucos*. They were little strips of dirt for gardening. They were real close to the barracoons, almost right in back. They grew everything there: sweet potato, squash, okra, corn, peas, horse beans, beans like limas, limes, yucca, and peanuts. They also raised piglets. And so those products were sold to the *guajiros* who came straight from town. Truth is that the blacks were honest. Since they didn't know much yet, being honest just came naturally. They sold their things very cheap. Full-grown pigs were worth an ounce or one and a half ounces in gold, which was the money back then. But they never liked to sell their 'taters. I learned from the old-timers to eat 'taters, which are very nutritious. During slavery the main thing was pig meat. They were given 'taters for food. Pigs at that time produced more lard than they do nowadays. I think it's because they lived a more natural life. You had to let the pig wallow around in the pigsty. That lard of theirs was sold in ten-kilo batches. Every week the guajiros would come for their supply. They always paid in silver half-pesos. Later on, that coin dropped to a quarter, or half a half. The centavo was unknown because Alfonso XII hadn't been crowned yet. It was after the coronation that the centavo came. King Alfonso wanted to change even the money. The copper *calderilla*, which I think was worth two cents, came to Cuba with other new money on account of the king.

Strange as it may seem, blacks had fun in the barracoons. They had their pastimes and their games. There were also games in the taverns, but those were different. One of the ones they played the most in the barracoons was *tejo*. You put a corncob, split in half, on the ground. You placed a coin on top of it. You drew a line on the ground a short distance away, and you threw a stone from the line toward the corncob. If the stone hit the corncob, and the coin fell on the stone, the man took the coin as his. If it fell close to the corncob, no coin. Tejo caused great disputes. In such cases, you had to measure with a straw to see if the coin was closer to the player than to the corncob.

That game was played in the patio like the game of bowling. But bowling wasn't played much. I seen it no more than two or three times. There were some black coopers who made the sticks in the shape of bottles and the wooden balls for playing. It was an open game, and everybody could join in. Except for the Chinese, who were pretty standoffish. You rolled the balls along the flat ground to try to knock down the four or five sticks at the other end. It was the same game as the one that's played today in the city, but the difference is that with the older one, there were fights over the bets. That surely didn't please the masters. That's why they prohibited some games, and you had to play them when the overseer wasn't looking. The overseer was the one who told the news, news and gossip.

The game of *mayombe* was linked to religion. Even the overseers got involved, hoping to benefit. They believed in ghosts so that's why no one today should be surprised that whites also believe in those things. You played mayombe with drums. You put a *nganga*, or big pot, in the middle of the patio.

All the powers, the saints, were in that *cazuela*. And mayombe was a useful game, but the saints had to be present. The players began to play the drums and to sing. They brought things for the ngangas. The blacks asked about their health, and their brothers' and sisters' health, and asked for harmony among them. They did *enkangues*, which were hexes made with dirt from the cemetery. With that dirt you made four corners in little mounds to resemble the points of the universe. They put star-shake, which was an herb, in the pot with corn straw to hold human beings. When the master punished a slave, all the others picked up a little dirt and put it in the pot. With that dirt they vowed to bring about what they wanted to do. And the master fell ill or some harm

came to his family because while the dirt was in the pot, the master was a prisoner in there, and not even the devil could get him out. That was the Congo
people's revenge on the master.

There were taverns close to the mill. There were more taverns than ticks
in the woods. They were a kind of a small general store where you could buy
everything. The slaves themselves traded in the taverns. They sold beef jerky
that they stored up in the barracoons. During the day and sometimes even in
the evening, the slaves could go to the taverns. But that didn't happen at all
the plantations. There was always some master who wouldn't give permission
for his slaves to go. The blacks went to the taverns for rum. They drank a lot
to keep their strength. A shot of good rum cost a half-peso. The owners drank
a lot of rum, too, and I can't begin to tell you about all the to-do there was.
Some of the tavern keepers were old men retired from the Spanish army who
got a little pension, some five or six pesos.

The taverns were made of wood and *yagua* palm fronds. None of that cement you see in stores nowadays. You had to sit on piles of jute sacks, or else
stand up. In the taverns they sold rice, beef jerky, lard, and all kinds of beans.
I seen hard-case tavern owners who cheated the slaves by charging them fat
prices. I seen brawls where a black was beaten up and couldn't return to the
tavern. In booklets they noted down all the purchases, and when a slave spent a
half-peso, they put down one mark, and when he spent two, two marks. That's
how the system worked for buying everything else, the flour cookies, round
and sweet, salt biscuits, different colored sweets the size of chickpeas made
of flour, water bread, and lard. The water bread cost a half-peso a loaf. It was
different from the water bread today. I preferred that older kind. I also remember that they sold some candy called *capricho*, made of white flour, sesame
seeds, and peanuts. Sesame seeds, you know, were a Chinese thing because
their salesmen went around the plantations selling them. Those Chinese ped-
dlers were old indentured workers who couldn't lift up their arms to cut cane
any longer, so they started selling things.

The taverns were smelly. They got that strong smell from the goods hanging from the beams, sausages, hams curing, and red mortadella. Even so, it was
where you could fool around to relax. Men spent all their time in that silliness.
Black men really wanted to be good in games. I recall a game they called "the
cracker." The way that game worked was that four or five hard salt crackers
were placed on the wooden counter or any board, and the men had to hit the
crackers hard with their dicks to see who could break the crackers. The one
who broke the crackers won. That game attracted betting and drinking. Blacks
as well as whites played it.

Another pastime was the jug game. They would take a big jug with a hole in the top and stick their doohickey through it. The one who reached the bottom was the winner. The bottom was covered with a little layer of ash so that when the man took his dick out it was easy to see if he had touched bottom or not. . . .

Sundays were the noisiest days on the plantation. I don't know where the slaves found the energy. The biggest fiestas during slavery took place on that day of the week. There were plantations where the drum began at noon or at one. At Flor de Sagua it started very early. At sunrise the noise began, and the games, and the children began to spin around. The barracoon came to life in a flash. It seemed like the world would come to an end. And, even with all the work, everybody got up happy. The overseer and his assistant came into the barracoon and started fooling around with the women. I noticed that the ones who were least involved were the Chinese. Those bastards didn't have an ear for the drums. They were standoffish. It was that they thought a lot. In my opinion they thought more than the blacks. Nobody paid them any mind. And folks just went on with their dances.

The one I remember best is the *yuka*. In the yuka three drums were played: *la caja, la mula,* and the *el cachimbo,* which was the littlest. Behind the drums someone played two hollowed-out cedar trunks with two sticks. The slaves themselves made them, and I think they called them *catá.* Yuka was danced in pairs, and the movements were dramatic. Sometimes they swooped like birds, and it even seemed like they were going to fly they moved so fast. They did little jumps with their hands on their hips. Everybody sang to encourage the dancers.

There was another more complicated dance. I don't know if it was a dance or a game because the punches given out were serious. That dance was called the *maní.* The maní dancers made a circle of forty or fifty men. And they began to slap at each other. The one who got hit went out to dance. They wore ordinary work clothes and put red kerchiefs with drawings on them around their heads and waists. Those kerchiefs were used to tie up the slaves' clothes to take them to be washed. They were known as *vayajá,* or red-checkered kerchiefs. So that the licks of the maní would be the most painful kind, their wrists were charged up with any old kind of witchcraft. The women didn't dance but made a handclapping chorus. They would shout from the scare they got because sometimes a black would fall down and never get up again. The maní was a cruel game. The dancers didn't bet on the challenges. At some plantations, the masters themselves bet, but at Flor de Sagua I don't remember them doing it. What the masters did do was to prohibit the blacks from hitting each other too much because sometimes they got so beaten up they couldn't work. Boys couldn't play, but they took it all in. Take me, for example, I will never forget it.

Every time the announcing drum started up, the blacks would go down to the creek to bathe. Near every mill was a little creek. There were cases where a woman waited behind and met a man as he went into the water. Then they fooled around and began to do their business. Or, if not that, they went to the reservoirs, which were pools at the mill made to store water. They played hide and seek there, and the men chased the women to have sex with them. . . .

In the plantations there were blacks from different nations. Each one had its own traits. The Congos were dark though you also had many lighter, fair-skinned mulattoes. They were short on the whole. The Mandingos were slightly reddish colored. Tall and very strong. I swear on my mother's grave they were crooks and a bad bunch. They always went their own way. The Gangas were good folks. Short and freckle faced. Many were *cimarrones*. The Carabalís were fierce like the Musungo Congos. They didn't kill pigs except on Sundays and the days of Easter. They were very good at business. They ended up killing pigs to sell, and they didn't even eat them. Because of that a song was made for them that went: "Carabalí very needy, kills a pig every Sunday." I got to know all these newly arrived Africans better after slavery ended.

At all the plantations there was an infirmary near the barracoons. It was a large wooden house where they took the pregnant women. Children were born there and stayed until they were six or seven years old, when they went to live in the barracoons to work like everyone else. I remember that there were some black nannies who took care of the little slave children and gave them food. When someone was hurt in the field or got sick, those black women would doctor him. With herbs and potions they cured everything. There was no need to worry. Sometimes the little *criollitos* wouldn't see their parents again because the master was the owner, and he could send them to another plantation. Then the nannies certainly would have to do everything. But who was going to worry about a child that wasn't even her own! In that same infirmary they stripped and bathed the children. The breed stock children cost some five hundred pesos. The thing about the breed stock children was that they were born of strong, tall blacks. Tall blacks were privileged. The masters kept an eye out for them to mate them with big healthy black women.

After they were together in a separate room in the barracoon, they were obliged to have sex, and the woman had to bear good babies every year. I tell you it was like breeding animals. Well, if the woman didn't bear the way they liked, they separated them and put her out in the field again to work. The women who weren't like little rabbits were sunk because they had to go back to breaking their backs. Then they could choose a husband at will. There were cases where a woman was after a man, and she herself had twenty women behind her. The witches tried to resolve those matters with powerful magic.

If a man went to a witch to ask for help getting a woman, the witch sent him to get some of the woman's tobacco if she smoked. You ground up the tobacco and a bottle fly, those green, stinging ones, enough to make a powder which you gave to the woman in water. That's how the woman was seduced.

Another treatment was taking the heart of a hummingbird and grinding it into powder. You put it in the woman's tobacco. And if you wanted to make fun of them, all you had to do was send off to the store for barley. Any woman would die of shame on account of that barley because a man would put a little where she was going to sit down, and no sooner than it touched her behind, the woman would begin to break wind. That was a sight to see — those women farting with their faces all powdered up.

The old blacks entertained themselves with that kind of nonsense. When they were over sixty, they stopped working in the fields. Though, truly, they never knew their real age. But it happened that if a black man got tired and set himself apart, then the overseers said he was ready to be a doorman. Then they put that old man at the gates of the barracoon or at the pigsty, where the big litters were produced. Or, if not that, he helped the women in the kitchen. Some of them had their conucos, and they spent their time gardening. Doing those jobs gave them time for their witchcraft. They weren't punished or paid much attention to. But they had to be quiet and obedient. That's for sure.

TRANSLATED BY NICK HILL

Fleeing Slavery

Miguel Barnet, Pedro Deschamps Chapeaux, Rafael García, and Rafael Duharte

Resistance and rebellion were inherent elements in every slave society. Slave resistance ranged from "informal" or "everyday" attempts to maintain one's culture and dignity without overtly challenging the social system, to escape, and, at times, to outright rebellion. In a round-table discussion among Cuban researchers published in the Santiago-based journal Del Caribe, *historian Pedro Deschamps Chapeaux (b. 1913) discusses escape as a form of resistance. Some slaves escaped on their own, and survived in the wilderness; others formed communities called palenques in areas outside of Spanish control.*

Pedro Deschamps Chapeaux (Researcher, Havana): Running away was a constant objective in the life of a man held in servile status. From the beginning of the slave regime in Cuba, and starting with the forced arrival on the island of the first enslaved Africans, the Spanish colonizers recorded in their chronicles the frequent escapes by their slaves. In many cases, the slaves joined with the indigenous inhabitants to create situations such that, according to one chronicler, "nobody dared to walk on the land."

The palenque, or runaway-slave community, grew out of these escapes. At first running away was an individual affair, but over the course of time, as the numbers of those enslaved grew, slaves began to escape in groups. Even though we cannot determine the date that these palenques were first established, we do know that for over three hundred years, during almost the entire slave period, the palenque was a bulwark of resistance where Africans of different ethnicities, languages, and cultures joined together under the common ideal of freedom. They were situated in the most inaccessible regions of the island and, as Germán de Granda writes in his work on maroons, palenques were "collective examples of resistance to slave society and its Euro-American culture." . . .

The history of maroons on our Island begins in the first decades of the colony or, to be more exact, in 1533. Several fugitive blacks were captured by the colonial forces raised to pursue them in Jobabo, in the east of the country. They were taken to Bayamo and executed, quartered, and their heads placed in the public plaza to serve as a lesson to others.

From then on, rebel slaves maintained their protest against servile status. No punishment — not the whip, the stocks, or shackles — could hold back this permanent struggle for freedom, in which individual escape was the most frequent method. On other occasions, the slaves who worked on the plantations near Havana made common cause with the corsairs and pirates who attacked the city, and joined in the sacking of the churches and the residences of the slave-owners. This occurred in 1538, when Havana was attacked by French corsairs. On that date, if we can engage in some historical speculation, we believe that a new type of *cimarrón* emerged: the maritime cimarrón, who found freedom by taking to the sea. How many of these slaves, after sampling piracy, would go back voluntarily to their masters? Surely none.

Historians, in examining Cuban slavery — a topic which deserves further attention — have always referred to the rural cimarrón, that is, to the slave working in the sugar mill, coffee plantation, cattle farm, or any kind of plantation. These slaves could take advantage of their proximity to the wilderness and flee, seeking refuge in the caves and hills near their former place of forced residence, giving birth to the palenque. Over the years this phenomenon would repeat itself all over the Island, in the west as well as in the rugged eastern zone.

Historians have forgotten what we call the urban cimarrón, that is, the slave who worked in domestic service and who escaped from his master's home to outside the city walls, in the neighborhoods beyond the walled center. These neighborhoods became an immense palenque, nourished by ethnic solidarity, where the fugitive could evade the city police. In the same way, many historians have ignored the important role played by female runaways in the palenques and in the rebellions.

In the western zone, known then as Vueltabajo, there were some twenty-five palenques between 1802 and 1857, mainly in San Diego de Núñez, San Marcos, and Lomas del Cuzco. In the eastern region there were some twenty-seven palenques between 1808 and 1864, among which those named El Frijol, Bumba, Maluala, and others stand out. The so-called Gran Palenque del Frijol was the most important one. In it lived some four hundred cimarrones, men, women and children, in approximately two hundred huts.

The total number of palenques on the island between 1802 and 1864 was seventy-nine, some of which survived until the Ten Years' War. They managed to elude the famous Royal Cavalry Lancers Regiment [Regimiento de

Caballería Lanceros del Rey] and the slave-hunting parties such as those commanded by Francisco Estévez, the Riverones, Domingo Armona, and others.

It is worth mentioning here that on 14 May 1870—right in the middle of the Ten Years' War—the newspaper *Gaceta de la Habana* reported that on his last expedition Lieutenant Colonel Cubas had discovered a kind of palenque: "In the middle of a thick forest they had taken over some two *caballerías* of land with huts, cultivations, and wells, and living like in primitive times. Their clothing is also primitive. Two narrow and torturous paths lead into this palenque. The settlement is so well-hidden that one could pass by many times without suspecting the presence of a living soul." . . .

To these urban and rural cimarrones we should also add the seafaring cimarrón, who allows us to appreciate the lengths to which the slaves' audacity went in their struggle for freedom. On many occasions, dockworkers or domestic slaves living near the ports sought refuge on merchant fleets, perhaps with the complicity of black sailors on the British ships who, out of solidarity or for some material benefit, would facilitate the slave's flight, turning him into a maritime cimarrón.

This type of escape was frequent enough for it to be included in the Police Ordinances [Las Ordenanzas de Comisarios] of 1769, published in Havana on 28 January 1799. The order punished anybody who aided the escape of slaves by sea.

Article 97 of the Ordinances states: "Given that it is a very frequent occurrence for slaves to escape on ships that dock at this Island's ports, I order that a fine of ten pesos will be imposed on any ship on which an escaped slave is apprehended, divided in thirds among the person who reports the crime, the apprehender, and the *cámara*. The above does not preclude the imposition of legal punishments against those who hide the slaves and their helpers."

The frequency with which slaves fled from the Island's ports reveals that these escapes were as important as those that occurred daily on the plantations or in the towns.

Among those whom we call "seafaring cimarrones," the case of the Havana mulatto Diego Grillo stands out. He attained notoriety as a pirate in the ranks of the Dutch pirate Cornelio Jol, alias Pata de Palo, who made him an officer in his forces. A few years later, Grillo was known as Captain Dieguillo, a pirate and slave trafficker along the coasts of Central America. This may be the only case of a cimarrón pirate who achieved the rank of captain. Historian Antonio Núñez Jiménez, in his book *Isla de Pinos*, writes, "Diego Grillo occupies a special place among the corsairs and pirates who passed through what is today called the Isle of Youth . . . [and he was] the most famous and intrepid of all Cuban pirates of all times."

TRANSLATED BY AVIVA CHOMSKY

For complete references and notes, consult the work as cited in the acknowledgment of copyrights section.

Santiago de Cuba's Fugitive Slaves

Rafael Duharte

Prior to the late nineteenth century, Cuba's sugar plantation system was based mainly in western Cuba. This meant that eastern Cuba contained a smaller but more hetero-geneous population, including many free blacks. When the sugar economy expanded into eastern Cuba in the twentieth century, black migrants from other parts of Cuba as well as from elsewhere in the Caribbean combined to give eastern Cuba much more of an Afro-Caribbean identity than the western portions of the island. The largest city in eastern Cuba, Santiago de Cuba, has continued to be a center of Afro-Caribbean culture and research, especially through the Casa del Caribe (a research and cultural institute that focuses on Cuba's Caribbean context) there. Rafael Duharte (b. 1947), a historian at the Casa del Caribe, documents the paths taken by runaway slaves in the city of Santiago in the nineteenth century and shows the diversity of the urban environment there.

The remarkable urban development of Santiago de Cuba in the middle of the nineteenth century, along with the presence of a significant population of free blacks and mulattoes, provoked widespread slave flight in the city.

Free people of color comprised a significant proportion of Santiago's population from the first decades of the nineteenth century. According to Emilio Bacardí, the 1808 census of the city showed the following results: 8,146 whites; 5,726 free mulattoes; 3,500 free blacks; 748 mulatto slaves; and 8,309 black slaves. As we can see, if we combine free blacks and free mulattoes, they outnumber whites in the city. In addition, we must add — according to the same source — the presence of 1,891 free mulattoes and 450 free blacks who had come from war-torn Haiti.

The intricate alleys of Santiago in the nineteenth century were the scene of the slave rebellions that shook the city. By the middle of the nineteenth century rural and urban slave escapes were so common that the newspaper *El Redactor* maintained a regular column entitled "Escaped Slaves." In this column, masters would announce the escapes of slaves, sometimes offering a reward in addition

Characteristic street scene. Maturin M. Ballou, *History of Cuba, or Notes of a Traveller in the Tropics* (Boston, 1854) opposite 201.

to payment for their capture and, invariably, threatening to sue anybody who hid them for damages.

A careful study of this section of *El Redactor* provides a window into this world of rebellion. The central figure in this drama was the urban slave, that is, the slave who worked for a master in the city as a domestic or in some urban trade and who, taking advantage of a favorable situation or when faced with the threat of being sent to a coffee or sugar plantation, decided to escape. In these cases, the rebel would usually change neighborhoods and, blending in with the population of free blacks and mulattoes, would succeed in passing for one of them.

In the innumerable announcements in the "Escaped Slaves" column we see clearly the presence of these urban *cimarrones* in the neighborhoods of Santiago. The escaped slaves generally dressed immaculately and resorted to numerous subterfuges to "pass for free." Let us examine a few examples [from the 1840s and 1850s]:

> Since the sixth of this month, the black Tomás, a cattleman, has been missing from his master's house. He is thin, tall rather than short, of very black color, he is missing one of his upper teeth, he is very insolent, and *he passes for free on some occasions by dressing himself very well, he has been known to work as a sailor or in factories*. Reply to 43 San Gerónimo. The person who brings

him back will be amply rewarded, while anybody discovered hiding him will be equally prosecuted by the law.

On the sixth of this month, the black woman Guadalupe escaped from 51 San Pedro Street, where she was the slave of D. Cipriano Casamadrid; she is wearing a *túnico de cuarto* [a long tunic or robe], she is bald, and *she may be roaming the streets selling with a tray of fruits and other items*. Whoever turns her in to this house will be compensated, and anybody hiding her will be prosecuted in accordance with the law.

The black named Isaac has been missing from his house for six days. He works as a tobacco worker [*tabaquero*], he is short, a Mandinga [Mandingo speaker from West Africa], *he may be in the neighborhood of Tiboli where the new church is*. Anybody returning him to his owner, D. Ramón C. Arango, will be rewarded in addition to being paid for his capture, while anybody hiding him will be held responsible for damages.

The black José Francisco (alias Pañuelito) has been sleeping away from his house. He is a tobacco worker, average height, aquiline face, *he is probably in the neighborhoods of Santa Ana and Guayabito*. The person who shelters him will be held responsible. Anybody who returns him to 60 San Tadeo Street will be rewarded.

Since the eleventh of this month, my slave José has been an escapee from my house. He is a creole, from twenty-five to twenty-eight years old, and he speaks French as well as Spanish. He is of normal size and sturdy, round faced and smooth faced. He works as a bricklayer and a cook. He has continually been employed, without permission, to work as a cook on the ships in this port. He usually hangs around the *port neighborhoods working in the warehouses and other public places around Tibolí, and I have been informed that he has rented a room to sleep in* without having permission to do any of this, nor to walk the streets. The person who apprehends him, in addition to his capture, will be rewarded, while he who shelters or hides him will be responsible for damages.

In these cases, it is clear that the escaped slaves have not fled to the *palenques* infesting the mountains around Santiago, but rather that they "passed" as free persons inside the city, and sometimes worked at trades that they had surely learned as slaves. Thus, we find Tomás working in factories in the port zone, or Guadalupe walking through the streets selling fruit and other items from a tray.

Sometimes, a piece of information offered by the slaveholder allows us to infer that he is referring to an urban slave. This is the case with the *china* of "advanced age" who escaped from 171 Enramadas St.:

> Three days ago a china of advanced age escaped from her master's house. She is of average height, a creole from Maracaibo with a large behind; she belonged to the administrator. Whoever returns her to 171 Enramada St. will be rewarded, while whoever is caught hiding here will be prosecuted under the law.

The fact that this china from Maracaibo was of advanced age absolutely precludes the possibility that she fled to the Sierra, where hunger, sickness, and the slave hunters made the lives of escaped slaves extremely difficult.

Sometimes the urban cimarrón resorted to different means to escape pursuit by the colonial authorities or the slave hunters seeking the rewards promised by the newspaper. In many cases, a false license or an expired paper from the master to seek another owner allowed a slave to live clandestinely in the city. If the master suspects that the slave has such documents, he invariably mentions this in his newspaper announcement in order to facilitate the slave's capture.

> The black Margarita has been missing from the house of D. Senón Boudet for fifteen days. *She carries no license, or a false license.* Anybody sheltering her in their house will pay for damages, while anybody who returns her to 2 Santo Tomás will be amply rewarded.

> Since Saturday the 6th of this month the black Nicholasa has been hiding. She is about thirty-two years old and is thin, short, dressed in Prussian blue, *she carries a license to seek an owner, which is expired.* Whoever presents her to 18 San Félix St. will be rewarded, while anybody hiding her will be prosecuted.

> The black Benito (alias Baracoa), who belonged to D. Domingo Sánchez and then to Lieutenant D. Isidro Prieto, has escaped. He is a tobacco worker, tall, good looking, dressed in a white shirt, pants, and shoes, and a hat of *yarey* [a plant of the palm family used for weaving hats]. He claims that he works in this city, he will show a license that he has, stamped by the police officer D. Cayetano Martínez, which only allows him to travel to the Arroyón tobacconist's. Anybody who informs me of his whereabouts, or who returns him to 51 San Félix will be rewarded, while anybody hiding him will be held responsible.

On some occasions, escaped slaves managed to get outside the limits of the city and hide in the towns surrounding Santiago. There it was easier to pass themselves off as free. This is what the slave Eduardo did. He was detained by the district lieutenant in the neighboring area of Brazo del Cauto carrying a false identification card. He was then returned to the Santiago Headquarters, as this document explains:

> I am sending a mulatto prisoner to this Headquarters. He is about twenty-one years old and has been passing for free according to a card that he carries. His name is Eduardo and the card he carries is that of Gumersindo Sosa. He has confessed to being the slave of Don Tomás . . . who lives on Enramadas Street at the corner of Gallo. I have the honor of reporting this and returning the said card along with the mulatto who says his name is Eduardo.

Most of these cimarrones were urban slaves, that is, slaves who had carried out tasks for their masters in the city. This explains why they remained in the city, for they were perfectly familiar with it and they had friends there. For these slaves, fleeing to the countryside would mean confronting an uncertain life in an atmosphere that was completely foreign to them. . . .

The preference of the slave for the urban environment in [some] cases could be a result of their partial knowledge of the city, if they had traveled there with their masters, or if they had been sent there by their masters to carry out errands. Nevertheless, it is unquestionable that the traumas experienced by the urban slaves were not comparable to the terrible existence awaiting runaways in the mountains. Many escaped slaves would certainly have preferred to hide in urban areas. In addition, the presence of many slaves in the city of Santiago—rented, or self-employed—who were under a less strict control than that imposed on the slaves on the sugar plantations, contributed to increasing the runaway phenomenon in the city.

TRANSLATED BY AVIVA CHOMSKY

For complete references and notes, consult the work as cited in the acknowledgment of copyrights section.

Rumba

Yvonne Daniel

With the growth of the population of the African born in the nineteenth century, many African cultural forms were re-created in the new Cuban context. Cuban rumba music had its origins among both free blacks and slaves in the middle of the nineteenth century. Dancer-anthropologist Yvonne Daniel has done an intensive study of the history of the rumba, sometimes identified as Cuba's national dance.

The Spanish words *rumba* and *rumbón* refer to a collective festive event, a gala meal, a carousal, or a high time. They are synonymous with some Bantu and other West Central African words used in Cuba, such as *tumba, marumba*, and *tambo*, meaning a social, secular gathering with music and dancing. Fernando Ortiz, the major scholar of Afro-Cuban folkloric traditions, defines *rumba* as a dance of Cuban origin with African antecedents and lists other derivatives that mean "to gather and dance" or "to have a party," e.g., *rumbanchear, cumbanchar*. Argeliers León and Olavo Alén, Cuban musicologists who have studied the music and dance of these events, agree that the precise meaning of *rumba* is difficult to determine, but it is found within those words of African origin that point to a collective party, unrelated to religious ritual.

Rumba developed during the 1850s and 1860s in places where free blacks gathered to communicate their feelings or comment on their struggles and where enslaved Africans were permitted to congregate after work. Particularly with the abolition of slavery in Cuba after 1886, *los negros humildes*, poor Afro-Cubans, moved to urban areas and joined poor white Cubans looking for jobs, which were more plentiful near the ports than in rural areas. Both light- and dark-skinned groups adjusted to the particular conditions of free women and men in a society based on color and class and participated together from time to time in communal gatherings such as rumba. This was the Rumba event, spontaneous, "real" rumba. . . . (For clarity, I refer to the Rumba event with uppercase *R* and to the dances and music with lowercase *r*.)

Rumba is also the name of a dance, a rhythm, and a group of related dances, together called the rumba complex, which evolved in the nineteenth century. . . . Types within the rumba dance complex were transported from Cuba through much of the world, to Spain in the nineteenth century, to the United States in the 1920s and 1930s, to Africa in the 1940s and 1950s. Related dances are found in other Caribbean and Latin American settings, but they are not part of the rumba complex of Cuba, though they share similar ambiences and movement patterns: the chase of the female or the bumping of a dancing couple, for example, as found to some extent in the samba of Brazil, *malambo* of Peru, *zembra* of Argentina, *porro* of Colombia, *cumbia* of Puerto Rico, and *bandamban* of Suriname.

Rumba was and is associated with African communities in the Americas; however, in its most commercial form it has also been associated with whites and a style of ballroom dancing called rhumba or *rumba de salon*. While both dance variations use traditional rumba rhythms, the popularized ballroom style does not resemble the original Cuban dance, sometimes contrasted as *rumba del campo*, or rumba from the countryside. Rumba dancing flourished in urban and rural areas where Cuban workers of all colors and from many occupations rendezvoused and shared their creole heritage in music and dance.

According to Ortiz and Rogelio Martínez-Furé, the current authority on Cuban dance traditions, rumba may have begun as remembered fragments of songs and steps from Africa among the Ganga or Kisi people in Cuba, generalized ethnic groups of West Central Africa. Jahn suggests that the dance came from the Sara peoples of northern Nigeria, who sometimes dance with rows of boys in front of rows of girls, getting closer and closer until they touch and then separate from one another. In present-day Zaire there seems to be a history of similar dances; an old traditional BaKongo dance called *vane samba* seems to relate directly to rumba's antecedents. In this dance, men and women dance in a circle with cloth strips attached to waistbands around raffia skirts. As the performer kicks and throws his or her legs, the cloth is thrown up in the air and toward a member of the opposite sex. The cloth is intended to touch a person and in this way to ask the person to dance in the circle. The last person chosen stays in the circle to choose the next performer by throwing or "giving" the cloth again.

The antecedent dances that most closely relate to rumba in Cuba are of West Central African or Kongo-Angolan origin — from what today comprises Zaire, Angola, and the Congo — and are called *yuka* and *makula*. Cubans refer to them as Congolese or Bantu dances. A characteristic feature occurs when the bodies of a dancing pair meet or almost meet at the navel, a movement that relates directly to rumba's *vacunao*. From the musical perspective, there are

Náñigo, prankster, member of an Afro-Cuban secret society. From Paquette, *Sugar Is Made with Blood*, following 46. Reprinted by permission of Wesleyan University Press.

additional connections between Kongolese traits and Cuban rumba. For example, drummers characteristically use wrist shakers in both yuka and rumba, particularly when boxes are played as drums.

It is believed that rumba grew out of the social circumstances of Havana, the capital city. Havana was the center for large numbers of enslaved Africans by the end of the eighteenth century, and slave barracks became focal points of anguish and protest. Rebellion was difficult and dangerous, but protest in a disguised form was often expressed in recreational music and dance. These recreational events occurred at prescribed times or on predetermined occasions during the era of slavery. In fact, throughout the Caribbean and plantation America, enslaved peoples often imitated and satirized elite society in dance and music for personal recreation.

With the end of slavery, poor black workers continued to lament their meager opportunities and depressing conditions and expressed their frustrations, as well as their joys, through dance and music. *Solares*, the large houses that were divided into crowded living quarters and where poor Cubans were forced to live, served also as meeting places to relax, play, and dream in song, dance, and poetry. These solares offered spatial solace as they distanced poor blacks from continuous racial prejudice and the unjust realities of political impotence.

Martínez-Furé says that rumba came from the solares and was "a vehicle of liberation and protest." From the solares, Afro-Cubans expressed their personal successes or failures in love relations, satirized government practices, and gradually fashioned the dance/music complex called rumba. Poor Cubans, both dark- and light-skinned, created a music and dance of their own, neither totally African nor totally Spanish, that utilized singing, drumming, and dancing in specific configurations and within specific rules.

Different types evolved depending on the circumstances of particular locales. One type, which developed in the urban areas of Havana and Matanzas provinces (there is much debate on exactly where), involved couple dancing. Another type, a male solo form, was produced in rural areas; it may have reflected the huge imbalance between males and females during the slave trade. In the rural areas of Matanzas Province, especially near sugar mills, large African populations congregated both during and after slavery. The male solo type of rumba may be the result of the influence of the Carabalí (southeastern Nigerian male secret societies), which brought a tradition of male dancing to Cuba. Or the solo rumba may be part of the continuum of competitive male dances from Africa.

The rumba complex spread slowly throughout and beyond the country. Almost seventy years after its supposed beginnings in Cuba, rumba was taken

Street Celebration on Día de los Reyes (Three Kings' Day), held on 6 January. Cabildos, Afro-Cuban brotherhoods marched in streets under tribal banners. Paquette, *Sugar Is Made with Blood*, following 46. Reprinted by permission of Wesleyan University Press.

to a trade fair in Seville, Spain. At the Chicago World's Fair in 1933–34, rumba gained its first recorded performance outside Cuba. Rumba, along with other Latin American dances, gained great popularity in the United States and Europe in the 1930s. Latin dance surfaced again in the international popular dance fads of the 1950s, and again in the 1970s and early 1980s.

In 1934 a movie called *Rumba*, starring George Raft, joined a series of feature films highlighting music and dance of Cuban origin as well as Raft's dancing ability. Filmed dance extravaganzas were created as part of the burgeoning U.S. interest in "exotic" dance, and Katherine Dunham's all-black dance company was commissioned to perform in a general Caribbean style, including rumba. The filmed dances were often variations on the original or traditional Cuban rumba.

For complete references and notes, consult the work as cited in the acknowledgment of copyrights section.

The Trade in Chinese Laborers

Richard Dana

As the slave trade was abolished under British pressure and the demise of African slavery began to appear inevitable, Caribbean sugar planters desperately sought new sources of cheap labor. In the nineteenth century, slaves were imported from the Yucatán Peninsula in Mexico; later planters brought in Chinese indentured laborers. Conditions were harsh. One Cuban historian calculated that the suicide rate among the Chinese "coolies" was some five hundred per one hundred thousand.[1] A contemporary observer (1815–1882) describes the importation and marketing of the Chinese in the next selection.

Yesterday I drove out to the Cerro, to see the coolie jail, or market, where the imported coolies are kept for sale. It is a well-known place, and open to all visitors. The building has a fair-looking front; and through this I enter, past two porters, into an open yard in the rear, where, on the gravel ground, are squatting a double line of coolies, with heads shaved, except a tuft on the crown, dressed in loose Chinese garments of blue and yellow. The dealer, who is a calm, shrewd, heartless-looking man, speaking English as well as if it were his native tongue, comes out with me, calls to the coolies, and they all stand up in a double line, facing inward, and we pass through them, preceded by a driver armed with the usual badge of the plantation driver, the short, limber whip. The dealer does not hesitate to tell me the terms on which the contracts are made, as the trade is not illegal. His account is this—The importer receives 340 dollars for each coolie, and the purchaser agrees to pay the coolie four dollars per month, and to give him food, and two suits of clothes a year. For this, he has his services for eight years. The contract is reduced to writing before a magistrate, and two originals are made, one kept by the coolie and one by the purchaser, and each in Chinese and Spanish.

This was a strange and striking exhibition of power. Two or three white men, bringing hundreds of Chinese thousands of miles, to a new climate and people, holding them as prisoners, selling their services to masters having an

Asian street peddler. Samuel Hazard, *Cuba with Pen and Pencil* (Hartford, Conn.: Hartford Publishing Company, 1871), 166; reprinted in Joan Casanovas, *Bread, or Bullets! Urban Labor and Spanish Colonialism in Cuba, 1850–1898* (Pittsburgh: University of Pittsburgh Press, 1998), 34.

unknown tongue and an unknown religion, to work at unknown trades, for inscrutable purposes!

The coolies did not look unhealthy, though some had complaints of the eyes; yet they looked, or I fancied they looked, some of them, unhappy, and some of them stolid. One I am sure had the leprosy although the dealer would not admit it. The dealer did not deny their tendency to suicide, and the danger of attempting to chastise them, but alleged their great superiority to the Negro in intelligence, and contended that their condition was good, and better than in China, having four dollars a month, and being free at the end of eight years. He said, which I found to be true, that after being separated and employed in work, they let their hair grow, and adopt the habits and dress of the country. The newly arrived coolies wear tufts, and blue and yellow, loose, Chinese clothes. Those who have been here long are distinguishable from the whites only by the peculiar tinge of the cheek, and the form of the eye. The only respect in which his account differed from what I heard elsewhere was in the amount the importer receives, which has always been stated to me at four hundred dollars. While I am talking with him, a gentleman comes and passes down the line. He is probably a purchaser, I judge; and I leave my informant to follow what is more for his interest than talking with me.

The importation has not yet existed eight years. So the question, what will become of these men, exotics, without women or children, taking no root in

Asian cigarette maker, Havana. Hazard, *Cuba with Pen and Pencil*, 149; reprinted in Casanovas, *Bread, or Bullets!*, 36.

the land, has not come to a solution. The constant question is — will they remain and mix with the other races? Will they be permitted to remain? Will they be able to go back? In 1853, they were not noticed in the census; and in 1857, hardly noticed. The number imported may, to some extent, be obtained from the records and files of the *aduana*, but not so as to be relied upon. I heard the number estimated at two hundred thousand by intelligent and well-informed Cubans. Others put it as low as sixty thousand. Certain it is that coolies are to be met with everywhere, in town and country.

So far as I can learn, there is no law in China regulating the contracts and shipment of Chinese coolies, and none in Cuba regulating their transportation, landing, or treatment while here. The trade has grown up and been permitted and recognized, but not regulated. It is yet to be determined how far the contract is enforceable against either party. Those coolies that are taken from the British East Indies to British islands are taken under contracts, with regulations, as to their exportation and return, understood and enforced. Not so the Chinese coolies. Their importers are *lege soluti* [operating outside the law]. Some say the government will insist on their being returned. But the prevailing impression is that they will be brought in debt, and bound over again for their debts, or in some other way secured to a lifelong servitude.

Mr. —, a very wealthy and intelligent planter, tells me he is to go over to Regla, tomorrow morning, to see a lot of slaves offered for sale to him, and asks me if I have ever seen a sale of slaves. I never have seen that sight, and accept his invitation. We are to leave here at half-past six, or seven, at the latest. All work is early here; I believe I have mentioned that the hour of 'Change for merchants is 7:30 A.M.

Note

1. Juan Pérez de la Riva, "Demografía de los culíes chinos en Cuba (1853–74)," *Revista de la Biblioteca Nacional "José Marti,"* no. 4 (1966).

Life on a Coffee Plantation

John G. F. Wurdemann

*Despite the importance of sugar in colonial Cuban society, many of the island's in-
habitants had lived outside of the direct reach of the sugar plantation. In his Notes on
Cuba, physician John G. F. Wurdemann (1810–1849) contrasts the industrial character
of the sugar plantation with the more idyllic pastoral view of a coffee plantation.*

On the San Patricio coffee estate, by one of the alleys through which I passed,
stood a small stone building, smoothly plastered, with a flight of steps leading
to its entrance; but it was roofless, and shrubs were springing from its floor
and portico, while the door and windows had long since been removed. This
had once been the study of Maria del Occidente, where she composed that
most fanciful of English poems, "Zophiel"; but deserted and ruinous as it was,
in the midst of an unlettered people, it still seemed, from the recollections that
hovered about it, like an oasis in the desert.

An English critic has expressed his surprise that such a poem could be composed on a Cuba coffee plantation. Why! it is by a quadruple alley of palms,
cocoas, and oranges, interspersed with the tamarind, the pomegranate, the
mango, and the rose apple, with a background of coffee and plantains covering every portion of the soil with their luxuriant verdure. I have often passed
by it in the still hour of night, when the moon was shining brightly, and the
leaves of the cocoa and palm threw fringe-like shadows on the walls and floor,
and the elfin lamps of the cocullos swept through the windows and door, casting their lurid, mysterious light on every object; while the air was laden with
mingled perfume from the coffee, and orange, and the tube rose, and night-
blooming cereus; and I have thought that no fitter birthplace could be found
for the images she has created. A coffee estate is indeed a perfect garden, sur-
passing in beauty aught that the bleak climate of England can produce.

Imagine more than three hundred acres of land planted in regular squares
with evenly pruned shrubs, each containing about eight acres, intersected
by broad alleys of palms, oranges, mangoes, and other beautiful trees; the
interstices between which are planted with lemons, pomegranates, cape jessa-

mines, tube roses, lilies, and various other gaudy and fragrant flowers; while a double strip of guinea grass, or of luscious pines, skirt the sides, presenting a pretty contrast to the smooth red soil in the center, scrupulously kept free from all verdure. Then the beauty of the whole while in flower. That of the coffee, white, and so abundant, that the fields seem covered by flakes of snow; the fringe-like blossoms of the rose apple; the red of the pomegranate and Mexican rose; the large scarlet flowers of the piñon, which, when in bloom, covering the whole tree with a flaming coat, is the richest of Flora's realm; the quaint *lirio's* trumpet-shaped flowers painted yellow and red, and bursting in bunches from the blunt extremities of each leafless branch; the young pineapples with blue flowerets projecting from the centers of their squares; the white tube roses, and double cape jessamines; the gaudy yellow flag, and a score of other flowers known to us only by the sickly tenants of the hothouse.

And when some of the flowers have given place to the ripened fruit; and the golden orange, the yellow mango, the lime, the lemon, the luscious *caimito* [a sweet fruit native to the West Indies], and sugared *zapote* [a sweet fruit that grows in the Caribbean and Central America]; the mellow alligator pear, the custard apple, and the rose apple, giving to the palate the flavor of otto of roses—when all these hang on the trees in oppressive abundance, and the ground is also covered with the overripe, the owner of a coffee estate might safely challenge the world for a fairer garden. Nor must this be thought the appearance it presents for only a short period. The coffee has successive crops of blossoms five or six times in the winter and spring; and on the orange, the ripe fruit and the blossom, and the young green fruit, are often seen at the same time; while several of the shrubs and plants bloom nearly all the year.

The coffee tree, however, merits a special notice. Passing from Ethiopia through Persia to Arabia, it reached the West Indies through Europe. Van Horn, in 1690, then governor of Batavia, having raised it in Java from seeds procured in Mocha, sent one plant to Nicholas Witsen, a burgomaster in Amsterdam, who placing it in the botanical garden of that city, other plants were propagated from its seeds, and were sent to the West Indies. In 1718 coffee plantations were first made in Surinam[e], and about 1728 by the French in Martinico [Martinique], at which time it was also introduced into Jamaica. When the French were driven from Santo Domingo, they brought with them into Cuba the cultivation of this plant, and estates from that period multiplied rapidly on the island.

The tree, if left to nature, attains a height of twelve or eighteen feet in the nurseries, and gives off horizontal branches knotted at every joint, which like the trunk are covered with a gray bark. The blossoms look like the white jasmine, and form thick, circular clusters around the branches; they appear from

December to June, and last only two or three days. The berries at first are green, but as they increase in size and ripen become white, then yellow, and finally bright red, closely resembling the cherry in size and appearance. The trees are often loaded with them in closely wedged circles around each joint of the branches; I have counted as many as ninety cherries on a single one two feet long. Each cherry contains two berries applied with their flat sides together, having a sweet, soft, mucilaginous pulp between them and the pellicle.

The nursery is made by cleaning away the undergrowth of a wood, leaving the high trees to protect the young plants by their shade. The cherries are here sown, and the young plants, when from one to four years old, are transplanted to the squares about six feet apart, each square containing ten thousand trees. They are cut off about two inches from the ground; from which point a new shoot springs and forms the future tree, that bears the third year. They are then kept pruned to the height of five feet, and are yearly trimmed of all their dead branches. Amid the shrubs rows of plantains are formed eighteen feet apart, and corn freely sown wherever the foliage permits the sun's rays to reach the ground; so that a coffee square produces also a crop of these two valuable bread stuffs.

The cherries ripen from August to December, and are all gathered singly by the hand; and as three or four different crops are often ripening at the same time on each tree, as many separate pickings are required. Brought in baskets from the fields, they are daily exposed to the sun on the *secaderos*, but are each night raked together in heaps, and covered by tents of rice straw to protect them from the heavy dews; after three weeks they become quite dried and are then fit for the mill. The secaderos often cover a large surface of the *batey*, or yard, an estate of four hundred thousand trees having twenty-five, each sixty feet long and fifty feet wide. They are made of stones plastered smoothly over with cement, with raised edges; through which openings, guarded by comb-like gates, permit the rainwater to escape and stop the berries. Sometimes, between the secaderos, plastered gutters are constructed to convey the water into a general reservoir; which is highly useful in a country, where every pailful of that necessary fluid has often to be raised from a well two or three hundred feet deep.

The storehouse is generally about one hundred feet long, fifty feet wide, and twenty feet high to the eaves of a high pitched roof. Within this large building is also the coffee mill, consisting of a large circular wooden trough two feet deep and in width tapering from two at the top to one foot at the bottom. A heavy, solid, wooden wheel plays in it, about six feet in diameter, and eight inches in thickness at its circumference, increasing to two feet at its center. The berries are thus permitted to roll between it and the sides of the trough, which is kept well supplied to prevent their being crushed by the wheel, which cleanses them chiefly by pressing them forcibly against each other. The shaft is fixed at one extremity by a ring to a central post, and to the other the horse or ox is attached. The dried cherries, conveyed through a funnel from the storeroom above, fall into the central space, whence they are thrown into the trough; from which, also, those already crushed are withdrawn, and sent into the cleansing room. Here they are put into a fanning mill, which not only separates the husk from the berries, but divides the latter into two sizes, the largest rolling over a wire sieve into another room, while the smaller grains with the pebbles fall through it on the floor. The latter are then spread in heaps on long tables, around which the Negroes are seated, and the broken and distorted grains are separated and set apart for the use of the planter. For this very quality, rejected by us and called *triage*, consists chiefly of the round small grains produced by old trees, and possesses the finest flavor. It is kept from year to year, and when old is equal to the best mocha coffee.

It is now fit for market, and is packed in bags of Manila hemp, the only material that can resist the force produced by the swellings of the grain from the absorption of the atmospheric moisture. Some pass the coffee a second time through the fanning mill, which polishes it. A few, before submitting it to this process, mingle it with husks that have been parched by fire; thus painting each grain a dark green, but this deception is readily detected by rubbing them on a white handkerchief. The grinding continues through December, and by the end of January the whole crop is generally sent to market.

The coffee tree has many enemies to contend with. A small worm sometimes destroys the tree by girdling it below the bark; another bores into the trunk, traversing it in every direction, and it falls by the first high wind. Two species of moths, one bluish white, the other brown, prey on the edges of the leaf; but the most destructive of all is a small fly which deposits its egg on the leaf, the caterpillar from which destroys all but the veins, leaving a lacework foliage. Young trees, by having all their leaves thus destroyed, frequently die, and the old ones are often thus stripped completely.

Besides coffee, the cultivator plants his grounds largely in maize and plantains, which he sells to sugar estates; and yams, yuca,[1] sweet potatoes, and rice, which yields well on the uplands, for his own consumption. A few acres of sugarcane and guinea grass are also grown for the cattle during the long drought of winter, when all the *portreros* [pastures] are void of herbage. He does not amass as large a fortune as the sugar planter, but he witnesses no overtasked labor of his slaves. Well fed, with sufficient time allowed them for rest and the care of their own live stock of fowls and hogs, compared to the destitute of even our northern states, they are happier; and many are enabled to save enough money to purchase their freedom, which is not unfrequently done.

They are generally up at four o'clock, when they feed the animals, their own included; they then work in the fields, pruning the coffee or transplanting it, or opening new plantations, until nine o'clock, when they breakfast. From half-past nine until twelve they again work, dine at noon, and return to the fields from half-past one until dark, when the animals are again fed, and they retire to their *baracons* [*sic*; barracoons]. This is a large building around a central square, into which all the doors of their rooms open. The one on the estate where I now am is 160 feet long, and eighty feet wide; it contains twenty-eight apartments, each fourteen feet square, and nine high to the eaves of a high pitched roof of tiles, and has besides its door a window with iron gratings opening outward. In the middle of the square is the general kitchen; but each Negro has at night a fire in his room, over which he smokes himself in the hottest weather, and cooks his private stores. The hospital is in a second story built over the entrance, which, by law, is guarded by a gate that is closed every night. The window near which I am seated commands a full view of it; they have just retired from their day's labor, volumes of smoke are issuing from the crevices of the tiled roof, and no one who listens to their cheerful voices and merry laughter, will believe that they come from heavy hearts.

Notes

For complete references and notes, consult the work as cited in the acknowledgment of copyrights section.

1. *Jatropha manihot*; the sweet species is cultivated, the fecula is named *casave*.

Cuba's First Railroad

David Turnbull

In this selection, nineteenth-century British abolitionist David Turnbull lauds the American-built railroad from Havana to Güines, and he notes the project's multinational labor force and financing.

The first line of railway of any consideration, which has yet been laid down in the West Indies, is that which now exists in this island, connecting the Havana with one of the most important of its sugar districts, and, having its inland terminus at the town of Güines, forty-five miles distant from the capital. The other points at which it touches are Almendares, Bejucal, San Felipe, and Melena. Before my final leave of the Havana the road was completed; and on the occasion of its being thrown open to the public, an entertainment was given in the spacious station-house at Güines at the expense of the contractors, who are supposed to have realized more than ordinary profits by the undertaking. The dinner and the ball which followed it were got up with all that disregard of expense, which seems to be the chief distinction of intertropical entertainments. The novelty of riding on a railroad, with the prospect of dancing at the end of it, was sufficient to overcome the delight of doing nothing, the *"dolce far niente"* of the fair señoras and señoritas of the Havana. The attendance of strangers was also considerable; and it was my fortune to be placed at table among a party of officers of the United States Navy, who seemed to agree in the expression of sentiments, which at that time were new to me, but which in the course of a subsequent tour in North America I heard repeated to satiety. On the question of war or peace, which had then begun to be agitated, they spoke with great animation, describing the advantage of a little bloodletting with the most edifying gusto. They were good enough to prefer an outbreak with any other country than with England, and to express the strongest disapprobation of the proceedings of the State of Maine, on the subject of the northeastern boundary, which had then begun to be agitated. The question of slavery having afterward been introduced, as it exists in the United States, I ventured to speak of it to these gentlemen in the way which I thought least calculated to give them any personal or national offence, by describing it as a sad inheritance from their British forefathers, of which it would be well for them to rid themselves at the earliest possible opportunity. To my extreme surprise and disgust the answer of the mouthpiece of the party to this pacific remark was such as compelled me to break up the conversation. "WE HOLD," he said, "ON THE CONTRARY, THAT IT WAS A GLORIOUS INHERITANCE!" These are the very gentlemen who, as will be seen in the sequel, had been sent to the Havana for the purpose of checking the abuses of the American flag, which were notoriously committed by parties most deeply concerned in the African slave trade.

The works of this railroad are exceedingly well executed, as compared, at least, with any thing I have seen in the New World, and do great credit to Mr. Alfred Cruger, of the United States, the directing engineer, more especially when we reflect for a moment on the difficulties he had to contend with, not so much in the nature of the ground, as of the human instruments by the aid of which his task was to be accomplished. Such is the baneful influence of slavery, that Mr. Cruger, although sufficiently accustomed to its effects in his own country, made no secret of the fact, that if he gave an order to a white man to do some specific piece of work, he found as soon as his back was turned it would be transferred to another, and by that other to a third, until in the end it was committed to a Negro, if at all within reach of a Negro's capacity.

Several thousand Isleños from the Canary Islands were brought to the Havana for the purpose of working on the railroad. A vast number of prisoners from the Cabaños, most of them transported convicts from Old Spain, but many of them *facciosos* [rebels] captured in the Biscayan war, were likewise placed at the disposal of the company; as was also a portion of the captured Negroes emancipated by British cruisers before the arrival of the Romney receiving ship, who till then were given up to the tender mercies of the captain general, and placed, therefore, in a much worse condition than ordinary slaves, making, as has been shown, the very word *emancipado* a term of reproach and a byword among the lowest of the Negro population.

To make up their numbers, or to show how much could be done for a little money, upward of a thousand Irishmen, who are to be found in every part of the world prepared with their lusty sinews to cheapen the price of labor, were tempted in an evil hour to go there from the United States, allured by promises on the part of the railroad company which were never fulfilled. They were to be furnished with suitable places to live in; they were to be provided for when sick, and were to be sent back from whence they came at the expense of the company when the term of their engagement should arrive. So far, however, from the fulfillment of these reasonable engagements, as soon as any of them fell sick or was maimed, as many of them were in the service, they were instantly paid off and left to their own resources or to beggary. I have reason to believe that our consul, Mr. Tolmé, did all in his power to obtain justice for them at the hands of the local government; but the only result of his interference was to obtain from the Captain General Tacón, an offer to receive them at the prison of the Cabaños, an establishment elsewhere spoken of, connected with the fortress of the Moro, on the shores of the bay of the Havana, nearly opposite the city; but although their sufferings must have been extreme, not a single individual accepted the offer, preferring, without exception, the precarious resource of the eleemosynary [*sic*] aid. The evil became so great, and lasted so long, that the British consul at New York, Mr. Buchanan, at the suggestion, doubtless, of his colleague Mr. Tolmé, found means to warn his countrymen of the great dangers to which they would expose themselves, by engaging in an enterprise conducted on such cold-blooded and iniquitous principles.

The Color Line

José Antonio Saco

Cuban intellectuals in the nineteenth and twentieth centuries devoted a great deal of energy to studying the impact of sugar on Cuban society. In the nineteenth century, intellectuals struggled with the questions of slavery and colonial status in a continent where both had become things of the past. In most of Latin America, independence had been achieved by 1820, slavery was abolished shortly afterward, and some form of representative government was established. The Haitian revolution (1791–1804), and the subsequent abolition of slavery in the British Caribbean (in the 1830s), meant that by the middle of the century, educated Cubans were questioning the sugar/slavery/colony complex in different ways. José Antonio Saco (1797–1879) exemplified the beginnings of nationalism among the creole elite, arguing that white Cubans should have more political authority on the island and that continued importation of slaves threatened the development of a white class of independent farmers.

We believe that the island of Cuba today has over eight hundred thousand inhabitants, and we do not fear erring if we state that the number of slaves is not below 350,000, and that of free people of color 140,000; that is, in a population with only a few more than three hundred thousand whites, there are almost five hundred thousand people of color.

These figures are in themselves enough to show that we are gravely ill, and if a cure is not applied with a firm hand, death could surprise us in the midst of the apparent happiness that we are enjoying.

Our situation is even worse if we turn our eyes to the horizon around us. There we can already see the smoke and fire spewing from the volcanoes that have erupted, and the horrendous fuel that devours the entrails of the Antilles threatens a general catastrophe in the American archipelago. Read, my compatriots, read the history of the future in the patterns that we place before you, and after considering them with the attention they deserve, tell us if you do not hear the profound wails of a dying fatherland. . . .

In 1823 the population was 40 percent slaves, 43 percent free coloreds, and 17 percent whites; that is, for every seventeen whites we had eighty-three people of color!!!

And if that was the population of the archipelago then, what will it be twenty years from now? Anybody who thinks that because of the ending of the slave traffic almost everywhere in the Antilles the population of the African race will decrease or remain stable, is fooling himself mightily. This may happen in one or another of the small islands, but the general mass of the population of the archipelago will grow daily. The current situation cannot be judged by the past: then slaves were little cared for, because their masters could recover their losses in an abundant market. But now that the circumstances have changed, economic interest more than humanity has compelled them to treat their slaves less harshly. . . .

If it were not enough to have at our doorstep nine hundred thousand Haitians and four hundred thousand Jamaicans, the North American republic, the freest country on the earth, presenting one of the strangest anomalies, also offers us, to complement our fears, a population of color almost exclusively concentrated in its Southern states, which are those that are closest to us. . . .

Would it not be advisable for us to carry out some experiments, to see what difference there is between using slave labor to cultivate cane, and other methods that we could adopt in the future? Because there is no obstacle to this except economic interest; and if our hacendados can be convinced that without slave labor they would make greater or equal profits, there is no doubt that they would voluntarily embrace any party who offered them an alternative. We would urge, then, that some mill owners dedicate one, two, or more cane fields, from the preparation of the land for sowing until the packaging of the processed sugar, to an experiment with waged labor. They would take into account the time spent, the investment and interest on capital, and all of the other elements that enter into this type of calculation, and draw a firm conclusion about the relative merits of the two systems. . . .

And without the need of paying wages, could not all or part of the mill's land be divided among free men who commit themselves to cultivating cane, in return for a portion of the sugar produced? This method is used in some parts of Asia, and we believe it preferable to the wage method, for if the land is divided into small plots, the cultivation will be more perfect; if there is a bad year, the hacendado will be spared paying the salaries which he would otherwise have to pay; and the farmer, identifying with the interests of the plantation owner, would work hard to increase the yield of the cane he cultivates. If all of our hacendados could realize the importance of these ideas, we would see them dedicated to promoting the introduction of white men, and preventing the introduction of Africans; and creating committees [juntas], collecting funds, and working heatedly for such an eminently patriotic objective. They would remove the obstacles that now block colonization by foreigners, and would instead invite them with the guarantee of the laws and the protection of the country. . . .

You have been very imprudent, many will cry, very imprudent, in taking up the pen to write about a matter that must always be buried in the most profound silence! This is the accusation that is generally made against anybody who dares to touch upon this topic. Unfortunately a disastrous opinion has been formed among us which we will call *silence*. Everybody recognizes the evils, everybody knows about the dangers, everybody wants to avoid them; but if anybody tries to apply a remedy, a thousand confused cries are launched at the same time, and the only voice that is heard is the one saying "be quiet, be quiet." Such behavior resembles that of certain timid people who, when they are attacked by an illness, hide it and move toward their death, to avoid hearing the details of their illness from the mouth of a doctor, nor finding a means of curing it. When we are confronting a terrifying precipice, and we stop on the road to retreat from the abyss that is going to swallow us, who are really the imprudent ones? Those who raise their voices to warn of the danger, or the timid and *silent* ones who watch a people plunge to their ruin? If our sufferings were incurable, then we would not open our lips, for we would deprive many of the comfort of a peaceful death; but when the patient, in spite of the gravity of his illness, has a vigorous temperament, and thanks to remedies that are easy to apply, could be relieved of his sufferings, it would be an unpardonable crime if we were to remain tranquil spectators. Let the selfish say what they want about us; let those who pride themselves on being discrete censure us; let the parricides accuse us; nothing, none of that matters to us. We yield before considerations of an exalted lineage, and honoring the noble mission of writers, we will not tire of repeating *let us save the fatherland; let us save the fatherland*.

TRANSLATED BY AVIVA CHOMSKY

Abolition!

Father Félix Varela

Félix Varela (1787–1853) was elected to represent Cuba before the Spanish Cortes in 1821. Among the proposals he presented to the Cortes were one for an autonomous government in Cuba, and one calling for the abolition of slavery. The following statement accompanied his abolition proposal. Although he took a more humanitarian position than Saco in his opposition to slavery, like Saco he associated greater political independence for the island with the abolition of slavery.

Nature's irresistible voice cries out for Cuba's happiness. The island's propitious location, its spacious and secure ports, its fertile lands crisscrossed with large and frequent rivers, all suggest Cuba's potential to play a key role in the world. In its earliest days, it was inhabited by a peaceful and simple people who, innocent of the politics of men, enjoyed the pleasures of frugality; the hand of the conquistador brought death everywhere, and created a desert that their warriors could not fill. The ancient race of Indians that lived on the continent . . . disappeared like smoke. Only a few areas remained populated: around the ports, where the horror of their own victory led the victors, surrounded by a small number of their victims, and the peaks of the distant mountains where a few miserable survivors sought a dreadful refuge, sadly contemplating their ruined homes, and the beautiful plains that not long before were gardens of delight.

I would not remind you of these facts, as disagreeable as they are true, if it were not absolutely necessary in order to understand the political situation of the island of Cuba. Those events were the first link in a great chain that today oppresses thousands of men, causing them to groan under a harsh slavery in the land where others went to their deaths, an ill-fated chain that preserves in this island, that nature seemed to destine for pleasure, the sad image of degraded humanity. . . .

The colonizers immediately declared a terrible war against the prosperity of the colonies, believing them to be destined by Providence to enrich the mother country, and unaware of the true sources of greatness for both, sources that were obstructed by the greed of the colonizers to the detriment of all.

This government conduct produced a backwardness in the population of that beautiful Island, and stimulated . . . England to the enterprise of offering us African laborers to cultivate our fields. . . . England introduced the beginning of so many evils onto our soil. She was the first who, to the scandal and abomination of all of the virtuous, did not hesitate to immolate humanity for her avarice, and if she has ceased in these barbarous sacrifices it is because those well-known benefits have ceased. . . .

I dare to state that the general will of the people of the island of Cuba is that there be no slaves, and that they only want to find another means of fulfilling their needs. Even though it is true that the custom of dominating a part of the human species inspires in some a certain insensibility to the sufferings of those unfortunates, many others are trying to relieve it, and act more as fathers than masters to their slaves. . . .

The African native would not be scorned in our land if the laws had not set him up to be so. Backwardness inspires compassion in just souls, and not scorn; but the laws, the tyrannical laws, try to perpetuate the misfortune of those unfortunates. . . .

When the issue of freedom is raised among slaves, it is natural that they make terrible efforts to break their chains, and if they do not succeed, jealousy devours them, and the injustice makes their situation even more unbearable. Whites in Cuba don't cease to congratulate themselves for having overthrown the former despotism, recovering the sacred rights of free men. Are we to hope that people of African origin will be calm spectators to these emotions? Rage and desperation will oblige them to raise for themselves the alternative of *liberty or death*.

I must warn the Cortes that among people of African origin there is a well-known discontent with the Constitution, for they have never given the slightest sign of happiness, when it is well known that in any fiesta or public celebration they are always the first to create a scandal. Sensible people observed that when the news of the reestablishment of the system arrived in Havana, it seemed as if the earth had swallowed the blacks and mulattoes, for one could count on one hand those that were in the streets, despite the general rejoicing, and for some time they maintained a somber and imposing air. Do not believe that they did this out of ignorance, or out of adherence to the old system, for we already know that they have tried twice to overturn it, declaring themselves free, and I am sure that the first person to mount the call for independence will have almost all of the people of African origin on his side. Let us not fool ourselves: Constitution, liberty, equality, are synonyms; these terms are polar opposites to the words slavery and inequality of rights. It is in vain to try to reconcile these opposites. . . .

Under such circumstances, there is no recourse except removing the cause of these evils, while trying not to create others that could compromise the peace of the Island. By this I mean, give freedom to the slaves in such a way that their owners will not lose the capital that they invested in their purchase, nor the people of Havana suffer new burdens, and the freedmen, in the heightened emotions that their unexpected good fortune will surely cause them, will not try to take more than what they should be given, and finally, assisting agriculture as much as possible so that it will not suffer, or at least will suffer the least damage possible, because of the lack of slaves.

TRANSLATED BY AVIVA CHOMSKY

Cecilia Valdés

Cirilo Villaverde

Nineteenth-century Cuban novelists also drew on slavery, abolitionism, and nation-alism as important themes in their work. Cirilo Villaverde (1812–1894) was exiled to the United States for having conspired against the Spanish colonial regime. He au-thored the first Cuban novel to be published in book form in 1838. His abolitionist novel, Cecilia Valdés, *was begun in Cuba in 1839 and completed in New York in 1882. He had been a romantic when he began but was a realist by the time he finished, some forty years later. Through the medium of the novel, Villaverde, as did so many Latin American novelists of the romantic period following the independence wars, cap-tures the society of his day—in this case, the horrors of slavery and the social and racial hierarchy of colonial society—with greater precision than many historians of that time.*

As the framework for the doomed love affair of Cecilia Valdés, a beautiful mulatta and her half-brother, Leonardo Gamboa, Villaverde creates an enormous canvas, a microcosm of Cuban society of the day. All of the social classes and types, from the slave-owning elite to the slaves, and everything in between, are represented, as are the ideals, pastimes, and prejudices of each, viewed through the prism of abolitionist thought.

The selection consists of a conversation between Leonardo and several of his law school classmates. It opens with discussion of how laws govern people and property rights, as well as the categories of people—slaves and their descendants—considered property under the prevailing legal code. The jokes and exchanges that ensue reveal the full scope of race and class prejudice from which even the elite is not exempt.

For the good of the criminal's soul,
As they lead him to the gallows!
"El Reo de Muerte" [Condemned to Death]—Espronceda

The student headed for the Plaza Vieja by way of the Calle de San Ignacio. At the corner of the Calle del Sol he met two other students of about his own age, who were evidently waiting for him. One of them is already known to the reader as Diego Meneses, who accompanied Leonardo to the *cuna* ball in the Calle de San José. The other was much less handsome and not so elegantly dressed; not only was he short of stature but he had a short neck and raised shoulders, between which his little round head appeared partially interred. His forehead was low and narrow, his eyes small and piercing; his nose was somewhat *retroussé*, his chin was pointed; his thick and moist lips were by far the most conspicuous of his diminutive features; his hair was curly and in his bodily movements as well as in his facial expression one detected a high degree of cunning animating a mischievous disposition. Addressing him as Pancho Solfa, Leonardo gave him a hearty slap on the back. Half amused, half annoyed, Pancho said, "Every animal has his own particular form of speech, Leonardo, and at times yours is a bit too expressive."

"It's because I love you that I beat you, Pancho. Would you like another caress?"

"That'll do, old man," and he made as if to ward off a second blow by raising his left hand.

"What time is it?" asked Leonardo. "I must have forgotten to wind my watch last night and it stopped."

"The clock of the Church of the Espíritu Santo just struck seven," replied Diego. "We were about to leave without you, thinking you were still stuck to the sheets."

"I very nearly didn't get up at all. Went to bed late and my father had me called at daybreak. He always rises early, as he goes to bed with the chickens. What do you chaps say to a stroll by Angel's Hill?"

"I'm against it," said Pancho. "For unless you're another Joshua, able to stop the sun in its course, there isn't time for it."

"You've got your citations mixed up, Pancho, am I right or wrong? Don't you know that the sun hasn't moved from the moment that Joshua commanded it to stand still? If you had studied astronomy you would know that."

"It would be more correct to say, 'if you had studied Biblical history,'" said Meneses.

"The fact is," observed Pancho, "that, without having studied either subject very deeply, I know that the case comes within both, and that you lads are not qualified to correct my examination paper."

"Be that as it may, *caballero*, what's the lesson for today? I missed class on Friday and haven't cracked a book in all this time."

"Govantes assigned title III for today. It deals with the rights of persons," replied Diego. "Open the book and you'll see."

"Well, I haven't even a nodding acquaintance with the subject," added Leonardo. "I only know that, according to Spanish law, there are persons and things and that many of them, although they think and speak, do not have the same rights as others. For example, Pancho, since you have a penchant for comparisons, you—in the eyes of the law—are not a person but a thing."

"I don't see any resemblance, since I am not a slave, which is what the Roman law regards as a thing."

"Granted, you aren't a slave, but one of your ancestors was, which amounts to the same thing. Your hair is suspicious, anyway."

"You're a lucky dog to have hair as straight as an Indian's. However, if you and I were to examine our respective family trees, we should find that some who pass for freeborn are only the children of freedmen."

"You are getting back at me because I offended you. Come now, it's no sin to tie the mule behind the door.[1] My father is Spanish and has no mule; but my mother is a creole and I can't guarantee that she is of pure Spanish blood."

"Even if your father is Spanish, that does not free him from the suspicion of having mixed blood. For I suppose he is Andalusian, and the Arabs, who ruled Andalusia more completely than any other part of Spain, were not pure Caucasians, but of African blood. And, in addition, the union of whites and blacks was common in those days, according to Cervantes and other contemporary writers."

"That little historical sketch is worth a Potosí.[2] It's obvious the racial question has given you a few headaches. It's too trivial to bother about. I don't think mixed blood has any particular importance or significance, one way or the other. But I will say, and I don't know whether it's because I may have a little colored blood myself, I do have a weakness for mulatto girls. I confess it without shame."

"What is bred in the bone will come out in the flesh. The goat is drawn to the hills."

"The saying is not apt unless you mean to imply that you don't like cinnamon, which is far worse, Pancho, for it means you like *coal*, which is an inferior substance."

At this point in the conversation they passed through Rosary Gate into the Plaza Vieja.[3] The gate is formed by the portals of four or five houses belonging to noble or wealthy families. The doorways and windows of these houses were covered during the day with hemp curtains, each one resembling the mainsail of a square rigger. The upper floors were usually occupied by the owners, or their tenants, who live on the income from their investments; but the rooms on the ground floor, for the most part dark and poorly ventilated, are used as shops by retail merchants, who sell new and secondhand furniture, clothing, jewelry, hardware, and the like. They are Spaniards to a man, and usually northerners.[4] Bolts of cloth and general merchandise are kept inside and, in front under the stone arches, are displayed what they call hardware in portable showcases, some of them glass covered; these cases rest on legs consisting of two pairs of crossed sticks of wood or sawhorses. They bring them out in the morning and put them back inside at night.

They usually open their shops for business at a little after seven in the morning. Two shopkeepers lift a showcase, one at each end, and the cases are carried out like so many coffins, for they are too heavy for one man.

Some of them were already on display, and the traders were walking up and down in their shirtsleeves in front of their wares, notwithstanding a cool morning breeze, when the students were passing by under the arcade.

Leonardo and Diego were in the lead, chatting and laughing, and paying no attention to the Spaniards who came and went, engrossed in placing their wares on display as early as possible. Behind them came Pancho, walking slowly and silently, his eyes fixed on the ground. Whether for this reason or because his somewhat bizarre appearance startled them, the first hawker he ran into clutched him by the arm, and said: "Hello! Blondie,⁵ don't you want to buy a pair of first-rate razors?"

Pancho freed himself with a jerk and another one grasped him, saying: "Right over here, cousin, I've got some excellent spectacles for sale."

A third vendor, up ahead, interrupted to offer him elastic suspenders; a fourth thrust some Spanish penknives, superior to those of English manufacture, before his eyes. Passing along from one hawker to the next, first smiling, then with a gesture of impatience, the student, now thoroughly exasperated, succeeded in advancing only a few steps. Finally, surrounded by a group of vendors more intent upon making sport of him than upon puffing their wares, Pancho stopped and folded his arms in defiance. Luckily, at that moment his companions missed him and, looking back, beheld him completely surrounded. Without waiting to inquire the cause, Leonardo, who was the most courageous of the party, ran back and forced his way into the circle, rescuing Pancho from his predicament. But when he learned from the latter what had occurred he gave a hearty laugh and said: "They took you for a country bumpkin, Pancho. You do look—."

"My appearance has nothing whatever to do with the case," Pancho interrupted, annoyed at being made the butt of his companions' ridicule. "It's because those Spaniards are more Jews than gentlemen."

Continuing along the Calle de San Ignacio, our students came out shortly into Cathedral Plaza. As they passed by the door of a shop known as the Nightingale they noticed a large and densely packed crowd of people entering through a second door on the opposite side, that is to say, from the Calle de Mercaderes and an alley known as El Boquete [the gap]. The vanguard was composed largely of colored people, men, women and children, dirty, ragged and barefooted. As they walked along they would stop every so often, and look behind them, twisting their heads round as if operated by springs. Two columns of soldiers marched in single file; the men were lightly equipped, their uniform consisting of blue cloth jacket, white breeches, and round hat. Cartridge boxes were attached to their belts in front, and they carried the short carbine used by the regular army. Between the two files of soldiers walked some dozen or so Negroes and mulattoes dressed in long, black serge gowns with white muslin hoods, the long points of which floated behind like pennants; each marcher carried in his right hand a black cross with long standard and short cross-arm. Four of these gloomy men, by crossing their arms to form a chair, carried on their shoulders what appeared to be a human being, whose face and body disappeared under the folds of a black, woolen cape, which fell down perpendicularly over the whole apparatus.

By the side of this mysterious being came a priest in black silk cassock and biretta, carrying a crucifix in both hands; on the other side walked a youthful Negro, of agile and robust appearance. The latter wore white breeches, round bat, and black cloth jacket, on the back of which was embroidered what looked like a yellow ladder. This was the emblem of his office, and he was nothing less than the executioner. He walked with measured tread and never lifted his eyes from the ground. Just behind came a white man wearing short breeches, silk stockings, cloth jacket, and three-cornered cocked hat, all of black. This was the clerk of the high court of justice. Next came a military officer of high rank, as indicated by the three twisted gold fringes on his coat, as well as his cocked hat with three gold points and a white ostrich feather.[6] Other Negroes and mulattoes in black cloth suits with the white hoods, already described, concluded the cortege, which was followed by more of the rabble, all moving in solemn and silent procession, the stillness being broken only by the sound of slowly marching feet and the snuffling voice of the priest intoning the prayers for the dying.

The Havana reader will have gathered from the foregoing description that a condemned criminal was being led to the gallows, accompanied by the Brothers of Faith and Charity, a religious order composed entirely of colored people and charged with aiding the sick and the dying, and attending to the burial of the dead, for the most part executed criminals. That Spanish justice carried its wrath to the brink of the grave is well known, and hence the need for a religious order to take possession of the body of the criminal and give it burial. This cannot be done by relatives or friends of the deceased, who are prohibited from so doing by law or custom.

The company that guarded the criminal in the scene just described, in

Havana if not in other parts of Cuba, was a detachment of the Armona Guard, which Captain General Vives established as a sort of civil guard, to perform the duties usually discharged elsewhere by police. The high-ranking officer, at that time the commander of the guard, was Colonel Molina, later governor of Morro Castle, in which office he died, charged with the odium of those whom he had oppressed and exploited while occupying the first of these positions. The individual whom they were carrying to the gallows in the manner just described, was not a man but a woman, and a white woman, the first of her kind, perhaps, to suffer capital punishment in Havana.

TRANSLATED BY SYDNEY GEST

Notes

1. Ashamed, because it is not a horse. Or, as we would say, "It's no disgrace to keep the skeleton locked in the closet."
2. The fabulously rich gold mines of Potosí, Bolivia.
3. Old Square, in the N.E. quarter of the city. Its weather-beaten houses were once the mansions of the great. It reminds one of Valencia or Cádiz.
4. Most of them from Galicia and Asturias.
5. Flattery, perhaps slightly tinged with sarcasm, for he was of mixed race.
6. Used in the Spanish army to designate colonels and general officers.

Sab

Gertrudis Gómez de Avellaneda y Arteaga

Gertrudis Gómez de Avellaneda, known as La Avellaneda (1814–1873), also spent a good part of her life in exile (in Spain and France). We include an excerpt from her antislavery novel Sab, *published in Spain in 1841.* Sab *was banned in Cuba and not published there until 1914. Yet it is an eminently Cuban novel, with its vivid and loving evocations of Cuban landscapes and its romantic heroes: Sab, the mulatto slave, son of an African princess and her Spanish master, and Carlota, a* criolla, *a "sensitive island girl" (37).*

Who are you? What is your homeland? . . .
The tyrannical influences
of my guiding star formed me
into a monster of such rare quality
that while I am of heroic lineage
in the endowments of my soul,
I am also the scorn of the world.
— Cañizares

Twenty years ago, or thereabouts, late on a June afternoon a young man of handsome bearing journeyed on horseback through the picturesque country watered by the Tínima River and in leisurely fashion guided his spirited sorrel along the path known in these parts as the Cubitas Road, leading as it did to the villages of this name, which were also known as the red lands. The young man in question was four leagues from Cubitas, from whence he appeared to have come, and three from the city of Puerto Príncipe, at that time the capital of the central province of Cuba, though only a few years earlier it had been but a humble township.

Perhaps because of his scant knowledge of the road, perhaps because of the pleasure he took in appraising the landscape before him, the traveler gradu- ally slackened his pace and from time to time reined in his horse as though to scrutinize the places through which he passed. Quite possibly his repeated stops had as their sole object the fuller savoring of the richly fertile earth of that privileged country, which most likely attracted him all the more if—as his fair, rosy skin, blue eyes, and golden hair seemed to indicate—he had been born in some northern region.

The brutal sun of the torrid zone was sinking into dusk among undulating clouds of purple and silver, and its last rays, already feeble and pale, bathed the virgin fields of that youthful nature in melancholy hues. It was a landscape whose vigorous and luxuriant vegetation seemed eagerly to welcome the afternoon's balmy breezes which began to flutter through the leafy crowns of the trees, parched by the day's heat. Flocks of swallows crossed and recrossed in all directions in search of their night's refuge; the green parrot, banded with gold and scarlet, the crow, distinctly black and lustrous, the royal woodpecker, of iron tongue and muted plumage, the blithe macaw, the swift *tomeguín*, the iridescent butterfly, and a whole host of native birds alighted in the branches of tamarind and aromatic mango trees, ruffling their variegated feathers as though to imprison therein the comforting breath of the gentle breeze.

After having crossed immense savannas where the eye encounters but the dual horizon of earth and sky, and pasturelands crowned by palms and gigantic ceiba trees, the traveler at last reached a fence, which indicated that this was someone's property. And indeed one could discern in the distance the white facade of a farmhouse, toward which the young man immediately directed his mount. But suddenly he reined in his horse and pulled him over to the side of the road, apparently intending to wait for a country fellow who was approaching with measured step, singing a folk tune whose last verse the traveler's ear was able to catch perfectly:

> A dark woman is my torment
> Have pity on me—
> For she whom my heart adores
> Has none at all for me.

When the man was but three paces from the stranger, noting that the latter was waiting expectantly, he stopped, and both men regarded each other for a moment before speaking. Perhaps the uncommonly handsome appearance of the traveler caused the local man to hesitate, while in turn the eyes of the former were just as strongly drawn to the latter.

The newcomer was a tall young man of average build but with striking features. He did not appear to be a white criollo; neither was he black nor could one take him for a descendant of the indigenous inhabitants of the Antilles. His face was a singular composite which revealed the mingling of two distinct races, an amalgam, it could be said, of the features of the African and the European yet without being a perfect mulatto.

His coloring was of a yellowish white with a certain dark undertone; his broad forehead was half hidden under irregular locks of hair as lustrous and black as the wings of the raven; his nose was aquiline, but his thick, purplish lips revealed his African heritage. His chin was triangular and somewhat prominent, his slanted eyes large and black under straight eyebrows; in them shone the fire of early youth, despite the slight lines that etched his face. The sum of these traits formed a face of distinctive features, one of those countenances which instantly attracts the gaze of others and which, once seen, is never forgotten.

The man's clothing was in no way different from that which is generally worn by farmers in the province of Puerto Príncipe and consisted of trousers of cotton ticking with wide blue stripes and a linen shirt, also striped, secured around the waist by a belt from which hung a wide machete, his head covered by a floppy hat woven of *yarey* leaves—quite informal clothing, but comfortable and indispensable in a scorching climate.

The stranger broke the silence and, speaking in a Spanish so pure and fluent that it seemed to belie his northern physiognomy, said to the farmer, "My good friend, would you be so kind as to tell me if the house that can be discerned from here is that of Bellavista plantation, belonging to Don Carlos de B—?"

The farmer bowed and answered, "Yes, sir, all the land you see down there belongs to Don Carlos."

"Undoubtedly you are this gentleman's neighbor and can tell me if he and his family have arrived at the plantation."

"They have been there since this morning, and I can be your guide should you wish to visit them."

The stranger showed by a nod of his head that he accepted the offer, and without awaiting a further response the farmer turned as though to take him to the house, which was now quite close. But perhaps the stranger did not wish to arrive quite so soon, for slowing his horse to a walk, he resumed his conversation with his guide, all the while casting curious glances around him.

"Did you say that Señor de B—owns all of this land?"

"Yes, sir."

"It appears to be very fertile."

"Indeed it is."

"This plantation must bring its owner a good income."

"As far as I know there have been times," said the young man, stopping to glance at the land under discussion, "when this plantation produced for its owner some three hundred thousand pounds of sugar every year, because then more than a hundred blacks worked in the cane fields. But times have changed, and since the present owner of Bellavista has only fifty blacks, his production does not exceed six thousand loaves of sugar."

"The slaves on these plantations must have a very hard life," observed the stranger, "and I am not surprised that their number has been so considerably reduced."

"It is truly a terrible life," said the farmer, casting a sympathetic glance at his questioner. "Under this fiery sky the nearly naked slave works all morning without rest, and at the terrible hour of midday, panting, crushed under the weight of the wood and the sugarcane he bears on his shoulders, scorched by the rays of the sun that burn his skin, the unhappy soul at last gets a taste of all the pleasures which life holds for him: two hours of sleep and a frugal meal. When night comes with its breezes and shadows to console the scorched land and all nature rests, the slave with his sweat and tears waters the place where neither the night has shadows nor the breeze freshness, because there the heat of firewood has replaced that of the sun and the unhappy black walks endlessly around either the machine which extracts the cane's sweet juice or the cauldrons in which the fire's heat converts this juice into molasses; hour after hour he sees go by, and the sun's return finds him there still. . . . Ah, yes! The sight of this degraded humanity, where men become mere brutes, is a cruel spectacle. These are men whose brows are seared with the mark of slavery just as their souls are branded with the desperation of Hell."

The farmer suddenly halted, as though aware that he had said too much, and, lowering his eyes while permitting a melancholy smile to touch his lips, added hastily, "But the principal cause of Bellavista's decline is not the death of the slaves: many have been sold, as has some of the property, yet it is still a valuable enough plantation."

Having said this, he resumed walking toward the house but stopped after a few steps when he noted that the stranger was not following, and when he turned to look back at him, caught an expression of distinct surprise fixed on the stranger's features. In effect, the bearing of that farmer seemed to reveal something great and noble which attracted attention, and what the stranger had just heard, expressed in a language and with an eloquence which belied the class his dress appeared to denote, increased his admiration and curiosity.

The young farmer had approached our traveler's horse with the demeanor of a man who waits for a question he knows will be directed to him, and he was not mistaken, for the stranger, unable to quell his curiosity, said, "I gather that I have the pleasure of conversing with a distinguished landowner of these parts. I know that when they are out on their country estates, the criollos like to dress as simple laborers, and I would be sorry to remain ignorant any longer of the name of the person who has offered to guide me with such courtesy. If I am not mistaken, you are Don Carlos de B—'s friend and neighbor. . . ."

Upon hearing these words the countenance of the one addressed showed not the slightest surprise but fixed the speaker with a penetrating glance; then, as though the mild and charming nature of the stranger's features had satisfied his inquiring gaze, he lowered his eyes and answered, "I am not a landowner, sir, and though within my breast beats a heart ever ready to sacrifice itself on Don Carlos's behalf, I am not in a position to call him my friend. I belong," he continued with a bitter smile, "to that unhappy race deprived of human rights. . . . I am a mulatto and a slave."

"So you're a mulatto?" exclaimed the stranger, who, once he had heard the speaker's declaration, assumed the tone of disdainful familiarity used toward slaves. "Well, I suspected as much in the beginning, but you have a look so uncommon to your class that it caused me to think otherwise."

The slave continued to smile, but his smile became increasingly melancholy and, at that moment, held a hint of scorn as well.

"It can happen," he said, again fixing his eyes on the stranger, "that at times the soul is free and noble though the body be enslaved and base. But night is coming on and I will guide Your Grace to the plantation, which is now very near."

The mulatto's observation was correct. As though it had been torn violently from the beautiful Cuban sky, the sun had ceased shining on that land it loves so well, though the altars once erected to it have long since been destroyed. The pale and melancholy moon slowly rose to take possession of its dominions.

The stranger followed his guide without interrupting the conversation.

"So you're Don Carlos's slave?"

"I have the honor of being the *mayoral* [overseer] of this plantation."

"What is your name?"

"I was christened Bernabé, but my mother always called me Sab, and that is what my masters have called me as well."

"Was your mother black or a mulatto like you?"

"My mother came into the world in a country where her color was not a mark of slavery. My mother," he repeated with a certain pride, "was born free and a princess. This was well known among all those who, like herself, were brought here from the coasts of the Congo by the dealers in human flesh. But although a princess in her own country, here she was sold as a slave."

The gentleman smiled indulgently when he heard Sab bestow the title of princess on his mother, but as the conversation appeared to interest him, he wished to prolong it further.

"Your father must undoubtedly have been white."

"My father! I never knew him. My mother was only a child when she was sold to Don Félix de B—, the father of my present master and of four other children. For two years she wept inconsolably, unable to resign herself to the bitter turn her fate had taken. But once this time was over, a sudden change took place within her; my mother was once again able to embrace life because she had fallen in love. A deep and powerful passion was kindled in her African heart. In spite of her color my mother was beautiful, and undoubtedly her passion was reciprocated because about that time I came into the world. My father's name was a secret which she always refused to reveal to me."

"Your fate, Sab, seems less deserving of pity than that of the other slaves, as the position you hold at Bellavista proves the esteem and affection which your master feels for you."

"Yes, sir, I have never suffered the harsh treatment which is generally meted out to slaves, nor have I been condemned to long and arduous labor. I was only three years old when my protector Don Luis, the youngest of Don Félix de B—'s sons, died, but two hours before that excellent young man departed this world he had a long and secret talk with his brother Don Carlos and, as was revealed later, entrusted me to the latter's kindness. And so I found in my present master the same good and pious heart of the kind protector I had lost. A short while later he married a woman—an angel!—and took me with him. I was six when I began to rock Miss Carlota's cradle, the first child of that happy marriage. As she was an only child for a period of five years, I became the companion of her games and her studies; her innocent heart disregarded the distance that separated us, and she bestowed upon me the affection due a brother. At her side I learned to read and write, for she refused to be instructed if her poor mulatto Sab were not with her. Because of her I grew to love reading; her own books and even her father's have always been available to me and have been my solace, though they have often stirred up disturbing ideas and bitter reflections in my soul."

The slave stopped himself, unable to hide the deep emotion which, to his sorrow, his voice revealed. Swiftly regaining control, he brushed his hand across his forehead, shook his head slightly, and added more calmly, "By my own choice I became a coachman for a few years; later I wanted to work with the land, and I have been helping on this plantation for two years now."

The stranger had smiled maliciously ever since Sab had mentioned the secret discussion which the late Don Luis had had with his brother. When the mulatto stopped talking, he said, "Strange that you are not free, seeing how much Don Luis de B—loved you. It only seems natural that his father should have given you your freedom, or that Don Carlos should have done so."

"My freedom! Freedom is doubtless very sweet . . . but I was born a slave, I was a slave from my mother's womb and so—"

"You are accustomed to slavery," interrupted the stranger, very pleased at having articulated what he thought the mulatto must be thinking.

The latter did not contradict him but smiled bitterly and, as though he derived pleasure from the words he slowly uttered, said in a low voice, "As a child I was signed over to Miss Carlota; I am her slave, and I wish to live and die in her service."

The stranger spurred his horse lightly, and Sab, who was walking ahead of them, had to quicken his pace as the handsome sorrel of Norman stock, on which his interlocutor rode, stepped out.

"That affection and your excellent feelings do you great honor, Sab, but Carlota de B—is about to marry, and perhaps dependence on a master will not be as pleasing to you as dependence on your young lady."

The slave came to a sudden stop and turned his penetrating black eyes on the stranger, who continued, momentarily reining in his horse.

"As you are a servant who enjoys the confidence of his masters, you cannot fail to know that Carlota is engaged to marry Enrique Otway, only son of one of the richest merchants of Puerto Príncipe."

A moment of silence followed these words, during which time there was no doubt but that an incredible upheaval was taking place in the slave's soul. Vertical lines creased his brow, from his eyes shone a sinister brilliance, like the lightning bolt which flashes from among the dark clouds, and then, as though a sudden idea had dispelled his doubts, he exclaimed after an instant of reflection, "Enrique Otway! That name, along with your appearance indicate a foreign origin. Doubtless, then, you must be Señorita de B—'s future husband!"

"You are not deceived, young man; I am indeed Enrique Otway, Carlota's future husband, the same who will try not to have his union with your mistress be a misfortune for you. Just as she has done, I promise to make your sad lot as a slave less arduous. But here is the gate; I can manage without a guide now. Farewell, Sab, you may go your way."

Enrique spurred his horse, which, after passing through the gate, departed at a gallop. The slave looked after him until he saw him reach the door of the white house. He then fixed his eyes on the sky, gave a low moan, and let himself fall upon a grassy bank.

TRANSLATED BY NINA M. SCOTT

An Afro-Cuban Poet

Plácido

In a slave society people of color, whether slave or free, had less opportunity for literary expression. Nevertheless, one of Cuba's great poets of the nineteenth century was the free mulatto Gabriel de la Concepción Valdés, popularly known as "Plácido" (1809–1844). Although most of his poetry eschews any explicit reference to the great political issues of his day, slavery and nationalism, Spanish authorities seemed to consider his very existence a threat to the social order. He was executed in 1844 for allegedly fomenting or participating in a conspiracy for a slave rebellion known as "La Escalera." The poem "The Pineapple Flower" is one of a series extolling Cuba's natural environment; "To a Comet" reveals a passionate commitment to freedom.

THE PINEAPPLE FLOWER

The most beautiful fruit
That is born in the Indies
The most esteemed
By all who look at it,
Is the sweet pineapple
That offers us nectar,
More pleasing and tasty
Than that which in the old
Ages the Olympic deities
Savored;
But the pineapple flower
Is more precious.

When above the stem
She presents herself erect,
Her head encircled
By a green crown
The fertile countryside
Proclaims her queen;

The dawn of pearls
With laughter salutes her,
Favonio [the wind] kisses her
And the star of the day
Contemplates entranced
The pineapple flower.

As if you were to weave
A small basket
Of rushes, twisted,
To form a pyre;
And in every distance
Like that of a pearl,
You were to place a ruby,
Imitating shells,
Like those small ones
That the sea places at its bank.
This is how the pineapple
Presents itself with flowers.

She is an emblem
Of living infancy
Fruitful in her trunk
Fertile in her path
And since young girls tend
To give birth to
Loving desires
because of what they see,
So that the finished image
Of love will remain in her eyes
Springing forth
Like a pineapple flower.

TO A COMET[1]

Unknown body, that spins
In the region of the air
Leaving behind your course
A long brilliant tail,
You, who for so many centuries
Traveled without stopping

Seeing generations
Born and buried,
You, who among so many worlds
That circulate, wandering
in space, you see the earth
Mansion of weeping and blood;
Tell me if you have seen a people
Where there is only one man,
And angels obey
What his voice commands.
Or on the opposite extreme,
Where in lasting peace,
The vassals are men,
And he who governs, an angel.
Tell me, I beg you
By the just and great Being
At whose voice you rise up
And at whose voice you decline.
Answer me, for if my unshakable
Star avoids me
It denies me the chance
To be able to inhabit you,
Let me be given, at least,
The invaluable good
Of knowing that there is a place
Where virtue rests
And that you shine more than the sun,
And because you are forever
You will become a dazzling crown
For your Supreme Maker.

TRANSLATED BY AVIVA CHOMSKY

Note

1. Because of censorship, the cry for liberty is only implied in this poem.

III

The Struggle for Independence

Economic crisis and political exclusion in Spanish colonial Cuba led various sectors of Cuban society to pursue different visions of autonomy, reform, annexation to the United States, and independence in the late nineteenth century. The Ten Years' War (1868–78) was a separatist uprising led by the Cuban-born creole elite of eastern Cuba, who felt marginalized both politically and economically. Reformist rather than revolutionary, the movement nonetheless attracted peasants, workers, and ex-slaves who sought more profound social change. The movements for abolition of slavery and for the end of colonial rule in Cuba became intertwined. However, the colonial government's gradual abolition of slavery in the 1880s did little to resolve the economic and racial divisions in Cuban society.

By 1895 Cuban nationalism took on a much more radical cast. The Cuban "nation," many argued, had to be a nation of blacks and whites together, avoiding both the Haitian and the U.S. models of independence and nation building. In Haiti, independence was achieved by rebel slaves, and the white planter class fled; in the United States, it was the white elite who obtained independence and forged the new country's institutions, maintaining slavery for almost a hundred more years. Cuban nationalism, as crystallized by its foremost spokesperson, José Martí, explicitly celebrated the country's multicultural heritage.

Spain's formal empire in the Caribbean was already giving way to a U.S. "informal" empire, as U.S. involvement and investment in the sugar industry grew rapidly in the late nineteenth century. Thus the United States played a large role in Cuban conceptualizations of what independence would mean, and, finally, in the actual struggle for independence, as U.S. forces intervened in 1898 and Cuba became a U.S. protectorate instead of an independent nation.

Freedom and Slavery

Carlos Manuel de Céspedes

In October of 1868, as the Ten Years' War against Spain broke out, sugar planter and independence leader Carlos Manuel de Céspedes (1819–1874) freed his slaves to fight with him in the battle for a free Cuba. His 27 December 1868 Decree on Slavery shows his attempt to negotiate a fragile alliance between different sectors of Cuban society willing to fight for independence: it condemns slavery, in theory, but accepts it in practice.

The Cuban Revolution, in proclaiming the independence of the fatherland, has with this proclaimed all liberties, and could hardly accept the great contradiction of limiting these to only one part of the population of the country. A free Cuba is incompatible with a slaveholding Cuba; and the abolition of Spanish institutions must include, and out of necessity and for reasons of the highest justice does include, the abolition of slavery as the most iniquitous of all. Thus this abolition is recorded among the principles proclaimed in the revolution's first manifesto. Full realization of this goal, resolved in the minds of all truly liberal Cubans, must be the first act that the country carries out as one of the rights it has gained. But the country can only fulfill this goal, as a general measure, when in full use of those rights it can, by means of free suffrage, agree upon the best manner to carry it out to the true advantage of both its old and its new citizens.

The object of these measures is not, thus, nor could it be, the arrogation of a right that those who today are at the front of revolutionary operations feel is far from being invested in them, to precipitate the outcome of such a transcendental question. But at the same time, the provisional government cannot oppose the use of the right that slave owners have in accordance with our laws, and which many of them want to use, to emancipate their slaves. The provisional government also agrees, at the same time, with the morality of using these freed slaves for now in the service of the common fatherland, and the need to act to ward off the dangers that could result for them and for the country from the lack of immediate employment. Thus we urge the adoption of provisional measures that will serve as a rule for the military chiefs who are operating in the different districts of this Department to resolve the cases that come before them in this matter.

Thus, and in accordance with the faculties invested in me, I have resolved that from now on, and until another agreement is made by the country, the following articles shall be followed:

1. Any slaves whose masters present them to the military chiefs to be freed are so declared. The proprietors who so desire reserve the right to indemnification as decreed by the nation and with the option of a higher rate than that fixed for those who emancipate their slaves at a later date.

Toward this goal, proprietors will be issued receipts.

2. These freedmen shall for now be used in the service of the fatherland in the manner that will be resolved.

3. To this end, a commission will be named to take charge of providing the freedmen with appropriate employment in accordance with regulations that will be created.

4. Outside of these cases, we will continue to treat the slaves of Cubans loyal to the Spanish cause, and those of neutral foreigners, in accordance with the principle of respect for property that the revolution has declared.

5. The slaves of those who are convicted of being enemies of the fatherland and openly against the revolution shall be confiscated along with the rest of their goods and declared free, with no right to indemnification, and shall be used in the service of the fatherland according to the terms already agreed upon.

6. To resolve the confiscations mentioned in Article 5, legal proceedings will be initiated for each case.

7. Proprietors who lend their slaves to the service of the revolution without freeing them for now, will conserve their ownership until the question of slavery reaches a general resolution.

8. Any slaves from the *palenques* who present themselves to the authorities will of course be declared free, with the right to live among us, or to remain in their settlements in the wilderness, recognizing and obeying the government of the revolution.

9. Individual runaways who are captured, or those who without the consent of their owners come before the authorities or the military commanders, will not be accepted without previous consultation with said owners, or in accordance with a resolution accepted by this government in a previous decree.

Fatherland and freedom. Bayamo, 27 December 1868. Carlos Manuel de Céspedes.

TRANSLATED BY AVIVA CHOMSKY

Memories of a Cuban Girl

Renée Méndez Capote

The testimonial novel arose in the 1960s as counterpart to the chronicles of the conquerors. Testimonies sought to give voice to those left out of the official documentation, the illiterate and powerless who were excluded from top-down historical accounts. In the climate of the 1960s, in which much that had been taken for granted was being questioned, testimonial narratives spurred historical inquiry. They also proposed active readership, involving the reader as a character in the life of the epoch, free to dispute and question the official version. Many of the testimonial novels of that decade were Cuban. Despite recent scholarly debate about the uses and abuses of testimonies, they remain an important source for understanding a history that goes beyond official voices.

Renée Méndez Capote's (1901–1988) Memorias de una cubanita que nació con el siglo (Memories of a Cuban girl who was born with the century) (1964) explores the world of the Cuban bourgeoisie at the turn of the century and through the early development of the republic. In it the author casts a glance back in rich detail but without nostalgia. The author evokes and recreates the world she was formed in — one of gender and class restrictions, with a legacy of slavery, cruelty, and hypocrisy.

Although set in the Cuban republic, many of the vignettes take the form of flashbacks to the recent colonial past, as in the following selection in which the narrator recounts an event of 1869, at the outset of the war, told to her by her mother.

It is the Havana of 1869. War has just broken out and the rich, aristocratic, and slave owning, who have amassed their wealth and bought their titles with the suffering of blacks, don't give a damn if Cuba is never free. Carlos Manuel de Céspedes horrifies them, and the burning of Bayamo seems to them a fatal precedent, for which all those madmen who squandered their fortune like that deserve to be punished. In Havana, the highborn families are on the side of Spain, which represents order and authority. The sound of the Demajagua has hurt their delicate ears, and so they choose not to hear it, continuing to live as if the Cuban countryside were not being bathed in heroic blood.[1]

On this cold December dawn, three singular people walk down Oficios Street:

Madroña, the good-looking marquise who hides her tiger eyes under a mantilla; elevated in status by the title bought for her by a slave trader, she makes up for her humble origins by scandalizing "proper society" with her insolence.

Jacinto, the trusted slave, elegant and flexible within his green livery coat with gold buttons.

María Mercé, the pretty young black woman, with her blue and white striped suit, on her head a silk lace mantilla like the one her mistress wears.

Jacinto carries a lantern to light the way.

They are on their way to dawn mass. With each difficult step on the narrow streets, an imperious voice calls out to Jacinto to light the way, to María Mercé to take her arm. Her long, pale hands hold the tortoiseshell breviary, around the fingers that emerge like lilies from the open-fingered lace gloves the heavy rosary of fine gold is wound, and that youthful, smooth hand is nevertheless claw-like.

Once the mistress is no longer in need of assistance, María Mercé returns to her place five steps behind her. The young black woman carries the folding chair, the large fan with which she will fan her slowly, standing to the right of her señora while she prays, and she will carefully hold up the small chiffon parasol with the long, carved ivory handle, so that the weak, early sun doesn't harm the lady's skin on the way back.

They proceed down the silent and still deserted street. The large palace doors are all shut. The blinds on the mezzanine where the slaves live are hermetically closed, just like the large windows on the first floor where the owners live. At the corner, the night watchman, bundled up in his cape, with his lantern and his handful of keys, waits in resignation for the night to end.

When they reach the Alameda, the sun begins to throw out small rays, breaking up the grayness of the quiet waters. The beautiful ships of the Royal Navy are anchored in the bay. The sails, and the red and gold flags, of liners, frigates, and brigs are outlined against the Antillean sky.

Madroña stops a moment to contemplate the *Imperator II*, which gently rocks, moored alongside the pier. She emits a clear song that pierces the new morning. On deck, watching over the coming and going of sailors busy emptying buckets of water and washing the decks until they shine, the *curro* sings.[2] Still agile, despite his seventy years.

The beautiful marquise takes the parasol from María Mercé's hands and waves with it in the direction of the pier, before turning down Acosta Street. The curro, from a distance, barely containing a cry of joy, returns her greeting.

The men stop working, raise their heads, and follow the formidable woman with their gaze. Lope, the *manchego*,[3] suffocated by desire whenever she comes on board, stands next to the mainsail.

"She is beautiful, but evil. . . . She takes after her grandfather, a brute who died mysteriously. He assassinated, tortured, raped, and sold the children he made with the slave women . . . and his granddaughter takes after him."

Morning is rising. The port begins to come alive. The ocean is covered in sparkling silver. The seagulls, shaking off sleep, come down to search the sardine stains for food. On Saturdays, the mornings are playful. On the ships, heads of tousled hair can be seen throwing buckets of water into the sea. The free black men who work as stevedores, arrive in crews, with their colorful striped suits. A group of Spaniards, having grown rich, now return to their homeland.

Meanwhile, the three who were making their way on foot up Acosta Street arrive at the Church of the Holy Spirit. Madroña has a predilection for the temple of the free blacks, perhaps because of how they mistreat their slaves.

"Her conscience drives her there to pray . . . ," María la O said quietly to María Mercé when the former went to the kitchen, before dawn, to prepare breakfast for her master who was going to mass. María la O was living proof of Madroña's cruelty. When she was still very young, she had had her tied to her cot, because she liked to sleep, and she left her tied there so long that when she was finally untied, she could never walk straight again.

"I think she's putting a spell on Father José Basilio. If you saw the way she looks at him when he's saying mass. The poor man breaks into a cold sweat because La Niña has him crucified with her evil eyes. . . . Forgive me Jesus, but the gentleman Juan Francisco is not man enough to control her. . . ."

María Mercé crosses herself hurriedly and picks up the heavy silver platter with the china cup holding steaming hot chocolate and the vanilla-flavored sponge cake on an etched crystal plate.

In the peace and quiet of the church, before the altar to Santa Bárbara, Father José Basilio says the daily mass.

Kneeling modestly on the tile floor, with her hands chastely intertwined, Madroña eats him up with her eyes.

Feeling her presence, the little priest becomes confused. He cannot escape the spell of her gaze. He feels so confused he could die, deeply ill at ease.

"Dominus vobiscum . . . orate, fratre . . . ," his voice breaks.

Before the kneeling woman in lace and silks, the drama of a tortured conscience is played out. The spectacle entertains her. For a moment, the poor priest believes he sees a mocking glint in the implacable eyes that torture him.

Madroña's eyes will drive him crazy . . . those eyes so strange, so hard, so cold and ardent, so beautiful . . . and so cruel. . . .

When the mass is over, she follows the priest to the vestry. He is shaking and, though he holds his hands together, they tremble.

"Take this, Father José Basilio, it's my alms for tomorrow's feast . . . since you haven't wanted to come to my house to get it, I've brought it to you. . . ."

As she hands him the twenty gold ounces, her smooth fingers brush up against his cold hand, and he suddenly grows pale as if all the blood were rushing from his face to his heart.

Large black wings seem to cast their shadow over the temple. María Mercé instinctively draws closer to Jacinto. Madroña catches a glance of infinite tenderness from one of the young people to the other. At the door to the church, the mistress's voice rings out metallic, inhuman.

"María Mercé, as soon as we get home, I want to speak with you!"

"Yes, mi ama . . . ," the young black woman lowers her head and opens the parasol.

Jacinto, who is walking behind them, casts a terrible glance at the white woman. His hand moves, in a habitual gesture, to his right cheek, where a deep scar interrupts the smoothness of his twenty-year-old skin. The iniquity of this woman will never be erased from his mind where the iron left an even deeper mark.

"Brand that Negro, he's too beautiful," she had said to the overseer on Three Kings' Day, as Jacinto sang, in the kitchen, waiting for his turn to join the chorus.

TRANSLATED BY PAMELA MARIA SMORKALOFF

Notes

1. La Demajagua was the sugar plantation belonging to Céspedes, where he freed his slaves and led them in rebellion against Spain in 1868.
2. An Andalusian émigré, a southern Spaniard living in America.
3. A person from the Spanish region of La Mancha.

José Martí's "Our America"

José Martí

José Martí (1853–1895), more than any other Cuban, is seen as the father of the Cuban nation. In exile in the United States, he successfully forged alliances and developed the ideologies of a popular, antiracist, and anti-imperialist nationalism that still has enormous resonance for Cubans today. His essay "Our America," originally published in 1891, became a touchstone for Latin American intellectuals and popular movements attempting to create a Latin American identity that could be celebrated for its differences from Europe and the United States, rather than seen as inferior to the more politically and economically powerful areas.

Only those born prematurely are lacking in courage. Those without faith in their country are seven-month weaklings. Because they have no courage, they deny it to others. Their puny arms—arms with bracelets and hands with painted nails, arms of Paris or Madrid—can hardly reach the bottom limb, so they claim the tall tree to be unclimbable. The ships should be loaded with those harmful insects that gnaw at the bone of the country that nourishes them. If they are Parisians or from Madrid, let them go to the Prado, to swan around, or to Tortoni's, in high hats. Those carpenter's sons who are ashamed that their fathers are carpenters! Those born in America who are ashamed of the mother who reared them, because she wears an Indian apron; and those scoundrels who disown their sick mother, abandoning her on her sickbed! Then who is a real man? He who stays with his mother and nurses her in her illness, or he who puts her to work out of sight, and lives at her expense on decadent lands, sporting fancy neckties, cursing the womb that carried him, displaying the sign of the traitor on the back of his paper frock coat? These sons of Our America, which will be saved by its Indians and is growing better; these deserters who take up arms in the armies of a North America that drowns its Indians in blood and is growing worse! These delicate creatures who are men but are unwilling to do men's work! The Washington who made this land for them, did he not go to live with the English, at a time when he saw them fighting against his own country. These unbelievers in honor who drag that honor over foreign soil like their counterparts in the French Revolution with their dancing, their affectations, their drawling speech!

For in what lands can men take more pride than in our long-suffering American republics, raised up among the silent Indian masses by the bleeding arms of a hundred apostles, to the sounds of battle between the book and the processional candle? Never in history have such advanced and united nations been forged in so short a time from such disorganized elements. The presumptuous man feels that the earth was made to serve as his pedestal because he happens to have a facile pen or colorful speech, and he accuses his native land of being worthless and beyond redemption because its virgin jungles fail to provide him with a constant means of traveling the world, driving Persian ponies and lavishing champagne like a tycoon. The incapacity does not lie with the emerging country in quest of suitable forms and a utilitarian greatness; it lies rather with those who attempt to rule nations of a unique and violent character by means of laws inherited from four centuries of freedom in the United States and nineteen centuries of monarchy in France. A decree by Hamilton does not halt the charge of the plainsman's horse. A phrase by Sieyès does nothing to quicken the stagnant blood of the Indian race. To govern well, one must see things as they are. And the able governor in America is not the one who knows how to govern the Germans or the French; he must know the elements that make up his own country, and how to bring them together, using methods and institutions originating within the country, to reach that desirable state where each man can attain self-realization and all may enjoy the abundance that Nature has bestowed in everyone in the nation to enrich with their toil and defend with their lives. Government must originate in the country. The spirit of government must be that of the country. Its structure must conform to rules appropriate to the country. Good government is nothing more than the balance of the country's natural elements. . . .

How can the universities produce governors if not a single university in America teaches the rudiments of the art of government, the analysis of elements peculiar to the peoples of America? The young go out into the world wearing Yankee or French spectacles, hoping to govern a people they do not know. In the political race entrance should be denied to those who are ignorant of the rudiments of politics. The prize in literary contests should not go for the best ode, but for the best study of the political factors of one's country. Newspapers, universities, and schools should encourage the study of the country's pertinent components. To know them is sufficient, without mincing words; for whoever brushes aside even a part of the truth, whether through intention or oversight, is doomed to fall. The truth he lacks thrives on negligence, and brings down whatever is built without it. It is easier to resolve our

José Martí, painted by
Jorge Arche in 1943. Juan
A. Martínez, *Cuban Art
and National Identity: The
Vanguardia Painters, 1927–
1950* (University Press of
Florida, 1994), 71. Courtesy
of Museo Nacional de
Cuba, Havana.

problem knowing its components than to resolve it without knowing them.
Along comes the natural man, strong and indignant, and he topples all the
justice accumulated from books because he has not been governed in accordance with the obvious needs of the country. Knowing is what counts. To know
one's country and govern it with that knowledge is the only way to free it from
tyranny. The European university must bow to the American university. The
history of America, from the Incas to the present, must be taught in clear detail and to the letter, even if the archons of Greece are overlooked. Our Greece
must take priority over the Greece which is not ours. We need it more. Nationalist statesmen must replace foreign statesmen. Let the world be grafted onto
our republics, but the trunk must be our own. And let the vanquished pedant
hold his tongue, for there are no lands in which a man may take greater pride
than in our long-suffering American republics. . . .

Thrown out of gear for three centuries by a power which denied men the
right to use their reason, the continent disregarded or closed its ears to the
unlettered throngs that helped bring it to redemption, and embarked on a government based on reason—a reason belonging to all for the common good,
not the university brand of reason over the peasant brand. The problem of
independence did not lie in a change of forms but in change of spirit.

It was imperative to make common cause with the oppressed, in order to secure a new system opposed to the ambitions and governing habits of the oppressors. The tiger, frightened by gunfire, returns at night to his prey. He dies with his eyes shooting flames and his claws unsheathed. He cannot be heard coming because he approaches with velvet tread. When the prey awakens, the tiger is already upon it. The colony lives on the Republic, and Our America is saving itself from its enormous mistakes—the pride of its capital cities, the blind triumph of a scorned peasantry, the excessive influx of foreign ideas and formulas, the wicked and unpolitical disdain for the aboriginal race—because of the higher virtue, enriched with necessary blood, of a Republic struggling against a colony. The tiger lurks against every tree, lying in wait at every turn. He will die with his claws unsheathed and his eyes shooting flames. . . .

We were a phenomenon with a chest of an athlete, the hands of a dandy, and the brain of a child. We were a masquerader in English breeches, Parisian vest, North American jacket, and Spanish cap. The Indian hovered near us in silence, and went off to hills to baptize his children. The Negro was seen pouring out the songs of his heart at night, alone and unrecognized among the rivers and wild animals. The peasant, the creator, turned in blind indignation against the disdainful city, against his own child. As for us, we were nothing but epaulets and professors' gowns in countries that came into the world wearing hemp sandals and headbands. It would have been the mark of genius to couple the headband and the professors' gown with the founding fathers' generosity and courage, to rescue the Indian, to make a place for the competent Negro, to fit liberty to the body of those who rebelled and conquered for it. We were left with the judge, the general, the scholar, and the sinecured. The angelic young, as if caught in the tentacles of an octopus, lunged heavenward, only to fall back, crowned with clouds in sterile glory. The native, driven by instinct, swept away the golden staffs of office in blind triumph. Neither the European nor the Yankee could provide the key to the Spanish American riddle. Hate was attempted, and every year the countries amounted to less. Exhausted by the senseless struggle between the book and the lance, between reason and the processional candle, between the city and the country, weary of the impossible rule by rival urban cliques over the natural nation tempestuous or inert by turns, we begin almost unconsciously to try love. Nations stand up and greet one another. "What are we?" is the mutual question, and little by little they furnish answers. When a problem arises in Cojimar, they do not seek its solution in Danzig. The frock coats are still French, but thought begins to be American. The youth of America are rolling up their sleeves, digging their hands in the dough, and making it rise with the sweat of their brows. They realize that there is too much imitation, and that creation holds the key to salvation. "Create" is the password of this generation. The wine is made from plantain, but even if it turns sour, it is our own wine! That a country's form of government must be in keeping with its natural elements is self-evident. Absolute ideas must take relative forms if they are not to fail because of an error in form. Freedom, to be viable, has to be sincere and complete. If a Republic refuses to open its arms to all, and move ahead with all, it dies. The tiger within sneaks in through the crack; so does the tiger from without. The general holds back his cavalry to a pace that suits his infantry, for if its infantry is left behind, the cavalry will be surrounded by the enemy. Politics and strategy are one. Nations should live in an atmosphere of self-criticism because it is healthy, but always with one heart and one mind. Stoop to the unhappy, and lift them up in your arms! Thaw out frozen America with the fire of your hearts! Make the natural blood of the nations course vigorously through their veins! The new Americans are on their feet, saluting each other from nation to nation, the eyes of the laborers shining with joy. The natural statesman arises, schooled in the direct study of Nature. He reads to apply his knowledge, not to imitate. Economists study the problems at their point of origin. Speakers begin a policy of moderation. Playwrights bring native characters to the stage. Academies discuss practical subjects. Poetry shears off its Zorrilla-like locks and hangs its red vest on the glorious tree. Selective and sparkling prose is filled with ideas. In the Indian republics, the governors are learning Indian. . . .

But perhaps Our America is running another risk that does not come from itself but from the difference in origins, methods, and interest between the two halves of the continent, and the time is near at hand when an enterprising and vigorous people, who scorn and ignore Our America, will even so approach it and demand a close relationship. And since strong nations, self-made by law and shotgun, love strong nations and them alone; since the time of madness and ambition — from which North America may be freed by the predominance of the purest elements in its blood, or on which it may be launched by its vindictive and sordid masses, its tradition of expansion, or the ambitions of some powerful leader — is not so near at hand, even to the most timorous eye, that there is no time for the test of discreet and unwavering pride that could confront and dissuade it; since its good name as a Republic in the eyes of the world's perceptive nations puts upon North America a restraint that cannot be taken away by childish provocations or pompous arrogance or parricidal discords among our American nations — the pressing need of Our America is to show itself as it is, one in spirit and intent, swift conquerors of a suffocating past, stained only by the enriching blood drawn from the scarves left upon us by our masters.

The scorn of our formidable neighbor, who does not know us, is Our

America's greatest danger. And since the day of the visit is near, it is imperative that our neighbor knows us, and soon, so that it will not scorn us. Through ignorance it might even come to lay hands on us. Once it does know us, it will remove its hands out of respect. One must have faith in the best in men and distrust the worst. One must allow the best to be shown so that it reveals and prevails over the worst. Nations should have a pillory for whoever stirs up useless hatred, and another for whoever fails to tell them the truth in time.

There can be no racial animosity, because there are no races. The theorist and feeble thinkers string together and warm over the bookshelf races which the well-disposed observer and the fair-minded traveler vainly seek in the justice of Nature where man's universal identity springs forth from triumphant love and the turbulent hunger for life. The soul, equal and eternal, emanates from bodies of different shapes and colors. Whoever foments and spreads antagonism and hatred between the races, sins against humanity. But as nations take shape among other different nations, there is a condensation of vital and individual characteristics of thought and habit, expansion and conquest, vanity and greed which could—from the latent state of national concern, and in the period of internal disorder, or the rapidity with which the country's character has been accumulating—be turned into a serious threat for the weak and isolated neighboring countries, declared by the strong country to be inferior and perishable. The thought is father to the deed. And one must not attribute, through a provincial antipathy, a fatal and inborn wickedness to the continent's fair-skinned nation simply because it does not speak our language, nor see the world as we see it, nor resemble us in its political defects, so different from ours, nor favorably regard the excitable, dark-skinned people, or look charitably, from its still uncertain eminence, upon those less favored by history, who climb the road of republicanism by heroic stages. The self-evident facts of the problem should not be obscured, because the problem can be resolved, for the peace of centuries to come, by appropriate study, and by tacit and immediate union in the continental spirit. With a single voice the hymn is already being sung; the present generation is carrying industrious America along the road enriched by their sublime fathers; from Río Grande to the Strait of Magellan, the Great Semí [a Taíno deity], astride its condor, spreading the seed of the new America over the romantic nations of the continent and the sorrowful islands of the sea!

TRANSLATOR UNKNOWN

Guantanamera

José Martí

José Martí (1853–1895) authored the poem "Yo soy un hombre sincero" more well known for its adaptation into the popular song "Guantanamera."[1] In it the narrator affirms both his eminently Cuban identity and attachment to the land, and his multiple origins ("I come from everywhere, and I am going everywhere").

I am an honest man
From where the palm grows
And before I die I wish
To fling my verses from my soul.
I come from everywhere
And I am going toward everywhere:
Among the arts, I am art
In the mountains, I am a mountain.
I know the strange names
Of the herbs and flowers
And of mortal deceits
And of sublime pains.
I have seen in the dark night
Rain over my head
The pure rays of lightning
Of divine beauty.
I saw wings born in men
Of beautiful women:
And coming out of rubbish
Butterflies flying.
I have seen a man live
With his dagger at his side,
Without ever saying the name
Of she who had killed him.
Rapid, like a reflection,

I saw my soul, twice
When the poor old man died,
When she said good-bye to me.
I trembled once — at the fence,
At the entrance to the vineyard —
When a barbarous bee
Stung my daughter in the forehead.
I felt joy once, such that
Nobody ever felt joy: when
The mayor read the sentence
Of my death, crying.
I hear a sigh, across
The lands and the sea
And it is not a sigh, it is
That my son is going to wake up.
They say that from the jeweler
I took the best jewel,
I took a sincere friend
And left love aside.

TRANSLATED BY AVIVA CHOMSKY

Note

1. "Guantanamera" was composed by José (Joseíto) Fernández Díaz; the song was popularized in the United States by Pete Seeger.

The Explosion of the *Maine*

New York Journal

The explosion of the U.S. battleship Maine *on 15 February 1898 off the coast of Havana was the ostensible trigger for the entrance of the United States into the war. The navy quickly announced that the explosion, which killed over 250 shipmates, had been caused by sabotage, although a 1970s navy investigation concluded that an internal coal combustion was more likely the cause. Remnants salvaged from the ship adorn the* Maine *monument overlooking Havana's harbor—though the eagle crowning the monument was removed in 1961—Arlington National Cemetery in Washington, and many historic parks in the state of Maine.*

The role of the U.S. media in sensationalizing the incident, and demanding a military response, is legendary in the era of "yellow journalism." William Randolph Hearst's New York Journal *competed with Joseph Pulitzer's* New York World *to give the most lurid accounts of events on the island. The following excerpt from Hearst's* Journal *gives a sense of the reporting of the time.*

SUNK BY TORPEDO OR MINE, THEY SAY

Naval Constructor Bowles and Others Declare No Internal Accident Destroyed the Maine

Harbor Covered by Mines

Merchant Pendleton, of Key West, Says He Heard a Spanish Consul Predict the Sinking of the War Ship

Naval men here are agreed that the explosion that wrecked the *Maine* was not caused by any accident on board the ship itself, but that the cause came from the outside—in other words, that the *Maine* was blown up by a torpedo or submarine mine. . . .

COULDN'T HAVE BEEN FROM INSIDE

An officer high in authority in the Navy Yard, and who has been closely associated with the *Maine*, said yesterday:

"The idea that the catastrophe resulted from an internal accident is preposterous. In the first place, such a thing has never occurred before that I have ever heard of either in the British navy or ours. There was an English ship that was lost several years ago, and it was theorized that an explosion may have occurred from volatile gases in the paint room, but, since then the paint room on war ships is open to the air, and the gases can escape freely.

"The only theory of the accident that is in the least tenable is that fire in the coal bunkers exploded in the shells. The coal bunkers on the *Maine* adjoin the ten-inch shell magazine, but these are really nothing more than pockets, the ones which are always emptied first, and I expect later investigation to show that no coal was in them at the time of the accident. This would dispose of that theory, supposing the explosion to have been in the bows, which all the reports seem to show.

"The ten-inch shell room I refer to is about eighty feet from the bow of the boat. Further than that, there are electrical appliances in all of the coal bunkers to show the evidence of fire, and even if these failed to work the smell of smoke would have been detected by the men on board, and there is no testimony to that effect from the survivors—a thing which would be mentioned first by a sailor.

"There is only one gun cotton magazine on the *Maine* and that is far to the aft, almost directly under the ward room and officers' quarters. This gun cotton is kept constantly wet and is regularly inspected. There is found to be not more than a half-ounce evaporation in a month, so that it remains moist of itself. Further than that the only thing that could explode it is fulminate of mercury.

"These magazines are surrounded by stores and water tanks to make explosion impossible. The ammunition is placed first in bags and then in hermetically sealed copper tanks. The rooms are kept locked, except when charges are wanted for target practice, and the keys are kept in the captain's room under his personal care. I do not know about the rules in this regard on the *Maine*, but generally these kegs are kept directly over the captain's bunk and are guarded by a special sentry.

"You can be almost absolutely sure that this thing did not happen within the boat. As to other theories I do not credit the idea of a torpedo having been sent against her or a boat loaded with high explosives set off under her bows. These, in my opinion, would not cause the great havoc and the almost instant sinking of the ship that followed.

A battery of the Second U.S. Artillery at Guard Mount, Captain General's Palace, Havana. F. Matthews, *The New-Born Cuba* (New York, 1899), 2.

"TO MY MIND THERE IS BUT ONE EXPLANATION, AND THAT IS — A SUBMARINE MINE

"Why the mine should be in that place, who put it there, and how and why it was fired, are beyond conjecture, but that the *Maine* anchored over a mine and that it exploded under her and sent her in a jiffy to the bottom seems the only explanation that bears plausibility.

"Now, a mine is not made in a minute, and neither is it placed in position by one man. There must be several who know the secret of this tragedy, and it should not be so difficult to run it down and place the blame where it belongs.

"I think the government will start at once to raise the ship and then the whole matter can be told. Divers will be put to work and a court of inquiry probably will be ordered immediately, and the disclosures will substantiate what I say." . . .

MAY HAVE BEEN A PLOT, SAYS PENDLETON

Key West Merchant Who Heard a Spanish Official
Boast the Maine *Would Be Blown Up*

Mr. C. B. Pendleton, a merchant of Key West, Fla., comes forward with a most remarkable story. He arrived in this city by steamer yesterday, AND WHEN HE LANDED FIRST HEARD THE NEWS OF THE *Maine*'s destruction. According to the story he tells there may have been a real plot to blow the vessel up.

"On Sunday morning last," said Mr. Pendleton, "Spanish Vice-Consul Fernández at Key West told me in the presence of witnesses that if the *Maine* ever trained her guns on Havana she would be blown out of the water in a minute. At noon I took the steamer for this port, and on landing today I heard the news of the explosion. I at once recalled the remark of the vice-consul, and I am almost satisfied in my own mind that the *Maine* was deliberately destroyed."

Mr. Pendleton is a merchant who has lived twenty years in Key West. He recently returned from Havana, and from what he knows of Spanish character the tide swinging the big ship so as to bring her guns to bear would be construed by the more rabid into training on the port.

"I met Fernández at breakfast in the Hotel Duval early Saturday morning," said Mr. Pendleton. "He sat at a table adjoining the one occupied by myself, United States Marshal John F. Horr, C. L. Roberts, my bookkeeper, and a young woman, also in my employ. The conversation started by the vice-consul's allu-

A U.S. mail cart in Havana. Matthews, *New-Born Cuba*, 167.

sion to the death of Ensign Breckinridge, who was lost from the torpedo boat *Cushing.*

" 'It is a good thing there is one more American gone,' said Fernández.

"We bantered him a bit, and then he got angry and said:

" 'That's all right, Let the *Maine* train her guns on Havana and she'll be blown to h—l in a minute.'

"Of course I cannot say that Fernández was aware of a plot, if one existed, but he spoke like a man who knew what he was talking about. On the trip up I told a number of passengers on the *Lampasas* of this threat and they attached much significance to it when we arrived and heard the news."

Mr. C. L. Roberts, one of the party at the table, to whom Mr. Pendleton refers, sent this telegram to the *Journal* from Key West last night:

"I heard Mr. Pendleton and Fernández talking on Saturday, and Mr. Pendleton was telling Fernández that the *Maine* had her guns trained on the city of Havana. Fernández remarked: 'If the *Maine* turns her guns on Havana, Spain will blow the ship into eternity.' "

U.S. Cartoonists Portray Cuba

John J. Johnson

In this selection of contemporary cartoons, U.S. newspaper artists deploy many of the most common images and devices that were used in representations of Cuba and, more generally, of Latin America. The cartoons reveal the awakening imperial pretensions of the United States following the defeat of Spain in 1898. Cuba and Cubans are portrayed as infants, carefree children, or rowdy, undisciplined youths, requiring the constant guidance and tutelage of the United States. Cubans are not only infantilized; they are frequently represented as blacks who are alternately cheerful, irresponsible, lazy, dim, and grotesquely deformed—reflecting racist stereotypes common in the United States in the period between the Civil War and World War I. The first cartoon reveals the sharp change in U.S. perceptions of the Cuban independence fighters after U.S. troops landed on Cuban soil—from a preintervention sympathetic portrayal of heroic freedom fighters fighting a barbaric Spain—to a representation of Cuban patriots as shifty, comic black men dressed in bizarre uniform. The second cartoon illustrates U.S. pride in international recognition of its new imperial maturity, while in the third cartoon, published three years after U.S. troops had left Cuban soil, Cuba is portrayed as an out-of-control, gun-toting delinquent, the blackness of the Cuban figure contrasting sharply with the polite, well dressed, young and very white Puerto Rican child.

This style of plaster will cure all their wounds. John J. Johnson, *Latin America in Caricature* (Austin: University of Texas Press, 1993), 165. Taken from *Detroit Journal*, 1899. Cartoon by Thomas May.

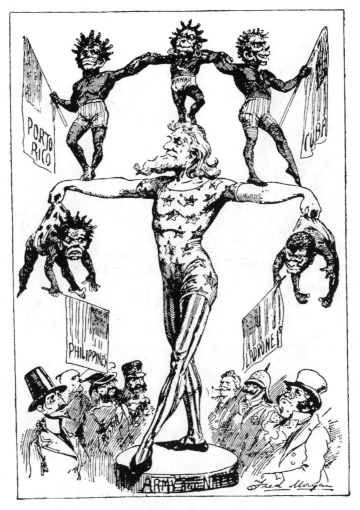

John Bull, "It's Really Most Extraordinary. . . ." Johnson, *Latin America in Caricature*, 163. Taken from *Philadelphia Inquirer*, 1898. The U.S. cartoonist is showing British recognition of U.S. imperial strength. Cartoon by Fred Morgan.

Uncle Sam to Puerto Rico. Johnson, *Latin America in Caricature*, 127. Taken from *Chicago Inter-Ocean*, 1905.

The Devastation of Counterinsurgency

Fifty-fifth Congress, Second Session

Although U.S. policy and opinion makers had reason to exaggerate Spanish atrocities, the destructiveness of these policies, and of the war, should not be underestimated. Some three hundred thousand Cubans died in the war, during the forced relocations (reconcentrations), and of starvation and disease. And as historian Louis Pérez points out, in some ways these wartime deaths were only the tip of the iceberg: houses, roads, and railroads were destroyed, mining, livestock, and agriculture devastated.[1] In addition, the island emerged from the war not independent, but under occupation by the United States. In Cuba U.S. consuls documented the horrors of the war, helping to set the stage for U.S. intervention.

Enclosure with dispatch No. 712, Mr. Lee to Mr. Day, Havana, 27 November 1897
Anonymous

Sir: The public rumor of the horrible state in which the *reconcentrados* of the municipal council of Havana were found in the *fosos* [ditches] having reached us, we resolved to pay a visit there, and we will relate to you what we saw with our own eyes:

Four hundred and sixty women and children thrown on the ground, heaped pell-mell as animals, some in a dying condition, others sick and others dead, without the slightest cleanliness, nor the least help, not even to give water to the thirsty, with neither religious or social help, each one dying wherever chance laid them, and for this limited number of reconcentrados the deaths ranged between forty and fifty daily, giving relatively ten days of life for each person, with great joy to the authorities who seconded fatidically the politics of General Weyler to exterminate the Cuban people, for these unhappy creatures received food only after having been for eight days in the fosos, if during this time they could feed themselves with the bad food that the dying refused.

On this first visit we were present at the death of an old man who died through thirst. When we arrived he begged us, for God's sake, to give him a drink. We looked for it and gave it to him, and fifteen minutes afterward he breathed his last, not having had even a drink of water for three days before. Among the many deaths we witnessed there was one scene impossible to forget. There is still alive the only living witness, a young girl of eighteen years, whom we found seemingly lifeless on the ground; on her right-hand side was the body of a young mother, cold and rigid, but with her young child still alive clinging to her dead breast; on her left-hand side was also the corpse of a dead woman holding her son in a dead embrace; a little farther on a poor, dying woman having in her arms a daughter of fourteen, crazy with pain, who after five or six days also died in spite of the care she received.

In one corner a poor woman was dying, surrounded by her children, who contemplated her in silence, without a lament or shedding a tear, they themselves being real specters of hunger, emaciated in a horrible manner. This poor woman augments the catalog already large of the victims of the reconcentration in the fosos.

The relation of the pictures of misery and horror which we have witnessed would be never ending were we to narrate them all.

It is difficult and almost impossible to express by writing the general aspect of the inmates of the fosos, because it is entirely beyond the line of what civilized humanity is accustomed to see; therefore no language can describe it.

The circumstances which the municipal authorities could reunite there are the following: Complete accumulation of bodies dead and alive, so that it was impossible to take one step without walking over them; the greatest want of cleanliness, want of light, air, and water; the food lacking in quality and quantity what was necessary to sustain life, thus sooner putting an end to these already broken-down systems; complete absence of medical assistance; and what is more terrible than all, no consolation whatever, religious or moral.

If any young girl came in any way nice looking, she was infallibly condemned to the most abominable of traffics.

At the sight of such horrible pictures the two gentlemen who went there resolved in spite of the ferocious Weyler, who was still captain general of the island, to omit nothing to remedy a deed so dishonorable to humanity, and so contrary to all Christianity. They did not fail to find persons animated with like sentiments, who, putting aside all fear of the present situation, organized a private committee with the exclusive end of aiding materially and morally the reconcentrados. This neither has been nor is at present an easy task. The great number of the poor and scarcity of means make us encounter constant conflicts. This conflict is more terrible with the official elements and in a special manner with the mayor of the city and the civil authorities, who try by all means to annihilate this good work. The result of the collections are very insignificant if we bear in mind the thousands of people who suffer from the reconcentrations; but it serves for some consolation to see that in Havana some 159 children and eighty-four women are well cared for in the asylum erected in Cadíz Street, No. 82, and ninety-three women and children are equally well located in a large saloon erected for them in the second story of the fosos, with good food and proper medical assistance, as also everything indispensable to civilized life.

According to the information which we have been able to acquire since August until the present day, seventeen hundred persons have entered the fosos proceeding from Jaruco, Campo Florido, Guanabo, and Tapaste, in the Province of Havana. Of these, only 243 are living now and are to be found in Cadíz Street—eighty-two in the saloon already mentioned and sixty-one in the Quinta del Rey and the Hospital Mercedes, the whole amounting to about 397, and of these a great many will die on account of the great sufferings and hunger they have gone through.

From all this we deduce that the number of deaths among the reconcentrados has amounted to 77 percent.

No. 97. Mr. Brice to Mr. Day.
Consulate of the United States, Matanzas, 17 December 1897

Sir: I have the honor to report the following Cuban news in this province, taken from personal observation and reliable sources of information:

CONCENTRADOS

Relief offered these and other poor people by Spanish authorities is only in name. I have personally visited (on several occasions) headmasters of distributing stations. Two thousand rations were given out, for a few days only, to eight thousand persons. . . . There are more than twelve thousand starving people in this city to-day. One out of four (or six) received the following ration: two ounces rice, one and one-half ounces *tassajo* (jerked beef), and sometimes a small piece of bread, per diem. Imagine starving people being relieved by such rations! Even this ration of food has been discontinued since eleven inst. [instant; of this month]. Death rate has diminished somewhat; now about sixty-three daily. There are less people to die.

The scenes of misery and distress daily observed are beyond belief. Here is one out of hundreds. In a family of seventeen living in an old limekiln, upper part of city limits, all were found dead except three, and they barely alive. . . . A few of the strongest of these people have been sent out to sugar plantations, which expect to grind. They get thirty cents per day and board themselves. General Blanco's order, allowing reconcentrados, owners of plantations and farms, to return and cultivate crops, etc., is inoperative and of no avail. Several of our American citizens, owners of land, have repeatedly asked the civil governor of this province for permission to return to their homes, and in every case refused or restrictions imposed making it impossible to comply with. . . .

I am, etc., A. C. Brice, United States Consul.

Note

1. Pérez, *Cuba*, 190–91.

IV

Neocolonialism

The newly independent Cuban Republic was inaugurated on 20 May 1902, under the presidency of Tomás Estrada Palma. But Cuban independence would be a fragile entity, interrupted by a series of U.S. military and political interventions and undermined by economic dependency on the United States and a succession of treaties and agreements that constrained economic initiatives; consolidated Cuba's sugar monoculture; and precluded the establishment of stable, strong, and self-confident governments.

United States troops entered Cuba on numerous occasions during the 1902–34 period, occupying the country between 1906 and 1909, in 1912, and between 1917 and 1920. During the abortive 1933 Revolution, U.S. warships circled the island, intimidating the weak nationalist coalition that briefly took power. From 1901, when the Platt Amendment was incorporated under duress in the Cuban Constitution, until its abrogation in May 1934, the amendment became a symbol of Cuban impotence and a constant reminder of U.S. self-declared authority to interfere in Cuban affairs. Article 7 of the amendment provided for the establishment of a U.S. base in Cuban territory and became the legal basis on which Guantánamo Bay was selected for a naval base that still remains, a reminder of Cuba's neocolonial past.

In its economic life, too, Cuban sovereignty was quickly weakened. The Reciprocity Treaty signed with the United States in 1903 privileged Cuban access to the U.S. sugar market but at a substantial cost. Reciprocity meant that U.S. manufactured goods and other products could enter the Cuban market, establishing an informal economic protectorate and consolidating Cuba's role as producer of a single crop (sugar). For the next fifty years, Cuban economic prosperity would be dependent on the outcome of a series of byzantine struggles over the fate of Cuba's tariff privileges in the U.S. Congress.

Economic dependency and U.S. military intervention and political hegemony did not promote good government. With opportunities for economic advancement blocked, Cuban politicians viewed a bloated, corrupt state as the only opportunity for acquiring wealth and social status. The United States responded with yet more vigorous efforts to tame and educate what it viewed as an uncivilized, irresponsible, and juvenile political class, sending plenipotentiaries (such as Enoch Crowder in the early 1920s) on special missions to supervise the conduct of economic life and the construction of honest cabinets. Even during the brief interregnum of constitutional and properly elected governments of the 1940s, unprecedented levels of corruption and political nepotism under the dominant Auténtico Party undermined public faith in government. The "politics of disappointment" facilitated the coup d'état launched by Fulgencio Batista in March 1952, which inaugurated seven years of increasingly repressive government.

Critics of Cuba's distorted economic and political development model emerged in large numbers in the 1920s, with students, army veterans, a newly unified labor movement, and a small but active Communist Party taking the lead. An attempt to remove a brutal dictatorship (led by Gerardo Machado) and implement a program of nationalist social and economic measures dominated Cuban life in the second half of 1933, although internal divisions among the revolutionaries and the opposition of the United States brought a rapid end to the experiment. The bold, heroic revolutionaries of the early 1930s would eventually become the tawdry corrupt politicians of the Auténtico governments of the 1940s—further reducing Cuban faith in liberal democratic politics. Few mourned the passing of constitutional government when Fulgencio Batista overthrew the Auténtico government of Carlos Prío Socarrás just before the 1952 elections were due to be held.

A new politics emerged early during the Batista regime (1952–59). Its key protagonist was Fidel Castro, who captured the imagination of the Cuban public (but not yet the world outside Cuba) with a daring assault on the Moncada Barracks of the Cuban Army in Santiago de Cuba on 26 July 1953. The Moncada assault was unsuccessful, and Castro was imprisoned and then exiled to Mexico. Although the tributaries of Fidel Castro's politics lay in the world of student activism and the Ortodoxo Party, the protests of the old political parties (Auténticos and Ortodoxos) were soon to be eclipsed by the action-oriented exploits of a variety of citizens groups. In the cities students battled the regime, and members of the Revolutionary Directorate of Havana University assaulted Batista's presidential palace in March 1957. Dissident segments of the armed forces mounted unsuccessful revolts in April 1956 and September 1957. Sugar workers, a sector that had long been a key actor in protest movements, paralyzed production and occupied regional towns in a spectacular series of strikes in December 1955.

Although the role played by armed struggle has been somewhat exaggerated by official histories of the 1959 Revolution, the arrival on the coast of southeastern Cuba of a group of rebels led by Fidel Castro on 2 December 1956 gave the anti-Batista movement new momentum. The cadres of the 26th of July Movement (M-26-7) undermined the regime on two levels. An urban underground practiced sabotage, distribution of propaganda, and armed resistance. The sierra wing of the M-26-7, with the help of country folk, established guerrilla-controlled zones—first in the Sierra Maestra and then, with the involvement of sugar workers, in northern Oriente Province. In the second half of 1958 the rebels moved westward into the plains of Camagüey and Las Villas provinces as the demoralized and increasingly ineffectual Batista army crumbled. In the early morning of 1 January 1959, Batista and his entourage fled the island for exile in the Dominican Republic. Havana was occupied by the rebel forces of Che Guevara and Camilo Cienfuegos while Fidel Castro began a slow march of victory from Santiago to Havana.

The Platt Amendment

President Theodore Roosevelt

The Cuban republic "with all and for the good of all" resolved neither the problem of national independence nor that of racial equality. Political dependence on the United States was enshrined in the Platt Amendment (passed by both houses of the U.S. Congress and signed by President McKinley in March 1901, and written into the Cuban Constitution as a condition for U.S. withdrawal in 1902). The political system set up by the U.S. occupiers and Cuban elites ensured that social inequalities remained.

That in fulfillment of the declaration contained in the joint resolution approved April 20th, 1898, entitled "For the recognition of the independence of the people of Cuba, demanding that the government of Spain relinquish its authority and government in the island of Cuba, and to withdraw its land and naval reserve forces from Cuba and Cuban waters, and directing the president of the United States to use the land and naval forces of the United States to carry these resolutions into effect," the president is hereby authorized to "leave the government and control of the island of Cuba to its people" so soon as a government shall have been established in said island under a constitution which, either as a part thereof or in an ordinance appended thereto, shall define the future relations of the United States with Cuba, substantially as follows:

I. That the government of Cuba shall never enter into any treaty or other compact with any foreign power or powers which will impair or tend to impair the independence of Cuba, or in any manner authorize or permit any foreign power or powers to obtain by colonization or, for military or naval purposes or otherwise, lodgment in or control over any portion of said island.

II. That said government shall not assume or contract any public debt, to pay the interest upon which, and to make reasonable sinking fund provision for the ultimate discharge of which, the ordinary revenues of the island, after defraying the current expenses of government shall be inadequate.

Hoisting the Cuban Flag over the palace, 20 May 1902. Albert G. Robinson, *Cuba Old and New* (New York: Longman, Green and Company, 1915), op. 137.

III. That the government of Cuba consents that the United States may exercise the right to intervene for the preservation of Cuban independence, the maintenance of a government adequate for the protection of life, property, and individual liberty, and for discharging the obligations with respect to Cuba imposed by the Treaty of Paris on the United States, now to be assumed and undertaken by the government of Cuba.

IV. That all Acts of the United States in Cuba during its military occupancy thereof are ratified and validated, and all lawful rights acquired thereunder shall be maintained and protected.

V. That the government of Cuba will execute and as far as necessary extend, the plans already devised or other plans to be mutually agreed upon, for the sanitation of the cities of the island, to the end that a recurrence of epidemic and infectious diseases may be prevented, thereby assuring protection to the people and commerce of Cuba, as well as to the commerce of the southern ports of the United States and of the people residing therein.

VI. That the Isle of Pines shall be omitted from the proposed constitutional boundaries of Cuba, the title thereto being left to future adjustment by treaty.

VII. That to enable the United States to maintain the independence of Cuba, and to protect the people thereof, as well as for its own defense, the government of Cuba will sell or lease to the United States land necessary for coaling or naval stations at certain specified points, to be agreed upon with the president of the United States.

That by way of further assurance the government of Cuba will embody the foregoing provisions in a permanent treaty with the United States.

Imperialism and Sanitation

Nancy Stepan

The United States military occupation of Cuba (1898–1902), which followed the defeat of the Spanish imperial army, set out to remodel Cuban society along North American lines. Making the new island republic safe for commerce and investment was one of the priorities of the U.S. occupying forces, and a commitment to reforming public health—sanitary imperialism—was built into the Platt Amendment.

The connections between the setting of agendas for scientific research and the urgent need to reinsert Cuba into the circuits of international trade, migration, and investment form the background to one of the most fascinating episodes in the history of medical research: the search for an explanation of how yellow fever was transmitted. Nancy Stepan shows how the pioneering research of the Cuban physician Carlos Finlay on the role of mosquitoes as carriers of the disease was discounted until the immediate needs of the U.S. military occupation made control of yellow fever an urgent priority.

Yellow Fever Research, Cuba and the United States

[When] the U.S. Yellow Fever Commission (usually called the Reed Board) triumphed over yellow fever in Havana in 1900, by confirming that yellow fever is transmitted by the *Aedes aegypti* mosquito, the result was a matter of immense satisfaction to the United States, and did much to enhance the prestige of North American medical research.

Yet in retrospect what is interesting is that almost all the ingredients of the mosquito theory had been in existence for nearly twenty years. In 1881 the Cuban physician Carlos J. Finlay proposed that the Aedes mosquito transmitted yellow fever from person to person through its bite; between 1881 and 1900 he experimented and published repeatedly on the subject. If, as I propose to demonstrate, Finlay had indeed provided the key to the scientific puzzle of yellow fever, one may well ask why there was a twenty-year delay in confirming his work. . . .

Until 1900 yellow fever was assigned low priority among the public health tasks of the United States. The low priority was the result of the fact that after

1878 no major scientific or political institution was directly threatened by the disease. Partly for this reason no organization representing the public health sciences was able to mobilize support for yellow fever research, particularly at a time when the role of insect vectors in disease lacked scientific credentials. . . .

General Wood, who succeeded General Brooke [in commanding U.S. forces in Havana] in December 1899, was confident that North American efficiency and honesty would restore order and that his plan of sanitation, based on the cleaning of houses and water supplies, the standard customs of disinfection and fumigation, and compulsory smallpox vaccination and quarantines, would improve the health of the city. To a large extent, indeed, North America's entry into the Cuban war against Spain, and the occupation of the island in 1899, was rationalized in North America by the belief that the United States brought to Cuba a moral, political, and technological superiority not to be found in a traditional colonizing power such as Spain; and, in Wood's personal opinion, not to be found among Cubans either. Much of the justification for the fight against Spain was seen as resting on North America's "modernizing" and "humanizing" mission, in which efficient technology would play a large part. In fact annexation of Cuba as a means of sanitizing a focal point of yellow fever in the Caribbean was a theme heard in North American medical debates long before the war of 1898 placed Cuba in North American hands.

America's presumed technological superiority, however, was abruptly challenged by yellow fever. Until the middle of 1899 the port of Havana, the main entry point for immigrants, the majority of them Spanish and not immune to yellow fever, was closed to ships, while a thorough job of cleaning the city streets was undertaken. All went well until the autumn, when the port was once again opened to immigrants. Some forty thousand people entered the city between the fall of 1899 and the end of 1900, 50 percent of whom remained in the city. By January of 1900 several cases of yellow fever were reported among the immigrants. Major Gorgas, who replaced John Davis as chief sanitary officer under General Wood, was at first certain that the sanitary program based on the careful identification and isolation of all yellow fever patients would halt the spread of the disease. But new cases continued to appear. By July, Gorgas had to report the appearance of 106 new cases of yellow fever in Havana, of which 30 died. In August a further 49 cases were found, in October a startling 396, in November 214, and finally in December 485. By January 1901, it was clear the army risked having an epidemic of alarming proportions on its hands. While it was admitted that tuberculosis, diarrhea, enteritis, meningitis, malaria, and pneumonia were responsible for more deaths than yellow fever, the fact remained that American troops, and the immigrants that many considered essential for the rapid recovery of the Cuban economy, were at risk. Both the imperial rationale and the North American military presence were threatened. These economic and political factors transformed yellow fever from a low priority disease to one of the highest priority. What was required to combat the epidemic was not to clear the city of dirt, but to make a scientific probe of the way in which the disease was transmitted.

Surgeon General Sternberg immediately ordered a high-level commission to Havana. Its members included several of the leading bacteriologists available in the United States, some commissioned as army officers for the purpose. Ironically, the first several months of the commission's inquiry were spent on bacteriological examinations, notably in rebutting the only scientific conclusion about yellow fever to have emerged as a direct result of the Cuban-Spanish-American war. The Marine Hospital Service had sent two scientists to Havana to test the claims of the scientist Sanarelli to have found the causative organism of yellow fever. Sanarelli's work was unfortunately confirmed by the Marine Hospital Service Commission; however, as Reed pointed out in 1899 and again in 1900, Sanarelli's "bacillus" was nothing but the bacillus of common hog cholera. Thus one of the few pieces of research financed by the federal government between 1888 and 1900 added in no wise to the understanding of yellow fever.

With the collapse of Sanarelli's claims, the Reed Board was faced with the question of what to do next. The U.S. Army had run out of options. It no longer had the alternative of depopulation, since as far as was known the entire island was an epidemic area and for security reasons troops could not be moved from Havana. It had also no plausible hypothesis about yellow fever except that of Finlay. Once circumstances forced the U.S. army physicians to consider Finlay's theory, the transmission of yellow fever by *Aedes aegypti* was proved within two months. Within six months following the Army's decision to back the recommendations of the board, and to reorient their sanitation measures toward the extermination of the Aedes mosquito and the rigorous isolation of yellow fever patients behind mosquito nets, the disease was under control.

Despite later claims, many errors in experimental procedures were made by the board's staff. Some board members, especially Gorgas, approached the hypothesis with a good deal of skepticism. According to McCullough's recent account, Walter Reed proceeded first to prove once and for all that yellow fever was not a disease of dirt. Much time was therefore spent in testing whether or not fomites spread yellow fever, experiments that had been undertaken a hundred years earlier. Of the first three positive cases of yellow fever induced by the bite of an Aedes mosquito, two had to be ruled out as evidence because of inadequate precautions to isolate the experimental subjects from possible infection from other sources. Throughout the work of the Reed Board, Finlay was at hand to offer advice. In all respects the research design was his, Finlay supplying the eggs of the Aedes mosquito and the techniques of inoculation. Most important was Finlay's correct identification of the species of mosquito; had the board screened the hundreds of species native to Havana their results would have been delayed for months. . . .

It remains now to ask what were the implications of the conquest of yellow fever for U.S. imperial interests and, more specifically, for the future of public health in Cuba. . . .

The United States's concern to control epidemic disease provided the Americans with a motive for monitoring Cuban domestic affairs. However, their interests could be served by a narrow "city-port" model of public health which was by no means adequate as a model of public health for the Cuban population.

The continued control of yellow fever, now a threat to the hundreds of non-immune laborers coming into the Panama Canal zone, was given high priority by the United States. The success of the sanitary engineers in Havana had indeed been impressive. By September 1901, yellow fever was eliminated from the city for the first time since its importation from Vera Cruz in the eighteenth century. Annual mortality rates, which had usually averaged over thirty deaths per one thousand in Havana under the Spanish, had been cut by the North Americans to less than twenty per one thousand. There was a determination on the part of the North Americans that vigilance against yellow fever should be maintained. The North Americans possessed a new policy instrument with which to ensure their goal, namely, the now infamous Platt Amendment, which the United States imposed on the Cuban constitution as the price of Cuban independence. The terms of the Platt Amendment gave the United States the right to intervene in the affairs of the country should events threaten U.S. life or property. What is less well known is that sanitation was made a special provision of the amendment. The threat of further military intervention in Cuba should sanitary conditions fall away from the standards set by the United States during the three years of military occupation between 1899 and 1902 ensured that the health priorities of Cuba would be those set by the United States, and that the control of yellow fever would continue to occupy a central place in the sanitation program of the island.

When the North Americans left Cuba in 1902 and handed over the sanitation program to the now aging but internationally recognized Carlos Finlay, the Cubans were well aware that they had inherited both a new and valuable tradition of sanitation and also a vulnerability to foreign interference and criticism.

A Child of the Platt Amendment

Renée Méndez Capote

The opening pages of Méndez Capote's (1901–1988) testimonial novel — a work that is part autobiography, part social history — situate us immediately and irrevocably in the Cuban republic that was marked by continuous U.S. intervention. Told from the perspective of a small child, Renecita, whose earliest memories are associated with the U.S. intervention permitted by the Platt Amendment, we seem to hear and feel the resounding hooves of the soldiers' horses that, by virtue of their constant presence, acquire a "supernatural power." Her narrative is a cry of liberation, as she was born of the struggle for independence, whereas her younger sister, born later at only four pounds, was "the daughter of the Platt Amendment." Disillusionment with the kind of independence finally gained after so many years of war mingles in these pages with a spirit of rebelliousness and the hope for change.

I was born immediately before the Republic. I was born in November 1901 and she in May 1902, but right from birth we were different: she was born amended, and I was born determined never to allow myself to be.

A family awaited me that was anxious for the arrival of a girl after two boys and, naturally, they expected a lot of me; it was inevitable that I would disappoint them in one way or another. I was born big and fat, healthy, rebellious, and strong. My mother could not understand why her *female* daughter, they used that term back then, was not delicate and pretty, since she was very delicate and very pretty. There was nothing delicate about me, and I wasn't pretty either. My father, who saw himself reproduced in me right down to the smallest details, except of course for the basic differences — the same chubby cheeks, fat legs, wide body, puffy, slightly almond eyes and fleshy mouth, decided that "the prettiest little girl in the whole wide world" had been born. He declared this so proudly to anyone within earshot, which was the "toute la Havanne," a multitude of well-mannered people who, upon noting the extraordinary resemblance, did not dare contradict him. Right away, he brought me into the living room, happy as could be, and, in between the bubbling glasses of champagne they were drinking, I was carried by Alberto Herrera y Franchi, who had been his aide-de-camp throughout the whole independence war and was, at the time engaged to my then nineteen-year-old sister, Teresa, and Joaquín Llaverías, who I suppose aspired to an important position at the National Archives, and was a close friend of the family's. Joaquín's face cured me of fear from that very moment on, and that is why I have never been afraid of anything.

When I was engendered, Cuba was in full effervescence. My embryo fed on struggle, hope, and combative force. I was the child of the Constitution, just as my sister who was engendered two months after I was born and weighed, at birth, less than four pounds, was the "child of the Platt Amendment" and was nourished, in the womb, by disappointment and bitterness, anxiety and impotence.

Despite all of the good conditions I brought with me into the world, I had been born under a terrible sign, and my first memories are associated with the intervention. I don't care what the historians say. I don't believe the history of Cuba has been written yet, because no one has really dug around in the dregs that were the cradle of the Republic. The shortness of vision and the grand personal ambitions which, like diapers, enveloped the Republic have yet to be fully explored. That will take an impartial historian, patient and without prejudice, and also very well-informed, not afraid of hurting anyone in the pursuit of justice. I don't pretend to be a historian of any kind, but I know that in the years that preceded 1902 and those immediately after, there was a shadow of malaise over everything, clouding events in a tenacious fog. I was, for my father, the lantern's light that cut through that fog, and that alone justified my existence in the world.

I was a child of open spaces, and the first place I found myself in life was on an enormous expanse of green grass, in front of a cheerful group of wooden houses with big, wide porches. Behind the houses, off in the distance, were large, low barracks which one entered by climbing a small set of stairs. You could hear the sound of the troops in exercises, of horses moving back and forth, their neighing, bugles at dawn, and on the solemn occasion of hauling down the new flag, the flag whose right to wave had cost so much and whose solitary star piercing a red triangle recalls all the blood shed. . . . It is Columbia, the camp established by the interventionists, where the first government spends its summer vacation.

In front of one of those houses, where she lives, right next to President Estrada Palma, the first president of the Senate, sits a little girl on a wooden bench. At her feet is a big, furry dog, so big that in all of canine history it has no equal. The dog is so frighteningly large that the little girl pulls up her little feet encased in red shoes, and hides them underneath her white skirt, edged with an embroidered strip of cloth.

Until I was more than four, my feet never wore anything but little red shoes. "The *niña* must always wear bright red shoes," Nana declared, and added mysteriously, "They suit her." And everyone came to agree with Nana's firm decision.

"Come on, Renecita. . . . You're not going to be afraid of Diana, are you? Diana is a child's friend! Go ahead . . . pet her."

Her chubby little hand does not budge, and Renecita can feel two huge tears trying to escape her almond eyes. Her heart is jumping around in her chest. She looks, and is surprised that the grown-ups can't hear the palpitations of her heart, and pats the dog with her hand to calm down. She doesn't want to cry because they are going to take her picture, and besides, next to her is a little boy with light eyes, wearing a silk cravat. A little boy who, because he is a boy, is not afraid. Guillermo Alamilla is serene, indifferent to the danger of being devoured by the monster with mouth, fangs, and four legs, whose ears perk up at the slightest thing.

TRANSLATED BY PAMELA MARIA SMORKALOFF

Spain in Cuba

Manuel Moreno Fraginals

Manuel Moreno Fraginals (1920–2001) argues that, paradoxically, political indepen-dence in some ways reinforced the social and demographic ties between Cuba and Spain.

We lost more in Cuba [Más se perdió en Cuba].
—Popular Spanish saying

United States intervention in the war in the long run built solidarity between Spaniards and Cubans. In part, it increased longstanding Spanish resentment over the U.S. policy to annex Cuba, since the middle of the century, and even attempts to purchase the island. In addition, the rapid defeat of the Spanish forces in only 112 days, with the loss of Cuba, Puerto Rico, and the Philippines, created a festering wound in Spain's national honor. On the Cuban side, the United States had the support and the sympathy of many people in the middle and upper sectors of creole society, who were influential in economic life, and who had always been open or covert partisans of annexation. This group was joined by many members of the creole exile community in the United States, who had adapted to the *American way of life*. But it seems evident that even though the Cubans initially accepted the intervention, the United States was rejected by the bulk of the independence army which, after a long struggle (for many of its members, in two wars), felt frustrated when they were shunted aside during the peace talks and the reordering of institutions. The national pride of these Cubans was also profoundly wounded. The frustrations of both Cubans and the Spanish merged at the base of society. In contrast to what the anarchist tobacco workers of Havana claimed at the time, a sense of nation-hood was not simply a bourgeois invention: it was a tough cultural residue. Nor was the war to create a Cuban nation simply a class struggle.

During the most critical and cruel moments of the colonial confrontation between Cuba and Spain (1868–1898), the island was filled with peninsular Spaniards. During those thirty years 464,503 civilians and 535,495 soldiers ar-

Street scene of turn-of-the-century Havana. Matthews, *New-Born Cuba*, 141.

rived, making a total of almost exactly a million people. A careful study of the numbers of soldiers who died and those who returned to Spain, added to the estimated number of Spanish travelers who returned home, leaves us a balance of seven hundred thousand immigrants who remained in Cuba.

This powerful wave of migration is typical of the great European population movements to America at the end of the nineteenth century; but it was also the result of a conscious policy to Hispanicize Cuba in order to check the independence movements. . . . The large Cuban cities (Havana, Santiago, Matanzas, Cienfuegos, Camagüey) filled up with men (the migration was essentially male) who gave a peculiar peninsular tone to white creole society. Cubans and Spaniards came into daily and unavoidable contact in the street, in cafés, in taverns, in shops, when they sought the services of a wagon or coach, and, in the end, in any activity, since there was a high proportion of immigrants at every social level, from the biggest businessmen to the lottery-ticket vendors. This daily communication among men of the two nationalities, united, besides, by a common origin, militated against a mutual rejection by reason of birthplace. We have already mentioned several times how Cuban popular speech never coined a derogatory term to refer to Spaniards. At the end of the nineteenth century Cubans called all Spaniards *gallegos*; but this was because of the preponderance of Galician immigrants at the time. Even the term *gallego* always contained a certain element of endearment.

This instinctive communication, at all levels of Cuban society, added to the thousands of marriages between members of the Spanish army and creole women, and the marriages and illegitimate unions between Spaniards and women from more humble strata, smoothed over boundaries of exclusion or political difference. In the rich documentation from the end of the century, incredibly, there are few mentions of personal conflicts based on differences in (Spanish or Cuban) origin at the end of the war. In our personal archive is a letter that illustrates what was occurring. Beatriz Masó Hecheverría was a creole descendant of the sturdy Catalan line of the Massós, natives of Sitges, whose uncle, Bartolomé Massó (the last name was Cubanized with a single *s*), was president of the Republic of Cuba in arms, and her brother was Lieutenant Colonel Carlos Masó Hecheverría, a member of General Calixto García Iñiguez's staff. In tandem with this extremely Cuban constellation was Beatriz's husband, Emilio Ventura, a colonel in the Spanish army, born in Galicia, with a brilliant military record earned in successive battles against the Cuban Army after 1877. In 1898, with the defeat of Spain, Colonel Emilio Ventura was repatriated with his army corps and stationed in Ceuta, where he took his Cuban wife and two daughters. The following year (1899), a third daughter was born in Ceuta; his wages were low and payments were late. Under these conditions he turned to his brother-in-law Carlos Masó, against whom he had fought for four years; the latter, although short of money himself, went into debt and saved Ventura with one hundred gold pesos, an extremely large sum given the salaries of the period. The letters between the victorious lieutenant colonel and the defeated colonel express all of the family warmth of people who were not separated by war. Family ties overcame political differences.

This is a representative story. With different variations there were thousands of cases in which a sense of family, fundamental in Spanish society, overcame the breaches opened by a war in which the presence of a third party, the United States, highlighted the extent to which elements of a common origin linked Spanish and Cuban identities. (In research currently underway, we have created a database of over two thousand marriages between creole women and Spanish soldiers, in just three Cuban cities and in the period from 1890 to 1894. Thus political-family conflicts like the one described above, or of different types, must have occurred thousands of times.)

General Miró Cardona, a Catalan who fought under the command of Antonio Maceo, commented in astonishment on the number of Spanish soldiers and officers who hid at the end of the war to avoid repatriation, revealing that for them Cuba was not an enemy territory, even under U.S. occupation. And in passing, he recounts an event of a different type that is emblematic of what was occurring in the realm of symbols. An Asturian owned a bodega which he had named after a crucial date in Spanish history: *The Second of May*. When the Cuban republic was inaugurated on 20 May 1902, the Asturian paid homage to the new date and the Cuban republic, in the cheapest and most expeditious way; he simply painted a o after the 2 in the old name.

Naturally, these events unfolded in a climate of mutual understanding. Over and above the subjective factors already mentioned, the institutional strength of the peace treaty guaranteed that there would be no expropriations or personal revenge in the island. Spanish capital, both large and small businesses, continued to operate under legal protection and, in addition, the North American intervention halted the march toward economic collapse. Since almost all of the major newspapers continued to publish, news of these measures, along with reports about the economic boom in North America, created a general climate of optimism. Logically, Spanish and Cuban capital felt more secure under a government of the United States (although they rejected the United States for other reasons) than in the hands of a republic of "machete-wielding blacks" (for the Spanish always referred to the Cuban troops as "blacks").

This cautious rapprochement between North Americans, Spaniards, and Cubans, had one drawback: the blacks. Cuba's identity was Spanish; but it also had black roots that did not seem to be taken into account officially, in spite of the fact that the "race war" bogeyman had been invoked for four years. In white culture, blackness, in a general sense, was assumed to be *lack* of culture. And at the end of the war elites tried to marginalize the "black problem" (a problem of whites and blacks), one of the entrenched realities of Cuban life. The profound racism of the North Americans also played a role in this process. Cuban blacks were not especially resentful of the United States. In fact, during the Civil War a black song, with its repeated chorus of "Advance, Lincoln, advance, for you are our hope," became famous in Cuba. Two versions of this song have been noted—by an astonished Spanish official in 1864 and by the great Cuban folklorist Rogelio Martínez Furé, who collected it from an informant in 1985! The vast majority of Cuban blacks were completely ignorant about the state of racial conflict in the United States.

Transfer of power from Spain to the United States occurred on 1 January 1899, and a few days later, on 6 January, the traditional Catholic celebration of the Three Kings took place. Three Kings' Day revived an old tradition in the cities of Cuba, in which slaves were allowed to parade in the streets, in costume, singing and dancing to the rhythm of their drums and other percussion instruments. On Three Kings' Day, which marks the day the kings brought gifts to the infant Jesus Christ, blacks would be given special gifts: money, drink, and, in a few cases, freedom. Slavery was over in 1899, but the African-inspired traditions of song and dance persisted. In the new political environment, voices were raised labeling any musical or dance expression of African origin "barbarous" and "savage" and demanding their official suppression. Among those who visited the seat of government to request the U.S. occupiers to definitively prohibit "this shameful spectacle" were the most senior members of the black societies, including Juan Gualberto Gómez. Prohibition led to the loss of much Afro-Cuban folkloric culture; other features simply went underground and resurfaced publicly years later.

The black question also emerged in other ways. When the war was over, the United States had a particular interest in disarming and dissolving the independence army, a force that was not under control, not officially recognized, but impossible to ignore. The solution was to disband the forces. Without going into details about this complex operation, one point should be mentioned. An extremely high percentage of the independence troops were black-mulatto; it is impossible to give precise figures, but whites were in the minority. The senior officers, who were mostly white, understood this situation, as did the North American administration.

Small conflicts, foreshadowing a future explosion, quickly began to emerge. A first, apparently innocent attempt to resolve the problem, was the decision not to mention skin color in the military discharge papers. This was an attempt to prevent the papers' being used to support Spain's claim that the war in Cuba was a race war. And it also precluded use of this politically dangerous data to encourage racial confrontation. In fact the discharge forms were the only ones used in Cuba at the end of the nineteenth century that did not indicate skin color, or "race" as it was called then. The entire archive and all of its data have been preserved and it has been impossible to measure race from this source. Historians have made their calculations by relying on the general information contained in the burial records (where race was recorded) of war veterans who died after 1900.

Ten years after the end of the war, there emerged a political party with the name "Independents of Color"; its membership consisted mostly of black and mulatto war veterans. For the first time in Cuba, this party published references to the racial composition of the independence army and the marginalization of its humble soldiers from public office. At the same time the "Independents of Color" attacked the new wave of Spanish immigration to Cuba (almost a million individuals) as a strategy of Hispanicization directed against blacks. The arguments they employed were very questionable, but they reveal the dual processes of conflict and convergence governing relations between the two Cuban ethnic races.

The War of Independence and the North American intervention in Cuba definitively separated Cuba and Spain politically, but they did not stop the process of Hispanicizing Cuban society. It was after the proclamation of the republic of Cuba that the Spanish regional societies reached their peak, Spanish anarchists dominated the Cuban labor movement (especially among tobacco workers), the Casa Hispano Cubana de Cultura was founded, and the gallego continued to be a key actor in the Cuban vernacular. The statue of José Martí, a man who had ignited the war, declaring that it was not waged against his Valencian father nor his Canarian mother, stood in a plaza surrounded by the Centro Gallego, the theatre of the Catalan Payret, the Centro Asturiano, and the very Spanish Manzana de Gómez, among other buildings.

TRANSLATED BY AVIVA CHOMSKY

The Independent Party of Color

El Partido Independiente de Color

In the aftermath of independence, Afro- and Euro-Cubans made clear their very differ-
ent interpretations of Martí's antiracism and association of Cuban nationalism with
an end to racial discrimination. Euro-Cuban elites consolidated their hold on politi-
cal and economic power, using the language of equality to cover up the continuity of
inequality. Education and property qualifications for jobs and public office limited op-
portunities for Afro-Cubans, and Euro-Cuban and Afro-Cuban elites condemned any
attempt at race-based organizing as a threat to national unity, especially after the
second U.S. occupation began in 1906.

The Partido Independiente de Color (PIC), founded in 1908, clearly called upon the
language of Cuban independence to promote its program. "We continue to love and
adore the goddess of slavery with the tunic of the Republic," the party's founder, Eva-
risto Estenoz (d. 1912), explained bitterly, associating racism with colonialism and
insisting on the association of independence with racial equality.[1]

POLITICAL PROGRAM OF THE
INDEPENDENT PARTY OF COLOR

The "Independent Association of Color" hereby constitutes itself as a national
organization in the entire territory of the Republic. We seek to maintain a balance among all Cuban interests, spread love for the Fatherland, develop cordial relations, and interest everybody in the conservation of Cuban nationality,
allowing everybody born in this land to participate equally in public administration.

Our motto is an egalitarian, sovereign, and independent republic, without
racial divisions or social antagonisms. All Cubans who are worthy should be
able to be named to the diplomatic corps, and, as a matter of important and
urgent necessity, citizens of the race of color should be named, so that the
republic can be represented in all of its hues.

We believe that all court trials that take place in the Republic should be trials
by jury, and that the duty of serving on the jury should be mandatory and free.

We call for

- The abolition of the death penalty, and for the creation of penitentiaries that fulfill the needs of modern civilization.
- The creation of correctional School-ships [*Barcos-escuelas*] for youthful offenders who, according to the law, cannot suffer greater penalties.
- Free and compulsory education for children from ages six to fourteen.
- The creation of polytechnic [vocational] schools in each of the six provinces, free and compulsory for adults, to be considered as the second stage of compulsory education, and consisting of Arts and Trades.
- Official, national, and free university education available to all.
- The regulation of private and official education, under the auspices of the state, so that the education of all Cubans will be uniform.
- The creation of a Naval and Military Academy.
- Free and faithful [*leal*] admission into military, administrative, government, and judicial services of citizens of color, so that all of the races can be represented in the service of the state.
- Immigration should be free for all races, without giving preference to any. The free entrance of all individuals who, within sanitary prescriptions, come in good faith to contribute to the development of the public good.
- The repatriation, at public expense, of all Cubans from foreign shores who want to return to their native land but lack the necessary resources.
- The creation of a Law to guarantee that in employment in all public enterprises, in Cuba and abroad, Cubans will be given preference to foreigners, until the latter are naturalized, and preventing new enterprises from being established in other countries.
- We will work to make the eight-hour day the norm in all of the territory of the republic.
- The creation of a Labor Tribunal to regulate any differences that arise between capital and labor.
- The promulgation of a law prohibiting the immigration of minors, and of women, except when they are accompanied by their families.
- The distribution of plots of land from State reserves, or from lands acquired by the state for this purpose, among veterans of the War of Independence who lack resources and who wish to devote themselves to agriculture, giving preference to those who are not suited for public office.

CONSTITUTIONAL ACT OF THE
AGRUPACIÓN INDEPENDIENTE DE COLOR

In the city of Havana, in the residence of General Evaristo Estenoz, 63 Amargura Street, on the night of 7 August 1908, after a long and well-thought-out discussion, those who have signed below unanimously approved the following:

That in light of the results of the elections of 1 August throughout the Republic to fill the positions of provincial governors, provincial councilors, municipal mayors, and municipal councilors, in which the candidates of color were excluded, with preconceived intent, from the candidate lists of the different political parties that participated in the election;

This being a self-evident demonstration that the black race cannot rely on the political parties for the betterment which it deserves for the services that it has lent and continues to lend to the national interest;

We solemnly agree, with our sights set on universal cordiality, on love for the progress of humanity, on the collective good of all of the inhabitants who make up the territory of the homeland, and above all, on the mutual respect and consideration that in accordance with human law, and with political and civil law should exist so that all who enjoy the light of the sun in this land can love each other and understand each other, and;

collecting the general sentiment of all of the elements of the race of color in the whole island, who have consulted us daily, showing their dissatisfaction with the current state of things;

we believe that in order to bring about an era of moral peace for all Cubans;

we resolve to present a candidate list made up of men of color, covering all of the elective positions.

This proposal is not based on hatred, nor animosity toward anybody, for all Cubans have the right to support us or to combat us. We simply say that we, inspired by a high and generous goal, have the duty to maintain the balance among all Cuban interests, and that the black race has the right to participate in the government of its country not with the objective of governing anybody, but rather with the aim that we should be well governed.

President Evaristo Estenoz
Secretary Gregorio Surín

TRANSLATED BY AVIVA CHOMSKY

Note

1. Tomás Fernández Robaina, *El negro en Cuba, 1902–1958: Apuntes para la historia de la lucha contra la discriminación en la necolonia* (Havana: Editorial de Ciencias Sociales, 1990), 61.

A Survivor

Isidoro Santos Carrera

In 1912 the PIC was crushed by armed attack by government troops and white militias, and thousands of Afro-Cubans massacred, including the party leadership. Eight years later, former PIC leader Isidoro Santos Carrera recalled the massacre and protested against the black organizations that showed support for President José Miguel Gómez and José de Jesús Monteagudo, who had led the government forces that carried out the massacre.

The Voice of a Survivor

We cried out, when the Independents of Color were imprisoned, after it became easy to capture or kill every Cuban with dark skin who happened to be out in the countryside or even in the cities and towns. We cried out when the society "Luz de Oriente," a society of blacks, who were persecuted, jailed, humiliated, and assassinated, sponsored a dance for that barbarous pack of wolves that is the perverse and heartless officers, made up of jackals and led by that vulture Monteagudo who, obeying the orders of José Miguel [Gómez], called the whites to arms to attack and defend themselves from the blacks. We cried out, I repeat, against the way that society celebrated that act, putting the waists of the unfortunate women, who had not yet finished mourning their earlier crimes and when we were still deprived of freedom, into the hands of the tormenters of hundreds of their sons, abandoned, without knowing what could have happened to them, and not a few of them heading toward exile, as the only means of escaping that conspiracy, of which José Miguel and his supporters were commander in chief.

The society Luz de Oriente presented Monteagudo with a sword, it sponsored a dance for his officialdom and it took a place at his banquet, it offered a toast thus, to the blood spilled and to the prisoners, since those blacks of the Luz were not tied by any family relationship then, and much less now, to those men who were assassinated and deprived of their freedom; nor did they

Street scene in turn-of-the-century Santiago. Matthews, *New-Born Cuba*, 307.

form part of those families who were humiliated and persecuted, simply for being black families, at the time of that sadly recalled government of barbarous events. . . . The world should know that we blacks who were — and many of us continue to be — Independents of Color take up the challenge of all of these outrages: we take note of these great injustices, we do not forget our tormentors, who perhaps some day will die by our hands, and in the public plaza we will display their cadavers and scatter their ashes. All is not lost, there are still worthy blacks, who do not gamble, who do not dance, who do not forget, who do not forgive, who live for an ideal and immolate themselves for it; there are still among us those who go smiling to the scaffold, and who leave their cell with a firm step to approach the gallows, with a prayer to Liberty, to Right, to Justice, to Democracy, and to the Fatherland where we were born and for whose independence we struggle, accepting the preachings of Martí the Apostle and running and fighting with machete in our hands with Maceo the Titan.

The dead of May! The black race of Cuba! Independents of Color! Blood is paid with blood, and you can all be sure, that neither the banquets, nor the degradation of some few of us, nothing, none of this frees José Miguel from the judgment of history, nor absolves him of our hatred and our vengeance.

Cuban Brotherhood

Eight years ago Cuban society as a whole was witness to great crimes; it saw stupendous outrages and abuses, without any kind of consideration or respect; it had rushed headlong into war; it saw poor unfortunates stoke the fire in which they were going to be immolated; baskets and containers of ears were paraded before Santiago society; people had their possessions stolen. All of what I have recounted stemmed from a single order: finish off everything black, destroy everything that blacks have, do away with anything that fulfilled, ennobled, and raised up blacks, just to spite a meek society, that obeyed José Miguel's frenzy and Monteagudo's thirst for blood. . . . Nature, at least in Oriente, added her contribution to the carnival with thunder, storms, downpours; the persecuted black of that time and his humiliated and jailed family received the monster, although only under pressure from the societies, there were smiles, motivated by vice, smiles and flattery dedicated to the executioner and his friends, even though their numbers were few everywhere. It should be said in passing that what is true, what is certain, what is accurate, is that emptiness accompanied him everywhere. Consider the Moncada Club in Guantánamo, presided over by José Asencio, the very same conscientious and proud Asencio of May who, in Boquerón, offered his life for the betterment of his race; who suffered the outrages and the humiliations in the Moncada Barracks, convinced then of the base plot of which we had all been victims. Nevertheless, he remained upright, always standing tall when faced with sacrifice. Many people may have been surprised by the attitude of the Moncada Club, but I was not in the least surprised. Rather, I expected that this, and only this, would be its stance. For those blacks, who take shelter under the name of Moncada, know how great he was, and do not forget his glorious deeds and they immolate themselves, but they do not bend; they sacrifice themselves, but they do not humiliate themselves, they swore and defended freedom, so as not to be slaves and much less to accept masters, whatever their power. . . .

This has not been a triumphant excursion, but rather a funeral procession. Gómez was attending his own burial. The Strong Man did not want to die without convincing himself that Ivonnet and Estenoz could not speak, because they had really been assassinated. Now, now that he is at peace, he can surrender to the hands of Eternity, within the memory of his bad government. He will never be able to forget his crimes, now that he has seen the nightmares of his victims, now that he has seen the scorn of the people, the pain of the mother who lost her son; of the wife and sons who lost their father and husband; of the friend who was seen leaving but never returned. José Miguel did not want to believe in his work, it was not good enough for him that others told him what had been done, so he came to witness his mistakes and he found what he had to find, the emptiness that we his victims made for him. He found that while he fought to separate brothers, he has instead found us more united; shoulder to shoulder we have told him, we have shouted to him "ACCURSED ONE, JUST LEAVE!"

TRANSLATED BY AVIVA CHOMSKY

Rachel's Song

Miguel Barnet

Like Biography of a Runaway Slave, *also by Miguel Barnet*, Rachel's Song *is a testimonial novel. Barnet uses the narratives of a series of cabaret dancers who worked at the Alhambra Theater to create an archetype, a single composite voice. The result is an X ray of the first three decades of the Cuban republic and the delusions that fed it. Rachel, the protagonist, though alienated and frivolous in the extreme, becomes a reliable witness to the degree that her own biases, shortsightedness, and internal contradictions mirror those of the Cuban republic itself.*

In the first excerpt we listen as Rachel defines herself in terms that are evasive, fragmented, and reductionist. In italics, the voices of anonymous witnesses to her life provide grounding for the reader with alternate versions to the one that Rachel offers. The second excerpt focuses on the "Little War" of 1912. In it, Rachel's version is corrected by that of Esteban Montejo, the informant for Biography of a Runaway Slave. *Rachel's "song" is the mythmaking apparatus of the republic, which dismissed that crucial struggle in Cuba's history as nothing but a "racist racket." For Montejo, it was a struggle that went to the core of the nation, and his interpretation of events puts into question the very basis of the republic, which Rachel has come to represent.*

Note: *An excellent film was made from the work, titled* La Bella del Alhambra *and directed by Enrique Pineda Barnet (1989). It is available on video.*

How small the world is in the eyes of memory.
—Baudelaire

Rachel's confessions, her troubled life during the scintillating years of the Cuban belle epoque, conversations in the cafés, in the streets, have made possible a book which reflects the frustrated atmosphere of republican life. Rachel was a sui generis witness. She represents the age. She is somewhat of a synthesis of all the showgirls who appeared at the defunct Alhambra Theater, a true gauge of the country's social and political activities. The characters who appear in the book, and who complement the central monologue, are by and large men of the theater, writers, lyricists, and inevitably, the ones behind the scenes. *Rachel's Song* speaks of the person, of her life, as she told it to me and as I then told it for her. — Miguel Barnet

Chapter One

This island is something special. The strangest, most tragic things have happened here. And it will always be that way. The earth, like humankind, has its destiny. And Cuba's is a mysterious destiny. I'm not a witch, or a reader of cards, or anything like that. I don't know how to read palms the way one should, but I've always said to myself that whoever is born on this piece of ground has his mission, for good or ill. Things don't happen here like in other places where loads of people are all born the same, behave the same, and live and die anonymously. No. Whoever is born in Cuba has his star assured, or his cross, because there are also those who are born to bang their heads against the wall.

Now, what you call a Milquetoast, who's not either one thing or another, a ninny, you don't see that type here.

This island is predestined for the divine commandments to be obeyed here. For that reason I've always looked on it with respect. I've tried to live on it the best way I can, caring for it and keeping myself as center. For that, the best thing is to work, to entertain yourself with something and don't give free rein to your mind because that's the worst. Cuba is my home. I was born here and I became a woman and an entertainer here. And here is where I want to die, because if there's a place I'd like to be buried it's in this little spot. I've seen other countries, all very beautiful, very modern, and very courteous, with very cordial people, but with the warmth of my homeland, not one. And I'm even of European descent. My mother was Hungarian and my father, German. She Hungarian and he German. She, short and freckled, very fun loving. A little lady with backbone. My father, I don't have any idea. I saw him, I used to see him every time Mama would show me his photograph. He seemed like a good-looking young man. At least in that portrait.

"He was German, little one," my mother would say. "You got that hard little head of yours from him."

My mother provided me with a good education. And above all, much love for your neighbor. She had this genuine gift of convincing you, and convince she did. Mama loved humanity. She spoke well of everyone so that they'd respect her. And she never got entangled with anyone. Not even with married men. On the contrary, she avoided marriage. I was her reason for being, the first and only thing in her life.

Mama's friends would come up to the house. And me: "Hello, how are you?"

and that was that, because as soon as one of them arrived, the little girl goes straight to her room to play and she's real careful not to stick even the tip of her nose out the door.

Mother knew how to be stern and sweet at the same time. There was no god who would disobey her. Even the servant girl was afraid of her. A servant who was more than that, a friend, a companion, and, still, everything was: "You called, madame, ma'am, please, Excuse me, ma'am, if madame wishes," and what not, so I, who was her daughter, her own blood, had to live terrified in spite of the fact that Mama was my only love, the only person I had in the world.

Sometimes I dreamed Mama came and wrapped me up in a quilt and we two would sleep together. I was happy in that dream. Other times Mama would take up the whole bed and I'd fall on the floor. Kaboom! Then I'd wake up and nothing had happened, because I would be sleeping alone, all alone. My habit of always sleeping with a little light on comes from those years.

The devil things are, because old as I am, as peaceful and mature, I haven't been able to put a stop to it.

Mother did everything for me. She sacrificed her life to give me a respectable career and she succeeded.

I live in the alleyway, What I know about Rachel is what there was between the two of us, and that's personal.

Better if we cross that bridge some other day. Not today, she's sick with the flu now. Just let her be. She died with the theater, she was left behind, and she has nothing to say about any of it.

Allow her to remain in her Parnassus; if you remove her, then certainly Rachel is no more.

In any case, tomorrow I'll let her know about some of this, We'll see what she says. She pays attention to me. We were husband and wife, and now it happens that by chance I live two steps from her house.

Thirty-five years without seeing her. Life is like that!

There are those of us who come into the world with just such an attraction. I believe that whatever destiny holds in store for you always comes about.

That's what I was telling her the other day: "Gal, you and I are like they say in the song: prisoners in the same cell."

Mama was not what you'd call a floozy, a loose woman.

Whoever talks like that is mistaken. My mother had her life, she lived it her way, she did with her body whatever she pleased. Walking a tightrope to survive and plenty of courage. That was my mother.

To tell the truth, I can't complain about her. I guess my native sense made me understand her all the way down to the particulars. She knew that even as a little girl, I had sniffed it out, but she never spoke of it openly. She was always slippery about that. She'd get away from me along the edges.

And since I was already smart, I kept quiet. Who better than from my mother was I going to hide her affairs, her secrets. There's not much that I could really say about my mother. It's not because she's under the ground and that we have to be respectful, no. It's more because she was like a saint with me; she devoted herself to my whims, to my foolishness. I'd ask for a bird on the wing, and off my mother would go to bring a bird on the wing.

Talking about her makes me sad, but it clears my mind. When you love that way, it's good to constantly talk about the other person because then the love grows.

There are days when I get to talking about my mother, and I go on without stopping.

Then days go by when I don't think about her. At night is when I think about her most. At night, Ofelia leaves and I lie down on the bed with those white pillows.

Ofelia is a great companion, she takes care of me, she puts up with what no one else does, but it's not the same as a mother. For Mama I was always the silly, the absentminded one, the doll.

I am alone, yes, alone. But I'm not a woman who makes a mountain out of a molehill. I'm not hysterical either. Dramatic, even less. The word wretch I never apply to myself. I'm a sad, melancholy person.

Listen to that. What is that woman thinking of. If they let her have her way, if they let her. . . .

She wasn't born with any silver spoon in her mouth, and that's not the way she's gone. She was brought up pretty poor, with a lot of twisting around by her mother, and a lot of hunger. I know because I was acquainted with the family. She always was quite self-centered. You pass by and see her dolled up and all, but to say she was raised from the cradle like that is really stretching it.

Rachel was born in a neighborhood whose name it's better not to even mention. Knifings, depravity, robbery.

She came out pretty clean.

She was never anything but a rumba dancer. The only thing she knew how to do was wiggle.

She wiggled all her life. She's ignorant, wild, and frivolous.

A frivolous woman and nothing more. No, I don't like to talk about her.

The loveliest thing is to look back with happiness. To see yourself like in a movie, as a playful child, just sitting straight up in an armchair, playing the piano. . . . I love that.

We were what has come to be called middle class. Not rich not poor.

Havana was beginning to take off, to become a city of progress, inspiring real admiration. The electric trolley was one of the big happenings. People stopped on the street, when I was a girl, and looked with their eyes wide, they were dazed watching it move pushed by electricity.

After the initial slight fear of getting on, they would ride it every day just for pleasure.

What I know well is that part of San Isidro, the neighborhood around the Train Terminal, the old city wall. That's the Havana of my youth: very pretty and lively.

We lived in a boarding house, in a cramped room that did have some ventilation. Mama wasn't fond of moving like a gypsy. She preferred staying in one place. To move is to change mood and that was upsetting to her, since we were alone and she was a foreigner and all, with her own brand of Cubanness. . . .

That war was carried out with a lot of rum. The leaders were drunks and vicious types. The best proof was given by General Monteagudo whose picture appeared in the press with two rebellious Negroes and several bottles of rum. Monteagudo was sent by President Gómez to clean up the area. Of course it took a lot of work but he succeeded. Mendieta is another of the officers who participated and who the whole country remembers gratefully. They knew that, with rum, the Negroes would be defeated. And from what I heard, the bottles climbed up the slopes so that the drunken Negroes would give up. Alcohol can do marvels.

They burned sugar mills and whole plantations but they couldn't win. They were in the minority and wrong besides. There was a lot of destruction in La Maya. The racists burned eight hundred houses, a town in flames. The train station, the inn, and the post office.

La Maya was left in ashes! Later a song came out that went "Alto Songo Burns La Maya" and I don't know what else. That's my country: after the war, a little bit of music.

Negroes, Negroes! What a headache they caused, my Lord.

The worst part of that stupid uproar was what they did to our flag. They took the shining star off the flag that had appeared in dreams to Narciso López and, in its place, they painted a colt as black as coal. Right there you can sum up the war: the colt against the star.

Whites got mixed up in it out of curiosity, and it cost them dearly. A group of disloyal islanders formed up with the troops of the two little generals, Estenoz and Ivonet, and they were all liquidated. More than one islander was dragged on palm fronds to the cemetery, to the pigsty, to the cesspool. . . .

The government's rage was so great that it has to be admitted that some indiscretions occurred. For instance, I remember in Santiago, it's said the same thing happened in Regla, that each time a white saw a Negro on the street he would shoot him. And so, many fell who most likely didn't even know who Estenoz or Ivonet were. Wars are like that. The just always pay for the sinners.

In Havana the fellows from Acera del Louvre flooded out into the streets, along Prado, down Zulueta, to the Malecón. Any Negro they saw who was sort of "prettied up," they cut his tie off. Now, to speak the truth, they were to blame. They threatened that this island would be colored territory, that Estenoz would be president and other monstrosities, that's why the white fellows revolted.

Under the custard apple tree in Prado, there was an old aristocrat, very refined, who had been one of the rebels. He told me the story of how the colored boys would sneak away each time they saw him. They'd lower their heads or cross the street. He stopped them good.

The agitation stirred up the whole island. There was no talk but of the racist racket. But since everything is the way it is, and no evil lasts a hundred years, the situation calmed down when the Americans arrived. The Americans certainly were respected. They anchored a ship in the bay and the storm ended. They also announced that something like five hundred lassoing cowboys would arrive, experts in roping wild steers.

If they came, it didn't say so in the papers, but I take it for granted that the bulk of the rebels were captured by them. A man with experience in roping a horse could rope four or five Negroes with one try.

That was what ended the little war of '12 here. Let them say the Cuban officers did their job, alright, let them. I'll put my hands in a flame if the Americans weren't the real saviors.

On the 24th of June, 1912, Evaristo Estenoz was killed. It was Saint John's day, that's why I remember it so clearly.

The death of the ringleader finished off the insurrection. I returned to Havana with the old man when train service was resumed again. I bought the newspaper and saw a cartoon that gave the key to understanding that binge. It was in the Political Funnies.

Two bumpkins wearing tropical shirts and straw hats were saying:

In Cuba's rich and happy nation,
Big shots too feed chicks their ration.

And you could see a field general in a corner, with a bag in one hand and a
sword in the other, tossing corn to a flock of crows. Who knows if it's true that
the Negroes received any money? No one. It stayed that way. And the ones
who sacrificed themselves were the ones who followed the leaders, Estenoz
and Ivonet.

Here you all have Ivonet
A dark-skinned Frenchie Cuban,
Put this land in a tourniquet,
'Cause he's the rebel's chieftain.
He sports the Haitian uniforms
Of general 'n commander,
And soon he'll be forsworn
To serve as our defender.

And the other couplet was dedicated to Evaristo. I can't forget it because I
sang it a lot for fun:

That valiant general
Black and independent
Proclaimed himself President

And now Emperor Tropical;
To see him so weighty
In his bright uniform
We must promptly inform You:
Why, this must be Haiti!

Just as I said, after the war, a little music.
Of course, there was no one who could replace the blood.
Stars of gold, boots with silver spurs, rough cotton drill pants. . . .
I should say! No country could put up with a war like that.
The Negroes were smashed for being ambitious and racist.

And what the hell did they think, that we were going to turn ourselves in like little
lambs, that we were going to put down our weapons and pull down our pants? Not
at all. And we showed them. They called us savages, little patent leather boys and a
thousand other insults, but since when in this country has a program more democratic
than that of the Independents of Color been brought before the people than when we

Cuba's lido, the beach at La Playa, Havana in the 1920s. A. Hyatt Verrill, *Cuba of Today* (New York: Dodd, Meade, and Company, 1931), 155.

fought tooth and nail to gain benefits for us Negroes, who had come out of the war barefooted and in rags, hungry, just like Quintín Banderas, who was killed later while he was getting water from the well in his house? Let's not hear any more cheap talk. The moment of justice has arrived. And none of us who risked our necks in that little war are going to keep our mouths closed.

Anyway, whoever comes here where I stand and talks about racism, saying that the Negroes were bloodthirsty, I'm going to give him a punch in the nose so he'll know who Esteban Montejo is.

I don't know what the journalists, the writers, and the politicians think about that. But as for me, as a man, as a citizen and as a revolutionary, I think that it was a just struggle. With its egotism and its errors, but necessary. The Negroes didn't have anything to cling to, they couldn't even breathe and they had been generals and men of letters, like Juan Gualberto Gómez. I'm not interested in what that woman says. I see things from another perspective. I knew her and she liked the good life, never had a social concern, or was interested in national politics. She did her little shows there and then she'd go home much pleased with herself. Do you believe that can be given value? In my mind what she says about the Negroes' insurrection is pure foolishness. A racist woman like her, opportunistic and . . . Better not to go into that. I declare my admiration for those men who tried to breathe freely. And if she says they're animals or were animals, I'm not concerned. She was the animal that took advantage of this Republic, that only knew how to accumulate wealth. Because she didn't have fame, much less glory. Rachel is the best example of the prostitution, the vice, and the lie wrapped in a red ribbon that reigned in this country. I say that and I affirm it. And as far as I know, I don't have a single drop of Negro blood. But I see things as they are, as they have to be. Listen to her, because she's nice, fun-loving, and she knows some trifles, but don't pay much attention. I'm telling you this and I've been plugging along in life for quite some time now.

TRANSLATED BY W. NICK HILL

Honest Women

Miguel de Carrión

After the events of 1898, which much of the Cuban intelligentsia experienced as a "giant leap" into the twentieth century, there was a long lull in literary production, with the notable exception of Miguel de Carrión's Las honradas *(Honest Women) and* Las impuras *(Immodest Women) of 1918 and 1919, respectively. Carrión (1875–1929) belongs to the generation that experienced the war in early youth and began their literary careers in the first three decades of republican life.* Las honradas *focuses on the situation of women in Cuban society—middle-class women in this case—portraying the vestiges of Spanish colonialism along with the growing influence of the United States and the opportunism of the class that Victoria, the protagonist, springs from.*

What I am about to do has caused me to hesitate many times, up until now, and put down the pen, already dipped in the inkwell, having decided to abandon the enterprise. That a woman, who has only written a few letters in her life—more or less celebrated by her relatives and friends—decides to write a book, which will never be published, might be considered by any sane person to be true insolence. But no one needs to know what I am doing, of that I am sure, and my innocent whim may remain among the extraordinary number of things we think, plan or do, without being able to tell anyone else about them.

Ever since my misfortunes taught me to know life, I do not feel a great enthusiasm for novels. I have read many, and I have not found a single one in which woman is really situated in the place she holds in society. The women writers themselves barely dare to develop types of women, as they really are, with their magnificence, their ugliness and their intimate miseries, always subjected to a humiliating subordination, regardless of their station and fortune. I do not know if it is because these authors have not dared to face the scandal of photographing themselves inwardly, with too much precision, an act that would be nearly the equivalent of standing naked before the public. . . . In any event, I don't believe the novel of a woman's life has been written yet, and in order to write it, the author would have to be a doctor, a priest or a woman, or, better yet, join together all three of those activities in a strange collaboration.

Society has attempted to divide civilized women into two large groups: the honest and the impure. Just what mysterious partition of the female heart forces us to belong to one band or the other is something the most detailed anatomical study has yet to determine. Balzac has only discovered that the honest woman has "one fiber too many or too few in her heart." This means that she either has a will superior to all temptations (more fibers), or that her way of experiencing love is extremely defective (one too few fibers). However you look at it, it is something that is outside the framework of normality. The great humanist was, of course, referring to real honesty. Yet, in society, it becomes necessary to group real and apparent honesty within the same category. From what corner of the human soul do the impulses spring which keep a woman in that state, almost always against all the laws of instinct? I have often thought about this, and come to the conclusion that an honest woman, real or apparent, is honest because of religion, because of ignorance, because of hypocrisy (you may read prudence there, if you like), or because of a complex and ill-defined sentiment in which ideas of all that is shameful, dirty, and should be hidden, are associated in a thousand different ways. Clearly, I am not speaking of the honesty that is the result of true love, which translates as faithfulness, and which is, of all, the only rational kind. In thinking this way, I do not attempt to be the advocate for my own cause. This book, I repeat, will never be published.

It is my misfortune to think too much, and because I do, and suffer, and feel, my ideas about good and evil have become extraordinarily mixed up. My whole life, since I now take it all in in a single glance, seems to me to be the result of a terrible external contradiction for which I have been the wretched plaything. I have done wrong, in the current meaning of the word, but I do not consider myself evil. Oh, I swear it, at this very instant that I am addressing myself just as I would address God's tribunal! And the only thing I regret, today, as I propose to write down, in a few pages, even the most minor incidents of that life, good or bad, is not having the freedom a man has, so that I might stamp, like Daudet, on the front of this manuscript, which no one but I will ever see, the following dedication, at once humble and arrogant, that seems to escape from my soul: "For my daughter, when she turns twenty."

But, will I ever really finish the work I have just begun? Is this not just a woman's passing fancy, fleeting like all of our determinations? Will I have the strength to finish a job that requires time, perseverance, thoroughness, and literary faculties that not everyone possesses? I do not know. But I do know that my memory, extremely lucid when it comes to the events of my own life, offers me up the past like a painting viewed in full light, without losing even the most insignificant of details. As far as time is concerned, I have plenty of it, whereas my husband, bent on making his fortune, spends the better part of the day far from me, developing plans for a grand sugar industry or busy with other more pleasant activities—who knows what men do when they are out in the streets?—about which he tells me nothing.

I will delay no longer, and pull up anchor. The only thing I will do is to divide my travels through life into three journeys which could be titled: "The Reign of Illusions," "The Death of Illusions," and "The Rebirth of Illusions." My book, if it is ever finished, will have three parts. . . .

In those old photographs the eyes give off sparks of curiosity, which has always been the most salient feature of my personality. I have always had an obsession with knowing everything, wanting to know, for myself, the how and why of each thing, not accepting as true anything that did not seem explicable to me. My mother would often grow impatient with my questions, and my father used to lovingly poke fun at me, calling me a little know-it-all, and a materialist. Other times, he would look at me with pride and let slip that I was very intelligent. That always elicited a rebuke from my mother, who didn't like for us to be praised like that, so that "we wouldn't grow too vain." As far as Alicia was concerned, she sometimes looked at me with her big, innocent eyes, surprised that so much indocility could exist in a little girl like me.

I can't say exactly when, but I know that very early in my childhood that headstrong spirit of mine began to perceive the injustice with which the rights of the sexes had been distributed. Gastón enjoyed certain prerogatives that irritated me and made me lament not having been born a boy, instead of a girl. He could run around and jump whenever he pleased and climb trees without Mamá appearing to notice. But when I wanted to imitate him, I would hear the terrible cry, "*Niña!, Niña!,*" which stopped me in my tracks. This only increased in him the pedantry peculiar to boys of his age. He made fun of our games, he hid our ribbons and sewing just to make us mad, or hung our dolls by their necks from the branches of the trees in the garden, taking advantage of the moments when he knew we were busy somewhere else. Alicia, less impetuous than I was, would patiently repair the damage done, and smile, or cry in silence. I, on the other hand, would furiously rebuke him, and sometimes even jumped on him like a fiend, pinching him. Mamá almost always intervened, before the fight could begin. And it seemed to me that she was much more tolerant with Gastón, as if so many more things in life were granted him than us. Sometimes her strictness would take the form of her calling Gastón "*mariquita*,"[1] and scolding him for taking part in girls' games. He would walk away from us in contempt and immediately go back to bothering us with his tricks. The poor boy, who was not allowed to play with other boys his age, would often get bored, and had to entertain himself somehow.

Even in the games we played together, and in times of harmony, the difference was pronounced. In a shady corner of the garden there was a swing, hanging from the horizontal branch of an old laurel. The branch was very high up, and as a result, the long ropes permitted the swing a wide range of movement. We loved that toy. Gastón made some fantastic flights on the swing, sometimes he would even get lost in the foliage of the neighbor's yard. My sister and I tried to imitate him, and Alicia, since she was much older, often succeeded, aided by Gastón, who pushed her furiously, panting, because he wanted to frighten her. But all of a sudden, in the liveliest moment of the scene, a white figure would appear in the door frame, and we would hear the peculiar whistle with which Mamá called us to order when we were being tumultuous.

"*Niña! Niña!* Alicia! Pull that skirt down and don't swing so hard," she ordered in a curt, dry voice.

"But, Mamá, Gastón is doing the same thing we are . . . ," my sister would dare to timidly retort, stopping, all the same, to pull down her skirt, blushing slightly.

"Gastón is a man, he can do it . . . ," my mother would insist in a harsh tone, "but you are little girls and must always know your place."

In the educational system employed by my parents, that place was always defined in the clearest possible manner. Little girls had to be modest, reserved, and sweet. Excessive happiness distressed them as much as all too visible bashfulness. Girls should know how to please, without being presumptuous. My mother had her ideas on the care and delicacy with which girls should be treated, ideas similar to those of a collector of fragile objects who had to move and put back daily the most valuable filigreed crystal. Often she preached to us sweetly, trying to infuse us with humility and moderation. "Little girls don't play certain games, they don't laugh loud, nor do they jump about like male children. You should strive to behave in such a way that anyone who sees you will say to themselves: 'What a modest little girl, and how sweet!' " When we were little, Alicia and I used to sing, no doubt to make sure we remained in "our place," this bitter little song:

Papers are papers,
letters are letters;
the words of men,
are all false.

Neither Alicia, Gastón, or I went to school. My mother would teach us, one by one, all that was indispensable. When we knew how to read, she gave the three of us classes every day for three hours in a row, just like if we had attended school. She was not a coarse woman. Before marriage she had studied to be a teacher, but had been rescued from the slavery of teaching by marriage to my father, before she applied for a position in the public schools. She was at the time more than twenty-five, and had suffered a great deal to remain an honest woman, since her family was very poor. Consequently, all she had to do was recall her former enthusiasm to become our governess. My father would perhaps have liked to save her the trouble and send us to a school nearby. But he was in the habit of respecting Mamá's wishes in all that concerned our upbringing, so he didn't insist. My aunt, for her part, was also an enemy of schools, where, according to her, the young were corrupted. It was agreed that Mamá would teach us grammar, arithmetic, geography, and a bit of history; and she would teach us our catechism, sacred history, and embroidery. In spite of her age, she had sprightly fingers for needlework, and excellent eyesight. But we hated her lessons, which had to be memorized and she would not tolerate the omission of a single comma, because of her short temper and the punishment she inflicted on us. After one hour of class with *tía* Antonia, it was unusual for one of us not to bear the mark of her pinches on our arm.

Our classes were held in a large salon, next to the kitchen, where the red and yellow squares on the floor appeared worn down by the feet of three or four generations of inhabitants. The tiles were so badly worn that water would collect in the center of the tiles after the floor was washed. That was where our school was improvised. There was a big pine table in the middle of the room, and on the walls were maps and small bookshelves. After noon, the sun would trace a large square of light on the floor, on which was drawn, like lace in motion, the shadow of the trees. There was no clock in the room, and we would gauge time by the dimensions of that bright square so that we would know almost exactly in each season, the moment when our work was finished.

Some Sundays, if we had been studious and good, Mamá would take us out to the ugly little square in front of the governor's palace, or for a visit to the homes of some of her friends. Those were the most relaxing days, because we enjoyed greater freedom and would often get together with other children like us. Some days there was a retreat or a dance at the Lyceum, and the music gave us such great pleasure that we remembered it all week long. My mother always went dressed in dark clothing, as was proper for a respectable married woman, and didn't let us away from her side for very long. Despite the rigid rules, we longed for Sundays, and studied zealously for the six days of the week so we wouldn't be deprived of our outing.

An educational system based on the most scrupulous isolation had to bring about the expected results. At age nine, my ears had never been wounded by a single word that could perturb the serenity of my innocence. In the house there were no paired animals, the servants had been there for years and years, and were absolutely trustworthy, and my parents would not have dared to touch even each other's fingertips in front of us. I am sure that Alicia, in spite of her thirteen years, was no wiser than I was, and that Gastón didn't know any more than we did about certain naughty things. Mamá took delight in contemplating us, satisfied with her work, and she watched over us always, driven by an innate distrust of everything that came from outside.

TRANSLATED BY PAMELA MARIA SMORKALOFF

Note

1. The diminutive form of slang expression meaning homosexual.

Generals and Doctors

Carlos Loveira

Carlos Loveira's Generales y doctores *is a novel in three parts about the Cuban republic, with the first devoted to life on the island in the years preceding the outbreak of the War of Independence, the second to emigration and the War of 1895, and the last section to life in the neocolonial republic.*

Loveira (1881–1928) emigrated to New York with his mother and the family for whom she worked as a maid. In New York, he learned English, working in a hotel and later as a fruit vendor until he enlisted, at sixteen, in the revolutionary army and returned to Cuba. In 1903 he became a railway worker, which led to a lifetime of commitment to international labor activism. Unlike the other major novelists of his generation, Miguel de Carrión and Jesús Castellanos, Loveira retained a sense of optimism based on his faith in the Cuban people who he believed would eventually rid the nation of the "fatal plague of generals and doctors." It is on that note of hope for the future that he concludes the novel.

In a highly symbolic passage, Loveira describes the passengers on the Camagüey-Havana express, a reflection of the state of affairs and power relations in the republic.

The train travels, fast, noisy, blowing smoke, through the plains of Colón, breaking the deep silence of the cane fields, an endless green ocean that grows iridescent under the dog day sun's rain of fire. Through the car's windows, avid for the illusion of some air, what blows in is smoke, slack, dust clouds, and suffocating furnace fumes. The reverberating atmosphere is blinding, and the landscape monotonous, except for a cluster of palm trees, the gray stain of a hut, or the far-off towers of a sugar mill standing out against the foliage of the grounds. Since, on top of all that, I have just read a volume by Pedro Mata, and was just about falling asleep in the middle of an editorial in *El Mundo*,[1] I take a look around the inside of the car, and thanks to my powers of observation and unfortunate penchant for philosophizing, I quickly discover that this first-class car on the Camagüey-Havana express, is a symbol.

In one of the seats in front of mine travels a North American, big and pink, dressed in khaki, a gray Texan hat on his head, on his feet, a pair of yellow leather spat-style boots. He is reading a thick, voluminous magazine full of puerile adventure stories and insipid serial novels. And among other things the giant wouldn't dare do in a Pullman car in his own country — like the khaki and the spats — he is sucking on a "Corrona de la Corrona" and occupying the entire seat facing him, with his feet up and a whole series of rolled-up maps and blueprints, labeled the Cuban Land Co., the Tropical Land Co., the West Indies Land Co., the Pan-American Land Co. In front of this geophagist are two creoles, a mulatto and a white man, both about forty. Underneath their brand-new hundred-thread count linen suits, you can make out the Herculean members, which one would say called out for the plow, the carpenter's bench, or the cane cutter's machete, traded in years ago for committees and electoral agencies. They sport identical wide-brimmed Panama hats, that cost one hundred pesos; their plump fingers, with square nails, exhibit sparkling stones of many colors; they are stretched out in their seats, so as not to be bothered by the discomfort of the enormous revolvers each carries on his hip, and they dialogue in loud voices, to dazzle everyone in the car.

"That's why I'm going to Havana: to tell the general if they don't find me a slot in the 1920 elections, there's going to be a terrible ruckus in the assembly."

"Me too. I've already told that to the doctor. If he can't even get me a miserable position as representative, then why are we in the Conservative Party?"

"Sure. And at the last minute, you'll come over to us."

"Yeah, I'll go, *chico*. Don't believe anything. When things no longer look clear, I'll go. Sure! With all the people I'll take with me from the slaughterhouse, I'll leave a big hole in the party!"

Above the train noises, repeated and jumbled together, the ritual words rise up; the committee, the assembly, the candidate, the voting slip, the reinforcements, the election results, the electoral college, and the names ending in *ist*. The seats in one corner of the train are black with nuns' habits. Three couples, humble Spaniards all, are traveling today in the first-class car. Right behind the nuns, a fat, placid, provincial bishop, chats in a brotherly manner with a liberal legislator. The rest of the car is filled with lordly señoras, covered in silk and diamonds; redheaded tourists who have divided up among themselves sections of the *Herald*, and now have reading material for the whole trip; a few *gallegos*, all wrapped up in cashmere, with the air of village bodega owners; a military man, tall and knotty, like a giant reed; a provincial, reeking of cologne, putting on airs, from his new horsehide shoes to his new straw hat, for the much talked about trip to the capital, and suitcases and bundles underneath the seats, on the seats, in the corners, and on the metal racks that hang above the passengers' heads.

The train whistles. It whistles for a long while. You can hear the sound of the brakes, gentle at first, then harsh and loud, causing the car to vibrate. Seconds later we stop in front of a station, elegant in style, with openwork planking painted green, minuscule and happy. Ingenio Iberia, says the large, flamboyant, gold sign. And here the picture of the train car is complete, summary and compendium of the sad reality that surrounds it.

TRANSLATED BY PAMELA MARIA SMORKALOFF

Note

1. Written in the days when Our Great Protective Forces were at war with the Hohenzollern.

A Crucial Decade

Loló de la Torriente

By the third decade of the twentieth century, Cuban intellectuals were beginning to develop a critique of their country's economic and social condition and to couch that critique in anti-imperialist (that is, anti-U.S.) terms. The Mexican Revolution of 1910 to 1917 was the first major Latin American upheaval to frame an explicitly anti-U.S. imperialist agenda. As U.S. intervention became entrenched in Central America and the Caribbean in the 1910s, popular, intellectual, and official anti-imperialism grew throughout Latin America.

In a fluid genre that fuses personal memoir and cultural history, Loló de la Torriente (1906–1983), journalist, essayist, and art critic, takes stock of the decade from 1920 to 1930. A crucial decade for Cuban history and culture, it witnessed the rise of organized social movements, with fierce political repression on the one hand, and creative fervor on the other.

In this passage, de la Torriente takes the pulse of artistic and intellectual life that was, at the time, inseparable from politics on the island and that gave rise to the influential Grupo Minorista and journals including Revista de Avance.

Those were the best years in the forging of our civic criterion. We were beginning a new era with a new style. The journal *Cuba contemporánea* had gathered around it, and held the interest of, the most select and advanced groups among the intelligentsia. Born in 1913, it was published until 1927, collecting in its pages the essays of Manuel Sanguily and the writings of Enrique José Varona, the chronicles of Jesús Castellanos and, in general, the work of a group of men interested in our collective self-betterment. It was at that time that the work of Martí became popular, when his disciple, Gonzalo de Quesada, published his papers, and a group of scholars read, revised, and annotated documents, all of which culminated in the magnificent collection of exhaustive biographies written about the Apostle.

Our tastes in literature broadened their horizons. The previous "new" generation had had their predilections: Santos Chocano, Leopoldo Lugones, Herrera y Reissig, the Spaniard, Juan Ramón Jiménez, and, naturally, Rubén

Darío; the Minorista group had other concerns, and the impressionism of Proust, the dissatisfaction with life expressed by Jean Cassou in *Curar la muerte*, and the "aesthetic atomism" of Joyce suddenly, and willingly, let loose a fount of inspiration among the new generation that was marching confidently ahead in the search for national values.

In the sociopolitical arena, Julio Antonio Mella had cast the first stone with his pamphlet: *Cuba, un país que nunca ha sido libre* (1923; Cuba, a nation that has never been free). A year later, Dr. Fernando Ortiz published *La decadencia de Cuba* (Cuba's decadence); while in 1926 Dr. Ramiro Guerra y Sánchez published *Un cuarto de siglo de evolución cubana* (A quarter century of Cuban evolution), a slim volume that gathered the articles which he had published in *El Diario de la Marina*. Among us circulated books as important as *Dollar Diplomacy*, by Scott Nearing and Joseph Freeman; *Our Cuban Colony*, by Leland H. Jenks; and *La isla encadenada* (Island in Chains), which Marcelino Domingo had published in Madrid, upon his return from a trip to Cuba.

The work of many of our writers had matured, like that of Francisco González del Valle, the most knowledgeable about the nineteenth century; and that of Gerardo Castellanos and Joaquín Llaverías, who devoted themselves to historiography. José María Chacón y Calvo, in Seville, researched the works of nineteenth-century writers; José Antonio Fernández de Castro and Félix Lizaso worked on a selection of modern poetry. Emilio Roig de Leuchsenring used archival materials in order to offer an interpretation of our diplomatic relations, while Medardo Vitier, in the province where he lived, passionately devoted himself to historical-philosophical scholarship, and Emeterio Santovenia and Enrique Gay Calbó studied, with a critical eye, the pages of newspapers and other publications.

The members of the Minorista Group, founded in 1923, were influential until 1927. Then, in 1927, the *Revista de Avance* emerged, a publication which, in some ways, filled in the gap left by *Cuba Contemporánea*. Its editors were certain they had embarked on a new journey, although they did not know what direction they had taken or where they would end up. It was their mistake. There was, however, in that publication, the noble gesture and gallant attitude of those who wanted our cultural life to take flight. The pages of *Avance* gave refuge to all that was new, that which had no documentation, that which was being born, painfully, and without stimulus.

While ongoing research was venturing new historical interpretations, the "social question" was being addressed in letters in order to incorporate itself in poetry. Blacks, as cultural element, began to be studied, enriching our culture with two manifestations directly related to it and which, until that moment, had ceased to be appreciated. The *economy*. Everything began to refer to the economy, to the ways of life of the Cuban people, with agricultural production defining the role of primary importance played by the peasant, in the inspiration of poets and painters as well as the research of scholars. Also considered was our condition as mestizos. Cuba is an island in which blacks and whites have mixed. The blacks, imported from Africa after colonization, have grafted onto our insular culture their rites, habits, and customs, maintaining, as well, in certain cases, their vital forms as ethnic group. These two "discoveries" marked the end of the provincialism which had plagued Cuban letters since the days of the colony.

From 1920 to 1930 the atmosphere began to change. With the aid of new interpretations, our cultural tradition began to impose itself as a great national reserve. Those who study, read, with love, [Félix] Varela, [José de la] Luz Caballero, [José Antonio] Saco, Domingo del Monte, [Manuel] Sanguily, and [Enrique José] Varona, trying always to assimilate the luminous words of José Martí. The new generations still read Ortega y Gasset, but they develop a passion for the men of America. [Florentino] Ameghino begins to be known, setting in motion a scientific system that strengthens the will toward spiritual liberation on the entire continent. He is not the only Argentine. There is also [Domingo Faustino] Sarmiento and Alfredo Palacios and, above all, José Ingenieros. Along with them, we are learning, almost by heart, the prose, as poetic as it is philosophical, that José Enrique Rodó unleashes in *Ariel*. The horizons of our culture are gaining altitude. [Friederich] Engels (*Origins of the Family*) is read by all scholars and, along with this fundamental work, the others pile up, those of Karl Marx and Vladimir Ilich Ulianov (Lenin), followed by the dense, difficult texts, first of Trotsky, then of Stalin.

The new philosophical predilections leave their mark on artistic and cultural activities. The plastic arts begin to shed their neoclassical darkness. Juan José Sucre, in Florence, studies sculpture, creating a magnificent *Head of the Apostle*. In painting, Leopoldo Romañach and Armando García Menocal are considered the ultimate masters in an age attached to Italianate Spanish taste. A colonial style of painting which, in full decadence, envelops itself, historically, in shadows and silence. Romañach, a master of color in San Alejandro, gives his students freedom, with regard to their vocation. And in Paris, Victor Manuel learns the great lessons of postimpressionism.

TRANSLATED BY PAMELA MARIA SMORKALOFF

Afrocubanismo and Son

Robin Moore

Anti-imperialism in Cuba was related to the growth of Afro-Cubanism, a movement mostly among white intellectuals that "discovered" Afro-Cuban culture in the 1920s and 1930s and developed an analysis that placed this culture at the center of Cuban identity. Ethnomusicologist Robin Moore describes the emergence of the son musical genre and its gradual acceptance by different sectors of the Cuban population.

Genres Antecedent to the Son

Afro-Cubans engaged in many kinds of musical activity during the first decades of the Republic. I have mentioned some of these practices, such as the sacred songs and drumming of *santería* and *abakuá* ceremony and noncommercial rumba events, to underscore the strength and extent of African-derived traditions in Cuba. The significant numbers of blacks and mulattoes involved in the performance of classical music, conversely, attest to the strong influence of European music on Afro-Cubans and to its attractiveness as a marker of cultural distinction and a source of employment. *Danzón* orchestra leaders Enrique Peña and José Urfé, composer Aniceto Díaz, opera singer Zoila Gálvez, and symphonic musician Virgilio Diago, among others, all established themselves as successful artists performing middle-class music. To this list might be added the many *trovadores* (troubadours, balladeers) of the period who wrote and performed songs strongly influenced by light classical music and art song.[1] Well-known Afro-Cuban trovadores included Pepe Sánchez, Sindo Garay, and Manuel Corona. These artists too performed in styles well within the confines of "acceptable entertainment music" as defined by the dominant society.

Straddling the boundary between "legitimate" musical practice and the clandestine sphere of African-influenced traditions performed in the home was a third sort of music making performed by the *coros de clave* and *guaguancó* (Afro-Cuban choral groups). These ensembles, associated primarily with the western provinces, represent an important precursor to and stylistic influence on early *son* bands in Havana. Surprisingly little is known about them. Urfé suggests that both began as Afro-Cuban imitations of the recreational choral societies established in Havana by the *sociedades españolas*. . . .

The years following the Wars of Independence witnessed a great deal of demographic movement in Cuba. Many rural families whose assets had been devastated as a result of military conflict moved to urban areas after 1898. Others were forced to leave their homes when the lands they farmed and lived on were sold to foreign investors. Unemployed agricultural workers frequently had to move to new provinces in search of work. The creation of the *ejército permanente* (permanent army) by the provisional U.S. government in 1908 also resulted in the displacement of large numbers of Cubans. American authorities during the 1906 military intervention, and later officials of the Gómez administration (1909–1912), deliberately stationed new Cuban soldiers far from their homes and families, so that they would be less likely to question orders if led into combat against the population. All of these factors combined to bring *son* musicians from Oriente to Havana and other cities in the 1900s and 1910s, where the genre grew in popularity among the Afro-Cuban working classes.

In contrast to the musically literate Afro-Cubans who played in danzón orchestras, military bands, and symphony orchestras, the emerging body of celebrated *son* musicians of the 1910s and 1920s had little formal education. Expertise among *soneros* derived for the most part from an active involvement with music making in homes, on street corners, and in local bars. *Son* became popular in poor neighborhoods of Havana at a time when nearly half of all Cubans were still illiterate. It is not surprising, therefore, that its first performers had little schooling. . . .

The Son *as Cultural Bridge*

Son can be viewed as a stylistically pivotal genre linking the culture of the Afro-Cuban underclasses with that of mainstream society. Musicians who performed *sones* publicly in the 1920s, for instance, also performed more markedly African-influenced genres in private. . . .

Son musicians of the 1940s and 1950s also performed noncommercial Afro-Cuban musics, with singers such as Beny Moré and René Alvarez singing rumbas and santería songs as children before they became commercially successful dance band entertainers. The emergence of *son* in the 1910s significantly widened the syncretic sphere mediating between realms of African- and Iberian-derived culture. It represented an important source of income and form of public recognition for many black musicians otherwise excluded from commercial performance. . . .

In Cuba of the 1910s, African cultural retentions of any sort were considered "barbaric" or vulgar. At a time in which even progressive intellectuals still subscribed to notions of white superiority and cultural evolution, African-influenced music represented little more to the majority than the senseless pounding of children. The growing popularity of sones among the black and eventually white working classes thus caused considerable anxiety among those devoted to European music. Conservatory-trained composers and critics characterized the period that gave rise to commercial *son* as one of "degeneracy" in which middle-class traditions were increasingly "tainted" by those of the street. As late as 1928, figures such as Eduardo Sánchez de Fuentes denounced urban *son* as a genre of African rather than Cuban origin, one representing *"un salto atrás"* (a leap backward) for the nation. He and others called for the suppression of musical activity by black street bands, claiming that their efforts were contributing to an overall decline in the quality of Cuban culture.

Spokesmen of the black middle classes also openly condemned the *son*. Members of the exclusive Club Atenas and the Unión Fraternal refused to allow *son* dancing as part of their recreational gatherings through the mid-1940s, longer than their white counterparts. Trumpeter Lázaro Herrera mentions that despite their international acclaim, top *son* groups such as the Septeto Nacional were never asked to play in these locations. Atenas and Unión Fraternal members continued to prefer genres such as the waltz, the fox-trot, and the danzón long after they had lost popularity among other sectors of the population.

Under the administration of Mario Menocal (1913–1920), ongoing condemnation of *son* by the middle classes resulted in a campaign against it by local authorities.[2] This was the same period that witnessed heated controversy over *comparsa* ensembles and the outbreak of the Guerrita del Doce in Oriente. Blanco cites an incident in 1913 in which residents of a *solar* [a poor urban residence, often divided among several families] in the Habana Vieja began playing sones in their central courtyard. Shortly after 10 P.M. a dozen policemen arrived and began to beat those taking part in the celebration with truncheons. The following day the same residents were fined for "immoral behavior" and the use of "illegal African instruments." Blanco describes a similar incident in 1919 involving the arrest of ten individuals in Guanabacoa for "dancing the immoral *son*." Even members of the relatively well-known Sexteto Habanero were thrown in jail on various occasions for playing sones at public gatherings.[3]

Throughout the 1910s, police routinely confiscated or destroyed instruments associated with *son* music such as the *bongó*, maracas, and the *marímbula*, or *botija*. Occasionally, they also shipped them to the Museum of Anthropology, at the University of Havana, as material evidence of the "inferior" behavior of "primitive" peoples.[4] Perhaps the instrument that aroused the most antagonism was the bongó. Because it was played with the hands and in that sense resembled instruments used in santería and abakuá ceremonies, police officials considered the bongó especially offensive. Carpentier and others note that municipalities including Havana eventually passed legislation specifically prohibiting its use. Sonero Antonio Bacallao remembers his father telling him that in the late 1910s, "You could usually play a little *son*, but you couldn't play it with the bongó."

Although the jailing and harassment of *son* musicians tapered off in the early 1920s, discrimination against them continued within the music establishment. Musicians' unions refused to accept *son* players as members until about 1935. Representatives of organizations such as Solidaridad Musical, formed in 1916, and the Unión Sindicato de Músicos de Cuba (USMC), created in 1923, maintained that only those performers with formal training and who could read music had a right to membership.[5] This position was apparently used to justify long-standing prejudices against black street culture and to maintain distinctions between condoned and "nonlegitimate" music making. . . .

National Acceptance of Son

The period from 1925 to 1928 constitutes a turning point in the history of *son*, one in which it was transformed from a marginal genre of dubious origins into the epitome of national expression. One of the first indications of changing attitudes came in May 1925 when president Machado publicly asked the Sonora Matancera, at that time a septet-style ensemble, to play at his birthday party. As mentioned, such invitations had been common for years but had typically been made in secret as part of semiclandestine *encerrona* gatherings. At roughly the same time, the first public *son* festival took place, and the Machado administration issued a public statement in support of *son* music. Machado's Secretario de Gobernación announced on 23 October that *son* music and dance would henceforth be permitted in hotels, cabarets, and restaurants as long as it was not "scandalous or immoral." Attitudes toward the *son* on the part of the Cuban middle classes remained decidedly ambivalent through at least 1927, but even the most outspoken critics could not deny its increasing popularity. The mid-1920s was also the first time that stylized *son* compositions for piano such as those used in the *teatro bufo* began to appear in middle-class leisure publications such as *Carteles* and *Bohemia*.

Popularization of the *son* in Cuba cannot be separated from international

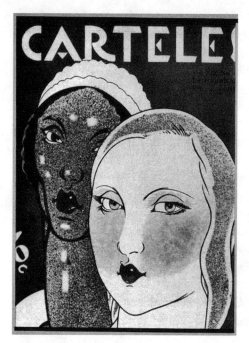

Carteles magazine front cover from 1933: black and white women in the new order. Reprinted in *Cuban Heritage* 2, no. 1 (1988): 26.

artistic currents in Western Europe and the United States. Recordings that facilitated the spread of sones in Cuba also spread them and other African American musics throughout Latin America and to many other parts of the world. Moreover, this dissemination of Afro-Cuban culture had its corollary in other art forms. In visual art, dance, poetry, and literature as well as music, the late 1920s witnessed an explosion of a rather superficial interest in African and African American culture among the Western middle classes as demonstrated by the celebrated figures of bohemian Paris and the Harlem Renaissance.

Cuban intellectuals and critics shaping public opinion during this period were highly aware of such international trends, having lived and studied abroad themselves. The international fashionableness of Africanisms undoubtedly contributed to a more tolerant stance on the part of many Cubans toward *son* music. Economic and political circumstances played a role as well. Increasingly violent protest against the pro-U.S. Machado administration and anger at the United States itself led to a strong nationalist campaign on the part of intellectuals. Changing attitudes toward *son* are in part due to their attempts to valorize and promote cultural forms viewed as uniquely Cuban. In the context of the barrage of North American merchandise, films, literature, sports events, and music that entered Cuba during these years, *son* represented an important symbol of national identity and a "weapon against [American] jazz." . . .

By 1930, *conjuntos de son* had achieved widespread popularity in Cuba, and government-funded organizations such as the Comisión de Turismo Nacional actively promoted musical events that featured them. If not yet unanimously heralded as "the Cuban music par excellence," *son* was recognized as the most influential new genre of the day. The early poetic works of mulatto Nicolás Guillén appeared in the conservative *Diario de la Marina* at this time, based in part on the formal structure of *son* music. In his collections such as *Motivos de son, Sóngoro cosongo*, and *West Indies, Ltd.*, Guillén fused themes of *son* music and dance, as well as lyrical segments based on the call-and-response structure of the *montuno* section, with images of everyday street life. His work represents one of the first attempts to incorporate Afro-Cuban musical themes into Cuban literature.

Liberal intellectuals such as Alejo Carpentier saw in the *son* a powerful symbol of the new Cuba he and others envisioned, one in which African-derived traditions would more directly affect, or at least inspire, national artistic production. *Son*, Carpentier wrote,

> is a product unique to us, as authentically Cuban as any *danza* or bolero. . . . What is more, in terms of pure lyrical expression, *son* . . . has created by means of its lyrics a style of popular poetry as genuinely creole as peasant *décimas* could ever be. . . . A whole Antillean mythology . . . lives in those couplets.

. . . Perhaps the most successful Afro-Cuban group of the mid-1920 in bridging the gap between *trova* and *son* was the Trío Matamoros from Santiago. Miguel Matamoros, the leader and author of a majority of the ensemble's original compositions, experimented early on with musical fusion and first popularized such hybrid genres as the *bolero-son*. "Lágrimas negras" (Black tears) is one of his better-known *bolero-sones*, shifting from an initial section in a moderate tempo to a brisk montuno call-and-response. Matamoros also wrote songs in styles more popular at the turn of the century than in the 1930s such as the *criolla* and habanera. An example of the latter is his "Mariposita de primavera" (Butterfly of springtime), part of the standard repertory of trovadores even today.

Finally, the *danzonete*, first introduced by Aniceto Díaz in 1929, serves as an example of *son*'s fusion with the danzón. Early *son-danzón* hybrids tended to be little more than *danzones* (typically an instrumental form) with added lyrics

Carteles magazine front cover from 1933, by García Cabrera: female figure represents the new Cuba. Reprinted in *Cuban Heritage* 2, no. 1 (1988): 26.

and possibly a repeated chorus. Later hybrids demonstrate more direct *son* influence through the inclusion of a *cencerro*, or cowbell, the addition of a final montuno section, and an emphasis on vocal and instrumental improvisation. Predominantly Afro-Cuban *charanga* ensembles such as Arcaño y sus Maravillas and La Orquesta Aragón became exponents of music of this type. They were among the first to perform upbeat *son*-like music on violin, flute, and other European instruments not initially associated with the genre.

The mass popularization of *son* music led to an increasing valorization of Afro-Cuban street culture and of the artists who created it. . . .

By the late 1930s, the heyday of "classic *son*" had largely ended. With important exceptions, especially ensembles performing in other countries such as the Cuarteto Machín in Spain, the sextetos and septetos that had enjoyed wide commercial popularity increasingly lost ground to jazz bands and amplified *conjuntos*. Street-corner *son* bands of past years found themselves unable to compete successfully for jobs in a market demanding full horn sections, sophisticated arrangements, and musicians who could read music. Members of El Septeto Munamar, La Sonora de Piñón, El Sexteto Liborio, and a host of other Afro-Cuban conjuntos that had enjoyed brief commercial success found themselves disbanding or performing solely in the Afro-Cuban community once again. . . .

By the late 1940s, *son* had lost its controversiality even among conservative Cubans and provided the basis for most dance music repertory on radio and records. In the process of mainstream appropriation, however, *sones* increasingly demonstrated the influence of jazz and ballroom dance music. Many successful soneros of later years maintained their popularity only by substituting the acoustic bass and piano for "folk" instruments such as the botija, replacing the bongó with the *timbal*, composing "sophisticated" arrangements with extended horn sections for their conjunto, and diversifying their performance repertoire to include genres other than *son*. Charanga orchestras popular in the 1940s developed dance music heavily influenced by *son* but performed on violin, flute, and other European instruments. Genres of the later 1940s such as mambo manifest many characteristics derived from *son* yet reflect the even stronger influence of North American big bands. *Son* was and continues to be a form of musical and stylistic bricolage, demonstrating the creative fusion of distinct traditions, national and international. It contains oppositional elements potentially liberating to the Afro-Cuban working-class community, as well as the constraints of middle-class influence, and thus illustrates the contradictions so prevalent in popular culture. It is a metaphor for the social order within which it developed, embodying and perpetuating emerging conceptions of Cubanness.

Notes

For complete references and notes, consult the work as cited in the acknowledgment of copyrights section.

1. The influence of art music on *vieja trova* repertory does not imply that its proponents received formal musical education. Unlike symphony musicians and directors, trovadores generally taught themselves to play and learned their repertory from other performers. One example is Sindo Garay, a poor and musically illiterate mulatto, who composed some of the most famous boleros of the early twentieth century. Interestingly, he virtually never wrote compositions directly influenced by African culture and in his biography expresses no interest in these traditions.

2. Countless authors refer to legislation specifically prohibiting *son* performance at this time, yet no one I interviewed has seen it personally or knows where to find it. My own attempts to locate such documents in the Archivo Nacional in Havana proved fruitless. It remains unclear whether *son* was actually banned by municipal decree or whether it merely became established practice for police officials and others to discourage its performance.

3. Such incidents proved to be of little consequence to the members of this group because they had influential white patrons who could negotiate their release within a few hours.

4. Fernando Ortiz began his personal collection of objects associated with Afro-Cuban cultural expression at this time by requesting them from the police.

5. Parodies of *son* musicians appear in *Bohemia*, 9 January 1927, 32–33. The caricature, en-

titled "The Manzanillo Symphony," depicts a group of twenty or thirty Afro-Cuban musicians, either a conjunto or an *estudiantina*, performing on numerous instruments. The faces have been altered to give the impression of brutishness, and the technically unsophisticated nature of many of the instruments has been emphasized to make the "symphony" seem ridiculous.

Drums in My Eyes

Nicolás Guillén

Born in 1902 in Camagüey, Nicolás Guillén came to earn the title of National Poet for his vast and varied oeuvre. The translators and editors of Man-Making Words, *Roberto Márquez and David Arthur McMurray, have observed that Guillén's poetic themes move "carefully and surely," "from the urban black themes of* Motivos de son *to a more general, national concern in* Sóngoro cosongo *(1931), then beyond to the broader Caribbean vision that shapes* West Indies Ltd. *(1934)" (xiii). His poetry later takes on the Spanish Civil War from an international perspective, and it ultimately embraces the entire world, with uncommon versatility and universality.*

"My Last Name" is an odyssey of self-discovery, a poetic treatise on race, identity, and the hierarchy of color that had characterized race relations in prerevolutionary Cuba.

"Cuban Elegy" and "Far-off . . ." examine U.S.-Cuban relations and the lack of sovereignty enjoyed by Cuba within that relationship. "Cuban Elegy" posits the island as a "sold-out palm grove," and "Far-off . . ." offers a revealing and seemingly endless laundry list of U.S. interference in the economic, political, and social life of the island nation.

MY LAST NAME
A family elegy

I

Ever since school
and even before . . . Since the dawn, when I was
barely a patch of sleep and wailing,
since then
I have been told my name. A password
that I might speak with stars.
Your name is, you shall be called . . .
And then they handed me
this you see here written on my card,

this I put at the foot of all poems:
thirteen letters
that I carry on my shoulders through the street,
that are with me always, no matter where I go.
Are you sure it is my name?
Have you got all my particulars?
Do you already know my navigable blood,
my geography full of dark mountains,
of deep and bitter valleys
that are not on the maps?
Perhaps you have visited my chasms,
my subterranean galleries
with great moist rocks,
islands jutting out of black puddles,
where I feel the pure rush
of ancient waters
falling from my proud heart
with a sound that's fresh and deep
to a place of flaming trees,
acrobatic monkeys,
legislative parrots and snakes?
Does all my skin (I should have said),
    Does all my skin come from that Spanish marble?
My frightening voice too.
the harsh cry in my throat?

Merci!
Merci bien!
Merci beaucoup!
But no . . . Can you believe it? No.
I am clean.
My voice sparkles like newly polished metal.
Look at my shield: it has a baobab,
it has a rhinoceros and a spear.
I am also the grandson,
great-grandson,
great-great-grandson of a slave.
(Let the master be ashamed.)
Am I Yelofe?
Nicolás Yelofe, perhaps?

Or Nicolás Bakongo?
Maybe Guillén Banguila?
Or Kumbá?
Perhaps Guillén Kumbá?
Or Kongué?
Could I be Guillén Kongué?
Oh, who knows! What a riddle in the waters!

II
I feel immense night fall
on profound beasts,
on innocent castigated souls;
but also on ready voices,
which steal suns from the sky,
the brightest suns,
to decorate combatant blood.
From some flaming land pierced through
by the great equatorial arrow,
I know there will come distant cousins,
my ancestral anguish cast upon the winds;
I know there will come portions of my veins,
my ancestral blood,
with calloused feet bending frightened grasses;
I know there will come men whose lives are green,
my ancestral jungle,
with their pain open like a cross and their breasts red with flames.
Having never met, we will know each other by the hunger,
by the tuberculosis and the syphilis,
by the sweat bought in a black market,
by the fragments of chain
still clinging to the skin;
Having never met we will know each other
by the dream-full eyes
and even by the rock-hard insults
the quadrumanes of ink and paper
spit at us each day.
What can it matter, then.
(What does it matter now!)
ah, my little name

of thirteen letters?
Or the Mandingo, Bantu,
Yoruba, Dahoman name
of the sad grandfather drowned
in notary's ink.
Good friends, what does it matter?
Oh, yes, good friends come look at my name!
My name without end,
made up of endless names;
My name, foreign,
free and mine, foreign and yours,
foreign and free as the air.

TRANSLATED BY ROBERTO MÁRQUEZ

CUBAN ELEGY

CUBA — an island of Central America, the largest of the Antilles, situated at the entrance to the Gulf of Mexico. . . . Illustrated Larousse

Cuba: sold-out palm grove,
drawn and quartered dream,
tough map of sugar and neglect . . .

Where, fine stag,
from forest to forest to forest pursued,
will you find the forest to stop and lick the blood
of your gaping flank?
Before the choleric chasm
of your tireless, shipwrecked breast
I stand and feel the somber
thrust of sleepless waters.
I feel each throb
as from expanding sea,
as from contracting sea,
as from concentric sea,
a sea which seems to crash upon itself.
They know it now, they've seen it:
black women with shoulders like mahogany,
guitars with bellies like black women.
They've seen it, they repeat it:
nights in the harbor

with a great tin sky above
a sailboat floating dead.
The drum and the crocodile know it,
like the drivers, the customs
man, and the tourist
with a militant surprise.
The bottle, in whose depth a star
is drowned, has learned it too.
They've seen it, they've learned it well:
the street with a centenary child,
the rum, the bar, the rose, the sailor,
and that woman who passes suddenly
with a dagger of cane-liquor
piercing her breast.

Oh, Cuba, I see your cane moan
and grow . . .
anxious and long, long as a heavy sigh.
In the air I breathe the acrid smoke of its burning.
There, the little demons which Ambition calls
together with her infinite trumpet
raise their horns, then quickly disappear
in myriad flashes of light.
There, cloaked in the black powder
of cowardly dynamite, is the youth
who murders with a smile.
There is the blustering *cacique* (brief Jupiter,
obsequious mandarin)
who suddenly explodes and rises . . . rises . . . rises
'til sparkling brightly at his peak,
an acrobat on the tip of a cloud,
he just as suddenly falls . . . falls . . . falls
to smash upon a rock:
a corpse without a discourse or a shroud.

And there the avaricious pig I see,
who wades in carnage to his knees;
and the cardboard general, his medals bright,
who scaled Olympus without a fight;
and the doctor with a mossy skull,
who thinks the joys of spring are dull . . .

Right next door our neighbor is seen,
who has the phone and the submarine.
He has a barbarous fleet, a barbarous
fleet. He has a mountain of gold,
the penthouse, and a chorus bold
of eagles: soldiers by the score
who, blind and deaf, are led to war
by hate and fear.
(Their banners,
plastered with blood, spread a physiological
stench which stops the very flies
dead in their tracks.)
Yes, the neighbor lives just off our coast,
surrounded by nocturnal ghosts.
He sends: ambassadors who plan,
pugilists, corned beef in cans,
bullets, builders of ships, screws,
ephebic onanists, convoys too,
chimneys full of smoke, gears for the machine,
the finest light tobacco, high-test gasoline,
gum for chewing, shoes of leather,
great cyclones, changes in weather,
and troops of fierce Marines, on top of all the rest:
he finds, from time to time, the bayonet speaks best.
What else? What else? Nothing but
a torn and blinded countryside, vomiting
its shadows on the road, beneath the lash
of a field boss; the fallen city
without a future; *el esmoquin* and *el club* . . .
nothing but slow, submerged, viscous peoples who die
like animals, in hospitals and delirium,
dreaming of life.

"And nothing else?" cry voices
and voices together.
Well, there's John Barefoot: his long night waits for dawn.
There's John Backlands: a verdant sigh
from his guitar,
and a song that's diverse and one.
There's John Black, brother

to John White: side by side they walk.
I'm saying, there's John People:
our own multitudinous blood;
and I with my poem,
and you with your rose,
and you with your smile,
and you with your gaze,
and you with your sharp
lament — a sword in every tear.
John People speaks; he cries,
"Great Martí, your blue star blazes yet.
Your clear voice divides the mist.
In the mountain your sacred fire glows."
John People speaks; he cries,
"Maceo of steel, friendly cane-knife,
lightning flash, bell, mirror — I follow
the scarlet path left by your wounds."
Oh, for another Peralejo
to brand with hot flames,
not the flesh of the old and beaten lion,
but the wing of the bloodthirsty eagle
that from the terrible North brings
death-maggots and death, a cross and death,
a tear and death, death and the grave,
death and microbes, death and the bayonet,
death and stirrup, death and horseshoe,
death by secret weapons,
death of the ambushed who die alone,
death of the young man crowned with laurels,
death of the innocent sextant:
predictable, a priori death,
rehearsed in Las Vegas
with a deluge of planes and blind bombs.
John People speaks; he cries,
"Midway on the road,
just yesterday, there came an evil blow
to halt our march, to break our spirit,
an evil blow to strike us down."
But the child — knowing little

of his father save a name on marble carved—
inheriting his chains,
he also bears his father's metal heart:
it glows, a flower of shining bronze,
upon his breast.
Sun-like, with his brilliance
armed, and crowned
by retribution's rose,
a child-hero takes up the ancient cry:
by the trench, turret, and wall of stone,
cold iron pierces, wounds to the bone,
and clean flames rise to meet the sky . . .
Maceo gleams from his zenith sure.
The blue star of Martí burns pure.

TRANSLATED BY DAVID ARTHUR MCMURRAY

FAR-OFF . . .

When I was a boy
(say, reader, fifty years back)
we had grand, ingenuous people
who over a row in the street
of a hell-raising crowd in a bar
would shudder. They'd exclaim,
"Good Heavens, what would the Americans say!"
For some folks
to be a Yankee in those days
was to be something almost sacred:
the Platt Amendment, armed
intervention, battleships.
Back then, what is today quite common
was unthinkable:
the kidnapping of a gringo
colonel, like in Venezuela,
or of four *agents provocateurs*,
like our brothers did in Bolivia,
and least of all things like decisive bearded ones from the Sierra.

Some fifty years ago
in the first section of the newspapers, no less,

they put the latest baseball scores
direct from New York.

Great! Cincinnati beat Pittsburgh!
St. Louis whipped Detroit!
(Buy Reich baseballs. They're the best.)

Johnson, the boxer,
was our model of a champ.

For kids, Fletcher's Castoria
was the remedy prescribed
in (rebellious) cases
of enteritis or indigestion.

One newspaper
in its table of contents listed
each day a page, in English, for the Yankees:
"A Cuban-American paper
with news of all the world."

Nothing like Walk-Over Shoes,
or the pills of Dr. Ross.

And the native pineapple juice
came no more from the plant:
the Fruit Juice Company
said it was *"huélsencamp."*

We would take the Munson Line to Mobile,
Southern Pacific to New Orleans,
and the Ward Line to New York.

We had Nick Carter and Buffalo Bill.
We had the immediate, greasy memory of fat Magoon:
obese gangster and governor,
the thief among thieves of thieves.
There was the American Club.
There was Miramar Garden
(when any fool can say *jardín* in Spanish).
To travel by train there was the Cuban Company.
There was Cuban Telephone.
There was that tremendous ambassador.

And above all there was, "Watch your step,
the Americans will intervene!"

Some folks, not so ingenuous
used to say,
"Hah! They'll intervene?
You mean they're not already here?"

At any rate,
they were great . . .
strong,
honest above reproach,
the cream of the crop,
and our model:
for quick elections without debate,
for buildings with many floors,
for presidents who did their duty,
for those who smoked light tobacco,
for those who used chewing gum,
for whites who wouldn't mix with blacks,
for those who puffed curved pipes,
for energetic and infallible functionaries,
for aborted revolution,
for a single strong tug on the chain
in the water-closet.

But it came to pass
that one day we were like children who grow up
and learn that the honorable uncle who bounced us on his knee
was sent up for forgery.
One day we came to know
the worst.

   How and why
they murdered Lincoln in a theatre-box of death.
   How and why
the bandits there become senators.
   How and why
There are many cops who're not in prison.
   How and why
there are tears in the stones of every skyscraper.

How and why
with one blow Texas was ripped-off and pocketed.
How and why
the vineyards and orchards of California no longer belong to Mexico.
How and why
Marines killed the soldiers of Veracruz.
How and why
Dessalines saw his flag torn from every Haitian staff.
How and why
our great General Sandino was betrayed and murdered.
How and why
they dirtied our sugar with manure.
How and why
they've blinded their people and torn out its tongue.
How and why
they're forbidden to know us and tell our simple truth.
How and why . . .

Oh, we came from far-off, from far-off.
One day we learned all this.
Our mind sorts out its memories.
We've simply grown up.
We've grown . . .
but we don't forget.

TRANSLATED BY DAVID ARTHUR MCMURRAY

Abakuá

Rafael López Valdés

The abakuá secret society is an important element in the heritage of slavery in Cuba. The society developed a major presence among dockworkers in Havana, Matanzas, and Cárdenas on the northwestern coast of the island. It functioned until the early 1940s as a mutual aid organization and self-defense body that was intricately bound up with the system of labor recruitment via contractors employed in Cuban ports. In the following extract, Cuban ethnographer Rafael López Valdés provides the first published account of the place of abakuá, or ñañiguismo, in the life of black port workers.

The "Abakuá" Secret Society among a Group of Cuban Dockworkers

At the beginning of the Republic and especially during the First American Intervention, foreign capital flowed into Cuba, eager to take over the wealth of the country. Its economic importance led to the port of Havana being quickly taken over by foreign investors. The North American administrations of different docks commenced in the early republican years, but the new owners did not change the labor structure of the docks but rather continued to recruit "free contract labor" through contractors and middlemen.

In the last century small numbers of abakuás entered the ports, first establishing themselves as a group and then expanding their ranks. According to Rivero Muñiz, by 1900, "It was rumored that many of the dockworker groups were controlled by devotees from different *potencias*, or *ñáñigo* societies, that were commonly found among the people, especially in working-class neighborhoods.

"There were repeated denials that being 'sworn in' as a member of one of these potencias was a requirement for being allowed to work on this or that pier, but this was in fact the case. On more than one occasion this gave rise to bloody fights between members of the societies and the people who were trying to earn their living by loading and unloading the ships that docked at the port of Havana." . . .

ACCESS TO WORK

The position of the foremen and contractors was, as we have seen, truly power-ful. "Whether one ate or starved"—that is, the decision about who worked and who didn't work—depended on these men. In this way contractors and foreman assembled a labor force whose loyalty was sustained by a common interest in obtaining and safeguarding its jobs.

Being a contractor or foreman implied exercising power over a group of workers and the abakuá, especially those who occupied a position within a par-ticular potencia, were socially and culturally well positioned to play this role.

This is why closed groups of the society could penetrate the port, and why they were not reluctant to use force when necessary to deal with anybody who challenged their power.

This was the mechanism which allowed the contractors to hire relatives and *ekobios* [members of the same potencia or *juego*] at the docks. Even though everyone was exploited by the contractor, these people enjoyed advantages denied to workers who were not family members or abakuá members. This group also enjoyed access to permanent work, while the most difficult jobs were reserved for those men who, not being ñáñigos, could only get work when there were more positions available than could be filled by the potencia to which the contractor or foreman belonged. On the other hand, when it was necessary to fill a better-paid position, like *cubiertero*, or foreman, promo-tions depended on the family, or *ekobiazgo* ties that sustained the relationship between contractor or middlemen and their trusted employees.

At the turn of this century, the neighborhoods most closely linked to the docks were Jesús María and Belén, inhabited by a large number of poor people. There were several abakuá potencias in these areas. The Bakokó society was based in Belén. Its *iyamba* [the title of a leadership position within a potencia] was Faustino, a contractor for the American Line, whose boats moored at the Ward Line's pier. The Kanfioró society was also in Belén, and its iyamba was the contractor for the Spanish Line. In Jesús María there were two potencias who served as contractors on three piers; the Vaccaro, Atarés, and Tallapiedra piers were controlled by the Equereguá and Uriapepá societies.

Each potencia is an organic unit operating over a fixed territory with its boundaries usually established by the neighborhood.

Neighborhoods have a tremendous importance for ordinary folk in the city of Havana. The neighborhood is where their life unfolds, shaped by intensely local traditions. People wear their origins in this or that neighborhood as a badge of pride, particularly if they come from one of the areas which make up the old quarter of the city, known as Old Havana.

The abakuá society was nourished by and developed in the neighborhoods.

This was where it attained its greatest status. Every juego [local-level abakuá society] was tightly linked to the neighborhood in which it had its roots. When we speak of a potencia, we assume a relationship with a particular neighborhood base. Its function in the neighborhood begins the moment an individual tries to join the society and goes to a potencia's leader to express this wish. If he seeks membership outside of his neighborhood, he will be asked why he didn't approach his own potencia, since admission requires knowledge of the most trivial details of his life, from infancy onward; just one example of weakness when confronting an enemy or danger could be a major obstacle to joining the society, and nobody knows all the details of a man's life better than the residents of his neighborhood.

The expression so common in those days, "this shipping line belongs to Jesús María" is rooted in the relationship between society, neighborhood, and contractor. It meant that people who lived in that neighborhood were the preferred workers there, especially those who belonged to the neighborhood's potencia.

During our research we repeatedly heard comments that "to be able to get work, you had to be an abakuá." . . .

So, even though members of different juegos might work on the same pier as happened in Zone 2, where we carried out our research, one juego always stood out as having the largest number of members. Thus, at the Harry Brother's pier (later the Vaccaro pier), during the first decade of the Republic, the potencia with the largest number of members among the workers was the Equereguá Momí, in the Havana Dock it was the Urianabón and Betongó, the former from the Colón neighborhood and the latter from Pueblo Nuevo; in the Ward Line it was Kanfioró, Bakokó, and Enyegueyé; in the White Fleet, Otán Efó; in Tallapiedra, Equeregué and Ibondá; and so on in each of the Companies. . . .

After the 1920s the most important contractors and middlemen were residents of Regla, and as we have seen, their status was usually derived from their double role as contractors and members of the abakuá society. When they came to work at the Havana docks with their people from the other side of the bay, they did so against the will of the Havana workers, displacing many of them or at least giving preference in hiring to men who were not closely related to the Havana workers.

Clearly it was economic factors which allowed the entrance of these contractors from Regla, since the Regla work force was cheaper, and because the Reglans were willing to work for less money, rather than have no work at all. We should also consider the situation in Cuba at the time. In 1912, the armed uprising led by Evaristo Estenoz and his Independent Party of Color tried to win rights that were being denied to dark-skinned men. This generated a wave of racism encouraged by those who were interested in maintaining discrimination, which had repercussions in many parts of the country, including Regla, where an attempt was made to use terror to "whiten" a population that was already mostly white.

Both conflicts, the local and the racist, had been present on the docks for some time, and were most evident during the 1920s when the Reglans entered the docks under the control of the contractors. They were used as strike breakers during these years and stayed on as workers.

Abakuá was no obstacle for the Reglans. On the contrary, many of them belonged to a juego of white ñáñigos, the Enyegueyé Efó, which had been founded in 1882 under the patronage of the white potencia Ekorio Efó Número Uno.

It was common for contractors to belong to an abakuá society. . . . Let us follow the experiences of one of these contractors, Manuel de Jesús Capaz, "Chuchú" Capaz, today a very old man and very attached to the old abakuá traditions, to the ancient rituals and initiation rites, which have relaxed a bit over time. Chuchú was known as "the man who knows most about abakuá in Cuba" according to his own words, a fact confirmed by the daily visits he received from ñáñigos belonging to all of the potencias seeking advice and instruction concerning the rites and religious formulas of the society.

Chuchú was born in 1881 in Regla and at the age of twenty-one, on 24 February 1902, joined the Efó Abakuá juego in Regla. From his earliest years Chuchú stood out as a powerful man in the special abakuá sense of manliness. So no one was surprised when the leaders of the Stevedores union, looking for somebody to help them scare an opponent "by firing a few shots" during a dock strike in 1904, chose Chuchú for the role. He was sentenced to several months in jail as a result. Once out of jail, he went to the leader of the Union asking to join, since the workers at this period were hired either by the contractors or by the union leaders. When he made his request, he was told that to join the union he would have to pay fifty pesos, spend six months as an apprentice, and six months observing. Manuel told them that he would not accept their conditions, and that "he was going to break their union."

In spite of these initial difficulties obtaining work on the docks, he finally succeeded, and began to work shoveling coal, one of the most difficult jobs at the dock.

Later, in 1909, when he held the position of iyamba in the Enyegueyé Efó juego, he became a foreman with the stevedores at the Harry Brothers pier.

In 1912, during the presidency of José Miguel Gómez a strike broke out among the dockworkers of Havana caused by problems in the loading of pineapples. The loading had to be carried out under special conditions determined by the size of the crates that the fruits were packed in. When the strike happened, Chuchú met with José Miguel Gómez, who was a personal friend, and with his help, he managed to speak to Mr. Smith, administrator of the Ward Line. He offered to solve the strike by bringing men from Regla to work. Things turned out just as he had promised. An old stevedore, crippled by age and hard physical work, has told us how they turned up to work at the docks in small boats from Regla, avoiding a confrontation with the strikers who were on the other side of the fences surrounding the dock, where the police were blocking their entry. In any case, the Reglans had come prepared for any eventuality, armed with knives and other weapons. Understandably, Chuchú's group consisted of men that he trusted implicitly, among them relatives and members of his potencia.

This strike in the bay coincided with Estenoz's uprising, known as the "little war of the blacks." The contractors exploited this coincidence, and Chuchú, in particular, launched the slogan "we have to take jobs away from Havana's blacks," a reference to the racial composition of the majority of stevedores on the Havana docks.

Manuel de Jesús Capaz was a councilor in the Regla city government during Gerardo Machado's first government, and he was president of the city government during Machado's second term in office (1929–33). It was not unusual for a prominent abakuá to hold political office, if we recall that abakuá had important ties to Cuban politics. A potencia might support particular candidates, sometimes even drafting electoral leaflets using the language they employed in their rituals.

When Machado fell in 1933 Chuchú not only lost his political positions, but he was also forced to retire from the docks. In his years as a middleman, he had accumulated a good deal of money, and from then on he played a role instructing people in the complex abakuá ritual.

This was how he lived until a few years ago in his native Regla. But the Socialist revolution was not a welcoming environment for this old political boss, strikebreaker, and exploiter of his own ekobios, and Chuchú Capaz left his country, his people, and his potencia.

ABAKUÁ AND THE NONINITIATED CONTRACTORS

Let us now look at the development of a contractor who was not an abakuá.

Angel Naya became a contractor of stevedores for the Munson Line around 1929 or 1930. What allowed him to obtain this position was his marriage to a daughter of Santa Marina, the owner of a "train" of barges and boats that operated in the Havana Bay. The barges played an important role in the unloading of the ships, serving as floating docks. As one of the contractors, who fought each other over contracts to exploit workers, Naya got rid of 150 workers, replacing them with cheap workers from Regla.

The pay rates set by law in 1920 were always ignored by the contractors. The contractors used many techniques to pay their workers less and thus increase their own profits. Moreover, competition among contractors, caused by the system of free "contracting," encouraged cost cutting. They convinced workers to accept lower wages by saying that another contractor would get the job because he paid less, or that the shipping line would move to Matanzas, because the workers there received lower wages.

When the contract began, Naya reduced his workers' daily pay from forty-five pesos for loading a thousand bags of raw sugar to twenty-eight pesos, and for refined sugar, from fifteen pesos per thousand bags to eleven. In addition, he paid three pesos for an eight-hour day, instead of four.

When the Havana workers were thrown out of work, they boarded one of the boats, trying to force Naya's workers off, but this attempt failed. This violent situation ended with Naya's death at the hands of dockworkers who we can assume were ñáñigos.

After Naya's death, those of his relatives who continued to hold the contract made a deal with the workers in which the work would be divided among the workers from both Regla and Havana.

A comparison between the two contractors, Chuchú Capaz and Angel Naya, reveals two contrasting figures. Chuchú, of humble origins, began as a worker, and became a contractor via abakuá, while Naya took advantage of his bourgeois origins, in particular, the important position that his father-in-law held as the owner of the barges.

The peak of the contractors' power was seen during the hiring of workers. The workers gathered on the docks in Regla or at the gates at the entrance to the Havana docks. There, the contractors called the workers by their names, or simply pointed at them. Many workers spoke to the contractors before the hiring on, asking for work because of their particular problems—they were being evicted, or some other reason. . . .

Frequently, in conversations about the dock contractors, the name of Blas Pérez Rojas comes up. He was one of the best-known contractors, for he controlled the White Fleet, one of the biggest shipping lines. "Blasito," as he was generally known, was a leader in the Regla potencia Otán Efó and he became a contractor in the 1930s. . . .

He started from "the bottom," as a stevedore, so he knew from experience about the work and its risks. He retained enough of this humble past to win a certain amount of support from workers. He frequently went down into the ship's hold, and he would occasionally invite certain trusted workers to drink with him. They say that some workers offered Blas women in exchange for work, until one day he stood up on the dock and told them not to bring him any more women, because he was exhausted. This is the most often-told story about Blas. . . .

The contractors opposed the development of union organizations that protected the rights of the workers, and they used their power to withhold work from men who went to political or union meetings. They were also strike-breakers, since strikes affected their earnings and made them look bad in the eyes of the companies.

TRANSLATED BY AVIVA CHOMSKY

The First Wave of Cuban Feminism

Ofelia Domínguez Navarro

Another social movement that contributed to the reformist surge of the time was feminism. Cuban feminists of the early twentieth century sought changes in the legal system, both in terms of political rights for women—namely, the vote—and for social goals such as protective labor legislation. Their sometimes dramatic achievements made prerevolutionary Cuba one of the most advanced countries in the hemisphere in terms of social and labor legislation. Progressive law is not the same as social change, however, and many of these laws were not enforced.[1]

The goals and ideology of the Cuban feminist movement were shaped both by Cuban culture and history and by the class position of the women who led the movement. Early-twentieth-century Cuban feminists based women's claim to rights on their special moral characteristics, in particular as mothers, which should enable them by their very presence to purify and humanize traditionally male spheres: "a feminism centered on motherhood, cooperative with patriarchy, and respectful of class ordering."[2] While the first wave of U.S. feminism used a language of "individual rights and social equality," Cuban feminists—reflecting their cultural heritage, the fragility of the newly independent Cuban state, and the uneasy relationship with their powerful northern neighbor—deliberately distinguished their feminism from that in the United States. Cuban feminists emphasized their patriotism and their commitment to complementary (rather than equal) roles for men and women.[3]

The following excerpts from the autobiography of socialist feminist activist Ofelia Domínguez Navarro give the flavor of the ideas and activism of a woman of the elite who was strongly committed to social change.

La Patria Potestad

In the past, the natural, and almost the only, fate of a woman was marriage, and for marriages that produced many daughters the great problem arose of placing their daughters, that is, finding other men who would protect them. Sometimes the problem resolved itself naturally without the dramas that took over some homes, darkening family life. Many parents went ahead on their

Eduardo Abela,
Guajiros (Peasants),
1938. Martínez, *Cuban
Art and National
Identity*, 61. Courtesy
Museo Nacional
de Cuba.

own, without considering their daughters' feelings, because the expedient thing to do was to get rid of them and, even better, if this could be done in order of age. This helped to resolve the problem before a long spinsterhood made a match, and thus marriage, a difficult prospect.

With respect to some parents' interest in marrying off their daughters in order of age without skipping any, I remember a friend's distress when he went to a father who had four single daughters, to ask for the hand of the youngest one. The father remained very serious in silence, as if hesitating to make a reply, which terribly distressed the prospective suitor. Finally the father, instead of responding to the request that the suitor made, suddenly made the following marvelous appeal: "Well, and why don't you ask me for the hand of my daughter Rosa, who is the eldest? Imagine the situation you would put the other sisters in, if the youngest of all was to be the first to marry." The youth had to argue for a long time to convince this father that he was actually in love with, and thus should marry, the youngest of his daughters.

The fate of a single woman was very uncertain. In general, in the best of cases, she had to spend the rest of her life living in the home of relatives, helping with domestic chores or in raising her nieces and nephews. Thus many parents became arbitrary in trying to impose their will, spurred by the conflict that was created at home and by the potential futures of their remaining single daughters.

Our women, accustomed to the obedience that law and custom imposed on them, accepted without protesting, even after they reached the age of majority, their parents' decision. In a few cases they attempted to undermine or influence parental decisions. If the suitor was what was called a *good catch*, many parents cared little if he was not to the girl's liking, and a family siege was put up to bring her to agreement. I knew a case that was repeated frequently, in which the suitor was a good man, son of a wealthy peasant family, a bit hunchbacked, illiterate, shy, and with rough manners; in short, he was not at all attractive. The girl, on the other hand, in addition to being pretty and pleasant, had successfully completed primary school; she was vivacious and motivated to improve herself, or at least, to marry a man whom she loved. But her family was dazzled by the suitor's fortune, and the father responded to his daughter's refusal telling her that if she did not accept, he would shoot her, because through this marriage the family would escape its poverty. There was weeping, threats, despair, begging on bended knee, . . . etc.

Finally the daughter accepted, but at her wedding night another intimate drama began. She had married a man who could not consummate the marriage physically, and she had to tolerate this situation for almost seven years, even though she let her family know about the realities of this matrimonial farce, which she repudiated with all her strength. But now the father, with the help of his son-in-law, had begun to emerge from his precarious economic situation, and he wanted to watch out for this advantageous marriage. . . . But one day all was lost. The girl fell in love with a poor man, who only earned a modest salary, and she ran away from home. I played a role as the divorce lawyer. After some time had passed, I ran into the couple and these were the girl's first words: "I am happy, I have four sons, which I could never have had with the other. In my house we don't have servants, nor abundance of anything, but there is love and, above all, my life has a purpose."

"And your family?" I asked her.

"Imagine, they have not come to terms with the fact that I left the man that they forced on me. But anyway, I feel content and happy. My husband and my children fulfill my life."

I have presented, through the case of one daughter, one of the multiple facets that the exercise of patria potestad created in the old system. The son was freed from paternal authority when he reached the age of majority, but both the mother and the daughters of the family had to tolerate it as long as they lived under the authority of the father or the husband. Article 154 of the Spanish Civil Code states that the father exercises patria potestad or, in his absence, the mother does. This, like other principles, prevailed in the Republic until 1959. In spite of the military orders imposed by the U.S. occupiers in 1898–1902, the different laws passed by the Republic, and the new Constitution, the lower status of women, with the fluctuations imposed by time, remained in place.

Bit by bit, a few rights for women were timidly recognized. Still, if we go back a few years in the colony, we find that the mother could not exercise patria potestad over her legitimate children, even if the father was absent or dead. Article 64 of the 1870 Marriage Law recognized for the first time the right of a woman to exercise patria potestad if her husband died. On 2 March 1883, this Article, and Articles 44 and 78, were extended to Cuba. However, it is also true that the patria potestad that devolved to the mother in the absence of the father almost always brought fatal consequences for the family inheritance and the integrity of the family.

This sense of inferiority took such deep root in the bodies and the minds of most women of the past, that they accepted it with resignation as something fatally inherent to their sex. One could frequently hear, before anything that affected a widow or single woman, in a pained tone: "Of course, the poor thing has no man! If she had had a man to take care of her. . . . They take advantage of her, because she does not have a man to protect her." Women did not recognize themselves as a social force. Women were terrified at the idea of independence. When one spoke of equal rights, many stood up against such nonsense and claimed their position as "real women." That is to say, the ballast imposed by law and reinforced by custom kept them tied to a fate that many accepted without protest.

Second National Women's Congress (1925)

[Thirty-one women's organizations participated in the First National Women's Congress in Havana in 1923; seventy participated in the second Congress in 1925. Ofelia Domínguez Navarro represented Santa Clara province at both. In 1924, she spoke out passionately on "The Need to Grant Illegitimate Children the Same Rights as Legitimate Children," provoking an impassioned debate.]

Dr. Camín: It seems impossible, Señora Domínguez, that you, being a lawyer, would be so sentimental.

Dr. Domínguez: I see no reason why a woman should have to dispense with feelings when she adopts a profession like this one, to which she should in fact bring all that is human and tender in her. And note, Dr. Carmín, that I do not support my thesis with sentimental arguments. I depart from the principal of justice that emanates from nature itself, which is more in accordance with human happiness than those that appear in legal texts, because nature does not differentiate among children. It is not, thus, a sentimental reason, although it is one of humanity and of justice, of that justice that humans have still not known how to bring to their law codes, but which is inscribed deep in all honorable consciousnesses.

Dr. Amelia de Vera: This would mean the destruction of the family, the introduction of concubinage, and besides, there is no woman who could agree to her husband taking part of what justly belongs to her legitimate children to distribute it among those others. (Murmurs of approval.) Someone who does not know how to be a mother in accordance with the law has to pay the consequences.

Srta. Hortensia Lamar (Miss Hortensia Lamar comes before the tribunal and standing beside Dr. Domínguez, amidst a salvo of applause, says energetically): Motherhood is so sacred, it is something that should be so respected and venerated, that it is neither legal nor illegal; all motherhood is as one and no matter where it is we are obliged to raise it up and protect it.

Let us raise up the mother! Let us raise up and protect her children! And more, if a mother responds to an impulse of her heart or a call of nature and has a child, that mother, who has done nothing but respond to the longings of her heart and the dictates of her conscience should be blessed.

(Shouts and applause in the room.)

Dr. Angela Zaldívar (with her arms raised and practically lifted by her comrades, climbs up on a chair and exclaims): Honorable women, let us abandon this Congress!

The president (energetically ringing the bell to call the room to order, and without directing her reply personally to Dr. Zaldívar, who was the one who had disturbed the order, says): I beg the Congress delegates not to get carried away when they have a reply to make.

Dr. Rosa Anders: I am here representing the Province of Camagüey. . . . I wanted to know the opinion of Camagüeyan women and bring them to the Congress, and I assure you that in Camagüey the women are emphatically opposed to the approval of this measure. I have visited over three hundred families before coming to this Congress, and that is what they told me.

Dr. Domínguez: . . . I cannot silence the sadness I feel at the opinion that the illustrious women of Camagüey uphold. The land of the most tender and beautiful women of Cuba; the land with an Indian, purely Ciboney, name, is that which today extends its accusatory finger toward the unfortunate child who has committed no crime except that of having been born. I prefer to remain convinced that Camagüey's women are ignorant about the painful problem that we are trying to remedy; I prefer to believe that those three

Eduardo Abela, logo for the exhibition of New Art, Havana, 1927. Martínez, *Cuban Art and National Identity*, 9. Reprinted from *Revista de Avance* (15 May 1927).

hundred families that you have visited to extract their opinions, have spoken lightly, without studying the issue in depth. A woman who is a mother cannot drown in her breast the longing that all children should be happy, even those who come into life in conditions that are not accepted by the social environment. . . .

Dr. Anders: Dr. Domínguez is inspired by reasons of false charity. Do not be deceived by them, because they do not have a solid basis and they are inspired by false sentiments.

Dr. Domínguez: May I speak, Sra. President?

President: Dr. Anders has the floor.

Dr. Domínguez: But Srta. Anders has put forth ideas that regard me, which I would like to clarify at once. I cannot accept her statement that my work is inspired by stupid sentimentalism. As I have already said, I do not ask for charity: I ask for justice and only justice, and if part of my heart is in this work, it is because I have never been able to separate my heart from my work with children. I can assure you that today we are on the side of what is truly just and human.

Dr. Amelia de Vera: And in a marriage in which the woman contributes more to the common earnings than the man, do you think that she could patiently accept her legitimate children being deprived of part of what she has contributed, so that it can be handed over to another who has been brought into life under irregular conditions?

Dr. Domínguez: Your reasoning appears logical as long as we do not stop to analyze it. In the case of an illegitimate child we are confronted with an evil that has to devolve upon somebody, and I do not think that somebody should be the most innocent of all: the child. And in addition, Dr. De Vera, these special cases should not be taken into account in establishing general rules. The partner who has children outside of the marriage should, logically, take financial responsibility. When one contributes more than the other to the common earnings, this should not affect the child's subsistence. The interest of protecting the child, and guaranteeing its future in equal conditions as the other children, should be above the interests of the adult.

Domínguez Navarro reflected on the significance of the Congresses: "Both the first and the second Congresses helped to create a national atmosphere of interest in the problems that were raised in the political, social, and economic order, highlighting the backward attitude of many groups of women, who perhaps without realizing it, and under the influence of old customs, opposed the just and forward-looking measures that were proposed by a small group of women who were obliged to leave the Congress. A few years later, all of these proposals that were then considered immoral and threatening to the family became both law and accepted norms in everyday life."

TRANSLATED BY AVIVA CHOMSKY

Notes

1. See K. Lynn Stoner, *From the House to the Streets: The Cuban Woman's Movement for Legal Reform, 1898–1940* (Durham, N.C.: Duke University Press, 1991), 183.
2. Ibid., 85.
3. Ibid., 1–3.

Life at the Mill

Ursinio Rojas

In the period from 1910 to the 1940s, sugar was harvested and processed in what analysts call "agro-industrial complexes." Field workers, many of them until the early 1930s
labor immigrants from Haiti and the British West Indies, cleared the land, prepared it
for planting, and, finally, harvested the cane during the zafra. The mills, or centrales,
were concentrated within and around the central yard, or batey, some of which took
on the characteristics of a small town. The mill complex incorporated the buildings
involved in the processing of sugarcane, electricity-generating plants, schools, and hospitals as well as retail stores, restaurants, and extensive housing for batey workers. The
spatial and architectural characteristics of the largest mills, especially U.S.-controlled
facilities, followed a common pattern—a so-called tropicalized Anglo-Saxon cluster-
ing of private schools, churches, recreational centers, and residential zones segregated
by ethnic and class lines.

    The cane harvest season signified more than an alteration to the tempo of life in
the cane fields, because in the sugar zones the zafra's impact was felt in virtually every
sphere of social, economic, and cultural life. Economic crises were common in the cycle
of booms and busts that the Cuban sugar industry experienced in the period 1910–1935.
The first major crash occurred in 1920 and 1921 when the wild rise of sugar prices that
Cubans call "The Dance of the Millions" ended in a period of mass unemployment
and bankruptcies of mills and sugar farms. But the worst crisis was still to come. The
drama of life for sugar workers and their families in the early 1930s, difficult years in
which the Depression cut the length of the zafra and decreased wages, is conveyed in
an extract from the memoirs of a former sugar worker (and later leading communist
trade unionist), Ursinio Rojas.

Workers' Struggles in the Tacajó Mill

In 1929, the year I began working at the mill, the Wall Street crash happened,
with disastrous consequences for world capitalism. As we've seen, the sugar
industry had already been falling into this crisis, since the world was producing
more sugar than it was consuming. Thus every year the price of sugar fell on the

world market. To solve this problem, the producing countries agreed to limit production. That was when the policy of restricting the harvests began, which meant lower wages and less work for the sugar workers, the cane cutters, and the small *colonos*. The falling income of some six hundred thousand workers and peasants also affected business and industries that produced clothes, shoes, cigarettes, cigars, and drinks—mostly industries owned by Cubans.

But the bulk of the population knew nothing of these economic problems. The workers and peasants, especially—a large proportion of whom were illiterate—did not read newspapers, nor did they own radios, or have any other way of obtaining information. A large portion of our people blamed these difficulties on "their bad luck" and other superstitions, and tried to solve them using spiritists or witchcraft, making vows, praying, or playing the lottery. The exploiters had no interest in seeing the people better themselves. On the contrary, they wanted to keep the people stupid, so that they could exploit them better.

In those times, the only way to get work and obtain a few pesos to buy some clothes or shoes, eat, and solve the main problems at home was the sugar harvest. After a long "dead season" of eight or nine months, during which only a few workers were employed making repairs for fifty or sixty days, the rest of the workers and their families, unemployed, suffered hunger and needs of all kinds.

On a very few occasions, the mill workers could find work in the sugar fields, where most of the work was carried out by Haitians, who were paid lower wages than the Cubans. The Haitians survived on sweet potatoes, flour, herrings, and salt cod; and with one change of clothes and one pair of sandals they could get by for months; they lived in *barracones* and slept in hammocks made of henequen bags; they healed themselves with herbs, which they could do for very little money. They provided serious competition for Cuban workers, which made the situation even worse. . . .

When the harvest began, in all of the mills and sugar zones, the military barracks and posts were reinforced with soldiers from the capital and the major cities. The mills' managers provided the soldiers with *motores de líneas* [motorized railcars] and horses so that they could patrol daily. At the mill gates and inside the mills, pairs of soldiers were stationed to search the packages that the workers used to carry in their lunch or snack.

On pay day pairs of rural guards were stationed in the offices to put down protests when workers received their wages. If a fire broke out in a cane field, many guards turned up to force the workers to help put it out, and afterwards they rounded up anyone who seemed at all suspicious, or who carried matches in their pockets. In this way, in an atmosphere of terror imposed by the rural guard and the corps of "sworn guards" organized by each company, the harvest was carried out. The *plan de machete*, blows with rifle butts, arrests, and the firings, were almost daily activities in the mills and the cane zones. . . .

[In 1930] the harvest was shorter, as had been announced, and it was over by the middle of April. Most of the workers could not buy clothes, or shoes, to replace what they had worn out. Much less could they repay the debts they had piled up over the previous year, which meant that in the upcoming dead season, they would not be able to obtain any credit.

When the milling and labor of cleaning up and dismantling the mill were finished, only a few office employees and the sworn guards and overseers remained working. A large part of the sugar that had been refined remained warehoused, and there was no news of new shipments. The mill and the batey returned to their traditional tranquility, with just a little activity in the *bodegas* and the shops. The cane fields were totally paralyzed, and people said that until June or July, after the spring rains, there would be no work in agriculture.

This is why my father got the overseer to let him sow several fire lanes near the house, and grow *boniatos* [a Cuban tuber similar to a sweet potato] and beans to feed us. In those months without work, we spent our time cultivat-

Central Manatí trilingual flyer, 1920. Reprinted in Carl Van Ness, "Gainesville's Sweet Archives," *Cuban Heritage* 1, no. 2 (fall 1987), p. 36.

AVISO AL PUBLICO

RESOLUCION No. 1.

Habiéndose acogido el **BANCO NACIONAL DE CUBA** a la Ley de Moratoria de 27 de Enero del corriente año, en cumplimiento de lo estatuido en el Art. 2º de dicha Ley, proceda el Banco sin demora a reintegrar a todas las personas que en 10 de Octubre de 1920 fueran depositantes del mismo hasta el 15% de sus créditos, debiendo computarse en ese tanto por ciento las cantidades que hubieren sido pagadas a dichos depositantes con posterioridad a dicha fecha, entendiéndose que los depositantes que hubieren percibido el 10% les será incluido en el 15%, de manera que los que estuvieren en ese caso solo percibirán el 5%.

Al propio tiempo y de acuerdo con lo preceptuado en el Art. 1º de la misma Ley, procédase al cobro de todas las Obligaciones de carácter mercantil contraídas antes del 10 de Octubre de 1920, que consten por medio de Letras de Cambio, Giros, Pagarés, Libranzas, Vales y demás documentos de créditos comprendidos en el Código de Comercio ya vencidas o que fueren venciendo dentro del término de vigencia de la citada Ley de 27 de Enero del año corriente, a no ser que esos deudores hayan abonado o abonen el 15% en efectivo de sus respectivas deudas pudiendo entregar el resto en cheques intervenidos y girados a cargo de esta Institución de crédito.

Fíjense estas reglas en lugar visible de este Establecimiento, circúlense a los deudores y remítanse a las Sucursales del Banco.

Febrero 12-1921.

Dr. Juan de D. García Kohly,

Interventor del Banco Nacional de Cuba designado por el Poder Ejecutivo.

Public notice of a bank closure in the 1921 crash. Reprinted in Carl Van Ness, "Gainesville's Sweet Archives," *Cuban Heritage* 1, no. 2 (fall 1987): 38.

ing our kitchen garden and taking care of our animals which, along with the credit we could get from the store and the butcher shop, allowed us to survive, barely.

My grandparents had a small farm in a neighborhood of Holguín called "Santa Rosa," and my father used to send me and my brother there for several weeks to help them. That year, my brother had waited at the gate of Tacajó, trying to be taken on as a substitute for a couple of shifts but he hadn't been successful, and he spent the harvest cutting cane, along with my father.

In 1930 the repairs began fairly late, towards the end of October and with fewer workers than in previous years. The 20 percent wage reduction imposed during the harvest was maintained during the period of repairs.

After the spring rains, work in agriculture was reduced substantially, since the cane was only cleaned once and there was hardly any replanting. There was a lot of cane left over, and there was no need for new plantings or replantings. Thus, for workers in both the industrial and the agricultural side of sugar production, the dead season was longer, there was little work, lower wages, less credit, and thus more hunger and suffering. . . .

At the end of January 1931, we found out that the harvest would begin in the middle of February, and Company spokespeople began to spread the word that the prospects were not good: "that the price of sugar had continued to fall, that the harvest would be restricted again," etc. This was how they created the psychological conditions for what they knew was going to happen. At the beginning of February, there were some moves to commence the harvest, but the better-informed skilled workers, technicians, and others, who came from the cities and towns of the interior, declared that this would be even shorter and that wages would surely be cut again.

Once again, the newspapers highlighted the news about the measures the government would take to protect the sugar zones and the harvest. The usual reinforcements of soldiers began to arrive, patrolling the *colonias* on horseback and publishing the traditional "military decrees" in public papers. A list with the names, positions, shifts, and wages of each worker was posted, showing that the wages of a large number of workers had been reduced by varying percentages. Skilled workers took the biggest wage cuts, and day laborers and less skilled workers had smaller cuts. Once again, jobs were eliminated. This time, almost all of the mechanics', carpenters', building workers', *paileros* [workers who tend the metal boiling pots], and solderers' assistants were eliminated, and every weighing crew and railroad crew lost a few of its workers.

By contrast, the wages of workers cutting and hauling the cane were cut more severely than those of the mill workers.

That year, the company introduced other changes to save money, like contracting the sugar-packing department to a contractor who paid the carters and stevedores for transporting a certain number of 325-pound bags per day, so that if the mill stopped for repairs and there wasn't enough sugar to carry or load, the workers earned nothing that day. Breaks for cleaning the mill would be announced the previous day, and only those workers needed for the task would work that shift. If there was a longer stoppage because of breakdowns in the machinery, the same thing would happen.

In the workshop, work was paid according to the time that it was supposed to take to complete it. In addition to these measures that were put into place during the harvest, the bosses became more and more demanding with the workers, reprimanding them constantly for any insignificant infraction, and even firing people for talking or for not paying enough attention to their work.

At the same time, the rural guards and the "sworn guards" were constantly patrolling the mill, and searching the workers' lunchboxes when they entered and exited.

With these methods, the company managed to carry out the 1931 harvest without major difficulties. When it was over, the only people still around were

Bullock cart loading cane in Cuba. Francis Maxwell, *Economic Aspects of Cane Sugar Production* (London: Norman Rodger, 1927), op. 14.

View of Agramonte Sugar Central. Maxwell, *Economic Aspects of Cane Sugar Production*, op. 107.

the guarda jurado who watched over the warehouses bulging with sugar and the other facilities.... Once the office work was finished, the offices were closed and the workers thrown out into the street, except for the night watchman.

The dead season that year was horrendous. In the sugar fields and in many of the houses around Tacajó (including mine), the workers built *"cunyayes."* This is the name we gave to a piece of wood that was buried in the ground, with a hole in it for another piece of wood which we used to press strips of sugarcane to extract the cane juice. This was then boiled to make *raspadura* and candies that children and grown-ups ate to deaden their hunger.

Around this time garden plots appeared everywhere, and almost all of the fire lanes were planted with vegetables, tubers, and grains. Thanks to this, many families managed to survive.

In the general stores, the shops, and the butchers', prices fell every year. So did the price of clothes and shoes, but even so very few could buy them, because nobody had a cent.

In the general stores, the peasants brought eggs and chickens to exchange for salt, coffee, and other products. The bodega sold rice for two centavos, lard for two, salt for one, salt cod for three, and offered an onion or a few cloves of garlic on credit, but even so, there were very few who could obtain those foods. The vast majority of the workers, their wives, and children went around with broken shoes, barefoot, with their clothes torn and patched. Begging rose to unprecedented figures, and not only in the sugar areas, but in the whole country.

The economic crisis had affected all sectors of the economy. Thousands of businesses folded and had to close their doors. Hundreds of factories were paralyzed and threw their workers into unemployment and poverty.

Many banks went bankrupt and customers lost their savings. Virtually every business cut wages and salaries, and lowered costs, like the sugar mills had. Peasants roamed the streets with their horses loaded, offering their products, but almost nobody could buy them.

Hunger and poverty took possession of the country, especially in the sugar zones.

This situation of misery was reflected even in the peasants' poetry. A poem from this time addressed to President Machado began:

Señor General Machado
Most illustrious compatriot
Today we send you this note
Regarding my sad state.
With my pockets emptied

I have ceaselessly sought
A place to work
Even if just for food
To sustain my life
And I have not been able to find it.

TRANSLATED BY AVIVA CHOMSKY

Migrant Workers in the Sugar Industry

Leví Marrero

The expansion of the sugar industry brought with it a new wave of immigrants, this time most of them Haitians, Jamaicans, and other West Indians. Between 1913 and 1933 tens of thousands migrated, some as temporary contract workers and some as permanent immigrants, some legally and some without formal permission, transforming once again the demography of eastern Cuba. Immigration became an issue of intense political debate, a debate not unrelated to racism, because virtually all of the migrant workers were black. As nationalist and anti-imperialist sentiment grew among different sectors of the population, it mingled with nativist reactions against the black immigrants whom the foreign-owned sugar industry was bringing into the country. Both Haitians and Jamaicans were subject to onerous working conditions and also racist attacks. In the following selection, Cuban economist Leví Marrero describes the conditions facing Haitian migrant workers in a 1934 article for the popular weekly Bohemia.

Hunting Haitians in Eastern Cuba: The Horrors of the Sugar Fiefdoms

Nick Halley looked like a guy who had been wrenched violently from the adventurous and cordial zoo of characters invented by Jack London. I met him when he was over forty, in a small town — no more than five hundred inhabitants — near a sugar mill in the province of Santa Clara. . . .

"I was twenty years old," Nick said, "when I left my family in Philadelphia. I was the youngest of three children. The others were content with their jobs, but not me; I wanted to explore the world at any price. One day I found myself on the coast of Florida and I signed up on a freighter. Not long after, it landed in Haiti, but it could just as well have ended up in Shanghai.

"I found many strange and interesting things that occupied my attention for several days. But the time came when I found myself without a cent. A friend that I had met suggested that I 'join the roundup,' and I agreed. The truth was that I had no idea what this was, but they promised me eighty pesos a month, for minimal work.

"The next day we were aboard a schooner. My friend was the assistant to a labor contractor who was charged with bringing several shipments of Haitians to work in the north coastal regions of Oriente, in Cuba.

"After several hours at sea we arrived at a cove, near a town. My friend had a large barrel of rum unloaded from the schooner. By then over one hundred Haitians had gathered around us, curious.

"The boss, thinking practically, took advantage of the occasion and disembarking with an interpreter, climbed up on the barrel and began a speech.

"In appalling English he talked about the misfortunes that those men, abandoned by God, were suffering. Why live like this? Cuba was only a hop, skip, and a jump away, an earthly paradise, as everybody knows. The streets were paved with gold. And to prove it, as the Haitians stared at him in awe, he took a pile of pennies and nickels out of a bag and threw them at the group. The crowd began to fight over the pennies, until finally, when they were all gathered up, he began to distribute rum.

"One hour later, when they were all completely drunk, the boss spoke again. They had to leave for Cuba immediately.

"Some refused to go; others quickly reached the same decision. And pushing against each other, amid shouts, blasphemies, blows, and terrible beatings with truncheons administered by the twelve crew members — who had an interest in the success of the expedition — over fifty of the poor wretches were brought on board.

"The schooner departed, to reach land, a few days later, in Sagua de Tánamo, Cuba."

I couldn't say exactly how long ago it was that I met Nick Halley, but his story is fresh in my mind today, as the newspapers are reporting the mass repatriation of Haitians as a "health" control measure.

Repatriations

These repatriations begun on the orders of the Grau's Secretary of the Interior, Antonio Guiteras. Immediately after the first orders to this effect were given, military "expeditions" to the plantations, in search of black workers, began, with the aim of returning them to their country.

Extreme circumstances explain the background to this measure: the sugar companies — which import the Antilleans en masse, almost always outside of the requirements set down by law and in a manner similar to that narrated by Nick Halley — do not send them back, as they should, according to the law — to their homelands when the harvest is over.

There are two causes. The companies, on the one hand, are interested in saving the return fare and what it would cost, a few months later, to contract other workers. In addition, the Antilleans want to stay. They are afraid to return home, where the welcome received by those who return empty handed is terrible, as they themselves recount. Their friends, their relatives, everybody pretends that they do not exist, or even attack them physically, beating them in gangs, as if to show them what an abominable mess they made in leaving their country.

The children, lacking food and hygiene, take care of the fighting cocks while their fathers and mothers pick the sweet crop in the fields far away. And suffering these conditions, during the "dead season," that is, when the harvest is over, with no money left—for their labor is almost always paid in the form of coupons that can only be used at the company store—and without any means of surviving, they turn to stealing, to attacking whomever they can, sowing terror among the peasants.

These events, repeated year after year, have created a state of mind that has earned them the enmity of all. In reality, these unfortunates are the victims of all of the injustices that rain on them daily, pursuing them relentlessly. They cannot figure out why they have to live this way, in complete barbarism.

The Arrival

The life of a Haitian laborer—who is regularly confused with the Jamaican, who being an English subject enjoys other advantages—is that of a slave. The Haitians are generally recruited in the same way as the seventeenth-century slaves from the Gold Coast—to supply Cuban "mills" and *colonias*. A few hours after their arrival in Cuba, the prosperity they had been offered fails to eventuate.

One of the areas where they are concentrated, because of the enormous sugar and banana plantations there, is the northern part of Oriente. The ships leave them in the proximity of Sagua de Tánamo, in Antilla and other points, after delivering this cargo of exploitable flesh to the sugar company that has ordered them.

On other occasions, in a more civilized manner, they are imported in boats sent especially to pick them up. Over the last few years, the crisis that has forced the Cuban worker to resort to working for wages formerly paid only to Haitians has led to a diminution of this trade, although it has not disappeared entirely.

When they arrive, these immigrants, who do not speak the language or know the fate that awaits them, are lined up and given a rough canvas change of clothing, a hat made of *yarey* [a type of palm], and a machete. In addition they are each given a card, with the name that they must use. Sarcastic and ridiculous names: Peter the Great, Alcibiades the Magnificent, Judas the Crunchy. Or common last names: Juan Pérez, Pedro Valdés.

During the harvest season, workers brought in this way cannot leave the fields. A specially organized guard enforces the law against flight whenever necessary. But the immigrant rarely takes this risk. He knows that away from the plantation, his life would be no better.

Dead Season

For Havana residents, a Haitian is practically an unknown being. In Pinar del Río and Matanzas, their numbers are also insignificant. But in the three eastern provinces, and especially in Oriente, the number of Antilleans—most of whom are Haitians—is enormous.

During the harvest they live in the infected barracks of the colonias. They eat what the "commercial departments" [of the mills] give them in exchange for their coupons. And they work from sunup to sundown. But work comes to an end. The company does not return them to their country, nor does it give them any means of surviving. Whatever they saved during the harvest disappears in only a few weeks. And the moment comes in which they find themselves without work and without food.

Then the thefts, the assaults, and even the rapes begin. In many areas life becomes impossible for the Haitian peasant. Pursued by hunger, by prejudice, and by the Rural Guard, they quickly turn into primitive cavemen. They live among the cane fields, they only come out at night, and their raids frequently have bloody results.

Legends about these cases abound. But there is not much truth to them.

Mass Expulsions

The worsening economic crisis, and the union movement among the sugar workers, which has generated anxiety and recent acts of protest in the mills and colonias and the ensuing consequences, have produced hasty measures to purge Cuba of Haitians.

As the social group most severely affected by the crisis, their reaction has been the most violent. While many Cuban workers had been hesitating to go on strike, fearing for their families, for their young children, and dreading immediate reprisals, the Haitian, realizing that he had nothing to lose except for his miserable life, was one of the elements that fought back most violently.

After the massacre at the "Senado" sugar mill, for example, ten of the dead were identified as Haitians.

This fact provoked the government's policy of expulsion. Cuban workers, who had suffered for years by losing their jobs to these people, actively supported the measure in many places, helping the army to capture the unfortunates. According to the news, in many areas posters had been put up offering a bounty of two pesos for each Haitian captured.

These persecutions have given rise to the most horrifying manhunts. In many areas the companies succeeded in bribing the hunters, to bring them the Haitians who were easiest to handle. But in other areas, explosions of inhuman fury and cases of naked barbarism have been recorded.

Many fleeing Antilleans, sure that they would be killed, or believing that there was another agenda behind the measures, have resisted, finally being killed.

Other times they have been iniquitously stripped of their possessions, with nobody to hear their protests.

In the vicinity of Santiago de Cuba and Guantánamo, where many Haitians had succeeded in becoming independent coffee growers and establishing their homes after many years of residence in Cuba, the most horrendous acts have been committed. They have been repatriated without being able to sell off their possessions, which have ended up in the hands of their unscrupulous captors.

After the monthly round-ups, in groups of one hundred, or two hundred, these poor unfortunates, men, women, and children, have been taken to Cayo Duan, in Santiago de Cuba, to be reembarked in groups of five hundred, or a thousand, after spending several months in prison. First they were crowded into barracoons where they were assembled; later they were placed in the barracks of the Guardia Rural.

And without the slightest hint of why, after years of working, of poverty, and of savage abuses, these unfortunates for whom "civilization" is a meaningless word, are being returned by violent force to their country, like tired beasts.

But with the passage of time, hundreds of Antillean workers will perhaps soon return to Cuba to replace those that have been expelled. Our semicolonial state makes slavery an eternal necessity.

Why isn't this disguised slavery the worst of all?

TRANSLATED BY AVIVA CHOMSKY

The Cuban Counterpoint

Fernando Ortiz

Fernando Ortiz's (1881–1969) Cuban Counterpoint: Tobacco and Sugar *argues that Cuban history has been fundamentally shaped by these two crops and by the different social complexes connected to their production. Ortiz joined other intellectuals in arguing that sugar was inevitably tied to exploitation and dependence, both in terms of labor relations on the plantation and in terms of Cuba's world position. Just as sugar had cemented Cuba's dependence on Spain and African slavery, now, in the twentieth century, it was supporting Cuba's dependence on the United States and the further misery of Cuba's working class. Hardworking, independent small farmers were far better suited to constitute the independent nation Ortiz and others so fervently desired.*

The outstanding feature of our economic history is in reality this multiform and persistent contrast between the two products that have been and are the most typical of Cuba, aside from that period of brief duration at the beginning of the sixteenth century when the conquistadors' gold-mining activities and the cultivation of yucca fields and stock raising to supply cassava bread and dried meat for the conquerors' expeditions took preeminence. Thus a study of the history of Cuba, both internal and external, is fundamentally a study of the history of sugar and tobacco as the essential bases of its economy.

And even in the universal history of economic phenomena and their social repercussions, there are few lessons more instructive than that of sugar and tobacco in Cuba. By reason of the clarity with which through them the social effects of economic causes can be seen, and because few other nations besides ours have presented this amazing concatenation of historical vicissitudes and this radical contrast, this unbroken parallelism between two coexisting orders of economic phenomena, which throughout their entire development display highly antithetical characteristics and effects, it is as though some supernatural teacher had purposely selected Cuba as a geographic laboratory in which to give the clearest demonstrations of the supreme importance of the basic economy of a nation in its continuous process of development.

The posing and examination of this deep-seated contrast which exists between sugar and tobacco, from their very nature to their social derivations, may throw some new light upon the study of Cuban economy and its historical peculiarities. In addition it offers certain curious and original instances of transculturation of the sort that are of great and current interest in contemporary sociological science. . . .

The social consequences deriving from tobacco and sugar in Cuba and originating in the different conditions under which the two crops are produced can be easily grasped. The contrast between the *vegas*, where tobacco is grown, and the sugar plantation, particularly if it is a modern *central*, is striking. Tobacco gave origin to a special type of agricultural life. There is not the great human agglomeration in the tobacco region that is to be found around the sugar plants. This is due to the fact that tobacco requires no machinery; it needs no mills, nor elaborate physical and chemical equipment, nor railway transport systems. The vega is a geographical term; the *central* is a term of mechanics.

In the production of tobacco intelligence is the prime factor; we have already observed that tobacco is liberal, not to say revolutionary. In the production of sugar it is a question of power; sugar is conservative, if not reactionary.

I repeat, the production of sugar was always a capitalistic venture because of its great territorial and industrial scope and the size of its long-term investments. Tobacco, child of the savage Indian and the virgin earth, is a free being, bowing its neck to no mechanical yoke, unlike sugar, which is ground to bits by the mill. This has occasioned profound economic and social consequences.

In the first place, tobacco was raised on the land best suited for the purpose, without being bound to a great indispensable industrial plant that was stationary and remained "planted" even after it had impoverished all the land about it. This gave rise to the *central*, which even in olden times was at least a village, and today is a city. The vega was never anything but a rural holding, like a garden. The vega was small; it was never the site of *latifundia*, but belonged to small property owners. The *central* required a plantation; in the vega a small farm was enough. The owners of a *central* are known as *hacendados* and live in the city; those of the vegas remained *monteros, sitieros*, or *guajiros* and never left their rural homes.

The cultivation of tobacco demands a yearly cycle of steady work by persons who are skilled and specialized in this activity. Tobacco is often smoked to kill time, but in the tobacco industry there is no such thing as "dead time," as is the case with sugar. This, together with the circumstance that the vega was a smallholding, has developed in the *veguero* a strong attachment to his land, as in the rancher of old, and made it possible for him to carry on his tasks with

Small tobacco factory (*chinchul*) in the 1860s. Hazard, *Cuba with Pen and Pencil*, 216; reprinted in Joan Casanovas, *Bread, or Bullets!*, 18.

the help of members of his family. Only when this is not feasible does he hire workers, but in small groups, never in gangs or by the hundred, as happens with sugarcane. The vega, I repeat, is merely a topographical denomination; the *colonia* is a term having complex political and social connotations.

For these same reasons, while during slavery Negroes were employed as sugar plantation hands, the cultivation of the vegas was based on free, white labor. Thus tobacco and sugar each have racial connections. Tobacco is an inheritance received from the Indian, which was immediately used and esteemed by the Negro, but cultivated and commercialized by the white man. . . .

Sugar was mulatto from the start, for the energies of black men and white always went into its production. . . . Sugarcane and Negro slaves arrived together in the island of Cuba, and possibly in Hispaniola, from across the sea. And since then Negro labor and sugarcane have been two factors in the same economic binomial of the social equation of our country.

For centuries the workers in the *centrals* were exclusively Negroes; often even the overseers were colored. This was true of the mill workers as well as of the field workers, with the exception of the technicians and the management.

It was not until the abolishment of slavery, the influx of Spanish immigrants after the Ten Years' War, and the introduction of the sharecropping system that white farmers were to be found on the Cuban sugar plantations.

. . . In the distribution of colored population in Cuba today the greatest density is to be found in the old sugar-growing sections, not in the tobacco-raising areas, which were settled in the main by white immigrants from the Canary Islands and peasants of old Cuban stock. Tobacco drew upon the free white population, whereas for sugarcane black slaves were imported. This also explains why there are no invasions of migrant seasonal workers in the tobacco industry, and still less of Haitians and Jamaicans, who were brought in to make the harvesting of cane cheaper. . . .

The seasonal nature of the work involved in sugar, in both the fields and the mill, is likewise very characteristic and of great social consequence. The cutting is not continuous, and whereas it used to last almost half a year, it is now almost never longer than a hundred days, and even less since legal restrictions have been placed upon it. All the rest of the year is "dead time." When it is finished, the workers who came to Cuba for the harvest in swallowlike migrations leave the country, taking their savings with them, and the native proletariat goes through a long stretch of unemployment and constant insecurity. A large part of the working class of Cuba has to live all year on the wages earned during two or three months, and the whole lower class suffers from this seasonal work system, being reduced to a state of poverty, with an inadequate, vitamin-deficient diet consisting principally of rice, beans, and tubers, which leave it undernourished and the ready prey of hookworm, tuberculosis, anemia, malaria, and other diseases. This does not occur to the same degree with the tobacco workers, for both the agricultural and the industrial activities require steadier work; but even so, unfortunately for the country, they are also coming to suffer from undernourishment.

The unflagging devotion of the tobacco grower to his field, his constant concern with weather and climatic conditions, the painstaking manual care the plant requires, have prevented the development of the vegas into great plantations, with great capital investments and submission to foreign control. González del Valle writes that "there is not one known case of an American or other foreigner who has grown rich cultivating tobacco in Cuba; as a matter of fact, foreigners who have tried it have lost most if not all of their capital." There are foreign landowners, but they are not the growers, with the exception of a few Spaniards who became quickly naturalized because of their easy adaptability to Cuban ways. Tobacco has always been more Cuban than sugar. It has been pointed out that tobacco is native to the New World, while sugar was brought in from the Old.

Foreign predominance in the sugar industry was always great, and now it is almost exclusive. Tobacco has always been more Cuban because of its origin, its character, and its economy. The reason is obvious. Sugar has always required a large capital investment; today it amounts to a veritable fortune. A century ago a well-balanced *central* could be set up with a hundred thousand pesos; today the industrial plant alone is worth a million. Moreover, ever since the *centrals* were first established in America, all their equipment, with the exception of the land, has had to be brought in from abroad. Machinery, workers, capital, all have to be imported, and this makes necessary an even larger outlay. If the sugar industry was capitalistic in its beginnings, with the improvement in mechanical techniques and the introduction of the steam engine more elaborate mills were required, more cane fields, more land, more slaves, greater investments and reserves — in a word, more and more capital. The entire history of sugar in Cuba, from the first day, has been the struggle originated by the introduction of foreign capital and its overwhelming influence on the island's economy. And it was not Spanish capital, but foreign: that of the Genoese, the Germans, the Flemings, the English, the Yankees, from the days of the emperor Charles V and his bankers, the Fuggers, to our own "good-neighbor" days and the Wall Street financiers.

TRANSLATED BY HARRIET DE ONIS

The Invasion of the Tourists

Rosalie Schwartz

As the importance of sugar in Cuban-U.S. relations diminished in the period after the late 1920s, tourism and investment in real estate came to the fore. Prohibition brought wealthy Americans to drink and gamble; an elaborate publicity campaign presented Havana as the "Paris of the Western Hemisphere"; in 1930 the jewel of Cuban hostelries, the $7 million luxury Hotel Nacional, opened its doors overlooking the Malecón. In the period of mass tourism after World War II, new investments by the Florida mafia transformed the industry into one that reveled in presenting Cuba as a strange, exotic, tropical environment filled with African-inspired rhythms and sexually uninhibited mulatas.

In this 1991 selection Rosalie Schwartz provides an overview of the tourist relationship between Cuba and the United States, and a selection of contemporary photographs and advertising posters reveals dimensions of the graphic representation of Cuba in the discourse of tourism during the first half of the century.

Thirty years ago Fidel Castro padlocked Cuba's fabulous gambling casinos and taught Havana's prostitutes new trades. Revolutionary Cuba effectively ended a financially profitable, but morally bankrupt, tourist industry in 1960. Now the Cuban government, facing economic uncertainty as a result of global political and economic realignments, is returning to tourism to earn the hard currency demanded in the international marketplace.

Cuba lured tourists of the 1920s and 1950s with romantic visions of a lush tropical paradise set in unparalleled blue seas. Now the island's vacation alchemy expects to transform Caribbean sunshine into real gold. Castro expects tourism to generate $500 million in foreign exchange in 1991 and to become Cuba's leading industry. In anticipation, the government has committed substantial resources to the tourist sector and will add several thousand new hotel rooms to accommodate visitors.

Cuba's leaders have made a considered judgment, working from a promising statistical base. More than four hundred million international tourists spent nearly U.S.$4 billion in 1989, representing 12 percent of the total world gross

national product and 7 percent of world trade. The worldwide tourist industry currently generates approximately seventy-four million jobs. With world
tourism increasing at an annual rate of 12 percent, the travel industry could
overtake petroleum as the premier international business.

The Beginnings of Cuban Tourism

Like the devastating hurricanes that sometimes hit the island, the 1920s
roared through Cuba. Sugar—Cuba's economic mainstay—took a dizzying
roller coaster ride of price and market fluctuations and forced Cuban and
North American entrepreneurs to seek alternative investments. Tourism promoters envisioned thousands of moneyed visitors who would spend their
dollars in Cuba's hotels, restaurants, shops, and nightclubs, or at the casino
and racetrack; see the sights from Havana's electric railway or Cuba's national railroad lines, drink Cuban beer, and build their own luxury bungalow in new residential developments surrounding the new Havana Country
Club.

Investors imagined an American Riviera, catering to wealthy and thirsty
U.S. travelers who would do for Cuba in the twentieth century what Europeans had accomplished for Monaco in the nineteenth. The high life on the
Mediterranean attracted affluent Americans, as well as Europeans, and why
should they go so far away for warmth and fun with Cuba so close?

Moneyed travelers wanted to escape cold weather and routine cares. Unemployment and political unrest, notable outcomes of Cuban economic hardship,
offered no appeal. So image makers ignored reality in favor of romance: dream-
like Havana offered sensuous women; its streets throbbed to rumba rhythms.
Seduced by suggestions of sunshine, sex, and rum, North Americans headed
for Cuba by the thousands.

United States businessmen intended to make Havana the Paris of the Western Hemisphere, particularly those merchants of leisure pursuits who saw
their enterprises threatened by a United States gone dry. Prohibition put a
damper on mainland pleasures, but was a gift to the nascent resort industry
ninety miles off the Florida Keys.

The Havana Success Story

United States hotel, restaurant, and resort interests welcomed Cuba's prospects as a condemned prisoner views his reprieve. Cuban legislation opened
the way for gambling and established a national committee to promote tourism. Encouraged by bankers, entrepreneurs, and government officials, Havana

United Railways of Havana advertises "Quaint and Beautiful Cuba," 1915. Collections of the New York Public Library — Astor, Lenox, and Tilden Foundations.

indeed became a playground for the wealthy — mostly North Americans and a few Europeans. A "Winter in Cuba Committee" distributed thousands of brochures in the United States, swelling the demand for accommodations that builders — predictably North American firms — scrambled to complete. Contractors rushed to bid on hotels and apartment houses, new residential developments, and roads.

In the city's bustling suburbs, the Havana Country Club attracted the sufficiently well-to-do with its landscaped golf course, rolling grounds, and winding brooks. Royal palm trees surrounded the clubhouse and terrace where fashionable men and women danced the Charleston, or the Cuban *danzón*, at late afternoon tea. The developers knew their market; they sold lots in nearby Country Club Park, a planned residential community complete with lakes and fountains, beautiful lawns and gardens, to club members who built handsome villas.

To make the new residents happy, a National Commission for the Promotion of Tourism prepared feasts and celebrations for the winter season and subsidized horse and boat races, as well as the opera. February 1924 set a record for

A *Carteles* magazine cover
from the 1940s: "The
Carmen Miranda Look."
Reprinted in *Cuban
Heritage* 2, no. 1 (1988).

tourists in Havana, a record that would be broken each successive year before
the end of the decade.

Tourism stimulated the creative imagination of entrepreneurs like Milton
Hershey, who owned a huge plantation and refinery complex east of Havana.
Hershey continued to ship sugar to his chocolate factory in Pennsylvania, but
he also turned his business into a tourist attraction. Three decades before Walt
Disney turned familiarity with a company name into a tourist bonanza, Milton
Hershey promoted trips on his Hershey Cuban Railway to see the Hershey
Mill and Model Town, where pleasant nights at the Hershey Hotel cost six
dollars a day, American Plan.

Tourists who enjoyed Havana's nightlife did so courtesy of Frank Steinhart's
Light and Power Company, and they saw the sights from the cars of Steinhart's electric railway as it went from Central Havana to the suburban casino
and racetrack, or to the beach at Marianao. Steinhart was also vice president
of a Havana brewery, an insurance company, and a mortgage company, all of
which profited from tourism.

The astute Mr. Steinhart saw more than trolley revenues and beer sales in

A *Carteles* magazine
cover from the 1940s:
"Sex and Tourism."
Reprinted in *Cuban
Heritage* 2, no. 1
(1988).

the tourism boom. He also became a partner in the Cuban National Syndicate,
spearheaded by two other dynamic deal makers. Syndicate partner Charles
Francis Flynn arrived in Cuba in 1914, used his knowledge of construction to
build Havana's Oriental Park race course, and then served as vice president
and manager of the Havana American Jockey Club.

Prohibition loomed just around the corner when Charles Flynn took New
York hotelman John McEntee Bowman to Havana in 1919. Flynn showed Bowman a ten-story office building and suggested he turn it into a hotel. Bowman
liked what he saw in Cuba — rum, for example — and Havana's best hotel of the
1920s, the Sevilla-Biltmore, opened on New Year's Eve, 1919–20. Cuban and
North American social elites made themselves at home in the Sevilla's salon,
when they weren't at the country club, the casino, or the racetrack. With the
hotel launched, Flynn put together the Cuban National Syndicate and introduced syndicate chief Bowman to Frank Steinhart and other Cuban investors.

John Bowman had a passion for horses as well as hotels, and the syndicate
took over operation of Oriental Park in Marianao, with a two-year option to
buy the track. Steinhart, as an officer of the Cuban-American Jockey Club and

A *Carteles* magazine
cover from the 1940s:
"Pet Love." Reprinted in
Cuban Heritage 2, no. 1
(1988).

syndicate investor (and owner of the trolley line to Marianao), made the announcement. The Syndicate also acquired the Casino Marianao and a tract of land on the coast west of the city on which to build the town of Biltmore. With its palatial clubs, hotels, golf, polo and tennis grounds, and yacht harbor, Biltmore would house racing fans much as Country Club Park accommodated golfers.

Whether horse racing, the casino, carnival, or rumba provided the incentive, tourists kept coming. From the opening of the racing season in December until the warmth of spring invited them back home again, North Americans enjoyed Havana. People whose names made headlines in U.S. newspapers sipped rum on the patio at the Hotel Sevilla or tea on the terrace of the country club: Astors, Biddles, Harrimans, Vanderbilts, and Whitneys, Will Rogers, New York Mayor Jimmy Walker, secretary of state Charles Evans Hughes, joined by a number of titled Britons. Havana had captured the captains of industry and social elites.

When John Bowman broke ground for the new Havana-Biltmore Yacht and Country Club early in 1927, Cuba's president Gerardo Machado turned the

Cuban Tourist Commission
poster from the 1940s by
Massaguer. Courtesy Center for
Cuban Studies Archives.

first spadeful of dirt and New York mayor Jimmy Walker the second. Among the Cubans participating in Bowman and Flynn's venture was Machado's son-in-law, José E. Obregón, the new club's "commodore."

The winter tourist season of 1927–28 broke all previous records. The Cuban tourist office in Miami, opened in December 1927, established contact with tourist agents in the United States and Canada and distributed pamphlets, post-cards and film. Then-president Calvin Coolidge visited Havana in January 1928 to address the Pan-American Congress, accompanied by a host of journalists who filed glowing stories about the city.

Everybody's hero of the decade, Colonel Charles A. Lindbergh, arrived in February. Pan American Airways had inaugurated passenger service between Key West and Havana the previous October, and while the reporters watched, Lindbergh flew Cuban officials around Havana aboard a Pan American plane. No wonder the hotels overflowed, and visitors filled the casino and racetrack to capacity.

Never mind that sugar prices continued to drop, that the economy as a whole floundered, that unemployment rose while wages plummeted, that

Bill Griffith's "Zippy" at the Hotel Riviera, 1995. Zippy copyright © 1995 Bill Griffith.

President Machado responded to Cubans' complaints with calculated violence. Tourists don't respond well to street demonstrations or labor stoppages; they want to enjoy themselves. Havana's mayor tried to keep the beggars off the streets in January 1929 so as not to annoy tourists or discourage investors. The 1928 Christmas season had disappointed retailers, and Havana needed tourists to make up the difference.

Construction was started on the $7 million Hotel Nacional in Havana, a partnership between the Cuban government and New York hotel interests. Further east, Irénee DuPont made plans to develop beautiful Varadero Beach as a resort for North American business executives. These projects had barely begun, however, when the tourist bubble burst.

The boom lasted only half a decade, brought precipitously to a close by the Depression, Cuba's 1933 Revolution, and the end of Prohibition. Aside from alterations to the Havana landscape, Cuba had changed little. The impact on traditional Cuban culture was minimal. Few Cubans relinquished cockfights for tennis or replaced the danzón with the fox-trot. Cubans continued to think the sea too cold for swimming in winter, tourist brochures notwithstanding.

Wild and Wicked: Havana in the 1950s

Circumstances surrounding Cuba's second tourist boom bore some striking similarities to the first. The rationale for tourism in the 1950s mirrored that of the 1920s: an alternative revenue source when sugar slumped at the close of the Korean War; foreign investment collaboration; collapse brought about by revolution and the loss of investors' cash.

On the other hand, the 1950s differed from the 1920s in the social base of tourism and its impact on Cuban society. Jumbo jets and package tours captured the middle and working classes who had acquired paid vacations and disposable income. Pan American Airways operated from sixty to eighty round-trip flights a week between Miami and Havana; the $40 fare attracted lots of customers. Steamers departed from Key West, and families used the car ferry service to drive to Cuba. New hotels accommodated the influx, and new restaurants reflected the new clientele—from the luxurious, strictly kosher Moishe Pipik, to the counter at Woolworth's (El Tencén).

Varadero Beach lost the elitism of an earlier era when Irénee DuPont had built mansions for himself and other corporate executives. In the 1950s the Greyhound bus brought tourists from Havana to enjoy the beaches. Millionaire's row remained at the southern end of town, but the less affluent crowd found their appropriate niche at various small hotels. . . .

North Americans flocked to Cuba by the thousands, geese headed south to find their winter paradise. To hipsters of the fifties, "strange, wonderful, and foreign" Havana was the "coolest." The Tropicana and Sans Souci nightclubs turned the backstreet rumba, originally danced in dimly lit bars by black Cubans who mimicked the animated mating of hen and rooster, into elaborately costumed showpieces, more appropriate for mass audience tastes. Few barnyard fowl would have responded to the cleansed gyrations, but the tourists loved it.

Dark-eyed Cuban women and local color never lost their attractiveness, but by the late 1950s casino gambling, plush hotels, beautiful beaches, and Hollywood stars drew most of the tourists to Cuba. For eastern seaboard residents, Havana was closer than Las Vegas.

Good times came in packages that looked more and more like the United States and less and less like an exotic foreign country.

A mixed blessing for Cuba, 1950s tourism undeniably contributed to anti-Batista sentiment. Nevertheless, when the revolutionaries chased Batista and the gangsters out, they tried to hold on to tourism.

Fidel Castro touted Cuba's friendliness toward travelers in 1959 and determined that tourism could become Cuba's biggest business even without gambling and prostitution. The government appropriated millions of dollars for beaches, highways, hotels, and to repair airport damages caused by the fighting. Castro welcomed more than two thousand travel agents to a meeting of the American Society of Travel Agents in October 1959, even as he railed against the United States. The Society made Castro an honorary member before they departed. But shortly, a U.S. trade embargo doomed tourism.

Or so it seemed. For now, Cuba is courting the traveler for yet a third cycle of investment, promotion, and construction intended to salvage the Cuban economy. Two previous waves of tourism ended in financial loss and revolution. History never repeats exactly, but it sometimes comes close.

Waiting Tables in Havana

Cipriano Chinea Palero and Lynn Geldof

Cipriano Chinea Palero, headwaiter at the Habana Libre (formerly the Hilton), describes working in this luxury hotel in the heyday of mob and gambling activity. (Sidney Pollack's 1990 film Havana, *starring Robert Redford, also gives a vivid picture of corruption and mob activity in Cuba at the time of the revolution, as does Graham Greene's* Our Man in Havana.*)*

Cipriano Chinea Palero

Chinea, as he is called, has a fine, chiseled face and a gravelly voice to match. He is from Las Villas Province and, unusually in Cuba, is a bachelor. He is forty-seven. He works in the Sierra Maestra restaurant in the Habana Libre Hotel, formerly the Hilton, where he would often stop and have a chat with me. This interview takes place in the echoing disco bar on the top floor of the hotel.

29 September 1988

I started as a cleaning boy. I had to clean all the floors of the hotel, clean the first lobby, the second lobby, and some other areas. And often, when, for example, Sra. Carmen Coll or La Fresneda came into the lobby and didn't see their faces reflected in the floor, I had to clean it all over again. And so I did.

They paid me 118 pesos, and I had to pay for my lunch out of that. I paid fifty centavos for my meal, so I was left with a total of seventy pesos.

But I always wanted to get on in life, and I became what is known as a *mochila*. Mochila is what you call in English a busboy, someone who does the heavy work. He has to put the water and bread and butter out on the tables, carry the dirty tray-loads, carry the plates — all the dirty work. In those days, he was the one who worked most and earned least. Then I became a waiter, which is up a scale in the hierarchy, better wages; I got around 148 pesos. But I still had to pay for my lunch and whatever else I ate or drank. Then I moved up, to the cabaret. The casino was beside this Cabaret Caribe, and what is today called the Solidarity Room was the old casino.

While I was there I saw and met a lot of the Mafia. They used to go to cabarets as a rule. In those days the Caribe, the Sans Souci, the Riviera, the Capri, the Nacional were all top-class cabarets and that's where those gents used to go. I know that their boss was a guy by the name of Charlie White. An American name but he wasn't American. He was Italian. This was 1961.

So, although the revolution had been won, there were still casinos and the Mafia?

Oh yes. Run by the Mafia. They controlled them. The casinos remained after the revolution until one day in the Plaza [Revolution Square] the Comandante en Jefe [Fidel Castro] said that from that day, in 1962 if my memory serves me correct, the casinos would be closed. That's when they nationalized, or rather they got rid of, the casinos. But until that time, the Mafia operated them.

That Charlie White guy lived in an apartment in the Focsa building, and he had a number two who controlled the Capri, a character by the name of Niceo Constanze. And another of them I knew was Santo[s] Traficante, and he controlled the Sans Souci and the Hotel Habana Libre; that's the casino here. They had a lyrical or classical singer called René Cabell — a Cuban, of Cuban origin — who collaborated with them. Charlie White's body was covered in scars according to those who looked after him, and he had to have a daily fix of drugs — morphine or cocaine or whatever — to function at all. His assistant injected him. He was short, thickset, with a ruddy complexion. About fifty years old. Niceo Constanze was big and tall and as fat as a fool. He was also about fifty. And Santo[s] Traficante was tall, thin, and white. They simply didn't get involved. They had their *palas*, their front women, or their dealers. The pala is the woman who sells you your chips and does the rigging. She rigs it up and then hides whatever cheating might be going on. Do you follow? So what they did then was, when the casino closed, they would come along, collect the loot, and head for their offices. I don't know who it was told me, a few years back, that the same Charlie White and Niceo Constanze killed Santo[s] Traficante in Las Vegas for something he did to them there. I don't know how they did their dirty deals; I only overheard ordinary conversations.

They were silent types. But always working out ways of getting the biggest cut. Extorting from others. How can I get rid of you so I can have it all? Do you follow me? They smoked marijuana in all the casinos in those days. There was coke, all kinds of drugs. They often worked while under the influence of drugs, drugged up to the eyes. They worked, they cruised around, but drugged. I never saw them with their wives because they always had someone different on their arm. Today they'd appear with one and tomorrow another and you couldn't tell if this woman was this fella's or the other fella's.

They'd arrive and say, "Bring me a Pernod," or, "Bring me a Johnny Walker on the rocks." And my job was to serve them. I would bring them the Johnny Walker on the rocks but I'd be listening as well. I overheard a conversation between Charlie and Traficante — "I rented an apartment on the top floors of Las Cibeles, 21 and N Streets." "I got one in the Focsa." "How do you think the night will turn out?" "Well, we'll see, let's see how things go." That sort of thing. And me bringing my gin and orange juice or my Johnny Walker on the rocks.

But these guys would circulate. And they would never let you take their photograph. They didn't like having their picture taken. They would circulate around their casino, check it out, and disappear. They might first come here to the Habana Libre casino, into the cabaret and then on to the Capri, the Riviera, always on the move, keeping an eye on their business. I can't honestly say I had any relationship with them; they would just ask me for a Pernod and I'd bring them the Pernod.

They didn't leave many tips because they were only passing through. They'd order their drink, have it, and go. They might leave forty cents, a dollar . . . not much. They would have a whisky, pay for it, and leave the rest, twenty or forty cents. They were about their business, on the move all the time. . . .

My childhood was one of poverty. My parents were very poor peasants who worked in the fields in Las Villas Province and had nothing. There were six of us and my parents, and they cultivated a patch of ground. First we had to give half of what we grew to the landlord, so if we grew four pumpkins we would have to give him two and keep two for ourselves. That later changed and we had to give him a quarter of our produce. But he always got his share. Like we grew tobacco, corn, beans, and the rest, and we had to give him a quarter of it all. And if by chance, as happened on one occasion, the weather ruined the tobacco, he would lend us money, but you would have to pay him back with interest. That was the way it was in the past all right. A desperate situation, with people living in alleys, in houses made of tin and palm leaves.

We lived in a palm-thatched hut made of planks of palm tree. You could make planks from the tree and the roof from the leaves and you had a dirt floor. That was our house. That's where myself and my brothers and sisters were raised. Toward the end of 1959, the beginning of 1960, a brother-in-law of mine began working here in the Habana Hilton Hotel and so I just packed my bags and came up here out of the blue. I was seventeen. I appeared out of the blue and went to look for him, and he got me the job.

The Brothel of the Caribbean

Tomás Fernández Robaina

Havana's reputation as the "brothel of the Caribbean" attracted foreign tourists as well as Cuban customers, and prostitution employed tens of thousands of women in the prerevolutionary period. In the following extract from interviews with three ex-prostitutes conducted by one of Cuba's leading historians, Tomás Fernández Robaina, we are given an exuberant evocation of carnival and sexuality.

Carnival was one of the times when we had the most work. Not all of the pimps let their women participate in the *comparsas* [Afro-Cuban dance group], because the time they spent rehearsing before the carnival began, and during the Saturday and Sunday parades along the streets of the neighborhood, took away from the time they were supposed to devote to their trade. But even so, there were women who, with or without their pimps, joined the comparsas.

But don't think that all of those joined the *congas* were people like us. Black women, white women, of all sizes and weights, who worked as maids, iron- ers in the Chinese laundries, and in many other places, joined the comparsas, either out of tradition, or just because they liked them.

Not every woman in the neighborhood liked to march around Prado, either. Some thought that it was just behaving like a monkey for people to gawk at. Others, on the other hand, really enjoyed it. For some, dancing in the com- parsa was something that gave them a certain cachet; especially, if they dressed up as a *figura* or as a queen, since every conga had a queen with her figuras, or courtiers.

The figuras were dancers whose skill and good looks allowed them to dance more freely than the couples who made up the dance troupe and even than the queen herself. The figuras did not have to follow the dance steps and patterns that had been rehearsed.

The Sultana troupe was the comparsa of the Colón neighborhood. It was one of the most exotic and most peculiar, because it included many "men" dressed up as women, who were generally taken to be women, because they did such a good job at hiding what they really were, with capes, turbans, and makeup. I remember the Queen of Italy; he was a very well-known *santero* who did a fantastic job disguising himself as a woman, but I don't remember whether he participated in the Sultana or in the Oxherds.

The Belén Dandys, the comparsa of the neighborhood of San Isidro, were usually quite different from La Sultana and other congas. The Dandys had a touch of elegance, some people thought it a bit contrived, but they weren't like other groups such as the Marquises, from the Atarés neighborhood, the eternal carnival rivals of the Dandys. The Marquises were also a very elegant comparsa, because they tried to imitate the costumes of a king's court with marquises and counts. The Dandys' costumes were always fashionable. What told you that it was a comparsa was not only the fact they all dressed in the same way, but also the canes and straw hats used by the men. The women wore simple long evening dresses, sometimes with a stole. The colors they wore were generally very discrete.

Among the queens in the Dandys' group, I recall two who are still talked about by the older people in the neighborhood: Candita and Teresa. Physically they were completely different, but both had a lot of personality and beauty.

Teresa was one of those typically Cuban neighborhood mulattas, tall, fleshy without actually being fat, narrow waist, a great behind, big and eye-catching breasts, always happy, flashing that special movie actress smile, very nice. She lived in a tenement in Paula Street, just at the corner of Paula and Damas. The rhythmic, majestic way she walked grabbed your attention; she was a real neighborhood aristocrat. The costumes she wore for the festivals sponsored by the Polar and Tropical beer gardens really made you stop, and her husband was proud and thrilled by that wonderful mulatta of his who everyone talked about because she was so gorgeous. When she dressed up as queen during carnival, her poise and elegance expanded as she paraded before the wildly applauding public.

Candita, the other queen who comes to mind, was a completely different type. For me, she was the most elegant of all of them, and she was the one who sported the most expensive dresses that a comparsa queen could have worn. She didn't have Teresa's body, she was more a Parisian type; nothing in front, nothing behind, but when she dressed up as queen and marched ahead of the couples, it looked like she had turned into a real blueblood aristocrat. Her greatest pride was to go out every Saturday, for the four Saturdays that the carnival lasted, with a different costume. . . .

Consuelo la Charmé danced for several years as a figura in different comparsas; she claims that she was once put up for queen, and she even emerged as the favorite in La Sultana, a comparsa that imitated a sultan and his harem, and of course, the main dancer in the conga was his favorite. She said she preferred being the favorite to being the queen, because she could dance more creatively, while the queen had to keep to the officially prescribed movements and steps. A figura, like the favorite, could move anywhere among the couples, use intricate dance steps, and grab the spectators' attention more.

Carnival time also attracted a lot of violence; the problems started with the rehearsals. Carnival time was when people took revenge on their enemies. When a man or woman's attention was diverted, they could be slashed or stabbed. When the conga came through the neighborhood, it was also a very dangerous period for robberies because people could snatch your necklace or wallet. It was hard for them to steal our wallets, though, because we didn't use them. . . .

Some men dressed up as women, not like in La Sultana, but in more ridiculous ways. I feel as though I can still see Guillermo, the one they called "the Jamaican," a tall black man, thin, but very graceful and who had good luck with women. He would begin to talk all funny and say that he was looking for his husband, and tell stories with doubles entendres that everybody listening to and watching found very funny. Other male dancers dressed up in grotesque costumes, imitating kings, or just tasteless or crazy people. They danced, and collected money handed out by the residents and businesspeople.

Even though I wasn't really much part of the comparsa, because I was always a bit of a rough peasant, I really enjoyed the comparsas and I even marched behind the congas and La Mojiganga. Then I really believed that the chorus lines sung by Los Dandys were true:

> I feel a drum, mamita, they're calling me,
> I feel a drum, mamita, they're calling me,
> Yes, yes, it's Los Dandys.
> Yes, yes, it's Los Dandys.

TRANSLATED BY AVIVA CHOMSKY

A Prostitute Remembers

Oscar Lewis, Ruth M. Lewis, and Susan M. Rigdon

The next selection, from a woman ("Pilar") interviewed in 1969 and 1970 by U.S. sociologist Oscar Lewis (1914–1970), gives a more sober view of life as a prostitute in prerevolutionary Cuba.

My friend was working in the Province of Pinar del Río, at a bar in Candelaria. At the beginning she didn't say it was a whorehouse, she only told me, "If you want to earn more money, come and work at the bar with me." She was almost certainly paid for taking me there — that's what they always did, and it's only natural, though I never tried to talk anybody into becoming a prostitute.

When I got to the bar I saw right away it was a brothel, and I didn't like the looks of it. It was a rundown old house where all kinds of men were allowed. The parlor was cramped, the six or seven bedrooms were tiny, the dining room and kitchen were small, and the furniture was old and shabby. The women were sitting in the parlor, fully dressed, and the men would go in, pick one out, then go to a room with her.

Most of the brothel owners were women or perverts; I never knew a real man to own one. My friend introduced me to the madam. "Here's a girl who wants a job."

"Delighted," said the madam. "Please consider this your home. As for work, there's plenty of it."

She explained that I was expected to talk with the men and be pleasant. Then when a man asked me to go to a room with him, I must accept and charge 1.50 pesos, half of which I could keep and the other half turn over to her. Every brothel owner gave a cut of his profits to the police so they'd look the other way.

"Here I'll have a place to live and plenty of food," I thought, "and I'll earn a lot more money to boot." How wrong I was! I managed to earn enough so my folks could eat, but that was all, and even for that I had to work hard.

I started the very day I arrived. I changed my name to Mercy, thinking it would be easier for me. At first I was terribly depressed and just sat without saying a word to anybody, but the madam soon saw to it that I had customers. When the first man asked me to go with him I went at once, but when we were alone in the room I was paralyzed. "Are you going to stand there?" he said roughly. "I didn't come here to look at your dress, I came to fuck." That horrible, filthy word! I wanted to run away — to vanish — but I obediently took off my clothes and did it.

Afterward I told the madam how I felt. "It's that way with everybody the first day," she said reassuringly. "It'll pass. Besides, where else are you going to get a job?" There was no answer to that, and I thought maybe I'd get over my revulsion. But that night was almost as bad as my wedding night. Most of my customers were like Eleodoro, rough and crude, and it wasn't a matter of education — a lot of cultured men went there. I think they had a morbid desire to humiliate a woman.

I slept, ate, and lived in that house, attending my clients in my bedroom. We closed at 3:00 or 4:00 in the morning and opened again for business sometime around noon. In between we slept. From the moment I became a prostitute I began to drink. I had to. I couldn't stand the men and suffered bitterly from shame. Unless I had a few drinks first, I didn't feel capable of going into that room.

After I became more or less adjusted to the style of life, though, it didn't seem so bad. At least my daughter had enough to eat and so did my brothers and sisters. . . .

To a girl like me who was not yet seventeen, being a prostitute was terrible, and I drank more all the time. I noticed the other women taking Benzedrine and Aktedrom pills with their liquor, so I began taking them too. With pills and drink, I was able to face the night. When I was high, though, I'd get into arguments with the men. Any little thing would make me angry. One day a young queer who cleaned the house used some of my new makeup. "You don't need it," he said. "It looks better on me." I struggled with him, and when I saw I couldn't take it away, I burned my bed and three new dresses. That's the way I let off steam — I'd burn my clothes. I did it about twice a month, sometimes once a week.

Some of the men thought they could do anything they wanted for the measly three pesos they paid. I fought with them all the time, especially when they wanted anal coitus, and with the ones who were a bit effeminate or who'd had too much to drink and tried to bite me. When I fought and screamed at them, the police would come and arrest me. Now and then men came in drunk and made a scene just for the fun of it, and when that happened, the madam called the police. . . .

Every single day in a brothel was a day of anguish. Once I started at 1:00 P.M.

and worked straight through till 5:00 A.M. the following day. I laid about twenty-five men, one after the other, twenty-five to thirty minutes apart. Drink and pep pills kept me going.

The longest I ever stayed with any client was a whole night, for which I'd get fifteen or twenty pesos. But I had to need the money pretty desperately to do it. If you agreed to spend the night with one man, you had to put yourself out to please him, even if you'd never met him before. Having several clients a night wasn't such hard work because you didn't have to pretend so much. I hated to pretend. . . .

I never went to any of the gambling casinos they had before the revolution, but I went to all the big hotels—the Riviera, the Capri, the Sevilla, the Hilton, the Deauville. Prostitutes weren't supposed to be allowed in places like that, but with money you could buy your way in anywhere.

Once I went to the Hotel Sevilla with an American, but they called up from the desk and told him he could only take a woman to his room if she'd checked in as his wife. "Very well, then," he said. "Bring down my luggage. I'm checking out." Then he took me to the Habana Libre—it was still the Hilton then—and signed me in as his wife. That was the only time I ever got into a big hotel legally, without having to hide.

I was wearing a flowered dress with a plunging neckline and a very tight skirt and I looked every inch a prostitute. The man at the desk gave me a look as if to say, "Some wife!" Of course he couldn't come right out and say anything, but what a look!

On the whole, my memories of Americans are very ugly. Oh sure, they'd take me places like the Hilton, but it was as if they did it to humiliate me. And there were some who'd threaten you with a bottle if you refused to comply with their whims. Most of our American clients brought drugs along with them. They'd arrive in Cuba loaded with cocaine and marijuana, and they'd pay you extra to take it with them. They'd put cocaine up their noses and sniff it, take it in their mouths, and some of them would rub it on their private parts. I tried not to take drugs but I couldn't avoid it. To refuse was asking for trouble.

As long as I was a prostitute, I hated the guts of every man I went to bed with. I never let a customer hang around afterward—no friendly farewells for him! If he didn't get up right away I'd say, "You got what you paid for. You're through. Beat it!" I loved to flaunt that in a man's face! I always got my money in advance, of course, so I could say whatever I pleased.

I had to be pretty worn out before I'd get any pleasure from sex with a client. The few times I was weak enough to react like a woman, I felt so soiled and degraded afterward that I wanted to die. Not all prostitutes feel that way. I've heard others say nothing is more normal than getting pleasure in bed, even if you don't care for the man. My reaction depended on the man; some are gentle, others are brutes. In a brothel you get maybe a couple of nice men to every ninety-eight brutes. . . .

I dreamed of getting out of the brothel and working at a decent job. I wanted to study. I wanted to be somebody. But that was before the revolution—and there was no hope of any such thing. One time I went to enroll in a school, but the first person I met was a man I'd slept with. I turned around and left.

Another time when I was about seventeen I made a vow to La Caridad to dress in yellow gingham. I kept my vow faithfully but the Virgin didn't help me. Finally in my desperation I went to a spiritist. Not that I believe in them. I think once you're dead and the worms eat you, there's nothing left. But I thought, "What can I lose?"

It was a farce. Like a psychologist, a spiritist knows that if you go there you must have some problem. So first she tries to draw you out to see what's worrying you. The things that woman read in my cards she'd practically dragged out of me first. When she was through I said, "None of this is news to me; after all, I told it to you."

Sugarcane

Nicolás Guillén

During the 1920s and early 1930s, intellectuals and social movements developed a powerful critique of post-independence Cuban society. They emphasized the corruption and brutality of the political elite, as well as the economic and political subordination of the island to the United States. The protagonists of this critique included students; veterans of the independence struggle; trade unionists and workers (sugar workers were organized for the first time in the early 1930s); a middle class frustrated by limited economic opportunities and (for government employees) by unpaid wages; and a group of young poets and writers, many of them engaged in a campaign to recover the roots of cubanidad in the heritage of Afro-Cuban rhythms and language.

Poet Nicolás Guillén (1902–1989) captures the interlocking threads that contributed to this movement in his brief poem, "Caña" (Sugarcane).

The Black
next to the cane

The Yankee
over the canefield

The earth
under the canefield

The blood
We are losing!

TRANSLATED BY ROBERTO MÁRQUEZ

Where Is Cuba Headed?

Julio Antonio Mella

From his exile in Mexico, Julio Antonio Mella (1903–1929), student leader and one of the founding members of the Cuban Communist Party, expressed the views of the nationalist and socialist Left in a 1928 document that circulated widely in his home-land, entitled "Where Is Cuba Headed?" Less than a year later, in January 1929, he was assassinated—a crime almost certainly committed on the orders of the Machado regime.

WHERE IS CUBA HEADED? *(Mexico, 1928)*

Only a New Revolution Will Liberate Her from Colonialism

The Constituent Assembly is meeting. This body has been illegally convened, not through free popular elections, but rather by government parties. Prior to this, laws had been passed preventing the forming of new parties or the re-organization of the official parties. The Assembly is acting illegally, because its only constitutional mission was to reject or accept the reforms agreed upon by Congress. But at the President's request, it is introducing new "reforms." Although we do not yet have firm news about the results, it seems clear that everybody who today fills a government position will be granted the right to "extend" their terms for two additional years. The President of the Republic, simply because he requested it, will "suffer" first a reelection and . . . then a new six-year term, that is, an "extension." The Vice President's position will be abolished so that the dictator can avoid dangerous rivalries among those who aspire to his post. The electoral campaign and the reform had been carried out in the name of abolishing the "crime" of reelection.

The "Sweet" Economic Situation

The true gravity of the situation lies in the economic organization of the coun-try, and this is where we must turn in order to answer the question. Observing

Picture of Julio Antonio Mella. Antonio Núñez Jiménez, *Cuba, cultura, estado y revolución* (Mexico City: Presencia Latinoamericana, 1984), p. 244.

both the economic and political situation, we realize how Cuba is at a historical crossroads.

Cuba produces between 20 and 25 percent of the world's sugar. Sugar, along with tobacco, is the only important industry. The entire life of the country depends on the price of sugar. A measure that reveals the Kindergarten level of our hacendistas' talents has worsened the situation. We are referring to the limits placed on sugar production, supposedly in order to raise the price.

The *machadista* talents ingenuously supposed that the other cane and beet-sugar producing countries were not going to increase production to fill the markets that Cuba was abandoning!

This is exactly what happened. Several paragraphs in the *New York Sun* of 10 April shed light on Cuba's economic situation. This U.S. newspaper states:

"Outside of Havana, *Cuban conditions are less prosperous than they have been at any other time since 1921*, when the price of sugar fell drastically by more than twenty cents a pound.

"*The opposition has grown, based on the belief that U.S.-owned mills have received better treatment than Cuban owners.*"

"Cuban government orders prohibit the preparation of new lands and *most producers do not have enough money even to sow the lands they have already prepared."*[1]

No comment is necessary. The U.S. newspaper tells us how Yankee and other sugar producers benefited. At the same time, it admits how exploited Cuban interests are, both those of the mills and those of the *colonos*. And the situation is like 1921!

The Cuban industrial bourgeoisie, which is the sector of Cuban capitalism that is in power, wanted to pass some *nationalist* laws establishing new protective tariffs. According to official economists, these would be the salvation of the country. But Cuban production cannot supply even the internal market, and the country had to resort once again to foreign imports. The United States, by means of a "special treaty," continued to be our "most favored nation." In short: national industry did not develop, and prices rose exorbitantly. The poor consumer—worker, peasant, middle class—is the one who suffers the effects the "nationalism" and "protectionism" of foreign capital's allies—the aforementioned Cuban industrial bourgeoisie.

Imperialist Penetration

Yankee imperialist penetration has continued. The $50 million that the United States had invested before declaring war on Spain, giving us "Independence," rose to $141 million after the second intervention, and $1.36 billion in 1924. Today, according to unofficial data, U.S. investment has reached some $1.7 billion.

The Government has resorted to the classical method of American despots: public works. Here these consist of roads, but not of projects to develop agriculture or to compete with the high rates charged by the railroads, but to give the Yankees a military advantage in the event of another war. In any case, although the Government issues denials, public works concessions always end up in the hands of imperialist capital. A short time ago U.S. capitalists gave the Government an "advance" of $9 million. . . .

Hope for the Nation can only arise from the nationalist and workers' movements. The nationalist movement managed to mobilize the entire Cuban people under its banners. The people were eager for something practical, in this case, a violent method, to end the despotic situation. But the majority current within the leadership insisted on exhausting legal means and waiting until the Government "moved outside of the law." The true division in the nationalist movement is between those who believe it is possible to overcome Machado by legal means, and those who recognize that the only hope is to respond to violence with violence. Among the latter are the important group of nationalist university students and some of the leaders.

The other important movement is the workers' movement. "The Confederation of Cuban Workers" had two hundred thousand members when it was founded in Camagüey. Neither Government terror, nor the treachery of several leaders, like the known secret police agent Juan Arévalo, has succeeded in destroying the workers' movement. The most recent railroad workers' strike lasted forty-five days and is a sign of the vitality of the workers' movement. The National Army was incapable of breaking it or protecting the scabs.

The Yankee Phantom

When a despot wants to enthrone himself he resorts to saying that he has the support of the United States. Some of the so-called revolutionaries have said the same thing. Any decision to abandon principles in Cuba is also justified by reference to the "Yankee threat." But there are sectors of the people for whom this terror is disappearing. Sandino has taught the timorous a lot. We should not believe in mechanical application of the experiences of other places. Nicaragua is on the mainland, which allows it to receive aid. But Cuba is an island. On the other hand, Cuba has six times the population of Nicaragua. But the deciding factor lies in the level of development of the productive forces. Cuba is one of the most industrialized countries of Latin America. Imperialism's gravediggers do exist and they can do their work. This is the key to the struggle: an exact appreciation of the role of the proletariat. The concentration of the working class in the cities encourages swift and effective action. An army cannot easily defeat the workers' ammunition: strikes, boycotts, sabotage of the sugar fields, etc. etc.

Given the limitations of a magazine article, we cannot exhaust the subject here. But we will set out the following points as a basis for discussion for those who want to study the "threat posed by imperialism":

1. Imperialism cannot dominate in a country without some kind of international support. In this case a complete military occupation of the territory would be required. This means war, which, naturally, is not out of the question.

2. When a regime, like the Machado regime, totally lacks popular support and is opposed by every social class, the main goal of imperialism — a peaceful arena to invest money and develop industry — cannot be achieved because of the "peaceful" or armed opposition that emerges.

3. The greater the imperialist investment, the more people are forced into the opposition: workers, the ruined middle classes, etc.

4. Problems like Cuba's, and anti-imperialist forces, can be found in Haiti, in Santo Domingo, in Puerto Rico, in Mexico, and in Central and South America. The struggle, which seems quixotic in isolation, can easily be internationalized if we focus on the practical revolutionary aspect of the problem. There are also contradictions among the imperialists and between different sectors of U.S. capitalism, as well as between U.S. capitalism and its working-class masses.

5. The slogan according to which the workers, in this case, the urban, rural, and intellectual workers, "have nothing to lose but their chains and have a world to win" is not demagoguery. *In our countries, more than in Europe, the stages of the progress of classes and nations are, given the character of our social relations and the violent penetration of imperialism, determined by periodic insurrections, which are not always mere caudillo movements, for they involve the masses.* This means that the proletariat must participate in these movements, even though it recognizes that in later stages Moncadas or Chang Kai-Sheks will emerge. This does not matter. Mexico can serve as an example of how much the masses can change things.

6. In the concrete case of Cuba there has been a victorious revolution. There have also been three periods of democracy (those of Palma, Gómez, and Zayas).

Where is Cuba headed? There is only one possible response: it is headed toward becoming a formal colony of the United States (like Puerto Rico and the Philippines), toward the destruction of everything on which a nation is based. This is the path taken by the Constituent Assembly, the extension to the presidential term, and the issue of reelection. But there are forces capable of taking Cuba down the path of a necessary democratic, liberal, and nationalist revolution, which is already latent in events. If this does not happen in the next two or three years, Cuba will fall, absolutely, under the yoke of imperialism until the era of proletarian revolutions in the continent, either in the so-called Anglo-Saxon area, or in the Latin regions.

TRANSLATED BY AVIVA CHOMSKY

Note

1. Emphasis added by Julio Antonio Mella.

The Chase

Alejo Carpentier

Carpentier's (1904–1980) novella El acoso *(The chase) is a reflection of the times surrounding the fall of the Machado dictatorship in the 1930s; it depicts the political struggles begun in the 1920s and the search for direction in political and historical outlook among students, workers, and intellectuals, as well as the contradictions within these groups. Through the interior monologues of one of the main characters, a scholarship student at the University of Havana, we experience the noble aspirations of a generation of young Cubans who want to eradicate corruption and bring down the Machado government. However, many grow impatient with organized resistance, abandon the university, lose their ideals and discipline, and ultimately resort to blind violence.*

In this monologue, the former student reflects on his shame about his provincial origins, his failed academic career, and the pressures of the times that led to both his heroic quest for social justice and his downfall.

Express Train

Departing from Sancti-Spíritus. The hand has let go of the useless shaving brush that was used to showily trace the words with India ink. In his refuge, the man looks at himself, in that decisive moment of his life. He sees himself busy placing things in the old trunk, brought to the island, so many years ago, by the immigrant grandfather. He is surrounded by the relatives and friends who will soon accompany him to the station and who, this morning, have stopped moving in the present. Their voices come to him from far away; from a yesterday in the process of being abandoned. He does not hear their advise, in order to better enjoy the delight of feeling himself in a future already vaguely glimpsed—and of detaching himself from the reality that surrounds him. At the end of the trip, the capital, with the Fountain of the Indian, Habana, all in white marble, just the way it looks in the color photograph from a magazine stuck on the wall with thumbtacks. The legend of the fountain recalls that in her shadow the poet Heredia once dreamt; Heredia for whom the fact of

having been born in a stupid little town, like this one, would not be an impedi-
ment to becoming a French Academic. At the end of the trip he will encounter
the University, the Stadium, the theaters; he will not have to account for his
actions; he will find freedom and perhaps, very soon, a lover, since the latter,
so difficult to come by in the provinces, is common to a place where there is
neither ironwork nor shutters over the windows, and no busybody neighbor
women. This idea makes him fold, with special care, the brand new suit which
his father had made for him according to the latest models, and which he plans
to wear for the first time, with the coordinated tie and handkerchief, when he
registers. Afterward he would walk into a café and ask for a Martini. He would
finally know what that mixture served in a cocktail glass with an olive in it tastes
like. Later he would go to the house of a woman named Estrella, about whom
the Scholarship Student had told him wonderful things in a recent letter. And
his father, who is telling him, at that precise instant, not to associate with the
Scholarship Student because it seems he lives a dissipated life and squanders
the fellowship awarded him by the town hall on parties "that leave only ashes in
the soul." The voices reach him from a distance. And seem even more distant
in the train station, surrounded by peasants shouting to each other across the
platforms, later, the passing of a cattle train that rolled through in a thunder-
clap of bellowing. At the very last moment, the father buys a few honeycombs
to send as a gift to the old woman who offered to put the son up where she
lives—it seems she has a mirador on the roof, a room, independent and com-
fortable for a student—and then the arrival of the express, with its locomotive
and bell, and the tumult of goodbyes. . . . And it was here he had arrived, late
at night, with the trunk he is staring at: to this mirador which his ancient wet
nurse made him visit, she who had come to the capital years ago, following a
rich family, owners of a once grand mansion transformed into neighborhood
lodgings. Right from the start he surmised, from the black woman's decidedly
maternal tone, that she would place fetters on his desire for freedom, keeping
track of his comings and goings, grumbling and making a fuss—preventing
him at the very least, of bringing women to the mirador. For that reason, he
decided to change lodgings, as soon as he was settled into his studies. And
now, after having forgotten about the old woman for months—is it she who
has been moaning like that since a moment ago, or is it the whimpering of
the dressmaker's son?—after deserting this room so long ago, it was here that
he found the most supreme refuge, the only possible refuge, along with his
provincial trunk, left behind when he moved, because it held things that had
ceased to interest him.

But today, when he opened the lid, he encountered once again the University he had abandoned, present in the case of large and small compasses his

father had given him; in the slide rule, ruling pen, and drawing triangles; in the bottle of India ink, long empty, that still gave off a scent of camphor. There was the Treaty of Viñola, with the five orders, and also a school notebook in which, as an adolescent, he had pasted photographs of the temple of Paestum and the dome of Brunelleschi, the "Casa de la Cascada," and a view of the temple of Uxmal. Insects had fed on the canvas on which he had made his first ink drawings, and of the spires and foundations, copied onto transparent paper, there remained only yellowed lace, which came apart in your hands. Then came the books on the history of architecture, descriptive geometry, and, at the bottom, on top of the high school diploma, the Party membership card. The fingers, lifting up that piece of cardboard, came into contact with the only barrier that might have protected him from the abominable. But in those days he had been surrounded by too many impatient for action. They told him not to waste his time in Party meetings, or reading Marxist tracts, or homages to remote collective farms, with photos of smiling tractor operators and cows endowed with phenomenal udders, while the best of his generation were falling under a rain of lead from the repressive police. And one morning, he was carried along by a vociferous demonstration that was moving down the grand staircase that leads to the University. A bit further on was the collision of forces, the mob, and the panic, with rocks and roof tiles flying above the faces, trampled women, wounded heads, and bullets hitting flesh. The vision of those who had fallen made him think that, in effect, the times demanded immediate action, and not the caution and constant postponement demanded by a kind of discipline that feigned ignorance of so much exasperation. When he switched over to the band of impatient youth, the terrible game began that brought him once again to the mirador, just days ago, in search of the ultimate protection, carrying the weight of a body being pursued, and which had to be hidden somewhere. Now, breathing in the smell of moth-eaten papers, the camphor scent of dried up ink, he found the trunk to be a kind of symbol, which only he could decipher, of Paradise before Guilt. And achieving, a moment here, a moment there, a degree of lucidity never imagined, he understood how much of it was owed to the confinement that made him sit down and talk to himself for hours on end, seeking, in a detailed examination of the connection of events, some relief from his present misery. There was a fissure, certainly; an infernal passage. But, considering the vicissitudes of that passage; admitting that almost all of it had been abominable; swearing that he would never repeat the gesture that caused him to stare so directly at a neck scarred by acne — that neck that obsessed him more than the howling face, glimpsed in the uproar of that terrible second — he thought it might yet be possible to live somewhere else, to forget the period in which he had gone astray. Spoken in moans were the words with which the tormented, the guilty, the repentant, approached the Holy Table, to receive the Body of the Crucified and the Blood of Bloodless Sacrifice. Under the Cala-trava Cross that adorned the little book of Christian Instruction for innocent children which his mother had given him, that pathetic cry could be heard, in the prayers for confession, the litanies to the Virgin, the supplications of the Blessed. With sobs and entreaties, the unworthy, the fallen, addressed them-selves to the divine mediators, too modest to speak directly to Him, who had for three days descended into Hell. Besides, it was not all his fault. It was the result of the times, the contingencies, of a heroic illusion: the work of the bril-liant words with which they drew him in, one afternoon — him, a high school graduate from the provinces, ashamed of his suit, poorly cut in his father's tailor's shop — behind the walls of the building on whose façade of majestic col-umns, stamped in bronze relief, below an illustrious surname, were the lofty Elzevirs of HOC ERAT IN VOTIS [this was in my prayers]. . . . He was looking now out toward the Concert Hall, whose capitals with squared volutes seemed to him a caricature of those that had been associated with his now abhorred ini-tiation. There he saw affirmed the condemnation imposed by that city on the orders which degenerated into heat and covered themselves with sores, offer-ing its astragalus [ankle] to hold up the examples of dry cleaners, barbershops, soda shops, and the hissing of fried food stands in the shadows of its pillars, wedged between display cases of empanadas, ice-cream freezers, and tamarind water. "I'll write something about this," he told himself, never having written anything, due to the urgent need to propose noble tasks for himself. He would emerge from the endless drunken bouts of those months, from the excesses to which those who take risks and pose challenges believe they are entitled, find-ing the first light at the end of the tunnel. He didn't know where he would go now, since the High Personage would determine, at his greatest convenience, the most expeditious route to be taken. He would never return to his study of architecture, abandoned in the first semester. He accepted, in advance, the roughest work, the worst pay, the sun on his back, the oil on his face, the hard cot and the soup bowl, as phases in a necessary atonement.

TRANSLATED BY PAMELA MARIA SMORKALOFF

The Fall of Machado

R. Hart Phillips

Critics saw the dictatorship of Gerardo Machado (1925–33) as the perfect expression of Cuba's failure to develop as an authentic nation. In the depths of a major economic depression, action groups such as the ABC and Revolutionary Student Directorate waged a violent struggle against the machadato. *The withdrawal of U.S. support for the dictator and a wave of mobilizations by urban and rural workers in the summer of 1933 led to the collapse of the Machado regime in August and the inauguration of a brief four-month-long experiment in economic and social reform during the "revolutionary" government of Grau San Martín.*

The following extract from the diary of Ruby Hart Phillips, a U.S. journalist resident in Havana, captures the popular anger and violence accompanying the fall of Machado.

August 14

Days and nights have so run together since the downfall of Machado that I shall merely put down what I can remember of the whole affair.

Machado resigned or rather asked for "leave of absence" and then fled for his life. The entire procedure was supposed to have been carried out in "legal form" according to the Constitution. That is the influence of Ambassador Welles. . . .

When Phil and I reached town about nine Saturday morning, people were beginning to venture out into the streets. Groups gathered here and there conversing in low tones. There were no streetcars, buses, or taxis as yet. The public could hardly believe that Machado had resigned. There were no newspapers, so the news went from mouth to mouth. Trucks filled with soldiers passed through the streets. Some of the soldiers made speeches and were cheered by the public. Slowly, the people realized that Machado was no longer head of the government. More people came into the streets; things began to assume a holiday air; the crowds were laughing, talking, and cheering in spontaneous bursts of enthusiasm. Soon Central Park, the Prado Promenade, and all adjoining streets and sidewalks were crowded.

Phil had gone to the airport to meet a German correspondent who was arriving that morning. I asked the elevator boy to take me up to the roof of the Manzana [a building called "La Manzana de Gómez" that overlooks Havana's central park] so I could see what was happening. I stood leaning on the parapet looking down six stories to the streets and Central Park thinking—"What a happy crowd." All at once people started running toward the upper end of the Prado, collecting at Virtudes and Neptuno Streets. A few seconds later there were scattered revolver shots, a fusillade, then two rifle reports. I couldn't see what happened but a few minutes later a group emerged into the street carrying a soldier on their shoulders and shouting and cheering. The killing of *porristas* [members of the Partida de la Porra, a government-sponsored paramilitary death squad] had begun. They had just killed Captain Jiminez, Chief of La Porra, and his Negro aide in the drugstore on the corner of Prado and Virtudes.

While this was going on an incident took place in Central Park which brought the tears to my eyes—the sheer pathos of it. A small group of boys of probably ten to twelve years, poorly dressed, some of them barefooted, came solemnly across Zulueta Street carrying a Cuban flag. They marched quietly up to Martí's statue in Central Park and waited while one of their number climbed the tall statue, no small feat in itself, and put the flag in Martí's outstretched hand. Then the small boy climbed down and they all walked quietly away.

We checked some twenty porristas killed that day. But that was only the beginning. One youth boasted that he had helped kill seventeen. Luis Fuentes came into the office on Sunday afternoon exceedingly drunk. When I scolded him he said, "Mrs. Phillips, I had to get drunk. I haven't killed any porristas. I couldn't kill a man in cold blood that way. But I've seen things I can't forget. I'll say one thing for them, they died fighting."

The terrible things which happened. Civilization was stripped away in one stroke. Relatives of boys who had been tortured and killed started on vengeance hunts and they knew the men they were seeking. The porristas never tried to keep it a secret as to whom they had killed. I remember in the killing of the seventeen-year-old student, Rubiera, that one of the secret operatives who had taken part in the murder returned to the police station and washed blood from the lapel of his coat while he described the killing to others at the station. The ABC terrorist organization knew his identity in twenty minutes. So now it was their turn to hunt the porristas.

The young terrorists seemed to have killed cleanly and with some justifica-

"Isle of the Lost Ships." This cartoon depicts the massive U.S. naval deployment of ships around Cuba in September 1933. Ruby Hart Phillips, *Cuban Sideshow* (Havana: Cuban Press, 1935), 117.

tion, if not with due process of law. But not so the crowd who gathered at the scent of blood, the same public who had shouted, "Viva Machado" only a few months ago in the streets. They demanded blood and more blood.

One porrista named Leblanc was killed in front of the Capitolio, that big white glittering building on the upper Prado. He left the Hotel Pasaje, apparently in an effort to escape. As he crossed the street someone recognized him. The horde was upon him. He drew his revolver, backed up against a light post, and prepared to die fighting. A huge stone smashed against the side of his head; a bullet struck him in the breast. He sagged, clinging to the post for support. The crowd, howling like devils, closed in. Across the street, on the balcony of the hotel, his wife and two children saw him beaten to death. Several soldiers standing on the sidewalk looked on. Finally one pushed his way through the mob and sent a bullet crashing through the brain of the victim. The body was completely unrecognizable when the mob finished its work.

Another porrista was trapped by several youths on the third floor of a building. They shot it out and the porrista was wounded. The crowd, attracted by the shooting, surged up the stairway, grabbed the wounded man, and hurled him from the third floor to the pavement below. They rushed down, picked him up, and repeated the performance. Still he did not die. One of the boys, who had wounded him, ran downstairs to the pavement in an attempt to kill the victim outright. He thrust his revolver against the head of the porrista, who had somehow struggled to his knees, his hands outstretched imploringly. A huge Negro knocked the revolver away, and, putting his foot in the face of the wounded man, kicked him violently to the pavement. He finally died. The boy who had shot the porrista told me this with tears in his eyes. He said he would never forget the incident so long as he lived. There is a curious ending to this story, for the boy died two weeks later. The diagnosis of the physician was that his heart simply gave out under the tremendous strain and excitement of that day. Those two incidents were told to me by people who saw them. Others equally fantastic and unbelievable occurred all over town and in the interior. What the total killings of the day were we shall never know. I am sure a lot of innocent people were ruthlessly slaughtered, people who probably had done nothing except talk too loud.

On that morning of the twelfth, I had remained on the roof a long while, watching the streets below. Some minutes after the small boys had placed the flag of Cuba in Martí's hand, a crowd began pouring down Zulueta from the direction of the presidential palace, many of them carrying queer articles. Boys ran along the street with ferns, uprooted cannas [lilies], and other shrubs offering them to anyone who would buy — loot from the lower floors of the palace.

Such a joyful looting! One huge Negro proudly pushed out of the palace grounds a watercooler on which reposed two bottles of mineral water; an old woman carried a couple of pillows, another a stalk of bananas — canned goods, chairs, typewriters, the side of a bed — someone else had the other side. They were perfectly useless articles to those who carried them, but the nation had gone mad. Every plant in the palace patio was uprooted, every shrub and flower. I suppose they would have carried away the palm trees if they could have.

The palace looting which yielded little of value spurred the crowd on to greater deeds. The home of every member of the cabinet was looted and wrecked. Fine collections of rare books were divided among those who could not read. Beautiful china, valuable objects of art were borne away. I saw an old Negro woman sitting on the curb on Twenty-third Street. Beside her was a beautiful radio, a birdcage, and a china vase. How she had managed to carry them all and what she would ever do with them was a mystery, but there she was.

Louis Hamburg, photographer, tells the story of the looting of the Averhoff residence. Averhoff was secretary of treasury under Machado for only a few months. He took the position in opposition to the wishes of his entire family, who wanted him to stay out of politics. Hamburg, intent on taking pictures of the looting and looters of the Averhoff home, located on Malecón Drive, started to enter the lower floor. He glanced up to see a baby grand piano tottering on the upper balcony. He didn't have time to run. The piano crashed, its beautiful mahogany and delicate wires a tangled mass. The looters later burned all the furniture that they had thrown into the street.

Some families of the Cabinet members had fled, taking in many cases not even a change of clothing. Personal effects, letters, jewelry, everything was grabbed by the looters. Beautiful things were destroyed. Irreplaceable things. The books of Senator Wilfredo Fernández, a lifelong collection of rare volumes, many of which he had bound with his own hands, a collection started in childhood, were completely destroyed.

Nor was it only the homes of officials of the Machado regime which were looted. The houses of the mistresses of various high officials were sacked and burned. A pet store, owned by Villapol, palace paymaster, was raided. Many of the animals were killed—canaries, puppies, kittens, rare tropical birds— crushed, strangled, many of them torn to pieces. . . .

August 15

The track down of porristas and minor officials continues, but more as a dark undercurrent in an atmosphere of happiness and bright new hopes, and quite in contrast with the grim desperation of Havana a few days ago. The Cuban people are like children who have suddenly entered fairyland. They have a new government making new promises, and now, to hear the Cubans tell it, all they have to do is sit back and wait for the miraculous recovery of business and watch the dollars roll in from the United States. They confidently expect a loan of fifteen million dollars, although the island cannot pay what it now owes. Foreign obligations total almost $160 million. They cannot understand that, in view of the many defaulted Latin American bonds now held by U.S. investors, the Yankee dollar may become scarce.

There is an unprecedented amount of drinking going on. Cubans are getting drunk day after day—something never seen before on this island. It has always been the American tourist whose drinking has provided the natives with considerable amusement. Now it is the Cubans, particularly the youths. The terrorists spend their days and nights—they never seem to sleep—drinking. Salon H, the café downstairs, is crowded with a hard-drinking crowd, all claiming they won the revolution. . . .

The students talk of reopening the university. Frankly, I think returning to Havana University will be impossible for many of them. One can't plant bombs, commit murders, become hunted outlaws, and then return to the atmosphere of the classroom. Luis Fuentes is an example. He was expelled from the university by presidential decree for a period of eight years, when he and other students in 1928 protested against the Prorogue Measure. He left home because he did not want to involve his family and bring down on them the wrath and vengeance of Machado. For years he did not have enough to eat. He slept on park benches and in flophouses. Once, when he was sharing a tiny room with two companions, he escaped arrest only because he had gone with a girlfriend to her home to spend the night. "Pure luck," he admitted to me, somewhat embarrassed. His girlfriend, a university student, later left her home because her family objected to her joining the ABC. There are many such cases, young girls of good families living as the mistresses of young men. It seems queer to see such a sudden change in a Latin country with century-old ideas concerning women. A way of life has vanished. Young girls who had been living a cloistered, sheltered life now speak with pride of the bombs they have planted.

I remember a story Phil told me. On the sidewalk near our office, he encountered several students he knew standing in a circle. In this group was a girl, quite young, with a package under her arm, and as Phil approached he heard them making a lunch date. The boys greeted Phil and began chatting with him. The girl looked at her wristwatch, held it to her ear to listen to it, and then said, laughing, "I've got to hurry or I'll be late." After the girl had walked away, one of the boys drew Phil aside and told him that the package was a bomb she was going to plant, and they were meeting in a nearby café to have lunch and wait for it to explode.

What is going to happen to the younger generation? Will they be able to readjust themselves to a normal way of life, to the pattern of daily life, to the society of their parents and relatives? Can they discard their present bloody ideals and their reckless disregard for authority? Frankly, I don't know. Undoubtedly they will have the same difficulties returning to civilized ways of living that every nation has following a war. But terrorism, in my opinion, more quickly and permanently undermines the morals of a country than does open warfare. War between nations, terrible as it is, leaves both the victor and the vanquished with a certain unity, a common bond. But terrorism is a form of mutilation that breeds distrust and hatred, severing a people into irreparable factions.

Soldiers are everywhere. Saturday night, following the orgy of killing porristas, a squadron of cavalry moved into Central Park. The park is now practically a stable, with bales of hay and sacks of oats piled high in front of the Manzana de Gómez. Machine guns are mounted on tripods. Troop patrols and night watches prowl the city with a businesslike manner. The khaki uniform is looked on with favor, but I cannot forget that it is the same army which killed under orders of Machado.

Colonel Perdomo, former chief of police, sat in a café today eating his lunch and conversing with friends. With tears running down his face, he expressed his sorrow for "pobre Cuba." He said the revolt of the army was the most terrible thing that had ever happened on the island. From now on the army would be the most important factor in Cuban life. From now on the army could never be trusted.

He is right. In the history of Cuba no president has ever before been ousted, nor any change of government brought about by a revolt of the army. The army never dared before because of the Platt Amendment. All previous revolutions in Cuba started in the outlying provinces and none of them had ever been successful. Now for the first time the people realize how easy it is for the army to force a change of government.

Sugar Mills and Soviets

Salvador Rionda

The insurrection of sugar workers and occupations of sugar mills in the summer and fall of 1933 alarmed local and foreign business interests and signaled the emergence, for the first time, of an insurgent working class and a small but vigorous Communist Party as important actors in Cuban politics. In the following extract Salvador Rionda (b. 1854), the administrator of a major U.S.-controlled sugar mill, describes the radicalization in the behavior of his workforce.

Manati, 25 Sept. 1933 AIR MAIL

Irving Trust Company, Receiver of
Manati Sugar Company,
New York, NY
Re: General Strike at Manati

Dear Sirs,

As we informed you by cable the men here went on strike Saturday, 16th September at about 10:30 A.M.

The writer after having spent around twenty-two years on plantations in Cuba has never seen anything like these strikes that seem to have been organized all on more or less on [sic] the same plan although at some places they have been more violent than at others. . . .

. . . the writer was informed by telephone that a U.S. destroyer had arrived at the bay and that the commander wanted to see him. . . . The writer left for the bay bringing back with him the commander of the destroyer, the medical officer, who talked Spanish, and one very large sailor. The two officers of the ship had lunch with the writer and toward the end of the lunch, three men broke into the dining room violently, accompanied by the chief of our company police (who had joined the strike). The men stated that they wanted the chief of the company police to hand over the company's arms. I stated to the men that the arms belonged to sworn deputies of the government and that they could only be turned over to the corporal in charge of our soldiers here. The result of all this was that the strikers (that had gone on strike while I was on the destroyer) took over the rifles, revolvers, and machetes of our police, the army corporal here not doing anything to prevent them.

. . . the property of the Manati Sugar Company has been in the hands of the strikers from Saturday (16th Sept.) morning until last Saturday (23rd Sept.) afternoon, one week. We have not been allowed to work in the office, the first few days we were not allowed to circulate in the *batey* [central area of the mill complex] on foot or automobile, our truck motors were used by the strikers without our permission, we could not talk by telephone to the wharf or any of the colonias, the long distance telephone was left but the line was tapped so that all of our conversations with Havana were heard, all the servants of our houses were told not to work or that they would be beaten up and all of us had to cook for ourselves. The strikers ran the electric plant at night as they needed water but we had no intervention and they gave us lights as they pleased, distributing ice among themselves but having the rest of us without any. A complete SOVIET REPUBLIC!!! The army soldiers here were of little use as you probably know what has happened in Cuba with students, soldiers, sailors, and workers!

With all of this going on, we have made every effort to bring men to their senses but the demands continued. On Friday . . . we signed a notarial document giving them as much as we could but leaving the solution of the port open; this was settled yesterday. On account of our having to accept the eight-hour day because of its now being a law. . . . We think that you are perfectly justified in asking for whatever the increase is from the banks. . . .

[signed] Salvador C. Rionda

The United States Confronts the 1933 Revolution

Sumner Welles and Cordell Hull

The fate of the Revolution of 1933 was greatly influenced by the hostile response of the United States to the economic and political nationalism of the Grau administration. United States attitudes toward the revolutionary government emerge clearly in the following extract from the diplomatic correspondence of the U.S. special envoy to Cuba, Sumner Wells. Wells's encouragement of the ambitions of Fulgencio Batista and the movement of noncommissioned officers that he had led in a "sergeants' revolt" against the officer corps in early September sealed the fate of Grau's administration in January 1934.

Document 7. Memorandum: Telephone Conversation between [Secretary of State] Cordell Hull and [Ambassador] Sumner Welles, 6 September 1933.

Secretary: How is everything looking?
Ambassador: I had four hours of sleep last night and I feel somewhat better.
Secretary: How are conditions?
Ambassador: There was some trouble in the city last night, but not as bad as might have been expected. I think the presence of the destroyer did a great deal to prevent more disturbance. The situation in the interior seems to be becoming very serious and while Santiago during the early night was quiet, there is no word as to what happened after midnight.
Secretary: We have been discussing this last evening and this morning as best we could. It seems to us that the whole thing down there revolves around the army, and the question comes up with us as to whether the landing of men before we are absolutely compelled to do so—if we should land a thousand men there—it would in all probability mean intervention, and while we will not hesitate to go in if compelled to, we do not want to unless compelled. Because if we have to go in there again, we will never be able to

Cuban Public—"Well Uncle Sam . . . ," 1933. Phillips, *Cuban Sideshow*, 177. Cartoon by Santee Haldero.

come out and we will have on our hands the trouble of thirty years ago. . . . Now if in the meantime some of our American friends should get unduly alarmed, we might consider dropping submarine destroyers in at such ports as Guantánamo, Santiago, and Cienfuegos for the time being. Everything is revolving around the army now and if they were to receive some cooperation from the different leaders, whether they are immediately a part of the army or not but had liberal ideas, that would be very helpful. . . .

Ambassador: I am in full accord with what you say.

Secretary: I am just getting these facts before you for what they may be worth, because we have implicit confidence in your judgment and in your ability to keep yourself ingratiated with all groups while we are giving Cuba and the dominant forces in it an opportunity to work out of the snarl or to take such steps as would make intervention by us unnecessary. I do not know whether I have said anything at all which would fit in there according to your judgment, but I wanted to get these things before you.

Ambassador: I agree absolutely with everything you have said. One or two members of the present group in power I know and one was here with me for an hour and a half last night. I will be in touch with them constantly,

"The Ringmaster
Colonel Fulgencio
Batista . . . ," 1934.
Phillips, *Cuban
Sideshow*, 309.

but for the time being we ought not even to consider recognizing any government of this character, in my opinion.

Secretary: Until it has shown its ability to preserve law and order.

Ambassador: What they want is an expression of opinion from me and I have
refused to give any opinion whatever except to insist on the maintenance
of order.

Secretary: It is natural that from their viewpoint they would be urging us, just
like our Chamber of Commerce friend last night, to rush in and intervene.
But of course you and I are keeping our eyes on the other side of the thing
as well and we can hope that those people will be patient and give such
cooperation as the dominant forces are willing to receive. . . .

Document 9. Sumner Welles to Cordell Hull, 18 September 1933.

. . . I am more than ever confident that the wisest policy for us to pursue is
to keep our hands off except insofar as the protection of American lives is involved. If the solution is long postponed it will be difficult to lift Cuba from
the economic and financial prostration toward which it is rapidly headed. It is
also within the bounds of possibility that the social revolution which is under
way cannot be checked. American properties and interests are being gravely

prejudiced and the material damage to such properties will in all probability be very great. All of these contingencies seem to me preferable to intervention. By intervention we not only would seriously jeopardize our continental interests but we also would once more give the Cuban people and particularly the Cuban leaders to understand that they do not have to assume the responsibility for their own lack of patriotism or lack of vision, and that the U.S. government stands always ready to repair the damage which they themselves cause their own country. It is my sincere belief that Cuba can never become a self-governing republic so long as this feeling persists.

Document 10. Sumner Welles to Cordell Hull, 7 October 1933.

I had a conference with Batista this afternoon. He advised me that he realized now fully that the present regime was a complete failure and that a concentration government in which the political groups and the commercial interests of the country could have confidence was an absolute necessity. He also stated that he appreciated the fact that recognition by the United States was essential before any improvement in conditions here could be expected.

He was deeply impressed by the fact that delegates of all of the important business and financial groups in Cuba had visited him this afternoon before I saw him to insist upon the creation of a government in which the public could have confidence.

He also assured me of his intention to proceed immediately with a firm hand in all of the American sugar plantations where labor troubles still existed, by arresting and removing all Communist leaders and by using the troops to restore order whenever it was necessary.

The Political Gangster

Samuel Farber

The impact of the Revolution of 1933 on future generations of Cuban intellectuals and political activists was enormous. Although the revolution "failed," political and economic agendas changed radically during the rest of the decade. The Platt Amendment was abrogated in 1934, the pleas of economic nationalists finally bore fruit in legislation that strengthened the position of Cuban sugar growers vis-à-vis the largely foreign-owned mills, and, in an extraordinary move, the éminence grise of the post-1933 period, Fulgencio Batista, embraced a program of radical nationalism and populism.

The decade of the 1940s was marked by the "Politics of Disappointment." Formal democracy prevailed during the first Batista government (1940–44) and the two Auténtico governments that followed under Grau San Martín (1944–48) and Carlos Prío Socarrás (1948–52). This was also a period in which the sugar economy prospered — during the Second World War. But it was also a decade in which the expectations of the generation of 1933 politics were dashed, as politics degenerated into a vortex of political violence, gangsterism, and corruption. The following extract from Samuel Farber's book discusses the emergence of the gangster in the politics of the 1940s.

According to William S. Stokes, during 1949 and 1950 the organized use of force in Cuban urban areas was characteristic of party factions, university terrorist groups, and labor unions, with the University of Havana being one of the principal sources of political power in Cuban politics. Assassinations and street battles were common. He writes, "The year 1949 began with the assassination of two students, supposedly for having participated in the shooting of a police sergeant, who in turn reputedly took part in the shooting of Manolo Castro, president of the Havana University Student Federation." Sessions of the social sciences faculty were once interrupted by a fusillade of revolver shots. In front of the coco [radio] broadcasting station assassins gunned down the vice-president of the University Student Federation, riddling his body with bullets. Police officers invaded the school of agronomy, arresting fourteen persons and confiscating machine guns, rifles, revolvers, and thousands of bullets. Observed Stokes, "The struggle for control of student offices in the university and for the spoils of government in the capital continues."

These Cuban gangs support Merle Kling's thesis that politics and the state are avenues of mobility and enrichment in Latin America. Although gang leaders and members seldom won much prestige, the financial and political stakes were increasingly high, and some of these gangs even branched out into areas other than state patronage. However, the groups still wanted to keep some form of political image, and their names and presumed "ideologies" bear witness to this desire: besides the UIR [Unión Insurreccional Revolucionaria], which pretended to anarchism, there were Acción Revolucionaria Guiteras (ARG) [named after Antonio Guiteras, a leader of the 1933 revolutionary government] and the Movimiento Socialista Revolucionario (MSR), whose names clearly indicate their ideological pretensions. Groups such as these were usually very crude and politically unsophisticated. Their leaders believed chaos to be "a wonderful thing for a revolutionary" and found it easier to do away with someone than to write a speech or formulate a political program.

The Auténtico administration encouraged gangster groups for another reason. As a result of the Cold War, a split was developing in the organized labor movement, with the Communists and the Auténticos forming two rival labor federations. Traditionally weak within the organized working class, the Auténticos desperately needed anti-Communist labor cadres. The gangster groups, particularly the ARG, helped to fill this role and eventually controlled various unions such as the Tramway Workers' Union. The ARG members were probably some of the fiercest opponents of the Communists inside the trade-union movement. They contributed to making the labor movement subservient to the interests of the Auténtico governments, which continued the tradition of trade-union-government collusion consolidated during the Batista years. Charles Page, a student of the Cuban labor movement, has described how the ARG, claiming a national membership of eight thousand (the great majority of whom appeared to be labor gangsters originally trained in the anti-Machado terrorist underground), did not attempt to reach the masses but tried to develop leaders, and even established the Georges Sorel School for Leadership. Their tactics were primarily direct action, particularly the slowdown. Yet they made a pact with the government, becoming the Communists' most bitter and violent enemies and the goons of the pro-Auténtico CTC [Confederación de Trabajadores Cubanos], known as the CTC(a). In this role, the ARG received $100 per month for each of two ARG *activistas* (agitators) in the six provinces of the island. Commented Page, "The alliance is an unnatural one, but at present is mutually advantageous." The ARG succeeded in placing nine of its members in the secretariat of the CTC(a) and twenty-three on the CTC(a) executive committee. An ARG member was even appointed to the Minimum Wage Commission of the Ministry of Labor as a delegate of the CTC(a).

The political gangs were a real obstacle to the work of serious political reformers and revolutionaries. At the University of Havana, for example, university reformers and political students who were serious about their views were forced to carry on long struggles against gangster domination of university politics. Eventually the gangsters disappeared, not so much because of the opposition of the students and faculty, but because, after the overthrow of the Auténticos by Batista in 1952, the gangster groups suddenly lost their political role: Batista, unlike the Auténticos, had no reason to appeal to or to pacify these particular elements. Some individual gangsters, such as Rolando Masferrer, joined the Batista regime and became well known for the atrocities they later committed on behalf of the government. Gangsterism similarly declined within organized labor, where Batista's suppression of both the Communists and other oppositionists left little need for the use of any such gangs. With the gangsters out of the way, the road was left open for the building of a serious movement of opposition to Batista, particularly among the students at the University of Havana. . . .

Political gangsterism was both cause and effect of the political demoralization and disintegration under the Auténtico governments. However, the climate of corruption also provoked a very different political phenomenon: the birth and growth of the Party of the Cuban People under the leadership of Eduardo Chibás.

The United Fruit Company in Cuba

Oscar Zanetti

In an extract from a study of U.S. sugar investment in northeastern Cuba, distin-
guished Cuban historian Oscar Zanetti (b. 1946) and his team outline how the United
Fruit Company's political influence extended well beyond the boundaries of its mill
towns and sugar estates during the 1940s and early 1950s.

United Fruit: Relations with the Cuban State and Cuban Politics

Among the North American monopolies which have operated in Latin America, it is difficult to find one that surpasses the United Fruit Company with
respect to intervention and meddling in the political life of the countries in
which it has operated. Openly or deceitfully, United Fruit has deposed governments, instigated frontier conflicts and forced the promulgation of shameful
laws, always managing skillfully to keep under its control groups of venal politicians who have faithfully served its interests. However, in the case of Cuba, a
series of factors of a different character combined so that the interventionist attitude of United Fruit was manifested on a more limited scale. In the first place
there was the fundamental question of size. Although United Fruit figured
among the great North American sugar enterprises that operated in Cuba, it
never came to occupy one of the first places on the list; the production of its
mills rarely represented more than 5 percent of the national output, and the
extent of its landholdings put it in fifth place among the North American sugar
monopolies. To this fact must be added others such as the secondary character of sugar production by the UFC enterprise on the international scale, the
relative remoteness of its properties, the more direct intervention of the imperialist North American state in the political control of Cuba, etc. All of these
circumstances determined that, on occasion, United Fruit kept itself surprisingly on the fringe of some of the most important political maneuvers of the
North American sugar interests in Cuba, causing its political influence to be
rather less than that of some other enterprises such as Cuba Cane (Atlántica

del Golfo), the Cuban American Sugar Mills Company, or the Cuban Company. . . .

The Mechanisms of Political Action

During its sixty years of activity in Cuba, the UFC spared no efforts to make sure that the state would faithfully serve its interests. Among its numerous techniques, the most blatant mechanisms of political pressure and blackmail were used, such as bribes, flattery, and the most cunning tricks. The techniques varied from case to case, adapting to the circumstances of the moment. . . .

Ideological Penetration

Propaganda and other forms of ideological activity were not absent from the political ploys of the UFC. However, those mechanisms appeared later, reaching a true development only in the decades of the 1940s and 1950s. From 1939 onward, the journal *El Pueblo* inserted in its pages, with considerable frequency, an announcement that the UFC had contracted with a powerful North American broadcasting station to transmit a program in Spanish, dedicated to Latin America. During those first years, the UFC propaganda was concentrated on demonstrating the beneficent character of its activities, employing for that purpose space in the daily press of [the town of] Banes and other publications.

Nevertheless, company propaganda began to take on a markedly political hue in connection with the development of the "Cold War" strategy of the U.S. government. In the heat of the Korean War and, particularly, after the measures taken by the Arbenz government in Guatemala seriously affected its interests, United Fruit fell into a truly hysterical anti-Communism.

The propagandistic activity of the UFC developed as much within the framework of the company as part of the ideological training of its management — as it did outside, with instructions to its agents to place a great quantity of pamphlets and other kinds of printed propaganda in offices, tobacco shops, barbershops, conference rooms, and other public places of their *bateyes* or the town of Banes. Some of these materials were official publications of the North American government — "Know Our Communist Enemy," of the Department of Defense, but also there were reprints of magazine articles or speeches of businessmen.

The UFC also applied its own creative efforts to the anti-Communist campaign, publishing on its own account books and pamphlets of diverse titles — *How a North American Company through Propaganda and Public Relations Has*

Cuban game show (1957) imitating U.S. TV format. Cuban television, which began in 1950, was highly developed by Latin American standards. Courtesy Center for Cuban Studies Archives.

Fought Communism in Latin America or *Why Don't the Soviets Like Bananas?*— also almanacs or other very visible media, like the plaque containing Eisenhower's definition of Communism, printed by the head office and sent in great quantities to their tropical divisions. In like manner, the company filmed documentaries — *The Living Circle*, dedicated to promoting the role of the UFC as a bridge of good relations between the United States and Latin America — for the purpose of special showings within its divisions.

Besides these activities, the UFC developed another, not less important, as an agent of ideological penetration in the service of official U.S. organizations. The manager of the UFC in Banes regularly received pamphlets and other materials sent by the North American consul in Santiago charging him to distribute them in the town of Banes and to forward names and addresses of persons to whom the embassy might send propaganda directly. The branches of the company, as much in Banes as in Macabí and Preston were utilized by the U.S. Information Service (USIS) to show documentaries with titles like *The Reason for Korea*, etc.

The administration of the UFC in both divisions also had the task of bringing about contacts between agents of the North American government and persons in the fields of education and the press.

Control of Local Politics

In the relations maintained by United Fruit with political institutions in the region in which it functioned, one perceives some of the basic lines of the "Banana Republic" attitude that characterized this company. As powerful as the UFC was in its influence on the central state organizations, at that level it was no more than one among ten North American sugar enterprises. But at the local level, among the lesser civil servants of the two or three municipalities in which the UFC properties were located, it was simply "the Company," embracing in this concept the tacit recognition of the decisive importance it had in the economy of the locality.

The total concentration of its properties in a single region permitted the UFC to exercise political control there by means of the whole gamut of sophisticated mechanisms previously examined and by the unquestionable weight of its economic power. On the other hand, the activities of the company contributed to the acquiescence of sectors within the regional society—top employees, big planters, tenants, etc.—who publicly and notoriously defended the company to which they had linked their destinies. . . .

[Banes was] the most submissive of the three municipalities in which the UFC operated. If one examines the bulging files of correspondence between the municipal branches and the division administration of the UFC in Banes, there is hardly a line concerning the extensive range of administrative services and necessities in which the city government or the other municipal institutions did not solicit the company's help. The petitions were of all kinds: security guards for special watch duty, material for paving streets, vehicles of all types, even a petition from the municipal judge asking for five meters of cable for the installation of a telephone extension. The abundance of these demands, as revealed in the files, suggest that the practice had degenerated into a vice. Nevertheless, this is perhaps the most superficial and anecdotal aspect of the dependence, since the municipality of Banes very early had incurred extremely grave obligations with United Fruit.

Thus, the city government of Banes incurred $50,000 of debt with the company in order to build its sewer system. This type of agreement was repeated on various occasions, for the paving of streets, for the construction of the slaughterhouse, etc. For all this "assistance" the municipality of Banes owed United Fruit in 1944 the considerable sum of $102,678, which was rather more than it could collect in taxes in its most prosperous fiscal year. In reality, the city government of Banes never succeeded in paying its debts, nor did United Fruit show any anxiety to recover them, deriving from this situation latent possibilities of blackmail, very convenient to the interests of the company. An article published by the journal *El Pueblo*, in July 1937, revealed the characteristics of the game: "It is certainly true that we have the sewer system, the slaughterhouse, etc. through the cooperation that the company has given us, but this cooperation costs us too much. With the amount of money the UFC should have paid in taxes to the municipality, according to informed persons, the sewer system of Havana could have been constructed."

The situation of Banes typifies the structural dependence inherent in the subordination of local political institutions to the interests of an enterprise. In this case, it is a political manifestation of a broader phenomenon, described in the preceding chapter, of the methods of control that United possessed over the life of the region.

The dependence of the remaining municipalities — Mayarí and Antilla — on United Fruit was manifested in varying forms. Although the UFC owned a considerable portion of the land of the municipality of Mayarí, its control there was not so extreme. There were various reasons: on the one hand, the relative distance of the Preston administrative center from the municipal seat, which tended to lessen its influence; on the other hand the existence in Mayarí of other important economic activities, especially the exploitation of nickel deposits from the 1940's, which somewhat counterbalanced the UFC's influence. The third municipality connected with United Fruit — Antilla — was created in 1921 through the separation of some districts from Banes to Holguín. Neither of the company's two mills was located in Antilla, but its immense landholdings covered a large part of that municipality's rural area. Nevertheless, Antilla was, above all, an important railroad terminus and a great sugar-exporting port, so that its economic dependence on the UFC was much less.

In Banes, the penetration of United Fruit led to the disappearance or the subjection of the once dominant social sectors in the region. The local landowners lost their holdings, totally or partially, either because they sold them to the company or because they were snatched from them by means of the fraudulent land appropriation process that took place in the whole Banes area. Those who succeeded in keeping any important property had to become *colonos* of the UFC [sugar growers who were suppliers to the mills], since the absolute control of the company over the regional infrastructure left no alternative. Beside this group appeared another, even more intimately tied to the company, composed of Cuban employees — generally middle-level functionaries, but with some exceptions in a higher category — in the service of United Fruit. In some cases these employees were descendants of the landowning group who had fallen on hard times—certain members of the Dumois family are typical—and in other cases, individuals who had come to Banes with the idea of finding an advantageous employment in the UFC complex.

Given the absolute economic control exercised by United Fruit in Banes, it was practically impossible for anyone or any group to arise to economic power outside the sphere of the company's influence. Therefore, for a long time those groups with the capacity to participate actively in local politics were, for the most part, tied to the company's interests.[1]

United Fruit could, therefore, complement the pressure mechanisms derived from its economic power with a wide network of personal relationships. At all times, it could rely on certain henchmen or, at least, persons obligated to the company, conveniently placed in various municipal offices. From the time Banes became a municipality, the company could always count on two or three councilmen who were also its employees and who were expected to look after its interests. Thus, for example, the project of the sewer system, promoted by the UFC, was presented to the municipal council by Ernesto Dumois, long-time trusted employee of the company, and Councilman Juan Campaña, a manager of the UFC who immediately asked his colleagues to approve it, without further discussion, in its entirety. In 1926, the mayoralty of Banes was occupied by Delfín Campaña, who was at the same time the highest-ranking Cuban of the Banes division of the UFC. Campaña was replaced in 1932 by Rafael Díaz Balart, lawyer of the company who did not complete his term because of the revolutionary movement of 1933.

TRANSLATED BY VIRGINIA HILDEBRAND

Note

1. Some of these groups—the cane growers, the local merchants, etc.—may have occasionally opposed the company, but their position was so fragile that in no case were they able to sustain their opposition.

Cuba's Largest Inheritance

Bohemia

The corruption of the Constitutional Period reached its peak in the late 1940s and early 1950s during the government of Prío Socarrás. A vivid exposé of illicit enrichment — focusing on the investments of Prío's minister of education, José Manuel Alemán — appeared in the leading news magazine Bohemia *in 1950; an extract appears below.*

CUBA'S LARGEST INHERITANCE

The Fortune Left by Alemán is Beyond Calculation

(Bert Collier of the Miami Herald *Estimates it at Seventy to Two Hundred Million Dollars.)*

Exclusive Report by Manuel Hernández Torres

It was the middle of 1946 — Cuba's midterm elections were already over — and a Cuban, just over forty, dark, elegant, and witty, turned up in a Miami Beach real estate broker's office and in person, and in cash, purchased a small house at the end of Alton Road, above a gentle hill leading to the golf course of a private club. It was a small property with few comforts and a lot of garden, facing onto the elegant street, and the purchase price could not have been more than fifteen to eighteen thousand dollars.

The new owner did not move in permanently and during the remaining months of 1946 he only occupied the house for a couple of weekends, when he was joined by family members and a few friends who visited him frequently. This man was José Manuel Alemán, the recently inaugurated minister of education in Cuba. Previously, he had been director of vocational education, and he had extensive experience and knowledge of the practical management of the Education Ministry's budgets.

That was his first adventure in Miami.

Three years later, in September 1949, the Miami and Miami Beach papers . . . published a sensational news item, based on information obtained from the federal offices in the state capital, Tallahassee. According to the report a group of Latin American investors had just completed a deal in Greater Miami worth over $100 million, involving the acquisition of hotels, buildings, industries, and other enterprises. The report highlighted the fact that the leader of the group was a Cuban politician: José Manuel Alemán, former minister of education in Dr. Grau San Martín's government and senator of the republic in absentia, now a voluntary exile in Florida and much more interested in his own businesses than in Cuban politics.

And this was the second great adventure in José Manuel's fabulous career as an investor, all exposed in broad daylight.

A few months later, only a few days ago in fact, José Manuel Alemán turned up again in the newspapers of the U.S. south, this time in an obituary which stated that his businesses in Miami were worth somewhere between seventy and two hundred million dollars, and that it was impossible to accurately establish the extent of this Caribbean politician's Florida fortune, because the huge empire was hidden under the cover of limited liability companies. Only meticulous research in the government's tax offices (an unlikely occurrence) could reveal the true scale of Alemán's wealth.

TRANSLATED BY AVIVA CHOMSKY

The Last Call

Eduardo A. Chibás

In August 1951, Eduardo Chibás (1907–1951), founder of the Cuban People's Party (Orto-doxo) and a fierce critic of administrative corruption, shot himself shortly after con-cluding his popular radio program. In his talk, "El último aldabonazo," Chibás made a final ringing attack on the corruption of the Prío government.

Five centuries ago the Court of the Inquisition shouted at Galileo: "Liar! De-ceiver! Show us the proof that the Earth moves around the Sun!" Galileo could not produce physical proof of this obvious fact, and was found guilty, but he continued repeating, firm in his moral conviction, "But it moves! But it moves!"

Five years ago I accused the minister of education, José Manuel Alemán, of stealing money from school materials and school breakfasts, and of building a real estate empire in Miami. Minister Alemán and all of his spokespeople filled the airwaves with cries of "Liar! Slanderer! Show us the proof!" I could not produce physical proof that they are stealing money from the National Treasury, but I continued repeating, firm in my moral conviction, "They are stealing! They are stealing!"

Now I accuse the government of Carlos Prío of being the most corrupt of all of the governments that the republic has had until the present, and his min-ister of education Aureliano Sánchez Arango—who has substituted the ASA for the BAGA—[that is, Aureliano Sánchez Arango (ASA) is as corrupt as his pre-decessor José Manuel Alemán, with his Bloque Alemán-Grau-Alsina (BAGA)] of stealing money from school materials and school breakfasts and of making great investments in Guatemala and other republics of Central America.

Last Sunday, from this same political platform, I presented the Cuban people with irrefutable material proof of the enormous corruption of Prío's regime: photographs of schools and hospitals in poverty, contrasted with the ostentatious estates and palaces of our rulers who a short time ago lived in poverty. Nevertheless, in spite of the fact that the continuous depredations of Machado, Batista, Grau San Martín, and Carlos Prío have not managed to blunt the moral sensibility of the Cuban people, which speaks loudly of the strength of their virtues, my words of last Sunday did not have the resonance that the grave situation required. Cuba needs to wake up. But my wake-up call was not, perhaps, loud enough. We will keep appealing to the conscience of the Cuban people.

Geographical position, rich soils, and the natural intelligence of its inhabitants mean that Cuba is destined to play a magnificent role in history, but it must work to achieve it. Other peoples, inhabiting islands that do not enjoy the privileged position of our homeland, have played a prominent role in history. The historical destiny of Cuba, on the other hand, has been frustrated, until now, by the corruption and blindness of its rulers, whose ideas—with a few exceptions—have never risen much above ground level.

The fortunate conjunction of natural factors so propitious for a splendid destiny, together with the great qualities of our people, only await the honorable and capable management of a team of rulers who are equal to their historical mission. The current government, corrupt to the bone, cannot fulfill this role although it tries new ways of covering up its thieving, smuggling, and shamelessness. The fake opposition led by Batista, who is calling for the return of the colonels, of the lash, the truncheon, and the *ley de fuga*,[1] is no use. And the angry bunch of people who hang around ex-President Grau are not up to the task either. The only political team capable of saving Cuba is the Cuban People's Party (Ortodoxos), with its commitment to rejecting political deals and to maintaining the kind of political independence which will not tolerate deals or compromises.

Comrades of Orthodoxy, let us move forward! For economic independence, political freedom, and social justice! Sweep the thieves from the government! People of Cuba, rise up, and move forward! People of Cuba, wake up! This is my last CALL!

TRANSLATED BY AVIVA CHOMSKY

Note

1. Shooting prisoners "while trying to escape."

For Us, It Is Always the 26th of July

Carlos Puebla

Cubans resisted the Batista government in a number of ways. Sixteen months after Batista seized power in 1952, Fidel Castro and a group of over one hundred young men and women, mostly workers and students, attacked the Moncada Barracks in Santiago de Cuba. The attack was a failure, but it served as a reminder that the tradition of armed action by Cuban youth (last seen in the student struggles against Machado between 1930 and 1933) was still alive. The Moncada assault on 26 July 1953 also introduced Fidel Castro to a national Cuban audience. The 26th of July remains Cuba's most important national holiday; Carlos Puebla's (1917–1989) song "Para nosotros siempre es 26" (For us, it is always the 26th [of July]) immortalizes the date.

The Moncada showed us
The way to go
And ever since that exalted example
For us it is always the 26th
Always the 26th, always the 26th
For us it is always the 26th.

The homeland is song and love
The homeland is struggle and duty
And in all that has to do with patriotism
For us it is always the 26th
Always the 26th, always the 26th
For us it is always the 26th.

Only creative work
Is the way to grow
And in the question of work
For us it is always the 26th
Always the 26th, always the 26th
For us it is always the 26th.

Ideology is the motor
For advancing and overcoming
And as far as ideology is concerned
For us it is always the 26th
Always the 26th, always the 26th
For us it is always the 26th.

Consciousness and strength
Triumphed over yesterday
And ever since that very instant
For us it is always the 26th
Always the 26th, always the 26th
For us it is always the 26th.

TRANSLATED BY AVIVA CHOMSKY

Three *Comandantes* Talk It Over

Carlos Franqui

Carlos Franqui (b. 1921) was one of Fidel Castro's earliest collaborators and propagandists and an important journalist in the first years of the revolution. His book The Twelve *is an oral history account of the anti-Batista struggle, and in the following conversation Franqui paints a vivid picture of the excitement and anticipation surrounding the planning of the assault on the Moncada Barracks in July 1953. Carlos Franqui now lives in exile.*

[*José*] *Ponce:* During the attack on Moncada, we were in different spots. I was in one of the first cars. Others were assigned to take over the nearby hospital. Moncada brought people together from many places. Afterward, too—in prison.

In the house at the suburb of Siboney, before the attack, there was a mess of unknown faces. In fact, nobody knew anybody else.

Here's how I joined the ranks of the Revolution. Or, rather, the insurrection, because back then I didn't know the meaning of revolution.

[*Juan*] *Almeida:* Let's begin at the beginning. I was a mason's helper. We had a work yard at Ayesterán. The boss was a good guy. Up to a point, anyway. Deep down he was decent but not about the job because, actually, he gave us starvation wages.

One day I got to know Comrade Armando Mestre, a high school student in Havana. A real sport. He lived near me and we got along well. We'd go out together and talk things over. He asked me if I was studying; I told him no, I'd quit school in the third grade and I didn't have a chance to keep up my studies. Then he said he'd try and help me so I could get back to school, because that would open up lots of things for me. I told him, sure, school would give me a lot but I had to make a living first, since I came from a big family and had to help my parents.

Our friendship had already lasted a few years when Batista's coup came on 10 March 1952. Armando came to tell me, "Let's go to the university.

They're mobilizing the people against this military coup and they are trying to save the country."

We went there. People were looking for weapons. There weren't any —weapons were coming, weapons weren't coming. . . . Finally, the first weapons I'd ever seen were the ones Fidel gave us in the Hall of Martyrs on University Hill, so that we could get the hang of the M-1. Springfields, too, but the M-1 without a stock or, I should say, with a removable stock, that was something everybody got to handle. Those were the rudimentary weapons with which we made our first steps, our first contact with firearms. Now, of course, everybody can use a gun. . . .

That's where I met Fidel. He began talking about the Revolution and explained the process of evolution and how the coup d'état was a step backward. He said that youth had to unite, that it was a vital force, that he was counting on elements which hadn't made any compromise with the past.

That was my first contact with Fidel. It wasn't long after 10 March. He was always carrying a volume of Lenin under his arm. A blue book with a picture of Lenin in relief on the cover. He wore a gray suit, a well-used shirt with a worn collar. He always had that same energetic way about him.

Ponce: Fidel? . . .

One evening, after I was acquitted, I met Pepe Suárez in the park and he told me what was going on. He told me about Fidel, that he was young and had new ideas, and how the movement had nothing to do with the past or with political hacks. So I said, "Fine, keep me informed." One Saturday morning he came and said, "Tomorrow wait for me. We're going to Havana." That's all he told me.

We went to Havana, to the offices of the Orthodox Party, and that was my first contact with the comrades. I got to know Andrés Luján and some of the others, too. That was the place where we received instructions from the University of Havana. . . .

All they had at the house on Prado Boulevard was a submachine gun and an M-1. At Artemisa some of us used to get together regularly also, but we never greeted each other in the streets. Our meetings took place at the Masonic lodge.

This was about the time I first saw Fidel. On the Central Highway, as I recall, Pepe Suárez said to me, "Stay in the car." An old jalopy. I found a book on the seat. It was by Martí.[1] It had a red cover and many of Martí's statements were underlined. Just then, Fidel, who had been in a house across the way, came over. That was in 1952.

In our group there were Ciro Redondo, Julio Díaz, Ricondo, Flores, and Labrador, a comrade who lost an eye in the attack on the Moncada Barracks.

And there were some comrades who later fell at Moncada, like those peasants from Pijiriga. I don't remember their names any more because we didn't have much contact with them. Well, that's how it goes. . . .

Almeida I met at Boniato. In the prison at Boniato.

Almeida: Yes. It was hard, those early days. But everybody understood what was going on: not one prisoner complained. The comrades helped each other and that was clear for all to see later in the courtroom. We were sentenced, some to ten years, others to three, in the penitentiary on the Isle of Pines. . . . And I remember that book of Lenin. It was the one they seized afterward at Moncada.

In those days I was always smiling, always gay. I had a, well, let's say an easier outlook on life. I remember when I went for shooting practice at Los Palos. An instructor there was teaching us how to shoot with .22 rifles. They put up an empty milk can and each of us had to fire at it. Six shots. I took my rifle without ever having fired before and bang! The first shot hit the can! The second shot in the can, bang! The third in the can, bang! . . . I began to jump around like a goat, yelling, "I'm terrific, just terrific!" Then the instructor said, "Now, now, comrade, it's crazy to be excited like that!" And I answered him right back, "Nope, I'm happy inside, I can't hold it back." He said to me, "I don't think you're going to be much of a revolutionary." And me: "Listen to me — if I had been born in '95 I would have been a veteran of the War of Independence. Okay, in today's war I can only be a good revolutionary."

When we left for the attack on Moncada, a special recommendation was made about me. My dossier must have said I was a bit wacky, because Fidel said to Comrade Alcalde, who was driving the car to which I was assigned: "Keep an eye on Almeida, he's some kind of a joker."

They took me to Santiago on the Central Highway practically like they would a prisoner. Comrade Alcalde must have thought I was going to take off. The last thing in the world I'd want to do, since I thought we were driving to the carnival at Santiago as a reward for my doing so well in our training exercises.

We arrived in Santiago about four-thirty, the afternoon of the twenty-fifth. We went into a house at Celda Street, then left for another address where Comrade Guitart came about midnight to lead us away. He took us to Siboney, and there they started passing out uniforms. Uniforms of Batista's army.

"Great," I thought. "They're going to give me a rifle, aren't they?" I waited for my rifle like the Messiah. When I saw that the one they gave me was a .22-caliber I froze up. . . .

From the moment I arrived at Celda Street I knew it wasn't a training exercise this time, but a real revolutionary mission. But honestly, I have to tell you that when I saw that rifle my heart sank. It just about stopped. Imagine—a .22! They passed out the bullets and I took my four boxes. And I waited. Before leaving, Fidel spoke to the comrades about the historic event we were about to live through.

I don't remember his exact words very well. But I do recall his saying that we would be remembered and even earn a well-deserved place in history books.

There were some comrades who had become frightened. Fidel gave them encouragement. For my part, I'd have shot them, because on account of them there was some confusion later on.

For the rest, all Cubans know what happened. The shooting, comrades killed, those who could manage it getting away, our stay in the mountains until 1 August. . . .

Fidel, Alcalde, and Pepe were captured in a hut. . . .

Comrade Mestre, who has died since, got the worst manhandling. They kept telling him, "Come over here. You a revolutionary? Don't you know Negroes can't be revolutionaries? Negroes are either thieves or Batista's supporters, but never revolutionaries!" As for me, they threw me down on the ground. When I got up they fired over my head. I had to get back down and then they told me to get up—I didn't know what to do. Then Sarria came in and told me to stay on my feet.

[*Efigenio*] *Amejeiras:* You weren't afraid?

Almeida: No, we weren't afraid. To tell the truth, numbness overtakes you in those cases, so you don't react to the danger. They loaded us on a truck, tied our hands, and took us to the bivouac area. There we met other men: Raúl Castro, Ramiro Valdés, and some whose names I've forgotten. Then there was the trial.

From the Boniato prison we were sent by plane to the Isle of Pines for twenty-two months.

TRANSLATED BY ALBERT B. TEICHNER

Note

1. José Martí (1853–95), Cuban writer, revolutionary, champion of the struggle for liberty in all Latin America.

History Will Absolve Me

Fidel Castro

On 16 October 1953, Fidel Castro (b. 1926) defended himself at his trial after the assault on the Moncada Barracks with what is probably his most famous speech, "History Will Absolve Me." The speech crystallized, for many, the goals of the 26th of July Movement and catapulted Castro into the limelight as one of its most eloquent spokespeople.

In terms of struggle, when we talk about people we're talking about the *six hundred thousand* Cubans without work, who want to earn their daily bread honestly without having to emigrate from their homeland in search of a livelihood; the *five hundred thousand* farm laborers who live in miserable shacks, who work four months of the year and starve the rest, sharing their misery with their children, who don't have an inch of land to till, and whose existence would move any heart not made of stone; the *four hundred thousand* industrial workers and laborers whose retirement funds have been embezzled, whose benefits are being taken away, whose homes are wretched quarters, whose salaries pass from the hands of the boss to those of the moneylender, whose future is a pay reduction and dismissal, whose life is endless work, and whose only rest is the tomb; the *one hundred thousand* small farmers who live and die working land that is not theirs, looking at it with the sadness of Moses gazing at the promised land, to die without ever owning it, who like feudal serfs have to pay for the use of their parcel of land by giving up a portion of its produce, who cannot love it, improve it, beautify it, nor plant a cedar or an orange tree on it because they never know when a sheriff will come with the rural guard to evict them from it; the *thirty thousand* teachers and professors who are so devoted, dedicated, and so necessary to the better destiny of future generations and who are so badly treated and paid; the *twenty thousand* small businessmen weighed down by debts, ruined by the crisis, and harangued by a plague of grafting and venal officials; the *ten thousand* young professional people: doctors, engineers, lawyers, veterinarians, schoolteachers, dentists, pharmacists, newspapermen, painters, sculptors, etc., who finish school with their degrees, anxious to work and full of hope, only to find themselves at a dead end, all doors closed to them, and where no ear hears their clamor or supplication. These are the people, the ones who know misfortune and, therefore, are capable of fighting with limitless courage! To these people whose desperate roads through life have been paved with the bricks of betrayal and false promises, we were not going to say: "We will give you . . ." but rather: "Here it is, now fight for it with everything you have, so that liberty and happiness may be yours!"

The five revolutionary laws that would have been proclaimed immediately after the capture of the Moncada Garrison and would have been broadcast to the nation by radio must be included in the indictment. It is possible that Colonel Chaviano may have deliberately destroyed these documents, but even if he has I remember them.

The first revolutionary law would have returned the power to the people and proclaimed the 1940 Constitution the supreme law of the state until such time as the people should decide to modify or change it. And in order to effect its implementation and punish those who violated it—there being no electoral organization to carry this out—the revolutionary movement, as the circumstantial incarnation of this sovereignty, the only source of legitimate power, would have assumed all the faculties inherent therein, except that of modifying the constitution itself: in other words, it would have assumed the legislative, executive, and judicial powers.

This attitude could not be clearer nor more free of vacillation and sterile charlatanry. A government acclaimed by the mass of rebel people would be vested with every power, everything necessary in order to proceed with the effective implementation of popular will and real justice. From that moment, the judicial power—which since 10 March had placed itself against and outside the constitution—would cease to exist, and we would proceed to its immediate and total reform before it would once again assume the power granted it by the supreme law of the republic. Without these previous measures, a return to legality by putting its custody back into the hands that have crippled the system so dishonorably would constitute a fraud, a deceit, one more betrayal.

The second revolutionary law would give nonmortgageable and nontransferable ownership of the land to all tenant and subtenant farmers, lessees, sharecroppers, and squatters who hold parcels of five *caballerías* of land or less, and the state would indemnify the former owners on the basis of the rental which they would have received for these parcels over a period of ten years.

The third revolutionary law would have granted workers and employees the right to share 30 percent of the profits of all large industrial, mercantile, and mining enterprises, including the sugar mills. The strictly agricultural enterprises would be exempt in consideration of other agrarian laws which would be put into effect.

The fourth revolutionary law would have granted all sugar planters the right to share 55 percent of the sugar production and a minimum quota of forty thousand *arrobas* for all small tenant farmers who have been established for three years or more.

The fifth revolutionary law would have ordered the confiscation of all holdings and ill-gotten gains of those who had committed fraud during previous regimes, as well as the holdings and ill-gotten gains of all their legates and heirs. To implement this, special courts with full powers would gain access to all records of all corporations registered or operating in this country, in order to investigate concealed funds of illegal origin and to request that foreign governments extradite persons and attach holdings rightfully belonging to the Cuban people. Half of the property recovered would be used to subsidize retirement funds for workers and the other half would be used for hospitals, asylums, and charitable organizations.

Furthermore, it was to be declared that the Cuban policy in the Americas would be one of close solidarity with the democratic peoples of this continent, and that all those politically persecuted by bloody tyrannies oppressing our sister nations would find generous asylum, brotherhood, and bread in the land of Martí; not the persecution, hunger, and treason they find today. Cuba should be the bulwark of liberty and not a shameful link in the chain of despotism.

These laws would have been proclaimed immediately. As soon as the upheaval ended and prior to a detailed and far-reaching study, they would have been followed by another series of laws and fundamental measures, such as the agrarian reform, the integral educational reform, nationalization of the electric power trust and the telephone trust, refund to the people of the illegal excessive rates these companies have charged, and payment to the treasury of all taxes brazenly evaded in the past.

All these laws and others would be based on exact compliance with two essential articles of our constitution: one of them orders the outlawing of large estates, indicating the maximum area of land any one person or entity may own for each type of agricultural enterprise, by adopting measures which would tend to revert the land to the Cubans. The other categorically orders the state to use all means at its disposal to provide employment for all those who lack it and to insure a decent livelihood to each manual or intellectual laborer. None of these laws can be called unconstitutional. The first popularly elected government would have to respect them, not only because of moral obligations to the nation, but because when people achieve something they have yearned for throughout generations, no force in the world is capable of taking it away again.

The problem of the land, the problem of industrialization, the problem of

Fidel holds a press conference. Lionel
Martin, *The Early Fidel: Roots of
Castro's Communism* (New York: Lyle
Stuart, 1978), between 160 and 161.

housing, the problem of unemployment, the problem of education, and the
problem of the people's health: these are the six problems we would take immediate steps to solve, along with restoration of civil liberties and political
democracy.

This exposition may seem cold and theoretical if one does not know the
shocking and tragic conditions of the country with regard to these six problems, along with the most humiliating political oppression.

Eighty-five percent of the small farmers in Cuba pay rent and live under the
constant threat of being evicted from the land they till. More than half of our
most productive land is in the hands of foreigners. In Oriente, the largest province, the lands of the United Fruit Company link the northern and southern
coasts. There are *two hundred thousand peasant families* who do not have a single
acre of land to till to provide food for their starving children. On the other hand,
nearly *three hundred thousand caballerías* of cultivable land owned by powerful
interests remain uncultivated. If Cuba is above all an agricultural state, if its
population is largely rural, if the city depends on these rural areas, if the people
from our countryside won our war of independence, if our nation's greatness
and prosperity depend on a healthy and vigorous rural population that loves
the land and knows how to work it, if this population depends on a state that
protects and guides it, then how can the present state of affairs be allowed to
continue?

Except for a few food, lumber, and textile industries, Cuba continues to be primarily a producer of raw materials. We export sugar to import candy, we export hides to import shoes, we export iron to import plows. Everyone agrees with the urgent need to industrialize the nation, that we need steel industries, paper and chemical industries, that we must improve our cattle and grain production, the technique and the processing in our food industry in order to defend ourselves against the ruinous competition of the Europeans in cheese products, condensed milk, liquors, and edible oils, and of the United States in canned goods; that we need cargo ships; that tourism should be an enormous source of revenue. But the capitalists insist that the workers remain under the yoke. The state sits back with its arms crossed and industrialization can wait forever.

Just as serious or even worse is the housing problem. There are *two hundred thousand* huts and hovels in Cuba; *four hundred thousand* families in the countryside and in the cities live cramped in huts and tenements without even the minimum sanitary requirements; *2.2 million* of our urban population pay rents which absorb between one-fifth and one-third of their incomes; and *2.8 million* of our rural and suburban population lack electricity. We have the same situation here: if the state proposes the lowering of rents, landlords threaten to freeze all construction; if the state does not interfere, construction goes on so long as the landlords get high rents; otherwise they would not lay a single brick, even though the rest of the population had to live totally exposed to the elements. The utilities monopoly is no better; they extend lines as far as it is profitable, and beyond that point they don't care if people have to live in darkness for the rest of their lives. The state sits back with its arms crossed, and the people have neither homes nor electricity.

Our educational system is perfectly compatible with everything I've just mentioned. Where the peasant doesn't own the land, what need is there for agricultural schools? Where there is no industry, what need is there for technological or vocational schools? Everything follows the same absurd logic; if we don't have one thing we can't have the other. In any small European country there are more than two hundred technological and vocational schools; in Cuba only six such schools exist, and the graduates have no jobs for their skills. The little rural schoolhouses are attended by a mere half of the school-age children—barefooted, half-naked, and undernourished—and frequently the teacher must buy necessary school materials from his own salary. Is this the way to make a nation great?

Only death can liberate one from so much misery. In this respect, however, the state is most helpful—in providing early death for the people. *Ninety percent* of the children in the countryside are consumed by parasites that filter through their bare feet from the ground they walk on. Society is moved to compassion when it hears of the kidnapping or murder of one child, but it is criminally indifferent to the mass murder of so many thousands of children who die every year from lack of facilities, agonizing with pain. Their innocent eyes, death already shining in them, seem to look into some vague infinity as if entreating forgiveness for human selfishness, as if asking God to stay wrath. And when the head of a family works only four months a year, with what can he purchase clothing and medicine for his children? They will grow up with rickets, with not a single good tooth in their mouths by the time they reach thirty; they will have heard ten million speeches and will finally die of misery and deception. Public hospitals, which are always full, accept only patients recommended by some powerful politician who, in turn, demands the electoral votes of the unfortunate one and his family so that Cuba may continue forever in the same or worse condition.

With this background, is it not understandable that from May to December over a million persons are jobless and that Cuba, with a population of five and a half million, has a greater number of unemployed than France or Italy with a population of forty million each?

When you try a defendant for robbery, Honorable Judges, do you ask him how long he has been unemployed? Do you ask him how many children he has, which days of the week he ate and which he didn't; do you investigate his social context at all? You just send him to jail without further thought. But those who burn warehouses and stores to collect insurance do not go to jail, even though a few human beings may have gone up in flames. The insured have money to hire lawyers and bribe judges. You imprison the poor wretch who steals because he is hungry; but none of the hundreds who steal millions from the government has ever spent a night in jail. You dine with them at the end of the year in some elegant club and they enjoy your respect. In Cuba, when a government official becomes a millionaire overnight and enters the fraternity of the rich, he could very well be greeted with the words of that opulent character out of Balzac — Taillerfer — who in his toast to the young heir to an enormous fortune said: "Gentlemen, let us drink to the power of gold! Mr. Valentine, a millionaire six times over, has just ascended the throne. He is king, can do everything, is above everyone, as all the rich are. Henceforth, equality before the law, established by the constitution, will be a myth for him; for he will not be subject to laws: the laws will be subject to him. There are no courts nor are there sentences for millionaires."

The nation's future, the solutions to its problems, cannot continue to depend on the selfish interests of a dozen big businessmen nor on the cold calculations of profits that ten or twelve magnates draw up in their air-conditioned offices. The country cannot continue begging on its knees for miracles from a few golden calves, like the biblical one destroyed by the prophet's fury. Golden calves cannot perform miracles of any kind. The problems of the republic can be solved only if we dedicate ourselves to fight for it with the same energy, honesty, and patriotism our liberators had when they founded it. Statesmen like Carlos Saladrigas, whose statesmanship consists of preserving the status quo and mouthing phrases like "absolute freedom of enterprise," "guarantees to investment capital," and "the law of supply and demand," will not solve these problems. Those ministers can chat away in a Fifth Avenue mansion until not even the dust of the bones of those whose problems require immediate solution remains. In this present-day world, social problems are not solved by spontaneous generation.

A revolutionary government backed by the people and with the respect of the nation, after cleansing the different institutions of all venal and corrupt officials, would proceed immediately to the country's industrialization, mobilizing all inactive capital, currently estimated at about 1.5 billion pesos, through the National Bank and the Agricultural and Industrial Development Bank, and submitting this mammoth task to experts and men of absolute competence totally removed from all political machines, for study, direction, planning, and realization.

After settling the one hundred thousand small farmers as owners on the land which they previously rented, a revolutionary government would immediately proceed to settle the land problem. First, as set forth in the constitution, it would establish the maximum amount of land to be held by each type of agricultural enterprise and would acquire the excess acreage by expropriation, recovery of the lands stolen from the state, improvement of swampland, planting of large nurseries, and reserving of zones for reforestation. Second, it would distribute the remaining land among peasant families with priority given to the larger ones and would promote agricultural cooperatives for communal use of expensive equipment, freezing plants, and single technical, professional guidelines in farming and cattle raising. Finally, it would provide resources, equipment, protection, and useful guidance to the peasants.

A revolutionary government would solve the housing problem by cutting all rents in half, by providing tax exemptions on homes inhabited by the owners; by tripling taxes on rented homes; by tearing down hovels and replacing them with modern apartment buildings; and by financing housing all over the island on a scale heretofore unheard of, with the criterion that, just as each rural family should possess its own tract of land, each city family should own its own home or apartment. There is plenty of building material and more than enough manpower to make a decent home for every Cuban. But if we continue to wait for the golden calf, a thousand years will have gone by and the problem will remain the same. On the other hand, today possibilities of taking electricity to the most isolated areas on the island are greater than ever. The use of nuclear energy in this field is now a reality and will greatly reduce the cost of producing electricity.

With these three projects and reforms, the problem of unemployment would automatically disappear and the task of improving public health and fighting against disease would become much less difficult.

Finally, a revolutionary government would undertake the integral reform of the educational system, bringing it into line with the projects just mentioned with the idea of educating those generations which will have the privilege of living in a happier land. Do not forget the words of the Apostle: "A grave mistake is being made in Latin America: in countries that live almost completely from the produce of the land, men are being educated exclusively for urban life and are not trained for farm life." "The happiest country is the one which has best educated its sons, both in the instruction of thought and the direction of their feelings." "An educated country will always be strong and free."

The soul of education, however, is the teacher, and in Cuba the teaching profession is miserably underpaid. Despite this, no one is more dedicated than the Cuban teacher. Who among us has not learned his ABCs in the little public schoolhouse? It is time we stopped paying pittances to these young men and women who are entrusted with the sacred task of teaching our youth. No teacher should earn less than two hundred pesos; no secondary teacher should make less than 350 pesos if they are to devote themselves exclusively to their high calling without suffering want. What is more, all rural teachers should have free use of the various systems of transportation; and, at least once every five years, all teachers should enjoy a sabbatical leave of six months with pay so they may attend special refresher courses at home or abroad to keep abreast of the latest developments in their field. In this way, the curriculum and the teaching system can be constantly improved. Where will the money be found for all this? When there is an end to the embezzlement of government funds, when public officials stop taking graft from the large companies that owe taxes to the state, when the enormous resources of the country are brought into full use, when we no longer buy tanks, bombers, and guns for this country (which has no frontiers to defend and where these instruments of war, now being purchased, are used against the people), when there is more interest in educating the people than in killing them, there will be more than enough money.

Cuba could easily provide for a population three times as great as it has now, so there is no excuse for the abject poverty of a single one of its present inhabitants. The markets should be overflowing with produce, pantries should be full, all hands should be working. This is not an inconceivable thought. What is inconceivable is that anyone should go to bed hungry while there is a single inch of unproductive land, that children should die for lack of medical attention. What is inconceivable is that 30 percent of our farm people cannot write their names and that 99 percent of them know nothing of Cuba's history. What is inconceivable is that the majority of our rural people are now living in worse circumstances than the Indians Columbus discovered in the fairest land that human eyes had ever seen.

To those who would call me a dreamer, I quote the words of Martí: "A true man does not seek the path where advantage lies, but rather the path where duty lies, and this is the only practical man, whose dream of today will be the law of tomorrow, because he who has looked back on the essential course of history and has seen flaming and bleeding peoples seethe in the cauldron of the ages knows that, without a single exception, the future lies on the side of duty." . . .

I know that imprisonment will be harder for me than it has ever been for anyone, filled with cowardly threats and hideous cruelty. But I do not fear prison, as I do not fear the fury of the miserable tyrant who took the lives of seventy of my comrades. Condemn me. It does not matter. History will absolve me.

TRANSLATED BY MARGARITA ZIMMERMAN

Reminiscences of the Cuban Revolutionary War

Che Guevara

The Argentine-born Ernesto "Che" Guevara (1928–1967) joined Fidel Castro and his fellow conspirators in Mexico where they were preparing their expedition to southeastern Cuba. The exiled revolutionaries (eighty-two men) set off for Cuba in the motorboat Granma in late November 1956. The guerrillas' initial experiences were disastrous, and only twenty-one of the expeditionaries survived the first weeks on Cuban soil. Guevara was one of the small band of survivors who managed to reach the mountainous terrain of the Sierra Maestra, where the guerrillas struggled to create a base of support among the peasant population. In this extract Guevara reflects on the special characteristics of the peasant inhabitants of the Sierra Maestra and on the crucial assistance they provided the expeditionaries.

To live in a continual state of war and to adapt to this new phenomenon creates an attitude of mind in the popular consciousness. The individual must undergo an adaptation to enable him to resist the bitter experience that threatens his tranquility. The Sierra Maestra and other newly liberated zones had to undergo this bitter experience.

The situation in the rugged mountain zones was nothing less than frightful. The peasant, migrated from afar, eager for freedom, working to root out his sustenance from the newly dug land, had by dint of his labors coaxed the coffee plants to grow on the craggy slopes where creating anything new entails sacrifice — all this by his own sweat, in response to the age-old longing of man to possess his own plot of land, working with infinite love this hostile crag, an extension of the man himself.

Soon after, when the coffee plants began to blossom with the fruit that represented his hope, the lands were claimed by a new owner. It might be a foreign company, a local land-grabber, or some other speculator taking advantage of peasant indebtedness. The political caciques, the local army chieftains, worked for the company or the land-grabber, jailing or murdering any peasant who was unduly rebellious against these arbitrary acts. Such was the scene of defeat and desolation that we found, paralleling our own defeat at Alegría de Pío, the product of our inexperience (our only misadventure in this long campaign, our bloody baptism of fire).

The peasantry recognized those lean men whose beards, now legendary, were beginning to flourish, as companions in misfortune, fresh victims of the repressive forces, and gave us their spontaneous and disinterested aid, without expecting anything of the defeated ones.

Days passed and our small troop of now seasoned soldiers sustained the victories of La Plata and Palma Mocha. The regime responded with all its brutality, and there were mass assassinations of peasants. Terror was unleashed in the rustic valleys of the Sierra Maestra and the peasants withdrew their aid; a barrier of mutual mistrust loomed up between them and the *guerrilleros*, the former out of fear of reprisals, the latter out of fear of betrayal by the fearful. Our policy, nevertheless, was a just and understanding one, and the *guajiro* population began to return to their earlier relationship with our cause.

The dictatorship, in its desperation and criminality, ordered the resettlement of thousands of guajiro families from the Sierra Maestra in the cities.

The strongest and most resolute men, including almost all the youth, preferred liberty and war to slavery and the city. Long caravans of women, children, and old people took to the roads, leaving their birthplaces, going down to the *llano*, where they huddled on the outskirts of the cities. Cuba experienced the most criminal page of its history for the second time: the Resettlement. The first time it was decreed by Weyler, the bloody general of colonial Spain, this time by Fulgencio Batista, the worst traitor and assassin known to America.

Hunger, misery, illness, epidemics, and death decimated the peasants resettled by the tyranny. Children died for lack of medical attention and food, when a few steps away there were the resources that could have saved their lives. The indignant protest of the Cuban people, international scandal, and the inability of the dictatorship to defeat the rebels obliged the tyrant to suspend the resettlement of peasant families from the Sierra Maestra. And once again they returned to the land of their birth, miserable, sick, decimated. Earlier they had experienced bombardments by the dictatorship, the burning of their *bohíos* [huts], mass murders; now they had experienced the inhumanity and barbarism of a regime that treated them worse than colonial Spain treated the Cubans in the War of Independence. Batista had surpassed Weyler. The peasants returned with an unbreakable will to struggle until death or victory, rebels until death or freedom.

Our little guerrilla band, of city extraction, began to don palm leaf hats;

An image of Alberto Korda's photograph of Che Guevara overlooks the Plaza of the Revolution in Havana. Photo by Jackie McCabe.

the people lost their fear, decided to join the struggle and proceed resolutely along the road to their redemption. In this change, our policy toward the peasantry and our military victories coincided, and this already revealed us to be an unbeatable force in the Sierra Maestra.

Faced by the choice, all the peasants chose the path of revolution. The change of mental attitude, of which we have already spoken, now showed itself fully. The war was a fact—painful, yes, but transitory, a definitive state within which the individual was obliged to adapt himself in order to exist. When the peasants understood this, they made the adjustments necessary for the confrontation with the adverse circumstances that would come.

The peasants returned to their abandoned plots of land; they stopped the slaughter of their animals, saving them for worse days; they became used to the savage machine gunning, and each family built its own shelter. They also accustomed themselves to periodic flights from the battle zones, with family, cattle, and household goods, leaving only their bohíos for the enemy, which displayed its wrath by burning them to the ground. They accustomed themselves to rebuilding on the smoking ruins of their old dwellings, uncomplaining but with concentrated hatred and the will to conquer.

When the distribution of cattle began in the struggle against the dictatorship's food blockade, they cared for their animals with loving solicitude and they worked in groups, establishing what were in effect cooperatives in their efforts to move the cattle to a safe place, giving over all their pastureland and their mules to the common effort.

It is a new miracle of the Revolution that the staunchest individualist, who zealously protected the boundaries of his property, joined—because of the war—the great common effort of the struggle. But there is an even greater miracle: the rediscovery by the Cuban peasant of his own happiness, within the liberated zones. Whoever has witnessed the timorous murmurs with which our forces were received in each peasant household, notes with pride the care-free clamor, the happy, hearty laughter of the new Sierra inhabitant. That is the reflection of his self-assurance which the awareness of his own strength gave to the inhabitant of our liberated area. That is our future task: that the concept of their own strength should return to the Cuban people, and that they achieve absolute assurance that their individual rights, guaranteed by the Constitution, are their dearest treasure. More than the pealing of the bells, it will be the return of the old, happy laughter, of carefree security, lost by the Cuban people, which will signify liberation.

One Year of Armed Struggle

By the beginning of 1958 we had been fighting for more than a year. A brief recapitulation is necessary—of our military, organizational, and political situation, and our progress.

Concerning the military aspect, let us recall that our troops had disembarked on 2 December 1956, at Las Coloradas Beach. Three days later we were taken by surprise and routed at Alegría de Pío. We regrouped ourselves at the end of the month and began small-scale actions, appropriate to our current strength, at La Plata, a small barracks on the banks of the La Plata river, on the southern coast of Oriente.

During this period between the disembarkation and prompt defeat at Alegría de Pío and the battle of El Uvero, our troop was composed primarily of a single guerrilla group, led by Fidel Castro, and it was characterized by constant mobility. (We could call this the nomadic phase.)

Between 2 December and 28 May, the date of the battle of El Uvero, we slowly established links with the city. These relations, during this period, were characterized by lack of understanding on the part of the urban movement's leadership of our importance as the vanguard of the Revolution and of Fidel's stature as its leader.

Then, two distinct opinions began to crystallize regarding the tactics to be followed. They corresponded to two distinct concepts of strategy, which were thereafter known as the *Sierra* and the *Llano*. Our discussions and our internal conflicts were quite sharp. Nevertheless, the fundamental concerns of this phase were survival and the establishment of a guerrilla base.

The peasantry's reactions have already been analyzed many times.

Immediately after the Alegría de Pío disaster there was a warm sentiment of comradeship and spontaneous support for our defeated troop. After our regrouping and the first clashes, simultaneously with repressive actions by the Batista army, there was terror among the peasants and coldness toward our forces. The fundamental problem was: if they saw us they had to denounce us. If the army learned of our presence through other sources, they were lost. Denouncing us did violence to their own conscience and, in any case, put them in danger, since revolutionary justice was speedy.

In spite of a terrorized or at least a neutralized and insecure peasantry which chose to avoid this serious dilemma by leaving the Sierra, our army was entrenching itself more and more, taking control of the terrain and achieving absolute control of a zone of the Maestra extending beyond Mount Turquino in the east and toward the Caracas Peak in the west. Little by little, as the peasants came to recognize the invincibility of the guerrillas and the long duration of the struggle, they began responding more logically, joining our army as fighters. From that moment on, not only did they join our ranks but they provided supportive action. After that the guerrilla army was strongly entrenched in the countryside, especially since it is usual for peasants to have relatives throughout the zone. This is what we call "dressing the guerrillas in palm leaves."

The column was strengthened not only through aid given by peasants and by individual volunteers but also by the forces sent from the National Committee and by the Oriente Provincial Committee, which had considerable autonomy. In the period between the disembarkation and El Uvero, a column arrived consisting of some fifty men divided into five fighting squads, each with a weapon, although the weapons were not uniform and only thirty were of good quality. The battle of La Plata and El Arroyo del Infierno took place before this group joined us. We had been taken by surprise in the Altos de Espinosa, losing one of our men there; the same thing almost happened in the Gaviro region, after a spy, whose mission it was to kill Fidel, led the army to us three times.

The bitter experiences of these surprises and our arduous life in the mountains were tempering us as veterans. The new troop received its baptism of fire at the battle of El Uvero. This action was of great importance because it marked the moment in which we carried out a frontal attack in broad daylight against a well-defended post. It was one of the bloodiest episodes of the war, in terms of the duration of the battle and the number of participants. As a consequence of this clash the enemy was dislodged from the coastal zones of the Sierra Maestra.

After El Uvero I was named Chief of Column Two, later called Column Four, which was to operate east of Turquino. It is worth noting that the column led by Fidel personally was to operate primarily to the west of Mount Turquino, and ours on the other side, as far as we could extend ourselves. There was a certain tactical independence of command, but we were under Fidel's orders and kept in touch with him every week or two by messenger.

This division of forces coincided with the July 26th anniversary, and while the troops of Column One, the José Martí Column, attacked Estrada Palma, we marched rapidly toward Bueycito, a settlement which we attacked and took in our column's first battle. Between that time and January 1958, the consolidation of rebel territory was achieved.

TRANSLATED BY VICTORIA ORTIZ

The United States Rules Cuba, 1952–1958

Morris Morley

The combination of a stubborn Batista who was reluctant to give up power and a nationalist Castro-led guerrilla movement that was articulating radical reformist and anti-U.S. sentiments placed the U.S. government in a difficult position as the events of 1958 unfolded. In the following extract Morris Morley discusses the key dilemmas facing the U.S. "imperial state" and identifies the increasing importance of the CIA in U.S. plans for a post-Batista transition.

The White House and the State Department "were not particularly interested in Cuba affairs" prior to 1958, a stance abruptly transformed by the evolution of a large-scale, antidictatorial nationalist movement with multiple class participants. This development contributed to a now pressing need to elaborate a coherent strategy that could influence the outcome of the political-military struggle and, thereby, limit the possibility of anticapitalist forces gaining control of the Cuban government and state. In this "crisis" context, the State Department, at the operational level, assumed the primary responsibility for ensuring an antistatist and procapitalist resolution of the struggle. . . .

The abrupt deterioration in the politico-military situation of the Batista dictatorship created initial confusion within the State Department and other involved agencies, forcing officials to hastily improvise new strategies under the pressure of very limited time constraints. Policymakers were now operating in an exceedingly fluid context which drastically weakened their capacity to anticipate and influence the outcome of events. The basic dilemma confronting Washington was articulated by a participant in the tactical debate: "The United States was caught in a dilemma. Nobody was all that enthusiastic about Batista. Everybody understood that he was unpopular, his government corrupt, etc. At the same time, one had great reservations about Castro. Earlier on there seemed to be other options — Castro was not the only anti-Batista movement — but by the summer of 1958 with the failure of the Batista campaign and the consequent rise in Castro's stock, he became the option and all other revolutionary groups had to fall in or fall out."

In early August, the American embassy in Havana transmitted to the State Department a confidential policy paper assessing the various U.S. policy options on a cost-benefit basis. The adherence to a policy of strict neutrality was viewed as "a drifting policy under which we would not use our influence to direct the course of events in Cuba." Political party fragmentation and the polarized social forces presented "overwhelming" obstacles to any effort to implement the electoral option. A strategy to "encourage moderate elements within the Armed Forces and the legal opposition to overthrow Batista and establish a provisional government" offered the greatest likelihood of a future regime "capable of maintaining law and order." The major drawback to a military-civilian coup, according to the policy paper, pertained to the risks and difficulties almost certain to be encountered at the "implementation" level: "How far the United States can go about promoting a change of government by this means is hazardous. Such steps would mean direct intervention for the overthrow of the government of Cuba, and the possibilities of success are problematical. Therefore, it is too risky to attempt." The final alternative, which was favored by Ambassador Smith, was to forego any tampering with the existing government-to-government relationship and "support the Batista government to the extent of complying with our commitments and contractual agreements and not give moral support to the revolutionary opposition."

The paramount concern of the Eisenhower administration was to deny political power to the nationalist forces under the leadership of Fidel Castro. The preferred alternative was a procapitalist government not identified with the excesses of Batista's rule, but oriented to the reconstruction of a more efficient and less corrupt state structure in the interests of external capital accumulation. As one State Department participant in the tactical deliberations explained: "I didn't know anybody in the State Department that thought Castro would make a good head of state. It certainly wasn't in our interest to have him get in. . . . Nobody in the State Department wanted Castro to get in." Within the executive branch, the possibility of a nationalist guerrilla-led regime reinforced the ever-present ideological concerns of U.S. policymakers at this time:

> What motivated the policymakers was the belief that the situation in Cuba could not continue without an explosion and the hope was that liberalization, modernization of what was hoped to be a gradualist process would avert an explosion which, in terms of East-West business, would provide opportunities for the growth of communism and, by extrapolation, the growth of Soviet influence. The result was a strong belief that Batista was no good, that the system was rotten, and that there was going to be a change

and it would be in our interest that the change be one of moderation and not an extreme change.

The problem of sifting through the various strategy options, and settling on an appropriate response, was made more difficult by Batista's intransigent refusal to capitulate to Washington's requests for his voluntary resignation in favor of a transitional antidictatorial, anti-Castro regime. Fearing that Batista's obstinacy would increase the chances of "a more extreme reaction, a government extremely hostile to the United States," State Department officials ultimately decided upon a multifaceted strategy to forestall, at one and the same time, the guerrilla challenge, oust Batista from political power, and impose an interim government composed of selected (anti-Castro) civilian and military individuals hostile to the Batista dictatorship. The CIA became the designated instrumentality in this "last gasp" imperial state effort to prevent a nationalist guerrilla victory. In a top-secret memorandum to President Eisenhower in October, acting secretary of state Christian Herter outlined the immediate strategic priorities:

> The Department has concluded that any solution in Cuba requires that Batista must relinquish power whether as chief of state or as the force behind a puppet successor. . . . The Department clearly does not want to see Castro succeed to the leadership of the government. . . . Therefore, we have been and are attempting in every appropriate way, through all means available, *without openly violating our nonintervention commitments*, to help create a situation in which a third force could move into the vacuum between Batista and Castro. . . .

U.S. Policy and the Role of the Central Intelligence Agency

The global "Cold War" "foundations" of the CIA dictated its overall view of Cuba during the 1950s: "[Cuba was assessed] largely in a geopolitical context. This was an area of the world that was guaranteed against foreign influence by American power." The CIA was a pervasive presence in Batista's Cuba, developing "assets" and "liaisons" throughout the political, social, coercive, and administrative fabric of Cuban society and its state structure: "A lot of people that the CIA worked with in 1958 — liaison contacts — were a part of the Cuban structure. The CIA penetrated all institutions during the Batista period, including the security forces and the labor movement, to build up 'plumbing' or propaganda outlets." For the duration of Batista's rule, the CIA performed basically as an instrument of executive branch policymakers. The deputy director of Central Intelligence, General Charles Cabell, described the relationship between the covert agency and the State Department: "whatever we were doing in Cuba was at the direction of, and with the authority of, the incumbent Secretary of State." In discussing the activities of agency field personnel, a Havana embassy official commented: "They did exactly what they were told to do."

After December 1956, the CIA began to reassess the notion of Cuba as a "safe precinct" and to advocate the construction of a long-range strategy to take account of the renewal of the historic guerrilla struggle for national liberation. During 1957 and 1958, agency field officers sided with those embassy "liberals" who expressed concern over the increasing fragility of the military regime's social and institutional supports, maximized the seriousness of the emerging guerrilla challenge, and raised the possibility that these rurally based nationalists might eventually threaten Batista's hold on political power:

> The CIA during this period was relatively alert to the fact that the Batista government was going to fall once Castro got into the hills. There was considerable dissension between the two CIA chiefs of station in a row and the Ambassadors, Gardner and Smith, over Castro. . . . CIA-Embassy relations in 1958 were split. . . . The CIA people, while conservative, joined the liberal Embassy clique of [Richard] Cushing, [Daniel] Braddock, and [John] Topping. . . . Ambassadors Smith and Gardner were both absolutely convinced that Castro wasn't going to come out of the hills. They believed what Batista told them and didn't see that changes were going to come.

In late 1958, as U.S. policy responses increasingly tended to embrace the clandestine option, the CIA began to assume an important policy advisory role in planning the most appropriate strategies to realize immediate imperial state policy goals. Acting Secretary of State Herter noted as much in his confidential October memorandum to President Eisenhower: "the Department has been given increased attention to the Cuban problem and what, if anything, this government might appropriately do to encourage a solution short of a blood bath which could result there. We are consulting regularly with the Director of the CIA and his staff in an effort to develop courses of action which might lead to a viable solution."

The CIA, according to deputy director of plans Richard Bissell, played an instrumental role in the executive branch efforts to apply the "intermediate solution": "We were quite involved in some efforts to persuade Batista to step down voluntarily in favor of a group that he might designate." The refusal of Batista to accede to these pressures led agency officials to lobby for an alternative (longer-term) strategy that would, at a minimum, limit the impact of a victorious antidictatorial movement under guerrilla leadership. As one covert agency official in Cuba at the time observed: "The CIA prediction was that

Castro would come out of the hills but into a vacuum in Havana. Better that he come into Havana into a coalition government. . . . The CIA wanted Castro in a context of checks and balances."

The agency envisaged, in other words, the development of imperial "satellites" within the amorphous nationalist movement that could substantially encumber and influence the direction of any Castro-led government.

This CIA notion of "checks and balances" was, to some extent, appropriated by the State Department in the waning days of Batista's rule. "With Batista out and an interim government in," a then-department Cuba specialist declared, "Castro and the 26th of July Movement would have been effectively, if not totally, isolated. Or they would have had to come into the picture with other elements." Ultimately, these and other belated attempts by the U.S. imperial state to take charge, and shape the direction, of events in Cuba were unable to derail the imminent success of a political revolution hegemonized by nationalist guerrillas—one historical "moment" in a complex ongoing process of societal transformation and socialist reconstruction. Castro's call for a revolutionary general strike at the end of December administered the coup de grâce to these imperial endeavors. In the struggle for state power after 1959, the ease with which the guerrilla political leadership, rooted in a mobilized working-class constituency, was able to destroy the fragile social-class institutions of the bourgeoisie and the old state structure decisively undermined the capacity of the U.S. imperial state to apply successfully the "checks and balances" strategy.

For complete references and notes, consult the work as cited in the acknowledgment of copyrights section.

The Cuban Story in the *New York Times*

Herbert L. Matthews

In early 1957, with the Batista government claiming that Fidel Castro was dead and his band of rebels defeated, New York Times *reporter Herbert L. Matthews (1900–1977) traveled to the Sierra Maestra to search out and interview the rebel leader. The interview, published in the* Times *on 24 February 1957, drew world attention to the rebellion and to the lies, brutality, and incompetence of the Batista government—which the United States was still publicly backing.*

Fidel Castro, the rebel leader of Cuba's youth, is alive and fighting hard and successfully in the rugged, almost impenetrable fastnesses of the Sierra Maestra, at the southern tip of the island.

President Fulgencio Batista has the cream of his army around the area, but the army men are fighting a thus-far losing battle to destroy the most dangerous enemy General Batista has yet faced in a long and adventurous career as a Cuban leader and dictator.

This is the first sure news that Fidel Castro is still alive and still in Cuba. No one connected with the outside world, let alone with the press, has seen Señor Castro except this writer. No one in Havana, not even at the United States embassy with all its resources for getting information, will know until this report is published that Fidel Castro is really in the Sierra Maestra.

This account, among other things, will break the tightest censorship in the history of the Cuban Republic. The Province of Oriente, with its two million inhabitants, its flourishing cities such as Santiago, Holguín, and Manzanillo, is shut off from Havana as surely as if it were another country. Havana does not and cannot know that thousands of men and women are heart and soul with Fidel Castro and the new deal for which they think he stands. It does not know that hundreds of highly respected citizens are helping Señor Castro, that bombs and sabotage are constant (eighteen bombs were exploded in Santiago on 15 February), that a fierce government counterterrorism has aroused the people even more against President Batista.

Throughout Cuba a formidable movement of opposition to General Batista has been developing. It has by no means reached an explosive point. The rebels in the Sierra Maestra cannot move out. The economic situation is good. President Batista has the high officers of the army and the police behind him, and he ought to be able to hang on for the nearly two years of his present term that are still left. . . .

Because of the complete censorship, Havana and the other Cuban cities crackle with the most astonishing rumors; one constantly encouraged by the government has been that Fidel Castro is dead. Only those fighting with him and those who had faith and hope knew or thought he was alive — and those who knew were very few and in the utmost peril of their lives if their knowledge was traced.

This was the situation when the writer got to Havana on February 9 to try to find out what was really happening. The censorship has been applied to foreign correspondents as well as Cuban. What everybody, even those who wanted to believe, kept asking was: "If Fidel is alive, why does he not do or say something to show that he is?" Since 2 December he had kept absolutely quiet — or he was dead.

As I learned later, Señor Castro was waiting until he had his forces reorganized and strengthened and had mastery of the Sierra Maestra. This fortunately coincided with my arrival and he had sent word out to a trusted source in Havana that he wanted a foreign correspondent to come in. The contact knew as soon as I arrived and got in touch with me. Because of the state of siege, it had to be someone who would get the story and go out of Cuba to write it.

Then came a week of organization. A rendezvous point and a time had to be fixed and arrangements made to get through the government lines into the Sierra Maestra.

After the first few weeks the army had given out the report that the remnants of Señor Castro's forces were being starved out in the Sierra. In reality the army had ringed the Sierra with fortified posts and columns of troops and had every road under heavy guard. The reports reaching Havana that frequent clashes were taking place and that the government troops were losing heavily proved true.

The first problem was to get through the government roadblocks and reach a nearby town that would be a jumping off place. Late on the afternoon of Friday, 15 February, Señor Castro's contact man got in touch with me in Havana with the news that the meeting was set for the following night in the Sierra and that Señor Castro and his staff would take the chance of coming a little way toward the edge of the range so that I would not have to do too much climbing. There are no roads there, and where we were to meet, no horses could go.

A pensive Fidel on the eve of victory. From Martin, *Early Fidel*, between 160 and 161.

To get from Havana to Oriente (more than five hundred miles away) on time meant driving all night and the next morning, so as to be ready Saturday afternoon to start for the Sierra.

The plan worked out to get through the army's roadblocks in Oriente was as simple as it was effective. We took my wife along in the car as "camouflage." Cuba is at the height of the tourist season and nothing could have looked more innocent than a middle-aged couple of American tourists driving down to Cuba's most beautiful and fertile province with some young friends. The guards would take one look at my wife, hesitate a second, and wave us on with friendly smiles. If we were to be questioned a story was prepared for them. If we were searched the jig would be up.

In that way we reached the house of a sympathizer of Señor Castro outside the Sierra. There my wife was to stay amid warm hospitality, and no questions asked. I got into the clothes I had purchased in Havana "for a fishing trip," warm for the cold night air of the mountains and dark for camouflage. . . .

Señor Castro was encamped some distance away, and a soldier went to announce our arrival and ask whether he would join us or we should join him.

Later he came back with the grateful news that we were to wait and Fidel would come along with the dawn. Someone gave me a few soda crackers, which tasted good. Someone else stretched a blanket on the ground, and it seemed a great luxury. It was too dark in the grove to see anything.

We spoke in the lowest possible whispers. One man told me how he had seen his brother's store wrecked and burned by government troops and his brother dragged out and executed. "I'd rather be here fighting for Fidel, than anywhere in the world now," he said.

There were two hours before dawn, and the blanket made it possible to sleep.

With the light I could see how young they all were. Señor Castro, according to his followers, is thirty, and that is old for the 26th of July Movement. It has a motley array of arms and uniforms, and even a few civilian suits. The rifles and the one machine gun I saw were all American-discarded models.

The captain of this troop was a stocky Negro with a black beard and mustache, a ready brilliant smile, and a willingness for publicity. Of all I met, only he wanted his name mentioned—Juan Ameda [Almeida], "One of the Eighty-two."

Several of the youths had lived in the United States and spoke English; others had learned it at school. One had been a professional baseball player in a minor league, and his wife is still in the United States.

The part of the Sierra we were in grows no food. "Sometimes we eat; sometimes not," one rebel said. On the whole they obviously keep healthy. Supporters send in food; the farmers help, trusted couriers go out and buy supplies, which the storekeepers sell them at great risk and against government orders.

Raúl Castro, Fidel's younger brother, slight and pleasant, came into the camp with others of the staff, and a few minutes later Fidel himself strode in. Taking him, as one would at first, by physique and personality, this was quite a man—a powerful six-footer, olive-skinned, full-faced, with a straggly beard. He was dressed in an olive-gray fatigue uniform and carried a rifle with a telescopic sight, of which he was very proud. It seems his men have something more than fifty of these, and he said the soldiers feared them.

"We can pick them off at a thousand yards with these guns," he said.

After some general conversation we went to my blanket and sat down. Someone brought tomato juice, ham sandwiches made with crackers, and tins of coffee. In honor of the occasion, Señor Castro broke open a box of good Havana cigars, and for the next three hours we sat there while he talked.

No one could talk above a whisper at any time. There were columns of government troops all around us, Señor Castro said, and their one hope was to catch him and his band.

The personality of the man is overpowering. It was easy to see that his men adored him and also to see why he has caught the imagination of the youth of Cuba all over the island. Here was an educated, dedicated fanatic, a man of ideals, of courage, and of remarkable qualities of leadership. . . .

Castro is a great talker. His brown eyes flash, his intense face is pushed close to the listener, and the whispering voice, as in a stage play, lends a vivid sense of drama.

"We have been fighting for seventy-nine days now and are stronger than ever," Señor Castro said. "The soldiers are fighting badly; their morale is low and ours could not be higher. We are killing many, but when we take prisoners they are never shot. We question them, talk kindly to them, take their arms and equipment, and then set them free.

"I know that they are always arrested afterward and we heard some were shot as examples to the others, but they don't want to fight, and they don't know how to fight this land of mountain warfare. We do.

"The Cuban people hear on the radio all about Algeria, but they never hear a word about us or read a word, thanks to the censorship. You will be the first to tell them. I have followers all over the island. All the best elements, especially all the youth, are with us. The Cuban people will stand anything but oppression."

I asked him about the report that he was going to declare a revolutionary government in the Sierra.

"Not yet," he replied. "The time is not ripe. I will make myself known at the opportune moment. It will have all the more effect for the delay, for now everybody is talking about us. We are sure of ourselves.

"There is no hurry. Cuba is in a state of war but Batista is hiding it. A dictatorship must show that it is omnipotent or it will fall; we are showing that it is impotent."

The government, he said with some bitterness, is using arms furnished by the United States, not only against him but "against all the Cuban people."

"They have bazookas, mortars, machine guns, planes, and bombs," he said, "but we are safe in here in the Sierra; they must come and get us and they cannot."

Señor Castro speaks some English, but he preferred to speak in Spanish, which he did with extraordinary eloquence. His is a political mind rather than a military one. He has strong ideas of liberty, democracy, social justice, the need to restore the Constitution, to hold elections. He has strong ideas on economy too, but an economist would consider them weak.

The 26th of July Movement talks of nationalism, anticolonialism, anti-imperialism. I asked Señor Castro about that. He answered, "You can be sure we have no animosity toward the United States and the American people."

"Above all," he said, "we are fighting for a democratic Cuba and an end to the dictatorship. We are not antimilitary; that is why we let the soldier prisoners go. There is no hatred of the army as such, for we know the men are good and so are many of the officers.

"Batista has eight thousand men in the field against us. I will not tell you how many we have, for obvious reasons. He works in columns of two hundred; we in groups of ten to forty, and we are winning. It is a battle against time and time is on our side."

[When Matthews published his book in 1961, he added the following caveats to the 1959 story:]

For the historic record, a few minor errors in the *Times* story should be noted. It was not true that the Archbishop of Santiago de Cuba, Monseñor Enrique Pérez Serantes, saved Fidel's life. This is a myth that still persists. Orders had been given to kill Fidel on sight when captured after the 26th of July attack. The man who caught him, Lieut. Pedro Sarría, disobeyed orders and brought Fidel in alive.

I overestimated the size of Fidel's forces in the Sierra Maestra at the time. When asked, I said I had seen about twenty-five rebels and knew there were others nearby — perhaps forty in all. This was correct, but I was wrong to think the group I saw was a part of a large force. As Fidel revealed in a speech to the Overseas Press Club in New York in April 1959, he had only eighteen men under arms at that time. The number I saw was swelled by those from the 26th of July Movement who had come in with me.

My story, in fact, came at the ebb tide of the flood that was to lead Fidel on to fortune.

Fidel and his men had done more than come down "a little way toward the edge of the range," as I wrote. They had come a long way — from Pico Turquino — and, as those who went up later to see him discovered, it took about two days of walking and climbing, not three hours, to reach him.

He had, in fact, put himself well into the region controlled by Batista's troops, taking a really great risk to contact me. The whispering was not histrionics; it was a necessity. Fidel told me years later in Havana that they did not wait a minute after I left to dash back toward the mountain tops, and they heard they had narrowly escaped an ambush.

My estimate that the rebels had "something more than" fifty telescopic rifles was way off the mark. At all times in the next two years the size of Fidel's forces was greatly exaggerated. He neither needed nor wanted large fighting forces. The technique he used was explained so well after the victory by Che Guevara in his *La Guerra de Guerrilla* (*Guerrilla Warfare*) that the book is now used as a text by the United States Special Forces units.

Finally, I would never again call Raúl Castro "pleasant."

V

Building a New Society

The Cuban Revolution of 1959 was one of the most profound revolutions in Latin American history — in many ways more profound than the nineteenth-century wars for independence, which, despite the enormous human and material destruction, and despite the winning of political independence, did not overturn the structures of Latin American society. The Cuban revolution was part of the worldwide anticolonial and revolutionary ferment that followed World War II. The post-Stalinist, Third World revolutionary Marxism that it helped to define was also a factor in the emergence of a youthful New Left in Europe and the United States.

The Cuban revolutionary experiment was nothing if not audacious. Not only would politics, economics, and society be completely transformed; human beings themselves would be re-created — the new society would seek to create a "new man." In some ways, the revolution revived independence-era ideologies that linked colonial domination with domestic inequality and oppression. But in the context of the 1950s and 1960s, Cuban revolutionaries learned from, and contributed to, a new anti-imperialist, antiracist dynamic that grew throughout the newly defined Third World.

In the United States, this dynamic tended to be perceived in Cold War terms — and indeed, the Soviet Union sought to present itself as a defender of colonial peoples struggling against capitalist oppressors (at least those outside of its own sphere of influence). While Cuba became a key player in this Cold War drama, it was also playing out a struggle that had its own domestic roots and logic, at the same time as it symbolized the need for Third World peoples to escape from U.S. hegemony and take their destiny into their own hands.

The locus of the Revolution shifted toward the Left in the first two years. This happened because of pressure from below from workers, agricultural laborers, and peasants anxious to broaden and deepen the initial cautious policies of the new government and as U.S. resistance to economic nationalism and social reform initiated a series of "tit-for-tat" political and economic retaliatory measures in foreign policy that led to the breaking of diplomatic re-

René de la Nuez, "En Cuba Sí" (In Cuba, yes), 1963. De Juan, *Pintura Cubana*.

lations. Along with these factors came a growing economic reliance on the Soviet Union, which increasingly through the late 1960s and 1970s shaped the path of the revolution politically and socially as well as economically.

The agrarian reform, enacted in the summer of 1959, set the stage for an aggressive commitment to redistribution of the country's wealth and for a new definition of patriotism that required sacrifice on the individual's part for the good of the nation as a whole. On announcing the agrarian reform, Fidel Castro stated—in one of the passionate and lengthy speeches that came to characterize his public presence—"Great landowners must understand that their duty is to adapt themselves to the new circumstances. . . . This measure is fair, because not a single Cuban must suffer from hunger. It is criminal that there be uncultivated land in a country where people are hungry. These landowners must not allow selfishness to blind them. No one has the right to be selfish when his people is hungry. No one who feels like a Cuban, no real patriot, can fail to understand that this measure will be of benefit to the Nation."[1] Nationalization as a policy gained strength until 1968, when the last remnants of the private economy were essentially abolished.

Observers have continued to debate the impact, and merits, of Cuba's growing dependence on the Soviet Union in the late 1960s and through 1989. In the economic sphere, it meant that Cuba reproduced the old, colonial pattern of reliance on exportation of a single crop—sugar—with the important difference that the USSR chose, for political reasons, to subsidize Cuba's economy, instead of profiting from it as had previous colonial powers. In the political sphere, Cuban leaders found themselves obligated to support the USSR when it might have been more in their interest not to, though they also continued to blaze their own trail and sometimes challenge Soviet policies on the international level. At home, Cuba's political leaders adopted many institutions and forms from the Soviets that both solidified the revolution and limited its possibilities. Culturally, however, the Soviets seem to have had little impact on the island. It is U.S. culture that continues to attract Cubans of all ages, whereas the Soviets are more often the recipients of rueful, or acid, humor.

Note

1. Fidel Castro, "On the promulgation of the Agrarian Law," 17 May 1959.

And Then Fidel Arrived

Carlos Puebla

To give some of the flavor of the heady early days of the revolution, we begin with two songs (this and the next selection). "En eso llegó Fidel" by Carlos Puebla captures the sense of "Fidelismo" and the ways that the revolution symbolized the death of the old, corrupt Cuba and the birth of a new one. Born in Manzanillo in 1917, poet and composer Carlos Puebla (d. 1989) made his debut on a provincial radio station but gained much greater popularity in 1952 when he formed the group Los Tradicionales. They often played at La Bodeguita del Medio, a Havana restaurant and bar famous for the artists, writers, and assorted Bohemian types that frequented it. Today the Bodeguita has become a popular tourist destination.

Aquí pensaban seguir
ganando el ciento por ciento
con casas de apartamentos
y echar al pueblo a sufrir
y seguir de modo cruel
contra el pueblo conspirando
para seguirlo explotando
y en esto llegó Fidel.
Coda:
Y se acabó la diversión,
llegó el comandante y mandó a parar.
(bis)

Aquí pensaban seguir
tragando y tragando tierra
sin sospechar que en la sierra
se alumbraba el porvenir
y seguir de modo cruel
la costumbre del delito
hacer de Cuba un garito
y en eso llegó Fidel.

Aquí pensaban seguir
diciendo que los cuatreros,
forajidos, bandoleros
asolaban al país
y seguir de modo cruel
con la infamia por escudo
difamando a los barbudos,
y en eso llegó Fidel.

Aquí pensaban seguir
jugando a la democracia
y el pueblo que en su desgracia
se acabara de morir
y seguir de modo cruel
sin cuidarse ni la forma,
con el robo como norma,
y en eso llegó Fidel.

They were planning to stay on here
earning 100 percent (on their investments)
with apartment houses and the like
while the people suffered
and to continue in a cruel manner
conspiring against the people
to stay on exploiting it
and then Fidel arrived
And that was the end of the party
the commander arrived and ordered (all that) to stop

They were planning to stay on here,
taking in more and more land
without suspecting that in the mountains
the future was lighting up
and to continue in a cruel manner
the custom of crime
to turn Cuba into a gambling den
and then Fidel arrived.

They were planning to stay on here
saying that cattle thieves,
outlaws, highwaymen,

were destroying the country,
and to continue in a cruel way
with infamy as their shield
defaming the bearded ones,
and that's when Fidel arrived.

They were planning to stay on here
playing democracy
and the people in its misery
was to end up their days
and to continue in a cruel way
without even bothering with appearances
with theft as their norm,
and that's when Fidel arrived.

TRANSLATED BY AVIVA CHOMSKY

Tornado

Silvio Rodríguez

"Rabo de nube" (Tornado) by Silvio Rodríguez, in less explicit and more abstract terms, addresses the same sense of doing away with the old order and creating the world anew. Rodríguez exemplifies the nueva trova, the Cuban version of Latin America's "New Song" movement of the 1960s and 1970s. All over the continent, this movement attempted to create a socially conscious and artistically original Latin American music, in part as a response to a growing domination of the airwaves by highly commercialized foreign music. Cuban singer-songwriters Silvio Rodríguez (b. 1946) and Pablo Milanés (b. 1943) gained worldwide acclaim for their contributions.

If they told me to make a wish,
I'd choose a tornado,
a whirlwind on the ground
and a great fury that rises.
A sweeper-away of sadnesses
a downpour in revenge
which when the sky clears would look like
our hope.

It they told me to make a wish
I'd choose a tornado
which would take away the ugly
and leave us the sweetness
A sweeper-away of sadnesses,
a downpour in revenge
which when it clears looks like
our hope.

TRANSLATED BY AVIVA CHOMSKY

Castro Announces the Revolution

Fidel Castro

On 1 January 1959 Fulgencio Batista and his government fled Cuba as the 26th of July Movement troops marched into Havana. One of the last bastions to fall was the infamous Camp Columbia military barracks outside of the city. On 9 January Fidel Castro exhorted the people of Havana to follow him to Columbia — quickly renamed Ciudad Libertad, or Freedom City, and turned into an educational complex that today houses Havana's main teaching college as well a network of primary and secondary schools. From the new Freedom City, Castro emphasized the peaceful, popular, and on-going nature of the revolution. The speech is vague in programmatic terms but strong in moral exhortations. The assumption of national unity around moral and political goals underlies some of the most profound contradictions of the revolution.

I recall, from my first impressions as a boy, those revolutionaries who went around wearing .45 pistols in their belts and wanted to do things their own way. One had to fear them because they were capable of killing anyone. They went to the officers of high officials, threatening them in order to obtain what they wanted, which these officials had to give them. And in fact, one wonders: where is the revolution they undertook? Because there was no revolution and there were very few revolutionaries. The first question those of us who undertook the revolution must ask ourselves is what our intentions were in doing so, and whether an ambition, an ignoble desire, was hidden in any of us. We must ask ourselves if each of the combatants in this revolution had a firm and heartfelt idea or thought because of some egotistical goal or in the pursuit of other unknown but inadmissible goals.

If we undertook this revolution thinking that if only the tyranny were overthrown, we could enjoy the advantages of power, planning to mount the throne and live like a king, in a little palace, expecting life to be a lark for us from then on, if this was why we became revolutionaries, if we thought of removing one minister in order to impose another, to remove one man to impose another, it would not have been worth the trouble undertaking the revolution. But I know that in each one of us there was a real spirit of sacrifice. I know that in each one of us there was a desire to do this, expecting no reward. And if we were ready to give up everything in advance, we were ready also to carry out our duty as sincere revolutionaries.

This question must be asked because the fate of Cuba, of ourselves and of the people, may depend to a great extent on this examination of our consciences. When I hear talk of columns, of battle fronts, of troops, I always reflect. Because here our strongest column, our best unit, the only troops capable of winning the war alone are the people.

No general can do more than the people. No army can do more than the people. I was asked what troops I would prefer to command, and I answered I would prefer to command the people. Because the people are unconquerable and it was the people who won this war, because we had no army, we had no fleet, we had no tanks, we had no planes, we had no heavy guns, we had no military academies or recruiting and training teams. We had neither divisions nor regiments nor companies nor platoons, but we have the confidence of the people, and with this alone we were able to win the battle for liberty.

The people have won this war. And I say this in case anyone believes that the people have been deceived. And therefore, the people are more important than anything. But there is something else: the revolution does not serve my interests as a person, nor those of any other commander or captain. The interests the revolution serves are those of the people. . . .

And I want to tell the people and the mothers of Cuba that I will resolve all problems without shedding a drop of blood. I tell the mothers that they will never, because of us, have to weep. I want to ask the people, all responsible men, to help us to resolve these problems and when we are threatened with an action . . . this is immoral. I say here, moreover, that we will not access [succumb] to these threats, because this would be to dishonor the revolution and to compromise its success and consolidation. Let those who are not members of the regular forces of the Republic return the weapons to the barracks, because there are more than enough weapons here now, and it has been proven that weapons are only needed when one has to defend the right and the people. They are not for committing misdeeds.

I want to tell the people that they can be sure that the laws will be respected, because there is no egotism or partisanship here. However, on the day the people order that weapons be taken up to guarantee their law, their peace and their right, then these weapons which are under my jurisdiction will be taken up again to fulfill their duty. . . .

As of the present, the military battles have ended. Tomorrow we will have another day of peace like all the rest. We have become accustomed to war. For a long time, we did not know what peace was. But we must learn to work to pay the rent, the electrical bills, etc. I know that the young people are deeply imbued with the enthusiasm which will change the Republic. I am certain of it, and also of the fact that there is a president who has the confidence of the people, because no danger threatens. The position of the president is established, and has now been recognized by almost all the nations in the world. Nothing can threaten him, and he has the support of the people, our support and that of the revolutionary forces. This is true support, support without revolution and without danger. For us, this step is above suspicion because we have fought without ambition and full of the greatest hopes, faith, and without the slightest doubt.

Thus, now we must work hard. For my part, I will do all I can to the benefit of the country. And I with all of my comrades stand with the president of the Republic and all the other Cubans. I hope that the triumph of consolidation will not be long in being achieved.

I see an extraordinary spirit of cooperation in all sectors of the people, among the journalists and in all the other sectors of the country. We will make a tremendous advance. The Republic will be free of all petty politicking, vice, and gambling. And now it is the Republic which will resolve all the problems. . . . Because I am not a professional military man or an army careerist. I was a military man as short a time as possible. I am not going to engage in military war undertakings with neighboring countries, because if it is desired to fire shots, I believe that there is plenty of room here in Cuba to do so.

If we do not resolve all these problems it means an incomplete revolution, because I believe that the basic problem of the Republic, following the triumph, is work, and this is the way to resolve the problems.

TRANSLATED BY FBIS (FOREIGN BROADCAST INFORMATION SERVICE)

How the Poor Got More

Medea Benjamin, Joseph Collins, and Michael Scott

Nutritionist Medea Benjamin lived in Cuba from 1979 to 1983, among other things, working with Joseph Collins and Michael Scott for a project for the Institute for Food and Development Policy about food and hunger in Cuba. After living for eight years in Africa and Latin America, Benjamin writes, "I had had my fill of starving children dying in my arms for want of clean water or a meager plate of food. . . . Landing in Havana, I remember feeling that I had entered the kingdom of heaven. The head of the Nutrition Institute laughed when I told her I wanted to work with malnourished children. . . . What an immense pleasure to live in a society that had abolished hunger!"[1] Indeed, Cuba's socially and economically redistributive policies have earned the revolution high praise from many international observers, whereas critics of the revolution have tended to focus more on political issues.

The following selection describes the basic redistributive logic of the revolution and why food rationing became a crucial component of government policy. The purpose of rationing was to ensure the poorest members of society adequate access to food. Despite ongoing problems with food production and availability, rationing has in fact guaranteed Cubans a basic minimum undreamed of by the poor elsewhere in Latin America and the world.

Suppose all of a sudden many people [in the Third World], especially the poor majority, had more money. This was the situation in Cuba in the first several years of the revolution. The revolution's leadership viewed inadequate income as the reason why people were undernourished, so it set into motion policies designed to boost the earnings of the poorer half of society as well as to enlarge the share of their earnings they could afford to spend on food.

But once people had more money to spend on food, it became clear that there was not enough food to go around. How could the government deal with the shortages? One simple solution would have been to let prices rise, thereby reducing the number of Cubans able to buy the food. That would have dealt with the shortages but not with people's hunger. As Prime Minister Castro recalled several years later, "A price policy to compensate for this imbalance [between supply and demand] . . . would have been nothing short of a ruthless sacrifice of that part of the population with the lowest income." Such a policy was acceptable for luxury and nonessential goods "but never for necessities," he added.

Not only would high food prices have contradicted the egalitarian philosophy of the new government, but it would have been counterproductive to winning the broadest possible support for the revolution. "What should we do with what we have, which is more than we had before but still isn't enough? The answer is simple: we must distribute it better," Fidel proposed. In an attempt to find a more equitable form of distribution—by need rather than income—the government opted for rationing.

Money in More Pockets

But let's take a closer look at the developments leading up to the decision to implement a rationing system, starting with efforts to increase the incomes of the poor.

Above all, the government sought to generate fuller employment. Job opportunities for farm workers soared. With the large estates converted into "people's farms" by the first agrarian reform law, there were 150,000 year-round jobs on these lands by August 1962 compared to fewer than fifty thousand in 1959. Sugar plantation workers, previously unemployed during the long "dead season," now found steady work on the construction projects that seemed to be springing up everywhere—roads, schools, clinics, government offices, housing, etc. Early on, the government raised the minimum wage in agriculture but then fought against further wage increases lest there be less money for job creation.

These and other measures made their mark: more and more of even the poorer farm workers had higher incomes than before the revolution. While only 29 percent of rural workers earned more than seventy-five pesos a month as of April 1958, two years later 44 percent did.

Thanks to the new government's policies, many poor farmers also found themselves with more money. By granting generous tracts of land to some one hundred thousand tenant farmers, sharecroppers, and squatters, the first agrarian reform of 1959 freed farmers from the obligation to hand over to absentee landlords as much as 40 percent of the value of their crops. Moreover, they could now obtain cheap credit from the government, as well as count on stable prices for their produce.

In urban areas, many workers won substantial wage increases, thanks to the strength of their unions. No longer did workers' demands for a larger share

Mural *Homage to Cuban Heroes*. Photo by Tania Jovanovic.

of the wealth their labor produced run up against the violent repression of the Batista dictatorship. Even the earnings of the poorest workers notched upward. By one estimate, the lowest 40 percent of income-earners enlarged their slice of the national income "pie" from 6.5 percent before the revolution to 17 percent by 1962.

Gains for the urban unemployed came more slowly, but by 1962 expanding state payrolls and productive investments were sharply cutting unemployment. Of those workers who had found employment for less than six months a year before the revolution, 86 percent were finding work for ten or more months three years later, according to one survey. Higher wages and reduced unemployment meant more money in the hands of poorer urban households, especially those with more than one wage earner.

The new government also sought to enable low-income households to spend more of their earnings on food. It made basic social services free for everyone. Included were not only schooling, medical care, medicines, and social security, but also water, burial services, sports facilities, even public phones. The government lowered the charges for electricity, gas, and public transport that had eaten up so much of working people's earnings. The numbers racket and other forms of gambling that preyed on the incomes of the poor were outlawed. In 1960 the government initiated its "urban reform" by decreeing bold rent reductions of up to 50 percent. A year and a half later, the maximum rent was set at 10 percent of the income of the head of the household. Since many poor families lived in tenement housing notorious for exploitative rents, rent reforms in particular left appreciably more money for them to spend on other things.

The net effect of fuller employment and expanded free or highly subsidized services was a historically unprecedented redistribution of income—the transfer of 15 percent of the national income from property owners to wage earners in the first year alone. In few other societies have the poor and middle classes so rapidly found themselves with "extra money" on their hands.

What did people do with so much extra money? Among the most pressing desires for the poor was to eat more and better. Rural families, freed from landlord obligations and moneylenders, could eat more of what they produced. Peasants who for years had raised pigs but could never afford to eat them, now could. Nationwide consumption of such coveted foods as pork and milk soared; beef consumption shot up by 50 percent in just two years. Even the

"Long live the 26th" (referring to the 26th of July Revolutionary Movement). Photo by Tania Jovanovic.

Demonstrators display the Cuban flag. Photo by Tania Jovanovic.

economically better off wound up consuming more locally produced goods since it was increasingly difficult to go on shopping sprees in Miami or buy luxury imports in Cuba.

Supply Lags Behind Demand

But supply failed to keep pace with the growing demand. Overall agricultural production was handicapped by the flight to the United States of administrative and technical personnel, an elite unwilling to adjust to the new changes. The consequent lack of organization and technical experience on the newly created people's farms and cooperatives lowered production. The Eisenhower administration's 1960 embargo on most exports to Cuba seriously disrupted the island's agriculture, which had become dependent on the United States for farm machinery, fertilizers, pesticides, seeds, and other inputs. In addition, the Central Intelligence Agency fostered acts of sabotage, including burning fields and slaughtering cattle. Such sabotage, as well as repeated military attacks culminating in the Bay of Pigs invasion in April 1961, forced Cuba to divert scarce human and material resources into defense, exacting a toll on production. As if all this were not enough, a severe drought in 1962 further aggravated food production problems. . . .

In a reversal of the pre-1959 pattern, shortages became more chronic in the cities than in the countryside. Finding ever fewer consumer goods to buy, especially imports from the United States, tenants and sharecroppers had little need for cash and thus produced less for the market. Consequently, there was less food in the cities. *Viandas* [starchy accompaniments to the staples—rice, beans, and meat—including plantains and various types of sweet potato] in particular began disappearing from city marketplaces. Plantains . . . were no longer trucked in daily to Havana but consumed in the eastern provinces where they were grown.

Shortages often triggered more shortages since the lack of one item meant greater demand for others. By mid-1961, when taro, a usually abundant root crop, became scarce, people bought out sweet potatoes, putting pressure on the supply of white potatoes, and so on.

The disruption of normal imports further aggravated supply problems. . . . Cuba had become dependent on the import of large quantities of food— wheat, rice, beans, lard, poultry, dairy products, and eggs, even onions and garlic. With over 70 percent of these imports coming from the United States, the abrupt embargo on U.S. trade with Cuba left the country in dire straits. . . .

The U.S. embargo created a myriad of additional import problems. Since Cuba was so close to the United States, its ports and warehouses had been designed for frequent short hauls by small ferryboats from Florida and New Orleans. Once those sources of supply were cut off, Cuba found itself ill-equipped for transoceanic trade. . . .

Cuba depended not only on imports of U.S. food, but also on importing the materials needed to package the food, the machines needed to process the food, the trucks needed to transport the food, and so on. The U.S. trade embargo revealed the true depth of Cuba's food dependence. In the famous Cuban novel *Memorias del Subdesarrollo* (better known outside Cuba in its film version *Memories of Underdevelopment*), the protagonist complains: "For the past few weeks there hasn't been a soft drink to be had anywhere. I never thought that the manufacture of soft drinks could be paralyzed just because there was no cork for the caps. Never . . . could I have imagined how many insignificant things are necessary to keep a country running smoothly. Now you can see everything inside out, all the hidden entrails of the system."

The irony of the mounting food crisis was apparent by the third year of the revolution. Prime Minister Fidel Castro, in a high-level national conference on production in 1961, responded to Western reports about Cuba's shortages: "The problem in Cuba is not one of hunger. That was the problem before, when three to four hundred thousand people didn't have a cent in their pockets. Our problem is precisely that now people have work and have money. . . . While production has gone up since the revolution, it hasn't caught up to the increase

Shoe shine at the port of Old Havana, San Pedro and Luz Streets. Photo by Tania Jovanovic.

in purchasing power. . . . The only way to produce more is to put everyone to work, but by putting everyone to work, we find that the goods and production capacity which existed fall short of the demand created."

Beyond the Free Market

Even in the revolution's first months, it was clear that the ground rules of the "free market" could have taken care of the shortage problem—with higher prices. Under that system, consumers with the highest incomes would pay whatever necessary to eat what they wanted, leaving the remainder to the next highest bidders, and so on down the income ladder until nothing was left. There would never be "shortages" because under the ground rules of the free market, there is no shortage when all effective (money-backed) demand is being satisfied. Thus from the free-market viewpoint, there would not have been a "shortage" of food in Cuba even if it were priced way out of the reach of many poor Cubans.

Cuba's new government knew that under free-market rules, profiteers would quickly corner every scarce commodity to speculate on skyrocketing prices, at least until food supplies caught up with the increased amount of money in people's hands. Whatever early gains in their living standards rural and urban workers had made would just as quickly be wiped out. Such a development was so unacceptable that the government knew it could not wait for the hoped-for production increases. Instead it tried price controls.

Just three months into the revolution the new government set official prices for rice, milk, bread, and beef products. Two months later, in May 1959, the Ministry of Commerce added to the list butter, pork, cheese, potatoes, and other items, including consumer goods such as soap. At the same time the Ministry placed ceilings of 10 and 20 percent respectively on wholesale and retail profit margins. In the subsequent months, the prices of children's foods and virtually all other staples were frozen and added to the list of price-controlled goods.

Still the situation was far from under control. Price controls are extremely difficult to enforce in a society with a multitude of small retailers and with the unwritten law that everyone looks out for him or herself. Speculation as well as hoarding were widespread enough for Fidel Castro to label speculators "the number-one enemy of the revolution."

In an attempt to stem speculation, the wholesale food business was nationalized and those retail stores accused of hoarding and profiteering were taken over by the government. By 1961, some eight thousand retail outlets had been taken over. And in August 1961 a law was passed prohibiting the resale of certain basic goods. At the same time, the government's agrarian reform agency set up *tiendas del pueblo* (people's stores) in the rural areas in an effort to improve the supply of basic consumer goods — at official prices. There were two thousand such stores spread throughout the countryside by 1961. These stores extended credit generously, in contrast to the usury that had been so common.

But try as the fledgling government might, speculators' prices reigned as supply problems multiplied; and it was poor Cubans who were getting the short end of the stick. What was amounting to rationing by income flew in the face of everything the revolutionary leadership stood for. The government might have opted simply to make certain basic staples available to the poor at low prices (and thus to create different diets for the rich and the poor), but they decided instead to institute a rationing system for *all* Cubans, covering the most important food items.

The first item rationed was lard. The neighborhood organizations, known as the Committees for the Defense of the Revolution, were instructed to conduct a "lard census." Based on the census and the total supply of lard, in mid-1961 the government set the maximum amount of lard that any person could buy at one pound per week. In March 1962, the National Board for the Distribution of Foodstuffs was created to ration rice, beans, cooking oil, and lard on a nationwide basis; soap, detergent, and toothpaste in the twenty-six major

Crumbling architecture of Havana. Photo by Tania Jovanovic, c. 1992.

cities; and beef, chicken, fish, eggs, milk, sweet potatoes, and other root crops in Havana only. All these items were eventually rationed throughout the country, and others were added: sugar, salt, bread, cigars and cigarettes, shoes, clothing, cloth, and numerous household items.[2]

Rationing was initially expected to be temporary. At the first National Production Conference, held when only lard was rationed, optimistic officials gave short shrift to problems. Not only would beef shortages be overcome, they predicted, but within eight years Cuba would be exporting $300 million worth of beef annually. With vast increases in pork, poultry, cattle, and dairy production, there would be "protein to spare" by 1963. In his closing address to the conference, Fidel Castro promised an end to lard rationing by 1963, as well as a quick solution to shortages of chicken, beans, root crops, and fish. In 1965, he predicted that food rationing would end the following year.

Cuban leaders were not alone in their optimistic projections during the early 1960s. French agronomist René Dumont, an early adviser to the revolutionary government (and later a strong critic), stressed in September 1960 that "underproduction was such, before the Revolution, that Cuban agriculture cannot but advance, even if errors are still committed." He pointed out that if Cuba were only cultivated with the same intensity as southern China, the island would be able to feed fifty million people, then over seven times Cuba's population. Economist Charles Bettelheim, also a foreign adviser, wrote of Cuba's "absolutely exceptional agricultural possibilities" and noted that "studies made by specialists in agriculture and livestock showed that within a relatively few years (generally from ten to twelve) it will be possible to multiply the production of many commodities by a factor of three, four, five, or even more, without any great investment effort." Such heady optimism emanating from these and other distinguished foreign advisers undoubtedly influenced the Cuban leadership in its conception of rationing as an interim measure.

But everyday reality proved to be far less generous. Rationing, as a way to equitably distribute scarce goods, continues to this day.

Notes

For complete references and notes, consult the work as cited in the acknowledgment of copyrights section.

1. Medea Benjamin, "Things Fall Apart," NACLA *Report on the Americas* 24:2 (August 1990): 13.
2. [Here] we are dealing only with the food ration book (*la libreta de comida*), which in addition to food contains detergent, soap, toilet paper, and cooking fuel. There is a separate ration card (*la libreta de ropa*) for nonfood items such as sheets, towels, shoes, toilet articles, and fabric, as well as ration coupons for gasoline. As with the food items, today [in 1984] many of these same goods are also available off the ration at higher prices (gasoline, for example, costs 1.03 pesos/gal. on the ration and 2.00 pesos/gal. off the ration).

Fish *à la Grande Jardinière*

Humberto Arenal

Novelist and author of numerous collections of short stories that capture, with great compassion and psychological insight, ordinary people's complex relationship to the society they live in, Humberto Arenal (b. 1926) worked as a theater director, traveled widely through Latin America and Europe, and lived in New York from 1948 to 1959, working at the magazine Visión, *before returning to Cuba.*

These pages capture in all their richness and pathos the contradictions unleashed by the passage from the republican to the revolutionary period. The shift to the Left in the program of the revolution in its first two years, which in addition to the (first) land reform included redistribution of urban incomes through rent reductions and the readmission to political life of Cuban Communists (whose party had been banned after Batista's 1952 coup), threatened sectors of Cuban society that had lived comfortably in the old order. In this short story by Arenal, an upper middle-class widow searches for all the imported ingredients—truffles, asparagus, Sensat olive oil, and Spanish sherry—needed to prepare swordfish à la jardinière. While she searches Havana in vain, on public buses, now without a chauffeur, the enormous fish undergoes a grisly process of decomposition in her kitchen. In a clear allegory, yet with humor and affection for the protagonist, Arenal chronicles the decomposition of a certain sector, the Cuban bourgeoisie, unable to adapt to social change, anchored to the past and afraid of the future.

Scale, clean, and rinse well a fish of 10, 20, or more pounds. Place in the pan a generous amount of oil or butter, a pound of veal cut into very small pieces, one quarter-pound of pork belly, a cup of sherry, and a dusting of bleached flour. Cook over a low flame until the meat is well done and tender, stirring constantly; press the veal and bacon through a sieve, squeezing the liquid out into the sauce.

I mean, try to catch the bus, you wait and wait and wait for the 22 and the stupid bus doesn't come, you can go crazy waiting for those damn buses, I mean, when one does come it's full and doesn't stop so you have to wait for the next one, I mean, you really have to be patient, then another one comes that's not so full but it doesn't stop either, and why the hell not?, I mean, so I try to be even more patient and wait, and after a while somebody tells me that they moved the bus stop to the other corner, now it's on Tenth Street, I walk to Tenth Street and wait, then catch the 22, it's full too, completely full, but I get on anyway, on all fours if I have to, to get to Marianao, I mean, and there's Cuca on the bus all the way in the back, I'm up front next to the driver, and she's deafer than ever, I can't understand a word she's saying, she asks me screaming if I know if Jorge is living in Miami, if he's well, if he has a new car or something like that, the truth is I don't know because I'm all upset, and I can't hear a word she's saying, she asks me, screaming, if I know what's going on, so I tell her I can't hear her, and she's on the moon, in a dream, she doesn't know what's going on, so I tell her I can't hear her could she move closer but it makes no difference, she keeps saying eh? eh? and she puts her right hand to her ear, I make signs for her to move closer but she doesn't, finally I get through to where she is and I tell her in a normal voice that I'm going to Marianao to look for some ingredients and she screams *whose parents? is somebody sick?* she says, and I say no, nobody's parents, that nobody's sick, that what I said was *ingredients, in-gre-di-ents for swordfish* and she yells *ingredients, for swordfish?*, looking really surprised when I nod yes with my head and she asks me again, yelling, INGREDIENTS? even louder than before and I mean, earth swallow me up, because everybody is looking at us and listening, especially the militiaman with the green beret and everything in front of us who hasn't taken his eyes off me, you'll see, I'm going to end up in La Cabaña prison, you know, and Cuca just stands there like an idiot waiting for me to answer her, so just to say something, anything, I ask her how Florentino's doing and she says he's much better although right after that she tells me something's wrong with his vision, cataracts or something, and he's going half blind and his heart is bad and he's got something in his prostate, a tumor or something but they can't operate because his blood sugar is high or something, I don't know, but I say, to my-self, how can he be much better with all that?, then I realize that I'm already at Crucero de la Playa so I say good-bye to her and she yells, when are you going to come over? soon, soon, I say and push my way to the door because the bus was starting to move again, and I scream, wait, wait, I'm getting off here, be-cause I wanted to get to that place in Marianao to buy some Sensat olive oil from Spain and a bottle of sherry, and I was thinking how I had to get the pork belly too or else the swordfish recipe wouldn't turn out right and the sun was sticking to my back like a cat because it was around noon and it turned out the guy was a black guy who used to have a sweets shop, an old guy who used to have a sweets shop in the Cerro, that's where I knew him from, but he didn't have olive oil or sherry or anything, just a couple of limes from a little tree he had in the backyard of his house.

In a separate receptacle, strain the juice of thirty cooked tomatoes, one cup of olive oil, two pureed onions, finely chopped parsley, one clove of garlic, crushed, ground pepper to taste, a pinch of nutmeg, sliced asparagus, mushrooms, petit-pois, sliced truffle, salt, the juice of one or two limes; fold this into the previous sauce, then pour the sauce into the kettle in which you are going to cook the fish, being careful to separate out the truffles, mushrooms, asparagus, petit-pois, etc., etc., etc.

"Señora Julia, we have to cook that fish. It's taking up the whole kitchen."

María Pepa was complaining because the fish took up all the available space in the refrigerator. The woman had taken out all of the shelves and put the fish in on the diagonal, occupying the whole space. The potatoes were rotting, the tomatoes as well. The bell peppers, garlic, onions, and limes were spread out all over the kitchen. Some of the potatoes had to be thrown out, and the tomatoes too.

"The smell of that fish is driving me crazy, señora. It's horrible, I can't stand it, it smells a bit off, I think it's rotting. When Niño Lindo comes near it, he smells it and runs away in horror. He knows, animals know these things.

"Be quiet, María Pepa, don't say another word. There's nothing rotten about it. It's a beautiful swordfish. Just the way Pepe liked them."

"I don't think so, señora, I really don't think so. It doesn't smell right to me. The gentleman . . ."

Place the fish in the kettle; cover it with the rest of the sauce and cook over a low flame.

So the driver says he used to be a teacher, and look at him now, I mean life, life you never know who you really work for, my husband used to criticize me for always wanting to save money but now I think he was right, life is hell, says the driver, and forgive me señora for using such a vulgar expression it's just that, and I say that he used to like to enjoy what he had and share it with others, he was a good man, a very good man, I say, too good, and the driver says that you can't be like that, people, forgive me, says the driver, but people are shit, pardon the vulgar expression, señora, the truth is, I say, he wasn't, he was a family man, that's all, everything for his family, and for his friends, he spent his whole life working to help other people, his mother, his brothers, his aunts, all his life he gave to others, that fish business is worrying me a little, but mostly I'm doing it for him since he liked a big baked fish, my cousin Arturo suggested that I prepare it *à la Grande Jardinière* and that's why I'm out looking for Sensat olive oil and sherry, the driver says if we don't find it in Arroyo Apolo we can go to Mantilla to see a woman he knows who has Spanish olive oil and wine and asparagus, asparagus too? I say, and he says, at the very least, I'll find everything for you, don't you worry, señora, in El Cerro, in Miramar, or wherever, we have to help each other out, that's right, I say, because he seems like a nice person and I feel like I can trust him.

. . . when you are ready to serve the fish, garnish it with slices of hard-boiled egg, cucumber, and pickled cocktail onions, the truffles, mushrooms, etc., and the rest of the sauce. Before taking out the sauce, thicken it with a bit of finely grated bread crumbs.

"Mamá is not well, I'm telling you," says the woman.

"It's because of what happened to Papá," says the man.

"I've told her so, you know, I'm tough on her to see how she reacts, I've told her so: if that's the way you feel, then why not just kill yourself, *chica*, and that's that. Why don't you go ahead and do it? The truth is she's more of a woman than a mother, you know what I mean?, and I'm just realizing that now.

"You shouldn't talk to her like that."

"It's so she'll react."

"She's not going to react like that. You're mistreating her."

The woman looks at him.

"And now this whole business with the driver. When she called me today I said, this is too much, and I called Jorge. He took her all over Havana and he charged her twenty-five pesos, twenty-five pesos that I ended up having to pay because she bought olive oil and wine and who knows what else. She spent all the money she had because she wanted to make that fish, you know how she is. You have to help me."

"I don't have a cent. You know I don't have any money, I'm not working now and I'm making what little I have last until I leave."

"And until you leave for Miami . . ."

"For New York."

"For New York or wherever, I'm the one who has to be in charge of everything. It's no good, you know. You and Marta are leaving and I'm left to deal with everything. It's no good."

"The fish wasn't my idea, that's your thing."

"Mamá's thing."

"Whatever, but you deal with it."

"Why don't you tell Mamá that. You're always the good son, the noble son, and I'm the bad one. But I'm the one who's staying here with her, when you and that woman take off."

"You and your husband are revolutionaries. You can keep all of this, sword-fish and all."

Calmly, no, first, rather slowly, perhaps even lazily, but not calmly, nor peacefully, nor with tranquility; and later, a little later, he began to move more hurriedly, with less tranquility, with less peace, with less serenity. The truth was, and the man knew it better than anyone, that he was always anxious, well, maybe not anxious but disgusted and annoyed from the moment the woman told him she had spent twenty-five pesos on a hired car looking all over Havana for Sensat olive oil and sherry and mushrooms and asparagus and all she came up with in Mantilla was a little bottle of sherry that cost ten pesos and the olive oil she bought was Spanish but it wasn't Sensat and the tiny tin of mushrooms she bought was in pretty bad shape. The woman had been crying and he had told her a moment ago that he would help her. He had called Jaime, the driver, and told him to get out the Rolls Royce and oil it, fill it with gasoline, put air in the tires, oil in the motor, and come get him. He had walked from the tele-phone to the table in front of it, one exactly three steps from the other, thinking of all the friends and acquaintances he was going to visit. Ramón in Miramar, and Cristina in Old Havana, and Sigifredo in La Víbora and Juan on Animas Street. They might have the truffles or the asparagus or the Sensat oil or would know of someone who did. They were difficult times and he had to help Julia who had always been like a sister to him. He climbed the stairs. More quickly than usual and when he got to the top he was panting more than usual. His wife was in the room when he went in and she noticed it. He told her he was going out. His wife noticed that he was panting and told him he shouldn't get so agitated. He had to help Julia find the ingredients, he told her. He felt good. It was something he had to do, for her and for all the others. His wife didn't really know who he was referring to, but she repeated that he shouldn't get all worked up. He sent her to get out his blue cashmere suit, his black patent-leather shoes, the white Irish linen shirt, the silk socks, and his red piqué tie. He took a bath and shaved. When he was almost finished shaving he felt a pain in his chest. He closed his eyes and brought his right hand up to the center of his chest. He breathed in deeply and slowly and the pain almost disappeared. He went to the medicine cabinet, took out a little bottle, shook out a pill, and took it. He went to the bedroom and got dressed. As he was going down the stairs he felt the pain again but didn't put his hand to his chest because his wife was coming up the stairs. He told her he was going to be out all afternoon and asked her if Jaime had come. Jaime wasn't there yet. He went to the garden and looked at the flowers. He didn't take care of the garden himself anymore and it wasn't as meticulously groomed as it used to be. He went up to the rosebush, picked a rose, and put it in the buttonhole of his jacket. He went to the gate and looked out to the corner and went back to the same rose bush. He went back to the gate. He opened it and walked out onto the sidewalk. He walked to the corner. Halfway there he felt the pain in his chest. That was, perhaps, the last thing he remembered. Jaime appeared at the corner. His wife, at that very moment, not a moment before or after, appeared at the corner too and saw him lying on the ground.

She was in the center of the kitchen looking at the refrigerator. From where she stood, which was not close, she could smell the stench but she did not want to open it to show la señora Julia the state the fish was in. She had told her a minute ago and the woman had screamed at her to leave her alone. That the fish was not rotten. That there was no stench in the house. That it was just an excuse so she wouldn't have to help her. That she would cook it all by herself. The woman was sitting in the living room, or on the terrace, the other woman didn't know exactly where, with her eyes closed and a napkin soaked in alcohol because she had a terrible migraine. Someone rang the doorbell and the other woman went to open the door. She approached the woman and touched her shoulder. She told her that someone, the next-door neighbor, needed to speak with her. The woman didn't answer. The other woman touched her shoulder again. The woman opened her eyes.

"What is it now, María?"

When she called her María, the other woman knew she was in a bad mood.

"It's the young man from next door, señora, he wants to see you."

She closed her eyes again.

"What does he want?"

"I don't know."

"Tell him I'm not here."

"It's about the fish."

She opened her eyes.

"What about the fish?"

The other woman pulled in her lower lip and crossed her arms.

"Well, the guy says. Look, señora—she had opened her legs and begun to sway—you talk to him. I'm sick of all this."

"I don't have to talk to anybody."

The other woman began walking.

"It's up to you and him, but the truth is that nobody can stand that smell.

That's the truth. Niño Lindo is lost and hasn't come back to the house since yesterday." When she was finished speaking she was almost to the kitchen, which was three or four meters away.

The seated woman stood up. Now she was walking fast. From the kitchen, the other woman could hear the grave, monotonous voice of the man and the now sharp, nervous voice of the woman without being able to make out the details of the conversation. She only heard when the woman began to scream.

"There is no stench, there is no stench, there is no stench!"

She stayed in the kitchen, heating up in a tin can the coffee she had made at lunchtime.

She heard the woman's footsteps and saw her stop in the doorway but she didn't turn around.

"I don't know why you bothered to call me, María. That stupid man has made my headache worse. Get me an aspirin."

When she returned, the other woman said:

"Señora" — she was looking at her, with the little tin can full of coffee in her right hand and the other resting on her waist. "The truth is nobody can stand it. The stench is horrible — she walked to the refrigerator and opened the door — look at this, look at that fish in the corner."

The fish was in pieces and had fallen down.

The woman couldn't see it from where she stood and began to yell:

"There's no stench, there's no stench!"

"It's rotten, señora, it's rotten, can't you see it's rotten," yelled the other woman.

"It's not rotten, there's no stench, it's not rotten, there's no stench, there's no stench. . . ." She walked over to the other woman and began to push her and closed the refrigerator door. "Go away, get out of here, everyone's against me because I'm alone, they're abusing me, there's no stench, Pepe is the only one who's on my side, he will never abandon me, he has never abandoned me. Get out, get out!"

The other woman was going to leave but then she looked at her. She was crying, she was pale, and her hair was a mess.

"Señora," she said, and reached out her hand.

"Just go, María, I tell you, just go!"

The other woman walked to the yard. Then she stopped and looked at her through the window. She had not moved. After that the other woman kept walking without looking back.

When the woman heard the iron gate close, she began to walk around, saying to herself:

"It's not rotten, it's not rotten. There's no stench. There's no stench. It's not rotten. It's not rotten."

She walked through the dining room, the hallways, the living room, the three bedrooms, the bathroom. Repeating:

"It's not rotten, it's not rotten. There's no stench. There's no stench. It's not rotten. It's not rotten."

Once again, she walked through the dining room, the hallways, the living room, the three bedrooms, the bathroom.

Then she went to her bedroom and lay down. For a while, for quite a while. She doesn't know for how long. She lay down on her right side and cried. Her tears dampened the pillow. Little by little she could no longer feel the dampness on the pillow.

María Pepa and Arturo stood next to the head of the bed to ask her if she would come with them to the kitchen. She was very tired, she said, very tired, she repeated, and she wanted to rest. She asked that they leave her alone. María Pepa insisted that she come, and pulled her by the foot. She protested. She was very tired. The other woman pulled her by the foot until she was forced to stand up. Arturo took her by the hand to lead her. María Pepa opened the refrigerator door. Niño Lindo was at her side, at María Pepa's side. The sword-fish was not inside, she told her. She did not want to look. María Pepa insisted. She got a little closer because Arturo pushed her from behind and spoke something right in her ear which she didn't understand but which nonetheless upset her because she perceived the name Bilina, which was what her husband Pepe used to call her. Arturo kept moving her closer, pressing her on with a hand on her back. María Pepa opened the door wider and she covered her face with her hands. They both shouted at her to look, to look. She looked behind her, where Arturo was standing, and he pointed to the refrigerator with his hand. Then she looked. She turned to look at Arturo once more and realized that the fish was no longer there. Then María Pepa screamed: "Look, señora, look." She took a good look. There, inside the refrigerator, was her husband's naked body. She leapt to remove it, and the body began to break up into pieces. She picked up the right hand, the right forearm, the left hand, the left foot, the right foot, the left forearm. The head detached itself from the trunk and fell to her feet. María Pepa ran over, picked it up very carefully and placed it on the table, all the while repeating, "the gentleman, the gentleman, the gentleman, the gentleman." The dog ran around, following her, barking and jumping up and down. She ran back to the refrigerator to extract the rest of the body. It was now breaking up into even smaller pieces, which she tried to pull out with the help of María Pepa who was standing right next to her: a shoulder, a thigh, a buttock, a foot, the other shoulder, part of the chest, the intestines, the heart. She was on her knees and now she stood up. She walked, with the heart in her hand, which was still beating, it was the only part of the body which she had felt warm and alive. María Pepa approached her and she clutched the heart to her breast, covering it with her hands and arms. Niño Lindo was running to her. The other woman asked her to give it to her. She told her that she wouldn't, that it was hers, that it was her husband's heart, all she had left of him. María Pepa ran to the table and picked up the head. The dog followed her, jumping up and down. She ran after her, screaming that she should give it back; María Pepa screaming "no." They kept on running and screaming. What with all that running around, she has no idea when, the heart fell to the ground and the dog picked it up with his teeth. Then it was gone. She let out a cry, a howl, a shriek. She no longer knew if she had been dreaming before or if this was the dream. The accelerated rhythm and sound of her own breathing brought her back to reality. She didn't get up for a little while. She began to smell the fish's odor. The stench she had failed to perceive until then. Right away, or almost right away, or perhaps after a while, she went to the kitchen. She put some paper down on the floor, in front of the refrigerator and opened it. She began to take out the pieces of rotten fish which were everywhere. She wrapped it up in the paper and took the large package out to the backyard, to the garbage can. She threw it in and walked away, without looking back. The flies immediately began to swarm around it, then alight. The silvery white fish was being covered in black.

She walked to her room. She would wait for María Pepa to arrive, and she would say to her:

"It was rotten, María Pepa, it was rotten. You were right."

"I could tell, señora, I could tell a while ago," the other woman would say.

She lay down on the bed, face up, legs stretched out, eyes closed, hands crossed, with fingers intertwined, on her chest. She was feeling herself breathe. Less. Even less. Less all the time. Until she couldn't feel anything.

TRANSLATED BY PAMELA MARIA SMORKALOFF

Women in the Swamps

Margaret Randall

*If the former upper classes viewed the profound redistribution of their society's re-
sources with horror, those sectors of society that had previously been marginalized and
dispossessed had a completely different experience. Even the U.S. government, while
opposing the process, acknowledged that the government's redistributive measures gave
it "enormous popularity" among some 75 percent of the population. "In view of the
government's policy of redistributing income away from foreigners and upper-income
groups to the lowest-income groups and the lower middle classes, it is anticipated that
the standard of living of the great majority of the population will show no serious
decline and may even improve," a U.S. official in charge of evaluating the economic
transformation in Cuba wrote grudgingly. "By such measures as price freezing, arbitrary reductions in rents and utilities, forced wage increases, forced maintenance of
employment, transfers of unutilized urban land, agrarian reform, and other pressures
on foreign and domestic companies, basic steps in the direction of a redistribution of
income have already been taken. In the eleven months that Castro has been in power
the standard of living of low-income groups appears, on the basis of available statistics, to have improved. . . . Income disparities in Cuba are very wide, and the present
trend can probably be maintained for an appreciable period of time."[1]*

*The firsthand accounts of author, photographer, poet, and activist Margaret Ran-
dall (b. 1936), who writes of women's lives in revolutionary Cuba and Nicaragua, have
become feminist classics. In the following selection, four women from the impoverished
Zapata swamp area describe the material, and also the spiritual and psychological,
impact of the revolution's commitment to social change and redistribution of resources
to the poor.*

La Ciénaga, the inhospitable swamp area which includes the Bay of Pigs beach-
head, was one of the areas with the lowest standard of living before the Revolution. Formerly belonging to the Province of Las Villas, it is now included in
Matanzas's easternmost edge.

The American and Cuban counterrevolutionary mercenaries didn't choose
Bay of Pigs carelessly as a place for their all-out attack in April of 1961: as the

poorest and most backward area of the island, they thought people would rally and join them without struggle. What they didn't count on, as is always the case, was the Revolution.

Fidel came to the Ciénaga several weeks after the triumph, in 1959. He landed his helicopter in one of the clearings where the charcoal makers build their huge furnaces and the mountains of wood slowly smolder in the swamp. That was the only possible access. Before the triumph of the Revolution the only entrance to the swamp was a narrow-gage track, which was itself unusably covered over with water more than half the time. An old train made the trip in once a day when it was possible. When it wasn't, the swamp's inhabitants were often cut off from the rest of the island for weeks at a time.

The exploitation wasn't all foreign; Americans had better places to loot. Most of the owners of the big charcoal furnaces and the wood industry were of the Cuban oligarchy; a few were Spaniards. Around their dominions, *caserías*, or collections of miserable thatched huts, sprung up on stilts out of the water. Their occupants were the swamp people: ignorant, backward, totally without schools, medical aid, newspapers, even radios. Sometimes the *cienagueros* heard about the world on the radios that belonged to the bosses. Children didn't wear shoes and their feet were always swollen and split from the wetness. Malaria was a common disease because of the insects bedded in the swamp. Asthma and bronchitis were frequent because of the constant dampness.

The life was incredibly hard; the men hauled the wood after chopping it out of the mountain country. The women helped their husbands watch the furnaces endless days and nights. Everything was black. Sometimes the women helped haul the wood on the flat *chalangas* barges poled through the dull water. The children helped too. Everyone was a part of the same dreary life. . . .

Just past the Australia Sugar Mill, there is a billboard to the right of the highway.[2] It says: EVERYTHING PAST THIS POINT HAS BEEN BUILT BY THE REVOLUTION. "Everything." That means everything: the road, the houses, every shack built near the side of the highway was brought by its peasant owner out from the forgotten in-country, to civilization. Everything. The highway itself was the hardest task; tons of rock and gravel were needed for each meter of marshy earth. A highway into the swamp was an expensive process. Once the road was constructed, the rest was fairly quick and total. By the time of the Bay of Pigs, there were already a fishing cooperative, several new villages, eight doctors on full-time call, polyclinics, schools, the beginnings of a crocodile hatchery. The crocodiles had been rounded up and controlled; up to then they were just another menace in the swamp.

We were eating lunch at La Boca, seaside restaurant and tourist center, where workers and honeymooners fill the stilted cabins reached by small motor boats through the marshy inlets; good food and an organized artisans' workshop testify to the productivity of the project. The natural landscape has been tamed; the swamp is clean and filled with flowers. The women with us were from the provincial and local chapters of the [Cuban] Women's Federation [FMC]. We talked over lunch:

What jobs do the women here do?

They work in the tourist centers, in Guama, at the boarding school, at the Oceanic Institute.

What kinds of jobs at the Oceanic Institute, for instance?

Well, there are teachers, cleaning women, some work in the laundry, telephone operators. The Bay of Pigs Exhibition is there, too.

Is there an FMC regional office here?

Yes, it takes care of the whole area. But now we've gotten to the point where we've become a municipality, with four sectional offices: Agramonte, Torriente, Ciénaga, and Jagüey; Jagüey's the central office.

This whole area used to be part of the Province of Las Villas?

Yes.

Was it hard getting the women to join the Federation in the beginning?

No, it was easy; from the very triumph of the Revolution there was support for everything the Revolution did, because here the change was immediate and radical. A few days after the end of the war, Fidel came here in a helicopter, because there were no roads here, no communication, nothing. Fidel explained the plans they had, where the highways were going to come through. We'd never seen a helicopter in our lives!

But everyone in the swamp knew who Fidel was, being so cut off from civilization?

Yes, we knew who he was. We were cut off from the national reality, but we knew about the struggle because there were a few portable radios in the area. We didn't have any fighters because it was impossible even to walk; you'd be eaten by the crocodiles. There was total ignorance around here, about the tortures, about everything, because there was no communication.

But the people connected the conditions they lived under with Batista's regime, with the oppression? Because, for example, there are many places in all our countries where people are made to believe that their misery is a punishment from God, things like that.

Well, both. There were those who understood the connection with the regime, and those who believed the backwardness was a punishment from above.

How did the women react at first to going to work?

Look, women around here were used to work, because the women made charcoal alongside the men in the hills, so it wasn't difficult for the women to incorporate themselves into the labor force. In the capital, for a woman who had never worked, that was hard, but here any job that the Revolution opened up in a tourist office was easier than working the ovens, burning your feet; that's a miserable job! The change was like night and day here. We had more trouble with the boarding school; the mothers didn't want to let their children go at first. That took a lot of political work, explanations, showing them the school. They saw the attention their children would receive, the hospital. We had to really convince them, because the little ones were barefooted, with swollen bellies, their feet cracked and bleeding. . . .

We turned to talk to Edita, an older woman we'd picked up along the highway, who had also accompanied us:

You've lived here all your life too?

Edita: All my life. We didn't have much to do with the rest of the country. Making charcoal, cutting wood.

Did your mother help your father in that kind of work?

Edita: In our house the women didn't do that kind of work. Only the women who lived farther into the swamp.

Did you study when you were young?

Edita: Where I lived there was a small school. I got as far as first or second grade. After that the teacher just up and left and we didn't have school anymore. Then we started going kilometers to a farm where there was another little schoolhouse, but imagine, when it rained. . . . So I went to work for some people who had money, for five pesos a month. . . .

Were you aware of the attack on Moncada?

Edita: Look, everyone here was very marginal to the Revolution. You might hear something or other, but you never knew directly.

What was the first thing you remember when the triumph came, the first thing that particularly impressed you?

Edita: The women who came in to organize the FMC, the militia, right away most of us joined up. That was because the change here was immediate, and enormous. That is, right after the triumph, right away they started building the highways, houses, right away the leaders came. We began to see that the city people cared about us; some of them hadn't even known we existed back here. The change was for everyone—the doctors who came in, the literacy campaign.

And the attitude of the rebels must have been very different?

Edita: Look, here the guards used to come around looking for pigs and they'd just carry them off. And chickens. That was the way the old army acted with the peasants. Then the change! The rebels were concerned about us, about sending the children to school; here the rebel soldiers did a lot for the peasants, built schools.

I wish you'd tell us more about how you got into this process, because the first thing we heard about you is that you're a primary school inspector; that's a pretty important job. And now I find out that when the Revolution came to power you had a third grade education!

Edita: OK, look, when the revolution triumphed, then they opened the adult schools. I went right off. Afterward I kept on taking the different courses they were giving.

Those were courses offered by the FMC, or by the work places?

Edita: Well, the FMC organized schools in all the different zones, and other organisms, the CDR [Comités de Defensa de la Revolución] shells. A nephew of mine went right out to the launches and we didn't see him again for eight days, and they killed one of his daughters, named Dulce María Martín: this FMC delegation bears her name. So when it cleared, it happened that they wounded one of our men in a leg. I'm telling the whole story.

Tell me how it all seemed to you then.

Amparo: Well, we understood what was happening, seeing all those ships out there, and everything lit up and all that gunfire. You knew you were being attacked.

You were already integrated into the Revolution by that time?

Amparo: Yes, I was organized since 1960, in all the organizations: the FMC, the defense, and later the CDR. They killed our secretary general there, Cira María García. So we went out in a truck and they attacked us there where you turn to go down to Playa Larga. Imagine, later they took us prisoner for twenty-four hours. You can imagine what that was like!

You were in the truck that was attacked by the mercenaries?

Amparo: Yes, we went out in the truck that was sent to get the boy who was wounded in the leg. They didn't even bother to look and see who was huddled there. They just opened fire with a bazooka, right off. They killed my sister, my husband, a niece of mine, and other people like the president of the FMC and others from the "339" from Cienfuegos.[3] That was a bloodbath; that's what it was. The boys from the "339" were in trenches but we were on the truck; it was a flatbed truck and they shot at it because they wanted to; later they told us their orders were to shoot anyone that didn't have their insignia. Even being women, they shot us just the same. They died right off, the ones hit; then the truck caught fire and there was nothing left but the motor. And then the mercenaries picked the rest of us up and took us where they had their headquarters. [She begins to cry] I'm ashamed, 'cause I get upset. . . .

But those were very heroic moments, and they've got to be recorded.

Amparo: Later, they took us in a truck to the dining room where the workers at Playa Larga eat; that's where they had their headquarters and they held us prisoner twenty-four hours.

How did they treat you during those twenty-four hours?

Amparo: Imagine, they started off by killing us; what were they gonna do after that? They talked about how they were entering Colón, how they'd come to liberate Cuba. Practically all of them were strangers; they were going to liberate Cuba from communism, and a whole bunch of atrocities. The next day, the next morning at seven, two more mercenaries came. Ah! First we were at their headquarters and around twelve at night they bombed the gas station and all around us it was burning, so they moved us to the cafeteria; they had the workers prisoner there, and other people too. And the mercenaries told us, "You people take these white sheets and go out on the highway and if you find a militiaman tell him we didn't do anything to you!" They didn't do anything to us! After all they'd done!

Were you wounded?

Amparo: Yes, I was wounded a little. One of the boys from Cienfuegos (later I found out, he was named José Luis Martínez Paredes), José Luis, when I passed him he pulled me down, pulled me by the skirt, and threw me to the ground. That's when they killed him and it seems I was wounded just a little; I lost my hearing, three years without hearing anything.

Without hearing absolutely anything?

Amparo: Yes. Later I was cured, with medicine in Havana. My brother took me, and they gave me electric current and all that because I was a little bad in the head. But later they cured me, completely.

Notes

1. Memorandum from the chairman of the Working Group on the Cuban Economic Situation (Young) to the assistant secretary of state for Economic Affairs (Mann). Washington, 14 December 1959, FRUS (*Foreign Relations of the United States*) 1958–60, p. 702.
2. The Australian Sugar Mill is a large refinery which also served as the high command post during the Bay of Pigs invasion.
3. The "339" was a combat unit that was key in repelling the attack.

Man and Socialism

Ernesto "Che" Guevara

Explicitly addressing the issue of the "new man," this excerpt is from an essay by the Argentinean Che Guevara, who fought in the revolution and contributed so much to shaping its direction in the early 1960s. He remains a very important revolutionary leader, martyr, and myth in Cuba today. Between 1962 and 1966 Cubans (and some foreign advisers) engaged in a wide-ranging debate over the economic, political, and ethical strategies involved in the building of a noncapitalist order. In what became known as the "Great Debate," Guevara maintained that a transition from capitalism to communism required the abandonment of market mechanisms and material incentives used to motivate workers. A true communist society, he argued, required the adoption of moral incentives by the "new man" and a radical diminution of the role played by money and markets.

The emphasis on promoting economic change via the radicalization of peoples' consciousness grew in the years following Guevara's departure from Cuba in 1965 and led to the campaign to produce ten million tons of sugar in 1970. The failure to reach this target and the damage done to the Cuban economy during the attempt led to a major reorientation of politics and economics in the 1970s and 1980s.

Critics have pointed out that Che's concept required a moral conformity and suggested a type of social engineering at odds with the humanistic rhetoric that accompanied it. Critics have also noted the "glorification of traditional masculine values" implicit in the "new man." Political scientist Ian Lumsden notes dryly that "there is scant evidence that the Cuban leaders have given much thought to the feminist critique of contemporary gender values . . . except for their negative judgments about capitalism's exploitative values."[1]

In capitalist society man is controlled by a pitiless law usually beyond his comprehension. The alienated human specimen is tied to society as a whole by an invisible umbilical cord: the law of value. This law acts upon all aspects of his life, shaping his course and destiny.

The laws of capitalism, which are blind and are invisible to ordinary people, act upon the individual without his being aware of it. He sees only the vastness of a seemingly infinite horizon before him. That is how it is painted by capitalist propagandists who purport to draw a lesson from the example of Rockefeller — whether or not it is true — about the possibilities of success. The amount of poverty and suffering required for a Rockefeller to emerge, and the amount of depravity entailed in the accumulation of a fortune of such magnitude, are left out of the picture, and it is not always possible for the popular forces to make these concepts clear.

(A discussion of how the workers in the imperialist countries gradually lose the spirit of working-class internationalism due to a certain degree of complicity in the exploitation of the dependent countries, and how this at the same time weakens the combativity of the masses in the imperialist countries, would be appropriate here, but that is a theme which goes beyond the aim of these notes.)

In any case the road to success is pictured as beset with perils — perils that, it would seem, an individual with the proper qualities can overcome to attain the goal. The reward is seen in the distance; the way is lonely. Furthermore, it is a contest among wolves. One can win only at the cost of the failure of others.

I would now like to try to define the individual, the actor in this strange and moving drama of the building of socialism, in his dual existence as a unique being and as a member of society.

I think the place to start is to recognize his quality of incompleteness, of being an unfinished product. The vestiges of the past are brought into the present in the individual consciousness, and a continual labor is necessary to eradicate them. The process is two-sided. On the one side, society acts through direct and indirect education; on the other, the individual submits himself to a conscious process of self-education.

The new society in formation has to compete fiercely with the past. This past makes itself felt not only in the individual consciousness — in which the residue of an education systematically oriented toward isolating the individual still weighs heavily — but also through the very character of this transition period in which commodity relations still persist. The commodity is the economic cell of capitalist society. So long as it exists its effects will make themselves felt in the organization of production and, consequently, in consciousness. . . .

In this period of the building of socialism we can see the new man being born. His image is not yet completely finished — it never will be, since the process goes forward hand in hand with the development of new economic forms.

Aside from those whose lack of education makes them take the solitary road toward satisfying their own personal ambitions, there are those — even within this new panorama of a unified march forward — who have a tendency to walk separate from the masses accompanying them. What is important, however, is that each day men are acquiring ever more consciousness of the need for their incorporation into society and, at the same time, of their importance as the motor of that society.

They no longer travel completely alone over lost roads toward distant aspirations. They follow their vanguard, consisting of the party, the advanced workers, the advanced men who walk in unity with the masses and in close communion with them. The vanguards have their eyes fixed on the future and its reward, but it is not a vision of something for the individual. The prize is a new society in which men will have different characteristics: the society of communist man.

The road is long and full of difficulties. At times we lose our way and must turn back. At other times we go too fast and separate ourselves from the masses. Sometimes we go too slow and feel the hot breath of those treading at our heels. In our zeal as revolutionists we try to move ahead as fast as possible, clearing the way. But we know we must draw our nourishment from the mass and that it can advance more rapidly only if we inspire it by our example. . . .

It is still necessary to deepen his conscious participation, individual and collective, in all the mechanisms of management and production, and to link this to the idea of the need for technical and ideological education, so that he sees how closely interdependent these processes are and how their advancement is parallel. In this way he will reach total consciousness of his social being, which is equivalent to his full realization as a human creature, once the chains of alienation are broken.

This will be translated concretely into the reconquering of his true nature through liberated labor, and the expression of his own human condition through culture and art.

In order for him to develop in the first way, work must acquire a new status. Man-as-a-commodity ceases to exist, and a system is installed that establishes a quota for the fulfillment of his social duty. The means of production belong to society, and the machine is merely the trench where duty is fulfilled.

Man begins to free his thinking of the annoying fact that he needs to work to satisfy his animal needs. He starts to see himself reflected in his work and to understand his full stature as a human being through the object created, through the work accomplished. Work no longer entails surrendering a part of his being in the form of labor power sold, which no longer belongs to him, but represents an emanation of himself, a contribution to the common life in which he is reflected, the fulfillment of his social duty.

We are doing everything possible to give work this new status of social duty and to link it on the one side with the development of technology, which will create the conditions for greater freedom, and on the other side with voluntary work based on the Marxist appreciation that man truly reaches his full human condition when he produces without being compelled by physical necessity to sell himself as a commodity.

Of course, there are still coercive aspects to work, even when it is voluntary. Man has not transformed all the coercion that surrounds him into conditioned reflexes of a social character, and in many cases he still produces under the pressures of his environment. (Fidel calls this moral compulsion.) He still needs to undergo a complete spiritual rebirth in his attitude toward his own work, freed from the direct pressure of his social environment, though linked to it by his new habits. That will be communism.

The change in consciousness does not take place automatically, just as the change in the economy does not take place automatically. The alterations are slow and are not rhythmic; there are periods of acceleration, ones that are slower, and even retrogressions. . . .

Now, I would like to explain the role played by the individual, by man as an individual within the masses who make history. This is our experience; it is not a prescription.

Fidel gave the revolution its impulse in the first years, and also its leadership. He always set its tone. But there is a good group of revolutionaries who are developing along the same road as the central leader. And there is a great mass that follows its leaders because it has faith in them. It has faith in them because they have known how to interpret its aspirations.

It is not a matter of how many kilograms of meat one has to eat, nor of how many times a year one goes to the beach, nor how many pretty things from abroad you might be able to buy with present-day wages. It is a matter of making the individual feel more complete, with much more internal richness and much more responsibility.

The individual in our country knows that the glorious period in which he happens to live is one of sacrifice; he is familiar with sacrifice. The first ones came to know it in the Sierra Maestra and wherever they fought; afterward all of Cuba came to know it. Cuba is the vanguard of Latin America and must make sacrifices because it occupies the post of advance guard, because it shows the masses of Latin America the road to full freedom.

Within the country the leadership has to carry out its vanguard role. And it must be said with all sincerity that in a real revolution, to which one gives his all and from which one expects no material reward, the task of the vanguard revolutionary is at one and the same time magnificent and agonizing.

At the risk of seeming ridiculous, let me say that the true revolutionary is guided by great feelings of love. It is impossible to think of a genuine revolutionary lacking this quality. Perhaps it is one of the great dramas of the leader that he must combine a passionate spirit with a cold intelligence and make painful decisions without flinching. Our vanguard revolutionaries must make an ideal of this love of the people, of the most sacred causes, and make it one and indivisible. They cannot descend, with small doses of daily affection, to the level where ordinary men put their love into practice.

The leaders of the revolution have children just beginning to talk, who are not learning to say "daddy." They have wives who must be part of the general sacrifice of their lives in order to take the revolution to its destiny. The circle of their friends is limited strictly to the circle of comrades in the revolution. There is no life outside of it.

In these circumstances one must have a big dose of humanity, a big dose of a sense of justice and truth in order not to fall into dogmatic extremes, into cold scholasticism, into an isolation from the masses. We must strive every day so that this love of living humanity is transformed into actual deeds, into acts that serve as examples, as a moving force.

The revolutionary, the ideological motor force of the revolution within his party, is consumed by this uninterrupted activity that comes to an end only with death, unless the construction of socialism is accomplished on a world scale. If his revolutionary zeal is blunted when the most urgent tasks have been accomplished on a local scale and he forgets about proletarian international-ism, the revolution he leads will cease to be a driving force and sink into a com-fortable drowsiness that imperialism, our irreconcilable enemy, will utilize to gain ground. Proletarian internationalism is a duty, but it is also a revolutionary necessity. This is the way we educate our people.

TRANSLATOR UNKNOWN

Note

1. Ian Lumsden, *Machos, Maricones, and Gays: Cuba and Homosexuality* (Philadelphia: Temple University Press, 1996), 119. Lois Smith and Alfred Padula, in *Sex and Revolution: Women in Socialist Cuba* (New York: Oxford University Press, 1996), draw similar conclusions (see especially 93).

In the Fist of the Revolution

José Yglesias

The revolution became a firm demarcation in most Cubans' minds that separated "then" from "now." For the rural poor—the majority of the Cuban population—the disappearance of the foreign sugar companies that had dominated their lands, their labor, and their lives, transformed everyday life in innumerable ways. Journalist and novelist José Yglesias (an American of partly Cuban ancestry) traveled to Cuba in 1967 with a contract from Pantheon Books to investigate everyday life in a Cuban village. He chose the town of Mayarí, in the heart of eastern Cuba's sugar lands, formerly surrounded by lands owned by the United Fruit Company. In a brief selection from Yglesias's In the Fist of the Revolution, *an elderly Cuban describes the change the Revolution brought to the meaning of sugar and labor in the sugar industry.*

It was in those days [the beginning of the century] that the United Fruit Company began to build the sugar mill and to buy up the land around here and plant cane. It was never all cane, you know; there was a lot of tobacco, it even had a certain fame, and now after the triumph of the Revolution some are planting it again. They have even started a little cigar factory. But what Mayarí was really famous for was its cedars and *caobas* [mahoganies] and pines. They had been there since time began, and two blocks from here, where the court building is, right there they began, east, west, and south, so that the little donkey lane to Cueto was a path among those enormous trees. Up into Los Pinares the trees went.

Do you know how much all that fine wood was worth? I estimate at least ten to twenty million pesos. La United sold them all to Las Bahamas, and they were cut down and rolled into the river after a railroad-tie nail was driven into the head of each log. In spring the river would rise and the logs floated all the way to the Bay of Nipe. It is a mystery to me—one of those things that nevertheless has its scientific explanation—why those big nails made it possible for those heavy logs to float, but that is what they did.

Those trees were marvels, and with some it took a few men holding outstretched hands to surround them. Once at an *arroyo* by the Guayabo—you know the little Guayabo River on the way to Los Pinares?—whose water is still pure and delicious, right near there I saw a caoba cut down, so large I thought it would take ten men to embrace it. Old man, I asked my father, why did they cut it down when this little arroyo does not get sufficient water in spring to float it? And my old man explained that they could quarter it and if it still did not move, they could slice it again. Do you know what I think such a tree would be worth now? I would say ten to twelve thousand pesos.

Those were the days when people were run off their own lands—though they had papers dating back to colonial days to show it was theirs—because corrupt officials would sell the land to La United. They began their measurements of huge tracts with just a millimeter off at the start, but when the line was extended to a distance that little millimeter widened out to become whole towns and farms. You may ask yourself what a pass we had come to that eventually we had to beg La United for a tiny bit of land to have a cemetery. It was these things that made me have a certain view of life.

I have always had ideas that have put me in the left wing, not Communist, you know, but left wing. I am what you could call a tame left-winger, for I have always known that what makes men is economic and political interests and passions of the heart, and that it is no use intervening in these factors. What do men seek but to dominate others and impose their wills? And I have known that it is futile to come between men and these aspirations. I have always wanted peace and reasonable fraternity between men, an end to those interests which create injustices. This was but a foolishness of mine, for it could not be.

Yet listen to how, being a tame leftist, I came to a laughable pass. I had been an *alzado*, a rebel, here in 1918, another foolishness, for there was no difference between the group in power and the group out of power; but some of us took to the *monte* in rebellion, not knowing that these were two bourgeois parties, whose differences were simply the different personal ambitions of the leaders. I did not know this then, I learned it later with the Revolution—the Revolution has taught Cubans many things. Cubans have never liked to work, for example, because we have always seen that to get ahead or to gain this or that you do not work; you do it through friends, never through sustained study or work but always by the proper cultivation of friendships and politicking.

It was not difficult to see this because men, by and large, speak what is on their souls. Sometimes they repeat what they have heard or what they think you want to hear, but in the main, men say what is on their hearts. And so it was, listening to men, that I thought all this will never end: it will always be these interests which will rule men. That is what it was like with my first experience of revolution and with the *machadato* in the twenties and again in 1933 and then with Grau and Batista. Why should I hope?

The Revolution triumphed here, and during the first months I said to myself, It is the same thing: so-and-so wanted to be mayor, and the judges were still the same ones who had been selling themselves, and all the same people were scurrying around to maintain their positions or change to another, for there were a lot of vacancies. And the time passed and before I noticed it, very intransigent things happened. The Revolution said to La United, You have to go, I say you have to go and you will go, man. And so it happened. La United went—incredible!

And Cubans who do not like to work go off in droves to cut cane for nothing, 50 percent real volunteers full of enthusiasm and 50 percent—well, they go, carried along by the others and catching some of their enthusiasm for the while. For it is wonderful how the government does this. It does not grab anyone and say, Here, you have to cut cane. Oh no, for no one is forced anymore. They go instead to a work center and say, It is our hope and need that three or four here will go cut cane. They say this to someone who is responsible, and they are the ones who by psychology and their own enthusiasm find three or four and even more to go.

So it was that three years ago I suddenly came to this laughable pass that all the things I had learned in a lifetime were superseded. There is a real revolution, and those woods will never again be cut down and shipped away to make money for someone else. Of course they are not there, you cannot replace that fine wood in a short time—it was the work of centuries—but they are planting everywhere and scientifically, and the pines and the fruit trees grow faster and bear sooner. See those houses behind you, old and crooked like me, they are going to be cut down and there will be a *malecón* [broad sidewalk or esplanade along seawall] to walk on and look at the view!

"I know what you are going to say," I said to Dr. Morales when we had left Felix Estol. "You are going to say that Mayarí has a reason for coming into being, but none for existing under socialism, right?"

"Right," he said.

The Agrarian Revolution

Medea Benjamin, Joseph Collins, and Michael Scott

A great paradox of Cuba's socioeconomic transformation since 1959 has been the enormously successful changes in the areas of distribution, versus the continuing stumbling blocks in the area of production. The agrarian reform was a major component of the government's successful program to turn peasants into citizens and to bring a decent standard of living to the countryside. Yet the goal of increasing or even maintaining production proved elusive. Medea Benjamin, Joseph Collins, and Michael Scott discuss the goals and the paradoxes of Cuba's agrarian reforms in the first decades of the revolution.

During the days of the guerrilla war in the Sierra Maestra mountains, Fidel Castro and his rebel army gradually won the hearts and minds of the peasants. The rebels treated the peasants with respect and, unlike most armed groups, paid for all the food and supplies they used. Gradually the guerrilla army was transformed into a peasant army — by 1959, three-fourths or more of the soldiers were peasants. . . .

Once in power, the revolutionary government instituted a series of reforms designed to improve life in the countryside. All land rents were abolished. Tenant farmers, sharecroppers, and squatters were given title to the land they worked, along with guaranteed fixed prices for their produce and low-interest loans. Many seasonal workers were given full-time employment. Rural salaries were raised. People's stores were created to bring cheap consumer goods to the countryside. In 1961, the government initiated a massive literacy campaign, sending urban students to the countryside not only to teach reading and writing, but to gain an understanding and appreciation of rural life. For the first time, rural communities were provided with schools, clinics, and recreational and cultural activities. Teams of projectionists traveled to remote villages showing movies, free of charge, to people who had never seen a film. . . .

The revolution's leadership assumed that private individual farming would eventually disappear. Many farmers, perhaps most, would move out of agriculture altogether. Others would join agricultural cooperatives, or sell their land to the state and take jobs on state farms. Both state farms and cooperatives (in that order) were thought to be superior to small private farms in terms of both productivity and the social benefits they could offer their workers. Ideologically, state farms were considered superior to cooperatives, since they were not privately owned and the wealth they generated benefited the public at large.

But paradoxically, by giving land titles to tenants, squatters, and sharecroppers, the agrarian reforms helped make small farmers more secure. Small farming represents virtually the only private sector that still exists in Cuba. Since Fidel Castro has personally and categorically promised that small farmers will never be forced to give up their land, the state finds itself in the awkward position of having to guarantee the existence of islands of small farmers in a sea of large state farms. A look at the evolution of state versus private agriculture should give us a better understanding of how this relationship stands today.

The First Agrarian Reform

The revolutionary government instituted its far reaching land reform law just five months after taking power. Symbolically, it was signed at the former headquarters of the rebel army in the Sierra Maestra. The maximum land area one person could own was set at one thousand acres, with exceptions made for particularly productive farms. Land ownership was so concentrated that by expropriating twelve thousand large farms, the government gained control of 44 percent of farm and ranch land. State farms became key to Cuban agriculture for both domestic and export production.

For those with too little land to make a living, a "vital minimum," defined as the amount of land needed to support a family of five, was set at sixty-seven acres. Peasants with less were given that amount free, plus the right to buy another one hundred acres.

Whether they owned the land or not, farmers were still a minority of the rural population. Wage-earning farmworkers on large estates outnumbered them four to one. Most observers, both foreign and Cuban, assumed the government would divide the large estates among the laborers who had worked them. Traditional wisdom among socialist thinkers was that even if the eventual goal was to collectivize agriculture, the first step was to divide up the land among the workers, then at some later point encourage them to pool their resources and work together. In the Soviet Union, China, and all of Eastern Europe, land reform programs were all based on this principle of "land to the tiller."

But the Cuban land reform did not divide up the large estates among the workers, converting them instead into state farms and cooperatives. Why? "I found upon the victory of the Revolution that the idea of land division still had a lot of currency," Fidel explained years later. "But I already understood by then that if you take, for example, a sugar plantation of 2,500 acres . . . and you divide it into two hundred portions of 12.5 acres each, what will inevitably happen is that right away the new owners will cut the production of sugarcane in half in each plot, and they will begin to raise for their own consumption a whole series of crops for which in many cases the soil will not be adequate." Castro believed dividing the land would lead to a decline in production, which would be disastrous for the whole country.

Castro offered the same explanation for not dividing up the large cattle ranches. During the guerrilla war, the rebels had confiscated herds and distributed them among the peasants. Within a few months, practically all the animals had been eaten. "The majority of the campesinos had killed their cows because they preferred the immediate benefit of being able to eat them to the longer-range value of having the milk," Castro explained. "This naturally fortified my conviction that the land of the *latifundistas* should not be divided."

Cuba's leaders understood that circumstances in Cuba were different from those of other countries which carried out significant land-reform programs. The workers on large estates in Cuba were not small farmers who aspired to own their own land, but rather a rural proletariat whose main concerns were job security, better working conditions, and a higher standard of living. Thus the decision to create cooperatives rather than divide up the land did not encounter resistance from the farmworkers.

How Was the Law Implemented?

Even with the exemptions for particularly productive land, the agrarian reform law still called for the expropriation of half of Cuba's cultivated land. The National Agrarian Reform Institute (INRA) was to determine where to start and how fast to move. . . .

INRA's first moves were timid. In ten months, only six thousand small farmers received redistributed land. French agricultural economist Michel Gutelman noted that, with 150,000 small farmers to be dealt with, "At this rate, it would have taken twenty years" to complete the redistribution. But as the large owners (both Cuban and American) began to actively oppose the reforms, INRA was forced to adopt a more radical position. . . .

Since one-fourth of the best land in Cuba was owned by U.S. companies, agrarian reform placed the Cuban government in direct conflict with U.S. interests and set into motion a series of moves and countermoves that eventually led to the Bay of Pigs invasion in April 1961. (Cubans themselves see the passage of the agrarian-reform law as "the beginning of the end" of Cuba-U.S. relations.) With history moving at lightning speed, the legal text of the agrarian reform law was soon left behind. In fact only one-quarter of the land taken over was actually taken under the terms of the law itself. The majority came from the nationalization of U.S.-owned sugar mills and agricultural enterprises after the U.S. cut its sugar quota and from the confiscation of land owned by persons who left the country or engaged in efforts to bring down the revolutionary government after the Bay of Pigs invasion.

Two years into the reform, nearly half Cuba's total land area had been affected. More than one hundred thousand peasants—mostly tenants, share-croppers, and squatters—had gained title to the land they worked. But having made the decision to keep the large estates intact, the big winner was the state, which now controlled 44 percent of the land.

The State Sector

Apart from the ranches, the rest of the state's land was converted into "cooperatives." The cooperatives set up by the first agrarian reform were more akin to state farms than to traditional self-administered cooperatives whose members receive a share of the profits. Cooperatives were accountable to INRA and had little autonomy. Production targets were set by INRA and produce was sold to the state purchasing agencies. The cooperatives selected their own coordinator, but the administrator was appointed by INRA, creating a two-tier power structure in which the appointed administrator had the upper hand over the elected coordinator.

Workers reportedly were not enthusiastic about the creation of cooperatives. Their experience as farmworkers left them ill equipped to take on administrative responsibilities. While their monthly wage was theoretically an advance on their share in the year's profits, in practice it was simply a wage. (Since no accounts were kept, it was never known if there was anything left at the end of the year to distribute.)

The cooperatives also posed two challenges to the government's commitment to equality. One was the increasing difference between rich and poor cooperatives. Some co-ops had advantages—in particular, fertile land and high-value crops such as tobacco—that gave them higher revenues independent of the work of the members. The other problem was the friction between cooperative members and temporary workers. Temporary workers received higher wages than members (3.00 pesos a day vs. 2.50), since cooperative wages were supposed to have been supplemented by yearly dividends. Cooperative members, though, had a host of other advantages, such as free health care, housing, schools, sick leave, and accident insurance. Temporary workers became, in the words of Fidel Castro, "second-class citizens."

By 1962, the cooperatives were converted into state farms. Like the cattle ranches, they were called *granjas del pueblo*. In part, this move was merely an acknowledgment of existing reality. But there were some important differences. Workers no longer even theoretically shared the farm's profit but received a fixed wage. All workers received the same wage. Planning and investments were made more centralized than before. Since state farms were often formed by combining cooperatives, purportedly to take advantage of economies of scale, the average size was larger. . . .

The Private Sector

While the state sector was being created, the private sector was being transformed. By giving titles to former tenants, sharecroppers, and squatters, the agrarian reform added about 110,000 peasants to the already existing forty-five thousand small farmer-owners. Thus two-thirds of Cuba's small farmers became farm owners thanks to the revolution.

The private sector included both small and large farmers. Defined as those with under 165 acres, the small farmers constituted 94 percent of the private farmers. Large farmers, while in the minority, still held 42 percent of the land in the private sector. Together they were important producers not only of food but also of foreign exchange, accounting for 85 percent of tobacco production, 80 percent of coffee, and 33 percent of sugarcane.

The small private farmers reaped the benefits of the government's first agrarian reform. With land rents abolished, their incomes grew dramatically. They were given low-interest loans, guaranteed fixed prices for their crops, access to low-priced "people's stores," schools for their children, free medical care, and more. Freed from exploitative intermediaries and price fluctuations—harvest prices were now fixed and guaranteed before planting—small farmers improved their material conditions considerably.

In May 1961, on the second anniversary of the agrarian reform law, the National Association of Small Farmers (ANAP) was formed. Membership was voluntary and restricted to farmers with fewer than 165 acres and larger farmers who had proven allegiance to the revolution. ANAP was to coordinate small farm production, mainly through the allocation of credit. Before the revolution, government credit was largely confined to the estates and large farms. Many small farmers were forced into the hands of loan sharks charging up to 30 percent interest. Now small farmers were given credit at 4 percent annual interest. (From 1967 to 1978, no interest at all was charged on loans.)

Excluding the larger farmers from membership in ANAP represented a critical step in differentiating the remaining large farmers from the small ones. Rich farmers were few in number; two years after the first agrarian reform law, only 592 farms over 1,000 acres remained. (The number of holdings between 165 and 1,000 acres had grown from 9,752 to 10,623, their ranks swelled by former large owners.) While small farmers received special support from the state, large private farmers were excluded from the mainstream of agricultural planning. With the nationalization of the banking, transport, and distribution systems, it became increasingly difficult for these farmers to obtain supplies and deliver their goods to urban markets. "Discrimination against this group of farmers was apparently official policy of the revolutionary leadership that wished eventually to nationalize these properties," according to Canadian economist Archibald Ritter. "It refrained from doing so immediately due to a scarcity of INRA administrators and to political factors, i.e., the wish to avoid creating another body of opponents to the regime."

But while the government made it difficult for large farmers both to produce and sell their goods, the increase in national consumption coupled with the inexperience of the newly created state sector made these farmers more important than ever in supplying the nation's food. Rather than sell to the state at fixed prices, these farmers preferred selling their produce privately to the highest bidder.

In an effort to force the farmers to sell to the state, serious errors were committed. A number of farms were illegally expropriated. The large farmers used these errors to make even small farmers fear expropriation. To quell the fears of the small farmers, the government was forced to hand back lands taken illegally. Fidel said at the time, "If the return of illegally confiscated farms is going to restore peace and quiet to thousands of people who must go along with the revolution, then they will have to be given back."

Although the government considered the remaining rich farmers incompatible with the revolution, it did not want to precipitate their downfall and affect the economy adversely. The idea was to organize the state sector for several years and then deal the death blow to the remaining large farmers. But once again, the course of events forced the revolution to speed up its plans. Many rich farmers sabotaged production. Others, particularly in the Escambray mountain region, were directly involved in counterrevolutionary activities. Perhaps even more critical were their efforts to convince small farmers that the government was out to do away with all private farmers, big and small alike. These problems, coupled with the need to control food supplies in the face of ever-growing demand and shortages, led the government to promulgate a second agrarian reform.

The Second Agrarian Reform

In October 1963, the second agrarian reform was instituted, expropriating the land of all farmers with more than 165 acres. The government believed that state farms would guarantee food for everyone as well increased exports. They would make resurgence of capitalism in the Cuban countryside impossible. INRA took over about ten thousand farms, comprising approximately 20 percent of the nation's farmland. This left the state in control of about 63 percent of the cultivated land, as well as all agricultural credit, inputs, and marketing facilities.

Now the small farmers were the only significant private sector remaining in the entire economy. The government went to considerable lengths to reassure them there would be no "third agrarian reform" and that all future steps at collectivization would be strictly voluntary. Fidel Castro himself made a strong and highly visible political commitment towards the small farmers and their style of production. Not until a small farmer personally believed it was advantageous to farm collectively would his farm be joined with others in a cooperative, Fidel promised. If a farmer chose to live out his years as an individual farmer, this was fine. . . .

During the late 1960s, however, there was a big push to persuade farmers to sell or lease their land to the government for its ambitious agricultural projects. (Undoubtedly the deal was attractive to some; others, we have been told, felt forced more than persuaded.) Between 1967 and 1970, the government purchased about twenty thousand farms, then slowed down to buying fewer than fifteen hundred a year. . . .

Private farmers are private only in the sense that they own their land and live mainly off the sale of their produce. But unlike private farmers in capitalist countries, they cannot freely sell their land, they must respond to the government's request as to what to grow, they are dependent on the government for inputs, and they must sell part of their produce to the government at prices the government sets. . . .

Virtually all private farm families are better off in food terms than other Cubans. Not only are small farmers able to grow much of their own food, but along with all other Cubans they purchase foods inexpensively through the ration system. In addition to receiving guaranteed prices for their crops and low-interest credits from the government, private farmers can take advantage of food shortages to sell part of their produce through nongovernment channels (mainly the black market) at high profits. Many farmers also have leased part of their land to the government in return for a lifetime monthly "rent check"—often higher than the average monthly wage. And all farmers and their families reap government benefits from free education and free health care. Little wonder that many joked that Cuba's small capitalist farmers were exploiting the socialist state.

For complete references and notes, consult the work as cited in the acknowledgment of copyrights section.

1961: The Year of Education

Richard R. Fagen

The Year of Education provided the revolutionary leadership with an opportunity to fulfill a long-standing commitment to eradicate illiteracy as part of the revolution's educational reform program. But the campaign was much more than an educational effort. Coinciding with the breaking of diplomatic relations with the United States and the Bay of Pigs invasion, the Literacy Campaign underlined the relationship among neocolonialism, underdevelopment, and educational backwardness. As Fidel Castro exhorted departing literacy brigade workers: "The battle to be won against ignorance will give our country more glory than the military battles already fought or still to be fought. . . . While imperialism wants to destroy us and our revolution, we are going to destroy imperialism with our example, our success."[1] The highly politicized nature of the Literacy Campaign and the ways in which it contributed to the transformation of political culture can be seen in the extract from one of the literacy texts used in the campaign. Richard Fagen, professor emeritus of political science at Stanford University, collected and translated these texts for a study he wrote on revolutionary political culture in Cuba.

Of the 18 employees of a business, 9 are militiamen, 5 belong to Committees for the Defense of the Revolution, and 4 form part of a Battalion of Voluntary Workers. How many employees of this business are contributing their efforts to the progress of the Fatherland during this period of sacrifices?

A family's bill for electricity used to be $8 monthly, and after the reduction in rates ordered by the Revolutionary Government it is $3 less. What is the family's present monthly expenditure for electricity?

Some residents of Havana sent the following gifts to a peasant family that they had met during the 1959 26th of July peasants' rally: a doll worth 3 pesos, a set of table linens worth 5 pesos, and a flower pot worth 1 peso. How much did they spend on gifts?

On 2 December 1956, Fidel Castro and 81 other expeditionaries disembarked near Belic, at Las Coloradas beach, facing the Sierra Maestra. By land and by sea the forces of the tyranny bombarded them; 70 men lost their lives. How many expeditionaries from the "Granma" began the epic struggle for the liberation of Cuba?

In the battle of La Plata, which took place on 17 January 1957 — 1 month and 15 days after the landing — the Rebel Army won its first victory. How many years have passed since then?

The Revolution is developing goat raising in the mountainous regions of Cuba in order to increase dairy production. If one goat gives 6 liters of milk every day, how many liters will 4 goats give?

To defend our Socialist Revolution, we Cubans have organized ourselves into Committees for the Defense of the Revolution. If in one block there are 4 committees, each one made up of 9 citizens, how many people are part of those 4 committees?

The Guaniguanico Mountain Range, which extends between Guane and Mariel, is some 150 kilometers long. The Sierra Maestra, a chain of high mountains which runs from Guantánamo Bay to Cape Cruz, is 250 kilometers long. How many kilometers longer than the Guaniguanico Range is the Sierra Maestra?

I have $50 in the bank and save $8 more. How much do I have?

If a spool of thread costs 5 cents, how much will 4 spools cost? . . .

At one People's Farm [Granja del Pueblo], 374 liters of milk were collected during the morning milking and 379 during the evening one. How many liters of milk were collected during the day?

If you pay 9 cents for a liter of gasoline, how much will 5 liters cost?

The Popocatepetl volcano in Mexico is 5,450 meters high and the Orizaba volcano, which is the highest mountain in that country, is 300 meters higher. What is the elevation of the highest mountain in Mexico?

Cuba's first city and capital was Villa de la Asunción de Baracoa, founded by Diego Velázquez in 1512. How many years ago was that ancient Cuban city founded?

La Paz, the capital of Bolivia, at 3,640 meters above sea level, is the highest capital in the world. Mexico City, the capital of Mexico, is located at an elevation of 2,252 meters. How many meters higher than Mexico City is La Paz?

The electric milking machine, which is used in our modern dairies, frees the dairyman from the exhausting job of hand milking. In milking by hand, it is necessary to squeeze the cow's teat about 98 times in order to get one liter of milk. How many times will the milker have to repeat the same motion in order to get 8 liters of milk?

Approximately 500 people go to the reading rooms of the Havana National Library every day. How many readers will go to the National Library during one week?

The Revolution has put books within reach of the people. In a Galiano Street bookstall a railroad worker bought Palevói's work *A Man of Truth* (*Un hombre de verdad*) for 1 peso and 10 cents,[2] the *Song of Great Achievements* (*Canción de gesta*) by Pablo Neruda for 50 cents, and *Bertillón 166* by José Soler Puig for 35 cents. How much did his purchase of books amount to?

A peasant who used to earn 70 cents a day before the Revolution now earns 2 pesos and 80 cents. How much more does he earn now?

A medicine which cost $4.75 before the Revolution now can be bought for $3.16. How much less do we pay for this product?

In the battle of El Uvero, which took place on 28 May 1957, some 120 rebel soldiers fought against the much superior armed forces of the tyranny [of Batista]. About one-third of the rebel soldiers were killed or wounded. What were the losses suffered by the Rebel Army in this memorable battle?

In the United States there are 6 million unemployed workers, of which three-tenths are white and the rest Negroes. What part of those 6 million unemployed men are Negroes? (Think of the number "1" expressed as ten-tenths.)

TRANSLATED BY RICHARD R. FAGEN

Notes

1. Fidel Castro's speech at Varadero to departing Conrado Benítez Brigadistas and their families, 14 May 1961. Havana Domestic Service FBIS Report Date 19610504; 19610515.
2. *Eds. note*: The correct English translation for this work is *A Story about a Real Man* by Boris Nikolaevich Polevoi.

The Literacy Campaign

Oscar Lewis, Ruth M. Lewis, and Susan M. Rigdon

The mobilization of Cuban youth for the literacy drive challenged a number of gendered and class assumptions about the relationship between city and countryside. The intrafamily and personal tensions aroused by the literacy campaign are well conveyed in the testimonial account of a young woman interviewed by sociologist Oscar Lewis (1914–1970) for his oral history of the Cuban Revolution.

In February 1961, I volunteered for the Literacy Campaign, which aimed to combat illiteracy in the country. Fidel had been asking for volunteers for several weeks, and I suggested to my friend Milagros that we join. She was reluctant at first but I argued until she agreed. The family made a terrible fuss about my decision but *mami* accepted it. My aunts and uncles, who were still here then, thought it would be a disaster. How could mami permit me to go alone to God knows where, to live among God knows who, in the countryside where there was no running water or electricity? Angela Rosa Collazo practically had a fit! "Beatriz, my child, you must be insane to let Mónica go out to the country!"—adding a phrase that was habitual with her, "The country is for the birds!"

Uncle Bernardo and Aunt Mercedes said to mami, "Well, Beatriz, you know how it is, one goes and two come back." Mami was such a stern moralist they thought the fear that I might come back pregnant would be the strongest deterrent. But mami is a fighter, especially when people insinuate things like that. She faced right up to them, saying she'd brought me up to be incapable of such a thing.

Mami let us make decisions ourselves, although she had very definite opinions about what we should do with our lives. She wanted us to grow up into independent human beings and often had to stand up against the family to give us children a measure of independence. She, herself, had more individuality than any of the others in her family. She dared to think for herself and to act on her beliefs. In that sense, she does have self-control and I admire her for it. . . .

You see, to me the Campaign was such a great thing, such a historic event.

I thought when I was a little old woman I'd be embarrassed to explain to my grandchildren, "No, I didn't join the Literacy Campaign; I was too eager to see my sister again, and meet my niece." It seemed to me that would be down-right immoral. Besides, it was a beautiful opportunity to experience perhaps one-thousandth of the things Fidel had been through.

I'd get to know the people and be independent of my family for the first time in my life. All those things were important to me. And then, after eight months to return and be able to say, "Seven or eight little old men and women know how to read and write because I taught them."

At last the day came when I was to go to the country. We spent the first week in Varadero,[1] learning how to use the phonetic syllabary to teach people to read. The first few days there was a sort of mild mass hysteria among us. Everybody got sick. We were all young girls who had never been away from home before, and there were so many different rules and regulations to follow. We were strictly segregated from the boys. They lived at Camp Granma and the girls at Kawama.

One day there was an incident. We were all taken to the movies and a net was hung in the auditorium between the boys' side and the girls'!

That created a lot of tension. Nothing provokes people more than to be for-bidden to do something. The boys tore down the net and rushed over to us. Immediately the supervisors gathered the girls together and made us file out, double-time.

The only men at Kawama were some very cute lifeguards, and we girls kept pretending to drown so we'd be pulled out. We'd talk of boys all day long. One of my roommates—she must have come from a lower-class family—startled me with her dirty jokes. It's true that in a convent school you hear more dirty jokes than anywhere in the world, but in Varadero I heard things I never dreamed of. This girl said her brother had relations with heifers. I was terribly shocked. I'd never heard of bestiality. It hadn't ever occurred to me that a human being would do such a thing.

One day mami came to visit. We were filling in our requests for the place we preferred to be sent. I wanted to put down the Sierra Maestra in Oriente, which was my dream, but mami said no, it was too far for her to visit me and I was too young to be away from home for eight months. Milagros's *mamá* made the same objection. But we didn't want to be too near Havana. What would be the point of leaving home if I was going to have my relatives on top of me as usual? So Milagros and I compromised and put down Las Villas, which was within visiting distance, but far enough away so our families couldn't be there every minute.

We'd been in Varadero only two days when we were taken to Havana in

"Territory free of illiteracy": The Literacy Museum commemorates the campaign (2002). On the wall are photographs of *brigadistas* killed by counterrevolutionaries. Photograph by Aviva Chomsky.

buses for the May Day parade. Arriving in the city I was overcome with emotion, as if I'd been away ten years. Many of us wept. The streets looked so beautiful after our absence! . . .

Our first stop was Santa Clara. Then they took us to Remedios, and from there the commissioner of Remedios took us to a tiny village near Guanabo in Las Villas.

"Is this where we get off?" I asked.

"This is it."

"Oh, but look, I wanted to go to the country—real country, you know what I mean, where there are earthen huts with no electricity. Villages I know; it's the country I want."

"If that's what you want, I can take you. It's no problem."

Milagros, two other brigadiers, and I were driven out into the country in a jeep. First they dropped off the other girls; then they took Milagros and me to houses very near each other.

It was night when I arrived where I was to stay. It felt strange, getting off there and being introduced as "the brigadier who is going to live with you."

"Ah. Very well," the family said.

"Then you're staying?" the commissioner asked.

"Yes." As he drove off in his jeep, I looked at all the people in the house and thought, "Oh, my God!"

There was a little old couple, a girl, Graciela, of about twenty-three, Elías, who was about twenty-one, Pedro, about nineteen, another boy who must have been fifteen or sixteen, a girl of fourteen or so, and a little boy of four or five. It was a fairly good country house, with a porch, a little dining room, and a small parlor with a bedroom on either side, all built of cement. The kitchen had wooden walls and an earthen floor, and was thatched with palm leaves.

It was about bedtime, so I lit my lantern as we had been taught to do. It was a Chinese lantern, something new to me, and when we were first taught to use it, I was surprised at the brilliant light it gave, almost like electricity. They told me I was to share a room with the two girls and they showed me my bed. I lay down at once.

That first night was very long. The house was surrounded by cane fields. I'd never heard the rustle of cane at night. It seemed very loud in the stillness of the country. Next morning I woke up with a bad cold and a fever. Sick on my first day in the country! I didn't know what to do. I was awfully far from civilization, too far to expect any doctor to get to me, and worse still, I was among strangers and didn't know how they'd react. Mami had warned me never, under any circumstances, to allow myself to be treated with home remedies. Above all, I was not to allow anybody to rub my stomach—that's the standard country treatment for indigestion, and if you happen to have appendicitis it can be very dangerous.

On the other hand, at Varadero I had been told to adapt to country customs. Our aim was to educate the people gradually, not directly oppose any of their beliefs. If the people were not revolutionaries I should try to convert them, but tactfully, without startling them.

I was terrified, which made me sicker, and that's when my asthma started, though I didn't know it was asthma. I'd always been subject to a runny nose and allergic sneezing fits. For three days I ran a high fever and could hardly breathe. Now I realize it was psychosomatic; I was reacting emotionally to my situation. . . .

As soon as I went back I took a census of illiterates, as we had been instructed. In the barrio assigned to me there were eight or nine illiterates, and there was also one little house that nobody told me about. I asked the family I was staying with, "Who lives in that little house?"

"Oh, just some blacks."

"Can they read and write?"

"I don't know, they're blacks."

"Well, I'll just drop in and see if they have illiterates in the house."

"No, no, you can't go there! I tell you, they're blacks."

"All right, I heard you, but I'm going."

They tried to stop me, but seeing my mind was made up, the old man said, "Elías will take you on horseback and wait for you outside."

It was then I realized that country people were a lot more prejudiced than city people. They discriminated brutally against blacks. They never visited them and feared for my safety. They hinted that the black boys might molest me and also said they practiced bestiality. Later I learned that this was true. After a time I realized everybody there practiced it. Frankly I was scared, but I said to myself, "Buck up, kid, be brave," and I went to visit them.

I found that nearly every one of the blacks was illiterate, so I decided to give two classes a day, and, wanting to make people go to the blacks' house, I chose that one for the afternoon classes. My hosts, of course, were shocked.

The most difficult part of the Campaign was living with the old couple and their children. As a family they had more schooling than anybody else in the barrio—they must have gone as far as the sixth grade—and had great natural intelligence besides. But the only person in that house who wasn't hostile to me was the old man. At least he was gentle in his ways, though when I tried to persuade him to join a cooperative, we'd argue and he always came out the winner.

He owned four cows and a jeep, as well as a small plot of land where he planted yucca and beans, and although he planted mainly for family consumption, he hired a farmhand. He was a very kindhearted man, quiet and reserved. The family treated him with respect when he was around but he was hardly ever in the house.

His wife was hard to get along with. At first she made a great show of affection for me, but I could tell it was hypocritical, and she soon showed herself for the harpy she was. It was her fault that the rest of the family was so totally evil, each child more difficult than the next. She was the twin sister of the lady of the house where Milagros was staying, but they had completely opposite temperaments. Milagros's hostess was a good, sweet-tempered woman; she had the same number of children but the two families lived in different worlds. It was so pleasant in Milagros's house, I felt welcome and at ease, and went there for lunch as often as I could. In that house there were no illiterates.

My habit of going to Milagros's house made my family even more unfriendly. They quite often remarked that I liked it better over there. In time I realized that their hostility arose from the fact that they were not revolutionaries but small landowners, afraid of what would happen to them.

At least I learned something living there. Everything I saw was new to me—their family structure, the kind of life they led. . . .

By the end of my eight months I had taught almost all the illiterates in my section to read and write. One little lady in her eighties couldn't write because her hand trembled so much, but the others did very well, and the day we finished our work, we hauled up our pink flag, declaring the area free of illiteracy. I often wonder whether our pupils have kept up their reading, or forgotten it all by now.

Note

1. A popular beach and resort in Matanzas Province. (For a broader description of the training program at Varadero and of the campaign itself, see Fagen, *The Transformation of Political Culture in Cuba*, pp. 33–68.)

The "Rehabilitation" of Prostitutes

Oscar Lewis, Ruth M. Lewis, and Susan M. Rigdon

One of the revolution's earliest programs in the area of gender was against prostitution, which was seen as a symbol of Cuba's degradation as a playground for tourists and of women's lack of opportunity under the old order. A 1961 law outlawed prostitution, and a support system of schools, day care, and jobs was put into place to "rehabilitate" former prostitutes. Many Cubans' viewed the elimination of prostitution, like the universalization of access to health, food, and education, as a point of pride in the nation's twin goals of social equality at home and dignity in the international sphere. (The return of prostitution in the 1990s is similarly viewed with intense shame and as a major social defeat, even though most Cubans are quick to say that they understand and sympathize with the women who make this choice under the current economic situation.) Here U.S. scholar Oscar Lewis (1914–1970) interviews a woman who had worked as a prostitute before the revolution.

[On the] day the Revolution was triumphant . . . I was too high on pills to know what had happened. But when I heard such enthusiastic crowds out in the street, I got excited too. I thought, "The Revolution can't be so bad when so many people are happy about it." But it was confusing. Madams and pimps spread rumors that the new government would be ruthless with prostitutes. They made a great deal of that kind of propaganda. They said prostitutes would be jailed if they were lucky enough to escape the firing squad. But others thought it was no more than a change of corrupt officials, and life would go on in the same old way. Never did I imagine everything would be so different!

Life in the brothel changed at once. Lots of the owners ran away, and exploitation by those who remained was stopped. We girls started working for ourselves — if I earned ten pesos they were all mine. Of course we had to make a contribution toward the upkeep of the house, servants' wages, and so on, but it wasn't anything like half the take.

Three months, more or less, after the triumph of the Revolution, the police went to each brothel and told the owner that all the women were expected at the station at 5:00 the next evening. Our madam hired a car to take us there, and the police photographed us full face and profile and took our fingerprints. Then they told us we were required to have periodic medical examinations—a general checkup, a blood test, and a vaginal smear—and carry a kind of health certificate. We had to show our card to the police every week, and if it wasn't up to date we wouldn't be allowed to work.

Some of the prostitutes resented the new rules and had a lot to say about being photographed, too, but like it or not, we all had to do it. The pimps had said we'd be shot, or jailed, or sent somewhere to pick tomatoes, and it all seemed possible.

Homosexuals who owned brothels or worked in them were also rounded up. Practically every brothel had homosexuals to do the cooking and cleaning and sometimes to go to bed with clients. I'm sorry for queers and always got along well with them. There's no excuse for what they are, but at least they're better than lesbians.

It seemed perfectly fair to me to throw brothel owners in jail. They were exploiters, one and all. When you brought them a lot of money they were all smiles, but when you had to fight to defend yourself they didn't stand by you— a scandal in the house was too inconvenient for them.

In my opinion the revolutionary government was taking some very necessary measures to make brothels less disgusting. They put an end to the selling of drinks, they required us to meet the customers fully dressed, and a madam who didn't make sure her girls complied with the medical rule would have had to shut the house down. They made drugs illegal, too, so I hardly ever smoked marijuana or sniffed cocaine anymore. At first some men continued to bring a little, but they were scared to death.

Abortions were more difficult to arrange after the Revolution. To get one you had to go to the doctor accompanied by a friend of his [the doctor's], or he wouldn't have dared take the risk. In 1961 I had an abortion that cost 150 pesos!

There had been a time, near the end of the dictatorship, when hardly anybody came to the brothels, and it was a bad time for us. But right after the Revolution business picked up. Not that lines formed at the door, but everyone earned more and the men began to come back. Of course with our working hours shortened, we could attend to fewer men in a day. We worked from 8:00 to 12:00 at night; we had a heavy workload on Fridays and weekends, but the rest of the time there weren't many clients, and some days I didn't earn a thing.

I still had problems with the police now and again, but they treated me very differently from the way Batista's force did. If I got into a fight they'd ask me to go to the police station, but they wouldn't sentence me or ask for bail, they'd just tell me it wasn't right to make such scenes and let me go. . . .

At the end of 1961, comrades from the ministry in charge of the rehabilitation plan began visiting the brothels, one by one, to offer us a fresh start. They told us the Revolution had decided to put an end to the horrible life we were leading. We were to spend some time at a rehabilitation school, and if we needed it, we'd be trained and given a job. They said if we were willing to study and work, our debt to society would be wiped out.

I couldn't believe it. I thought, "A chance to study? They'll support my daughter while I go to school? Give me money without my earning it? These promises can't be true!"

Of course the pimps campaigned strongly against it. They said the revolutionary government was a monster of hypocrisy—no ministry could possibly be so generous. When had we ever known any government to help anybody? There must be a catch to it. "When they put you to forced labor you'll be sorry!" That was what the pimps said. But to my way of seeing it I had nothing to lose. Anything was better than a brothel. . . .

The school I was sent to had been a rich man's home and was not really suitable for a school building. The ministry planned to remodel it, but so many women were anxious to quit prostitution, it was decided to start school at once and fix it up little by little, so at first there were no workshops, machine shops, or schoolrooms—those things came later.

The school was only for former prostitutes. When I arrived, there were very few women there, but after a couple of weeks there were fifty, and by the time I graduated seven months later there were about three hundred. All who wanted to attend were admitted.

From the very first day I realized that all the things I'd heard against the revolutionary government were lies. Everyone, from the director to the most humble employee, treated us kindly. They were concerned about our children's welfare, they wanted us to have enough clothes and good, well-balanced meals. And we had excellent medical care from a doctor on call and a full-time nurse. When we first enrolled we were given a medical checkup to see if any of us had syphilis. The only thing they found wrong with me was the way my uterus was tipped, so they sent me to another doctor for treatment. They gave me vitamins, too.

One of the girls was found to have the lung sickness. Measures were immediately taken to protect the rest of us. The poor girl was so afraid we'd be repelled by her illness she wouldn't talk to anyone, but in time she was cured and lived a normal life.

Three other girls and I had completed the sixth grade, so we were excused from classes and housework and given the first jobs, at a textile factory. We rose at 5:00 in the morning, made our beds, and went to breakfast. Some days we did exercises and marched around before starting to work. The factory was quite a distance away, so we were taken in a school car and our lunch was brought to us. Sometimes the lieutenant in charge of us came to fetch us in her own car, and we'd sing all the way home.

We had two different uniforms: blue slacks and pink blouses for school, gray skirts and pink blouses for street wear. The director thought the uniforms set us apart too much from the other comrades at the factory, but I didn't mind. If you go to school, you wear a uniform. That's only proper.

School was a wonderland! The director was a kind, affectionate woman, and our group was so small at first that we could eat out together sometimes, or go to the movies. That was something new to me! For the first time, too, I was free from family worries, and I began to take more of an interest in things, and to read.

Naturally a certain amount of discipline had to be maintained; you couldn't just take off whenever you felt like it. Saturdays and Sundays were our days off, and occasionally we got a weekday pass as a reward for good behavior. If you overslept, came late to the workshop or class, or were disrespectful to a teacher, you lost your pass, but I never broke a rule so I never lost mine.

Lots of the women didn't like getting up early, or going to classes and workshops. One said, "This is all very well, but I can't bear studying."

"Well, then, don't study," I told her. "Tell them you'd rather be assigned to a workshop."

"Oh no! I don't want anybody ordering me around. I want to earn money my own way. Besides, I hate to be shut in here all the time. I need to be out in the street."

Finally, a few of the girls said they wanted to leave. They were perfectly free to go, but first they were asked to talk it over with the rest of us, and we persuaded them to stay. Thanks to that they're now happy women.

All the same, there were some who sneaked out at night to avoid our talks, and some, influenced by pimps, went to the United States, where they're still prostitutes. I know because they write to people here.

The Family Code

Margaret Randall

In 1975, after a year of nationwide discussion in workplace and neighborhood as-
semblies, the revolutionary government passed a comprehensive "Family Code" that
was both revolutionary and, in some ways, traditional. In guaranteeing equality for
women, legitimizing consensual unions and the rights of all children (regardless of
whether their parents were officially married), and requiring equal responsibility and
opportunity of partners inside the home and out, the code fundamentally challenged
many traditional Cuban ideas about men's and women's roles. In promoting monoga-
mous, heterosexual marriage as the ideal, it adhered to other traditional values — even
though outright repression of homosexuals eased in the 1970s. In both respects, the
code coincided with the institutionalization and bureaucratization of the revolution
in other spheres and reflected a state project to solidify its dominion.

The Family Code began to be discussed by the Cuban people early in 1974,
and the original idea was that it become law in time for the FMC Congress.
At the same time, the importance of this code made it imperative that discussions be thorough and far reaching. Blas Roca, now a member of the party's
Politburo and president of the National People's Assembly and then member
of the party's Secretariat and head of the committee to draft new laws, spoke at
the Women's Congress and explained the process of debate and discussion. He
noted tendencies, offered anecdotes about ingrained unconscious sexism on
the part of leadership, and made a plea for long-term ideological work in this
respect. He told us how junior high school students were discussing the law,
the first law to be discussed by this age group because of its importance to their
future. He brought statistics from the discussions held by Cuban diplomatic
delegations overseas, military units, and comrades involved in international
missions.

The Code, like all of Cuba's most important laws, had been published in
draft form in a cheap tabloid edition so that virtually every man, woman,
and young person could have a copy to read and study. In meetings through
the trade unions, the CDRs, the FMC, the schools, and the like, people have a

Women in the Territorial Troop Militia, Havana. Photo by Tania Jovanovic.

chance—often more than one chance, as most citizens attend more than one of these meetings—to discuss the Code point by point, ask questions, suggest additions, changes, or deletions. The way this process works is that a record is kept of each meeting, the results are sent through the respective organizations to their highest level, where they are tabulated, computed, and turned over to the original committee (adjacent, at that time, to the party's Central Committee, now adjacent to the National Assembly). The Code is then modified according to the people's attitudes around specific issues and their participation in this process. For example, in the original draft of the Family Code, the marriage age for men had been higher than that for women. The people made them the same. The Code was finally returned to the Cuban people on International Women's Day, 8 March 1975.

The Family Code covers marriage, divorce, marital property relationships, recognition of children, obligations for children's care and education, adoption, and tutelage. Basically, the Code stipulates a new equality between women and men in their social relationships. Child support is not now automatically expected of the man, but, instead, might be expected of the woman in cases

Women rolling cigars. Photo by Tania Jovanovic.

A bust of José Martí overlooks workers in a cigar factory. Photo by Tania Jovanovic.

where the man is studying and the woman working. Custody of children is not given over to one parent or another, but provisions are sought through which both must continue to assume responsibilities in the event of divorce.

The clauses in this Code receiving the most attention and discussion are those stipulating both parents' equal responsibilities for child care and housework. The five clauses (24 through 28) covering this aspect have also been incorporated into the Cuban marriage ceremony and are read by judges performing all civil marriages, the only kind recognized by Cuban law.

Clauses 24, 25, 26, 27, and 28 read as follows—

24. Marriage is constituted on the basis of equal rights and duties of both spouses.

25. The spouses must live together, be faithful to one another, consider and respect each other, and each mutually help the other.

The rights and duties established by this Code will subsist in their entirety as long as the marriage has not been legally terminated, in spite of the fact that for justifiable reasons a common household cannot be maintained.

26. Both spouses are obligated to care for the family they have created and cooperate with each other in the education, formation and guidance of their children in line with the principles of socialist morality. As well, each to the extent of his or her capabilities and possibilities, must participate in governing the home and cooperate toward its best possible care.

27. The spouses are obliged to contribute toward satisfying the needs of the family they have created in their marriage, each according to his or her faculties and economic capacities. Nevertheless, if one of the spouses contributes only through his or her work in the home and child-care, the other spouse must provide full economic support without this meaning that he or she be relieved of the obligations of cooperating with the housework and child-care.

28. Both spouses have the right to exercise their professions or crafts and must lend each other reciprocal cooperation and aid to this effect, as well as in order to carry out studies or perfect their training, but in all cases they will take care to organize their home life so that such activities be coordinated with the fulfillment of the obligations imposed by this Code.

How does this Code work in practice? That's the question asked by most visitors to Cuba, and many seem to imply that, unless an overnight close-to-total change be effected, the Code doesn't work.

The Family Code is a law. It is also an educational tool. At this point, I believe the latter is the most important of the two aspects. The very discussions over the period of eight months when people grappled with these ideas stimulated an emerging consciousness or gave voice to a series of previously unarticulated concepts. The discussions were not only those officially staged by the political and mass organizations; some of the most intense took place on buses, in waiting rooms, in supermarket lines, and on the streets!

One example of this occurred in the discussion held through the CDR on my block. An elderly male neighbor had this to say: "You know . . . I've always believed in helping my wife. We've been married a long time, and I cook, clean, have taken care of our children and our grandchildren . . . but one thing I never felt right about doing was hanging the clothes on the line. I was afraid people would see me and laugh. Now I guess the time has come to get over these complexes. . . . We're all in this together!" In a second incident, in our local supermarket, one day when Family Code discussions were at their height, a man in the meat line mumbled something about ". . . this really is women's work. . . .Women are so good at this kind of thing . . . !" A woman directly in front of him turned around, and, with her face as close to his as possible, responded: "and some men are good at eating shit!"

The judicial repercussions of the Code, needless to say, depend on women themselves actually taking their husbands to court for violations. How many women are willing to take this step? Not enough. Clearly, many, for a long time to come, will allow themselves to be conned by the dozens of mechanisms men all over the world have developed to keep things the way they have always been. The important thing, at this point, is that women have state and party support in their struggle. A woman can go to the president of her CDR, or to the leadership of her own or her husband's trade union, and she has a legal, and not simply a subjective, basis on which to request help in an unequal home situation. There are no statistics familiar to me of cases actually brought before judges. In close observation of this whole process, I think it is fair to say that in places like the Isle of Youth, where many young couples live and work without the proverbial grandmother or aunt in the house, there is a stronger definition and a more aggressive attitude on the part of the women than, say, in situations where it is easier to fall back on the oppression of older retired, mostly female, family members.

It's also important to note that prevalent attitudes around these issues vary greatly from the older to the younger generations. Cuban young people, provided with a new and more progressive type of education than their parents and grandparents, view sexual equality as a normal, natural part of their lives. Speaking with junior and senior high school students, you won't find many young women who see their futures dependent on marriage or a future husband's career. Their central goal in life is their own development and their potential contribution to society.

Mother and daughter. Photo by Tania Jovanovic.

My own two teenage daughters and their friends expect absolute agreement and support from boyfriends around their logical political participation, and they insist upon full social integration at all levels. One of my daughters attends a special school, the Lenin School, for above-average students going into scientific and technological fields. Of the 4,500 students, slightly more than half are young women. Girls excel in the traditionally male areas such as math, physics, chemistry, and biology. Several years ago at this school, some of the boys in one of the dorms tried to get their girlfriends to wash and iron their uniforms. This was clearly a ploy for status control. It wasn't only the small group of girls approached who resisted and refused, but, within days, a movement had developed through which the vast majority of the school's female students made it clear that this was an issue of principle for them all—a case of spontaneous ideology in action!

Although the law states that Family Code articles 24 through 28 are applicable only in cases where a man's wife works or studies, Vilma Espín, at a press conference following the official establishment of this Code, took the issue quite a bit further. She emphasized the fact that, although legally the Code only applies in the aforementioned cases, it will be important for all men, whether or not their wives remain in or work outside the home, to share these obligations. This will be the only way, she pointed out, that future generations will grow up with a new morality gleaned from a changed image of how men and women should interact.

Homosexuality, Creativity, Dissidence

Reinaldo Arenas

In this excerpt from the Reinaldo Arenas (1943–1990) memoir Before Night Falls, *upon which Julian Schnabel's 2000 film of the same title was based, Arenas recalls the early 1960s. Those years were, for him, a time of revolution on all levels, unleashing unlimited sexual and creative energies. That was the period in which he received his initiation into the literary world as well as the world of gay sex. As he reminisces, the two pleasures—literary and sexual—seem to meld into one. Later, when the repression began and gays were hauled off to "re-education camps," Arenas came to view homosexuality as "a protest against the regime," a conspiracy, that "began to flourish with ever-increasing defiance." The fevered pitch of his sensual life was matched only by that of his literary production, hammered out on his beloved old mechanical Underwood typewriter.*

My erotic adventures were not limited to beaches and military camps; they also occurred in universities and university dorms where hundreds of students slept. Once I met a student whose name was Fortunato Granada. He was Colombian and had come to Cuba in the hope of studying medicine. In those years the Revolutionary government had invited many young people from all over Latin America to study at Cuban universities. Once enrolled at the universities, they were subjected to political indoctrination and finally they were told that their country had to be liberated, that it was a victim of U.S. imperialism, that they had to return home as guerrillas.

Fortunato told me all this while we were making love on a bunk mattress in the dorm basement. He wanted to be a doctor—his reason for coming to Cuba—not to go back as a guerrilla. When he refused, his passport was taken away, and now they were threatening to expel him from the university. He was trying desperately to figure out what to do in Cuba after being expelled from the university and deprived of any ID.

We continued making love for a year; he finally had to enlist as a guerrilla fighter. I don't know if he got killed, because I never heard from him again.

When I wrote *The Palace of the White Skunks*, I wanted to pay tribute in a small way to this great lover of mine; the hero's name in my novel is Fortunato.

The guerrillas who were lucky returned to Cuba. One of them, Alfonso, had met Fortunato. One day Alfonso knocked at my aunt's door asking for me, and he identified himself as Fortunato's friend. I realized right away what he wanted. We became good friends and excellent lovers. He had belonged to the guerrillas and now worked for the Ministry of the Interior in Cuba. He had an official role at diplomatic affairs attended by Fidel Castro, as part of his security guard. Perhaps his homosexual inclination was forgiven because he was a foreigner; or perhaps the government didn't find out about it. He kept coming to me for years. Of course, he came only now and then and, frankly, behaved in a very masculine way. Then suddenly he disappeared; maybe he was transferred to another country on a special mission. God knows where he is now.

In addition to the pickups during the day, which generally took place at the beaches, there was another powerful homosexual scene in Havana, underground but very visible. There were pickups at night all over La Rampa, at Coppelia, on Prado Boulevard and along the Malecón Shore Drive, and at Coney Island in Marianao. These areas were full of recruits and students, single men who were locked up in barracks or schools and went out at night eager for sex. They were willing to settle for the first thing that came along. I always tried to be one of the first they met in these places. Hundreds of them ended up in my room. Sometimes they did not want to go that far, in which case we had to risk going downtown, to Old Havana, where we would walk up some stairway to the top floor and lower our pants. I think that in Cuba there was never more fucking going on than in those years, the decade of the sixties, which was precisely when all the new laws against homosexuals came into being, when the persecutions started and concentration camps were opened, when the sexual act became taboo while the "new man" was being proclaimed and masculinity exalted. Many of the young men who marched in Revolutionary Square applauding Fidel Castro, and many of the soldiers who marched, rifle in hand and with martial expressions, came to our rooms after the parades to cuddle up naked, and show their real selves, sometimes revealing a tenderness and true enjoyment such as I have not been able to find again anywhere else in the world.

Perhaps deep down they realized they were breaking into the realm of the forbidden, the dangerous, and the damned. Perhaps that is the reason why, when that moment came, they showed such fullness, such radiance, and enjoyed every instant in the awareness that it might be their last, that it could cost them many years in jail. There was, moreover, no prostitution. It was pleasure for pleasure's sake, the craving of one body for another, the need to find fulfillment. Sexual pleasure between two men was a conspiracy, something that happened in the shadows or in plain daylight, but always forbidden; a look, a wink, a gesture, a sign, was enough to start the sequence that resulted in such full enjoyment. The adventure in itself, even if fulfillment did not come with the desired body, was already a pleasure, a mystery, a surprise. To enter a movie theater was to figure out whom we would sit next to, and whether that young man over there would stretch out his leg toward us. To reach over slowly with one hand and touch his thigh, and then to dare a little more and feel the part of his pants where that penis wanted to break through the fabric; to masturbate him right then and there during an old American movie, to see how he would ejaculate, and then leave before the movie ended; and perhaps I would never see him again, after having seen his face only in profile. What does it matter, he was surely a wonderful guy.

People would really get sexually aroused on interstate trips. If you took one of those buses crowded with young men, you could be sure that some erotic games would take place during the trip. The driver would turn out the lights, and the bus would be moving on those highways full of potholes; with each lurch of the vehicle one had the opportunity for contact, for touching an erect penis, a young thigh, a strong chest; hands could move over a body, feel for the waist, unbuckle the belt, and then, cautious and eager, reach for the spot where that terrific member lay hidden. Those adventures, and the people with whom one had them, were great. Those men enjoyed their roles of active miles; they wanted to be sucked and even to fuck right on the bus.

Later, in exile, I found that sexual relations can be tedious and unrewarding. There are categories or divisions in the homosexual world. The queer gets together with the queer and everybody does everything. One sucks first, and then they reverse roles. How can that bring any satisfaction? What we are really looking for is our opposite. The beauty of our relationships then was that we met our opposites. We would find that man, that powerful recruit who wanted desperately to fuck us. We were fucked under bridges, in the bushes, everywhere, by men who wanted satisfaction while they penetrated us. Either conditions here are different, or it is just difficult to duplicate what we had there. Everything here is so regulated that groups and societies have been created in which it is very difficult for a homosexual to find a man, that is, the real object of his desire.

I do not know what to call the young Cuban men of those days, whether homosexuals who played the male role or bisexuals. The truth is that they had girlfriends or wives, but when they came to us they enjoyed themselves thoroughly, sometimes more than with their wives, who often would refuse to suck or had inhibitions that made lovemaking less pleasurable.

I remember an extraordinary mulatto, married and with several children, who escaped his family once a week to fuck me on the iron chair in my room. I never saw a man enjoy sex so much. He was, nevertheless, an excellent father and exemplary husband.

I think that the sexual revolution in Cuba actually came about as a result of the existing sexual repression. Perhaps as a protest against the regime, homosexuality began to flourish with ever-increasing defiance. Moreover, since the dictatorship was considered evil, anything it proscribed was seen in a positive light by the nonconformists, who in the sixties were already almost the majority. I honestly believe that the concentration camps for homosexuals, and the police officers disguised as willing young men to entrap and arrest homosexuals, actually resulted in the promotion of homosexual activities.

In Cuba gays were not confined to a specific area of a club or beach. Everybody mingled and there was no division that would place the homosexual on the defensive. This has been lost in more advanced societies, where the homosexual has had to become a sort of sexual recluse and separate himself from the supposedly nonhomosexual society, which undoubtedly also excludes him. Since such divisions did not exist in Cuba, the interesting aspect of homosexuality there was that you did not have to be a homosexual to have a relationship with a man; a man could have intercourse with another man as an ordinary act. In the same way, a real gay who liked another gay could easily go out and live with him. But the gay who liked real macho men could also find one who wanted to live or be friends with him, without in any way interfering with the heterosexual life of that man. It was not the norm for one queer to go to bed with another queer; "she" would look for a man to fuck "her" who would feel as much pleasure as the homosexual being fucked.

Homosexual militancy has gained considerable rights for free-world gays. But what has been lost is the wonderful feeling of meeting heterosexual or bisexual men who would get pleasure from possessing another man and who would not, in turn, have to be possessed.

The ideal in any sexual relationship is finding one's opposite, and therefore the homosexual world is now something sinister and desolate; we almost never get what we most desire.

That world, of course, also had its dangers. Along with other homosexuals, I was robbed and blackmailed a number of times. Once, after I received my monthly pay from the National Library, just ninety pesos, which was not much but had to cover all of my expenses for the month, I was foolish enough to go straight to the beach. I met a marvelous youth who had caught a crab, tied it to a string, and was walking it on the sand as if it were his dog. I praised the crab while looking at the legs of the youth, who then quickly came with me to my booth. He was wearing a tiny bathing suit. I don't know how he did it, but during his sexual gymnastics, which he handled with practiced skill, he managed to steal all my money from my pants pocket and hide it in his small bathing suit. The truth is that after he left I realized that I had been cleaned out; I did not even have a nickel for the bus fare home. I looked for him all over La Concha Beach. In one of the open booths I found a smashed crab. He was evidently a violent person. The carapace was all that was left of the crab. The beautiful adolescent had disappeared without leaving a witness: not even a crab.

That afternoon I walked home. Once in my room, I continued writing a long poem. I entitled it "Morir en junio y con la lengua afuera" (To Die in June, Gasping for Air). A few days later I had to stop working on the poem because somebody had entered my room through the window and stolen my type-writer. This was a serious theft; to me that typewriter was not only the one object of value in my possession but also the thing I treasured the most. To me, sitting down at the typewriter was, and still is, something extraordinary. I would be inspired (like a pianist) by the rhythm of those keys and they would carry me along. Paragraphs would follow one another like ocean waves, at times more intense, at others less so; sometimes like huge breakers that would engulf page after page, before the next paragraph. My typewriter was an old iron Underwood, but to me it was a magical instrument.

Guillermo Rosales, then a good-looking young writer, lent me his type-writer and I finished the poem.

Some time later a mulatto police officer, rather handsome in fact, showed up at my home. He told me my typewriter was at the police station. The thief had been caught burglarizing another home, and his house had been searched. They found many stolen items, my typewriter among them. Apparently the thief himself told the police that the typewriter was mine. After many bureau-cratic formalities, it was returned and I had to carry it home in a bus full of people; it seemed to weigh a ton, but I got it back where it belonged. I was afraid it would be stolen again, and my friend Aurelio Cortés had the bright idea of bolting it to its metal table.

A number of times hoodlums—that is, the boys with whom I had made love—entered my room and tried to steal the typewriter, but to no effect; it was impossible to carry both typewriter and metal table. From then on I felt safer, better able to continue my love life without endangering the rhythm of my literary production. That rhythm has always been part of me, even during periods of the most intense lovemaking or of the greatest police persecution. Writing crowned or complemented all other pleasures as well as all other calamities.

TRANSLATED BY DOLORES M. KOCH

The Original Sin

Pablo Milanés

Although the revolution did make a conscious commitment to gender equality, there was no parallel drive to end discrimination on the basis of sexual orientation. In fact, the revolutionary government went through periods (especially in the late 1960s and 1970s) of harsh and sometimes violent repression against homosexuals. Tomás Gutiérrez Alea's 1993 film Strawberry and Chocolate *reflects on the contradictions between conformism and liberation in Cuban culture and in the Cuban revolution. Set in 1979, the film critiques both the intellectual restrictions of this period of "Sovietization" and the insistence on sexual conformity. One of the heroes is a dogmatic Young Communist; the other is an intellectual, religious, and sexual nonconformist who insists that the revolution needs to include him too. The film was enormously popular in Cuba in the 1990s when the shift toward Sovietization seemed, in retrospect, to have been a socially and economically costly route to have taken. (The film — and most public discussion in Cuba — nonetheless avoided discussing the period of most intense official repression against homosexuals in the 1960s, which could not be attributed to any "outside" influences.)*

Also in the 1990s, the immensely popular Cuban singer Pablo Milanés (b. 1943) wrote "El pecado original" explicitly celebrating (male) homosexual love and decrying societal and legal repression of homosexuality.

Two souls
two bodies
two men who love each other
are going to be expelled from the paradise
that they lived in.
Neither of them is a warrior
who celebrated his victories with youths.
Neither of them has riches
to calm the wrath of his judges.
Neither of them is president.
Neither of them is a minister.

Neither of them is a censor of his own mutilated desires . . .
and they feel that they can, each morning,
see their tree,
their park,
their sun,
as you and I do;
that they can tear out their hearts
in the sweetest intimacy with love
just as I always sink my flesh
desperately into your belly
also with love.
We are not God.
Let us not make the mistake again.

TRANSLATED BY IAN LUMSDEN

Where the Island Sleeps Like a Wing

Nancy Morejón

In a recent essay, "Race and Inequality in Cuba, 1899–1981," Alejandro de la Fuente outlines some of the complexities in trying to evaluate the impact of the Cuban Revolution on race relations in Cuba. He notes the various schools of thought to which different Cuban and Cuban American scholars have subscribed: "the revolution inherited and solved the racial problem"; "the revolution did inherit a racial problem, but has reinforced it"; "the revolution has had a positive impact on race relations, but . . . pre-revolutionary Cuban society had already opened paths of social advancement for blacks"; "although the revolution has had a strong impact on race relations and has eradicated the most important aspects of inequality, some forms of racism and discrimination still persist."[1]

There are at least three conceptual issues that make the debate about race and racism in contemporary Cuba a complicated one. First, as with virtually everything about contemporary Cuba, the topic is politicized. Evaluations of the condition of blacks in today's Cuba are not unrelated to evaluations of the Cuban Revolution as a whole: in general, observers sympathetic to the revolution tend to argue that there has been improvement in race relations, whereas observers opposed to the revolution highlight examples of racism and racial inequality in Cuba today. Second, as we have learned from biologists and anthropologists, race is a social, cultural, and historical concept, rather than a scientific one. That is, racial categories and identities have different meanings in different societies, and these meanings have changed over time. (The very meaning of progress in race relations is still subject to debate inside the United States today, as can be seen in the ongoing discussions over the merits of integrated versus separate schools.) Thus Cubans of all skin colors have frequently chided U.S. observers for mechanistically applying categories and ideas from the U.S. context to the Cuban context and thus missing crucial aspects and nuances of Cuban race relations.

Finally, we must recognize that structural/material and ideological/cultural changes do not always go hand in hand. This, in the end, is de la Fuente's conclusion: the revolution's structural approach to reducing inequality has been quite successful in some areas (particularly in health and education), but "the persistence . . . of a

racist mentality should not be underestimated. . . . Still, when someone hears about
a robbery in Cuba, the customary comment is: 'It was probably a Negro.' "²

The poems of poet, essayist, and literary translator Nancy Morejón (b. 1944) are
at once universal and intensely Cuban. In some, she celebrates Havana, her city. In
others, the nation's historical figures come alive in a telescoping of time that links past
to present and that relates episodes in Cuban history to popular struggles across the
globe. "Barely a Hero" revisits Rosa de Castillas, an episode in the struggle against
Batista, in an expansive gaze that also takes in Teruel, one of the bloodiest battles
of the Spanish Civil War. "Rebirth" and "Madrigal for Runaway Slaves" exhibit the
same telescoping of time, and they celebrate collective memory, the oral history that
resurrects the lives of unsung heroes. "Black Woman" is a denunciation of colonial-
ism, slavery, and the sugar cycle that carries the reader through the entire trajectory
of Cuban history, from the slave trade and arrival through the horrors of the planta-
tion, maroon life, the war for independence from Spain, and, ultimately, the Sierra
Maestra, all from the perspective of an Afro-Cuban woman.

REBIRTH

Daughter of ocean waters,
asleep in that womb,
I am reborn out of the gunpowder
sown over the mountain
by a guerrilla rifle
so the world in its turn
might be reborn,
and the vast sea
and all the dust,
all the dust of Cuba.

BARELY A HERO

Still further than the hills
and their jungle thickets
glints the quiet water of a pool.
The soldier, leaning over a book,
lives on where valleys fill with light.

Bullets no longer fly in Rosa de Castillas.
No hymns, no tomb, no battle of Teruel
encircle the earthen shadow

dozing, stretched on the rugged ground,
barely more than a child, disheveled and slow.

Now, rain falls over the village
through the sheet of aromas and orange trees.
The wet trees shed their drops over the hero.

     There he is now.
I see a red hole
embossing his breast.
Let life be born again from his nature!

MADRIGAL FOR RUNAWAY SLAVES
for Miguel Barnet

Head and hands dangling, flaring,
mocking the Slave Tracker's clue.
Their sweating bodies dive into the tangled wet brush.

What a hard beauty their hearts have.
On their machetes as on slender branches
pigeons and tropical mice nest.
And days of suns,
and days of moon,
and days of will
resurrect their lives, and they are like children,
sweet children of a liberty already won.

BLACK WOMAN

I still smell the foam of the sea they made me cross.
The night, I can't remember it.
The ocean itself could not remember that.
But I can't forget the first gull I made out in the distance.
High, the clouds, like innocent eyewitnesses.
Perhaps I haven't forgotten my lost coast,
nor my ancestral language.
They left me here and here I've lived.
And, because I worked like an animal,
here I came to be born.
How many Mandinga[3] epics did I look to for strength.

      I rebelled.

His Worship bought me in a public square.
I embroidered His Worship's coat and bore him a male child.
My son had no name.
And His Worship died at the hands of an impeccable English *lord*.

     I walked.

This is the land where I suffered
mouth-in-the-dust and the lash.
I rode the length of all its rivers.
Under its sun I planted seeds, brought in the crops,
but never ate those harvests.
A slave barracks was my house,
built with stones that I hauled myself.
While I sang to the pure beat of native birds.

     I rose up.

In this same land I touched the fresh blood
and decayed bones of many others,
brought to this land or not, the same as I.
I no longer dreamt of the road to Guinea.
Was it to Guinea? Benin?
To Madagascar? Or Cape Verde?

     I worked on and on.

I strengthened the foundations of my millenary song and of my hope.

     I left for the hills.

My real independence was the free slave fort
and I rode with the troops of Maceo.

Only a century later,
together with my descendants,
from a blue mountain

     I came down from the Sierra

to put an end to capital and usurer,
to generals and to bourgeois.
Now I exist: only today do we own, do we create.
Nothing is foreign to us.

The land is ours.
Ours the sea and the sky,
the magic and the vision.
Compañeros, here I see you dance
around the tree we are planting for communism.
Its prodigal wood resounds.

TRANSLATED BY KATHLEEN WEAVER

Notes

1. Alejandro de la Fuente, "Race and Inequality in Cuba, 1899–1981," *Journal of Contemporary History* 30 (1995): 132–33.
2. De la Fuente, "Race and Inequality in Cuba," 161–62.
3. From the Mandingo-speaking people of West Africa.

Silence on Black Cuba

Carlos Moore

In 1988 Carlos Moore published a devastating, and widely disseminated, critique of the Cuban Revolution. Unlike the majority of the genre of antirevolutionary literature, Moore's claimed to come from below, from the oppressed black majority of Cuba. Instead of being published by right-wing institutions such as Freedom House or the Cuban American National Foundation, Moore's Castro, the Blacks, and Africa *was published by the University of California, Los Angeles's Center for Afro-American Studies. Nevertheless, Moore himself has in turn been criticized for using a "narrow racialistic framework" in his analysis and being unwilling "to recognize class, nation, and international political economy as equally important agents in history."*[1]

Like many studies of race relations in Latin America, Moore's analysis was based on dissecting the myths of racial harmony that have been used as a weapon to discredit blacks' legitimate struggles for racial justice. Moore argued that Castro's "silence on Black Cuba" continued a longstanding Cuban elite refusal to address racial issues. When Castro repeated José Martí's slogan that "to be Cuban is more than being White, more than being Black" and insisted that "a Cuban is simply someone who belongs to no race in particular." Moore concluded that he was actually "tacitly condon[ing] white supremacy."

Fidel Castro had assumed mastery over a population estimated at 6.7 million, of which conceivably about 50 percent were of African descent. . . .[2] Racial segregation both in public and private establishments was still pervasive when the Revolution overthrew Batista. Some Afro-Cuban soldiers who had risked their lives alongside Castro encountered discrimination at hotels and restaurants where their white counterparts were welcomed. Castro nonetheless pointedly minimized the racial question in Cuba in those early weeks of euphoria. In answer to a foreign journalist's question during a press conference on 23 January, he even reiterated standard white Cuban platitudes. "In Cuba we do not have the same problem as, for example, in the South of the United States," he said. "There is racial discrimination in Cuba, but to a much lesser degree. We feel that our Revolution will help to eliminate those prejudices and injustices

Men sitting in a doorway. Photo by Tania Jovanovic.

that remain latent. For the time being, we have given proof in our revolutionary struggle of an absolute identification and brotherhood with men of all skin colors. In that sense, ours are the thoughts of [José] Martí and we would be neither revolutionaries nor democrats if we were not free of all types of discrimination."

However, an opinion survey among Blacks conducted independently in late February by *Revolución*, the publication of Castro's Movimiento directed by Carlos Franqui, brutally contradicted Castro's appraisal. Racism in Cuba was not a "latent" phenomenon, but a veritable plague on the black population, according to the survey. One of the interviewees, Irene Fernández, complained: "We colored people have many problems . . . because many things are denied us in Cuba. That's why we are suffering a great deal." The general tone of the sample survey was voiced by Cristobalina Sardinas: "Fidel wants the truth told, since lies are worthless. Well, we want to tell him the truth: The black race has always lived under extreme oppression. It is high time that justice be done. Equal opportunities must be given us to exist. If one goes to rent a home and they see you're Black, they refuse to rent. It's an injustice and *we expect the Revolution to do away with it"* [italics added by Carlos Moore].

Two months after Castro's victory, Black Cuba was still unsure of its status with the regime. The racial question remained perilously unanswered. The predominantly black rural and industrial workers, the unemployed, and the

Sidewalk game in front of the Bacardi Building. Photo by Tania Jovanovic.

Men at work. Photo by Tania Jovanovic.

Cutting cane. Photo by Tania Jovanovic.

white peasantry were the true social base of the regime. But they continued
to have no say in the affairs of the exclusively Hispanic Cuban state.[3]

Grassroots and middle-class Blacks were uneasy about the still-unstated intentions of the new white men in power regarding the race question. Fidel
Castro's icy silence on anything remotely touching the plight of Black Cuba,
both before and immediately after 1959, was not reassuring. In those early
months of the Revolution there was widespread fear among Afro-Cubans that,
as in the past, *la gente de color* (the people of color) would be subtly marginalized
by the political establishment. . . .

Essentially, Castro's speeches reconfirmed two permanent features of his
approach to race relations: a commitment to an integrationist stance steeped
in white liberal paternalism and a firm refusal to allow the racial question to
escape that framework. In other words, it was out of the question for Blacks
themselves to define the content of their own oppression, or define the terms
of their ethnic emancipation. David Booth seems to have grasped that situation when he wrote that "in those two speeches in the early months of 1959
Fidel Castro not only identified the aspirations of his movement in relation
to domestic racial discrimination but also established the limits beyond which
it could not go. Henceforth he referred to the color problem in his speeches
only in passing and implying that, with the campaign to end discrimination

in workplaces and social centers completed, there was little if anything that remained to be done."

In other words, the government was intent on banning discrimination based on race or color, while racism itself could remain a sort of discretionary ethical question. Implicit in this policy was that Cuba's new white leadership tacitly condoned white supremacy but frowned on racial segregation.

At no time between March 1959 and the Third Congress of the Cuban Communist party in February 1986, *twenty-seven years later,* did Castro or any of his top lieutenants attempt to open Cuba's racial Pandora's box again. Rather, from that point on, the Castro leadership would resist and even repress attempts by black dissenters to force the issue into the open. "When Fidel approached the racial question in 1959," remarked a Haitian Communist, "his words were received enthusiastically. It would have befitted the situation to have pursued that theme further. . . . What made him come to a halt while in such a good position?" An overview of Fidel Castro's racial attitudes before he came to power is in order to give even a tentative answer to this question.

Notes

For complete references and notes, consult the work as cited in the acknowledgment of copyrights section.

1. Lisa Brock and Otis Cunningham, "Race and the Cuban Revolution: A Critique of Carlos Moore's 'Castro, the Blacks, and Africa,'" *Cuban Studies* 21 (1991): 171–86.

2. The question of how many Blacks there are in Cuba remains highly controversial. In his only public statement on this subject, however, Fidel Castro reported to foreign journalists in 1966 that *half* of Cuba's population was of African descent.

3. *Eds. note*: That is, controlled by people of Spanish origin.

Black Man in Red Cuba

John Clytus

Black activists from the United States and elsewhere in the world have frequently looked to the Cuban Revolution as either an example of hope for revolutionary change in their own societies, or, conversely, as an example of the failure of a revolution to effectively address racial issues, because it identified socioeconomic change as its top priority. American black activist John Clytus (b. 1929), in Black Man in Red Cuba, *describes his conversations about race with a Cuban prison guard after Clytus was arrested there for trying to cross into the Guantánamo Naval Base. Clytus had been on the island for two and a half years. Clytus argues that "communism . . . bodes no good for either the 'Negroes' or the blacks. . . . Cuba taught me that a black under communism in a white-oriented society—any society where whites hold or have held power—would find himself in a white society that would persecute him for even intimating that he had a love for black."*

"This is G-2 headquarters, the secret police," he announced, watching for my reaction.

I guess now I'm supposed to jump through the ceiling, I thought. "That doesn't impress me. I haven't done anything," I said.

"You haven't done anything," he mocked. "From the moment they locked you up in Santiago, we've been checking on you—you've been going about with counterrevolutionaries."

Even if he had spoken as though he believed that, I still would have laughed in his face. I explained that I didn't go about with anybody. The counterrevolutionaries hated all foreigners—any foreigners getting along in Cuba were, undoubtedly, rendering services for the government—and the revolutionaries, or so-called revolutionaries, were afraid that anyone from the United States might turn out to be a CIA agent. The only Cubans, I told him, with whom I had even a casual friendship were two or three who identified themselves as Afro-Cubans.

"Why do you say 'Afro-Cubans'?" he asked.

That had been a mistake. Anyone identifying with his blackness was considered a divisionist, a counterrevolutionary.

"Because all black people are of African descent," I answered.

He looked at me for a long moment, then asked, "if you return to the States, what group are you going to join?"

"An all-black group."

"You're a racist," he said.

"Black people are surrounded by racists," I retorted.

"We had that problem in Cuba before the revolution. My wife is Negro, a mulatta." He took out her picture and handed it to me.

I wondered if he were so stupid as to believe that people who had been racists all their lives, had a country with a history of racism, and were still under the culture of the racist Western world, could suddenly stop being racists.

I looked at the woman in the picture, noting the blood of the black race in her full lips and her heavy hair. Her skin was not a pale white, but light enough to put her into the *"mulata avanzada"* class, the group that evolved through women of the black race coupling with men of the white race, generation after generation.

"Before the revolution, I could not accompany her to dances at the black social clubs, and she could not go with me to the white social clubs," he went on.

You're breaking my heart, I thought.

"You should visit the day nurseries here," he continued. "White and black children together, without regard to race."

"I've seen them," I said, "but I don't believe in assimilation. The black man's going to disappear in Cuba. Miscegenation's going to wipe him out."

"What you say is true," he replied dryly, and then started the interrogation.

He began by asking me my place of birth and kept going on the history-of-my-life theme until an hour or so had passed. Then he called a guard and had me taken back to my cell. It was dark, and for a time I lay awake recalling all the officer had said to me. There had been nothing in his conversation or action to make me nervous, but neither had he indicated what I could expect to happen to me. Yet, for having at least talked with the higher-ups, I felt better. If they had turned on the lights in the cell I would have felt better still. But it was only around eight o'clock, and I told myself that perhaps they were conserving electricity. Eventually I was able to fall asleep. . . .

Epilogue

Using Cuba as a yardstick to measure the "delights" of communism, I am convinced that the latter bodes no good for either the "Negroes" or the blacks.

Communism is purported to be a system that will end the exploitation of man by his fellow man. It proposes to accomplish this phenomenon by ending the class society of the capitalist system and by creating a classless society under communism. What it actually does is reverse the direction of the exploitation — and this only when it is convenient.

If under capitalism the "haves" have because they take from the "have nots," under communism the "have nots" have because of what is taken from the "haves." Communism, championing equal treatment for all, would end the exploitation of just the poor and exploit all, rich or poor, who did not dance to the dictatorial tune of its ruling hierarchy.

Cuba taught me that a black under communism in a white-oriented society — any society where whites hold or have held power — would find himself in a white society that would persecute him for even intimating that he had a love for black. Periodicals, books, television, and other media of communication would no longer be permitted to carry his voice of dissent against injustice.

Communism, with its benevolent method of ending the racial problem by condensing all races into one-big-happy-humane-race, would ring down the final curtain on black consciousness. Nor would "Negroes," in spite of their love for integration with whites, find themselves in their expected paradise. The "Negroes" that constitute the "bourgeoisie of color" in white-oriented societies would suddenly find such capitalist "luxuries" as their homes and businesses, paid for with sweat and hard-earned money, taken from them for the "convenience" of the State.

Their protest marches, used so loosely by "Negroes" to publicize their problems in order for whites to solve them, would become their death marches. The only people who "overcome" in protest marches in Communist societies are those in the tanks and with the machine guns.

After three years in Communist Cuba, I am convinced that a "Negro" Communist is an absurdity and a black Communist is an impossibility.

Post-modern Maroon
in the Ultimate *Palenque*

Christian Parenti

For other African Americans, Cuba's experiment with socialism — despite its flaws — represented the hope for radical social change that seemed impossible in the United States. Sociologist Christian Parenti dubbed Assata Shakur — former activist in the Black Liberation Army, who escaped from prison in the United States and settled in Cuba — as a "post-modern maroon in the ultimate palenque" — drawing on the imagery of the times of slavery to depict Cuba as a refuge of freedom outside of U.S. domination. For Shakur, the vibrancy of Afro-Cuban culture in Cuba poses almost as stark a contrast to the United States as do the political and economic differences. This vibrancy is due more to the continuation of the slave trade until late in the nineteenth century, which meant that African culture was constantly renewed, than to the revolution — but it certainly plays an important role in the differences in racial ideologies and racial consciousness between the two countries.

What happens to old Black Panthers? Some wind up dead like Huey P. Newton. Some join the Moonies and the Republican Party, like Eldridge Cleaver. Some, like Mumia Abu Jamal, languish in prison. But a few, like Assata Shakur, have taken the path of the "maroon," the runaway slave of old who slipped off the plantation to the free jungle communities known as palenques.

Two decades ago Shakur was described as "the soul of the Black Liberation Army (BLA)," an underground, paramilitary group that emerged from the rubble of east coast chapters of the Black Panther Party. Among her closest political comrades was Ahfeni Shakur, Tupac Shakur's mother. Forced underground in 1971, by charges that were later proved false, Assata was accused of being the "bandit queen" of the BLA; the "mother hen who kept them together, kept them moving, kept them shooting." The BLA's alleged actions included assassinating almost ten police officers, kidnapping drug dealers (one of whom turned out to be an FBI agent), and robbing banks from coast to coast.

Throughout 1971 and 1972 "Assata sightings" and wild speculation about her deeds were a headline mainstay for New York tabloids. Then, in 1973, Shakur and two friends were pulled over by state troopers on the New Jersey Turnpike. During the stop, shooting erupted. A trooper and one alleged BLA member were killed, another trooper was slightly hurt and Assata—or Miss Joanne Chesimard, as authorities preferred to call her—was severely wounded by a blast of police gunfire. Left to die in a paddy wagon, she survived only to be charged for the trooper's death and sentenced to life in prison.

During the next six years (much of it spent in solitary confinement), Shakur beat a half-dozen other indictments. In 1979—after giving birth in prison, only to have her daughter taken away in less than a week—Assata Shakur managed one of the most impressive jailbreaks of the era. On the day of the escape, [a] team of three met in the waiting room at the prison entrance. . . . One member of the team went ahead. . . . Meanwhile . . . one of the [others] drew a gun and took the guard hostage. Simultaneously, the man visiting Shakur . . . ordered the officer to open the . . . door. . . . From there Shakur and "the raiders" took a third guard hostage and made it to [a] parked van. . . . Shakur . . . disappeared without a trace.

For the next five years authorities hunted in vain. Shakur had vanished. Numerous other alleged BLA cadre were busted during those years, including Tupac's uncle, Mutula Shakur. In 1984 word came from ninety miles off the coast of Florida. The FBI's most wanted female fugitive was living in Cuba, working on a masters degree in political science, writing her autobiography, and raising her daughter.

Cut to 1997. It's a stunningly hot summer afternoon in Havana, Cuba—the ultimate palenque—and I am having strong, black coffee with Assata Shakur who just turned fifty, but looks more like thirty-six. She keeps a low profile; security is still a big concern. She's finishing her second book. Given how much the Feds want this woman locked up, I feel strange being in her house, as if my presence is a breach of security.

Parenti: How did you arrive in Cuba?

Shakur: Well, I couldn't, you know, just write a letter and say "Dear Fidel, I'd like to come to your country." So I had to hoof it—come and wait for the Cubans to respond. Luckily, they had some idea who I was, they'd seen some of the briefs and UN petitions from when I was a political prisoner. So they were somewhat familiar with my case and they gave me the status of being a political refugee. That means I am here in exile as a political person.

How did you feel when you got here?

I was really overwhelmed. Even though I considered myself a socialist, I had these insane, silly notions about Cuba. I mean, I grew up in the 1950s when little kids were hiding under their desks, because "the communists were coming." So even though I was very supportive of the revolution, I expected everyone to go around in green fatigues looking like Fidel, speaking in a very stereotypical way, "the revolution must continue, *compañero*. Let us triumph, comrade." When I got here people were just people, doing what they had where I came from. It's a country with a strong sense of community. Unlike the U.S., folks aren't as isolated. People are really into other people.

Also, I didn't know there were all these black people here and that there was this whole Afro-Cuban culture. My image of Cuba was Che Guevara and Fidel Castro, I hadn't heard of Antonio Maceo [a hero of the Cuban War of Independence] and other Africans who had played a role in Cuban history.

The lack of brand names and consumerism also really hit me. You go into a store and there would be a bag of "rice." It undermined what I had taken for granted in the absurd zone where people are like, "Hey, I only eat uncle so-and-so's brand of rice."

So, how were you greeted by the Cuban state?

They've treated me very well. It was different from what I expected; I thought they might be pushy. But they were more interested in what I wanted to do, in my projects. I told them that the most important things were to unite with my daughter and to write a book. They said, "What do you need to do that?" They were also interested in my vision of the struggle of African people in the United States. I was so impressed by that. Because I grew up — so to speak — in the movement dealing with white leftists who were very bossy and wanted to tell us what to do and thought they knew everything. The Cuban attitude was one of solidarity with respect. It was a profound lesson in cooperation.

Did they introduce you to people or guide you around for a while?

They gave me a dictionary, an apartment, took me to some historical places, and then I was pretty much on my own. My daughter came down, after prolonged harassment and being denied a passport, and she became my number one priority. We discovered Cuban schools together, we did the sixth grade together, explored parks, and the beach.

She was taken from you at birth, right?

Yeah. It's not like Cuba where you get to breast-feed in prison and where they work closely with the family. Some mothers in the U.S. never get to see their newborns. I was with my daughter for a week before they sent me back to the prison. That was one of the most difficult periods of my life, that separation. It's only been recently that I've been able to talk about it. I had to just block it out; otherwise I think I might have gone insane. In 1979, when I escaped, she was only five years old.

You came to Cuba how soon after?

Five years later, in 1984.

I know it's probably out of bounds, but where were you during the intervening years?

I was underground. But I don't talk about that period. To do so would put a lot of people who helped me in jeopardy.

Right, I hear you. You've talked about adjusting to Cuba, but could you talk a bit about adjusting to exile.

Well, for me exile means separation from people I love. I didn't, and don't miss the U.S., per se. But black culture, black life in the U.S., that African American flavor, I definitely miss. The language, the movements, the style, I get nostalgic about that.

Adjusting to exile is coming to grips with the fact that you may never go back to where you come from. The way I dealt with that, psychologically, was thinking about slavery. You know, a slave had to come to grips with the fact that "I may never see Africa again." Then a maroon, a runaway slave, has to—even in the act of freedom—adjust to the fact that being free or struggling for freedom means, "I'll be separated from people I love." So I drew on that and people like Harriet Tubman and all those people who got away from slavery. Because, that's what prison looked like. It looked like slavery. It felt like slavery. It was black people and people of color in chains. And the way I got there was slavery. If you stand up and say, "I don't go for the status quo." Then "we got something for you, it's a whip, a chain, a cell."

Even in being free it was like, "I am free but now what?" There was a lot to get used to. Living in a society committed to social justice, a Third World country with a lot of problems. It took a while to understand all that Cubans are up against and fully appreciate all they are trying to do.

Did the Africanness of Cuba help; did that provide solace?

The first thing that was comforting was the politics. It was such a relief.

You know, in the States you feel overwhelmed by the negative messages that you get and you just feel weird, like you're the only one seeing all this pain and inequality. People are saying, "Forget about that, just try to get rich, dog eat dog, get your own, buy, spend, consume." So living here was an affirmation of myself, it was like "Okay, there are lots of people who get outraged at injustice."

The African culture I discovered later. At first I was learning the politics, about socialism—what it feels like to live in a country where everything is owned by the people, where health care and medicine are free. Then I started to learn about the Afro-Cuban religions, the Santería, Palo Monte, the *abakuá*. I wanted to understand the ceremonies and the philosophy. I really came to grips with how much we—black people in the U.S.—were robbed of. Whether it's the tambours, the drums, or the dances. Here, they still know rituals preserved from slavery times. It was like finding another piece of myself. I had to find an African name. I'm still looking for pieces of that Africa I was torn from. I've found it here in all aspects of the culture. There is a tendency to reduce the Africanness of Cuba to the Santería. But it's in the literature, the language, the politics. . . .

What about race and racism in Cuba?

That's a big question. The revolution has only been around thirty-something years. It would be fantasy to believe that the Cubans could have completely gotten rid of racism in that short a time. Socialism is not a magic wand: wave it and everything changes.

Can you be more specific about the successes and failures along these lines?

I can't think of any area of the country that is segregated. Another example, the Third Congress of the Cuban Communist Party was focused on making party leadership reflect the actual number of people of color and women in the country. Unfortunately by the time the Fourth Congress rolled around the whole focus had to be on the survival of the revolution. When the Soviet Union and the socialist camp collapsed, Cuba lost something like 85 percent of its income. It's a process but I honestly think that there's room for a lot of changes throughout the culture. Some people still talk about "good hair" and "bad hair."

Some people think light skin is good, that if you marry a light person you're advancing the race. There are a lot of contradictions in peoples' consciousness. There still needs to be de-eurocentrizing of the schools, though Cuba is further along with that than most places in the world. In fairness, I think that race relations in Cuba are twenty times better than they are in the States, and I believe the revolution is committed to eliminating racism completely.

I also feel that the special period has changed conditions in Cuba. It's brought in lots of white tourists, many of whom are racists and expect to be waited on subserviently.

Another thing is the joint venture corporations which bring their racist ideas and racist corporate practices, for example, not hiring enough blacks. All of that means the revolution has to be more vigilant than ever in identifying and dealing with racism.

A charge one hears, even on the Left, is that institutional racism still exists in Cuba. Is that true? Does one find racist patterns in allocation of housing, work, or the junctions of criminal justice?

No. I don't think institutional racism, as such, exists in Cuba. But at the same time, people have their personal prejudices. Obviously these people, with these personal prejudices, must work somewhere, and must have some influence on the institutions they work in. But I think it's superficial to say racism is institutionalized in Cuba.

I believe that there needs to be a constant campaign to educate people, sensitize people, and analyze racism. The fight against racism always has two levels; the level of politics and policy but also the level of individual consciousness. One of the things that influences ideas about race in Cuba is that the revolution happened in 1959, when the world had a very limited understanding of what racism was. During the 1960s, the world saw the black power movement, which I, for one, very much benefited from. You know "black is beautiful," exploring African art, literature, and culture. That process didn't really happen in Cuba. Over the years, the revolution accomplished so much that most people thought that meant the end of racism. For example, I'd say that more than 90 percent of black people with college degrees were able to do so because of the revolution. They were in a different historical place. The emphasis, for very good reasons, was on black-white unity and the survival of the revolution. So it's only now that people in the universities are looking into the politics of identity.

From Utopianism to Institutionalization

Juan Antonio Blanco and Medea Benjamin

If the 1960s were characterized by debate and experimentation, the 1970s saw an in-creasing shift toward "Sovietization," a return to material incentives, and reliance on the export of sugar to the Eastern bloc. In a series of interviews conducted in 1993, Cuban historian and philosopher Juan Antonio Blanco (b. 1947) talks about the con-trast between the 1960s and the 1970s. Blanco is the epitome of a Cuban-style public intellectual. He travels, works with international agencies, and has spoken frequently in the United States, as well as published several books in English. He is a Communist Party member and a strong supporter of the revolution, though he has had frequent disagreements with Cuban government policies over the years and lost his position at the University of Havana in the late 1960s due to his disagreement with the Sovietiza-tion of the curriculum. In 1993 he founded the Centro Félix Varela, a nongovernmental organization in Havana. Named after a nineteenth-century priest whose work con-tributed to Cuba's independence movement, the center conducts research and publishes a journal on politics and ethics.

Can you talk a little more about those different visions and the different stages the revolution has gone through?

In the first stage, during the sixties, it was basically the ideas of Fidel Castro and Che Guevara that prevailed. Che's criticism of the Soviet Union and the socialist camp was that they were obsessed with the economic construc-tion of socialism and that they were disregarding the moral and spiritual factors of socialist societies. Che once said in an interview that he was not interested in economic socialism. If you disregard the spiritual factors and only attempt to deal with economic factors, you are not going to get rid of alienation. For both Che and Fidel, socialism was not simply a matter of developing a new way of distribution. It was a question of freeing people from alienation at the same time.

This was a crucial and very clear distinction between the kind of socialism we wanted to build and that which was already in progress in the Soviet Union and the Eastern bloc at that time.

What made it possible for this alternative vision to prevail during the sixties?

The sixties was a time of questioning and upheaval all over the world, giving us more space for experimentation. There was the Vietnam War and the anti-war movement in the United States. It was the time of student insurrections in places like Berkeley and Paris and the time of the Cultural Revolution in China. It was the time of the Soviet invasion of Czechoslovakia. There were revolutionary struggles being waged throughout Latin America. There was Che Guevara himself and his vision of creating a new person with a new set of values.

The sixties was a time when we attempted to create a totally new way of organizing the economy that would promote solidarity and cooperation between both individuals and economic enterprises instead of competition. It was also a time of discussing freedom—intellectual freedom, individual freedom, the way to secure individuality within the context of a communist society.

You speak with great nostalgia about the sixties.

It was a crucial time for our revolution and for the world as well. I think one of the things we should all do one day is to sit and discuss the sixties and what it all meant—especially as we approach the closing of the century.

Yet you say that the vision of the sixties, even in Cuba, lost out. What happened?

Several things happened to derail this vision. On the one hand, there were internal factors. The Cuban economy became mismanaged after Guevara left Cuba in 1965 for the internationalist mission that he was committed to. His ideas were not discarded after he left, but many of them were actually pushed too fast after his departure. This brought about a degree of mismanagement of the economy that produced a critical situation for Cuba at the end of the sixties.

Could you explain that? What do you mean when you say that his ideas were pushed too fast?

For example, a campaign to reduce bureaucracy—a valid idea—turned into the destruction of the accounting system that Che had left behind. Without accurate and reliable data, no capitalist enterprise could operate, and this lack of data was even more devastating for a socialist centralized economy.

Another issue is that of material versus moral incentives. Che believed that social consciousness should become the main motivation for production, but after his departure this idea was really carried out by decree and not by long-term policies. It is one thing to try little by little to plant the seed of the new consciousness within the population by education and another to say that starting tomorrow there will be no more extra pay in the factory and everybody will work on the basis of moral incentives. And that's basically what happened. We pushed too fast and the people were not ready for it.

What about the 1968 ofensiva revolucionaria, the revolutionary offensive that banned all private selling? Isn't this another example of pushing too fast? Instead of trying to eliminate the worst excesses of the marketplace, the government eliminated the market itself.

Exactly. In 1968 we wiped out private enterprise, from the woman running a hamburger stand to the guy selling snow cones on the street corner. It was again done by decree, forbidding people from entering into market relations, rather than through a slower process of both educating the population and setting up an alternative to replace the vacuum created by this loss of private enterprise.

I think there was a valid concern that market relations should not run the society, that the society should be run on a more humane basis to guarantee the basics to everyone. I understand the nationalization of the nation's major industries. But in terms of small businesses, I think that instead of eliminating them they could have been regulated in their transactions, making sure that market relations did not become the general trend of the economy. By [the government's] pushing them aside in one fell swoop, the Cuban economy never recovered from that blow. Goods became scarce, inflation resulted because people had a lot of money and not much to buy, and the problem of poor services continues to haunt us today.

Another economic disaster in the late 1960s was the push for the ten-million-ton sugar harvest. This self-imposed goal of producing ten million tons of sugar in 1969–1970 was designed to take advantage of the relatively high price of sugar in the international market at that time and to get Cuba enough money to launch a major development program. The goal was not only too ambitious (representing about three million tons more than Cuba had ever produced) and was not achieved, but it also produced tremendous dislocations in the rest of the economy. This all-out drive for sugar meant that other sectors of the economy, including food production, were neglected. This failure must have been a major factor in the reassessment of the socialist path Cuba had been following.

Yes, it certainly was a major setback. But in addition to these internal factors we've been discussing, there were also a number of international setbacks that forced us to realign our policies. Guevara's death and the defeat of the guerrillas in many parts of Latin America at the end of the sixties left Cuba more isolated. In Vietnam, the replacement of U.S. troops by South Vietnamese troops and by more intensive bombing allowed the United States to end the draft, which led to a demobilization of the antiwar movement in the United States and allowed Washington to focus more on other foreign policy "problems" like Cuba. In general, the more conservative atmosphere that followed the 1960s unrest in many parts of the world was not beneficial to the Cuban process.

So with an international environment that was not exactly supportive of the Cuban revolution, we were obliged to reassess both the situation and the perspectives of the Cuban revolution. During that debate, which took place in the early 1970s, it was said that the only possibility of defending Cuba in that adverse environment was to strengthen our alliance with the Soviet Union and Eastern Europe. And with this alliance, throughout the 1970s and the first half of the 1980s, little by little we began to import the Soviet model of socialism into different areas of the Cuban society.

You say you were forced to strengthen your alliance with the Soviet bloc. Relations with the Soviets must have been quite poor after the 1962 Missile Crisis, when Cuba was angry with the Soviets for having negotiated with the United States for a solution to the crisis behind Cuba's back.

Cuban-Soviet relations suffered after the Missile Crisis, but improved afterward when Fidel went to the Soviet Union and spoke to Khrushchev. But this rapprochement was affected by the radical policies Cuba was following internationally, its support for the guerrilla movements in Latin America and in Africa.

Against the will of the Soviets?

Against the wisdom of the Soviets. And internally, our notions about constructing socialism in a different way were creating tensions in the relationship. The worst years were 1964–1967. I remember in 1967 when Premier Kosygin came to Cuba the relations were as cold as could be.

But by the early 1970s, the Cuban revolution was in trouble both because of internal economic problems and a less hospitable international climate, and those who favored closer ties with the Soviets won out. Can you describe this second phase of the revolution, and what elements of the Soviet model were incorporated into the Cuban system?

This second stage of the revolution was characterized not so much by creativity or imagination or the search for a unique Cuban identity but by the political and economic institutionalization of the Cuban revolution under the increasing influence of the Soviet model. Sure, we made adjustments to our reality and came out with some unique institutions such as our legislative body, called People's Power. But basically we copied the essential elements of the Soviet model in its overall conception of the economy, its relationship with politics, and the pervasive view of dogmatic Marxism as universal truths. We also created an unnecessary overdependence on the Soviet Union that was not healthy.

In our economy, we copied an absurd model that was based on a stupid, theoretical concept of creating "values" and on fulfilling your yearly plan to create these values, instead of actually creating useful goods. Let's say that you were the head of a construction company and you were told by the government that this year you had to create values of three million pesos. Fine. They didn't say that you had to construct three bridges and two schools; they said you had to create values of three million pesos. Their concept of creating values was spending that amount in labor and resources. So you could create three million pesos in values by moving land, digging ditches, putting in some columns here and there, but having nothing finished or useful in the end.

It's like in the Soviet Union where they were measuring the productivity of a chair factory not by the number of chairs it made, or how comfortable those chairs were, or how cost-effective they were in producing them, but by the total weight of the chairs. So you go to the Soviet Union and you need a crane to carry a chair, because they would make furniture as heavy as possible to "overfulfill" their yearly plan.

One of the funniest things in Cuba is that you could be driving along a highway and see a bridge built up on one side and on the other side, but nothing connecting them.

And the construction group that did it probably successfully completed its plan.

Oh yes, they probably overfulfilled their plan. They probably even got an award for being good workers, for creating a lot of "value."

Another irony of this Soviet model is that it disregarded social needs. Under this system, things such as child-care centers, schools, and hospitals — social services in general — were listed as unproductive expenditures and the orientation was to spend in productive areas. So construction for social needs was disregarded and we were accumulating more and more social problems in terms of lack of housing, child-care centers, schools, hospitals, etc.

Another problem we found is that unlike the focus on moral incentives in the 1960s, material incentives had become the motivating force for workers. Not only were people losing the sense of working for the common good, but these material incentives usually had little to do with the final outcome of their work. So people were making a lot of money, but not producing more or more efficiently.

Didn't this mentality of divorcing the work from the final results also affect the education system? I remember during this time that the teachers' main interest was promoting all the students so they could reach their yearly promotion goals. The quality of education suffered because students who should have been left behind were promoted to reach these abstract goals.

Yes, with this Soviet model, quality and concrete results suffered. So this kind of madness existed throughout our system and after some fifteen years it became obvious that something was very wrong.

In fact, I would say that the worst error we committed, the one with the most dramatic and lasting effects, was the decision to follow the Soviet model of socialism. Those fifteen years of "Russification" of our socialism left us with problems in almost every realm of Cuban society.

In the economy, it introduced the notion of state socialism and vertical command based on a primitive and incompetent style of authoritarian central planning. In politics, it promoted the bureaucratization of organizations that were once full of creativity and initiative by transforming them into formal extensions of the Party machinery, while restricting the limits of pluralism in society as a whole. Socially, an attempt to legitimize special privileges for a new managerial bureaucratic strata negatively affected the revolutionary spirit of our process. Culturally, it certainly killed the possibility of using social science—and Marxism for that matter—as a useful tool in the construction of the new society when they were transformed into a religious creed for the apologetic praising of official policies.

Several generations of cadre and professors were inculcated with this adulterated and manipulative version of socialism. The rectification campaign was launched in the mid-1980s to overcome some of these problems that were perverting our process.

This third stage of the Cuban revolution, what you call the rectification process, was talked about in Cuba as Cuba's own form of perestroika. It took place years before the Soviet Union began its reform process and involved "delinking" from the Soviet model. Did Cuba begin to decouple itself from the Soviet bloc solely because you were looking at problems within Cuba itself, or were you also looking at problems within the Soviet Union when you began the rectification campaign?

We did not attempt to wean ourselves economically from the Soviet sphere. We were instead concerned that the Eastern European model was not a good model for constructing socialism in Cuba. We distanced ourselves from the idea that what worked for the Soviets would necessarily work for the Cubans, and yes, we also started to realize that this model was not even working that well for the Soviets. I think Fidel himself had the wisdom of seeing what was going to happen in the Soviet bloc before it started. Remember, he launched the rectification process well before perestroika even existed.

When was that?

Officially speaking, the rectification process in Cuba began in April 1986 when Fidel Castro gave a speech calling for a revamping of many of our economic and political policies. But this process really started in 1984 after the U.S. invasion of Grenada, and it started in the military field with a reassessment of the defense doctrine of Cuba.

What happened in Grenada to cause this reassessment? Did the fact that the United States invaded Grenada make Cuba more concerned about a direct invasion? I remember that Alexander Haig, who was Reagan's secretary of state at the time, was making hostile statements about going to the source of revolutionary upheaval in the region, by which he meant Cuba.

Yes, and it was not only the invasion of Grenada that concerned us. The United States was also seriously considering intervening in El Salvador and Nicaragua. So we had to take the threat of a possible invasion very seriously.

In this process of reexamining our defense system, we reached the conclusion that we had wrongly copied the defense model of the Soviet Union and the Eastern bloc of relying on a regular army, which is only a small segment of the population. We decided to revise that approach, going back to our earlier notions of the 1960s when we thought that the defense of the Cuban revolution should be the task of the entire population. . . .

I think that this 1984 reassessment of our defense system was historically very important. It reactivated our original concept of the importance of the people's participation in defending their revolution and stressed our vision of an "armed democracy" as evidence of respect for Cuba's sovereignty.

How did rectification play out in the economy?

After reshaping the island's system of defense, we entered a process of reassessing our economic policies. First, we scrutinized our strategy of development and, second, the manner in which our economy had been structured according to the Soviet model.

For example, we decided to change our concept of state planning, to make sure that planning did not mean—as it used to—a total centralization of decision making at all levels. We were trying to strike a balance between centralized and decentralized decisions in a planned economy and to debureaucratize our planning process.

This is also the time that we geared our development to high technology. This had long been a Cuban position which had always clashed with that of the CMEA [the Council for Mutual Economic Assistance], the socialist trading bloc. A number of countries within that bloc tried to impose a traditional international division of labor that mimicked the division of labor in the capitalist world, with Cuba and other Third World socialist countries producing raw commodities and the more industrialized socialist countries producing manufactured goods. . . .

Starting around 1982, we began to invest heavily in biotechnology, as well as other high-tech areas. By the end of the 1980s, we had already invested the equivalent of several billion dollars in these areas. The three key areas we have been developing are biotechnology, pharmaceuticals, and computerized medical equipment and software.

How did the rectification process address this long-standing controversy of material versus moral incentives?

As part of this process we began to rectify the essence of the economic mechanisms we had been using. We realized that we could not develop an alternative society based on solidarity and feelings of love for your neighbor while using capitalist economic incentives, which foster a dog-eat-dog mentality. So we recaptured the use of moral incentives, which had been set aside for nearly 15 years. We did not discard material incentives; we understood that material incentives were also important to motivate people. But little by little we began to recover the idea that the revolution was not only a matter of a more just distribution of wealth, but also a spiritual project to release people's creativity and give them a greater degree of participation in society. . . .

Getting back to rectification, what effect did it have on the political system?

Rectification led us to a careful review of our political system, with a serious search for ways to get people more involved in the political process. In early 1991 we opened a national discussion with an open agenda in every single workplace, school, university, and neighborhood, so that people could openly and freely discuss the problems of Cuban society and how they felt those problems should be dealt with. Their criticisms and suggestions were actively solicited. During the several months of this nationwide discussion, more than a million opinions, criticisms, and proposals were recorded.

All these contributions were processed and circulated to delegates of the Communist Party Congress, who also were elected in a more democratic manner than ever before. For the first time there were direct delegates proposed by the rank-and-file party membership rather than a list of possible candidates presented to the rank and file for voting. This time people were selected by their peers to attend the Congress.

The Fourth Party Congress in 1991 was also a peculiar congress if you compare it with any of those previously held. It was a very open, democratic discussion. Normally, the party congress — this was the tradition in the Soviet Union and the Eastern bloc — is opened by the first secretary of the Communist Party (in this case Fidel), who gives his assessment of everything that happened during the past five years. Typically, he also presents his ideas as to how the Congress should proceed. Fidel decided that he was not going to do that, because he didn't want to preempt the discussion. He simply made some opening remarks on the current situation we were facing, and then opened the floor to debate.

For those who have a picture of the Cuban revolution from the outside, especially as it is portrayed in the international media, the notion of democracy within the Cuban party is a very difficult one to accept. They think that a one-party system, per se, precludes the possibility of democracy. Moreover, they think that Fidel Castro decides the outcome of every issue the country faces. But this just isn't so.

During the second stage of the revolution, from the 1970s to the first half of the 1980s, Fidel Castro's views on more than one issue represented, in fact, a minority within the party and he has acknowledged that he was overruled on several political and economic issues. He has always accepted the majority opinion, even if he disagreed with it.

That's not new. During the fight against Batista he also had this style of accepting collective decisions. For instance, he never thought that the idea of calling for a general strike against Batista in April 1958 was a sound one, but he accepted it because it was the criteria of the majority. The strike was a disaster, and the very existence of the revolution was put in jeopardy.

Fidel sometimes criticized what was going on in the 1970s — I remember one speech in which he said that some things in this revolution were legal but they were not moral. But he didn't try to impose his will, because he knew that democracy and unity were more precious for us than imposing a view even if it was a correct one.

So how did Fidel manage to start the rectification campaign? What was happening in the mid-1980s that allowed his view to prevail?

It had become obvious to many people at that time that the model of development that we imported from the Soviet Union had begun to reach the point of stagnation. Therefore, it was easier for Fidel Castro and those who sympathized with his point of view to present the problems we were facing and to propose a reexamination of our own roots in an effort to put our socialist process back on a more authentic path.

Carlos Puebla Sings about the Economy

Carlos Puebla

In a different vein, singer Carlos Puebla (1917–1989) takes a humorous look at the many inefficiencies in the way society and economy function. This grouping of his works reflects, with humor and compassion, the contradictions of revolutionary society as they were experienced by ordinary men and women and that shaped the texture of their daily lives. A sensitive antenna, Puebla picked up what people were saying on bus lines, at markets, and in front of the television, and through the troubadour's poetic imagination he turned it into a popular art form.

CINEMA ON TELEVISION *(Cine en televisión)*
(A program they stopped showing a few years ago)

Rodríguez Alemán, my friend:
TV seems unpleasant to me
since after listening to your serenade
I don't even get the chance to say "gee."

You take off navigating a river
of technical terms with which you unleash
a well-meaning but long, boring speech
that leaves the viewers cold.

After all that energy's been wasted,
the evening's movie begins
and you depart with neither shame nor glory,

it turns out the film you're offering, we can tell from the start
is so old and has been shown so many times
that we know it by heart.

Street scene. Photo by Tania Jovanovic.

LIKE IT IS *(Cosa ocurrida)*

I live here, right next to Havana,
in the borough of Chibás,
and for the twenty-two years
that I've been living here,
never, ever, has the newspaper *Granma*,
of which I've been, in parenthesis, a subscriber
since the very first day,
arrived before three in the afternoon,
and that, *compay*, burns and burns,
like a bad wound . . .

But one day,
one lucky day,

Laborers. Photo by Tania Jovanovic.

Cutting cane. Photo by Tania Jovanovic.

the record for lateness
was broken:
when the man on the scooter appeared,
in a hurry and with great cheer,
before eight in the morning . . .
Imagine,
the scandal it caused on our block,
my grandchildren hauled out their horns
the neighbors' kids, their tin cans,
sticks and wooden rattles,
until the racket could be heard all the way to Guanabacoa.
We picked the man up
and carried him on our shoulders
all around the block
all the way up and all the way back,
and the man, with longing in his face,
and his hair all messed up,
begged us to let him speak,
and we said no,
us first . . .
And we made a grand speech in his honor
about the value of the worker
who gets the job done
bar none,
and we made him a special cup of coffee,
and the only reason we didn't pin a medal on him
was,
because that was out of our hands.

II
But a little while later, and still very proud of ourselves
all of the hullabaloo having died down
we asked the man:
What was it
you wanted to say. . . ?
And he answered us: Yes, just wanted to let you know
that the newspaper is from yesterday . . .

THE WAIT (*La espera*)

No one has ever felt the pain I've felt,
the terrible anguish of waiting . . .
The heart waits and grows desperate
for her . . . —it is late and she has not arrived—.

She has beautiful coloring,
moves swiftly and with grace,
I wait for her, as always
and ask her fervently:
to cast off the distress
that your delay produces in me
please don't take so long this time
I beg of you, please be on time.

Every afternoon, like this one,
I wait to see her, to find her, anxiously,
but she makes me suffer bitterly,
but she makes me suffer bitterly,
that bus that is always late.

NEW HOPE (*Otra nueva ilusión*)

I'm in love again,
and it's so glorious to be in love
that even though my lot is cast
this fresh, new hope is dazzling.

Life is almost, almost always unfair,
I say, repeat and affirm;
it's true I like the one I have,
but I don't have the one I'd like.

Yet there is always the pleasant possibility
crying out to me in the light of a smile
that the shirt which every day in the shop window I see
will in the end belong to me.

TRANSLATED BY PAMELA MARIA SMORKALOFF

VI

Culture and Revolution

Art was, and is, an integral element in the Cuban revolutionary project of national vindication and social justice. The revolutionary government dedicated enormous resources toward promoting and democratizing the arts. The literacy campaign and the revolution's emphasis on education were one element; the promotion of institutes such as the Casa de las Américas and the Cuban Film Institute is another. Also important have been Cubans' explorations of the issue of revolutionary art. Following the advice of Che Guevara, who in the 1960s rejected both Stalinist "socialist realism" and Western individualist "personal expression" as the goals of art, many Cuban artists, writers, and filmmakers have been truly revolutionary in both the artistic and the social sense of the word. Films such as Tomás Gutiérrez Alea's *Strawberry and Chocolate* (1993) have given U.S. viewers a glimpse of the ways that art and cultural expression in Cuba have been products of, comments on, and active participants in the social revolution.

Promoting Cuban and Latin American culture, achieving an international cultural status, and placing culture at the reach of the masses were made into revolutionary priorities by the government. New cultural, literary, and artistic institutes were founded to promote different forms of artistic expression. Critic Roberto González Echevarría argues that the Cuban Revolution played a pivotal role in the development of Latin American literature, because of Cuba's own investment in and promotion of the arts and because Cuban actions prompted U.S. investment in Latin American culture. "Without this background," he writes, "it is difficult to conceive of the boom of the Latin American novel."[1]

Culture has frequently been a battlefield for struggles over the limits of artistic freedom. The revolution's policies toward intellectual freedom were summarized by Fidel Castro in 1961 in an oft-quoted speech entitled "Words to Intellectuals." In this lengthy speech, Castro addressed fears expressed by intellectuals that the government would attempt to control the content of their artistic production in the interests of the revolution. While asserting the revolution's commitment to artistic freedom, he also cautioned that no citizen had the right to threaten the existence of the revolution itself. "What are the rights of revolutionary or non-revolutionary writers and artists?" he asked rhetorically. "Within the Revolution, everything; against the Revolution, no rights at all."[2] This position, however, leaves much room for interpretation, and in fact the boundaries of what is considered "within the revolution" and what is "against the revolution" have changed considerably over time. Many Cuban writers and artists have encountered doors closed, works censored, books unpublished, and recognition denied. Some of them have stayed in the country and struggled—sometimes successfully—to find spaces to produce their work. Others, especially writers, have chosen exile and have continued to produce a vibrant Cuban literature abroad. A third group of intellectuals has settled overseas, particularly in Latin America, for a variety of economic and political reasons while not breaking with the goals of the revolution.

At the same time, Castro emphasized that the revolution's cultural goals went beyond fostering the cultural production of intellectuals. "Bringing culture to the countryside" through the literacy campaign, and making art, music, dance, literature, and theater accessible to the entire population, to "create the conditions that will permit every artistic, literary, scientific, or any other kind of talent to be developed" for *all* Cubans was just as crucial. Cuban cultural policies included major investment and innovations in dance, sports, visual arts, theater, and film as well as in literature. Just as with the social and economic changes, virtually all Cubans were affected by the changes in the sphere of culture brought about by the revolution.

Notes

1. Roberto González Echevarría, "Criticism and Literature in Revolutionary Cuba," *Cuban Studies / Estudios Cubanos* 11:1 (January 1981): 1–17; reprinted in Sandor Halebsky and John M. Kirk, eds., *Cuba: Twenty-five Years of Revolution, 1959-1984* (New York: Praeger, 1985), 154–55.
2. Source: Pamphlet entitled "Palabras a los intelectuales" (Words to intellectuals), Havana, National Cultural Council, 30 June 1961. Translated by FBIS (Foreign Broadcast Information Service), available online at lanic.utexas.edu/la/cb/cuba/castro/1961/19610630. Both quotes by Castro cited in this introduction come from this speech.

Caliban

Roberto Fernández Retamar

In his famous essay "Caliban," Cuban poet and essayist Roberto Fernández Retamar (b. 1930) argues that the literature of the colonized has to reject and overturn the political and artistic conventions of the colonizers. It is a 1960s response to Ariel, *by José Enrique Rodó (1900), who had interpreted Shakespeare's* The Tempest *by positing a Latin American identification with Ariel (representing the spiritual essence of idealism) as opposed to the crass, materialistic sensuality of Caliban. Rodó's Prospero, in turn, is seen as the wise, guiding master. Retamar reformulates the analysis once again, arguing that rather than being embodied in Ariel, the handmaiden of colonialism, Latin America was better represented by Caliban, the colonized, indigenous slave. From this standpoint, the redemption of the slave (thus of Latin America) must come through pride and self-assertion of this identity. Prospero now becomes the European imperialist, and Ariel becomes the intellectual slave who must choose which master to serve.*

In proposing Caliban as our symbol, I am aware that it is not entirely ours, that it is also an alien elaboration, although in this case based on our concrete realities. But how can this alien quality be entirely avoided? The most venerated word in Cuba — *mambí* — was disparagingly imposed on us by our enemies at the time of the war for independence, and we still have not totally deciphered its meaning. It seems to have an African root, and in the mouth of the Spanish colonists implied the idea that all *independentistas* were so many black slaves — emancipated by that very war for independence — who of course constituted the bulk of the liberation army. The independentistas, white and black, adopted with honor something that colonialism meant as an insult. This is the dialectic of Caliban. To offend us they call us mambí, they call us black; but we reclaim as a mark of glory the honor of considering ourselves descendants of the mambí, descendants of the rebel, runaway, independentista black — *never* descendants of the slaveholder. Nevertheless, Prospero, as we well know, taught his language to Caliban and, consequently, gave him a name. But is this his true name? Let us listen to this speech made in 1971:

> To be completely precise, we still do not even have a name; we still have no name; we are practically unbaptized—whether as Latin Americans, Ibero-Americans, Indo-Americans. For the imperialists, we are nothing more than despised and despicable peoples. At least that was what we were. Since Girón they have begun to change their thinking. Racial contempt—to be a creole, to be a mestizo, to be black, to be simply, a Latin American, is for them contemptible.

This naturally, is Fidel Castro on the tenth anniversary of the victory at Playa Girón.

To assume our condition as Caliban implies rethinking our history from the *other* side, from the viewpoint of the *other* protagonist. The *other* protagonist of *The Tempest* (or, as we might have said ourselves, *The Hurricane*) is not of course Ariel but, rather, Prospero. There is no real Ariel-Caliban polarity: both are slaves in the hands of Prospero, the foreign magician. But Caliban is the rude and unconquerable master of the island, while Ariel, a creature of the air, although also a child of the isle, is the intellectual—as both [Aníbal] Ponce and [Aimée] Césaire have seen.

This conception of our culture had already been articulately expressed and defended in the last century by the first among us to understand clearly the concrete situation of what he called—using a term I have referred to several times—"our mestizo America": José Martí, to whom Rodó planned to dedicate the first Cuban edition of *Ariel* and about whom he intended to write a study similar to those he devoted to [Simón] Bolívar and [José] Artigas, a study that in the end he unfortunately never realized.

Although he devoted numerous pages to the topic, the occasion on which Martí offered his ideas on this point in a most organic and concise manner was in his 1891 article "Our America." I will limit myself to certain essential quotations. But I should first like to offer some observations on the destiny of Martí's work.

During Martí's lifetime, the bulk of his work, scattered throughout a score of continental newspapers, enjoyed widespread fame. We know that Rubén Darío called Martí "Maestro" (as, for other reasons, his political followers would also call him during his lifetime) and considered him the Latin American whom he most admired. We shall soon see, on the other hand, how the harsh judgments on the United States that Martí commonly made in his articles, equally well known in his time, were the cause of acerbic criticism by the pro-Yankee [Domingo Faustino] Sarmiento. But the particular manner in which Martí's writings circulated—he made use of journalism, oratory, and letters but *never published a single book*—bears considerable responsibility for the relative oblivion into which the work of the Cuban hero fell after his death in 1895. This alone explains the fact that nine years after his death—and twelve from the time Martí stopped writing for the continental press, devoted as he was after 1892 to his political tasks—an author as absolutely ours and as far above suspicion as the twenty-year-old Pedro Henríquez Ureña could write in 1904, in an article on Rodó's *Ariel*, that the latter's opinions on the United States are "much more severe than those formulated by two of the greatest thinkers and most brilliant psycho-sociologists of the Antilles: Hostos and Martí." Insofar as this refers to Martí, the observation is completely erroneous; and given the exemplary honesty of Henríquez Ureña, it led me, first, to suspect and later, to verify that it was due simply to the fact that during this period the great Dominican had not read, *had been unable to read*, Martí adequately. Martí was hardly published at the time. A text such as the fundamental "Our America" is a good example of this fate. Readers of the Mexican newspaper *El Partido Liberal* could have read it on 30 January 1891. It is possible that some other local newspaper republished it, although the most recent edition of Martí's *Complete Works* does not indicate anything in this regard. But it is most likely that those who did not have the good fortune to obtain that newspaper knew nothing about the article—the most important document published in America from the end of the past century until the appearance in 1962 of the Second Declaration of Havana—for almost twenty years, at the end of which time it appeared in book form (Havana, 1910) in the irregular collection in which publication of the complete works of Martí was begun. For this reason Manuel Pedro González is correct when he asserts that during the first quarter of this century the new generations did not know Martí. "A minimal portion of his work" was again put into circulation, starting with the eight volumes published by Alberto Ghiraldo in Madrid in 1925. Thanks to the most recent appearance of several editions of his complete works—actually still incomplete—"he has been rediscovered and reevaluated." González is thinking above all of the dazzling literary qualities of this work ("the literary glory" as he says). Could we not add something, then, regarding the works' fundamental ideological aspects? Without forgetting very important prior contributions, there are still some essential points that explain why today, after the triumph of the Cuban Revolution and because of it, Martí is being "rediscovered and reevaluated." It was no mere coincidence that in 1953 Fidel named Martí as the intellectual author of the attack on the Moncada Barracks nor that Che should use a quotation from Martí—"it is the hour of the furnace, and only light should be seen"—to open his extremely important "Message to the Tricontinental Congress" in 1967. If Benedetti could say that Rodó's time "was different from our own . . . his true place, his true temporal homeland was the nineteenth century," we must say, on the other hand, that Martí's true place was the future and, for the moment, this era of ours, which simply cannot be understood without a thorough knowledge of this work.

Now, if that knowledge, because of the curious circumstances alluded to, was denied or available only in a limited way to the early generations of this century, who frequently had to base their defense of subsequent radical arguments on a "first launching pad" as well intentioned but at the same time as weak as the nineteenth-century work *Ariel*, what can we say of more recent authors to whom editions of Martí are now available but who nevertheless persist in ignoring him? I am thinking, of course, not of scholars more or less ignorant of our problems but, on the contrary, of those who maintain a consistently anticolonialist attitude. The only explanation of this situation is a painful one: we have been so thoroughly steeped in colonialism that we read with real respect only those anticolonialist authors *disseminated from the metropolis*. In this way we cast aside the greatest lesson of Martí; thus, we are barely familiar with Artigas, Recabarren, Mella, and even Mariátegui and Ponce. And I have the sad suspicion that if the extraordinary texts of Che Guevara have enjoyed the greatest dissemination ever accorded a Latin American, the fact that he is read with such avidity by our people is to a certain extent due to the prestige his name has even in the metropolitan capitals—where, to be sure, he is frequently the object of the most shameless manipulation. For consistency in our anticolonialist attitude we must in effect turn to those of our people who have incarnated and illustrated that attitude in their behavior and thinking.[1] And for this, there is no case more useful than that of Martí.

I know of no other Latin American author who has given so immediate and so coherent an answer to another question put to me by my interlocutor, the European journalist whom I mentioned at the beginning of these lines (and whom, if he did not exist, I would have had to invent, although this would have deprived me of his friendship, which I trust will survive this monologue): "What relationship," this guileless wit asked me, "does Borges have to the Incas?" Borges is almost a reductio ad absurdum and, in any event, I shall discuss him later. But it is only right and fair to ask what relationship we, the present inhabitants of this America in whose zoological and cultural heritage Europe has played an unquestionable part, have to the primitive inhabitants of this same America—those peoples who constructed or were martyred by Europeans of various nations, about whom neither a white nor black legend can be built, only an infernal truth of blood, that, together with such deeds as the enslavement of Africans, constitutes their eternal dishonor. Martí, whose father was from Valencia and whose mother was from the Canaries, who wrote the most prodigious Spanish of his—and our—age, and who came to have the greatest knowledge of the Euro–North American culture ever possessed by a man of our America, also asked this question. He answered it as follows: "We are descended from Valencian fathers and Canary Island mothers and feel the inflamed blood of Tamanaco and Paramaconi coursing through our veins; we see the blood that fell amid the brambles of Mount Calvary as our own, along with that shed by the naked and heroic Caracas as they struggled breast to breast with the *gonzalos* in their iron-plated armor."

I presume that the reader, if he or she is not a Venezuelan, will be unfamiliar with the names evoked by Martí. So was I. This lack of familiarity is but another proof of our subjection to the colonialist perspective of history that has been imposed on us, causing names, dates, circumstances, and truths to vanish from our consciousness. Under other circumstances—but closely related to these—did not the bourgeois version of history try to erase the heroes of the Commune of 1871, the martyrs of 1 May 1886 (significantly reclaimed by Martí)? At any rate, Tamanaco, Paramaconi, "the naked and heroic Caracas" were natives of what is today called Venezuela, of *Carib blood, the blood of Caliban*, coursing through their veins. This will not be the only time he expresses such an idea, which is central to his thinking. Again making use of such heroes, he was to repeat sometime later: "We must stand with Guaicaipuro, Paramaconi [heroes of Venezuela, probably of Carib origin], and not with the flames that burned them, nor with the ropes that bound them, nor with the steel that beheaded them, nor with the dogs that devoured them." Martí's rejection of the ethnocide that Europe practiced is *total*. No less total is his identification with the American peoples that offered heroic resistance to the invader, and in whom Martí saw the natural forerunners of the Latin American independentistas. This explains why in the notebook in which this last quotation appears, he continues writing, almost without transition, on Aztec mythology ("no less beautiful than the Greek"), on the ashes of Quetzalcoatl, on "Ayachucho on the solitary plateau," on "Bolívar, like the rivers."

Martí, however, dreams not of a restoration now impossible but of the future integration of our America—an America rising organically from a firm grasp of its true roots to the heights of authentic modernity. For this reason, the first quotation in which he speaks of feeling valiant Carib blood coursing through his veins continues as follows:

> It is good to open canals, to promote schools, to create steamship lines, to keep abreast of one's own time, to be on the side of the vanguard in the beautiful march of humanity. But in order not to falter because of a lack of spirit or the vanity of a false spirit, it is good also to nourish oneself through memory and admiration, through righteous study and loving

compassion, on that fervent spirit of the natural surroundings in which one is born—a spirit matured and quickened by those of every race that issues from such surroundings and finds its final repose in them. Politics and literature flourish only when they are direct. The American intelligence is an indigenous plumage. Is it not evident that America itself was paralyzed by the same blow that paralyzed the Indian? And until the Indian is caused to walk, America itself will not begin to walk well.

Martí's identification with our aboriginal culture was thus accompanied by a complete sense of the concrete tasks imposed upon him by his circumstances. Far from hampering him, that identification nurtured in him the most radical and modern criteria of his time in the colonial countries.

Naturally, Martí's approach to the Indian was also applied to the black. Unfortunately, while in his day serious inquiries into American aboriginal cultures (which Martí studied passionately) had already been undertaken, only in the twentieth century would there appear similar studies of African cultures and their considerable contribution to the makeup of our mestizo America (see [Leo] Frobenius, [Maurice] Delafosse, [Jean] Suret-Canale, [Fernando] Ortiz, [Arturo] Ramos, [Melville] Herskovits, [Jacques] Roumain, [Alfred] Métraux, [Roger] Bastide, [José Luciano] Franco). And Martí died five years before the dawning of our century. In any event, in his treatment of Indian culture and in his concrete behavior toward the black, he left a very clear outline of a "battle plan" in this area.

This is the way in which Martí forms his Calibanesque vision of the culture of what he called "our America." Martí is, as Fidel was later to be, aware of how difficult it is even to find a name that in designating us defines us conceptually. For this reason, after several attempts, he favored that modest descriptive formula that above and beyond race, language, and secondary circumstances embraces the communities that live, with their common problems, "from the [Río] Bravo to Patagonia," and that are distinct from "European America." I have already said that, although it is found scattered throughout his very numerous writings, this conception of our culture is aptly summarized in the article-manifesto "Our America," and I direct the reader to it: to his insistence upon the idea that one cannot "rule new peoples with a singular and violent composition, with laws inherited from four centuries of free practice in the United States, or nineteen centuries of monarchy in France. One does not stop the blow in the chest of the plainsman's horse with one of Hamilton's decrees. One does not clear the congealed blood of the Indian race with a sentence of Sieyès"; to his deeply rooted concept that "the imported book has been conquered in America by the natural man. Natural men have conquered the artificial men of learning. *The authentic mestizo has conquered the exotic creole"* (my emphasis); and finally to his fundamental advice:

> The European university must yield to the American university. The history of America, from the Incas to the present, must be taught letter perfect, even if that of the Argonauts of Greece is not taught. Our own Greece is preferable to that Greece that is not ours. We have greater need of it. National politicians must replace foreign and exotic politicians. Graft the world onto our republics, but the trunk must be that of our republics. And let the conquered pedant be silent: there is no homeland of which the individual can be more proud than our unhappy American republics.²

TRANSLATED BY EDWARD BAKER

Notes

For complete references and notes, consult the work as cited in the acknowledgment of copyrights section.

1. Nonetheless, this should not be understood to mean that I am suggesting that those authors who have not been born in the colonies should not be read. Such a stupidity is untenable. How could we propose to ignore Homer, Dante, Cervantes, Shakespeare, Whitman, to say nothing of Marx, Engels, or Lenin? How can we forget that even in our own day there are *Latin American* thinkers who have not been born here? Lastly, how can we defend intellectual Robinson Crusoism at all without falling into the greatest absurdity?

2. *Eds. note*: This quote (in a different translation) also appears in the selection from José Martí's "Our America" in this volume.

For an Imperfect Cinema

Julio García Espinosa

In an essay whose title appears to refer to Chilean poet and Nobel laureate Pablo Neruda's poetic manifesto "Sobre una poesia sin purezas" (On an impure poetry) Cuban film director Julio García Espinosa lays the foundations for an ars poetica of the new Cuban cinema. Although written in 1969, García Espinosa's essay is strikingly current in that it envisions the technological advances we are experiencing today— an era in which mass production and lower costs permit a large number of spectators to own video recorders and thus to become artists too; the advent of cable television, which grants space to a technologically "imperfect" cinema, but one rich in creative energy, tension, and doubt. Julio García Espinosa (b. 1926) studied film direction in Rome, has directed numerous short and feature-length films in Cuba, and is considered to be one of the founders of the new Cuban cinema.

Nowadays perfect cinema—technically and artistically masterful—is almost always reactionary cinema. The major temptation facing Cuban cinema at this time—when it is achieving its objective of becoming a cinema of quality, one which is culturally meaningful within the revolutionary process—is precisely that of transforming itself into a perfect cinema.

The "boom" of Latin American cinema—with Brazil and Cuba in the forefront, according to the applause and approval of the European intelligentsia— is similar, in the present moment, to the one which the Latin American novel had previously been the exclusive benefactor. Why do they applaud us? There is no doubt that a certain standard of quality has been reached. Doubtless, there is a certain political opportunism, a certain mutual instrumentality. But without doubt there is also something more. Why should we worry about their accolades? Isn't the goal of public recognition a part of the rules of the artistic game? When it comes to artistic culture, isn't European recognition equivalent to worldwide recognition? Doesn't it serve art and our peoples as well when works produced by underdeveloped nations obtain such recognition?

Although it may seem curious, it is necessary to clarify the fact that this disquiet is not solely motivated by ethical concerns. As a matter of fact, the motivation is for the most part aesthetic, if indeed it is possible to draw such an arbitrary dividing line between both terms. When we ask ourselves why it is we who are the film directors and not the others, that is to say, the spectators, the question does not stem from an exclusively ethical concern. We know that we are filmmakers because we have been part of a minority which has had the time and the circumstances needed to develop, within itself, an artistic culture, and because the material resources of film technology are limited and therefore available to some, not to all. But what happens if the future holds the universalization of college level instruction, if economic and social development reduce the hours in the workday, if the evolution of film technology (there are already signs in evidence) makes it possible that this technology ceases being the privilege of a small few? What happens if the development of videotape solves the problem of inevitably limited laboratory capacity, if television systems with their potential for "projecting" independently of the central studio render the ad infinitum construction of movie theaters suddenly superfluous?

What happens then is not only an act of social justice—the possibility for everyone to make films but also a fact of extreme importance for artistic culture: the possibility of recovering, without any kinds of complexes or guilt feelings, the true meaning of artistic activity. Then we will be able to understand that art is one of mankind's "impartial" or "uncommitted" activities [*una actividad desinteresada*]. That art is not work, and that the artist is not in the strict sense a worker. The feeling that this is so, and the impossibility of translating it into practice, constitutes the agony and at the same time the "pharisee-ism" of all contemporary art. In fact, the two tendencies exist: those who pretend to produce cinema as an "uncommitted" activity and those who pretend to justify it as a "committed" activity. Both find themselves in a blind alley. . . .

Popular art has absolutely nothing to do with what is called mass art. Popular art needs and consequently tends to develop the personal, individual taste of a people. On the other hand, mass art (or art for the masses) requires the people to have no taste. It will only be genuine when it is actually the masses who create it, since at present it is art produced by a few for the masses. Grotowski says that today's theater should be a minority art form because mass art can be achieved through cinema. This is not true. Perhaps film is the most elitist of all the contemporary arts. Film today, no matter where, is made by a small minority for the masses. Perhaps film will be the art form which takes the longest time to reach the hand of the masses, when we understand mass art as popular art, art created by the masses. Currently, as Hauser points out, mass art is art produced by a minority in order to satisfy the demand of a public reduced to the sole role of spectator and consumer.

Popular art has always been created by the least learned sector of society, yet

this "uncultured" sector has managed to conserve profoundly cultured characteristics of art. One of the most important of these is the fact that the creators
are at the same time the spectators and vice versa. Between those who produce
and those who consume, no sharp line of demarcation exists. Cultivated art,
in our era, has also attained this situation. Modern art's great dose of freedom
is nothing more than the conquest of a new interlocutor: the artist himself.
For this reason it is useless to strain oneself struggling for the substitution of
the masses as a new and potential spectator for the bourgeoisie. This situation,
maintained by popular art, adopted by cultivated art, must be dissolved and
become the heritage of all. This and no other must be the great objective of
an authentically revolutionary artistic culture.

Popular art preserved another even more important cultural characteristic:
It is carried out as but another life activity. With cultivated art, the reverse is
true; it is pursued as a unique, specific activity, as a personal achievement. This
is the cruel price of having had to maintain artistic activity at the expense of
its inexistence among the people. Hasn't the attempt to realize himself on the
edge of society proved to be too painful a restriction for the artist and for art
itself? To posit art as a sect, as a society within society, as the promised land
where we can fleetingly fulfill ourselves for a brief instant—doesn't this create the illusion that self-realization on the level of consciousness also implies
self-realization on the level of existence? Isn't this patently obvious in contemporary circumstances? The essential lesson of popular art is that it is carried
out as a life activity: man must not fulfill himself as an artist but fully; the artist
must not seek fulfillment as an artist but as a human being.

In the modern world, principally in developed capitalist nations and in those
countries engaged in a revolutionary process, there are alarming symptoms,
obvious signs of an imminent change. The possibilities for overcoming this
traditional disassociation are beginning to arise. These symptoms are not a
product of consciousness but of reality itself. A large part of the struggle waged
in modern art has been, in fact, to "democratize" art. What other goal is entailed in combating the limitations of taste, museum art, and the demarcation
lines between the creator and the public? What is considered beauty today, and
where is it found? On Campbell's soup labels, in a garbage can lid, in gadgets?
Even the eternal value of a work of art is today being questioned. What else
could be the meaning of those sculptures, seen in recent exhibitions, made of
blocks of ice which melt away while the public looks at them? Isn't this—more
than the disappearance of art—the attempt to make the spectator disappear?
Don't those painters who entrust a portion of the execution of their work to
just anyone, rather than to their disciples, exhibit an eagerness to jump over

the barricade of "elitist" art? Doesn't the same attitude exist among composers whose works allow their performers ample liberty?

There's a widespread tendency in modern art to make the spectator participate ever more fully. If he participates to a greater and greater degree, where will the process end up? Isn't the logical outcome — or shouldn't it in fact be — that he will cease being a spectator altogether? This simultaneously represents a tendency toward collectivism and toward individualism. Once we admit the possibility of universal participation, aren't we also admitting the individual creative potential which we all have? Isn't Grotowski mistaken when he asserts that today's theater should be dedicated to an elite? Isn't it rather the reverse: that the theater of poverty in fact requires the highest refinement? It is the theater which has no need for secondary values: costumes, scenery, makeup, even a stage. Isn't this an indication that material conditions are reduced to a minimum and that, from this point of view, the possibility of making theater is within everyone's reach? And doesn't the fact that the theater has an increasingly smaller public mean that conditions are beginning to ripen for it to transform itself into a true mass theater? Perhaps the tragedy of the theater lies in the fact that it has reached this point in its evolution too soon.

When we look toward Europe, we wring our hands. We see that the old culture is totally incapable of providing answers to the problems of art. The fact is that Europe can no longer respond in a traditional manner but at the same time finds it equally difficult to respond in a manner that is radically new. Europe is no longer capable of giving the world a new "ism"; neither is it in a position to put an end to "isms" once and for all. So we think that our moment has come, that at last the underdeveloped can deck themselves out as "men of culture." Here lies our greatest danger and our greatest temptation. This accounts for the opportunism of some on our continent. For, given our technical and scientific backwardness and given the scanty presence of the masses in social life, our continent is still capable of responding in a traditional manner, by reaffirming the concept and the practice of elite art. Perhaps in this case the real motive for the European applause which some of our literary and cinematic works have won is none other than a certain nostalgia which we inspire. After all, the European has no other Europe to which to turn.

The third factor, the revolution — which is the most important of all — is perhaps present in our country as nowhere else. This is our only true chance. The revolution is what provides all other alternatives, what can supply an entirely new response, what enables us to do away once and for all with elitist concepts and practices in art. The revolution and the ongoing revolutionary process are the only factors which make the total and free presence of the masses possible—and this will mean the definitive disappearance of the rigid division of labor and of a society divided into sectors and classes. For us, then, the revolution is the highest expression of culture because it will abolish artistic culture as a fragmentary human activity.

Current responses to this inevitable future, this uncontestable prospect, can be as numerous as the countries on our continent. Because characteristics and achieved labels are not the same, each art form, every artistic manifestation, must find its own expression. What should be the response of the Cuban cinema in particular? Paradoxically, we think it will be a new poetics, not a new cultural policy. A poetics whose true goal will be to commit suicide, to disappear as such. We know, however, that in fact other artistic conceptions will continue to exist among us, just like small rural landholdings and religion continue to exist. On the level of cultural policy we are faced with a serious problem: the film school. Is it right to continue developing a handful of film specialists? It seems inevitable for the present, but what will be the eternal quarry that we continue to mine: the students in Arts and Letters at the University? But shouldn't we begin to consider right now whether that school should have a limited life span? What end do we pursue there—a reserve corps of future artists? Or a specialized future public? We should be asking ourselves whether we can do something now to abolish this division between artistic and scientific culture. . . .

We should endeavor to see that our future students, and therefore our future filmmakers, will themselves be scientists, sociologists, physicians, economists, agricultural engineers, etc., without of course ceasing to be filmmakers. And, at the same time, we should have the same aim for our most outstanding workers, the workers who achieve the best results in terms of political and intellectual formation. We cannot develop the taste of the masses as long as the division between the two cultures continues to exist, nor as long as the masses are not the real masters of the means of artistic production. The revolution has liberated us as an artistic sector. It is only logical that we contribute to the liberation of the private means of artistic production.

A new poetics for the cinema will, above all, be a "partisan" and "committed" poetics, a "committed" art, a consciously and resolutely "committed" cinema—that is to say, an "imperfect" cinema. An "impartial" or "uncommitted" (cinema), as a complete aesthetic activity, will only be possible when it is the people who make art. But today art must assimilate its quota of work so that work can assimilate its quota of art.

The motto of this imperfect cinema (which there's no need to invent, since it already exists) is, as Glauber Rocha would say, "We are not interested in the problems of neurosis; we are interested in the problems of lucidity." Art no

longer has use for the neurotic and his problems, although the neurotic continues to need art—as a concerned object, a relief, an alibi, or, as Freud would
say, as a sublimation of his problems. A neurotic can produce art, but art has
no reason to produce neurotics. It has been traditionally believed that the concerns of art were not to be found in the sane but in the sick, not in the normal
but in the abnormal, not in those who struggle but in those who weep, not
in lucid minds but in neurotic ones. Imperfect cinema is changing this way of
seeing the question. We have more faith in the sick man than in the healthy one
because his truth is purged by suffering. However, there is no need for suffering
to be synonymous with artistic elegance. There is still a trend in modern art—
undoubtedly related to Christian tradition—which identifies seriousness with
suffering. The specter of Marguerite Gautier still haunts artistic endeavor in
our day. Only in the person who suffers do we perceive elegance, gravity, even
beauty; only in him do we recognize the possibility of authenticity, seriousness,
sincerity. Imperfect cinema must put an end to this tradition.

Imperfect cinema finds a new audience in those who struggle, and it finds
its themes in their problems. For imperfect cinema, "lucid" people are the ones
who think and feel and exist in a world which they can change; in spite of all
the problems and difficulties, they are convinced that they can transform it in
a revolutionary way. Imperfect cinema therefore has no need to struggle to
create an "audience." On the contrary, it can be said that at present a greater
audience exists for this kind of cinema than there are filmmakers able to supply
that audience.

What does this new interlocutor require of us—an art full of moral examples worthy of imitation? No. Man is more of a creator than an innovator.
Besides, he should be the one to give us moral examples. He might ask us for
a fuller, more complete work, aimed—in a separate or coordinated fashion—
at the intelligence, the emotions, the powers of intuition.

Should he ask us for a cinema of denunciation? Yes and no. No, if the denunciation is directed toward the others, if it is conceived that those who are
not struggling might sympathize with us and increase their awareness. Yes, if
the denunciation acts as information, as testimony, as another combat weapon
for those engaged in the struggle. Why denounce imperialism to show one
more time that it is evil? What's the use if those now fighting are fighting primarily against imperialism? We can denounce imperialism but should strive
to do it as a way of proposing concrete battles. A film which [portrays] those
who struggle against the evil deeds of an official who must be executed would
be an excellent example of this kind of film-denunciation.

We maintain that imperfect cinema must above all show the process which
generates the problems. It is thus the opposite of a cinema principally dedi-

cated to celebrating results, the opposite of a self-sufficient and contemplative cinema, the opposite of a cinema which "beautifully illustrates" ideas or concepts which we already possess. (The narcissistic posture has nothing to do with those who struggle.) To show a process is not exactly equivalent to analyzing it. To analyze, in the traditional sense of the word, always implies a closed prior judgment. To analyze a problem is to show the problem (not the process) permeated with judgments which the analysis itself generates a priori. To analyze is to block off from the outset any possibility for analysis on the part of the interlocutor.

To show the process of a problem, on the other hand, is to submit it to judgment without pronouncing the verdict. There is a style of news reporting which puts more emphasis on the commentary than on the news item. There is another kind of reporting which presents the news and evaluates it through the arrangement of the item on the page or by its position in the paper. To show the process of a problem is like showing the very development of the news item, without commentary; it is like showing the multifaced evolution of a piece of information without evaluating it. The subjective element is the selection of the problem, conditioned as it is by the interest of the audience — which is the subject. The objective element is showing the process — which is the object.

Imperfect cinema is an answer, but it is also a question which will discover its own answers in the course of its development. Imperfect cinema can make use of the documentary or the fictional mode, or both. It can use whatever genre, or all genres. It can use cinema as a pluralistic art form or as a specialized form of expression. These questions are indifferent to it, since they do not represent its real alternatives or problems, and much less its real goals. These are not the battles or polemics it is interested in sparking.

Imperfect cinema can also be enjoyable, both for the maker and for its new audience. Those who struggle do not struggle on the edge of life, but in the midst of it. Struggle is life and vice versa. One does not struggle in order to live "later on." The struggle requires organization — the organization of life. Even in the most extreme phase, that of total and direct war, the organization of life is equivalent to the organization of the struggle. And in life, as in the struggle, there is everything, including enjoyment. Imperfect cinema can enjoy itself despite everything which conspires to negate enjoyment.

Imperfect cinema rejects exhibitionism in both (literal) senses of the word, the narcissistic and the commercial (getting shown in established theaters and circuits). It should be remembered that the death of the star-system turned out to be a positive thing for art. There is no reason to doubt that the disappearance of the director as star will fail to offer similar prospects. Imperfect cinema must start work now, in cooperation with sociologists, revolutionary leaders, psychologists, economists, etc. Furthermore, imperfect cinema rejects whatever services criticism has to offer and considers the function of mediators and intermediaries anachronistic.

Imperfect cinema is no longer interested in quality or technique. It can be created equally well with a Mitchell or with an eight-millimeter camera, in a studio or in a guerrilla camp in the middle of the jungle. Imperfect cinema is no longer interested in predetermined taste, and much less in "good taste." It is not quality which it seeks in an artist's work. The only thing it is interested in is how an artist responds to the following question: What are you doing in order to overcome the barrier of the "cultured" elite audience which up to now has conditioned the form of your work?

The filmmaker who subscribes to this new poetics should not have personal self-realization as his object. From now on he should also have another activity. He should place his role as revolutionary or aspiring revolutionary above all else. In a word, he should try to fulfill himself as a man and not just as an artist. Imperfect cinema cannot lose sight of the fact that its essential goal as a new poetics is to disappear. It is no longer a matter of replacing one school with another, one "ism" with another, poetry with antipoetry, but of truly letting a thousand different flowers bloom. The future lies with folk art. But let us no longer display folk art with demagogic pride, with a celebrative air. Let us exhibit it instead as a cruel denunciation, as a painful testimony to the level at which the peoples of the world have been forced to limit their artistic creativity. The future, without doubt, will be with folk art, but then there will be no need to call it that, because nobody and nothing will any longer be able to again paralyze the creative spirit of the people.

Art will not disappear into nothingness; it will disappear into everything.

TRANSLATED BY JULIANNE BURTON

Dance and Social Change

Yvonne Daniel

Rumba is at the heart of dance culture in Cuba. Originally a dance anchored in the lives of lower-class black Cubans in the colonial era, rumba was quickly elevated into a symbol of Cuba's new popular culture after the 1959 Revolution. Rumba has now become one of Cuba's most potent national symbols. U.S. anthropologist and musicologist Yvonne Daniel provides a detailed description of a rumba performance. She argues that the revolution transformed rumba from "a spontaneous, improvisational event that included a set of rumba dances and other dance forms to a choreographed public performance executed regularly in cultural programs throughout the island."[1] The Ministry of Culture actively promoted and professionalized rumba "to assist overarching national principles that would benefit all sectors of the population. Rumba, apparently more than other Cuban dance traditions, expressed an identification with African-derived elements that make up Cuban culture, represented the interests of workers, and solidified the participation of the Cuban artistic community in the social advance of the new political system."[2]

The first time I saw rumba danced in Cuba was at the National Folkloric Company's studio in Havana during a regular Friday afternoon rehearsal before Sábado de la Rumba (Rumba Saturday). The entire company of about forty dancers entered the warm, shaded room and took prescribed positions: the younger technicians in the first rows, the veteran soloists at the rear. The battery of five percussionists and three singers formed a curved line on a stage at the far end of the studio, facing the dancers. Another five or six musicians were seated farther back on the stage, ready to take any part or any instrument on a simple cue. The *claves* (wooden sticks of a Latin percussion ensemble) announced the slow, repetitive basic rhythm, answered by a deep throat of the *hembra* (the lowest-pitched drum) and followed by the *macho* (middle-register drum); then I heard the sparse, terse commentary of the *quinto* (the falsetto of the drum trio) in playful percussive harmony. The *catá*, or *guagua* (a bamboo or wooden cylindrical instrument played with wooden sticks), and the *madruga* (a metal shaker) joined in the musical conversation, and a singer was inspired to begin the syllabic melisma of the *diana*, the introductory portion of rumba singing.

Immediately the dancers began to move in their places. As they waited for instructions from the two leaders of the class, the dancers were trying to maintain their prepared attention stance, but they could not help responding subtly to the rhythms. The movement came from deep within their torsos, through their chests, through their shoulders and arms, and ultimately involved their necks and heads. Their rocking, swaying, and undulating were an accompaniment to the antiphonal singing of a small chorus of men. Suddenly, for my uninitiated ears—but really at the beginning of the compelling rhythmic phrase—dancers' knees bent and the full force of the rules of the dance consumed the dancers: they began dancing rumba. The instructors had signaled for the performance of rumba to start.

The rhythm was hypnotic as rows of dancers advanced toward me and the musical ensemble on the raised stage. Six dancers proceeded in a single horizontal line, amply spaced across a huge mirrored studio. Their movements brought my attention to the very subtle undulations from the lower spine. The undulations flowed upward and laterally through the sea of bodies. I saw feet moving forward with many subtleties, even within the uniformity of unison movement. The basic footwork appeared like a touch to the side and a return to normal standing position, repeated on alternating sides. In reality, there was a small, weighted push of one foot to the side and a step in place with the same foot, alternating from one side to the other. With succeeding rows of dancers, however, the step was embroidered with small, passing steps as the pattern continued to alternate from side to side. Then I began to notice the dancers' arms, which opened outward and slightly upward, accenting, ever so smoothly, the alternating foot pattern.

The dancers were singing a refrain with the chorus of singers, a short vocal response to the solo singer. Occasionally the shoulders of a woman or man, or of several dancers, vibrated quickly. No knees were straightened; all male and female bodies were slightly lowered in a forward tilt (about a forty-five-degree hip flexion), responding to the rhythmic pulse of the claves. The rhythm acted like an injection that affected the body deeply and traveled upward through the spine, laterally through the hips, and forward and backward in the chest, creating sensuous polyrhythms within the body.

The drums began to speed up, and the instructors signaled a change from the horizontal lines to a large semicircle facing the drums. The dancers' bodies were glistening as they raised their voices in song, smiled, and danced. One instructor, in the closed circle under the resounding drumming, told dancers to watch the *informante*, the other dance specialist who also taught the class.

Music and dance performers. Photos by Tania Jovanovic.

One quiet dancer, who had danced in the back row earlier, came to the center, lifted the edges of her skirt, and began to articulate multiple minute movements of the shoulders, chest, hips, feet, arms and head. With the slightest bits of energy, she demonstrated the moving elaborated step, gradually building spatial and emotional dynamics and a sense of a soloist's drama. She was in her inner world; intermittently her eyes closed with feeling as she listened and responded to various signals from the quinto. The instructor signaled one of the younger men, and immediately, but slowly, the intense dynamics of a skilled and fiercely expressive body deepened toward the floor with a forward tilt and encircled the dancing diva.

The two dancers smiled at one another constantly, and I noticed how intensely they concentrated. They danced apart spatially, with different steps, but together in relation to one another and in relation to the music. The music was relatively slow, and their accentuation on the after pulse of the movement, the rebound to a musical accent within the body, was strikingly sensual. Even though they did not make large movements or dynamic changes, the movements grew in intensity. The man circled the woman slowly, deliberately. The woman watched constantly while alternating her body undulations to each side. They danced very close together without touching. He placed a large scarf around her shoulders, still holding two of its edges. They danced even lower to the floor, watching each others' eyes, smiling. They alternated their knees from side to side in unison while slowly rising from the ground. At the same time, the upper body was demonstrating the multidirectional ability of the human torso: forward to backward, side to side, up and down. The man was making wide claps with his knees, and he raised one arm over the woman's head. Now she held the scarf and turned her back toward him, still looking for him across her shoulders.

The rumba music shifted subtly, becoming faster, but the same dance movements prevailed. The instructor signaled the informante again, and she danced momentarily alone. Another young man saw his cue and dramatically advanced toward the dancing diva, holding his head high, his back straight, and rapidly traveling forward on his toes, firing his feet swiftly and tightly, one in front of the other (*pisao* steps). The two dancers watched each other, miniaturizing the basic movements momentarily as they sensed each other, the calls of the drums and the singers, and what I later came to understand as the impending choreographed attack. At that moment, no one knew exactly what was

about to happen in the repetitive, undulating, intermittently vibrating kinesthetic exchange. They danced close to one another, he reached to embrace her waist lightly, and both dancers deepened their knee bends even farther toward the ground together. They twisted from side to side and came upward. The man reached to hold the woman's shoulders, bouncing his knees together with wide rebounds. The woman was standing almost upright, slightly tilted and bent forward, noticeably alert, when suddenly there was a pelvic thrust from the man, even from his low position. The dancing diva gracefully but speedily slapped her skirt over her pelvic area, smiled, and spun around, leaving the man undimmed, pleased, and eager to advance again.

Several other couples took turns looking for the possibilities of the pelvic thrust, or *vacunao*. I later learned that this word came from the Spanish verb *vacunar*, meaning primarily "to vaccinate." Cubans coined it to signify the erotic pelvic gesture, the object of male pursuit and female flight that is the

aim of the dance. Sometimes it was not the pelvis or hips but a foot, a hand, even a scarf, that made the male's symbolic vaccination of the female. No matter what body part was used, the dancers reveled in mounting the attack and in preparing a defense. Some women came into the circle laughing, holding only one side of their skirts, almost daring the men to attempt a vacunao. When the accented gesture happened, the women adeptly covered themselves with their hands or skirts.

After a time of singing and faster-paced dances, the instructor signaled a tall, handsome man, who was slightly older, more dignified, and seemingly more respected than the earlier partners of the dancing diva. His movements were tight, rapid, and intricate as he traveled around the circle. He would freeze momentarily in implosive holds and quickly start again. His actions answered the beckoning pitches of the leading improvisational drum. The drummer and the solo male dancer conversed in a synesthetic dialogue. The other dancers

were quite animated, not only in dancing but also in vocalizing. Challenging comments and encouraging exclamations of amazement rippled around and across the dancing space. At last the tall, handsome dancer pointed a finger toward the floor and grandly exited from the center.

Several male dancers entered the circle in succession. One dancer used his shoulders in a steady vibratory motion as he slowly bent forward to display how evenly he matched the drums with his rhythmic movements. He too used quick locomotor patterns and interspersed them with designs that were momentarily frozen in space. Sometimes he raised both arms high, curving them slightly above his head as he focused downward, listening intently, grimacing with emotion, like a fiery flamenco stance. At other times his body crouched low over a blur of legs in rhythm. One second he was on the ground on his side; the next he was upright, swinging one leg over the other. He was challenged also, but this time by a young female dancer, who had apparently dropped her skirt for this type of dancing. She wore a leotard and tights that clearly showed both the full range of shapes that were the result of expressed rhythm in her body and a female version of the men's gestures.

At this moment the entire circle was filled with excited laughter and shouts; everyone encouraged the young woman to continue her skilled and unexpected display. She followed the drum solo and complemented the rhythmic calls. As she danced, the men were particularly vocal, answering her movements in ridiculing gestures; but when she proved her speed and technical proficiency, they quickly slapped the outstretched hands of one another in fraternal approval. The women cheered her on approvingly, and one woman, older, gave the accepted gesture of challenge, the pointed finger, and entered the center.

Everyone was having fun, competing, flirting, exhibiting their sensuality and skill. The instructor and the informante, the dancing diva, both captivated and pleased, made eye contact after a time and walked toward the drums. The two teachers conversed with the lead musician for a minute, then the drummers played an ending. There was loud and enthusiastic applause for the drummers, kisses and approving touches for the final two female dancers, and much discussion among all the dancers about style and the details of arm and leg placement or agility in the vacunao. I was amazed and puzzled by the analytical exchanges about dancing that followed the almost possessed or totally concentrated states, now so quickly abandoned. . . .

The company director, who was sitting with me, noticed my puzzled expression and told me that what I had just seen was distinct within the Cuban dance experience. Though rumba is technically difficult and is danced mainly by one social class and one "racial" group, it is cherished by many and acknowledged as intimately and fundamentally "Cuban" by most Cubans. It is one of four popular and representative creations from Cuban social dance of the nineteenth century (the others are *conga, danzón,* and *son*). A movie called *Rumba* made by Cubans Oscar Valdez and Héctor Vitaria and distributed fairly widely in the United States in recent years, documents the pervasive popularity of rumba as a well-known and specially regarded dance among old and young, dark- and light-skinned, rural and urban Cubans. Even more important for my analysis of social change, however, is that rumba has been selected by Cuban authorities (either the Ministry of Culture, the directors of the national dance companies, or the organic educational process of the Cuban Revolution—no one is quite sure which entity is fully responsible) as important dance material. Since the Revolution of 1959, rumba has emerged as a symbol of what Cuba stands for among its own people and what Cubans want the world to understand when the international community envisions Cuba and Cubans.

Notes

For complete references and notes, consult the work as cited in the acknowledgment of copyrights section.

1. Yvonne Daniel, *Rumba: Dance and Social Change in Contemporary Cuba* (Bloomington: Indiana University Press, 1995), 13.

2. Ibid., 16.

Revolutionary Sport

Paula Pettavino and Geralyn Pye

Cuba's impressive performance in the international sporting arena, symbolized by the achievements of Cuban boxer Teófilo Stevenson and Olympic gold medallist runner Alberto Juantorena (Cuba's vice minister of sports since 1984) was made possible by the removal of social, cultural, and economic barriers to participation in physical culture after 1959 and by the egalitarian and participatory features of the political culture of the new revolutionary state. In the following extract from the conclusion to Paula Pettavino and Geralyn Pye's study of sport in revolutionary Cuba, the authors examine some of the achievements and problems experienced by Cuban sport, paying particular attention to sport's ongoing dialog with the political, military, and foreign policy history of the revolution.

Domestic Policy

Cuba's economic problems together with the antagonism of the Reagan and Bush administrations led to an increased use of physical culture to promote fitness and military preparedness. The role of athletes as a vanguard for the revolution and the use of sports successes to create national pride and international prestige may be expanded [by the Cuban government]. On the domestic front, the use of physical culture for socialization and perhaps for social control could intensify. These aspects of physical culture, however, are unlikely to have much impact if discontent continues to grow in the face of economic hardship and political isolation.

MILITARY PREPAREDNESS

The use of physical culture within military training is common to all countries. In the socialist countries, sport was encouraged to promote fitness for defense among the population as a whole in the face of often hostile environments. This has certainly been the case in Cuba. It is not surprising that, in times of perceived or actual security threats, vigilance—including the use of physical culture for fitness and readiness purposes—has increased. The antagonism of the Reagan administration led to the formation of military sports clubs, which taught civilians basic military skills in combination with recreational activities. Should Cuba be threatened again (not an altogether unrealistic fear given the recent capture of armed Cuban Americans on Cuban shores), it seems probable that the use of physical culture for military preparedness will be maintained, if not increased.

POLITICAL ROLES

Athletes may also be called upon to intensify their role as revolutionary role models and as sources of national pride. Cuba's sports stars have already played a significant role in the revolutionary process, as has physical culture as a whole. Sport has affected three very important political factors: nation building, socialization, and political integration.

As Alberto Juantorena said, "Americans live in a country; we Cubans are building a country." Through sports, Cubans are able to feel personally involved in the process. This creates strong feelings of national pride. People who feel they have helped to create something identify more closely with it. The goals of mass participation were to break down class differences and to promote cohesiveness. The result, it was hoped, would be a system or network between government and people and among the people as a whole that was mutually supportive. Certainly, the people's participation in numerous activities and their administration (including physical culture) may serve this purpose. On the other hand, the fact that decision making in physical culture (as in other areas) is highly centralized in the upper levels of the state and party structures — and, in the case of physical culture, at the top levels of INDER [National Institute for Sports, Physical Education, and Recreation] — may have undermined, to some extent, the goal of political integration and national unity.[1] . . .

Foreign Policy

Physical culture has traditionally been significant in Cuban foreign policy in the postrevolution period. With the prospect of growing political isolation, this role is quite likely to grow in importance, although funding problems may well undermine this avenue of foreign policy.

Sport can serve as a powerful international political tool, a fact that is not lost on many countries today:

> For this land, whose boundaries are set by the sea, sports has become a kind of Cuban equivalent of nineteenth-century American [U.S.] Manifest

Destiny. The Olympics are their Oregon Trail, their Northwest Territory, their visible evidence of national accomplishment and a rallying point for morale.

Surely the value of a victory in the Olympics, the Pan American Games, or any international sporting contest goes beyond the gold medal. It is but a short distance from an individual athlete in his or her national uniform to the strong symbol of the country being represented.

There are many uses for sport, some of which are closely interrelated. [Four] of these are described below.

DIPLOMATIC RECOGNITION

One of the most concrete uses of sport is as a means of diplomatic recognition or nonrecognition. Sport is a clear but indirect way to communicate government policy. The most obvious examples have been relationships between East and West Germany, the People's Republic of China and Taiwan, South Africa and New Zealand, and South Africa and the British Commonwealth. At the 1966 Central American Games, for example, Puerto Rico denied Cuban athletes visas to attend the games and would not guarantee safe participation. The Cuban team was sent by sea on the *Cerro Pelado*, and despite a hostile reception and harassment, was allowed to compete. Cuban athletes dominated the games. Cuba's impressive victory in those games further enhanced the Cubans' political point. The U.S.-Cuban tensions at the 1987 and 1991 Pan American Games are further examples. The Cubans made political statements by boycotting the 1984 and 1988 Olympic Games. The 1991 Pan American Games may also have played a part in Cuba's current attempt to further break its isolation in Latin America.

PROPAGANDA

Sport provides a convenient stage for displaying the physical prowess (and superiority) of a country's athletes. The implication is clear: only a superior social system could produce such dazzling champions (the inferiority of the loser is implicit). So important was this function to the socialist countries that meetings were held regularly among the leaders of the propaganda sections of the sports associations of the entire bloc. The 1977 meeting was held in Cuba.

The revolutionary government has not lost the opportunity to capitalize on its sporting successes. After all, probably most people throughout the world identify Cuba first with the 1962 Missile Crisis, and second with Alberto Juantorena or Teófilo Stevenson, rather than Moncada, Granma, or even the Bay of Pigs. To the Cubans, sports success as propaganda is important throughout the world, but nowhere more so than in the rest of Latin America. Castro said, "I can assure you that one of the things most admired by our Latin American neighbors is our sporting successes. We can say that our athletes are the children of our Revolution and, at the same time, the standard-bearers of that same Revolution."

What gives Cuba more credibility with the less developed countries is that Cuba is still "one of their own," a neighborhood kid made good. This position was strengthened as Cuba moved into a leadership role and gained the ability to provide technical assistance to other countries. "Cuba thus provides a powerful example of the potential of a small country whose resources are rationally deployed under what the Cuban leadership described as a 'superior social system.'"

The collapse of most of Cuba's socialist allies means that this propaganda effort may be substantially weakened. The economic chaos in the former USSR and in Eastern Europe makes it harder for people and nations to believe Cuban claims to a superior social system. This also applies to Cuba's own domestic audience. The reduction of technical and economic aid will probably mean it will be harder for Cuba to maintain its current status as a world-class performer. Nevertheless, there will continue to be prestige in victories such as the ones at the 1991 Pan American Games and the 1992 Olympics.

PRESTIGE

Closely tied to propaganda is the function of sports in the search for national prestige. Athletes are sources of pride; victories are a bonus. Since the mid-1970s, Cuba has been a respected member of the international sporting community. This can be accredited not just to the nation's athletes, but also to the government officials and trainers who support the actual contestants. In 1976, Raudol Ruiz, a former prominent sports official in Cuba, became the first Latin American to be awarded the Philip Noel Baker prize for scientific investigation by the International Council for Sport and Physical Education [*sic*; International Council of Sport Science and Physical Education, ICSSPE]. In Cuba this was considered a high honor.

Ruiz began his career as an athletic trainer. After the revolution, he moved in to direct Manuel Fajardo (ISCF [Instituto Superior de Cultura Física]). With further study, he received his Ph.D. from the GDR. In 1982, he was vice-president for Latin America for [ICSSPE] and a professor at INDER. Ruiz's response upon receiving the award was in typical Cuban fashion:

I think that in the first place although my name is on the award, this distinction corresponds to those who in the last fifteen years have given their cooperation to the development of national sport. Implicit here is the tremendous privilege of learning what the Revolution has given to us, and for this recognition, we are obliged to improve our work every day.

Whether Cuba is able to maintain its sporting strength and the resulting prestige in the future remains uncertain, just as Cuba's important role in sports cooperation appears threatened by economic crisis. Both sporting strength with prestige and a role in sports cooperation, however, have been, and will remain, valuable tools of foreign policy.

COOPERATION

Perhaps the function of sport that carries with it the most hope is that it encourages cooperation among nations. The assumption is that any contact fosters understanding, perhaps even improved relations. Cooperation, which was especially valuable to Cuba, certainly occurred within the former socialist bloc, but since 1970 Cuba has also extended sports cooperation to less developed countries—notably Jamaica, where the Cubans have built sports facilities (including one for free). Jamaicans and many other people from poor countries in Africa and Latin America have also received sports training in Cuba.

Since 1977, Cuba's overseas sports program has been greatly expanded: Africa, Algeria, Angola, Benin, Congo (since 1984), Guinea (until the end of 1986), Guinea-Bissau, Malagasy Republic (up to early 1987), Mali, Mozambique, Nigeria, and Tanzania have all received Cuban sports aid. Iraq, South Yemen, Vietnam, Nicaragua, Panama, Peru, Brazil, and Venezuela have also been included in Cuba's sports program. In 1983, ninety Cuban sports specialists were working in a total of fifteen countries. By 1987, eighteen countries were assisted by forty-eight specialists. In 1990, there were four hundred foreign students from thirty-three countries on scholarships. Also in that year, there were a thousand technicians working overseas, and thirty-nine countries received technical aid. Hence, despite U.S. pressures to reduce Cuba's international influence in the 1980s, Cuba was assisting numerous countries in sports as well as in health and education.

Cuba's commitment to socialist internationalism is promoted through such sports links. With the current concerns with internal problems and, indeed, the very survival of Cuba's socialist system, it will be harder for Cuba to sustain this sports aid to less developed countries.

Notes

For complete references and notes, consult the work as cited in the acknowledgment of copyrights section.

1. Juantorena has important positions both in INDER and on the Central Committee of the PCC [Cuban Communist Party], so he feels he takes a part in the building of his country. This feeling may be less strong among those who do not have so much power.

Mea Cuba

Guillermo Cabrera Infante

Although the revolution has enormously expanded the physical infrastructure of culture in Cuba and increased people's access to cultural resources, the relationship between intellectuals and the revolutionary state has often been tense. The political culture of the revolution emphasizes, even demands, a high degree of commitment from citizens, as well as a certain subordination of individual needs to the achievement of collective goals. And though the worst excesses of Soviet-style "socialist realism" have been avoided, dogmatic and intolerant positions adopted by cultural functionaries have placed limits on artistic and cultural expression and given rise to censorship, self-censorship, and other forms of cultural exclusion. The clash between the logic of revolutionary unity and cultural and intellectual autonomy was observed most clearly during the first decade of the revolution as Cuban artists and writers adjusted to the opportunities and challenges posed by the new state. The following selections reveal some of the issues involved. Guillermo Cabrera Infante (b. 1929), one of the most distinguished Cuban writers living outside of the island, provides a characteristically humorous and sharply drawn account of several moments in the contest between cultural innovation and bureaucratic obscurantism during the 1960s.

Revolución had been the voice from the underground of the 26th of July Movement, the organization which did more to put Fidel Castro in power than the puny guerrilla he has made everybody believe did the job. Above ground now, *Revolución* became a very powerful newspaper indeed, the first in Cuba and the only one that had access to the innermost recesses of power in the Government and in Cuban political life in general. Moreover, it had, for Cuba — at the time a country of some seven million people — an enormous circulation. *Lunes* profited from all this and became the first literary magazine in Latin America or Spain to boast of a circulation of almost two hundred thousand copies. *Lunes* had a lot of pull — and not merely literary push.

My first mistake as an editor was to try and clean out the Cuban literary stables by sweeping the house of words with a political broom. That's called an inquisition, and it can induce writer's block by terror. The magazine, with the heavy weight of the Revolution and the government behind it plus the 26th of July Movement's political prestige, literally blasted many writers into submission — or oblivion. We had the Surrealist credo as our catechism and Trotskyite politics as our aesthetics, mixed like bad metaphors — or heady drinks. From this position of maximum strength, we proceeded to annihilate respected writers of the past, like Lezama Lima, simply because he dared to combine in his poems the anachronistic ideologies of [Luis de] Góngora and [Stéphane] Mallarmé, now joined in Havana to produce disjointed verse of a magnificently obscure Catholicism. We actually tried to assassinate Lezama's character. There were other, older casualties, like the Spanish dentist who wanted to be a Dantist and whose recently published novel was pulled from its Asturian roots with laughing gas. At the same time, the magazine exalted Virgilio Piñera, a man of Lezama's generation, to the position of a Virgil out of double hell. He who had always been a pariah in his own country, a novelist who was terribly poor, almost destitute, became our favorite father figure, the house-writer. Another mistake. Besides being an excellent short-story writer anthologized by Borges, a playwright of genius (he penned a play after the fashion of the theatre of the absurd when Ionesco hadn't yet staged *The Bald Prima Donna* [*Soprano*] and long before Beckett wrote *Waiting for Godot*) and a pleasant poet, Virgilio had a particular fault. As with San Andreas, it was a very visible one. Virgilio, like his Roman counterpart, was a pederast. Perhaps the epitome of the literary queen, a Cuban Cocteau known not for his plays but for his playmates. That was food for gossip in Paris, but this was revolutionary Havana and there was no room left for queens shouting "Off with his head!" in a revolution: all Cuban queens ended up with no head, not even their own, especially not their own.

Third original sin in a row: there were too many talented people grouped around *Lunes*, each one supporting the Revolution in their fashion. José Baragaño, the Surrealist poet who came back from his exile in Paris where he was befriended by André Breton himself, who hated Sunday painters and minor poets, was pet poet and pet pest on the magazine. Heberto Padilla, born in the same town as Baragaño (the funnily named Puerta de Golpe in Cuban tobacco country: Puerta de Golpe literally means, as if Larry Grayson had named it, "Shut the Door"), came from exile in the Berlitz Academy in New York, and cultivated an easygoing but mordant style of verse. Padilla was a powerful poet in *Lunes*. Both Baragaño and Padilla, pugnacious poets, were out to get the older generation, many of them civil servants from Batista times and even before, as was the case with Lezama. Calvert Casey, who, in spite of his name and having been born in Baltimore, was not only a Cuban but a true *habanero*, delicate and precise in the exquisite concealments of his homosexual prose, though he had a mulatto lover, openly a couple. Antón Arrufat was a disciple of Piñera—and not only in playwriting. Pablo Armando Fernández, a minor poet but an accomplished diplomat capable of extricating the magazine from any critical jam, was our pint-size Sebastian, a moving target. He is still in Cuba, still a diplomat but no longer a poet, minor or otherwise. He is professionally dedicated to being host to political tourists from the United States, where he lived in a closet in Queens, before returning to Cuba, already married, in 1959. Like Padilla and Hurtado, I persuaded Pablo to come back to Cuba from the States. Oscar Hurtado, also an economic exile in New York, was a dear giant of a man, like the family elephant, but an incredible shrinking poet, inimical to Lezama and his Orígenes group, and died not only unrecognized but unrecognizing in an asylum, suffering silently and alone from a varicose brain. And, never allowed to leave the boat when it was listing (*Lunes* was on all the lists of the security service, the counterespionage service, and the police), there was I, who, though an inveterate smoker, couldn't share the peace pipe because I smoked only cigars then. The magazine, as you can see, was manned by a manic crew of pederasts (wait and you'll see why this fact of life became crucial to our demise), the happy few, as Che Guevara labeled us, who were not real revolutionaries, with a skipper who, no doubt due to myopia, saw the danger signals very, very late. Too late, in fact. I discovered that we had no true power when we hit what seemed a mere sectarian wave but was the tip of the totalitarian iceberg. *Lunes* should have been called the *Titanic*, for very soon we were in deep, cold waters. Before sinking, I saw clearly that we had tried to make the Revolution readable, therefore livable. Both tasks proved utterly impossible.

In its heyday, however, *Lunes* expanded quickly. Soon we had branched out into a publishing house (Ediciones R), whose first published book was *Poesía, revolución del ser* ("Poetry, being's revolution," though, only a few months earlier, its author, José Baragaño, still the Paris Surrealist, had titled it *Being Is Nothingness*). This collection of poems was, in 1960, a rehashing of all the Surreal formulas of the preceding twenty years, but now sang a song to the Revolution and to the Heideggerian being for death. Though now, instead of nothingness, it offered everythingness. Opportunism, thy name is poetry. Then we had an hour, at peak time, on television, second channel to the left. We formed a record company, called Sonido Erre, or Sound R, *R* for Revolution. Our publishing venture—quite successful, by the way—was at the time the only independent publishing house left in Cuba. All the rest had already been nationalized. But it was no privilege, this solitary printing-press under private ownership. It was, in fact, as ominous as a smoke signal in Apache territory. It was then that I committed a mistake which proved to be a blessing in disguise. I helped Sabá, my brother, with the completion of a documentary he was making with the cinematographer Orlando Jiménez-Leal—at the time the youngest photographer in Cuba, capable of handling a CinemaScope camera when he was fifteen, quite a film feat. As its title suggests, *P.M.* would be a view of Havana after dark, the camera peeping into the small cafés and bars and dives patronized by the common Cuban having a last time before the political night closed in. I liked the idea. I gave them the money to edit the documentary, print two or three copies, and design the titles. All this was done outside the Film Institute—that is, officialdom—in our TV channel labs but quite openly. *Lunes* got the exclusive rights to show the picture on its program and we showed it. There was no censorship for us on television. As in my magazine, we were our own boss. After all, we were the offspring of *Revolución*, the newspaper of the Revolution, the voice of the people. We were omnipotent—sort of.

But a spectacle needs spectators, and the filmmakers wanted to show their little night film of music to a live audience. There were still two or three cinemas not yet nationalized in Old Havana. One of them specialized in documentaries. The owner agreed to run the film: the next step was to obtain permission from the Comisión Revisora to show the picture in public. The Comisión Revisora was the same censorship office as in Batista's time and further back: at headquarters you could see *The Great Train Robbery* and even Edison's *The Kiss* was under the control of the Film Institute, which is nothing like the British Film Institute but a state monopoly which controls everything that has to do with films—from making pictures to importing, distributing, and exhibiting them. The Cuban Film Institute owns all the cinemas, drive-ins, and movie houses in Cuba—and you must go to them even to get a roll of film for a snapshot camera. On top of that, they had a long-standing feud with *Lunes*, which they labeled as decadent, bourgeois, avant-gardist, and, the worst epithet in the Communist name-calling catalogue, cosmopolitist [cosmopolite]. In turn, we saw them as despicable bureaucrats, a bunch of ignoramuses with artistically reactionary ideas and no taste at all. The director of the Film Institute, Alfredo Guevara (no relation to Che Guevara), was the worst Communist commissar to deal with films this side of Stalin's Shumyavsky. To take *P.M.* to the Film Institute for approval was a naive and daring thing to do—like Little Red Riding Hood drilling the wolf's teeth. But, you see, it simply had to be done. Some time later, *Revolución* was going to be killed and reborn under the name of *Granma*—and it has indeed shown big bad teeth ever since. Nevertheless, we didn't expect such a brutal bite. The Comisión Revisora not only refused to give any seal of approval to *P.M.*, but banned the film, which was accused of being counter-revolutionary and dangerous rubbish and licentious and lewd. Furthermore, they seized the copy sent for approval.

This was more than we could stomach—even if there was to be a purge at the end of it. We had been expecting a showdown with the Film Institute. But it was to become a shoot-out. The banning of *P.M.* occurred in June 1961, in what could be termed a period between two wars. In April that year the Bay of Pigs invasion took place. All the invaders had been impressively routed in less than forty-eight hours and, rather hastily, Fidel Castro had declared Cuba a socialist republic, though the country would be neither. The times were auspicious for the Communist Party (now merged with the remnants of the 26th of July Movement and the ghost of the Revolutionary Directory into one single party called ORI [Organizaciones Revolucionarias Integradas]), so much so that its Council for Culture had decided to stage a writers' congress in Havana and to invite a few foreign novelists of note, such as Nathalie Sarraute, who were sympathizers of the Revolution but not necessarily Communists. In the meantime, in some kind of political montage (hooves of Klansmen's horses galloping, then cut to damsel in distress, then cut to threatening blackamoor), *Lunes* was seen busily collecting signatures to protest about the sequestering of *P.M.*, the little night film. This was going to have wider implications, with the Communist congress about to take place.

When they saw us coming and knew we meant business the Council for Culture panicked. They asked us please not to turn the letter against the Film Institute into a manifesto by making the statement public. In turn, they promised to postpone their congress and wash our dirty linen indoors by orchestrating a meeting (of all the factions concerned) with Fidel Castro and almost the entire Government. It was a sneaky ambush, the varmints. They invited all the intellectuals involved—and then some. The meetings took place every Friday for three consecutive weeks and were held in the spacious hall of the National Library, built by Batista but claimed by Castro.

The day of the first meeting came like doom. On the rostrum were Fidel Castro, President Dorticós (since deposed), the Minister of Education Armando Hart (now Minister for Culture), his wife Haydée Santamaría, head of the Casa de las Américas (later a suicide), Carlos Rafael Rodríguez, then an influential Communist leader, now the third man from Moscow in Havana, his former wife Edith García Buchaca (then the head of the Communist cultural apparatus, who later lived under house arrest for fifteen years), Vicentina Antuna, boss of the Council for Culture (under the political spell of Buchaca), Alfredo Guevara, no Che at all but a tropical Machiavelli giving advice not only to the Prince but also to the King. Then bringing up the rear came the scapegoats, lambs feeding with lions: Carlos Franqui, editor *of Revolución*, and I, as editor *of Lunes*. . . .

It became evident to everyone (defendants, prosecutor, jury, judge, and witnesses) that this was a show trial held in private: it was not only *P.M.* but *Lunes* (and everything it stood for in Cuban culture) that was in the dock. Kafka in Cuba, Prague in Havana. Most of the people who took the stand were sworn enemies of the magazine — and some had reason to be. Like the fat woman who sent in some sonnets that were published in the magazine with the title: "From the Fat Lady of the Sonnets." The pained dentist who thought he was Dante al dente complained bitterly. He not only complained but cried and prayed (he was a Catholic convert) and called us chartered murderers who assassinated writers as if they were so many characters. We were the hit-and-run men of culture. The Marxian Mafia perhaps? It was an impassioned though toothless speech — and he got what he wanted all along: a job as Ambassador to the Vatican as a consolation prize.

There were other witnesses, all for the prosecution, and a masked witness took off his mask for everyone to see his face: Baragaño, the Surrealist poet who instigated all the attacks against Lezama and his disciples, had turned on us! There was an expected enemy, though: Guevara, by now a guerrilla speaker who couldn't say his *r*s, delivered a blow below the belt at both *Revolución* and *Lunes*. Before I was an *infante terrible*; now I was a babe in the wood. Fidel Castro himself talked to us. Characteristically, he had the last word. Getting rid first of the ever-present Browning 9 mm fastened to his belt — making true a metaphor by Goebbels: "Every time I hear the word *culture*, I reach for my pistol" — Castro delivered one of his most famous speeches, famous not for being eight hours long, but for being brief and to the point for the first time since he became Cuba's Prime Minister. His deposition is now called "Words to the Intellectuals," and it ends with a résumé which Castroites everywhere claim to be a model of revolutionary rhetoric but which is really a Stalinist credo: "Within the Revolution, everything," he thundered like a thousand Zeuses. "Against the Revolution, nothing!" Everybody applauded, some in good faith. Though not I. I *had* to applaud even when I knew full well what he meant by his slogan. It had been the case of a sentence without a verdict: through-the-looking-glass justice.

The outcome of the trial was that the Film Institute gave back the seized copy of *P.M.* to its makers, but the film remained censored. *Lunes* was banned, too, and barely three months later ceased appearing. There was an official explanation for the stay of execution: an acute shortage of newsprint. A likely story. Three more literary publications saw daylight after the meetings: *Unión*, a monthly from the Writers' Union, dedicated to Communist culture, *Gaceta de Cuba*, a weekly published by the Writers' Union that resembled *Lunes* like Cain resembled Abel, and an illustrated magazine issued by the Council for Culture that looked like a tattered *Tatler*. Three red reviews all in a row. The Communists had their congress (why do they need congresses so much?—is it a fixation or a fix?) with foreign writers as guests. In a typical gambit I was made one of the seven vice-presidents of the newly formed Writers' Union, so I wouldn't complain. I didn't. I never intended to. You see, I had been in the Soviet Union the year before and found out what happened to all the writers who dared displease Stalin, even sotto voce. A tropical version of Stalin, even behind beards, could be tropically lethal.

TRANSLATED BY KENNETH HALL

In Hard Times

Heberto Padilla

In the late 1960s and early 1970s the poet Heberto Padilla (1932–2000) was one of the most articulate critics of the demands made of intellectuals by the revolution. In March 1971 Padilla was detained by the police, questioned, and obliged to sign a four-thousand-word document of self-criticism in which he acknowledged his counterrevolutionary errors. The "Padilla Affair" attracted enormous attention outside of Cuba, causing European, North American, and Latin American intellectuals to accuse the Cuban government of practicing a form of cultural and literary Stalinism. Padilla's poem "In Hard Times" conveys the flavor of the writer's opinions, zeroing in on the issue of the intellectual and the scale of commitment required of him in a revolutionary setting.

They asked him for his time
so that he [might] join it to the time of History.
They asked him for his hands
because during hard times
there is nothing better than a good pair of hands.
They asked him for his eyes
that once had shed some tears
so that he could see the clear side
(especially the clear side of life)
for when it comes to horror
one single eye will do.

They asked him for his lips
—which were parched and dry—
so that they [might] issue an affirmation
and with each affirmation build the dream
(the high dream).
They asked him for his legs
—which were knobbly and hard—

because during hard times
is there anything better than a good pair of legs
for building or for trenches?

They asked him for the woods
that nourished him as a child
with its obedient trees.
They asked him for his chest, his heart, his shoulders.
They told him that it was strictly necessary.
They explained to him later
that all these donations would be useless
unless he also surrender his tongue
because during hard times
nothing could be more useful
for stopping hatred or lies.
And finally they asked him politely
to start moving
because during hard times
this is, no doubt, the decisive test.

TRANSLATED BY JORGE GUITART

The Virgin of Charity of Cobre, Cuba's Patron Saint

Olga Portuondo Zúñiga

Like Cuba's population, Cuba's religions reflect diverse origins, yet have been shaped by many common experiences. Under Spanish colonial rule Catholicism was the official religion, but Cuban Catholicism (like other Latin American forms of Catholicism) took highly syncretic forms, transforming and being itself transformed by, in the case of Cuba, West African–based religions, which themselves drew on different African origins and were shaped by the experience of forced migration and slavery. In the early twentieth century U.S. Protestant sects also flocked to and set down roots in the island, through U.S. settlers and missionaries. British West Indian, Haitian, Chinese, and European Jewish immigrants also brought their own religions.

The story of the patron saint of Cuba, La Virgen de la Caridad del Cobre (the Virgin of Charity of Cobre), exemplifies some of the popular and syncretic nature of Catholicism in Cuba. These selections from a recent study by Cuban historian Olga Portuondo describe the origins of the legend and the saint, and the twentieth-century resonance of her power.

In the popular imagery of most contemporary accounts of the discovery of the Virgin of Cobre by three fishermen sailing a boat along the waters of Nipe Bay, the man in the center is black and the two people on either side of him are shown as white; the black man seems to be praying, while the two white men are rowing the boat.

If you ask the devotees who found the image of the virgin on the waters of Nipe Bay, they will almost all answer that it was three fishermen, Juan the White, Juan the Black, and Juan the Mulatto, also known as the Indian. In earlier times the fishermen have been seen as all black, or all white. People who are well versed in the gospel of the Catholic Church in present-day Cuba will tell you that there were one or two Indians in the canoe along with Juan Moreno. In his 1687 declaration, Juan Moreno announced that his companions were two Indians employed in hunting and searching for salt. Why have the color and the occupation of the travelers in the canoe that navigated the waters of Nipe Bay changed? . . .

Cachita, the One Whom Liborio Honors (1900–1995)

Anyone who knows anything about Cuban culture knows that Liborio is the symbol of the Cuban people, a simple, country man, the living image of the suffering caused by political trickery and irreverent interventionism, "mischievous, mocking, skeptical, but at the same time naïve and even pathetically gullible." How did Liborio see the Virgen del Cobre during the first decades of the republic? What did she mean to him?

My reply takes the form of a hypothetical interview with the Liborio of that time:

"Liborio, are you a follower of the Virgin of Cobre?"

"Of course, I called on her, and she came with me and protected me when I was fightin' for Cuba in the Liberation Army."

"Do you go to church regularly?"

"Well, I went once when Rufina's and my oldest boy was baptized; but I haven't gone back because there are no priests in the countryside, and the church is a long way off."

"And how is it that you feel such a strong devotion to the Virgin of Charity of Cobre?"

"Look, one thing has nothing to do with the other. I believe in her because that's the way it is; my mother taught me to pray to her because she is a miracle worker. When I was little she gave me an amulet with the image of the Virgin and I always keep it with me, so that when my son is older I can give it to him."

"Have you been to El Cobre?"

"No, I haven't. But Rufina, my wife, went there once to respect the promise she made when our little one was so sick with fever, and recovered."

The Catholic Church and the Cult of the Virgin of Cobre

For the Catholic Church, Spain's loss of the island also signaled the definitive loss of its religious monopoly. Beginning in the last quarter of the nineteenth century, Protestant churches lured away many of its followers, mostly from among the U.S. immigrants who arrived after the Ten Years' War ended in 1878. Masonry and Afro-syncretic cults also undermined the absolute primacy that the Catholic Church had maintained for four centuries.

After 1898, the church's commitments to the Spanish Crown meant that Catholicism lost ground to other forms of religious expression. Some Spanish

An engraving/representation of the Virgen de la Caridad del Cobre appearing to the three fishermen in the middle of a storm. Olga Portuondo, *La Virgen de la Caridad del Cobre: Símbolo de la cubanía*. (Santiago de Cuba: Editorial Oriente, 1995), 24.

priests, like the chaplain of El Cobre in 1896, had even been cheerleaders for the Spanish Army and paramilitaries.

At the same time, some of the new republic's political strongmen were Free-masons and Protestants or Protestant sympathizers, or Theosophists, so that during the first years of the republic there wasn't much chance of Catholicism winning back its supporters, especially among the rural people whom the church had long since abandoned in any case. The result was the construction in 1945 of a Baptist Church in Barajagua, birthplace of the cult of the Virgin of Charity of Cobre.

The private and elitist Catholic Church schools, which continued under the control of Spanish priests, gave preference to other Marianist devotions: Santa Teresita, the Virgin of Lourdes, etc. Especially in the west of Cuba, upper class people associated devotion to the Virgin of Charity with black *beatas* [holy women]. The Virgin's dark color contributed to lowering her class status. In 1902, a Brotherhood of Charity consisting exclusively of black women was organized at the Church of the Holy Spirit in Havana.

The hierarchy of the Cuban Catholic Church debated the role to be played by a native clergy. Many felt that a native clergy was essential if a church with a Cuban flavor was going to become involved in the reshaping of the Cuban people. Some Cuban priests began to raise their voices, drawing attention to the cult of the Virgin of Charity of Cobre noting "her decisive and benevolent influence in shaping the character of the nation. . . . Today the power that the "Mambisa Virgin" exercises over the soul of the Cuban people is the best guarantee of national unity and the survival of the Catholic tradition." . . .

The Virgin of Cobre, Santería, and Other Popular Cults

The renewed popularity of the celebrations of the Virgin of Cobre involved the Santo Tomás church, which housed one of the oldest, most interesting, and most enigmatic replicas of the Virgin. In Santo Tomás, the origins of her veneration were closely tied up with Conga religious syncretism.

In the west of the island, the Virgin del Cobre had occupied a place equivalent to that of Ochún in the Yoruba pantheon. Voluptuous and sensual, this *orisha* ruled the waters, and legends and myths identify her as the maternal virgin of religious syncretism: a Cuban mulatta quadroon, with thick, kinky hair. Ortiz noted the widely held belief that the Patron of Cuba was mestiza because of her African blood, a product of frequent and long-standing interbreeding between Europeans and Africans which was such an important factor in the creation of a popular Cuban identity.

Caridad-Ochún was worshiped via ritual—altars filled with lights, overflowing with flowers, food, and drink—and African dances. This reveals the depth of belief in her, and the importance of the position she had obtained within santería because of her attributes as a mother-god. There is a recipe for avoiding bad luck called "Baths of Charity," in which the person must be submerged in water mixed with basil, fresh flowers and incense, bees' honey and two eggs.

In the festival processions of the town of Regla, the four saints—borne by women—who take part are the Virgin of Regla, the Virgin of Mercedes, Santa Bárbara, and Caridad del Cobre, who leads the procession. The four figures with their features and altar finery represent Yemayá, Obtalá, Changó, and Ochún.

This blending of the Virgin of Charity of Cobre into santería may go back to the end of the nineteenth century, in the Havana-Matanzas region.

When the Yoruba religion began to penetrate eastern Cuba around the 1930s, the Virgin del Cobre was incorporated into its beliefs. . . .

At least in the eastern part of the country, we cannot talk about an assimilation of the cult of the Virgin of Cobre into the Yoruba god Ochún; the two coexist in parallel and interrelated forms. For example, in 1936, in the home of a woman santería practitioner, the Havana secret police found, among other objects, a likeness of the Virgin of Cobre, and some yellow-colored ribbons.

View of the New Shrine to the Copper Virgin. Sydney Clark, *Cuban Tapestry* (New York: National Travel Club, 1936), following 246.

In any case, the involvement of the Virgen de Caridad in santería and other popular cults is an expression of the strength of Cubanness within these beliefs.

A study of a sample of votive offerings in the Miracle Room [Cuarto de los Milagros] in the Virgin of Cobre Sanctuary (María Nelsa Trincado and I have analyzed over a thousand) reveals the presence of beliefs that are outside of orthodox Catholicism, but which are related to magical and ritual performance within popular belief systems. Santería predominates, but we have also found expressions of the *regla conga*.

I do not believe that the adoption of the Virgin of Cobre's identifying yellow clothing in the 1930s is merely a coincidence. Rather, it reveals the growing influence of santería in the religious beliefs and practices of the people.

Within spiritism, which has deep roots and is widespread throughout the province of Oriente, the Virgin of Charity is regarded as such a powerful figure that she requires another spirit in order to communicate with men. Her position as patron of Cuba is expressed in the following terms: "The people of Cuba today offer the purest and most sincere homage to this ideal reality which is the sum and compendium of the high spiritual virtues that beat in the Cuban soul, to this little Virgin of Charity of Cobre, to this divine power where faith, charity, and love united under the diadem of Hope."

The figure of Mamá Chola, in Regla de Palo or Palo Monte, is the manifestation of Mother Water and, in some way, is identified with the Virgin of Cobre. The white saint Ercilí of Cuban vodú, covered with jewels and goddess of love, water, and birth, is also paired with the Patron of Cuba.

In his notebooks Fernando Ortiz describes a very revealing experience: "In a procession of *ñáñigos* in Matanzas, in 1929, we witnessed a statue of the Virgin of Charity being carried by four *abakuá* practitioners. This is the only time that we have seen such a complete example of syncretism among the expressions of Catholic, ñáñigo, and Nigerian or Lucumí religions in Cuba. This example proves that devotion to the Virgin of Charity is growing among our people."

There are no indications that Chinese religions contributed to the construction of the myth and the legends of the Virgin del Cobre, because the tradition had already taken shape when the Asians arrived in Cuba, in the middle of the nineteenth century. This does not mean that there aren't some small points of contact currently. A 1977 inventory of the Colonia China association in Caibarién includes an altar to the Virgin of Charity and a Saint Fang Kong, which could suggest a certain ambivalence in beliefs among the Creole descendants of the Chinese. . . .

Responses to a survey carried out in recent months can offer our readers a composite view of the Virgin of Charity cult among Cuban believers today:

Why are you a follower of the Virgin of Charity of Cobre?

> Because I am a believer. My *mamá* taught me. She used to say, "Virgin of Charity, you lead and I'll follow." My mother worshiped her because she had six sons and they all died, and I was the first that survived and that was the work of the Virgin.

How do you picture the Virgin del Cobre?

> I see her dressed in white with a blue robe, a gold crown on her head; but my sister says that she dresses in golden yellow because she is Ochún, a mulatta with her special hair, with a round face. The baby is white and wears a crown.

Who is in the boat?

> Juan the White, Juan the Black, and Juan the Mulatto; according to the age-old story. She saved the three fishermen from a certain death when they were drowning. My mother told me that it was the Three Juans.

What do you know about the legend of the Virgin of Cobre?

> That she appeared on a plank of wood, and the silver nails have been pre-served, in Nipe Bay. From there it was brought to Regla, and she appeared once again in El Cobre where the three men were.

Have you made any requests or promises to the Virgin?

> When my son was sick I offered to take her a silver boy-statue and dress the boy in blue for a month; I have gone with my daughter to give her hair as an offering, because when she was born she looked very bad at the birth. I dressed in white and went deliberately one 8 September to Cobre to light a candle that I had promised her if my nephew returned home alive from Angola.

When do you ask her for things?

> When I am in trouble, I believe in her. My belief is spiritual; my favorite saints are Charity and San Lázaro. I sing to her; I give her her candle and her cup of clear water.

Do you see any relation between the Virgin of Cobre and the religion of the dead?

> All of the saints are in the altar. One prays to all of the dead and calls upon all of them. If I am going to purify my house [*despojar mi casa*], I mention the Virgin and the others, like San Lázaro and the Virgin Mary, but the main one is the Virgin of Cobre.

Why should she be the Patron of Cuba?

> Because she is the mother of all Cubans, she chose Cuba to appear, they even called her the Mambisa Virgin. She has helped Cuba.

How is the Virgin of Cobre connected to Ochún?

> I don't know anything about Ochún. To me she's an African saint, who has nothing to do with the virgin. Ochún is for the *santeros*, my mamá related her to Ochún and sang to her and danced for her during the ceremony: 'Ochún vere, ochún African vere.' There are many saints who are also spiri-tual [in Santería]. This is the song of the Virgin of Charity of Cobre:
>
> If a mother claims her children,
> And if children claim their mother,
> that mother is the Virgin of Cobre
> who comes with Ochún, with faith

hope and charity
the three Divine Powers."

Why is El Cobre the National Sanctuary?

Because the Patron of Cuba is there, that is her home and she wanted to stay here in El Cobre."

Some young people still spend their time searching for little pieces of copper, to sell to pilgrims who visit the Sanctuary, as a constant reminder of the ancient links between the origins of mining and of the Virgin del Cobre, which has brought worldwide fame to the small eastern town. The Miracle Room continues to receive large numbers of votive offerings from all over the country, and every year on 8 September large numbers of pilgrims visit. When the homily is over they sing the National Anthem and the lines written by the composer Miguel Matamoros:

And if you go to El Cobre
I want you to bring me
A little Virgin of Charity
I don't want flowers
I don't want prints
What I want is the Virgin of Charity

TRANSLATED BY AVIVA CHOMSKY

For complete references and notes, consult the work as cited in the acknowledgment of copyrights section.

A Conversation on
Santería and Palo Monte

Oscar Lewis, Ruth M. Lewis, and Susan M. Rigdon

The following dialogue, recorded by anthropologist Oscar Lewis in 1970, gives insight into the gender, racial, and political, as well as religious, aspects of two syncretic religions that draw on different west and perhaps central African religious roots, as well as on Spanish Catholicism: Santería, and Palo Monte. Both religious traditions grew among the slave population in the nineteenth century and flourished in Afro-Cuban communities after the abolition of slavery. Today Cuban popular Catholicism is heavily flavored with Santería. Lázaro Benedí is a follower of Palo Monte, Amalia Carranza a follower of Santería. They discuss their marriage, the differences between their religions, and the place of religion in the first decade of the revolution.

Benedí: The way I see it, Amalia's life and personality make it very clear she's a daughter of Ochún. I have a great respect for Ochún; they say she's a very protective mother. Many aspects of Ochún are not at all what they first seem to be. She's always smiling and friendly, but take care! She smiles a lot at her enemies to fool them. Then, the next day, the person she smiled at is found dead and nobody knows why. Ochún's no softy. She can tear a person limb from limb and laugh while she's doing it. She has no pity; she'll take anybody's child away from him.

Amalia may seem like a very soft and mild person, but with me she's as inconsistent as Ochún. Of course, she's not as bad as some of the daughters of Ochún. They bear a grudge a long time, but hide their anger and lead the offender wherever they want. Ochún's daughters hate to tell anybody that they need anything, no matter what it is. They won't communicate such things in words but others can see it by their sadness.

As a daughter of Ochún, Amalia is faced with many problems other women don't have. For one thing, she's in constant danger of betrayal. We have argued that point often. I tell her, "*Chica*, I've lived many years and gone to many places. Besides, I know about *santería* and I've seen that you daughters of Ochún are too trusting. If anybody smiles at you, you immediately think, 'She's my friend.' It never occurs to you that somebody pleasant might want to harm you."

Amalia has the generous openhanded ways of Ochún's daughters. If there are leftovers, she will immediately think of somebody that needs it. She waits till I'm out of the house to slip over to that person and say, "Here, take it." It's not that I'm hardhearted, but frequently Amalia gives away things we could use and her kindness isn't even appreciated. People think that since Ochún is the mistress of gold, her daughters are wealthy. This just isn't true. But this false belief causes a lot of trouble, because instead of being grateful, people think a daughter of Ochún should help them even more.

Another reason why daughters of Ochún are in constant danger is that they have a certain unstudied attractiveness about them. Even though they may not be beautiful or wear elegant clothes, they have a natural grace that makes anything they wear look good on them. A cheap pair of shoes, a simple little dress, a pair of earrings, an attractive hair style — everything becomes them.

Amalia has this natural grace. She isn't pretty and she doesn't have a figure — she doesn't even have any sparkle because she's rather reserved. But when she walks into a crowded room there are more eyes on her than if she were a millionaire. That kind of thing makes the daughters of Ochún victims of other women's envy. Yet Ochún's daughters are so simple and openhearted it never occurs to them that anybody might envy them.

Often when one woman refers to another as a "daughter of Ochún," she really means she's a whore. That's because Ochún managed to make Ogún come out of hiding. Ogún is a strong black, a laborer in fields and mountains, who knows all about plants. Many had tried to bring him out of hiding with no success. But with a little bit of honey and a smile, Ochún found him and gradually charmed him out of the mountain. What other woman could have made such a conquest? That's why people sometimes say Ochún is a whore.

I'm a son of Yemayá, but when Yemayá can't help me, Ochún does. In return, when Ochún can't come out, Yemayá takes care of whoever called for Ochún. There are many legends about this, but only someone completely involved in the religion can understand how it works.

Sometimes the marriage between a daughter of Ochún and a son of Yemayá lasts in a way that is impossible for an outsider to understand. A lot of times I foresee some danger in Amalia's life and am impelled by Yemayá to warn her. "Listen," I say, "one must use a bit of psychology in dealing with people. Keep your troubles to yourself. If you don't want to tell me about them, don't tell anybody, unless you want people to laugh at you."

Unfortunately, Amalia seldom listens to me. It's a rare daughter of Ochún who escapes having the dagger of treason plunged into her back, but just try to tell them so! They are very obstinate on that point and protest, "Who, me? Oh no! The person hasn't been born who can play any dirty tricks on me!"

Most of the time Amalia is easy to get along with, but all I have to say is, "Now look, Amalia, this is thus-and-so," and she gets huffy and refuses to listen. It isn't that Ochún doesn't pay attention to Yemayá. It's Amalia who doesn't pay attention to Lázaro. I say to her, "You must realize what your situation is, not as a *santera* but as a daughter of Ochún. Also, you don't know your guardian angel. If you did, you'd admit that lots of times I'm right when I warn you about things."

But Amalia is blind to evil. And she's too proud to ever admit that I was right. She answers my warnings, saying, "I'm a daughter of Ochún and we are the way we are."

Whenever I'm mistaken about anything, Amalia throws it back to me, saying, "Look at that—an illiterate like me has to teach a wise man like you!"

"Anyone can make a mistake, but don't you go believing that the illiterate can teach the wise," I answer. "An illiterate has nothing but his natural wits."

Then she laughs disagreeably, "And you think I'm the stupid one!" But I forgive her because she has little knowledge of the philosophy of life.

I've done a lot to help Amalia in her spiritual progress. For instance, when she was presented to the *santo*,[1] she was one hundred pesos short of the sum she needed to get her things, so I gave her the money. Amalia had to go through that ceremony to be a complete member of her religion. Until she did she was like an unborn child as far as her religion was concerned. So the money I gave her was very important to her religious development.

During the ceremony to become a *santero* certain people tear herbs and say words over them. These herbs are living bodies with powers of their own. The amount of time it takes to become a santero depends on how rapidly the person feels the effect of the ceremonies. It's just like medicine. A doctor may prescribe the same pill to two patients and one might get well with the first pill while the other doesn't.

Following the ceremony, the santeros must dress in white for a full year, because white is Obatalá's color and it symbolizes the peace that people seek when they make themselves santeros. A woman who has completed the whole ritual is called a *yabó*.

In spite of the fact that I gave Amalia the money to complete this ceremony, she fails to be appreciative. If only she had the philosophy of life to understand what this means! I wish she had a bit more education. Not that I want a woman who's done too much studying, but I'd like more than a *guajirita*, an ignorant country girl.

Amalia Carranza: Lazarito and I argue a lot about religion because our beliefs are different. And yet, all religions are the same in a way, like different paths leading to the same place. When Lazarito looks down on me from his superior knowledge, I feel he's belittling me. He speaks in tongues and knows many aspects of the saints that I know nothing about. But I have faith and love for the saints, too.

Lazarito used to practice the religion when he lived in Las Yaguas. I've been told that many people went to his house for consultations and he was very good at it. Lazarito has given up all that consultation business, so far as I know. I've never seen him throw the shells, in fact he doesn't keep any at home, but he knows how to do it. I've seen him consult coconut shells though. Sometimes when I get home I find him busy at those things, but I never ask him what he's doing because he wouldn't tell me. He's a strange man.

Lázaro's guardian angel is in El Palo, mine is in Regla Ocha. Actually, Lazarito has never told me that he's a *palero*. I found out by his warnings not to touch this or that. I've asked him more than once if he ever was an [Abakuá]. He answers with a question, "Why do you want to know?"

"Never mind," I tell him. "The day you die, I'll find out."

If Lázaro had told me he belonged to Abacuá, I'd never have married him. Well, maybe I would have, considering the way I felt and the situation I was in, but at least I would have known what I was getting into.

I've never known Lazarito to do anything bad with his religion, but I'm terrified of the paleros. I've heard that the people in that religion are terribly impulsive and if they get annoyed at any little thing they're apt to kill. Actually, I'm not so much afraid as I am wary. I keep my distance, not that I believe all those stories. After all, if the paleros were as violent as they say, wouldn't untold numbers of people have disappeared?

Lázaro despises women because of Palo Monte. There are women in El Palo, sure, but when a woman is menstruating, she's not allowed even to look in the door where they're gathered. I never touch Lazarito when I'm menstruating, not because he forbids it but because I'm cautious. I know it weakens a man if he touches a woman then.

I know that Lazarito hasn't called down a santo, because a number of people have told me they were waiting to do it together with him. He has such deep knowledge of the religion that they wanted him to be their *padrino*.[2] But they say he dropped his religious activities after the Revolution.

My religion is very different from Palo Monte. But it's very powerful and worthy of respect because it also knows how to make itself felt. I can't understand why Lázaro, who is such an intellectual, belongs to Palo Monte instead of to Regla Ocha, which has more instruction and is more intellectual. I guess it must be because of his guardian angel and because he has learned more about Palo Monte.

I joined the religion for a number of reasons. I was very ill and consulted several doctors but they prescribed remedies that made me unconscious. I met a man who told me I needed to be presented to a santo. No one in my family ever went in for that kind of thing, not even *mamá*, and I was scared. But since it was a matter of my health, all my folks, especially my son, agreed that I should give santería a try. In 1953 I started going to places where it's practiced. I called down a santo in 1965 and right away I felt like a different person.

Practically nobody who's integrated belongs to the religion, because the Revolution forbids it. So Lazarito doesn't want me to practice it. He shows his opposition by forbidding me to go where the religion is practiced. But it isn't my religion Lázaro objects to, only my going out. If he goes out in the morning, I can leave the house, so long as I come back that same day before dark.

One can't keep up with the religion if one has to get home too early. Suppose somebody is calling down a santo—the ritual could go on all night. According to the rules it should last three days, but I never stay that long so as not to provoke Lázaro. Whenever I go, I come back home the first day. If I have a chance, I go back the second day, but I never stay through the night.

I go to those santo ceremonies when friends of mine are in them. This is an act of friendship, because the ritual can't be carried out with only the one person. Several people are needed to carry out different tasks. For instance, on the day of the washing, seven basins of water are used and seven persons must sit there to perform different parts of the ritual. They have to pray while they crush certain aromatic herbs and so on, then the person who is to be the santero goes into a separate room to have the bath. Not everybody is allowed to witness the bath. There may be as many as fifteen santeros present at this part of the ritual, but they must be complete santero before they can lay hands or look on.

When I decided to become a santera, Lazarito told me to go ahead and do it if I wanted to, but not at home. I didn't argue. Our house is too small and the water goes off now and then, so taking all things into account, I did it at my godfather's house.

I waited almost five years before doing it. I'm not sure exactly how long the ceremony took. When one is in a fiesta, the hours fly and one can't keep track of them. I left home around 9:00 at night on the twenty-eighth and returned two and a half days later, on the afternoon of the thirty-first.

For a full year afterward I dressed in white. They cut my hair off completely. It cost me a lot of trouble to get all the things necessary for the fiesta because I wasn't allowed to keep animals where I lived. The goat and the sheep were the most difficult to get. The fowl were no problem because I was allowed to raise those and I already had pigeons and hens.

I needed money for the ceremony so I asked Lázaro's permission to go work in El Cordón. He refused because it's bad for my health to work on the land. So I had to ask him to lend me the money. The trouble I had before I got him to agree! I wept tears for that money. He wouldn't give it to me all at once. I had to get it in installments. For instance, I'd buy an animal, and when it was delivered I'd say to him, "Here, give the sixty pesos I owe for it." So he'd fork out the dough because he couldn't help it. That way I finally got together all the things I needed.

As soon as I returned from the ceremony he said, "All right, now pay me back my money."

"I can't," said I. "You know I didn't go there to get paid." We quarreled about that.

He knew I still had fifty pesos in my bank account and he wanted me to give them to him right away. I argued until I got so mad I was on the point of leaving him for good. His attitude disgusted me, and to top it off, he said what he always says, "Naturally you have to be stupid, you're illiterate."

"All right," I said, "I agree. But I can go further on my stupidity than you can with all your knowledge and wisdom. Illiterate as I am, I have to explain to you things that should be clear to anybody. Knowing where I just came from, you shouldn't ask me to go straight to the bank and get you the fifty pesos. It takes an awfully stupid person to say that, especially considering that it was almost 8:00 at night when I got home."

It wasn't as if he were putting obstacles in my way because he didn't want me to become a santera. He said he wanted me to. But he didn't want to fork out even one miserable little *kilo*[3] to pay for it. He's stingy—that's the whole problem.

Lázaro didn't need the money—he has a bank account, and for all I know he may have money right here in the house. I have no idea what his bank balance is. If I wanted to pry I could find out in a minute by getting hold of his bankbook. But what good would that do me? Anyway, it's his money and I don't need it or want it. Whatever money Lázaro lends me, I have to pay back. He loaned me almost three hundred pesos for my santo and I still owe him a bit over 130. I don't know just when I'll pay that back but I will, I will.

Notes

1. Ceremony by which the novice in santería calls upon an *orisha* and becomes its spiritual descendant.
2. Godfather.
3. One centavo.

The Catholic Church and the Revolution

Ernesto Cardenal

The Catholic Church was weaker in Cuba than elsewhere in Latin America, and the upper classes predominated among those affiliated with official Catholicism. Nevertheless, official Catholicism retained the strongest institutional religious presence in Cuba — in part because the Catholic Church answered to and depended upon an international hierarchy, whereas most of the other religions (including popular Catholicism) tended to take local, autonomous forms. Like virtually all of Cuban society, the institutional church initially greeted the revolution with enthusiasm, emphasizing the commitment of the church to the poor and to the revolution's project of social justice. In part because of its international and institutional ties, and in part because official Catholicism was most deeply rooted in the upper and middle classes of Cuban society, the revolution and the church soon clashed. By the middle of 1960, church authorities had decided that the revolution was not "Christian." "We Catholics are not against the revolution," wrote the auxiliary bishop of Havana in late 1960. "We are helping the revolution enormously, and we want the great social transformations that Cuba needs, but we cannot want nor support the materialist and totalitarian Communism which would be the most blatant negation of the ideals for which so many Cubans fought and died."[1]

Ernesto Cardenal (b. 1925), the celebrated Nicaraguan revolutionary poet and outspoken, often controversial Catholic priest, chronicled his months on the island from 1970 to 1971 in a book-length collection of essays, interviews, and sketches titled simply En Cuba. *In it, Cardenal offers a refreshingly objective and lucid view of that society, a decade into the revolution, through his contact with a wide variety of Cubans whose comments he records. Overall, the book sheds light on a topic of central importance to Cardenal: the situation, beliefs, and degree of isolation or integration experienced by Cuban Catholics and clergy. The result of his inquiries and observations is a compelling, multifaceted portrait of the Cuban Revolution and its internal conflicts and tensions.*

The Archbishop

At the door of the Archbishop's palace I met a priest, he was introduced, and he told me that he was the parish priest of Guantánamo (the Cuban Guantánamo). He was surprised that I had come to Cuba, and I was surprised by what he said: "What a coincidence. Not long ago the workers in a Guantánamo factory had in their study circle a weeklong seminar on your poetry. Yes, of course. They have their study circle, right in the factory"—he was amused at my surprise. "They invited me to attend this seminar on you, and I went to the last days of it. You must come to Guantánamo, even though we are in the farthest corner of Cuba. The workers will be delighted to see you."

And since in the rest of Latin America my poetry is known only among certain literary circles, I said to myself while climbing the ancient stairs in the big old house of the Archbishop: "Cuba is incredible!" The Archbishop of Havana, Monsignor Francisco Oves, is a cheerful young man, with neither the costume nor the manners of a bishop—he wears a sport shirt. He told me that he was very glad that the episcopal "palace" was this big old tumbledown house with almost no furniture, which they were now repairing so that it wouldn't tumble all the way down. He also told me: "The leaders of the Revolution live austerely; it would be absurd if the leaders of the Church lived in any other way."

"Food? It's the ration card food, like that of everyone. And it is meager. You can't invite anyone to a meal, because there isn't enough." Oves is on the side of the Revolution. He told me that the conflicts between the Revolution and the Church had ended. He added: "We have another way of thinking." He was named Bishop a short while ago. And he was recently from Rome, with a [post–Second Vatican Council] frame of mind. "There have to be conflicts at times. There is always intransigence on both sides. For example, now that I was going to the Isle of Pines, I could try to see some seminarists who are there in a Social Disgrace Unit, with marijuana smokers and homosexuals and other delinquents, working in the marble quarries. . . ."

"Forced labor?" "Practically. Under very harsh conditions. It's very annoying for them to be with homosexuals, sneak thieves, and other antisocial types. It would be great if you could encourage them, tell them to cheer up and work with good spirits and keep up their social studies circles and not to stop being revolutionaries even though they are treated that way. I have encouraged them, too. I don't want them to have a martyr complex."

Oves thinks that the new revolutions in Latin America are not going to bring conflicts with the Church. There wouldn't have been conflicts in Cuba, either, if the Council had taken place a little sooner or the Revolution a little later. The Revolution occurred just on the eve of the renovation of the Church.

This renovation, for Cuba, came too late. We were in a huge, almost empty room which I supposed to be the Bishop's office. Several priests in shirtsleeves came up and sat down to talk while we had small cups of thick black coffee and smoked Cuban cigarettes made of strong black tobacco.

"Is there persecution?" One priest laughed: "There is a persecution mania among many Catholics." The Rector of the Seminary, Father Carlos Manuel Céspedes—a descendant of General Carlos Manuel de Céspedes, leader of Cuban independence—thought that the Revolution would not have been possible if it had not become Marxist. And that the differences between Christianity and Marxism were less and less important. And that the People of God must support this Revolution. He was a young man, about the age of the Bishop. His family did not think as he did. His mother was in exile. An uncle of his was serving a twenty-year jail sentence. A girl cousin was sentenced to six years.

Father Angel Gaztelú, an important Cuban poet who belonged to the Orígenes group, told me that he used to go to say Mass for Fidel and the other Moncada prisoners in the Isle of Pines jail. He was certain that they were Catholics and not Marxists. And some of them took communion. And he told me also that not long ago he had celebrated Mass in the street in memory of José Antonio Echeverría, the Catholic student leader who was a martyr of the Revolution. A Mass in the open air, in front of the monument to José Antonio, attended by many Catholic students. Nobody interfered with it.

As far as I can tell, Cuba is the only place in the world where Catholicism is not going through a crisis of vocation. The Archbishop told me that in the Major Seminary there were nearly seventy seminarists, more or less the same number as before the Revolution. And there was no crisis of celibacy among the priests, or of authority, or of faith—none of the crises through which the post-Council Church is struggling throughout the world. I said to them: "There is no post-Council crisis not because the Church is very good but because it is very bad: because here the Council hasn't even entered." Oves laughed, and I think he agreed with me.

Oves also told me: Before the Revolution there were twenty-three hundred religious [members of religious orders]; about two thousand left (mostly through their own decision, not because they were expelled). There used to be about a thousand priests; now there are about 250. Those who get baptized are 25 or 30 percent of the population. Those who get married in the Church are about 5 percent. The Sunday school attendance is about half of what it used to be. The Archbishop is happy that Catholicism should be a minority and not a mass phenomenon. Let people enter the Church because of personal convictions and not because of atmospheric pressures. I observed: Christ wanted his

Church to be a ferment in the dough, and here it was just the opposite: Catholicism was the dough, and the ferment was the non-Catholics: the revolutionary vanguard. . . .

TRANSLATED BY DONALD WALSH

Note

1. Mos. Eduardo Boza Masvidal (auxiliary bishop of Havana), "Is the Social Revolution in Cuba Christian?" *Quincena*, 30 October 1960.

Havana's Jewish Community

Tom Miller

Cuba also became home to a small Jewish community, mostly Eastern European immigrants from the late nineteenth and early twentieth centuries. Many Jews were among the middle- and upper-class Cubans who fled for Miami in the early years of the revolution, but a small community has remained. American journalist Tom Miller describes his encounter with Havana's Jewish community in the early 1990s.

Fidel Castro thinks he's Jewish. Or at least part Jewish, buried in his past. "Castro" is among the more common names of Marranos, Spanish Jews who took on Christian identity during the Inquisition to avoid certain death at the stake. Fidel mentioned his heritage in private to Ricardo Subirana y Lobo, a chemical engineer and financial backer of the Revolution to whom he gave a diplomatic post in Israel in 1960. Castro, historian Maurice Halperin has written, "apparently was convinced that some of his ancestors were Marranos."

If Castro is a Jew, he's not a very good one. He doesn't attend Rosh Hashanah services, nor does he shop at Abraham Berezniak's kosher meat market on Cuba Street in Habana Vieja, which has messages to the Jewish community on its walls.

Every Cuban is entitled to a certain amount of meat and fish every couple of weeks in the ration system. (Entitlement doesn't guarantee availability, of course.) Each household, theoretically, has one ration book, called a libreta, which lists every occupant by age, name, and sex. I can't imagine that the ration books of any three neighbors selected at random would be entirely accurate. Relatives come and go, friends move in and out, some keep their *libreta* residence at one house and drink their morning *cafecito* at another. One entry in the libreta allows for special diets for medical reasons, age, or other reasons; those who qualify are assigned to special markets. To be a practicing Jew is another reason. Instead of going to their local butcher, Jews may go to Abraham Berezniak's place on meat days. To spend the afternoon at Abe's is to watch a remarkable flow of black, mulatto, and white Sephardim, Ashkenazim, and their descendants pass through the door with two metal Stars of David on it and chat about the state of the world.

On the wall:

Dear patron, to conclude the kosher process for the meat you are getting here, you should observe the following rules: (1) soak the meat in water for a half an hour. (2) Salt it on an inclined board with holes for one hour to let the excess blood run off. (3) Rinse off the salt—the biblical prohibition of consuming blood requires that the meat be thoroughly rinsed.

Kosher chickens will come the fifth of next month. After that date you will lose your right for that particular ration cycle.

Attention children—the Organization of Young Cuban Jews invites you to watch an Israeli film in Spanish called *From Toledo to Jerusalem* with Yehoram Gaon, the best Israeli singer.

Berezniak, balding and stocky, with a slight limp, has the personality to work behind the counter at the Carnegie Deli in New York or Goldenberg's in Paris. He wears nice loafers. A black fellow walked in, exchanged some doo-wah-diddy with Abe, and picked up his meat as Abe carefully marked his libreta. (Whenever Cuban Spanish sounded like high-speed mashed potatoes, I wrote "doo-wah-diddy" in my notebook.) A fellow of eighteen came in next for his family's allotment, then an elderly woman. A couple who looked like modestly successful retirees from Miami were next. As his assistant whacked at a carcass, loudly punctuating our conversation, Abe introduced me to the patrons, each of whom would invariably mention an old friend or relative who had abandoned Cuba for the States.

"Tell me, is there anti-Semitism there?" Abe asked. I thought for a moment, then said, a little, yes. "We have none here. For years we were called *polacos*, 'Poles,' even the ones who came from Spain. The Catholics gave us the space for this butcher shop in the early 1940s." A character in *Passing through Havana*, a novel by Felicia Rosshandler about one girl's coming of age in Havana's Jewish immigrant community during World War II, explains, "All Jews are called polacos here because Poles immigrated by the thousands after the turn of the century. Yiddish, believe it or not, is called *el idioma polaco*, the Polish language."

Berezniak is also the administrator of Adath Israel, a temple around the corner from the butcher shop. He toots the shofar, the ram's horn, on Rosh Hashanah. As he explained this, a young man in glasses walked by and waved. "That's Elpidio. He works in the church next door, but he's interested in Jewish things."

Elpidio came back in and took me to his church. "Two hundred people come here every day, more for Sunday mass. The first mass was said here in

1674. This is the oldest church in Havana. There are catacombs down below. We no longer use them." He ticked off the well-known people who have prayed at his church, "José Martí's sister, too."

Back at Abe's, a short, thin woman who appeared to be at least in her mid-sixties walked in. A damp stogie drooped from an ill-shaped smile on her gnarled face. She looked around the small store and walked over to me. Suddenly she grabbed my crotch and gave a forceful squeeze. Then with a loud cackle she threw her head back and walked out.

"She comes by now and then. She's meshuggenuh!" Everybody else in the place laughed, me last. Brief and crude as it was, I wasn't entirely offended.

Abraham Berezniak's neighbors that afternoon included a bare-chested man tinkering under the hood of his dirty green '48 Dodge. I went across the street to inspect the car. "It's got its original six-cylinder engine," he bragged. Clean, it would be the pride of any collector, a comment that gladdened him. Then he shook his head and drew a line through the dirt on the hood. "Think of this as an imaginary line. That's what it's like here. It's impossible to transfer private property like a car from one side to the other, but people do it all the time. For example, if this were your car and I wanted to buy it, we could make the transaction. But the next morning you want it back, so you take me to the authorities. Well, you have the ownership papers, and there's nothing I can do." Old American cars can only legally be turned over to a state agency, which will give you a Soviet Lada or pesos in return. The agency then sells the car—for dollars—to foreign collectors. An enormous lot full of old U.S. machines waiting for buyers sits at the end of Fifth Avenue. Paradoxically, the cars cannot go back home; for an American to buy one would be Trading with the Enemy.

A poster on the wall behind the bare-chested Dodge owner promoted the Sistema Unico de Exploración, a national program to watch for foreign invaders. A drawing showed a man looking out into the horizon, his hands cupped over his eyes. *When you see or hear parachutists jumping or landing*, the caption read, *or buildings collapsing, or anything that looks like aircraft carriers at sea, or suspicious airplane or helicopter activity, or Counterrevolutionary Proclamations or explosive devices, call this phone number of the People's Power Council.*

A few lots away kids romped in a playground with swings, seesaws, and slides. Abraham Berezniak's life revolved around this immediate neighborhood—his home, synagogue, and butcher shop were all within three blocks of one another.

I learned about Abe's kosher butcher shop from Adela Dworin and Maritza Corrales. The two are daily fixtures at the city's Jewish community center, the Patronato, on the ground floor of the synagogue in Vedado . . . Adela is executive secretary of the Patronato. Maritza is writing a book about the history of Jews in Cuba. Is there discrimination against Jews here? I asked. "There is no anti-Semitism in Cuba," Adela stated flatly. "We all get along. Even the PLO has an embassy here. They send thousands of students to Cuba every year. We coexist. There wasn't discrimination against Jews even before the Revolution. I've never seen anyone throw an egg at a synagogue. Never."

The Central Committee of the Communist Party has an office of religious affairs, Adela told me, "headed by Dr. José Felipe Carneado. He was a member of the first Communist Party in Cuba. He was a mulatto lawyer, so he knows what discrimination is. Of course, if you are a member of a religion, you can't join the Communist Party, so we have people who come here but don't claim to be Jewish, and some who even give money, but with no record of it. They come on the traditional holidays, and they're interested in reading about Judaism. Fidel said that someday believers will be members of the Party."

Maritza said Marxism wouldn't allow religion.

"But," countered Adela, "at Llamamientos some people have brought up the question—why can't believers be Party members? Believers feel discriminated against."

The two spend their afternoons in the Patronato library, a room filled with works in Hebrew, Spanish, German, and English. A calendar from the Jewish National Fund of Canada hangs on the wall next to photographs of Jewish writers. A list of Jewish winners of the Lenin-Stalin prize hangs nearby. I wouldn't have been surprised if the books on the Einstein shelf had been autographed by the Nobel physicist himself during his brief stopover in Havana during Chanukah, 1930. The Jewish community celebrated his visit, an event sandwiched between a dozen stops, including the Academy of Science, the Yacht Club, and a mental asylum. The morning after Einstein visited the synagogue, he insisted on touring Havana's poor neighborhoods. An account in the Cuban Geographic Society's magazine said he went to "the most wretched homes in the disordered yards of the tenements and the boarding houses." In his diary, Einstein recalled "luxurious clubs side by side with atrocious poverty, which mostly affects the people of color."

After the Revolution, Havana had a rabbi who commuted on weekends from Miami, an arrangement that ended when the United States severed relations with Cuba in 1961. Adela said, "Jews don't need a rabbi for services. Someone simply has to know how to read the Torah. We've had rabbis visit us from Mexico and Venezuela." And what if a graduate of a foreign rabbinical college wanted to come?

"He'd have to live like us. Would he be willing to do that? He'd probably have a different standard of living. He'd have to take a room in a Jewish house and eat what we eat. You can't find kosher pickles in a Communist country.

"We used to get Passover wine and products like matzo early. This year we didn't, so we sent a cable to a rabbi in New York. He shipped us the things we needed on the daily charter flight from Miami—wine, canned gefilte fish, matzo. The man at the Party said we could do the paperwork later. The people at the customs house know about Jews. So after Passover I went to see the customs officials and legalized it all."

A German gentile graduate student working on her doctorate about Jews in Cuba came into the Patronato library and took her regular seat. She lived in a room rented from the University of Havana in a house near the Soviet embassy. Despite all the problems, she said, she'd consider staying if she could only find a place that carried black bread.

Adela continued. "This building was originally a cultural center. We had Sunday school classes, ping-pong, everything. At the old synagogue we had a mikva—it's like a sauna. There used to be five Jewish schools in Havana. After the Revolution we were allowed one Jewish school. They permitted the children to take Hebrew classes. The government gave us a bus for that school. It was in Santos Suárez. Then they decided that it wasn't in the interest of the government for children to learn Hebrew, so we held the classes ourselves on Saturday afternoons. We had forty to fifty children. Well, one teacher died and the other went to Israel. The president of the Jewish Community was a widower. He taught his maid Hebrew, and also how to play the accordion. Eventually he went to Israel, and she followed shortly afterward. She knew Hebrew better than anyone in Havana. When she left in 1981, the school closed."

Moisés, twenty years old, walked in for a few minutes. Adela motioned toward him. "See? We have some young ones, too." "Three years ago we decided to open Sunday school for children. We had ten or twelve children. We have a few more now. The Jews in Venezuela have been very helpful. A rabbi from Caracas came three years ago and asked us what we needed. We told him, a small van—a microbus to pick up the children for Sunday school and take the elderly to services. Ten months later we got the van. But now we can't use it the same way because of the fuel problem.

"Well, that's not our only problem. Most marriages now are mixed marriages. There is practically no circumcision because not only do we not have a mohel, the hospitals won't perform them either."

VII

The Cuban Revolution and the World

Revolutionary Cuba played an important role on the world stage, for a number of reasons. The revolution's perhaps inevitable conflict with the United States and its alliance with the Soviet Union made it a significant player in Cold War politics, especially in the 1960s and 1970s. Both the United States and the USSR had their own agendas, and Cuba was sometimes used as a pawn. But Cuba also took initiative and became an actor in its own right. The Cuban government emphasized internationalism and foreign policy, taking a leading role in the Non-Aligned movement, sending thousands of foreign aid workers to the Third World, and providing military support to African and Latin American liberation movements.

Cuba's relations with its neighbor ninety miles to the north necessarily played an enormous role in its history from the nineteenth century on. Given the level of U.S. economic and military involvement in Cuba, it was perhaps inevitable that the Cuban Revolution would have a strong nationalist and anti-imperialist element, and inevitable that it would clash with established U.S. interests. When did the United States turn against the Cuban Revolution, and why? When did the revolution turn against the United States, and why? Did U.S. hostility drive Fidel Castro into an alliance with the USSR, or was it this alliance that provoked U.S. hostility? Which country was the aggressor and which the victim? Which posed a threat to the national security of the other? These and other questions have, predictably, elicited very different responses among politicians, analysts, and ordinary people in the two countries.

As relations with the United States soured in the first years following the revolution, Cuba's relations with the Soviet Union grew warmer. Economically, Cuba became increasingly dependent on Soviet trade and aid, and this relationship shaped Cuba's economic options and led to a shift away from the experimentation of the 1960s and toward a return to reliance on the exportation of sugar by the end of the decade. In some ways, this economic dependency mirrored the relationship Cuba had formerly shared with the United States: Cuba produced and exported sugar in exchange for manufactured goods. However, the Soviet Union had political and strategic reasons for supporting Cuba — unlike the classic economic dependency relationship in which a powerful country seeks to profit economically from a colony or neo-colony. The Soviet Union was willing to lose money on Cuba, in exchange for political loyalty.

Although Cuba was economically dependent on the USSR, it maintained a certain degree of political autonomy. Cuba could be counted on to support Soviet policies in Eastern Europe and Afghanistan, but Cuba's involvement in Latin America and Africa frequently challenged official Soviet policy. Cuba's military involvement in Africa is fairly well known. Cubans fought with Africans seeking an end to colonial rule from Algeria to Angola, and they confronted the United States as these independence struggles became flash points of the Cold War, especially in Angola in 1975–76. Less known, in the United States at least, is the huge commitment that Cuba made in sending doctors, teachers, and aid workers to the Third World, particularly Latin America and Africa.[1]

The Cuban Revolution had a global impact because of Cold War geopolitics, and because of the Cuban government's explicit efforts in the international sphere. In addition, the Cuban Revolution became a part of Third World and anticolonial consciousness worldwide because of its example in being a radical revolution in the backyard of the United States, and because its social policies addressed some of the Third World's most pressing problems in new and radical ways, with unprecedented success.

Note

1. "Cuba had more doctors working abroad [in 1985] (fifteen hundred in twenty-five countries) than did who. . . . By January 1985 Cuba had one civilian international aid worker for every 625 inhabitants and by January 1990 one civilian aid worker for every 228 inhabitants. In 1985 on the other hand, the United States had only one Peace Corps or Agency for International Development (AID) worker for every 31,023 inhabitants." Julie Feinsilver, *Healing the Masses: Cuban Health Politics at Home and Abroad* (Berkeley: University of California Press, 1993), 157–58.

The Venceremos Brigades

Sandra Levinson

Despite the well-known hostility between the two governments, the Cuban Revolution initially aroused sympathy from many sectors of the U.S. population, a sympathy encouraged by the daring reporting of Herbert L. Matthews in the New York Times. *The Cuban government encouraged U.S. citizens to express their solidarity by coming to Cuba to provide physical labor for the Revolution—often by cutting sugarcane in specially organized "Venceremos Brigades." (Venceremos means "we shall overcome" or "we shall triumph.") This selection in this section samples the testimonies of U.S. citizens who went to Cuba to work in the Venceremos Brigades in the early 1960s. Sandra Levinson is now the director of the Center for Cuban Studies in New York.*

It was difficult to relate to a culture in which it was good to support the government, in which the police and military served a positive function, and the alienated were a negative instead of creative force. The few alienated "hippies" in Cuba were really confused, emulating the U.S. drug culture, refusing to work or study, vandalizing the free telephones, seeking out special privileges for themselves.

Our own society had become violently insane. Total rejection of everything Amerika stood for (and killed for) was as natural as breathing, and cynicism a hard habit to break. —*Glenda Cimino*

I'm trying to understand exactly why the political discussion that goes on here in Cuba is different from that we know in the States. There is such enthusiasm, involvement, and general satisfaction among the people here that all of those old dreams that we had written off as being utopian can be seen, not as fantasies, but as victims of our own pessimism—a whole fuckin' *country* full of Marxist-Leninist revolutionary fighters! —*Chris Camarano, letter*

During the *merienda*, Howie and Ron and Angela were talking about the cultural revolution in the States. I don't think that Angela quite understands how much the cultural revolution is a rejection of some of the things the Cubans are striving for. Howie knocked television as being unnecessary; Angela saw it as something that everybody eventually ought to be able to have. Ron criticized the car for perpetuating individualism, and for creating pollution. I don't think Angela understood this at all. Ron and Howie envisioned the day in which man will no longer have to work. Angela said, "Don't worry; after the revolution there'll be plenty of work for everyone to do." —*June Erlick*

I remember that GIS in Vietnam speak of the United States as "the World," counting the days they must remain wherever they are, speaking the poem and prayer, "There's no hope without dope," and it flashed before me: No, *this* is the World. The United States is something, else, a bad movie or an indigestible nightmare or a cursed phantasm. This is real. —*Jeff Van Pelt*

Some of us are having a little trouble realigning our ideas about what constitutes bourgeois culture. When we first arrived at this hotel, for instance, we instinctively shrank from the opulence of the place—such bathhouses and mosaics, furniture, bases, chandeliers—but it's important for us to overcome this. The people deserve the best. Nothing is bourgeois by virtue of its physical composition; things are bourgeois through the intentions surrounding their use and ownership. When railroad workers and bus drivers walk on marble floors with their kids, there's nothing that makes those floors or chandeliers or silverware less than totally revolutionary. —*Chris Camarano, letter*

Q. How did you feel when you first got to Cuba?
A. I felt kind of shameful that I could fuck around with drugs and sort of take advantage of all the leisure and abstraction—what everyone is into in the United States. And it's so easy to get into those things, the cultural diversions, and not do political work. Here you see that the politics penetrates the culture, it's a positive culture, it's something that's moving. You see *Van* all over the place. You just get a feeling of motion, that there is positive motion as opposed to the kind of motion going on at home which is really, at this point, about the most decadent, just down-in-the-depths trip. —*Steve Kramer, interview*

"Do you want to learn a rhumba?"
"Sure."
"You want to learn everything!"
"Of course, but that's impossible."
"No! Listen, the most important thing is to be a revolutionary—that comes first. To be that you must know how to dance and sing." —*Tarnel Abbott*

Do the Cubans ever get tired? On four, five, six hours of sleep all they do is cut cane and dance. Singing while they cut, while they sweep the floor, and then dancing with the broom.

We've just come back from the beach and the Cubans have been whooping it up all the way, the Americans completely fagged out from the sun, the rum, the beer, dancing in circles, food all day, and, of course, cutting cane all week. The Cubans are like superthyroid freaks; the men will make music and dance and screw around at the drop of a hat. Where did Dad get the absurd notion that no one could do any work here because it's too hot? They're insane and the most unalienated people I've ever seen. Be it also mentioned that they're all Communists and would die for their Revolution at the same drop of the hat.

At lunchtime, we were being served up an elegant lunch with china from China, white tablecloths, floral centerpieces, and paper napkins, when "Happy Birthday to You" cascaded into "Los Cubanos ni se rinden ni se venden,[1] Malembay!" and everyone was off again, screaming, bottles crashing to the ground, people chugging beer up on their chairs, absolute Marx Brothers madness, the huge snake about to be born again, *"Chocolate!,"* glasses spilled, flowers thrown, everyone pounding with their fists on the tables, tinkling silverware on beer bottles, hands on shoulders, the waiters diligently trying to continue serving, the whole crowd spilling out onto the lawn, falling down sweaty, screaming at the top of their lungs, rolling down the hill. The air is absolutely pounding with their song, "Los COMUNISTAS ni se rinden ni se venden!" Commies don't cop out.

And it's all there right out front; that much unadulterated emotional give is almost unbearable. I begin to really conceive of being part of a current, that in the process of a revolution you are both very important and very small; we're talking about something bigger than all of us, and that is the transformation of an entire people, the liberation of that kind of energy we saw this evening, the beginning of building the new man. So that whether you as an individual live or die in the struggle is "relatively unimportant." This afternoon *Granma* announced the discovery by the Soviets of antimatter. So if our mass becomes energy, anyway, what is our ego? Fantastic thoughts. High on the People! Wooiiieeeeeeeee!! — *Anonymous*

We heard two stories on the ship down that depressed us: some crew members had drunk all the rum intended for the Brigade; some American guys had stolen a small birthday cake.

The Cubans explain such incidents as improper *concientización*, a word which implies simultaneously the notions of conscious awareness and conscience. He who is aware is moved to act by his conscience. "After all, you can't build a Communist society in one day," a Cuban comrade commented. "We must lift ourselves out of underdevelopment. We have the 'inheritance of capitalism' to overcome." Part of this inheritance which interferes with the creation of the new socialist man are the lessons of capitalism-individualism, competition, scarcity, putting oneself first. But the changes are coming. The political revolution of violence is only the beginning, the necessary tearing down of the old structure in order to create the new. — *Glenda Cimino*

Note

1. "Cubans neither yield nor sell out."

Photos from the Third Venceremos Brigade,
Brigadistas from Wisconsin and Minnesota,
August–September 1970.

Coffee break while doing agricultural labor. Photo by Teresa Meade.

Brigadistas on their day off. Photo by Teresa Meade.

Brigadistas pictured with a visiting Vietnamese guerrilla fighter, along with some Cubans from the brigade. Photo by Teresa Meade.

Members of a work brigade posing with Cuban and Southeast Asian visitors. Photo by Teresa Meade.

Meeting of the work brigade with its Cuban leader (white T-shirt). Photo by Teresa Meade.

The Cuban Revolution and the New Left

Van Gosse

In Where the Boys Are: Cuba, Cold War America, and the Making of a New Left, *historian Van Gosse argues that Cuba's Revolution played an important role in the development of what came to be known as the "New Left" in the United States in the 1960s. In the context of a generation of Cold War anticommunism, and disillusionment with actually existing socialism, the Cuban experience showed that alternative ways of imagining social change were possible and inspired a new generation of activists who contributed to building a new kind of leftist movement in the United States.*

Years before "The Port Huron Statement" was issued in August 1962, even before black students started sitting down at southern lunch counters in February 1960, disparate U.S. citizens — gun-toting teenagers, diehard liberals, excited reporters, stray adventurers, even Errol Flynn — had taken up the revolutionary cause championed by CBS News in a prime-time May 1957 special called "Rebels of the Sierra Maestra: The Story of Cuba's Jungle Fighters." In contrast to those team-playing organization men who were the fifties' explicit role models, the ragged *barbudos* led by Fidel Castro, chomping their cigars and darting down green mountain slopes to ambush Batista's garrisons, were every teenage boy's dream of gun-fighting, personal heroism, and nose thumbing at received authority. Two years of enthusiastic U.S. press coverage and solidarity both vicarious and practical climaxed when Batista fled Cuba on New Year's Eve 1958, leaving an entire column of would-be Yankee guerrillas stranded in Miami.

The popular fascination in the United States with Castro hung on, even as official hostility congealed, so that Fidel himself was greeted by ecstatic crowds in New York and Washington, D.C., and at Princeton and Harvard during his triumphal U.S. tour in April 1959. But as tensions steadily heightened over the rest of that year, all the voices that had once hailed Cuba's liberation rapidly stifled, and Castro became the latest case study in Latin betrayal and instability. As Cuba refused to accept North American dictates and the revolution defined itself, the Fair Play for Cuba Committee (FPCC) was organized across the country during 1960, a campaign that took place spontaneously and conspicuously outside the traditional divisions within the U.S. Left's shrunken ghetto. Over the next two years, thousands of people were pulled into the orbit of the FPCC and related efforts to defend the Cuban Revolution, as best symbolized by C. Wright Mills's runaway bestseller, *Listen, Yankee.*

Beyond its considerable reach, this "fair play movement" encompassed not only principal New Left theorists like Mills, I. F. Stone, William Appleman Williams, Paul Sweezy, and Leo Huberman; but also the most celebrated Beats and bohemians of the day — Allen Ginsberg, Norman Mailer, and Lawrence Ferlinghetti; many key black radicals and early nationalists, including LeRoi Jones, Harold Cruse, the once-notorious Robert F. Williams, and even Malcolm X; and the radical wing of a renascent pacifism led by Dorothy Day and Dave Dellinger. Perhaps even more important, a cadre of student activists came to the fore at a handful of campuses like Berkeley and Madison, many of whom would in the next decade play leading roles in the antiwar movement and the revival of the intellectual Left. In sum, virtually every current of the later sixties upsurge briefly cohered around the defense of Cuba.

Yet the excitement and admiration generated by Fidel Castro in the United States in 1957–59, let alone the existence of the Fair Play for Cuba Committee in 1960–62, are completely absent from the accounts published after the downturn of "the Movement" in the mid 1970s, and only recently have diplomatic historians noted the evidence of pro-Castro sentiment in assessing U.S. policy toward Batista. If the Fair Play for Cuba Committee is mentioned at all, the reference is usually to the claim made immediately after President Kennedy's assassination that Lee Harvey Oswald was a card-carrying member, and to the widespread anxiety on the Left that there would be a new witch-hunt for anyone who had manifested pro-Castro inclinations.

It is important therefore to stress that the Cuban Revolution was not always seen as extraneous to the formation of the New Left, just as the latter was not always defined as it is now, as a movement consisting solely of white college students. In one of the earliest books on the "new radicalism," Paul Jacobs and Saul Landau noted in 1966 that "by 1960, this new generation was throwing itself against American society, both literally and figuratively. They found a new hero in Castro, the man of action, the man without an ideology, whose only interest seemed to be bettering the life of the Cuban people. They responded to the youthful Castro with enthusiasm and demanded 'fair play' for the Cuban Revolution."

Similarly, in that same year the SDS (Students for a Democratic Society) veteran Jack Newfield published his influential *A Prophetic Minority,* which like others placed the Cuban Revolution near the center of events: "A New Left then began slowly to take root, nourished by the pacifist and socialist British New Left of the Aldermaston Marches and the *New Left Review*; by the Beats' private disaffection from and rage at the Rat Race; by the Cuban Revolution; and by the writings of such men as C. Wright Mills, Albert Camus, and Paul Goodman."

As late as 1976, Ronald Radosh edited a book-length collection, *The New Cuba: Paradoxes and Potentials*, that documented from a "critically supportive" position the relation of "the North American and Western European Left" to Cuba. In the introduction, he remarked with a distinct note of pride that "this small and often isolated Left had raised the banner of solidarity with the Cuban Revolution at an earlier moment, the era of the Bay of Pigs."

Of all those who once pointed to Cuba's influence in the United States, however, only the historian and activist Staughton Lynd hinted that this inspiration predated the appearance of a New Left in 1960: by any measure, that was the year when North American youth, black and white, first embarked on mass action, thereby spurring a revival on the noncampus Left. Writing at the height of the sixties, he linked the twin crises of informal apartheid and informal empire in defining this movement in the United States. After detailing the events touched off by Khrushchev's indictment of Stalin and the Soviet invasion of Hungary in 1956, he pointed out that "that same year . . . contrasting New Left charismas were launched in the Western Hemisphere. Fidel Castro and his handful of followers landed from the *Granma* to conquer their Cuban homeland, and Martin Luther King led the successful Montgomery bus boycott."

The question of what happened between 1956 and 1960, which Lynd describes accurately as an "incubation period," becomes crucial, and the Cuban revolutionary struggle, including Fidel Castro's sheer "charisma," comes to the fore as one of several circuitous routes toward radicalization.

My objective is to understand why the first effects of the Cuban Revolution were felt in the United States well *before* any idea arose of a "new" Left, and not coincidentally before Castro was seen as a direct threat to U.S. interests. The evidence suggests that Cuba's influence was felt primarily among those most insulated from political discontent: middle-class youth, especially males, in their teens and twenties, for whom World War II was at most a faint memory and the Affluent Society was the overwhelming tangible reality. Most of these young people had no practical idea of what the Left had been or could be, outside of the stylized paranoia of J. Edgar Hoover's *Masters of Deceit*. Nor had they inherited any vibrant traditions of cultural opposition, as both the "people's culture" of the Popular Front Left and the various avant-garde bohemias had been subsumed into the new high culture championed by repentant leftists, from Sidney Hook to Clement Greenberg. For many of these young men,

Cuba became an important early interstice between 1956 and 1960, akin to the struggle of African Americans in the demands it placed upon Cold War ideology. Ironically, it was certain Cold Warriors' very investment in Fidel as a "safe" guerrilla warrior that positioned Cuba as a wedge of radicalization; when the main body of North American liberals pulled back from the revolution in 1959–60, not everyone retreated with them. It is therefore not sufficient to look merely at the Fair Play for Cuba Committee, the events leading up to the Bay of Pigs, and the revelation of Kennedy's great-power cynicism as influences upon a New Left. Solidarity with Cuba in the early 1960s must be judged in the light of Fidel Castro's indisputable popularity in the United States before the fall of Batista.

For complete references and notes, consult the work as cited in the acknowledgment of copyrights section.

The U.S. Government Responds to Revolution

Foreign Relations of the United States

The U.S. government greeted the Cuban Revolution with caution. Internal U.S. government correspondence reveals an interlinked set of concerns regarding Cuba's new government. Castro himself was an unknown quantity — U.S. officials hoped that he would be open to what they termed "moderate" and "stabilizing" influences, rather than "anti-American," "communist," and "nationalist" tendencies. The U.S. government identified its interests closely with those of U.S. investors and an economy based on foreign investment. The next selection consists of recently declassified State Department correspondence published in Foreign Relations of the United States (FRUS).

249. Memorandum by the Assistant Secretary of State for Inter-American Affairs' Special Assistant (Hill). Washington, February 6, 1959.

Briefing Memorandum — Cuba
Foreign relations

The new regime's attitudes and intentions towards the United States are still in the formative stage. There is no question that Castro and especially some of his rebel lieutenants bitterly resent what they consider to have been the hostile attitude of the U.S. Government, and they have publicly attacked this Government and fomented anti-American feeling. On the other hand, Castro professes an admiration for the American "people" and a desire for good relations, a line followed by the titular government with perhaps greater sincerity and consistency. To date no concrete action has been taken or formally proposed against the United States or its interests (we took the first official steps with respect to the withdrawal of the military missions), and the Cuban rebels who have taken over have generally been cooperative with our representatives in Cuba. . . .

Likewise, the Cuban Government's and Castro's attitude towards Communist activities is still in the formative stage. On the one hand, the technically illegal Communist Party has come into the open and is working actively in the field of labor, press and propaganda, etc., and Guevara and a few other Castro leaders have given them help. On the other hand, Castro followers have moved to exclude Communists from the national labor leadership while the Government of Cuba has taken the position it does not intend to recognize the Communist countries.

U.S. Objectives in Cuba, for the present, may be summarized as strengthening the moderating and stabilizing influences on Castro and the Cuban Government. Diplomatic and other U.S. Government operations in support of this objective are in a particularly delicate stage since intimation of U.S. official pressures in the present atmosphere would tend to play into the hands of the anti-American elements.

362. Memorandum of a Conversation, Department of State, Washington, September 18, 1959

Subject: Our Future Relations with Cuba
Participants: R. R. Rubottom Jr., Assistant Secretary; Ambassador Bonsal; CMA [Office of Caribbean and Mexican Affairs, Bureau of Inter-American Affairs, Department of State]— William A. Wieland; ARA [Bureau of Inter-American Affairs, Department of State]—J. C. Hill; CMA—R. A. Stevenson, R. B. Owen

The meeting was called to decide what tactics we should employ in our future relations with Cuba. The following points were raised by the participants.

Ambassador Bonsal: A number of factors are more readily apparent on the scene in Cuba than they perhaps are in Washington. (1) That the purely Cuban objectives of the revolution have tremendous support and many of the things that worry us in the situation there are very minor as far as the Cubans are concerned and have little support. . . .

Mr. Hill: There are indications that if the Cuban Revolution is successful other countries in Latin America and perhaps elsewhere will use it as a model and we should decide whether or not we wish to have the Cuban Revolution succeed.

376. Attachment. Paper Prepared in the Department of State.
Washington, October 1959

Current Basic United States Policy towards Cuba (October 1959)

1. The immediate objective of the United States with respect to Cuba is the development of a situation in which, not later than the end of 1960, the Government then in control of Cuba should, in its domestic and foreign policies, meet at least minimally the objectives and standards indicated in the OCB [Operations Coordinating Board] Regional Operations Plan for Latin America which sets for the basic U.S. policy objectives for Latin American countries. . . .

a. Actions, policies, and statements tending to consolidate the Castro regime, in its present form and with those of its present policies and programs which run counter to U.S. objectives for Latin America, or tending to increase the chances of success of such programs and policies should be avoided.

b. Actions, policies, and statements tending to encourage and coalesce opposition to the Castro regime's present form and policies by elements presently or potentially acceptable to the Cuban people should be undertaken to the extent possible. Actual or potential opposition elements both within and without the government should be encouraged, but in case of conflict, priority or emphasis should normally be accorded to lines of action, policies, or statements tending to encourage opposition by suitable elements presently outside of the Castro regime with a view towards a step-by-step development of coherent opposition.

c. Actions, policies, and statements designed to emphasize throughout Latin America the U.S. concepts of genuine representative democracy, sound economic development, nonintervention, and inter-American solidarity within the free world should be undertaken whenever appropriate, as part of an effort to prevent the spread of the objectionable features of the Castro regime and program to other Latin American countries and to undercut within Cuba the support which Castro's present program derives from such popularity as it retains elsewhere in Latin America.

d. Avoidance of actions which would fundamentally damage the mutuality of interests of Cuba and the United States and of their respective peoples, and avoidance of actions, policies, or statements which would significantly affect adversely the viability of an acceptable Cuban regime, whether a reformed Castro regime or a successor to it.

409. Memorandum from the Chairman of the Working
Group on the Cuban Economic Situation (Young) to the
Assistant Secretary of State for Economic Affairs (Mann)

Washington, December 14, 1959
Subject: Estimate of Economic Outlook for Cuba

. . . The Cuban national income for the foreseeable future is likely to decline moderately, or, at best, remain at about the present level. This will result mainly from a reduction in export earnings because of lower sugar prices, the loss of tourist earnings, and the virtual disappearance of foreign capital inflows. It is estimated that for the foreign sector alone Cuba will suffer a decline of about $195 million in total income in 1959 as compared with 1958. . . .

In view of the government's policy of redistributing income away from foreigners and upper-income groups to the lowest-income groups and the lower middle classes, it is anticipated that the standard of living of the great majority of the population will show no serious decline and may even improve. By such measures as price freezing, arbitrary reductions in rents and utilities, forced wage increases, forced maintenance of employment, transfers of unutilized urban land, agrarian reform, and other pressures on foreign and domestic companies, basic steps in the direction of a redistribution of income have already been taken. In the eleven months that Castro has been in power the standard of living of low-income groups appears, on the basis of available statistics, to have improved. Although such apparent increases in incomes cannot be indefinitely maintained by purely redistributional measures not accompanied by increased overall output, income disparities in Cuba are very wide, and the present trend can probably be maintained for an appreciable period of time.

414. Memorandum from the Assistant Secretary
of State for Inter-American Affairs (Rubottom) to
the Under Secretary of State (Dillon)

Washington, December 28, 1959
Subject: Action Program on Cuba

Agreement was reached in ARA early in December that the United States Government could no longer tolerate the continued harassment of American property owners in Cuba, the failure of that government to respond in a positive way to our repeated efforts to seek a friendly solution to the problem of expropriation, and the vicious, unjustified attacks by the Castro government on the United States.

Although our attitude of patience and forbearance in the conduct of our relations with Cuba has generally won approval in Latin America and in the United States press, it is believed that in the face of these continuous provocations the time has come for the United States Government to assume a more openly critical and challenging posture vis-à-vis Cuba in order that our attitude to date may not be considered a sign of weakness and thus give encouragement to communist-nationalist elements elsewhere in Latin America who are trying to advance programs similar to those of Castro. Such programs, if undertaken, could only result in undermining United States prestige abroad, exposing United States property owners to treatment similar to that being received in Cuba, and, in general, prejudicing the program of economic development espoused by the United States for Latin America which relies so heavily on private capital investment.

423. Memorandum of Discussion at the 432d Meeting of the National Security Council, Washington, January 14, 1960, 9 A.M.

. . . [Mr. Merchant stated that] Our present objective was to adjust all our actions in such a way as to accelerate the development of an opposition in Cuba which would bring about a change in the Cuban Government, resulting in a new government favorable to U.S. interests. Mr. Merchant then called on Mr. Rubottom.

Mr. Rubottom said our policy objectives toward Cuba included friendship, mutual respect, and U.S. support for Cuba as one of the American republics; a sound and growing Cuban economy; receptivity to U.S. and Free World capital and increasing trade; the development of democratic government; a maximum limitation on Communist influence; participation in and support of hemisphere defense; access by the U.S. to essential Cuban resources; and Cuban support of regional cooperation. When Castro first came to power we had to wait for a period of time to see what he would do. The upper classes of Cuba supported Castro because he had been against Batista. The lower classes supported him because of their desire for social advancement. There had also been some support for Castro in the U.S., including such respectable sources as the National Education Association and the New York Times. This kind of support illustrates the difficulty of identifying the menacing nature of the Castro movement before Latin American and U.S. public opinion.

Mr. Rubottom then summarized U.S.-Cuban relations since January. He said the period from January to March might be characterized as the honeymoon period of the Castro Government. In April a downward trend in U.S.-

Cuban relations had been evident, partly because of the preparation by Cuba of filibustering expeditions against the Dominican Republic, Nicaragua, and Panama. In June we had reached the decision that it was not possible to achieve our objectives with Castro in power and had agreed to undertake the program referred to by Mr. Merchant. In July and August we had been busy drawing up a program to replace Castro. . . . On October 27 we delivered a statement of our views to Cuba, which had a noticeable effect, even though the propaganda barrage continued. On October 31, in agreement with CIA, the Department had recommended to the President approval of a program along the lines referred to by Mr. Merchant. The approved program authorized us to support elements in Cuba opposed to the Castro Government while making Castro's downfall seem to be the result of his own mistakes.

Castro Calls on Cubans to Resist the Counterrevolution

Fidel Castro

A speech by Fidel Castro in October 1959 gives the flavor of the Cuban response to U.S. policies and actions.

Workers, farmers, students, all Cubans: . . .

These are the questions we should ask ourselves: Why are we being attacked? Why have we had to meet here together again? Why are there traitors? Why is there an attempt to make the Revolution fail? What accusations are being made against the Revolution? Why are certain charges made against us? What ends are being sought? How should the people contend with these maneuvers and motives? How can the success of the Revolution be assured? What measures have we taken and what measures are we willing to take in order to defend the Revolution?

Before going further I want to read the following:

"UPI 3:38 P.M. Officials of the customs of Miami are investigating the news that six or seven airplanes are in flight from the Miami area toward Havana to drop counterrevolutionary leaflets over the rally in support of Castro being carried out in Havana. Customs official Joseph Portier said that he had information that these flights were being made but he did not know what success they may have had.

" 'We are trying to place agents in these possible flights,' Portier said. He also said that he had sent agents to various airports of the meridional region of Florida and that some of the airplanes that took part in the alleged flight to Havana were rented and others were private property."

I read this bulletin for the simple reason that I know that the people are not afraid.

But at the same time while we have been here on this platform, we have received the following communication from the head of the regiment of the

Rebel Army in the Province of Pinar del Río: "Be advised that an avionette [small plane] has flown over the city and [from it] were thrown handmade grenades as well as an incendiary bomb at the Niagara Sugar Mill. A house was set on fire between the post office and the Army garrison. It was at six-thirty in the evening. They also dropped pamphlets."

That is to say, the very authorities of Miami recognized that six or seven airplanes left from that area en route to Cuba and that they were still waiting for the results of the flights.

Very well. Now we can give the first report of the results. And we beg them, if they will be so kind, to go ahead and send along the official war communiqué letting us know the pilots' tally of this daring sortie against the people of Cuba.

This is the limit. We cannot be sure whether it is shamelessness or whether it is complete impotence on the part of the United States that the authorities should report news of the fifth aerial bombing mission over our territory. How is it possible that the authorities of a nation so powerful, with so many economic and military resources, with radar systems which are said to be able to intercept even guided missiles, should admit before the world that they are unable to prevent aircraft from leaving their territory in order to bomb a defenseless country like Cuba?

I wonder—and this is a question we should all ask ourselves in order to find an explanation for what is happening. . . . I wonder if the authorities of the United States would be so negligent as to permit Russian emigrants from Alaska to carry out bombing raids over cities and villages of Russian territory. I ask myself if they would be so careless as to permit that act of aggression from their territory.

Next I ask myself how it is possible then that the authorities of the United States should be so careless that on the other hand they do permit these aerial attacks against a country of their own continent—permit this aggression against a small and weak country that has no resources to defend itself from those attacks, and has no military power. I ask myself if the cause for this neglect is that we are a weak nation. Are the authorities of the powerful nations careful not to permit acts of aggression against other powerful nations, and yet do they on the other hand permit these acts against nations like us? I can see no other explanation.

I cannot conceive of any explanation other than the fact that Cuba is a small nation unable to defend itself from those attacks, a country that is not a world power. I am unable to find—and I do not believe that there is—any other explanation, because the honorable attitude for powerful nations would be to make certain to prevent their territory from serving as a base for aggression against a smaller country . . . as well as to prevent raids against a powerful country. . . .

On one hand, Cuba is being threatened by economic strangulation, that is to say, the loss of the sugar quota which provides our principal income. On the other hand, we are being subjected to aerial attacks that have the objective of terrorizing us so that we will renounce our magnificent revolutionary reform program and give up our hope of creating social justice here in our island. What has the Revolutionary Government of Cuba done to deserve this aggression against us? Our internal problems and our international problems simply result from opposition to the Revolution itself. It is our process of revolutionary reform that has caused aggressions from outside Cuba as well as treason inside Cuba.

What has the Revolutionary Government done? The only accusation that can be made against the Revolutionary Government is that we have given our people reform laws. Everything we have done can be reviewed with pride by our people. Why are the people of Cuba with us? Not just for purely sentimental reasons. The people support the Revolutionary Government because we have passed revolutionary reform laws.

Why do the farmers support the Revolutionary Government?

Why do the workers support the Revolutionary Government?

Why do the immense majority of the people support the Revolutionary Government?

Who do the people defend the Revolutionary Government?

Simply because we have been defending the people, because we have been carrying out reforms in Cuba. . . .

The problem is if we plant rice, we interfere with foreign interests; if we produce lard, we interfere with foreign interests; if we produce cotton, we interfere with foreign interests, if we cut down the electric tariffs, we interfere with foreign interests; if we make a Petroleum Law, like the one which is about to be decreed, we interfere with foreign interests; if we carry out a Land Reform, we interfere with foreign interests; if we make a Mining Law, like the one which is about to be announced, we interfere with foreign interests; if we create a Merchant Marine, we interfere with foreign interests. If we try to find new markets for our country, we interfere with foreign interests. If we attempt to sell at least as much as we buy, we interfere with foreign interests.

Because our Revolutionary Laws have an adverse effect on privileged classes inside Cuba and outside Cuba, they attack us and attack us and call us Communists. They accuse us, trying to find some pretext to justify aggression against our country. . . .

We must defend our country. Since we must defend our people, since we must defend our school children — the same children that I saw parading and singing on their way to this impressive concentration — since we must defend them; since we have been harvesting only evil; and since our enemies have become so audacious, it is good for us to let the world know that the Cuban people have decided to defend themselves.

Before the Cuban people are annihilated, the Cuban people are ready to annihilate as many enemies as are sent against them. Before allowing themselves to be murdered, the Cuban people are ready to die fighting.

The reactionaries, the invaders, and the counterrevolutionaries, both inside Cuba and outside Cuba, whether numerous or few, will find a nation that is proud to declare that we do not wish to do harm to anyone; that we do not wish to jeopardize any other people in any part of the world; that we wish only to live by our own labor; we wish only to live from the fruits of our own intelligence and wish only to live by the work of our own hands, but in order to defend our aspirations; in order to fulfill our destiny in this world; in order to defend rights that are the inalienable rights of any people of the world, big or small, today, yesterday, or tomorrow, in order to defend our honest aspirations, the Cuban people are ready to fight.

TRANSLATED BY FBIS (FOREIGN BROADCAST INFORMATION SERVICE)

Operation Mongoose

Edward Lansdale

In the aftermath of the U.S. defeat at the Bay of Pigs, the State Department autho-
rized the top secret "Operation Mongoose" with the goal of infiltrating, destabilizing,
sabotaging, and ultimately overthrowing the Cuban government. The most controver-
sial parts of Operation Mongoose involved direct acts of sabotage against Cuba. In
July 1962 Edward Lansdale, the director of the program, summarized its first year of
activities; in August 1962 a second stage was approved.

This is the Operations report at the end of Phase I. It has been compiled to
assist you in reviewing Operation Mongoose thus far and in determining the
best course of U.S. action for the future. . . .

My assessment of the organization, planning, and actions to reach the goals
in Phase I:

Intelligence

CIA had the main assignment to acquire the "hard-intelligence" desired. The
headquarters and field staff of CIA are now well organized for a major effort
for this aspect of Operation Mongoose, being strengthened by a number of
CIA officers experienced in "denied area" operations elsewhere in the world.
Planning and actions rate superior, in a professional sense of intelligence collection.

CIA established the Caribbean Admission Center at Opa-Locka, Florida [less
than one line of source text not declassified]. It undertook a priority plan to collect information on the target from third country areas in Latin America and
Europe. Inside Cuba, the recruitment and placement of third country nationals
and initiation of Cuban collection nets, particularly in urban centers, has made
Operation Mongoose numerically the largest U.S. intelligence agent effort inside a Communist state. However, the effort in more remote provincial areas
of Cuba, where guerrilla resistance was expected to be spotted, recruited, and
organized, was short of the hoped-for goal; this was due to the regime's secu-

rity precautions and, to some degree, to policy limitations on the risks to be assumed.

Defense contributed the majority of personnel to staff the Caribbean Admission Center, stepped-up SIGINT [Signal Intelligence] collection under NSA [National Security Agency] despite changes and improved sophistication of Cuban communication procedures, and brought into play the available assets of Service intelligence organizations, in coordination with CIA. State stepped up its information collection from diplomatic and refugee organization sources. Justice (FBI and INS) and USIA [U.S. Information Agency] provided significant support to the Caribbean Admission Center.

Guerrilla

CIA had the main responsibility for assessing resistance potential inside Cuba and to start quietly organizing such resistance as feasible. The CIA plan has been to set about doing this through introducing small teams into the Cuban countryside, "over the beach" from boats. Each team is tasked first to stay alive, while getting established in an area. Once able to live in an area, it then starts a cautious survey of potential recruits for a resistance group. Names of such recruits are sent to CIA for checking. As recruits join, they are trained on the ground by the team, and then continue the survey. This is slow and dangerous work.

CIA reports that eleven teams will have been infiltrated by the end of July and that nineteen maritime operations have aborted. Of the teams in, the most successful is the one in Pinar del Rio in western Cuba; its success was helped greatly by a maritime resupply of arms and equipment; the fact that it is a "going concern" and receives help from outside has attracted recruits. Its potential has been estimated at about 250, which is a sizable guerrilla force. With equally large guerrilla forces in other Cuban provinces, guerrilla warfare could be activated with a good chance of success, if assisted properly. However, the teams in other provinces have not been so successful; our best hope is that we will have viable teams in all the potential resistance areas by early October. Bad weather, high seas, and increased security patrols will make the infiltration of teams and their resupply from small boats a hard task.

Sabotage has not taken place, on a U.S.-sponsored basis. Planning for such action by CIA has been thorough, including detailed study of the structures and vulnerabilities of key targets. Sophisticated actions, such as the contamination of POL [petroleum, oil, and lubricants] has been frustrated by lack of cooperation of nations where POL would be vulnerable to action. Commando type raids would take maritime means which now have priority use in support of CIA teams being infiltrated inside to survey and create a guerrilla potential. CIA has reported that there is now some capability inside Cuba for sabotage action, that target selection has been under further careful review, and that a proposal is forthcoming to be submitted for policy approval.

Intervention Planning

The JCS [Joint Chiefs of Staff] were given the responsibility for planning and undertaking essential preliminary actions for a decisive U.S. capability for intervention in Cuba. This "Guidelines" objective has been met, fully. Also, U.S. military readiness for intervention in Cuba has been under continuing review within Defense, being improved wherever feasible. In addition, rumors during June of a possible uprising inside Cuba led to further planning for a contingency where a non–U.S. inspired revolt might start inside Cuba; inter-agency staffing of U.S. planning for such a Cuban contingency is being completed, under Defense leadership.

Assets

Whatever we decide to do in the future depends, to a large degree, on the assets available to us. Our own U.S. assets in organization, personnel, and equipment are sufficient to liberate Cuba, given the decision to do so. Assets among the Cubans, to liberate themselves, are capable of a greater effectiveness once a firm decision is made by the United States to provide maximum support of Cubans to liberate Cuba, and the Cubans start being helped towards that goal by the United States. There are enough able-bodied and properly motivated Cubans inside Cuba and in exile to do the job. There is widespread disaffection in Cuba, with strong indications that economic distress and demoralization of population is causing real concern and strain for the regime's control officials. Firm U.S. intention to help free Cuba is the key factor in assessing the Cubans themselves as an operational asset for Operation Mongoose.

At the close of Phase I, my concern is strong that time is running out for the United States to make a free choice on Cuba, based largely on what is happening to the will of the Cuban people. Rightly or wrongly, the Cubans have looked and are looking to the United States for guidance on what to aspire to and do next. They wonder if we are not merely watching Cuba closely, as a matter of our own security, undertaking some economic proscription, and isolating the Castro/Communist gang from contaminating the Hemisphere. Along with recognition of our humanitarian sympathies, this seems to be the fear among Cuban refugees, although they are still hopeful.

If Cubans become convinced that the United States is not going to do more than watch and talk, I believe they will make other plans for the future. The bulk of Cuban refugees in the United States are most likely to start getting serious about settling down for life in the United States, dulling their desire to return home with personal risk involved. The bulk of disaffected people inside Cuba will lose hope and incentive for futile protests against the regime and start accepting their status as captives of the Communists. Some Cuban activists will not accept the loss of their homeland so easily and may seek release from frustration by liberation operations outside U.S. territory and control. The recent wildcat Cuban scheme to bomb Habana from Central America is an example.

Our probes of the guerrilla potential inside Cuba have been hampered by similar morale factors. Cubans sent to risk their lives on missions inside Cuba feel very much alone, except for their communications link back to the United States. They are unable to recruit freedom fighters aggressively by the time-proven method of starting an active resistance and thus attracting recruits; U.S. guidelines to keep this short of a revolt have made the intention behind the operation suspect to local Cubans. The evidence of some intent is seen in the recent maritime re-supply of the team in Pinar del Rio. We brought in extra weapons, for which there were immediate recruits; if we were to exploit the evident guerrilla potential in this province, it appears likely that we would have to furnish supplies by air and probably open the United States to strong charges of furnishing such support to Cuban resistance elements.

Therefore, we have been unable to surface the Cuban resistance potential to a point where we can measure it realistically. The only way this can be done, accurately, is when resistance actually has a rallying point of freedom fighters who appear to the Cuban people to have some chance of winning, and that means at least an implication that the United States is in support. Word-of-mouth information that such a freedom movement is afoot could cause the majority of the Cuban people to choose sides. It would be the first real opportunity for them to do so since Castro and the Communists came to power. There was little opportunity for the Cuban people to join an active resistance in April 1961; there is less opportunity today. If the Cuban people are to feel they have a real opportunity, they must have something which they can join with some belief in its success.

Offensive Missiles on
That Imprisoned Island

President John F. Kennedy

The U.S. public knew nothing about CIA and Mongoose activities in Cuba until much later. In October 1962, however, President Kennedy shocked the world with his announcement that the Soviet Union was installing missiles in Cuba and that the United States intended to establish a naval blockade around the island. The crisis brought the United States and the USSR to the brink of nuclear war. The next document is U.S. President Kennedy's speech to the nation announcing the blockade.

Good evening, my fellow citizens:

This Government, as promised, has maintained the closest surveillance of the Soviet military buildup on the island of Cuba. Within the past week, unmistakable evidence has established the fact that a series of offensive Missile sites is now in preparation on that imprisoned island. The purpose of these bases can be none other than to provide a nuclear strike capability against the Western Hemisphere.

Upon receiving the first preliminary hard information of this nature last Tuesday morning at 9 A.M., I directed that our surveillance be stepped up. And having now confirmed and completed our evaluation of the evidence and our decision on a course of action, this Government feels obliged to report this new crisis to you in fullest detail.

The characteristics of these new missile sites indicate two distinct types of installations. Several of them include medium-range ballistic missiles, capable of carrying a nuclear warhead for a distance of more than one thousand nautical miles. Each of these missiles, in short, is capable of striking Washington, D.C., the Panama Canal, Cape Canaveral, Mexico City, or any other city in the southeastern part of the United States, in Central America, or in the Caribbean area.

Additional sites not yet completed appear to be designed for intermediate-range ballistic missiles capable of traveling more than twice as far — and thus capable of striking most of the major cities in the Western Hemisphere, ranging as far north as Hudson Bay, Canada, and as far south as Lima, Peru. In addition, jet bombers, capable of carrying nuclear weapons, are now being uncrated and assembled in Cuba, while the necessary air bases are being prepared.

This urgent transformation of Cuba into an important strategic base — by the presence of these large, long-range, and clearly offensive weapons of sudden mass destruction constitutes an explicit threat to the peace and security of all the Americas. . . .

Our unswerving objective, therefore, must be to prevent the use of these missiles against this or any other country, and to secure their withdrawal or elimination from the Western Hemisphere.

Our policy has been one of patience and restraint, as befits a peaceful and powerful nation, which leads a worldwide alliance. We have been determined not to be diverted from our central concerns by mere irritants and fanatics. But now further action is required — and it is under way; and these actions may only be the beginning. We will not prematurely or unnecessarily risk the costs of worldwide nuclear war in which even the fruits of victory would be ashes in our mouth — but neither will we shrink from that risk at any time it must be faced.

Acting, therefore, in the defense of our own security and of the entire Western Hemisphere, and under the authority entrusted to me by the Constitution as endorsed by the resolution of the Congress, I have directed that the following initial steps be taken immediately:

First: To halt this offensive buildup, a strict quarantine on all offensive military equipment under shipment to Cuba is being initiated. All ships of any kind bound for Cuba from whatever nation or port will, if found to contain cargoes of offensive weapons, be turned back. . . .

Second: I have directed the continued and increased close surveillance of Cuba and its military buildup. . . . Should these offensive military preparations continue, thus increasing the threat to the hemisphere, further action will be justified. I have directed the Armed Forces to prepare for any eventualities. . . .

Third: It shall be the policy of this Nation to regard any nuclear missile launched from Cuba against any nation in the Western Hemisphere as an attack by the Soviet Union on the United States, requiring a full retaliatory response upon the Soviet Union.

Fourth: As a necessary military precaution, I have reinforced our base at Guantánamo, evacuated today the dependents of our personnel there, and ordered additional military units to be on a standby alert basis.

Fifth: We are calling tonight for an immediate meeting of the Organ of Consultation under the Organization of American States, to consider this threat to hemispheric security and to invoke articles 6 and 8 of the Rio Treaty in support of all necessary action. The United Nations Charter allows for regional security arrangements — and the nations of this hemisphere decided long ago against the military presence of outside powers. Our other allies around the world have also been alerted.

Sixth: Under the Charter of the United Nations, we are asking tonight that an emergency meeting of the Security Council be convoked without delay to take action against this latest Soviet threat to world peace. Our resolution will call for the prompt dismantling and withdrawal of all offensive weapons in Cuba, under the supervision of UN observers, before the quarantine can be lifted.

Seventh and finally: I call upon Chairman Khrushchev to halt and eliminate this clandestine, reckless, and provocative threat to world peace and to stable relations between our two nations. I call upon him further to abandon this course of world domination, and to join in an historic effort to end the perilous arms race and to transform the history of man. He has an opportunity now to move the world back from the abyss of destruction — by returning to his government's own words that it had no need to station missiles outside its own territory, and withdrawing these weapons from Cuba — by refraining from any action which will widen or deepen the present crisis — and then by participating in a search for peaceful and permanent solutions.

Inconsolable Memories:
A Cuban View of the Missile Crisis

Edmundo Desnoes

The missile crisis is the catalyst for Edmundo Desnoes's (b. 1930) novel, translated as Inconsolable Memories. *In it, a well-off young man decides to remain on the island after the revolution, though his wife, family, and friends have all left. The nameless protagonist observes the revolution, the changes occurring all around him, from a distance and attempts to remake himself as a writer. The upheaval unleashed in the aftermath of revolution has liberated him from his preordained future as a furniture store owner. With this newfound freedom, and a monthly check as compensation for nationalized property his family once owned, he decides to become a writer but finds he has nothing to say. The novel is structured in the form of a journal, a writer's diary. In this selection, the missile crisis presents the narrator with a real crisis that distracts him from his ennui and forces him to confront the force of history and the need "to go beyond words." The novel was made into a film,* Memories of Underdevelopment, *directed by Tomás Gutiérrez Alea, in 1968.*

Up above, the stars were lighting up insignificant dots in the now pitch-dark sky. The stars are no comfort to anyone, they ignore us from afar. They're completely indifferent. Have nothing to do with us. It's impressive how much romantic babble a revolution can destroy! You get rid of your illusions and are left with nothing, vulnerable all around.

The idea of bombings, invasion, blood, stinking corpses, mutilated, rotten, is worse than accepting nuclear destruction. Yes: I'd rather be blown up all of a sudden in a brilliant flash of light, devoured, evaporated by roaring flames than lose a leg, bleeding to death in the street. Dying at the center of a clean bomb, as Eisenhower, I think, called it first. A clean bomb. Before, I had thought it was a stupid and macabre idea invented by puritanical hypocrisy, but now I find it comforting; it's a stupendous solution, a clean death, artificial, without pain or blood; a clean bomb without much fallout.

Another long truck went by like a train with another huge amorphous mass covered by an opaque and greasy tarpaulin. I thought I saw a hand waving at me as I turned to look.

We're already a modern country, we have twentieth-century weapons, atomic bombs, we're no longer an insignificant colony, we've already rushed into history, we have the same weapons that the Russians and the Americans rattle at each other. Our power of destruction makes us an equal for a moment to the two great world powers. Still, I'm sure they'll never accept us on equal terms, they'll take our weapons away, ignore us, crush this island.

I haven't heard anything from Noemí, is she coming by tomorrow? I don't care about tomorrow. I can't love anyone, everything is paralyzed. I feel impotent to desire her. Life has ended, I must really let go of everything now: the world is opening up under my feet, it swallows me, I'll lose my body.

Last night I couldn't sleep. Today I went out into the street again. A biting north wind is blowing. The waves hit the seawall and fling themselves over the barrier, crash down on the trucks and cars, against the iron rails and the pock-marked facades. The air gets all powdery with water then. It's cold. Several watery bursts crashed down on us, scattering dark pieces of water-soaked wood onto the street.

I saw a butterfly in an open lot, and I felt suddenly like stopping, things were coming to an end in that very minute. Flying silently and yellow through the air — everything seemed suspended, dead.

Out in the street I felt worse, more vulnerable. Walking around doesn't solve anything. Everything is much more dangerous out in the street; I can't do anything. I'm a victim. I can't explain it, but seeing the butterfly was the most terrible hallucination I've had, and I don't know why.

The phone rang, it sounded like long distance, and when I picked up the receiver I heard a strange conversation. "I didn't tell her anything, she doesn't know anything. She didn't notice all the coming and going in the hospital," the man's voice said; then a woman asked: "She didn't ask you anything?" "When they started putting all those strange wooden tables in the hall, for the bodies, it was frightening, Irene, long tables with tags to tie around the ankles of the corpses, with a number or a name or something, that's what the nurses told me; when she saw the tables, she asked me about them." "What did you tell her?" "I told her it was a hurricane. The sky was gray and this north wind gave me the idea, I told her we were expecting a hurricane." "Yes, she can understand that much better, she lived through the hurricane in '26 and in '44, but never, she's never seen a war." "Neither have you." "Are you afraid?" "They'll have to kill me." "Don't you even mention it, sacred heart of Jesus, that's asking for bad luck." "There's no such thing as bad luck, I'm a revolutionary, revolutionaries don't believe in religious superstitions like that." "Anyhow, you should respect my . . ." "¡Patria o muerte! ¡Venceremos!" he screamed. I hung up. It was the only violent reaction I had heard during these last terrible days. People in general are very calm.

They called back, again the prolonged long-distance rings, but when I answered there was no one on the line. Might be Laura or my old man trying to get in touch with me from New York. I'm not going to answer. I don't want to talk to anybody. I have nothing to say, what could I say? I don't want to hear anything from anyone.

After clicking down the phone I went into the kitchen and took a bowl of rice out of the refrigerator, but I couldn't swallow it, the cold grains of rice stuck in my throat.

I don't know what I'm doing. I just stuck my thumb into my mouth and started tapping the nail on the edge of my teeth. Several minutes of that. My finger came out with a transparent string of saliva. I wiped my thumb off on the rough fabric of my khaki pants.

I want to put it all down. Everything I do seems weird to me. I pulled a pack of cigarettes out of my soft damp and drooling shirt, a blue and white pack of cigarettes, Dorados. I pulled out a cigarette and thumped the end of it on the table. The fire consumed the green match head while I watched it and almost burned my fingers. I drew in the smoke, a mouthful of hot smoke went into my lungs. I stared at the tip of ashes and the white stick leaning into the ashtray. I picked up the cigarette, exhaled the smoke over the table, over the books and my diary. A piece of tobacco dropped onto the table.

I looked down at the floor and saw a ball of lint, of hair and a spider web and dust under the bookcase.

I got into bed and put the light out: but I couldn't sleep. The missiles are there, in Pinar del Río, Santa Clara, in Oriente. . . . The island seems to be covered with missiles all over. They'll brush us away, put us out, they're going to sink this alligator island into the bottom of the Caribbean. Then the battleships will sail over us and say: "This is where Cuba used to be." And the waves, the tides, will sweep over the island that had sunk into the bottom of the sea.

The Pentagon must already have a plan to destroy us. They'll crush us with the sheer weight of their arms and men. And if the Russians fire their missiles the earth might split in two. All because of Cuba. Never have we been more important nor more miserable. Fighting the United States — we're so small — might have a touch of greatness, but I reject that fate. I would rather go on being underdeveloped. Not interested, a fate that must face death each minute is not for me. Revolutionaries are mystics of this century: willing to die for an implacable social justice. I'm a mediocre man, a modern man, a link in the chain, a worthless cockroach.

The slightest sound can be the end of the world. A car going by in the street, someone starting a motor, if they slam a door. . . . Every sound is the beginning of the end. No, can't conceive nuclear destruction, it's something completely blank to me. The unknown. Have no way of relating myself to the phenomenon. I will become hot breath. No use complaining: I live here in Cuba and will die like the rest. They've pinned me down. No way out, none, I can see myself among the ruins of Vedado, a speck of dust, a smudge. . . .

I don't want to sleep nor do I feel like staying here. Have to go downstairs and get a glass of water, eat something; not even that. If I go down into the street, it could be worse. People, just to see people. What's the use, hanging on like this?

Let go, let go.

But I don't want to die, there's always the stupid hope of breaking through, of being happy some day. Fucked up. Never learn. Now, now is all that I have.

Why? Fear of losing my shitty personality, my memories, my desires, my sensations. Mine.

This diary is useless.

Underdevelopment and civilization. Never learn.

I take myself too seriously.

Everything I say oozes out and shoves me down. Still here. Go away. Leave.

If they drop the bomb, if we survive. My head. No, I don't want it. Makes no difference. It's a lie, it does make a difference. I do care.

And what if at this very moment the bombing were to start?

Everything breaking into hell. I get more tangled up. Scream. Scream for what. Why should I put down a question mark. Periods, semicolons, letters.

Accept, accept, accept. Not even that. My head's a trap. I'm tied down. Thought. Separates me from everything. Me, me nothing. I'm still here, here, here. Everything is painful and not what it should be.

I'm going to die and that's all. All right, I accept it. I'm not going to try to sneak away through the cracks like a cockroach. There aren't any more cracks left. Cracks and holes and shelters are over.

The October Crisis is over. The Caribbean Crisis. The missile crisis. To name huge things is to kill them. Words are small, meager. If I had died, everything would have been over. But I'm still alive. And staying alive also means destroying any deep moment of intensity. (What damned silly words!)

Want to preserve the clean and empty vision of the days of crisis. Things around me and fear and desires choke me. It's impossible. Beyond this, I have nothing to add. Finished. Man is sad, but wants to live. . . .

Go beyond words.

TRANSLATED BY EDMUNDO DESNOES

The Assassination Plots

Select Committee to Study Governmental Operations
with Respect to Intelligence Activities

Even after the missiles were withdrawn, the Kennedy administration continued its attempt to overthrow the Cuban Revolution. In 1967, the CIA conducted an internal investigation into its own assassination attempts against Fidel Castro. This classified report was available to U.S. Senate investigators in 1975, when they conducted a public investigation of U.S.-organized assassination plots against foreign leaders, and the report was finally declassified in 1994. In addition, the Senate investigators interviewed many of the players involved in the assassination attempts, from the highest levels of the CIA down to the Mafia hit men they had hired. The record reveals a surreal series of botched and unsuccessful schemes.

We have found concrete evidence of at least eight plots involving the CIA to assassinate Fidel Castro from 1960 to 1965. Although some of the assassination plots did not advance beyond the stage of planning and preparation, one plot, involving the use of underworld figures, reportedly twice progressed to the point of sending poison pills to Cuba and dispatching teams to commit the deed. Another plot involved furnishing weapons and other assassination devices to a Cuban dissident. The proposed assassination devices ran the gamut from high-powered rifles to poison pills, poison pens, deadly bacterial powders, and other devices which strain the imagination.

The most ironic of these plots took place on 22 November 1963—the very day that President Kennedy was shot in Dallas—when a CIA official offered a poison pen to a Cuban for use against Castro while at the same time an emissary from President Kennedy was meeting with Castro to explore the possibility of improved relations.

The following narrative sets forth the facts of assassination plots against Castro as established before the Committee by witnesses and documentary evidence. The question of the level and degree of authorization of the plots is considered in the sections that follow.

(a) Plots: Early 1960

(I) PLOTS TO DESTROY CASTRO'S PUBLIC IMAGE

Efforts against Castro did not begin with assassination attempts. From March through August 1960, during the last year of the Eisenhower Administration, the CIA considered plans to undermine Castro's charismatic appeal by sabotaging his speeches. According to the 1967 Report of the CIA's Inspector General, an official in the Technical Services Division (TSD) recalled discussing a scheme to spray Castro's broadcasting studio with a chemical which produced effects similar to LSD, but the scheme was rejected because the chemical was unreliable. During this period, TSD impregnated a box of cigars with a chemical which produced temporary disorientation, hoping to induce Castro to smoke one of the cigars before delivering a speech. The Inspector General also reported a plan to destroy Castro's image as "The Beard" by dusting his shoes with thallium salts, a strong depilatory that would cause his beard to fall out. The depilatory was to be administered during a trip outside Cuba, when it was anticipated Castro would leave his shoes outside the door of his hotel room to be shined. TSD procured the chemical and tested it on animals, but apparently abandoned the scheme because Castro cancelled his trip.

(II) ACCIDENT PLOT

The first action against the life of a Cuban leader sponsored by the CIA of which the Committee is aware, took place in 1960. A Cuban who had volunteered to assist the CIA in gathering intelligence informed his case officer in Havana that he would probably be in contact with Raul Castro. CIA Headquarters and field stations were requested to inform the Havana Station of any intelligence needs that the Cuban might fulfill. The case officer testified that he and the Cuban contemplated only acquiring intelligence information and that assassination was not proposed by them.

The cable from the Havana Station was received at Headquarters on the night of 20 July. The duty officer, who was summoned to Headquarters from his home, contacted Tracy Barnes, Deputy to Richard Bissell, CIA's Deputy Director for Plans [DDP] and the man in charge of CIA's covert action directorate. The duty officer also contacted J. C. King, Chief of the Western Hemisphere Division within the Directorate for Plans.

Following their instructions, he sent a cable to the Havana Station early in the morning of 21 July, stating: "Possible removal top three leaders is receiving serious consideration at HQS." The cable inquired whether the Cuban was sufficiently motivated to risk "arranging an accident" involving Raul Castro and advised that the station could "at discretion contact subject to determine willingness to cooperate and his suggestions on details." Ten thousand dollars was authorized as payment "after successful completion," but no advance payment was permitted because of the possibility that the Cuban was a double agent. According to the case officer, this cable represented "quite a departure from the conventional activities we'd been asked to handle."

The case officer contacted the Cuban and told him of the proposal. The case officer avoided the word *assassinate* but made it clear that the CIA contemplated an "accident to neutralize this leader's [Raul's] influence." After being assured that his sons would be given a college education in the event of his death, the Cuban agreed to take a "calculated risk," limited to possibilities that might pass as accidental. Immediately after returning to the station the case officer was told that a cable had just arrived stating: "Do not pursue ref. Would like to drop matter." This cable was signed by Tracy Barnes.

It was, of course, too late to "drop the matter" since the Cuban had already left to contact Raul Castro. When the Cuban returned, he told the case officer that he had not had an opportunity to arrange an accident.

(III) POISON CIGARS

A notation in the records of the Operations Division, CIA's Office of Medical Services, indicates that on 16 August 1960, an official was given a box of Castro's favorite cigars with instructions to treat them with lethal poison. The cigars were contaminated with a botulinum toxin so potent that a person would die after putting one in his mouth. The official reported that the cigars were ready on 7 October 1960; TSD notes indicate that they were delivered to an unidentified person on 13 February 1961. The record does not disclose whether an attempt was made to pass the cigars to Castro.

(b) Use of Underworld Figures — Phase I (Pre–Bay of Pigs)

(I) THE INITIAL PLAN

In August 1960, the CIA took steps to enlist members of the criminal underworld with gambling syndicate contacts to aid in assassinating Castro. . . .

The earliest concrete evidence of the operation is a conversation between DDP Bissell and Colonel Sheffield Edwards, Director of the Office of Security. Edwards recalled that Bissell asked him to locate someone who could assassinate Castro. Bissell confirmed that he requested Edwards to find someone to assassinate Castro and believed that Edwards raised the idea of contacting members of a gambling syndicate operating in Cuba.

Edwards assigned the mission to the Chief of the Operational Support Division of the Office of Security. The Support Chief recalled that Edwards had said that he and Bissell were looking for someone to "eliminate" or "assassinate" Castro.

Edwards and the Support Chief decided to rely on Robert A. Maheu to recruit someone "tough enough" to handle the job. Maheu was an ex-FBI agent who had entered into a career as a private investigator in 1954. A former FBI associate of Maheu's was employed in the CIA's Office of Security and had arranged for the CIA to use Maheu in several sensitive covert operations in which "he didn't want to have an Agency person or a government person get caught." Maheu was initially paid a monthly retainer by the CIA of $500, but it was terminated after his detective agency became more lucrative. The Operational Support Chief had served as Maheu's case officer since the Agency first began using Maheu's services, and by 1960 they had become close personal friends.

Sometime in late August or early September 1960, the Support Chief approached Maheu about the proposed operation. As Maheu recalls the conversation, the Support Chief asked him to contact John Rosselli, an underworld figure with possible gambling contacts in Las Vegas, to determine if he would participate in a plan to "dispose" of Castro. The Support Chief testified, on the other hand, that it was Maheu who raised the idea of using Rosselli. . . .

The Support Chief testified that Maheu was told to offer money, probably $150,000, for Castro's assassination. . . .

POISON IS PREPARED AND DELIVERED TO CUBA

The Inspector General's Report described conversations among Bissell, Edwards, and the Chief of the Technical Services Division (TSD), concerning the most effective method of poisoning Castro. There is some evidence that Giancana or Rosselli originated the idea of depositing a poison pill in Castro's drink to give the "asset" [the person who will poison the drink, then leave before it takes effect] a chance to escape. "The Support Chief recalled Rosselli's request for something "nice and clean, without getting into any kind of out and out ambushing," preferably a poison that would disappear without a trace. The Inspector General's Report cited the Support Chief as stating that the Agency had first considered a "gangland-style killing" in which Castro would be gunned down. Giancana reportedly opposed the idea because it would be difficult to recruit someone for such a dangerous operation, and suggested instead the use of poison.

Edwards rejected the first batch of pills prepared by TSD because they would not dissolve in water. A second batch, containing botulinum toxin, "did the job expected of them" when tested on monkeys. The Support Chief received the pills from TSD, probably in February 1961, with assurances that they were lethal, and then gave them to Rosselli.

The record clearly establishes that the pills were given to a Cuban for delivery to the island some time prior to the Bay of Pigs invasion in mid-April 1961. . . . The Report concludes that yet another attempt was made in April 1961, with the aid of a leading figure in the Cuban exile movement. . . .

Rosselli told the Support Chief that Traficante believed a certain leading figure in the Cuban exile movement might be able to accomplish the assassination. The Inspector General's Report suggests that this Cuban may have been receiving funds from Trafficante and other racketeers interested in securing "gambling, prostitution, and dope monopolies" in Cuba after the overthrow of Castro. The Report speculated that the Cuban was interested in the assassination scheme as a means of financing the purchase of arms and communications equipment.

The Cuban claimed to have a contact inside a restaurant frequented by Castro. As a prerequisite to the deal, he demanded cash and $1,000 worth of communications equipment. The Support Chief recalled that Colonel J. C. King, head of the Western Hemisphere Division, gave him $50,000 in Bissell's office to pay the Cuban if he successfully assassinated Castro. The Support Chief stated that Bissell also authorized him to give the Cuban the requested electronics equipment.

. . . If the Inspector General's conclusions were correct, the funds which Bissell allegedly authorized were probably the advance payment to the Cuban, and not the $150,000 that was to be paid to him after Castro's death.

The record does clearly reflect, however, that communications equipment was delivered to the Cuban and that he was paid advance money to cover his expenses, probably in the amount of $10,000. The money and pills were delivered at a meeting between Maheu, Rosselli, Trafficante, and the Cuban at the Fountainebleau Hotel in Miami. As Rosselli recalled, Maheu:

* * * opened his briefcase and dumped a whole lot of money on his lap and also came up with the capsules and he explained how they were going to be used. As far as I remember, they couldn't be used in boiling soups and things like that, but they could be used in water or otherwise, but they couldn't last forever. * * * It had to be done as quickly as possible.

Cuban Refugee Children

Monsignor Bryan O. Walsh

Emigration has been a fact of life in the entire Caribbean in the twentieth century. Caribbean laborers have migrated to work on the Panama Canal, on Central American banana plantations, and in the barrios and factories of New York and the rest of the eastern United States. After the revolution the U.S. government, eager to promote its view of the revolutionary government as repressive, opened its door, and substantial government largesse, to Cuban "refugees." Until 1995, all Cubans arriving on U.S. soil were virtually automatically granted refugee status. A lesser-known aspect of this policy was Operation Pedro Pan, in which the U.S. Immigration Department worked with the Catholic Welfare Bureau to "help Cuban parents send their children unaccompanied to the United States to avoid Communist indoctrination." Monsignor Bryan O. Walsh (1930–2001), Episcopal vicar for Spanish-speaking peoples for the Archdiocese of Miami, who helped to coordinate the project, wrote the following account.

About 4:30 P.M. on 26 December 1960, Pan American World Airways Flight 422 from Havana touched down at Miami International Airport. There were few passengers, if any, on that flight who did not experience a real sense of relief as they descended from the airplane. Events in Cuba were rapidly moving toward a climax and those who could were joining the increasing exodus to Miami. Two teenagers, a Cuban brother and sister, were among the passengers. Sixto Aquino and his sister, Vivian, must have shared in the general relief, but they still had reason to be apprehensive. No friends or relatives waited for them outside the doors of U.S. Customs. They had left their parents behind not knowing when they would see them again; and they were going as aliens into a new adult world where almost everything would be strange and new, including the language. Although Sixto and his sister did not know it, they were the first of a long line of youths who would make this same trip during the following twenty-three months.

Waiting for them at the desk of U.S. Immigration was a social worker, Mrs. Louise Cooper, from Miami's Catholic Welfare Bureau. The day before, in response to a cryptic message from Cuba, Mrs. Cooper and I, as Catholic Welfare Bureau Executive Director, had begun what was to become a daily vigil at the immigration desk. Thus it was on Christmas Day 1960 that the program of the Catholic Welfare Bureau for the care and protection of unaccompanied Cuban children in the United States actually got under way.

News reporters, sworn to secrecy, would christen it Operation Pedro Pan. Before it ended it would involve thousands of families, Cuban and American, several foreign governments, numerous officials of federal and state government, well over one hundred child welfare agencies, and the three major faiths in a unique effort of cooperation to help children, the innocent victims of power politics and clashing ideologies. Even though Operation Pedro Pan itself would only last less than two years, the Cuban Children's Program would go on for many years and would have a very real influence on the development of cooperative programs between government and voluntary child welfare agencies in the United States.

It is important to understand the difference between Operation Pedro Pan and the Cuban Children's Program. The Cuban Children's Program was inaugurated to provide foster care for Cuban refugee children who found themselves in the United States without the care and protection of their parents. Operation Pedro Pan was developed to help Cuban parents send their children unaccompanied to the United States to avoid Communist indoctrination. Both programs developed at the same time but, while operation Pedro Pan terminated with the missile crisis, the Cuban Children's Program is still in operation at the time of writing [1971]. Between the 3 January 1961 break in Cuban-U.S. diplomatic relations and the October 1962 Missile Crisis, 14,048 Cuban students were helped by Operation Pedro Pan to enter the United States; 6,486 of them received foster care in the Cuban Children's Program — either on their arrival or shortly thereafter. . . .

It was to help such families that Mr. James Baker came to Miami from Havana about the second week of December 1960. Mr. Baker was the headmaster of Ruston Academy, an American school in Havana, whose pupils were drawn from U.S. residents and upper-class Cuban families. Mr. Baker was joined in Miami by several U.S. businessmen formerly of Havana, and they set out to seek some way of providing shelter and education in Miami for those children who did not have relatives or friends here. Mr. Baker had sent one of his teachers to Miami and Washington the previous month to look over the situation. As a result of that visit, the decision had been made to open a boarding school in Miami for such children, and this was the purpose of the December trip. While looking for a suitable building for his school, Mr. Baker heard about the plans of the Catholic Welfare Bureau to provide care for unaccompanied refugee children and came to see me on 12 December 1960.

Mr. Baker talked about his plans and told me about the fears of many of his Cuban friends for the welfare of their children. He also explained that some of these friends were active in the anti-Castro underground and were afraid that their children would be taken by the government and used as hostages.

I recall our conversation very well. I had become convinced by this time that uncoordinated and scattered efforts would only do damage to the cause. Believing also that only licensed child-placing agencies should care for unaccompanied refugee children, I thought that even the best boarding school would only be a partial solution. I pointed out to Mr. Baker that this was a job for a social agency which could plan for the total care of the child, including the legal questions of custody, which were bound to come up sooner or later. I also pointed out that some children, especially the younger ones, belonged in foster families, not in institutions. I noted that the question of religious heritage would be very important in the minds of most Cuban parents, Jewish and Protestant, perhaps even more than Catholics, if the separation should prove to be lengthy. I was also able to tell him that Mr. Voorhees had indicated that funds would be available for the care of the children. As a result Mr. Baker agreed to work with us. He would get the children out of Cuba and we would see that they were met upon arrival in Miami and that they would receive proper care. He estimated that approximately two hundred children would be involved in this operation. Thus began Operation Pedro Pan, our project to fly the children out of Cuba. . . .

Mr. Baker's visit had brought a new dimension to the problem, mainly the question of children coming to us directly from Cuba, without any friends or relatives to meet them. In agreeing to work with Mr. Baker, we were accepting responsibility for the reception of the children right at the point of entry, Miami International Airport, and we were agreeing to provide foster care for those who had neither friends nor relatives able and willing to take them into their own homes. . . .

Thirty-nine days after the first fruitless wait at the airport on Christmas Day, the Cuban Children's Program and Operation Pedro Pan were now in full swing. We were taking care of children already in Miami; we were helping children leave Cuba directly for Miami and via Jamaica; we were placing children in foster care throughout the country; and our relationship with the federal government was about to be placed on a formal basis. Come what might our program was now on a firm foundation.

We could not read the future. We still shared the common hope that it would not be too long, maybe a year at the most, until these children could be reunited with their parents. We still were thinking in terms of a few hundred children coming from Cuba. We were pretty sure that sooner or later the Cuban authorities would discover what was going on, and put a stop to the exodus. It was too early for us to realize that all these assumptions would within a few months be proved wrong. In the meantime, however, we had a job to do. The next period would be one of expansion.

We would continue to grow in all aspects of the program during the following twenty-one months. We would receive more than fourteen thousand children at the airport. We would take 7,464 children under care. We would place them in foster care in thirty-five states under the auspices of ninety-five different child welfare agencies. We would set up three large reception centers in Miami and establish two group-care facilities for teenage boys in Miami with a State Department of Public Welfare authorized population of fifteen hundred children and a total staff in Miami of 465 persons. We would do all of this before the Cuban Missile Crisis shut off commercial air traffic on 22 October 1962.

From Welcomed Exiles to
Illegal Immigrants

Félix Roberto Masud-Piloto

Félix Masud-Piloto, a Cuban American who is married to one of the children brought to the United States under the auspices of Operation Pedro Pan, adds a poignant personal account to his description of the postrevolutionary exodus.

Over thirty-three years have passed since my father and I left Cuba with a mixture of sadness, anxiety, and hope. Although our departure, like most others during the period, was clouded in fear and seeming urgency, we felt confident of a successful outcome. My parents, like thousands of others, were certain that the revolution would last only a few months or at the most a few years. Thus they decided to emigrate to wait for political changes in Cuba.

My father, who was forty-nine years old at the time, was at the peak of his career in Cuba and had much to lose if our stay in the United States were to be prolonged. He was considered a sort of "Cuban success story." Coming to Cuba as an eight-year-old immigrant from Beirut, Lebanon, in 1920, he rose from poverty to fame and relative wealth in a few years. His highly successful and visible career as a popular trainer of boxers and baseball players made him well known in sports, political, and show-business circles. He had traveled widely with boxing champions and baseball teams. Yet he decided to risk fame and stability for the uncertainty of exile.

Years later I discovered that I had been the principal reason for my family's exile. Impressed by rumors making the rounds in Cuba, my parents, and many others with young children, became worried. My parents were fearful that I would soon be indoctrinated by the new socialist government and eventually be inducted into the army to defend the revolution. I was ten years old then and oblivious to the dangers my parents foresaw. In fact, I was quite excited by the atmosphere of change brought on by the revolution. Batista's overthrow, Castro's triumphant march into Havana, the literacy campaign, the agrarian and urban reforms, the explosion of La Coubre in Havana Harbor, the "El Encanto" burning, and the Bay of Pigs invasion were still vivid in my mind when I said good-bye to dear friends, my three sisters, and my mother.

On 15 October 1961, a small number of Cuban friends greeted us at Miami's International Airport with the often-heard phrase: "We'll be back in Cuba in six months." One of our friends even insisted that I go live with his family for that short period to avoid extra expense. My father declined the offer.

Our first few weeks in Miami were spent anxiously awaiting news from Cuba of Castro's "certain" downfall. I took the period as an extended vacation, missing home but confident that I would soon return. Six months passed and Castro's power grew stronger. Instead of returning to Cuba, we were joined by my mother and two sisters in 1962. By the time my other sister joined us in Miami in 1969, a deep sense of permanency had set in.

Compared to thousands of other Cuban families, our immediate family was reunited rather quickly, and slowly the rest of our extended family joined the constantly growing Cuban community in Miami. Two paternal uncles arrived with their families in the late 1960s; a maternal aunt arrived via Madrid in the early 1970s. Most recently, the Mariel boatlift brought us twelve relatives: a paternal aunt, three cousins, and their families. Yet we still have relatives in Cuba whom most of our family in Miami have not seen in more than thirty years.

Life in exile has been difficult for all of us, but particularly for our parents. My father never regained the status he enjoyed in Cuba. Nor was he ever able to practice his profession, since to do so he needed to pass a revalidation examination offered only in English, which he never learned. Like thousands of other exiled professionals, he worked at menial jobs to survive and provide for his family. He died in Miami at the age of eighty-one, still dreaming of returning to the "old" Cuba.

My mother, Victoria, although always a lively and robust woman, was simply overwhelmed by Cuban political events of the late 1950s and early 1960s. The constant turmoil, family separation, and the imprisonment of a brother and sister (Leonel was sentenced to twenty years and Emilia to fifteen) affected her deeply. By the time she came to Miami in 1962, she was suffering from hypertension and was often ill with related ailments. Mother never felt at home in Miami. She constantly missed Cuba and her loved ones, especially her brother and sister in prison. Emilia was released after serving six years of her sentence, and she joined us in Miami a few months later. Mother never saw Leonel again; he died in Cuba just a few months after serving his twenty-year term.

After a long illness Mother passed away in a Miami hospital on 23 January 1984. Like tens of thousands of other Cubans, she died dreaming of going back to Cuba to her familiar surroundings, to what she had left, presumably for just a few months, almost twenty-two years earlier.

The 15th of October 1961, will remain in my mind as the day I unsuspectingly started a new life in a foreign country where everything, including the language, was unknown to me. Sad and difficult as I found it, I was not alone; almost one million Cubans have faced similar circumstances since 1959. . . .

The Cuban Children's Program

The most bizarre episode of the Cuban migration to the United States during the Eisenhower administration was the Cuban Children's Program, a scheme to rescue Cuban children supposedly escaping Communist indoctrination. The program began in 1960 as the result of wild rumors circulating in Cuba and the exile community in Miami about Castro's revolutionary programs. One of the most sensational and powerful of those rumors was the one about the *patria potestad*, or the rights of parents over their children.

According to copies of a purported new Cuban decree that circulated through the underground network in Cuba:

> All children will remain with their parents until they are three years old, after which they must be entrusted to the Organización de Círculos Infantiles [state day-care centers]. Children from three to ten would live in government dormitories and would be permitted to visit their parents no less than two days a month. . . . Older children would be assigned to the most appropriate place and thus might never come home.

Other stories related that children were picked up off the streets and never seen again; that orphanages, such as Casa Beneficiencia, had been emptied and all children sent to the Soviet Union for indoctrination, and that in the town of Bayamo, fifty mothers had signed a pact to kill their children rather than hand them to Castro.

Despite Castro's public declarations that the "patria potestad" document was "a forgery put out by the Cuban underground and the United States Central Intelligence Agency to discredit his regime," the rumors continued. In the meantime, secret talks began between Monsignor Bryan O. Walsh and State Department officials, in an attempt to "save the children." Out of those discussions came Operation "Pedro Pan," designed to "help Cuban parents send their children unaccompanied to the United States to avoid Communist indoctrination." The operation later evolved into the Cuban Children's Program, intended to provide foster care for Cuban refugee children sent unaccompanied to the United States by their parents. According to Walsh, the operation was granted "blanket authority to issue visa-waivers to all children between the ages of six and sixteen."

The Eisenhower administration's decision to undertake the Cuban Children's Program broke with traditional U.S. immigration policy. Never before had the United States government funded foster care of refugee children in the United States. Previous child refugee programs had been supported by private organizations, church groups, and individual donations.

News of a U.S. government–funded foster service for children escaping "Communist indoctrination" spread throughout Cuba like wildfire. Soon there were thousands trying to get their children out, some for no apparent reason. On 26 December 1960, the first unaccompanied children — ten teenage boys — arrived in Miami. By the summer of 1961, about two hundred children reached Miami each week.

Alarmed by the large number of unaccompanied children arriving in Miami, and concerned about the causes for the unexpected migration, the U.S. Senate held hearings on the Cuban Children's Program. Unfortunately, the hearings produced little more than a number of emotional and unsubstantiated allegations about the Cuban indoctrination program. For example, Wendell N. Rollerson, director of the Inter-American Affairs Commission, which was organized in 1959 to assist the Miami community with the Cuban refugee influx, testified that some children were being sent to the Soviet Union for Communist indoctrination. He provided little or no evidence to support the charges in his testimony. Rollerson said only that he knew sixteen hundred Cuban children had been taken to the Soviet Union in one shipload, and that some parents had received letters of disaffection from them. The allegation was never verified.

The United States mass media rose to the occasion and dramatically pointed out the urgency of the matter. The *U.S. News & World Report*'s treatment of the children's exodus provides a good example of the political tone given to the sensitive human tragedy: "Why do Cubans send their children into exile? The big reason is to get them away from the Communist brainwashing that is universal in Cuban schools. It starts with the alphabet, and it extends through every school activity."

In the same fashion, the *New York Times* emphasized the parents' determination to prevent their children's indoctrination: "These parents would rather entrust their children to relatives, friends or strangers in the United States than permit them to be indoctrinated with Communist ideas. Castro's Cuba Communist indoctrination starts in the kindergarten and has to a great degree been substituted for education in all schools of the island."

Little was said, however, about the dramatic, and in most cases traumatic, situation the children faced: separation from their parents, arrival in a strange land, a language barrier, and adaptation to a new culture and environment. These emotional transformations went largely unnoticed by the media, as the children were quickly scattered in more than a hundred communities from Miami, Florida, to Yakima, Washington.

Most children who participated in the Cuban children's program were told by their parents that their separation would last only a few weeks or months. But events in Cuba (the Bay of Pigs fiasco in April 1961 and the missile crisis of October 1962) extended the separation for longer than anyone anticipated. Many of the 14,048 children who came to the United States during the program waited up to twenty years for family reunification.

For complete references and notes, consult the work as cited in the acknowledgment of copyrights section.

Wrong Channel

Roberto Fernández

Large numbers of Cubans from the middle and upper classes left the island for Miami in the early years of the revolution. Fearful for their own futures and social status in the rapidly changing political and economic context, many professionals fled, intending their stay abroad to be temporary. These early exiles formed a somewhat unique enclave among Latinos in the United States. They were generally better-educated, wealthier, and whiter than other Latinos, and they were welcomed by the U.S. government. Many were also resolutely right-wing and anticommunist, such as Cuban American novelist Cristina Garcia's Lourdes Puente, who runs a chain of "Yankee-doodle Bakeries" and spends hours conversing with her dead father about the "Communist threat to America." "Why can't the Americans see the Communists in their own backyards, in their universities, bending the malleable minds of the young? The Democrats are to blame, the Democrats and those lying, two-timing Kennedys. What America needs, Lourdes and her father agree, is another Joe McCarthy to set things right again. He would never have abandoned them at the Bay of Pigs."[1]

Cuban American Roberto Fernández was born in 1951 in Sagua la Grande. All his fiction, whether novels or short stories, captures the rarified and exclusive limbo of the Cuban enclave; a world of exile unto itself. The English and Spanish that the characters speak are peppered with references to the mythology of the "American Dream" and that of the Cuban exile, respectively, making both languages practically incomprehensible outside the enclave and making communication all but impossible. With biting humor, compassion, and critical distance, Fernández holds a rigorous historical mirror up to the distorted reality of his characters' lives and allows them to be seen clearly. Here, the tragicomic miscommunication between a U.S. doctor and his Cuban émigré patient is brought about by the pronunciation and meaning of two loaded consonants.

Barbarita waited impatiently for her ride as beads of sweat dripped from her eyebrows into her third cup of cold syrupy espresso. She was headed for the toilet when she heard the knocking sounds of Mima's old Impala. "About time you got here," yelled Barbarita from the Florida room.

"It wouldn't start this morning."

Barbarita got in, tilted the rearview mirror, and applied enough rouge to her face for a healthier look. She wanted to make a good impression on the doctor who would approve her medical records for her green card. On the way to Jackson Memorial, Mima talked about her grandchildren.

Barbarita knocked down all the Bibles and *Readers' Digest*s on the table when the nurse finally called her name.

"Sorry, ma'am, but you can't come in," the nurse said to Mima.

"I'm her interpreter," replied the polyglot.

"No bueno," said the doctor grimly as he walked in with Barbarita's X rays. He told Mima, "Ask her if she had TB."

Mima turned to Barbarita. "He says, if you have a television?"

"Tell him yes, but in Havana. Not in Miami. But my daughter has a television here."

Mima told the doctor, "She says she had TV in Cuba, not in Miami, but her daughter has TV here."

"In that case we need to test her daughter for TB too."

Mima translated, "He says he needs to test your daughter's television to make sure it works; otherwise you cannot get your green card."

"Why the television?" asked a puzzled Barbarita.

"How many times did I tell you you needed to buy one? Don't you know, Barbarita? This is America."

Note

1. Cristina Garcia, *Dreaming in Cuban* (New York: Ballantine Books 1992), 171.

We Came All the Way from Cuba So You Could Dress Like This?

Achy Obejas

The title of Achy Obejas's (b. 1956) short story alerts the reader that in it she will tackle generational difference among Cuban Americans, exploding along the way the mythology of exile that, she asserts, has become a set of false and static memories. The nameless, female, first-person narrator cuts back and forth in time across significant events in the shaping of her consciousness, beginning with her arrival at age ten from Cuba with her parents. She grows up and grows away from her parents. Displacement pushes her historical imagination back toward Cuba, across the years she was absent, though she was too young to have chosen that absence. And she wonders, as her parents would never dare to, what her life would have been like if she'd never left, thus connecting the timeline of her life with the island's historical present. In Miami, where her parents' journey has ended, hers begins. That journey is a complex, nuanced exploration of what it means to be Cuban American in the United States today, one that shatters the myth of the monolith.

I'm wearing a green sweater. It's made of some synthetic material, and it's mine. I've been wearing it for two days straight and have no plans to take it off right now.

I'm ten years old. I just got off the boat—or rather, the ship. The actual boat didn't make it: We got picked up halfway from Havana to Miami by a gigantic oil freighter to which they then tied our boat. That's how our boat got smashed to smithereens, its wooden planks breaking off like toothpicks against the ship's big metal hull. Everybody talks about American ingenuity, so I'm not sure why somebody didn't anticipate that would happen. But they didn't. So the boat that brought me and my parents most of the way from Cuba is now just part of the debris that'll wash up on tourist beaches all over the Caribbean.

As I speak, my parents are being interrogated by an official from the office of Immigration and Naturalization Services. It's all a formality because this is 1963, and no Cuban claiming political asylum actually gets turned away. We're evidence that the revolution has failed the middle class and that communism is bad. My parents—my father's an accountant and my mother's a social worker—are living, breathing examples of the suffering Cubans have endured under the tyranny of Fidel Castro.

The immigration officer, a fat Hungarian lady with sparkly hazel eyes and a perpetual smile, asks my parents why they came over, and my father, whose face is bright red from spending two days floating in a little boat on the Atlantic Ocean while secretly terrified, points to me—I'm sitting on a couch across the room, more bored than exhausted—and says, We came for her, so she could have a future.

The immigration officer speaks a halting Spanish, and with it she tells my parents about fleeing the Communists in Hungary. She says they took everything from her family, including a large country estate, with forty-four acres and two lakes, that's now being used as a vocational training center. Can you imagine that, she says. There's an official presidential portrait of John F. Kennedy behind her, which will need to be replaced in a week or so.

I fold my arms in front of my chest and across the green sweater. Tonight the U.S. government will put us up in a noisy transient hotel. We'll be allowed to stay there at taxpayer expense for a couple of days until my godfather—who lives with his mistress somewhere in Miami—comes to get us.

★   ★   ★

Leaning against the wall at the processing center, I notice a volunteer for Catholic Charities who approaches me with gifts: oatmeal cookies, a plastic doll with blond hair and a blue dress, and a rosary made of white plastic beads. She smiles and talks to me in incomprehensible English, speaking unnaturally loud.

My mother, who's watching while sitting nervously next to my father as we're being processed, will later tell me she remembers this moment as something poignant and good.

All I hold onto is the feel of the doll—cool and hard—and the fact that the Catholic volunteer is trying to get me to exchange my green sweater for a little gray flannel gym jacket with a hood and an American flag logo. I wrap myself up tighter in the sweater, which at this point still smells of salt and Cuban dirt and my grandmother's house, and the Catholic volunteer just squeezes my shoulder and leaves, thinking, I'm sure, that I've been traumatized by the trip across the choppy waters. My mother smiles weakly at me from across the room.

I'm still clutching the doll, a thing I'll never play with but which I'll carry with me all my life, from apartment to apartment, one move after the other. Eventually, her little blond nylon hairs will fall off and, thirty years later, after I'm diagnosed with cancer, she'll sit atop my dresser, scarred and bald like a chemo patient.

*   *   *

Is life destiny or determination?

For all the blond boyfriends I will have, there will be only two yellow-haired lovers. One doesn't really count — a boy in a military academy who subscribes to Republican politics like my parents, and who will try, relatively unsuccessfully, to penetrate me on a south Florida beach. I will squirm away from underneath him, not because his penis hurts me but because the stubble on his face burns my cheek.

The other will be Martha, perceived by the whole lesbian community as a gold digger, but who will love me in spite of my poverty. She'll come to my one-room studio on Saturday mornings when her rich lover is still asleep and rip T-shirts off my shoulders, brutally and honestly.

One Saturday we'll forget to set the alarm to get her back home in time, and Martha will have to dress in a hurry, the smoky smell of my sex all over her face and her own underwear tangled up in her pants leg. When she gets home, her rich lover will notice the weird bulge at her calf and throw her out, forcing Martha to acknowledge that without a primary relationship for contrast, we can't go on.

It's too dangerous, she'll say, tossing her blond hair away from her face.

Years later, I'll visit Martha, now living seaside in Provincetown with her new lover, a Kennedy cousin still in the closet who has a love of dogs, and freckles sprinkled all over her cheeks.

*   *   *

At the processing center, the Catholic volunteer has found a young Colombian woman to talk to me. I don't know her name, but she's pretty and brown, and she speaks Spanish. She tells me she's not Catholic but that she'd like to offer me Christian comfort anyway. She smells of violet water.

She pulls a Bible from her big purse and asks me, Do you know this, and I say, I'm Catholic, and she says that, well, she was once Catholic, too, but then she was saved and became something else. She says everything will change for me in the United States, as it did for her.

Then she tells me about coming here with her father and how he got sick and died, and she was forced to do all sorts of work, including what she calls sinful work, and how the sinful work taught her so much about life, and then how she got saved. She says there's still a problem, an impulse, which she has to suppress by reading the Bible. She looks at me as if I know what she's talking about.

Across the room, my parents are still talking to the fat Hungarian lady, my father's head bent over the table as he fills out form after form.

Then the Catholic volunteer comes back and asks the Colombian girl something in English, and the girl reaches across me, pats my lap, and starts reading from her Spanish-language Bible: Your breasts are like two fawns, twins of a gazelle that feed upon the lilies. Until the day breathes and the shadows flee, I will hie me to the mountain of myrrh and the hill of frankincense. You are all fair, my love; there is no flaw in you.

★   ★   ★

Here's what my father dreams I will be in the United States of America: A lawyer, then a Judge, in a system of law that is both serious and just. Not that he actually believes in democracy — in fact, he's openly suspicious of the popular will — but he longs for the power and prestige such a career would bring, and which he can't achieve on his own now that we're here, so he projects it all on me. He sees me in courtrooms and lecture halls, at libraries and in elegant restaurants, the object of envy and awe.

My father does not envision me in domestic scenes. He does not imagine me as a wife or mother because to do so would be to imagine someone else closer to me than he is, and he cannot endure that. He will never regret not being a grandfather; it was never part of his plan.

Here's what my mother dreams I will be in the United States of America: The owner of many appliances and a rolling green lawn; mother of two mischievous children; the wife of a boyishly handsome North American man who drinks Pepsi for breakfast; a career woman with a well-paying position in local broadcasting.

My mother pictures me reading the news on TV at four and home at the dinner table by six. She does not propose that I will actually do the cooking, but rather that I'll oversee the undocumented Haitian woman my husband and I have hired for that purpose. She sees me as fulfilled, as she imagines she is.

All I ever think about are kisses, not the deep throaty kind but quick pecks all along my belly just before my lover and I dissolve into warm blankets and tangled sheets in a bed under an open window. I have no view of this scene from a distance, so I don't know if the window frames tall pine trees or tropical bushes permeated with skittering gray lizards.

★   ★   ★

It's hot and stuffy in the processing center, where I'm sitting under a light that buzzes and clicks. Everything smells of nicotine. I wipe the shine off my face with the sleeve of my sweater. Eventually, I take off the sweater and fold it over my arm.

My father, smoking cigarette after cigarette, mutters about communism and how the Dominican Republic is next and then, possibly, someplace in Central America.

My mother has disappeared to another floor in the building, where the Catholic volunteer insists that she look through boxes filled with clothes donated by generous North Americans. Later, my mother will tell us how the Catholic volunteer pointed to the little gray flannel gym jacket with the hood and the American flag logo, how she plucked a bow tie from a box, then a black synthetic teddy from another and laughed, embarrassed.

My mother will admit she was uncomfortable with the idea of sifting through the boxes, sinking arm deep into other people's sweat and excretions, but not that she was afraid of offending the Catholic volunteer and that she held her breath, smiled, and fished out a shirt for my father and a light blue cotton dress for me, which we'll never wear.

*   *   *

My parents escaped from Cuba because they did not want me to grow up in a communist state. They are anticommunists, especially my father.

It's because of this that when Martin Luther King Jr. dies in 1968 and North American cities go up in flames, my father will gloat. King was a Communist, he will say; he studied in Moscow, everybody knows that.

I'll roll my eyes and say nothing. My mother will ask him to please finish his *café con leche* and wipe the milk moustache from the top of his lip.

Later, the morning after Bobby Kennedy's brains are shot all over a California hotel kitchen, my father will greet the news of his death by walking into our kitchen wearing a "Nixon's the One" button.

There's no stopping him now, my father will say; I know, because I was involved with the counterrevolution, and I know he's the one who's going to save us, he's the one who came up with the Bay of Pigs — which would have worked, all the experts agree, if he'd been elected instead of Kennedy, that coward.

My mother will vote for Richard Nixon in 1968, but in spite of his loud support my father will sit out the election, convinced there's no need to become a citizen of the United States (the usual prerequisite for voting) because Nixon will get us back to Cuba in no time, where my father's dormant citizenship will spring to life.

Later that summer, my father, who has resisted getting a television set (too cumbersome to be moved when we go back to Cuba, he will tell us), suddenly buys a huge Zenith color model to watch the Olympics broadcast from Mexico City.

I will sit on the floor, close enough to distinguish the different colored dots, while my father sits a few feet away in a La-Z-Boy chair and roots for the Cuban boxers, especially Teófilo Stevenson. Every time Stevenson wins one — whether against North Americans or East Germans or whomever my father will jump up and shout.

Later, when the Cuban flag waves at us during the medal ceremony, and the Cuban national anthem comes through the TV's tinny speakers, my father will stand up in Miami and cover his heart with his palm just like Fidel, watching on his own TV in Havana.

When I get older, I'll tell my father a rumor I heard that Stevenson, for all his heroics, practiced his best boxing moves on his wife, and my father will look at me like I'm crazy and say, Yeah, well, he's a Communist, what did you expect, huh?

★   ★   ★

In the processing center, my father is visited by a Cuban man with a large camera bag and a steno notebook into which he's constantly scribbling. The man has green Coke-bottle glasses and chews on a pungent Cuban cigar as he nods at everything my father says.

My mother, holding a brown paper bag filled with our new (used) clothes, sits next to me on the couch under the buzzing and clicking lights. She asks me about the Colombian girl, and I tell her she read me parts of the Bible, which makes my mother shudder.

The man with the Coke-bottle glasses and cigar tells my father he's from Santiago de Cuba in Oriente province, near Fidel's hometown, where he claims nobody ever supported the revolution because they knew the real Fidel. Then he tells my father he knew his father, which makes my father very nervous.

The whole northern coast of Havana harbor is mined, my father says to the Cuban man as if to distract him. There are *milicianos* all over the beaches, he goes on; it was a miracle we got out, but we had to do it — for her, and he points my way again.

Then the man with the Coke-bottle glasses and cigar jumps up and pulls a giant camera out of his bag, covering my mother and me with a sudden explosion of light.

★   ★   ★

In 1971, I'll come home for Thanksgiving from Indiana University where I have a scholarship to study optometry. It'll be the first time in months I'll be without an antiwar demonstration to go to, a consciousness-raising group to attend, or a Gay Liberation meeting to lead.

Alaba'o [Praise the Lord], I almost didn't recognize you, my mother will say, pulling on the fringes of my suede jacket, promising to mend the holes in my floor-sweeping bellbottom Jeans. My green sweater will be somewhere in the closet of my bedroom in their house.

We left Cuba so you could dress like this? my father will ask over my mother's shoulder.

And for the first and only time in my life, I'll say, Look, you didn't come for me, you came for you; you came because all your rich clients were leaving, and you were going to wind up a cashier in your father's hardware store if you didn't leave, okay?

My father, who works in a bank now, will gasp — ¿Qué qué? — and step back a bit. And my mother will say, Please, don't talk to your father like that.

And I'll say, It's a free country, I can do anything I want remember? Christ, he only left because Fidel beat him in that stupid swimming race when they were little.

And then my father will reach over my mother's thin shoulders, grab me by the red bandanna around my neck, and throw me to the floor, where he'll kick me over and over until all I remember is my mother's voice pleading, Please stop, please, please, please stop.

★   ★   ★

We leave the processing center with the fat Hungarian lady, who drives a large Ford station wagon. My father sits in the front with her, and my mother and I sit in the back, although there is plenty of room for both of us in the front as well. The fat Hungarian lady is taking us to our hotel, where our room will have a kitchenette and a view of an alley from which a tall black transvestite plies her night trade.

Eventually, I'm drawn by the lights of the city, not just the neon streaming by the car windows but also the white globes on the street lamps, and I scamper to the back where I can watch the lights by myself. I close my eyes tight, then open them, loving the tracers and star bursts on my private screen.

Up in front, the fat Hungarian lady and my father are discussing the United States' many betrayals, first of Eastern Europe after World War II, then of Cuba after the Bay of Pigs invasion.

My mother, whom I believe is as beautiful as any of the palm trees fluttering on the median strip as we drive by, leans her head against the car window, tired and bereft. She comes to when the fat Hungarian lady, in a fit of giggles, breaks from the road and into the parking lot of a supermarket so shrouded in light that I'm sure it's a flying saucer docked here in Miami.

We did this when we first came to America, the fat Hungarian lady says, leading us up to the supermarket. And it's something only people like us can appreciate.

My father bobs his head up and down and my mother follows, her feet scraping the ground as she drags me by the hand.

We walk through the front door and then a turnstile, and suddenly we are in the land of plenty — row upon row of cereal boxes, TV dinners, massive displays of fresh pineapple, crate after crate of oranges, shelves of insect repellent, and every kind of broom. The dairy section is jammed with cheese and chocolate milk.

There's a butcher shop in the back, and my father says, Oh my god, look, and points to a slab of bloody red ribs thick with meat. My god my god my god, he says, as if he's never seen such a thing, or as if we're on the verge of starvation.

Calm down, please, my mother says, but he's not listening, choking back tears and hanging off the fat Hungarian lady who's now walking him past the sausages and hot dogs, packaged bologna, and chipped beef.

All around us people stare, but then my father says, We just arrived from Cuba, and there's so much here!

The fat Hungarian lady pats his shoulder and says to the gathering crowd, Yes, he came on a little boat with his whole family; look at his beautiful daughter who will now grow up well fed and free.

I push up against my mother, who feels as smooth and thin as a palm leaf on Good Friday. My father beams at me, tears in his eyes. All the while, complete strangers congratulate him on his wisdom and courage, give him hugs and money, and welcome him to the United States.

★   ★   ★

There are things that can't be told.

Things like when we couldn't find an apartment, everyone's saying it was because landlords in Miami didn't rent to families with kids, but knowing, always, that it was more than that.

Things like my doing very poorly on an IQ test because I didn't speak English, and getting tossed into a special education track, where it took until high school before somebody realized I didn't belong there.

Things like a North American hairdresser's telling my mother she didn't do her kind of hair.

Like my father, finally realizing he wasn't going to go back to Cuba anytime soon, trying to hang himself with the light cord in the bathroom while my mother cleaned rooms at a nearby luxury hotel, but falling instead and breaking his arm.

Like accepting welfare checks, because there really was no other way.

Like knowing that giving money to exile groups often meant helping somebody buy a private yacht for Caribbean vacations, not for invading Cuba, but also knowing that refusing to donate only invited questions about our own patriotism.

And knowing that Nixon really wasn't the one, and wasn't doing anything, and wouldn't have done anything, even if he'd finished his second term, no matter what a good job the Cuban burglars might have done at the Watergate Hotel.

★   ★   ★

What if we'd stayed? What if we'd never left Cuba? What if we were there when the last of the counterrevolution was beaten, or when Mariel harbor leaked thousands of Cubans out of the island, or when the Pan American Games came? What if we'd never left?

All my life, my father will say I would have been a young Communist, falling prey to the revolution's propaganda. According to him, I would have believed ice cream treats came from Fidel, that those hairless Russians were our friends, and that my duty as a revolutionary was to turn him in for his counterrevolutionary activities—which he will swear he'd never have given up if we'd stayed in Cuba.

My mother will shake her head but won't contradict him. She'll say the revolution uses people, and that I, too, would probably have been used, then betrayed, and that we'll never know, but maybe I would have wound up in jail whether I ever believed in the revolution or not, because I would have talked back to the wrong person, me and my big mouth.

I wonder, if we'd stayed then who, if anyone—if not Martha and the boy from the military academy—would have been my blond lovers, or any kind of lovers at all.

★   ★   ★

And what if we'd stayed, and there had been no revolution?

My parents will never say, as if somehow they know that their lives were meant to exist only in opposition.

I try to imagine who I would have been if Fidel had never come into Havana sitting triumphantly on top of that tank, but I can't. I can only think of variations of who I am, not who I might have been.

In college one day, I'll tell my mother on the phone that I want to go back to Cuba to see, to consider all these questions, and she'll pause, then say, What for? There's nothing there for you, we'll tell you whatever you need to know, don't you trust us?

Over my dead body, my father will say, listening in on the other line.

Years later, when I fly to Washington, D.C., and take a cab straight to the Cuban Interests Section to apply for a visa, a golden-skinned man with the dulled eyes of a bureaucrat will tell me that because I came to the U.S. too young to make the decision to leave for myself—that it was in fact my parents who made it for me—the Cuban government does not recognize my U.S. citizenship.

You need to renew your Cuban passport, he will say. Perhaps your parents have it, or a copy of your birth certificate, or maybe you have a relative or friend who could go through the records in Cuba for you.

I'll remember the passport among my mother's priceless papers, handwritten in blue ink, even the official parts. But when I ask my parents for it, my mother will say nothing, and my father will say, It's not here anymore, but in a bank box, where you'll never see it. Do you think I would let you betray us like that?

*   *   *

The boy from the military academy will say oh baby baby as he grinds his hips into me. And Martha and all the girls before and after her here in the United States will say ooohhh ooooohhhhh ooooooohhhhhhhh as my fingers explore inside them.

But the first time I make love with a Cuban, a politically controversial exile writer of some repute, she will say, *Aaaaaayyyyyyaaaaaayyyyaaaaay* and lift me by my hair from between her legs, strings of saliva like sea foam between my mouth and her shiny curls. Then she'll drop me onto her mouth where our tongues will poke each other like wily porpoises.

In one swift movement, she'll flip me on my back, pillows falling every which way from the bed, and kiss every part of me, between my breasts and under my arms, and she'll suck my fingertips, and the inside of my elbows. And when she rests her head on my belly, her ear listening not to my heartbeat but to the fluttering of palm trees, she'll sit up, place one hand on my throat, the other on my sex, and kiss me there, under my rib cage, around my navel, where I am softest and palest.

The next morning, listening to her breathing in my arms, I will wonder how this could have happened, and if it would have happened at all if we'd stayed in Cuba. And if so, if it would have been furtive or free, with or without the revolution. And how — knowing now how cataclysmic life really is — I might hold on to her for a little while longer.

*   *   *

When my father dies of a heart attack in 1990 (it will happen while he's driving, yelling at somebody, and the car will just sail over to the sidewalk and stop dead at the curb, where he'll fall to the seat and his arms will somehow fold over his chest, his hands set in prayer), I will come home to Florida from Chicago, where I'll be working as a photographer for the *Tribune*. I won't be taking pictures of murder scenes or politicians then but rather rock stars and local performance artists.

I'll be living in Uptown, in a huge house with a dry darkroom in one of the bedrooms, now converted and sealed black, where I cut up negatives and create photomontages that are exhibited at the Whitney Biennial and hailed by the critics as filled with yearning and hope.

When my father dies, I will feel sadness and a wish that certain things had been said, but I will not want more time with him. I will worry about my mother, just like all the relatives who predict she will die of heartbreak within months (she has diabetes and her vision is failing). But she will instead outlive both him and me.

I'll get to Miami Beach, where they've lived in a little coach house off Collins Avenue since their retirement, and find cousins and aunts helping my mother go through insurance papers and bank records, my father's will, his photographs and mementos: his university degree, a faded list of things to take back to Cuba (including Christmas lights), a jaundiced clipping from *Diario de las Américas* about our arrival which quotes my father as saying that Havana harbor is mined, and a photo of my mother and me, wide-eyed and thin, sitting on the couch in the processing center.

My father's funeral will be simple but well attended, closed casket at my request, but with a moment reserved for those who want a last look. My mother will stay in the room while the box is pried open (I'll be in the lobby smoking a cigarette, a habit I despised in my father but which I'll pick up at his funeral) and tell me later she stared at the cross above the casket, never registering my father's talcumed and perfumed body beneath it.

I couldn't leave, it wouldn't have looked right, she'll say. But thank god I'm going blind.

Then a minister who we do not know will come and read from the Bible and my mother will reach around my waist and hold onto me as we listen to him say, When all these things come upon you, the blessing and the curse . . . and you call them to mind among all the nations where the Lord your God has driven you, and return to the Lord your God, you and your children, and obey his voice . . . with all your heart and with all your soul; then the Lord your God will return your fortunes, and have compassion upon you, and he will gather you again from all the peoples where the Lord your God has scattered you.

*   *   *

There will be a storm during my father's burial, which means it will end quickly. My mother and several relatives will go back to her house, where a TV will blare from the bedroom filled with bored teenage cousins, the women will talk about how to make *picadillo* with low-fat ground turkey instead of the traditional beef and ham, and the men will sit outside in the yard, drinking beer or small cups of Cuban coffee, and talk about my father's love of Cuba, and how unfortunate it is that he died just as Eastern Europe is breaking free, and Fidel is surely about to fall.

Three days later, after taking my mother to the movies and the mall, church, and the local Social Security office, I'll be standing at the front gate with my bags, yelling at the cab driver that I'm coming, when my mother will ask me to wait a minute and run back into the house, emerging minutes later with a box for me that won't fit in any of my bags.

A few things, she'll say, a few things that belong to you that I've been meaning to give you for years and now, well, they're yours.

I'll shake the box, which will emit only a muffled sound, and thank her for whatever it is, hug her and kiss her and tell her I'll call her as soon as I get home. She'll put her chicken-bone arms around my neck, kiss the skin there all the way to my shoulders, and get choked up, which will break my heart.

Sleepy and tired in the cab to the airport, I'll lean my head against the window and stare out at the lanky palm trees, their brown and green leaves waving good-bye to me through the still coming drizzle. Everything will be damp, and I'll be hot and stuffy, listening to car horns detonating on every side of me. I'll close my eyes, stare at the blackness, and try to imagine something of yearning and hope, but I'll fall asleep instead, waking only when the driver tells me we've arrived, and that he'll get my bags from the trunk, his hand outstretched for the tip as if it were a condition for the return of my things.

When I get home to Uptown I'll forget all about my mother's box until one day many months later when my memory's fuzzy enough to let me be curious. I'll break it open to find grade school report cards, family pictures of the three of us in Cuba, a love letter to her from my father (in which he talks about

wanting to kiss the tender mole by her mouth), Xeroxes of my birth certificate, copies of our requests for political asylum, and my faded blue-ink Cuban
passport (expiration date: June 1965), all wrapped up in my old green sweater.

When I call my mother—embarrassed about taking so long to unpack her
box, overwhelmed by the treasures within it—her answering machine will pick
up and, in a bilingual message, give out her beeper number in case of emergency.

A week after my father's death, my mother will buy a computer with a
Braille keyboard and a speaker, start learning how to use it at the community
center down the block, and be busy investing in mutual funds at a profit within
six months.

★   ★   ★

But this is all a long way off, of course. Right now, we're in a small hotel room
with a kitchenette that U.S. taxpayers have provided for us.

My mother, whose eyes are dark and sunken, sits at a little table eating one of
the Royal Castle hamburgers the fat Hungarian lady bought for us. My father
munches on another, napkins spread under his hands. Their heads are tilted
toward the window which faces an alley. To the far south edge, it offers a view
of Biscayne Boulevard and a magically colored thread of night traffic. The air
is salty and familiar, the moon brilliant hanging in the sky.

I'm in bed, under sheets that feel heavy with humidity and the smell of
cleaning agents. The plastic doll the Catholic volunteer gave me sits on my
pillow.

Then my father reaches across the table to my mother and says, We made
it, we really made it.

And my mother runs her fingers through his hair and nods, and they both
start crying, quietly but heartily, holding and stroking each other as if they are
all they have.

And then there's a noise—a screech out in the alley followed by what sounds
like a hyena's laughter—and my father leaps up and looks out the window,
then starts laughing, too.

Oh my god, come here, look at this, he beckons to my mother, who jumps
up and goes to him, positioning herself right under the crook of his arm. Can
you believe that, he says.

Only in America, echoes my mother.

And as I lie here wondering about the spectacle outside the window and the
new world that awaits us on this and every night of the rest of our lives even
I know we've already come a long way. What none of us can measure yet is
how much of the voyage is already behind us.

City on the Edge

Alejandro Portes and Alex Stepick

The city of Miami was utterly transformed by the influx of Cubans. In City on the
Edge: The Transformation of Miami, *Alejandro Portes and Alex Stepick discuss
the 1980 Mariel boatlift and its impact on the Cuban community, as well as on defini-
tions of Cuban identity and ethnicity, in Miami. It was Mariel, they argue, that turned
Cubans in Miami into Cuban Americans and led to the formation of organizations
such as the Cuban American National Foundation, which was aimed at influencing
U.S. policies. An excerpt from this book examines the "moral community" of Cubans
in Miami and the origins and nature of its legendary right-wing character.*

The Moral Community

"Miami: The World in Black and White," read the title of an editorial by a famous Cuban poet after spending a few months in the city. He summarized his
impressions in a few poignant words: "You have to live in Miami, sleep in it
each day, to really know how it is and how it has forged [the] profile [it has].
It isn't easy without a long historical recounting to understand the roots of so
much incomprehension."[1]

His last word referred to the peculiar political intolerance that accompanied
the rapid economic growth of the Cuban enclave. In Miami, an appearance by
Jane Fonda had led to a boycott and a series of threatening calls to Burdines, the
sponsor of her visit and the region's largest department store. Latin American
artists who had visited Cuba at some point or another were barred from performing at the annual Calle Ocho Carnival. And the Miami City Commission
permitted the Haitian community to celebrate the investiture of Haitian president Father Jean-Bertrand Aristide only provided Fidel Castro was not invited
to the home-country ceremony in Port-au-Prince.

As the Cuban community gained political power it imposed a monolithic
outlook on the city, often with little regard for the concerns and interests of
other segments of the population. A play by a New York–based Cuban writer
suspected of being sympathetic to the regime in the island had to be removed

from the program of the Miami Theater Festival after the organizers received numerous local threats. A Cuban businessman defended the protesters' point of view:

> When so many persons have been affected by communism, when so many had to abandon the land in which they were born, when people could not visit the cemeteries where their loved ones rest, we do have to protest this kind of thing. Why not? Why do they have to impose on us such a painful thing? A person who has not suffered, who has not had relatives killed, can say coolly that there must be freedom of expression. We know better. It is too hard that they come here, to our center, to tell us these things.

The play in question did not have much to do with conditions in Cuba, nor did it defend the regime. The exiles' objections were exclusively to the assumed political sympathies of the author. The expression *our center* in the above testimony encapsulated the belief that Miami was, above all, the capital of the Other Cuba. But other segments of the city resented the exiles' political intolerance. The *Miami Herald*, in particular, waged a relentless campaign against what it saw as the rising power of the Cubans and the threat that they posed to civic freedoms. Even before the Mariel confrontation, the paper castigated on numerous occasions the exile community's extremism.

During the 1970s, such attacks could be made with impunity, but after the exile community became organized for domestic political action in the aftermath of Mariel, the story changed. This is what the Cuban-American National Foundation had to say about the *Herald*'s campaign in a full-page paid advertisement, published in the *Herald* in 1987:

> All our achievements have been accomplished with a national press coverage that has often portrayed us as extremists. This has been the most unfair and prejudiced perception we have experienced in America. . . . The *Miami Herald* bears tremendous responsibility for this injustice. . . . The *Miami Herald* is aggressive in its ignorance of our people. It refuses to understand that Cuban Americans see the struggle between totalitarianism and democracy as a personal, ever-present struggle. We live the struggle daily because our friends and families enslaved in Communist Cuba live it daily.

As the enclave economy grew, so did the reach of this distinct political perspective, one that set the refugees sharply apart from the fairly liberal views of American journalism. The Cubans saw themselves as more militant in their defense of American values, more aware of the perils surrounding them, than the laid-back natives. The popular radio station wQBA, La Cubanísima (The "Cubanest"), for example, greets its listeners every day with this refrain: "It's noontime. Let us give thanks to God for living in a country of full liberty and democracy."

Anglo Miamians who cared to listen reacted to such fervor with alarm, if not scorn. The effect was to sharpen the contours of the refugee community and increase its internal solidarity. Little Havana is no mere immigrant neighborhood, not even a lively business hub, but a moral community with its own distinct outlook on the world. If from the outside the exiles' political discourse appeared as raving intolerance, from the inside it helped define who was and was not a true member of the community. To be a Miami Cuban, it does not suffice to have escaped from the island; one must also espouse points of view repeated ceaselessly by editorialists in Miami's Spanish radio and press—the same voices that take care of denouncing any member of the community who strays too far from the fold.

The political fallout of this ferocious right-wing frame has been generally negative with regard to the exiles' outside image, but its economic consequences are enviable. The consolidation of a moral community permeated imperceptibly the relationships between buyer and seller, lender and borrower, employer and worker in the ethnic enclave. A heightened sense of "we-ness" clarified the limits to which bounded solidarity would apply, while intensifying its hold. Cuban refugees bought from each other and sponsored each other's businesses to an extent seldom seen among Latin immigrant groups. Membership in this community defined, to a large extent, who was eligible for business loans and who was not. "Cubanness" by itself did not suffice.

Union organizers similarly reported that whereas Cuban workers in mainstream firms would join unions, the same workers in Cuban-owned firms would be next to impossible to organize. The adversarial union-management relationship appeared inimical to the bond between workers and owners created by a common past and common political outlook. For this reason, firms like Diego Suárez's Inter-American Transport could remain indefinitely union free.

If the exiles' political discourse had been more tolerant and less militant, it probably would not have been as effective in reinforcing the social capital on which their collective business advancement was cemented. The sense of having the truth but few allies with whom to share it strengthened considerably the moral bonds and self-reliance of this community: Cubans were in America, but not really of it, even after becoming U.S. citizens. Many feared that their situation and current well-being would be jeopardized by the moral laxity with which the nation's leaders were conducting the fight against communism. The following excerpt from a query by a Hialeah resident was published in *El Nuevo Herald*, the Miami Herald's Spanish-language edition, in 1988:

Hundreds of Cubans live in fear after the changes in the Immigration Law following the Pact between Mikhail Gorbachev and the government of the United States with regard to Fidel Castro.

I have been in the U.S. for twenty-five years. I am married and have children. My wife and I have been American citizens for fifteen years. My question is this: If we were deported to Cuba as a consequence of this Pact, would we still have a right to our Social Security pensions? Our children were born in this country, could we still have some rights as retirees with their consent?

It had never occurred to this old Cuban that U.S. citizenship would protect him from deportation, even if the U.S. government came to an understanding with Castro and the Soviets.

Origins of the Moral Community

There is a Black-Cuban element in this dispute and there has been since 26 June. That's the day that Mayors Gilda Oliveros of Hialeah Gardens, José Rivero of Sweetwater, Pedro Reboredo of West Miami, Julio Martínez of Hialeah, and Xavier Suárez of Miami signed a letter unwelcoming Nelson Mandela. "We, Cuban-Americans . . ." it said. With these words, the five mayors made this in part a Cuban issue.

The episode in question occurred in the summer of 1990, a few days before Nelson Mandela's arrival in Miami. The hero's welcome planned for the South African leader quickly turned into indifference and then opposition following acknowledgment of his friendship with Fidel Castro during an ABC television interview. Over the strenuous objections of Black community leaders, the Cuban-American mayors "uninvited" Mandela. Although the South African came to Miami only for a brief speech at a union convention and never accepted any local invitation, the mayors' action profoundly hurt the sensitivities of Miami's Black community. Black leaders responded by declaring a boycott of their own city, asking outside conventioneers not to come to Miami until the mayors formally apologized to Mandela.

None of them did. To have done so would have been tantamount to losing the next election. Political power in these cities rested with Cuban, not Black voters, and the exile community was monolithic in its repudiation of anyone having anything to do with Fidel Castro. Although the Black boycott could easily have been prevented with a minor gesture of conciliation, elected Cuban-American politicians were unable to take that step. Any sign of an apology would have been immediately denounced by the Spanish radio stations as un-Cuban and a sign of weakness in the face of the enemy.

Where did this fierce Rightism come from? It was not a foregone conclusion that escapees from Castro's leftist regime would move to the opposite end of the political spectrum. Indeed, the dominant political viewpoint among exiles during the days of active military struggle in the early sixties was very different: the revolution, embodying the legitimate aspirations of the Cuban people, had been betrayed by Castro and his henchmen; the fight, therefore, was to get them out in order to restore the country's constitution, organize free elections, and promote economic growth with social equality—in all, a social democratic or at least mildly centrist stance.

Three successive events undermined this position and opened the way for the hegemony of extreme right-wing politics. First, the exiles' Assault Brigade 2506 was trained and financed by the CIA only to be abandoned to its fate at the Bay of Pigs. The decision to leave the men stranded, which directly contradicted earlier guarantees made by the U.S. government, was taken by the liberal Kennedy administration. The exiled leaders duped by these promises were also, by and large, members of the old liberal and centrist wing of Cuban politics.

Even after the Bay of Pigs, these leaders still heeded the promises of the White House; one year later, however, the Kennedy-Khrushchev accord during the Missile Crisis put an end to all hopes. The military deactivation of the Cuban community was a liberal Democratic feat, and the exile leaders who had tolerated it were of a similar political persuasion. Shortly after the Missile Crisis, the head of the Cuban Revolutionary Council, José Miró Cardona, resigned in protest, and the council, the exiles' umbrella organization, was disbanded.

There was one more chance for Cuban progressives to prevail as the moral watchdogs of the exile community. It took the form of an organization built by former revolutionary leaders and militants and led by an ex-minister of one of Castro's first cabinets, Manuel Ray Rivero. They called themselves the People's Revolutionary Movement (Movimiento Revolucionario del Pueblo, or MRP) and for a long time maintained their distance from the CIA-supported Cuban Revolutionary Council, which they saw as excessively centrist and pro-American. The MRP reaffirmed the theme of the "revolution betrayed" and sought the overthrow of the regime through internal mobilization and the support of friendly Latin American governments. In the end, however, financial need forced Ray and his followers to accept covert U.S. support for their plans to launch a new invasion of the island. As with the Bay of Pigs three years before, political expediency again prevailed and the civil wing of Lyndon Johnson's Democratic administration betrayed its new clients. British authorities were notified as to the location of the would-be invaders in a Bahamian key, and Ray and his group were easily apprehended.

The ignominious end of the MRP and the repeated betrayals of exile aspirations by Democratic Party leaders in Washington paved the way for extreme-right elements to occupy center stage in Miami. Formerly discredited Batista supporters reemerged from the shadows with a claim to political foresight. "We told you so," they proclaimed; "Fidel has always been a communist, and his comrades of yesterday like Ray are not much better." Along with other conservatives, they forged a coherent interpretation of the exiles' plight. For them, the revolutionary triumph in the island had not been the result of social inequality or political oppression, because Cuba before Castro was already a quasi-developed country with enviable standards of living and economic opportunities for all. Rather, Castro's triumph was the result of an international communist conspiracy. The Cuban people had been deceived by Castro and his clique and then betrayed again by fellow travelers who had infiltrated the liberal Democratic establishment in the United States.

Liberalism, according to this view, was nothing more than a convenient disguise, a front for communist objectives. Accordingly, leftists of all stripes had to be resolutely opposed; intransigent anticommunism was the only valid position for the exile community. This discourse had two significant advantages. First, it absolved earlier Cuban governments, including Batista's, of all responsibility for the ascent of Fidel Castro to power. Second, it provided a coherent interpretation for the immensely depressing fact that the U.S. government had repeatedly abandoned its fervent Caribbean allies at key moments in their struggle. Communist influence was everywhere, even at the highest levels of the American government. Cubans, who had suffered in their own flesh the consequences of such deceit, had the mission of opposing it everywhere and alerting others as to its terrible consequences.

The Cuban liberal discourse, labeled by the conservatives "Fidelism without Fidel," simply disappeared from view. It had always had a difficult time reconciling its progressive claims with militant opposition to the Cuban Revolution. For left-leaning intellectuals and politicians in Latin America and for liberal academics in the United States, Fidel Castro symbolized the anti-imperialist struggle. His defiance in the face of Yankee hostility gained him much sympathy, which exiled liberals were hard put to counteract. In contrast, the conservative discourse was exceedingly coherent: since all these liberal academics and politicians were communist sympathizers anyway, there was no point in trying to persuade them on the appalling facts of the matter.

Instead, Cubans should line up with militant anticommunist forces and seek their support to liberate the island.

The hegemony of extreme conservatism did not emerge all of a sudden but evolved gradually, growing in tandem with the business enclave. The two developments thus became intertwined, with militant Rightism coming to define the vocabulary in which exile entrepreneurs expressed their views and with which they signaled membership in the bounded Cuban community. Even those who took exception to the extremist views aired ceaselessly on local radio had to keep their doubts to themselves for fear of the consequences. The moral community had taken firm hold, and its ideological trappings were unmistakably those of the far right, a direct outgrowth of the failed liberal promises of the early sixties.

Notes

For complete references and notes, consult the work as cited in the acknowledgment of copyrights section.

1. *Eds. note*: bracketed text is in the original.

Singing for Nicaragua

Silvio Rodríguez

Cuban internationalism has also been expressed in its music. In 1980 Silvio Rodríguez (b. 1946) wrote "Canción urgente para Nicaragua" (An urgent song for Nicaragua) using traditional Nicaraguan country rhythm and style, affirming Cuban solidarity with the 1979 revolution there, and alluding directly to the evil designs of "the eagle" — the United States — for Latin America. Unlike most of his music, which is notable for its multilayered complexities, this song is simple, direct, and explicitly political: the song is "urgent," the revolution is recently victorious and the United States is threatening.

AN URGENT SONG FOR NICARAGUA

In Nicaragua another branding iron
that the eagle once used
for imposing its will on the people
has been shattered.

In Nicaragua another rope
the eagle used
to tie the worker by the neck
has been broken.

The grass has been set on fire
all over the continent
the borders kiss each other
and catch fire.

I remember a man
who was dying for this
and seeing this day
—like a ghost from the mountain—
he laughed jubilantly.

The ghost is Sandino
with [Simón] Bolívar and Che [Guevara]
because the three of them walked
the same road.

These three walkers
with the same fate
have now become giants
they've outwitted death.

Now the eagle has
its greatest pain
Nicaragua hurts it
because love hurts it.

And it hurts it to see a healthy child
going to school,
because with that kind of wood
of justice and tenderness
it can't sharpen its spurs.

Nicaragua will go along
its way in glory
because it was wise blood
that wrote its history.

A brother tells you this
who has bled with you
a Cuban tells you this
a friend tells you this.

TRANSLATED BY AVIVA CHOMSKY

Cuban Medical Diplomacy

Julie Feinsilver

In Healing the Masses: Cuban Health Politics at Home and Abroad, *Julie Feinsilver argues that "medical diplomacy" has been a key element in Cuban foreign policy. Developing a health care system that provided access for the entire population, and the concomitant dramatic decrease in the infant mortality rate and increase in average life span, both of which rival the levels of First World countries, have been important points of pride and legitimacy for the revolution. Feinsilver's study shows the extraordinary commitment of Cuban health resources abroad as well, and the moral, ideological, and political implications of this commitment.*

Medical diplomacy has been overlooked in analyses of Cuban foreign policy, yet it has been an integral part of almost all the cooperation and aid agreements that Cuba has used historically to strengthen diplomatic ties with other Third World countries. Dozens of countries have received long-term Cuban medical assistance, and many others have received short-term aid in response to specific emergencies. Cuban medical aid affects millions of Third World people annually through the direct provision of medical care, and thousands annually through medical education and training programs both in Cuba and abroad. The positive impact of this aid on the health of Third World populations has vastly improved Cuba's relations with other countries and has increased Cuba's symbolic capital among governments, international organizations, and intellectuals who, in the Third World, often play an important role in the formation of public opinion and public policy.

Cuba has been particularly adept at using medical diplomacy to further its political and economic objectives and accumulate symbolic capital. Medical diplomacy or "collaboration between countries on health matters for the purposes of improving relations with one another . . . [produces] humanitarian benefit while simultaneously developing improved relations." Because all peoples consider health necessary for personal as well as societal development, medical aid may be a more effective foreign policy instrument than other, more traditional, ones.

Domestic success in the medical field led the Cuban leadership to capital-ize on accumulated symbolic capital and to make health an important part of its foreign policy. Since 1963 Cuba has provided civilian assistance to many Third World countries, despite its own economic difficulties. This assistance has taken the form of direct medical care and medical education both in the host country and in Cuba; donation of equipment, medicines, and supplies; disaster relief; epidemic control and epidemiological monitoring; facility con-struction; organizational, administrative, and planning advice; scientific re-search and exchanges; vaccination and health-education campaigns; and pro-gram design for both the development of human resources and the provision of specific medical services, among other things. Early cooperation agreements were bilateral, but over time Cuba also became a party to multilateral aid agreements and began to provide assistance to other Third World countries under the auspices of various United Nations agencies and regional organiza-tions.

The first beneficiary was Premier Ahmed Ben Bella's newly independent Algeria, to which Cuba sent a group of fifty-six physicians and other health workers for fourteen months in 1963. This was done despite the fact that half of Cuba's physicians emigrated (mostly to the United States) shortly after the revolution, reducing the number of Cuba's physicians from about six thousand to three thousand. Interestingly, this first program of medical assistance was known as the "Plan Fidel," presaging Castro's later daily involvement in and concern for health care. The growth of medical diplomacy and other civilian aid programs increased dramatically beginning in the mid to late 1970s, so much so that Cuba had in 1985 what the *New York Times* called "perhaps the largest Peace Corps style program of civilian aid in the world," with approxi-mately sixteen thousand doctors, teachers, construction engineers, agrono-mists, economists, and other specialists serving in twenty-two Third World countries. In fact, Cuba had more doctors working abroad then (fifteen hun-dred in twenty-five countries) than did WHO.

Throughout the 1980s Cuban foreign policy dictates sent between two thou-sand and three thousand medical workers abroad each year for two-year stints; at least half of them were doctors. In July 1991 over one thousand Cuban doc-tors were donating their services abroad, and up to that date more than ten thousand physicians had done likewise, as had another twenty thousand other health workers. These medical personnel have served in over thirty-six coun-tries on three continents, furthered Cuba's foreign policy goals, and contrib-uted significantly to Cuba's symbolic capital.

According to an unsubstantiated but published Cuban source, the global reach of Cuban civilian aid expanded in the five-year period from 1985 to 1990,

"The life of a single human being is worth more, millions of times more, than all of the wealth of the richest man in the world." Hospital, El Vedado, Havana, 2001. Photo by Emily Uddin-Alves.

when Cuba supplied sixty countries with more than forty-six thousand civilian aid workers per year, primarily doctors, teachers, and construction crews. These workers served in thirty-seven African and Middle Eastern countries, thirteen Asian and Oceanian countries, and ten Latin American and Caribbean countries. A Cuban official claimed that over a twenty-five-year period ending in January 1990, more than half a million Cubans provided civilian assistance abroad, a figure equivalent to approximately 10 percent of Cuba's economically active population at that time. These numbers appear to be high in light of other, better-known estimates.

Symbolically even more significant, by January 1985 Cuba had one civilian international aid worker for every 625 inhabitants and by January 1990 one civilian aid worker for every 228 inhabitants. In 1985, on the other hand, the United States had only one Peace Corps or Agency for International Development (AID) worker for every 31,023 inhabitants and in 1990 one for every 35,760 inhabitants. Whereas U.S. Peace Corps workers often work alone, Cubans generally work in teams or brigades, which makes their presence more visible. Moreover, Cuba has often sent more highly skilled personnel than the United States has. According to the Agency for International Development, "In general, the Peace Corps supplies technical assistance at a much lower level in

"A couple's best friend."
Sex education poster in a
family doctor's office. Photo
by Emily Uddin-Alves.

terms of expertise and experience than the technical assistance provided by
other donors."

The large number of international aid workers sent by Cuba compared with
that sent by the United States not only signifies Cuba's emphasis on civilian aid
as a foreign policy tool but also makes Cuba appear to provide more humanitarian aid than the United States despite the latter's much greater financial
assistance. Recognizing this visibility problem, the General Accounting Office
has suggested that the United States decrease the number of projects it finances
and concentrate on larger, more visible ones to improve its image. This visibility problem is particularly important because in the early 1980s, the United
States ranked seventeenth among the eighteen Development Assistance Committee member countries of the Organization for Economic Cooperation and
Development (OECD) in foreign aid as a percentage of gross national product.
By 1988–89 the United States was tied with Ireland for last place, providing
only 0.18 percent of its GNP in development assistance.

Cuba, by contrast, when compared with its former allies and benefactors
in the Soviet Union and eastern Europe, has sent a disproportionately large
number of international economic technicians to developing nations. Cuba
supplied 19.4 percent of the total Soviet, Eastern European, and Cuban eco-

nomic technicians abroad in 1979 . . . yet Cuba's population was only 2.5 percent of the combined populations of these countries. More importantly, Cuba was and still is the least developed of all these countries. Although the USSR and the eastern European countries had more economic technicians abroad than the Cubans, most were contract workers earning hard currency for their countries, whereas most of the Cubans were aid workers. Once again, Cuba demonstrated its commitment to civilian aid as a means of improving its international relations.

Moreover, Cuba's development of doctors as an export commodity is unprecedented. The Soviet Union, the eastern European countries, and China have provided some medical assistance to developing nations, but it has been a small part of their aid programs and they did not train surplus doctors specifically for export as Cuba did. For example, China, the other communist country that has primarily provided aid, had almost four times the number of economic technicians abroad that Cuba did in 1977, but in 1979 Cuba provided slightly more economic technicians than did China. During that two-year interval, China had decreased its aid by 50 percent and Cuba had doubled its aid. In medicine alone, Cuba also far outpaced China in the provision of international aid, sending almost as many health workers abroad from 1983 through 1985 (7,544) as China sent abroad between 1963 and 1986 (8,000). This achievement alone has made Cuba a world medical power in the eyes of many international organization officials and Third World intellectuals and policymakers, and as a result it has contributed substantially to Cuba's symbolic capital.

For complete references and notes, consult the work as cited in the acknowledgment of copyrights section.

VIII

The "Período Especial" and the
Future of the Revolution

Cuba's economy was clearly thrown into crisis with the collapse of the Soviet bloc and the accompanying loss of the trade and aid — in three years the country lost 70 percent of its import capacity. Industry and agriculture, moreover, have been paralyzed by the loss of imported fuel. The Cuban Revolution was built within, and depended on, an international economic order that no longer exists. Yet the revolutionary regime did not disintegrate as many observers, especially Cuban exiles in Miami and elsewhere, expected. Instead, the Cuban Revolution began to reinvent itself, evidence of the revolutionary order's continuing resilience and growing pragmatism under conditions of severe economic and political crisis.

In 1990 the Cuban government declared a "Special Period in Time of Peace" to deal with the national emergency. Since then, the government has carried out a series of economic changes that, at least superficially, resemble the kinds of structural adjustment programs being imposed by the IMF on other Third World countries. Changes have included allowing Cubans access to dollars, and opening state-run "dollar" stores with imported items not available elsewhere, opening farmer's markets where private as well as state farmers can sell to the public, allowing certain types of private enterprise, and seeking foreign investment and tourism. But Cuban economists have termed Cuba's path a "process of creation" that has tried to carry out an adjustment without following traditional IMF prescriptions such as privatization and drastic cutbacks in social services.

The changes that seem to go in the direction of capitalism are the most visible. The Cuban government has made investment in tourism a cornerstone of its economic recovery plan. Hotels, many of them run by joint ventures with Spanish, Italian, Canadian, Mexican, or other foreign capital, are being renovated, and tourists from Canada, Latin America, and Europe are provided with First World luxuries that Cubans have long lived without. Tourism has come to rival sugar as Cuba's primary source of income. Its impact on society has been enormous, and it has ranged from official promotion of Afro-Cuban culture as a tourist attraction, to the restoration of Old Havana, to the growth of tourism-affiliated business including prostitution and drugs, as well as taxicabs, private front parlor restaurants, or *paladares*, and home rentals.

The government has also welcomed foreign investment in other key sectors, such as telecommunications and oil exploration. Over a hundred categories of "self-employment" have been legalized, and Cuban artisans can now privately produce and sell their works, run storefront restaurants, or operate taxis, albeit under a regime of increasingly stringent taxation.

But other economic measures don't fit the pattern of encroaching capitalism. Food rationing, for example, continues to ensure that scarce goods such as milk go to the sectors that most need them: children are still guaranteed milk up to age seven. Health and education continue to be national priorities, and despite scarcities, indicators such as infant and child mortality and life expectancy continue to rival or surpass those of other wealthy industrialized countries, including the United States.

Finally, shortages of hard currency and imported goods have spurred experimentation along "small is beautiful" lines. For several years bicycles largely replaced automobiles on Havana's streets. International experts have hailed the "green experiment" in Cuban agriculture, a sector once highly dependent on imported fuel and pesticides, where now oxen are replacing tractors. City residents are planting backyard gardens and raising their own chickens and pigs. Doctors are experimenting with herbal medicines.

At an aggregate level, these policies have had a certain success; since 1994, the economy has been growing. However, the changes have also brought inequalities that are very painful to Cuban society, where, since the revolution, egalitarianism has been a key social value. Some people have access to dollars (through remittances or through the workplace); others do not. Prices at the farmers' markets are high by Cuban standards, and sellers there—and others who work in the gray or black market—make more than university professors or doctors. Dollars mean access not only to luxuries but also to basics—cooking oil and soap, for instance—that have not been available in the peso economy. Prostitution, begging, and other phenomena not seen since the early years of the revolution have indeed returned, as Cubans seek access to foreigners' dollars.

Although the economic landscape has undergone some dramatic changes, Cuba's political structure remains virtually intact, at least on the surface. Yet there have been some significant changes. The hegemony of the Communist Party is an ever-present reality, but mass mobilization organizations, such as the Committees for the Defense of the Revolution and the Federation of Cuban Women, have lost much of their resilience and relevance to ordinary

Cubans. Religious life has become revitalized both among traditional Catholics and adherents of Afro-Cuban religious traditions. There has been a steady growth in the number of nongovernmental organizations that make up civil society, although the Cuban state still reacts harshly against individuals and associations who reject socialism or are close to exile communities or to the U.S. government.

These and other developments suggest that there has been a decline in the Cuban state's capacity to dictate the direction of social and political debate. They also indicate an expansion of the spaces in which Cubans are attempting to reconcile the market, social solidarity, and the need for activities and debates that are more independent of the state. Yet domestic political change continues to be tightly controlled in Cuba. Although many Cubans are cynical about their government's insistence that U.S. hostility is the primary cause of their economic crisis, and justifies limits on political freedom at home, Washington's actions toward Cuba have continued to play an important role in Cuba's domestic politics. A more open and less aggressive stance in Washington's relations with Cuba is now an indispensable prerequisite for the opening of an entirely new and more democratic phase in the development of the Cuban Revolution.

Silvio Rodríguez Sings of the Special Period

Silvio Rodríguez

With a mixture of irony, pain, hope, and humor, singer-songwriter Silvio Rodríguez (b. 1946) continued to chronicle the revolution in the 1990s, along with the economic and social contradictions that are so ubiquitous now.

The song "Disillusionment" refers to the temptations inherent in the introduction of capitalism, through foreign investment and tourism, into Cuba. If people lose faith in the possibility of constructing a different, better kind of society, he warns, that in itself will contribute to the country's return to the corruption of the 1950s.

In "El necio" Rodríguez reflects on the pressures felt by Cubans, especially well-known Cubans like himself, to defect. If only he would "undefine" himself, he would be admitted into the altars of international commercialism and wealth. Still, an almost religious faith—in the face of apparent evidence to the contrary—that humans are capable of higher, unselfish motives keeps him committed to his vision. The last stanza refers to the fate of revolutionary artists such as Víctor Jara, who was tortured and murdered by the Chilean military after the 1973 coup that overthrew Salvador Allende's socialist government. When Cuba's revolution falls, Rodríguez's imaginary interlocutor suggests, he will suffer the same fate. Nevertheless, he prefers the "foolishness" of faith to the temptations of giving up.

"The Fifties Club" comments on the growing commercialization of Cuban society in the 1990s. As the government became less able to supply citizens' needs, access to the private economy—and to dollars from abroad—became almost a necessity for survival. Here Rodríguez decries not the material scarcities but the moral impoverishment that accompanies competition and materialism.

The song "Flores" (Flowers) refers to the recrudescence of prostitution, especially along the elegant Fifth Avenue of the Miramar neighborhood in Havana, where many foreigners and especially businessmen live or stay in the city's new hotels. Rodríguez seems to sympathize with the spiritual poverty of those—both buyers and sellers—who have turned sex into a commodity.

DISILLUSIONMENT

Like coins
Disillusionment jingles its theme
Disillusionment.
With a red mouth
And big droopy breasts
Disillusionment
Smoking light tobacco
And exhaling alcohol
The owner of the bed embroidered
In underwear.

What frenzy in interrogation
What suicide in investigating
A brilliant fashion show
Disillusionment.

It opened a business
Reviving leisure
Disillusionment.
Like tourism
It invented the abyss
Disillusionment
It touched the diamond
And turned it to coal
And it planted a good-for-nothing
In the administration.

THE FOOL

To keep my icon from being smashed,
To save myself among the few and the odd ones,
To grant me a space in their Parnassus,
To give me a little corner in their altars,
they come to invite me to repent,
they come to invite me not to lose out,
they come to invite me to undefine myself,
they come to invite me to so much bullshit.
I can't say what the future is,
I've always been what I've been,

Only God, up there, is divine.
I will die just as I've lived.

I want to keep on betting on the lost cause,
I want to be with the left hand rather than right,
I want to make a Congress of the united,
I want to pray deeply an "our son."
They'll say that craziness has gone out of fashion,
They'll say that people are evil and don't deserve it,
but I'll leave with my mischievous dreams
(perhaps multiplying bread and fish).
I can't say what the future is,
I've always been what I've been,
Only God, up there, is divine.
I will die just as I've lived.

They say that I'll be dragged over the rocks
when the Revolution comes crashing down,
that they'll smash my hands and my mouth,
that they'll tear out my eyes and my tongue.
It may well be that I'm the child of foolishness,
the foolishness of what today seems foolish:
the foolishness of accepting one's enemy,
the foolishness of living without a price.
I can't say what the future is,
I've always been what I've been,
Only God, up there, is divine.
I will die just as I've lived.

THE FIFTIES CLUB

I arrive at the club of the fifty-year-olds (1950s)
and one hand brings the bill
The sum (addition) calls my attention
from back to my cradle
Every fire, every undertaking [with the implication of something you really
    want to do]
comes with a price tag next to it
in spite of what has been paid.

I wonder what kind of business this is
in which even desire becomes an object of consumption
what will I do when the sun sends its bill?
But I keep turning my face to the east
and order another breakfast [using an Anglicism; that is, the word *order* isn't
     really used like that in Spanish]
in spite of the cost of love.

Let debts and inflation come,
ious, fines, recessions.
Let the pickpocket try to grab
the taste of my bolero.
Whoever the boss may be
Let him charge me diligently
(that cruel hand will find out
when I send him my bill).

FLOWERS

The night flowers of Fifth Avenue open
For those poor gentlemen who go to the hotel
Flowers that break in the darkness
Flowers of winks of complicity
Flowers whistling suicides
Flowers with a fatal aroma

What gardener has sown our Fifth Avenue
With such a precise nocturnal variety
What is their species, what is their country
What fancy fertilizer nourished their root
Giving them a wild tone
Where could their womb be?

Flowers that go through forbidden doors
Flowers that know what I'll never know
Flowers that string their dream of life
In garlands without faith
Flowers of sheets with eyes
Disposable flowers
Doorbells of desire
Flowers eating the leftovers of love

They sprout, they bounce, they explode on our Fifth Avenue
They are pulled up and depart with swift air
They say that a flower's job is hard
When its petals wither in the sun
Pale nocturnal flowers
Flowers of disillusionment.

TRANSLATED BY AVIVA CHOMSKY

Bill Griffith's Zippy Goes to Cuba,
1995 (based on 1994 visit). Zippy
copyright © 1995 Bill Griffith.

Just passing through.

A tour.

A Cuba Libre, please. (A Cuba Libre is rum and cola.)

Tourist attractions.

Can I have the next dance?

Do you have a light?

A room with a view.

A place in the shade.

From Communist Solidarity to Communist Solitary

Susan Eckstein

For Cuban intellectuals, the economic crisis of the Special Period provoked much soul-searching regarding the different economic paths open to the country. To American sociologist Susan Eva Eckstein, however, the economic decisions of the Special Period seem to be guided more by pragmatism than by ideology. In Back from the Future: Cuba under Castro, *Eckstein argues that since the 1970s, Fidel Castro and his advisors have made rational decisions based on the options available to them and have been guided more by a realistic assessment of their options than by blind commitment to theory. Thus in the crisis of the Special Period, Eckstein sees emergency measures drawing on capitalist, socialist, and precapitalist strategies. Eckstein's research was carried out from 1990 to 1993 and published in 1994. Although the statistics have changed (generally for the better), the broad trends that she identifies continue into the twenty-first century.*

Castro responded to the crisis created by the changed world situation by calling, in late 1990, for a "special period in peacetime." The Special Period, a euphemism for a siege economy, involved sacrifices and reforms "to save the revolution." Though "Socialism or Death" became Castro's slogan of the time, policy initiatives drew . . . on features associated with not merely ideal-typical socialist but also capitalist and even precapitalist societies. Noted Castro at a Congress of the Federation of University Students, "This is no time for theorizing but instead for advancing, resisting, and overcoming." With the revolution's future at stake, Carlos Lage, executive secretary of the Council of Ministers in charge of the Special Period economic policy, assumed an importance surpassed only by Fidel (although Raúl remained titularly second in command and next in line).

Socialist-Style Strategies

. . . The government began by promoting an ambitious "Food Program" designed to make the country as self-sufficient as possible and to offset the island's declining import capacity. Here Castro appeared to "revert" to the agricultural diversification strategy he had promoted during his first years in power, a project abandoned within four years because of the balance-of-payments problem it caused. But in contrast to the earlier effort, the new program had decades of experience on which to draw.

The program centered on an expansion of irrigation facilities; an expansion of rice, banana, plantain, root and green vegetable production (partly through irrigation-based increases in land productivity, partly through converting some twenty thousand hectares of land from sugarcane cultivation to vegetable production); fish breeding; fifty new hog-breeding centers; eighteen hundred new poultry sheds; and one thousand new dairies (about two hundred per year). Illustrative of the scope of the program, the new poultry farms were to raise egg and chicken meat production by 10 percent and vegetable production by 50 percent. Yet as Castro admitted with dismay, the project had to be developed without feed, without fertilizer, and almost without fuel, and for these and other reasons its results were disappointing (except for vegetables and tubers).

The Food Program targeted the distributive system as well as production, for about one-third of all crops rotted before reaching consumers. Transport and storage facilities were extremely inadequate. Consequently, the government constructed new distribution centers, storage facilities, and canneries.

Energy conservation was another central component of the Special Period, owing to the massive cutbacks in former Soviet-bloc oil deliveries and the rise in the price charged Cuba. When launching the austerity program, the government reduced petroleum supplies to both the state sector and private consumers by 50 percent, it cut back state investments, and it closed down a number of oil-guzzling factories, most notably cement and nickel plants. It also called for a 10 percent cut in domestic electricity consumption (though, independently of the mandate, power cuts soon became routine). . . .

The launching of the Special Period was also associated with stepped-up rationing, and with gradual reductions over time in official allotments. . . . The government had very deliberately reduced the role of rationing since 1970. However, as goods became scarce it sought, in its own words, "to equalize sacrifice" and to keep goods at prices everyone could afford. Rationing was confined, in the main, to basic necessities. . . .

Without rationing, scarcities would have caused prices to spiral beyond the means of low-income earners. But not one citizen, according to Castro, was

Agromercado (agricultural market), Havana, 2000. Photo by Jackie McCabe.

to go without sustenance. "How could a capitalist country accomplish this?" he asked rhetorically. Special Period rationing, however, followed on the heels of cutbacks already in effect for milk, petroleum, textiles, and kerosene, and on hikes in prices charged for consumer goods, transportation, and electricity just a few years before, in conjunction with "rectification." The new and more draconian austerity measures were largely the direct and indirect result of the near-total collapse of trade with former Soviet bloc countries. Cutbacks in Soviet grain deliveries, for example, meant less grain-based feed for chicken and cattle, and less wheat for bread, although the loss of the Soviet bloc market for citrus meant more fruit for islanders.

However principled government rationing was, people came to spend hours in queues for meager pickings. And they were forced to make numerous trips to stores just to attain their paltry official allotments, because on any one day not all items were available. Under the circumstances shopping became an obsession and caused people to miss work. A family typically spent fifteen hours a week in food lines, the burden of shopping falling disproportionally [*sic*] on women (in 1993, however, it became legal to pay someone to stand in the *colas*, the lines, and time spent in lines stabilized as distribution became better organized and there was less to buy). Although the Family Code specified that spouses were to share housework when wives worked, men continued to leave most family matters to women, even as household responsibilities became more onerous.

Despite the crisis, Castro remained committed to providing social services. He prided himself in speeches for not closing a single school, day-care center, or hospital, and for not leaving a single person destitute. But circumstances led him to call for no expansion of social services and no new housing construction, and to cut food allotments—in quality and quantity—to schools and day-care centers. Said Castro, "If in five years we don't build housing, if that's the price for saving the revolution, then we'll spend five years without building them." . . .

From a comparative vantage point, Cubans could afford no expansion of social services. . . . Cuba offered more low-cost institutional day care than any country in Latin America, and it had the lowest infant mortality and highest life expectancy rates in the region. Moreover, Cuba's primary and secondary school pupil/teacher and enrollment ratios were exceptionally high by Latin American standards at the eve of the Special Period. Yet the lid on social investment followed on the heels of . . . social consumption cutbacks, during the period of "rectification" [after 1986], and the halt in housing construction occurred despite pent-up demand and despite overseas sales of cement. The government gave hard currency exports priority over islanders' needs and wants as its deficit rose.

Not surprisingly, termination of construction projects, plant shutdowns and slowdowns, and investment cutbacks reduced employment opportunities. . . . At first Castro called for a reduction of the work week (but not the workday), to prevent layoffs. Particularly popular was the suspension of work on Saturday. "At worst," he said, "the worker will get more free time but he will never be left out in the street without a job or penniless." "Everyone will be assured of income sufficient to meet his needs." Castro sought to keep Cubans from experiencing the insecurities and destitution that economic recessions had in market economies.

With the contraction of job opportunities the government announced a change in its unemployment policy, which had it gone into effect according to plan would have reintroduced a labor scheme more consonant with an ideal-typical capitalist than ideal-typical socialist society. Workers who lost their jobs were given the right, according to the new policy, to select from three alternative jobs. If they refused the options, they were entitled to unemployment insurance, first for three and later for one month. Previously Castro had placed no limits on unemployment compensation. . . .

While changing compensation regulations the government concealed how pervasive unemployment was. A *Granma* headline in May 1991, for example, denied the problem altogether in noting that "There Is No Unemployment in Cuba." Yet one university professor informed me that about half the labor force in the light-industry sector and about half the workforce in many ministries around that time had been let go.

By 1993 underemployment was much more widespread than unemployment: Cuban economists estimated one-third of the labor force to be underemployed compared to only about 7 percent (in 1989) unemployed. . . .

To meet labor needs in the one sector where the demand for labor increased, agriculture, the government made use of a variety of collective and voluntary work strategies, consistent with socialist and Guevarist strategies previously deployed. For one, it set up agricultural brigades, or *contingentes*. The thirty brigades operating in 1991, with two hundred cadre each, were modeled after the privileged productive Blas Roca construction contingents. And Blas Roca contingents were redirected to agriculture. Contingentes signed up for two-year stints. They were expected to work twelve-hour days, six days a week, as model workers. In return for waiving the historically won labor right to an eight-hour workday, they were rewarded with relatively good living conditions and wages (68 percent above the average wage) and certain control over the work process. Contingentes (in all sectors) were up to 52 percent more efficient than ordinary workers.

Urban volunteers supplemented the work both of contingentes and of the permanent agricultural workforce, especially around Havana. But because they proved to be costly and inefficient, by the end of 1993 they were phased out.

The mobilizations outwardly resembled those of the latter 1960s, which the government had halted for both economic and political reasons. However, the Special Period's voluntary brigades differed in important respects. Most urban workers in the 1990s did not have to cut cane, despised arduous work, and their rural stints were shorter. Also, the mobilizations were much better organized, and they had their attractions. Many of the *campamentos* that housed the volunteers had the ambience of a summer camp, a diversion for city folk who otherwise could not easily get away, given the stringent gas rationing. Further, food at the campamentos was more plentiful than back home, and volunteers might establish informal food-supply networks to draw on subsequently. At the same time, though, the idealism of the 1960s was nowhere to be found. Islanders did not feel that they were helping to construct a utopian communist society, and the government did not try to convince them that they were. . . .

Marketlike Reforms

To "save the revolution" the government also introduced market-type reforms. It did so in both the externally and the domestically oriented sectors.

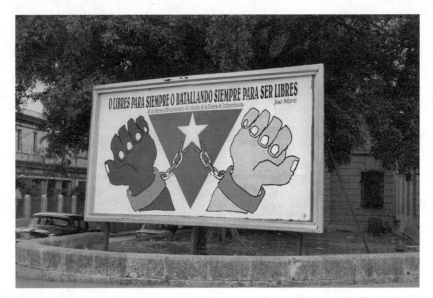

Billboard quoting José Martí: "Either free forever, or forever fighting to be free." Photo by Jackie McCabe.

All trade relations, first and foremost, came to be contracted in hard currency, though not by Cuba's own doing. Cuba, as a consequence, was pressed to develop internationally competitive products and new marketing networks. As of 1991 the island's hard currency exports amounted only to an estimated $3.3 billion. Though a 9 percent increase over the preceding year, they did not begin to compensate for the decline in Soviet-bloc trade and they did not begin to cover import needs; hard currency imports increased 45 percent, and more imports would have been desired.

To compete in the "new world order," Castro courted foreign investment as never before. He publicly defended the "creeping privatization" and economic "denationalization" involved. Said he, the revolution will make no concessions on principles. Capitalists could contribute capital, experience, and markets. "We're not dogmatic, no, we're realistic. . . . We do all this with a practical attitude, we're not violating any principles of socialism." "Capital yes, capitalism no" became the slogan of the day. . . .

Granma, in the process, took on a tone expected of a *Business Week*, not a "vanguard party" newspaper. Stories began to appear almost weekly on potential or actual hard currency deals. Front-page headlines like "Negotiations with Italian Business to Increase" or "Incentives for Mexican Firm in Cuba and Vice Versa" became commonplace.

The government encouraged mainly hard-currency-generating cooperative, or "associated production," agreements, along with joint ventures and marketing deals. . . .

Private foreign investment was courted in nearly all sectors. The government sought foreign investment both for existing as well as new ventures. But the "antediluvian" nature and scale of Soviet bloc–built factories, plus Special Period uncertainties, were disincentives to potential investors. In the main, plants built with Soviet-bloc assistance ran the risk of becoming tombstones of bygone "Communist solidarity." To offset such obstacles, the government exempted investors from compliance with labor laws, and it allowed for unlimited profit repatriation for up to ten years. The government also agreed to bear construction and infrastructural costs.

Foreign ownership crept up not only from zero to 49 percent, in compliance with the 1982 Investment Code, but in some instances to majority ownership. Accordingly, both labor and the government were "squeezed," to "save socialism." The CTC, the labor confederation, supported the economic restructuring. It did not, at least publicly, contest the concessions workers were called upon to make. As in the past, it took the *oficialista* position.

Foreign investment concentrated in the hard-currency-earning sector. . . . The main initial sector to attract investment was tourism. Billed as an "industry without smokestacks," the government hoped its beautiful beaches would generate even more hard currency than in the latter 1980s. The sector grossed an estimated $500 million in 1992 and $700 million the following year, up from $200 million in 1989. Cubanacán boasted 100 percent returns to investments in five years. Over 424,000 tourists came, and the government aimed to more than double the number by the mid-1990s. However, the government netted no more than half of gross earnings, and the sector was import-intensive.

Sociedades anónimas (SAS), such as Cubanacán, aggressively promoted foreign investment in tourism. Cubanacán also sought foreign hotel management contracts. Designed to ensure quality management, the contracts (along with foreign investor rights to repatriate profits) cut further into the money Cuba made from such ventures. At the same time, Cubanacán diversified its involvements, indicative of the new role SAS had begun to assume in the latter 1980s. Aside from building hotels and related infrastructure, it organized conventions, managed restaurants and shops, and operated taxis, rent-a-car services, and tours. It also developed import enterprises and represented twenty-seven foreign firms whose products it promoted, while continuing to serve since the latter 1980s as the exclusive exporter of certain medicines and to export some other products on a smaller scale.

But other sectors attracted foreign investment as well. Cuba negotiated production-sharing contracts with French, Brazilian, Swedish, and Canadian firms for offshore oil exploration, with Italian, Spanish, and Latin American companies to retool the steel industry (the private Cuban bank, Banco Financiero, also becoming a shareholder in the steel enterprise, Siderúrgica Acinox), and with a Canadian firm to develop the nickel industry. The state also contracted Benetton, of Italy, to set up hard currency clothing stores. Desperate for capital and people with entrepreneurial talent, the government even talked of allowing Cuban-American investment. . . .

In its drive to attract tourists the government played on the image of the "old Havana." Three of the main Cuban organs that operate resorts—Cubatur, Cubanacán, and Cimex—hosted a Playboy trip around the time the Special Period was launched. The government allowed the magazine to feature an article on the "girls of Cuba," contingent on coverage of the island's tourist facilities. Even the Ministry of Tourism began to run travel advertisements abroad featuring string bikini–clad sexy Cuban girls. If that were not enough, in 1991 the government opened a Tropicana nightclub in Santiago de Cuba, a club capitalizing on the name of Havana's most famous prerevolutionary nightspot. The government's interest in hard currency led it to play on its prerevolutionary reputation and to reverse its earlier puritanical stance on such matters. . . .

Tourism contributed to an officially sanctioned two-tier economy. Cubans referred to the disparity between the high life of tourists and their own austere, declining standard of living as economic apartheid. Foreign tourists, who frequented dollar restaurants and dollar stores and used dollar taxis, ate food and used transportation that Cubans could not, and they spent no time in queues for goods and services. The government's need for hard currency led it not only to reverse its initial puritanical antitourist stance but also to give foreigners preferential treatment. . . .

In its aggressive pursuit of convertible currency, the government expanded dollar stores that sold food, clothing, and other items. Initially it only allowed tourists and other foreigners to patronize the stores, though they could shop for islanders not permitted to hold dollars. In mid-1993, however, the government decriminalized islanders' possession of dollars. Since then, Cubans have been able to shop on their own in special stores, the government thereby appropriating hard currency that until then had been illegally circulating in the economy. . . .

While remaining publicly committed to "equality of sacrifice," Cubans with close ties to émigrés were the main beneficiaries, along with tourist-sector workers, of the dollar stores. Émigré contacts became a major material asset in other ways as well. On visits to Cuba exiles brought suitcases full of consumer goods for their island relatives, whom they also gave money (the remittances

Artisans' market for tourists, in dollars, Havana, 2000. Photo by Emily Uddin-Alves.

estimated to exceed net tourist earnings). Émigrés who never struck it rich in the United States complained of how expensive it was to visit their Cuban kin. No longer were exiles a source of political disgrace, the *gusanos* [lit., worms; a derogatory term applied to exiles who have allied themselves politically with the U.S. attempts to undermine or overthrow the revolution] of the early revolutionary years. . . .

Along with tourism, the government promoted biotechnology for hard currency. Initially the sector was developed without foreign investment, but foreign support came to be important for the overseas marketing of products. No other country, with the possible exception of Japan, assigned such high priority to biotechnology. Exports of the sumptuous Center of Genetic Engineering and Biotechnology rose from zero in 1988 to an estimated $800 million two years later. In 1991 the center received the National Export Prize, a prize introduced that year to encourage export excellence. Products of the center and other research institutes came to include epidermal growth factor (which helps to regenerate skin), a drug (PPG) that washes cholesterol out of the blood, and meningitis and hepatitis B vaccines. . . .

In the early 1990s, Cuban economists were optimistic about biotechnology's future prospects. In 1991 the sector was self-financing, and it generated capital for its own development. However, purchases from the former Soviet Union became unpredictable, and export prospects were constrained by international competition and the oligopolistic nature of the international pharma-

Restoration in Old Havana, 2000. Photo by Emily Uddin-Alves.

ceutical market, by difficulties in marketing products in countries that recognized U.S., European, and Japanese patents, and by Cuba's weak marketing skills. Under the circumstances the island's best hope for developing the sector rested not in fighting but in allying with its overseas competitors, through joint ventures.

The government, meanwhile, did not neglect traditional commodity exports for hard currency. Shortages of fuel, fertilizers, and spare parts, combined with labor demoralization and adverse weather conditions, however, made the eight-million-ton sugar yields of the 1980s a matter of history and the projected eleven to fourteen million tons for the 1990s an unfulfilled utopian dream. The 1992 harvest yielded seven million tons, the 1993 harvest only 4.2 million tons. The 1993 drop cost Cuba about $500 million in hard currency, equivalent to 1992 tourism earnings. The harvest had not been so low in three decades. But the problem with sugar was not merely the volume; it was also the value the commodity commanded in the world market. Castro referred to the price as the "garbage heap of the world market" (nine cents per pound in 1991 and 1992, and only slightly higher in 1993). In the fall of 1992 he claimed the purchasing power of sugar to be at its all-time post-1959 low: a ton of sugar being worth 1.4 tons of oil, in contrast to 7.5 tons thirty years earlier. Cuba had to spend half to two-thirds of its sugar earnings to import about half as much oil as just a few years earlier, when not dependent on world market dealings.

Meanwhile, hard currency nickel export earnings improved, though not to the point that they offset Soviet-bloc purchasing losses. The island's hard currency export potential continued to be jeopardized by U.S. pressure on other countries, along with the Soviet Union, not to purchase the Cuban mineral.

The government also promoted nonsugar farm exports. To do so it opened the sector to foreign investment, though not land ownership. A joint citrus venture with a group of Chilean companies, considered a model for other investors, centered on the modernization of pack houses, new machinery, improved packing, and worker training. Cuba had the potential of becoming a leading world citrus producer, but Castro had in years past failed to break into hard currency markets. The country had, by default not design, relied almost exclusively on sales to Soviet-bloc countries—where the quality of products did not have to be internationally competitive.

While relying increasingly on foreign investment, technology, and markets, Castro portrayed foreign capital as the source of island problems, as well as the basis of their solution. He was quick to blame, for example, the March 1993 "storm of the century," estimated to have caused a billion dollars in damage, on "capitalism, imperialism, and consumer society" and their environmental effects. Here Castro incorporated the growing international concern with environmental matters into his political discourse, just as he capitalized on that concern in the development of the tourist sector. . . .

The "market opening" also affected the organization of work. In the tourist sector not only were foreign managers entitled to fire workers; workers in the sector also became eligible for new bonuses, tied to the quality of the services they provided. Moreover, in the prime tourist area, Varadero, the government allowed workers . . . to retain tips (though they were to share them collectively).

In turn, in agriculture the government offered material incentives as never before. It paid Havana residents who committed themselves to work two years in agriculture more than four hundred pesos a month, the top of the state's wage scale; it extended bonus payments to farmers who exceeded average deliveries to the state; it initiated yield-related wages in sugar, rice, pig, and dairy farming, and an across-the-board 20 percent productivity bonus; it raised the average wage paid farm workers to the point that they no longer were the poorest-paid sector; and it raised the amount it paid for produce sold to the official collection agency. Although these measures increased government expenditures at a time of fiscal belt-tightening, they were designed to improve farm production and productivity, address subsistence needs, and, where possible, generate much-needed export earnings. "You can't have agricultural workers," conceded Castro, "unless you pay them adequate wages, unless they are properly taken care of, unless they have homes and day-care centers for their children." Castro recognized that if moral incentives did not work in the 1960s, a time of idealism, then they would not work now.

The government, meanwhile, transformed thousands of its holdings into cooperatives with unprecedented autonomy. It rescinded control over land use and labor, as well as revenue appropriation, to minimize its costs and losses at a time of crisis. The cooperatives received few subsidies. (By contrast, the cooperative moment of the 1970s and 1980s had targeted private independent farms.)

Castro even hinted at incentives for all workers "who do more, and a little less in the rationing card to those who do less." A subsistence threat was a far cry from the 1960s utopian communist principle of rewarding people "according to need."

Castro also became more tolerant of domestically oriented private economic activity. The 1991 Party Congress, as detailed below, relegalized private family-based service work, and the government authorized private pig breeding in Havana Province (though, in principle, for family consumption, not commercialization). Pork is Cubans' favorite meat, and a source of much-loved lard. Said Castro in a speech before the National Assembly, "We've declared a general amnesty for pigs." The measure was designed to help people supplement the paucity of rationed meat and undermine a huge black market in pork that had developed. Some fifteen thousand people reportedly bought pigs within days after the authorization. Pig raising until then, however, had been outlawed not merely because it was inconsistent with "socialist principles" but also because it was considered a health hazard; the crisis therefore led the government to sacrifice health and not just ideological principles.

The government "conceded" to contained private activity partly in response to "popular pressure"; but it did so also in recognition that the private sector succeeded at times where the state sector did not. The government even turned to the private sector for advice. In 1991 high-yield farmers received certificates accrediting them as advisers for the Council of Ministers' committee for the Food Program. They were to serve as consultants. As of 1991 private farmers still accounted for over half the bean, tobacco, and garden vegetable production, though for under 20 percent of all cane and citrus production. There remained 144,000 private farmers on 22 percent of the cultivated land and 34 percent of the pastureland. They concentrated on labor-intensive crops where they continued to have a comparative advantage relative to state farms. . . .

Finally, remaining state enterprises were encouraged to adapt new marketlike features. The government introduced, in early 1991, a profit-sharing scheme in about one hundred enterprises that had previously been applied in

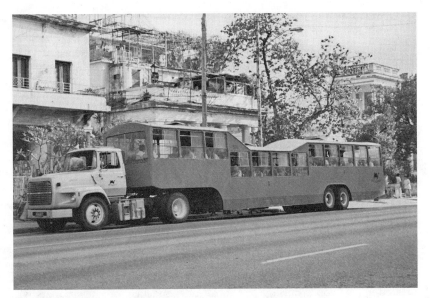

"Camel-hump" bus. Havana, 2000. Photo by Jackie McCabe.

enterprises run by the armed forces. The scheme involved higher earnings for increased output at the enterprise, not the individual, level. And self-financing, especially in hard currency, became the order of the day for about one-fourth of all enterprises (as of 1993). In conjunction with the self-financing mandate, the government allowed firms to negotiate trade deals on their own. Even academic and sports institutes became mini hard currency hustlers, marketing publications and services in convertible currency markets.

Precapitalist Survival Strategies

Castro also "reverted" to precapitalist-type strategies to deal with the crisis. He did so in a variety of ways, at the level of discourse as well as policy. He went so far as to plan "Option Zero," the survival strategy to be pursued under conditions of total economic isolation.

Castro, for example, turned to nineteenth-century symbolism to legitimate Special Period reforms. He portrayed the Special Period as but one additional struggle in the country's long history — dating back to the struggle for national independence — to control its destiny. In speech after speech Castro portrayed the country's independence and not merely the revolution and socialism to be at stake. A speech commemorating the anniversary of the Bay of Pigs invasion was indicative:

We will tell the imperialists, no, you can't do what you want with us! . . . And if we have to put up with material deprivation we will put up with it, because we can never forget that those who began our independence struggle spent ten years in the woods . . . and when some of them got tired and thought that it was impossible to fight under such difficult conditions . . . and wanted the Zanjón Pact's peace without independence, [Antonio] Maceo said "No!" And along with Maceo, the best representatives of that heroic people said "No!" and the eternal Baraguá Protest was born to confront the Zanjón Pact. That is who we are: the heirs of Maceo, the heirs of Baraguá, the heirs of Martí. . . .

Castro made use of historical symbolism to justify policies both reformist and restrictive in nature. He drew an analogy between austerity measures caused by cutbacks in Soviet imports and the country's nineteenth-century independence struggle. When the once superpower slashed newsprint deliveries, Castro proclaimed that "even if it were like the times of *El Cubano Libre*, printed in the woods during the war of independence, our newspapers will keep coming out, even if it's just one page once a week."

Farmers, meanwhile, were required to substitute manual labor and draft animals for the mechanized equipment the government had proudly manufactured and made available to state farms and cooperatives since the 1970s. The national leadership aimed to harvest 70 percent of the sugar crop by hand in 1993, the very percentage it had succeeded in mechanizing in a twenty-year drive. The machinery required petroleum now better reserved, in its view, for other purposes. Farmers of all crops were pressed, in turn, to weed manually again, once Soviet-bloc pesticides stopped arriving. Here too Castro made virtue of necessity, pointing out how much better the "new" methods were for the environment—and here too Castro incorporated contemporary international environmental discourse into his seemingly "hard-line" Communist orthodoxy. He went on to tell the National Assembly in March 1993 that the revolution and socialism had to be saved with a machete in hand, with lathes to make spare parts, and with hoes for weeding.

The crisis, moreover, contributed to deindustrialization, by default not design—to an unraveling both of Castro's "History Will Absolve Me" and of Che's industrial developmental vision. Nearly half of all factories were shut down or forced to operate on a much reduced scale, for lack of imported raw materials, spare parts, and petroleum. Until the . . . Mexican joint venture, the textile and apparel industry, for example, had come to a complete standstill. Cement, nickel, construction material, and chemical plants, among others, that the Soviets had helped build were hit by the drastic cutback in Soviet (and then CIS [Commonwealth of Independent States]) imports, by irregularities in deliveries, and by the exodus of some twelve hundred technicians in 1990. And the opening of the nearly completed Soviet-assisted nuclear power plant was put on hold when Moscow insisted on hard currency payments. Though controversial, the plant was expected to have lowered oil import needs by 1.2 million tons a year. Cuba had invested around $1.2 billion of its own in the project, a project that Raúl Castro acknowledged stood like an abandoned Egyptian pyramid. . . .

For transportation people had to turn to bicycles in place of buses, trucks, and cars. The government purchased a million two-wheelers from China, which it sold to students for sixty pesos and to workers for 120 pesos. By the close of 1992 *habaneros*, as Havana residents are called, relied on bicycles for one-third of all their trips; about half of all households had one or more bikes, mainly acquired since the start of the Special Period; and one-fourth of all bicycle owners used their two-wheelers to commute to and from work. The government, deciding that bicycles would be the mode of transportation "of the future," set up among the few new factories five that were to produce half a million two-wheelers within five years. And for transport of goods the government aimed to replace half the truck fleet with sixty thousand Chinese cargo tricycles. Symbolic of the transportation mode "of the future," the armed forces began to ride bicycles in the annual May Day parade.

Granma referred to bicycle use as the "transportation revolution," and the government organized an international bicycle conference in 1993 which it called "Bikes: Vehicle for the Twenty-first Century." Bicycling, the leadership claimed, was good both for islanders and for the environment. It guaranteed "health for all" and contributed to a modern "ecotopia" by not polluting. "We've entered the bicycle era," noted Castro, "but after this Special Period disappears we mustn't abandon this wonderful custom because of what it means to our health." Here too Castro drew on contemporary industrial-country discourse.

The transportation "revolution" created new problems while reducing dependence on oil-guzzling cars and buses. Bike riding increased people's appetites just when food became more scarce. With bikes in short supply, theft of two-wheelers also rose, and people were angered over having to carry their forty-eight-pound mode of transport up flights of stairs to their offices and apartments for security purposes.

Horse-drawn carriages even became "fashionable." They carried people who could not bike, and were used for cargo transport and rubbish collection. The main newspaper reported that in Bayamo, in Granma Province, nine million people used such carriages for travel in 1992. . . .

Meanwhile, the government, which had aimed to become a "world medical power," exhorted the ill to make use of "grandmother remedies." Doctors were encouraged to prescribe such cures, and even to grow their own supplies. Modern university–trained doctors, a source of revolutionary pride, were to transform themselves, when possible, into old-fashioned medicine men (and women). The government urged islanders to rely on traditional herbal cures at the same time that it assigned high priority to the production of pharmaceuticals for export. As it sought to address its own hard currency needs, islanders were left without such basic medicines as aspirin.

For complete references and notes, consult the work as cited in the acknowledgment of copyrights section.

The Revolution Turns Forty

Saul Landau

Over the years the revolution has brought a large number of foreign observers and com-
mentators to the island. One of the most frequent visitors is the U.S. filmmaker and
journalist Saul Landau, who has been documenting the Cuban Revolution since its
earliest years. In this extract from an article published on the fortieth anniversary of
the revolution, Landau, a friendly but increasingly critical observer of the Cuban scene,
provides a series of vivid glimpses of a Cuba transformed by nearly a decade of Special
Period policies. Like most observers, Landau is struck by the myriad ways in which
dollarization and the expansion of individual enterprise have upset the revolution-
ary landscape, devaluing the status of revolutionary elites and creating new oppor-
tunities for entrepreneurial individuals. Landau holds the Hugh O. La Bounty Chair
of Interdisciplinary Applied Knowledge at California State Polytechnic University in
Pomona.

As the Aerocaribe DC-9 began to descend into Havana forty-five minutes after
it took off from Cancún, I had an acute sense of déjà vu. It was almost thirty-
nine years since my first visit to revolutionary Cuba. Up until the last few years,
I returned to the island regularly to document the story of Fidel Castro's revolution. I'd landed on the old Havana airstrip countless times. This time when
I arrived I was jolted out of my reverie by the new, European-looking airport,
complete with decorative plastic bars crisscrossed under the ceiling, a newly
tiled floor, and vast spaces for travelers. . . .

The young, rash, and absolutely zany revolution that I first knew in 1960
has turned forty.

The cab driver is guarded for the first five minutes, until he satisfies himself that I am neither a fanatic Fidelista nor a government informant. Then he
talks freely. An economist for more than twenty years, he drives a tourist taxi
because "it pays better. I have three kids, you know."

We stop at a light in front of an ad for foreign products—something new in
the last few years, although the road still passes signs covered in revolutionary

slogans as well. "Nothing changes here," he declares. "Very peculiar to live in a revolutionary society that stays the same year after year."

And how's the tourist business? "They say we had 1.7 million last year. Must be good. Who knows? They say it brings in much more revenue than sugar. But I don't have to tell you that with tourism comes a lot of unpleasantness that we Cubans would rather not have to deal with: the *jineteras* [hookers], of course, and the foreigners who come in and enjoy the hotels we built that were supposed to be for us. But we're in a special period, which Fidel announced almost ten years ago, and we may stay in that special period until I die and then some."

He laughs. He is referring to the speech Fidel made after the Soviet Union collapsed and Cuba lost its multibillion-dollar-a-year subsidy. Since 1990, the Cuban government, without outside support, has fought just to stay afloat, to retain basic medical and social services, as well as its vast education complex, and to provide some subsidized food and other goods to the population.

The U.S. government dealt Cuba an extra blow by passing two brutal laws. In 1993, the Cuban Democracy Act sponsored by then-Representative Robert Torricelli (now a Democratic Senator from New Jersey) tightened the embargo and attempted to destabilize Cuba by supporting dissidents. The Helms-Burton Act of 1996 impedes foreign investment by opening U.S. courts to lawsuits against foreign companies that do business in Cuba.

I ask about Fidel. "Coho, Fidel is wise beyond belief," says the cab driver / economist. "But between you and me, you shouldn't put people in jail because they disagree with you. It's not natural for anyone to stay in power for more than forty years." He gives a resigned shrug.

The cab driver says that he would choose Carlos Lage to succeed Fidel. The vice president who manages the economy is a humble man in his forties, a medical doctor known for patiently explaining the logic of government economic policy on TV and radio. "Lage wouldn't put people in prison for opening their mouths or printing a newsletter. He wouldn't destroy our chance to watch HBO movies like those *malvados* [villains] do." He was referring to the recent decision by the Communist Party ideology chief to eliminate the ingenious devices Cuban citizens invented to pick up satellite TV and augment their own two channels. . . .

The dollar economy hurts much of the working population, since unskilled workers earning Cuban money make the equivalent of only about ten dollars a month, which doesn't buy much. You're in bad shape unless you can get a job in the tourist sector, which has replaced sugar as Cuba's leading foreign-exchange earner—a troublesome fact for Fidel and for most Cubans.

The TV set shows short clips from various economists. The bartender and the musician discuss globalization intelligently with others seated at the bar—Cubans and foreigners.

How informed and educated Cubans are for a people without a free press! Never mind free, there's no press to speak of in Cuba. Sure, *Revolución*, *Trabajadores*, *Juventud Rebelde*, and *Bohemia* call themselves papers and magazines, but they are no more than organs of government information. Yet people on the street, on the bus, in the barber shop, at the hotel, and on the university campus discuss a wide range of current issues with knowledge and insight.

"Life isn't easy," is the common refrain. Daily life in Cuba amounts to people coping with basic problems of food, housing, transportation, and aging household appliances. Yet most Cubans wear clean clothes and have shined shoes with no holes.

I talk to a thirty-nine-year-old friend of my daughter's who earns the equivalent of twelve dollars a month and has to support herself and her eight-year-old son. She works as a professional by day and does typing at night for foreigners—for dollars. "Without the *libreta* [government ration book]," she says, "life would be much worse. With six pounds of rice and two pounds of beans, we can stretch my salary. But when the shower head breaks and I need forty dollars to fix it. . . ."

Some women began to turn tricks to make extra money. Others became part of a more organized prostitution racket. Over the last decade, I've seen increasing numbers of beautiful young women and men (children, really) waiting for male tourists.

But on this visit, I note that most of the jineteras have disappeared from the hotel zones. A lone, scantily clad woman ambles coyly on Fifth Avenue, near a traffic light, making eye contact with drivers of rented cars—presumably tourists. But the recently declared Cuban war on crime is also proceeding apace. Thieves, muggers, and hookers have been arrested and sent away for "social rehabilitation" or reeducation camp, says Cuban Attorney General Juan Escalona. Crime was beginning to worry the people who run the tourist industry, so Fidel announced the new crackdown policy in January, as he commemorated the fortieth anniversary of the revolutionary police force. He called for Communist Party members to fill the ranks of the police.

Cuban officials attribute the growth in crime to the hardship of the special period, the growth of foreign tourism, and the presence of foreign businesspeople. I've never seen so many cops on the streets of Havana as I saw on this visit. I admit, I felt more secure with them out there. In 1992, thieves broke into a rented beach bungalow near Havana and stole various items from me. In 1994, I helped lead a delegation of 130 Americans to Cuba; twelve were mugged in a week. . . .

Recently, the state and the party, faced with the downward spiral of the economy, have had to make concessions in their ideology and practice. This meant more than yielding to the temptation of becoming a tourist mecca, dollarizing the currency, and inviting foreign investors to exploit Cuba's labor and resources (albeit with controls that other nations lacked the will to impose). The state could no longer maintain its vast bureaucracy. It began to fire all of its mid-level ministers.

I met an old friend, a former official who had attained high rank and who had also lived what I considered a noble life. As a major in the Cuban army in 1973, he faced complicated child-care arrangements because he refused to consider using his status to place his kid in a day-care center. He and his wife cooked on a two-burner stove and lived in a crumbling, working-class neighborhood in Havana. I never saw him use his rank to crash a line at a restaurant, as others did.

In the early 1990s, his ministry, like many others, "retired" thousands of people—not based on years of worthy service or value to the government. It was a wholesale dumping. Unlike my friend, many others who were let go had enjoyed the traditional perquisites and privileges of office—state cars, special stores, vacation resorts. They found themselves reduced to the standards of the majority. But these former officials, many members of the Communist Party, didn't lose their connections, or their knowledge of how the system works. Nor did they lose the resources they had acquired during service in the bureaucracy. As the special period—read, hardship—developed, they gained an edge making the transition from secure civil servant status to the risky world of the job market.

Some of the former civil servants reemerged as members of the small, newly propertied class. Some have opened *paladares* (small, private restaurants), pizza parlors with delivery, or B&Bs with chauffeur service. Others rented rooms or apartments, made out of their garages, to foreigners who are doing long-term research projects in Cuba.

Because Fidel has always opposed the emergence of a propertied and privileged class, the government has cracked down on those working independently—on *cuenta propia*. The state has taxed them and regulated them. But their persistent presence demonstrates the rise of civil society in Cuba. (Recall that by "civil society" Rousseau meant the bourgeoisie.) These petty entrepreneurs are joined by private repair services for cars, TVs, appliances, computers, and by tailors, shoemakers, seamstresses. Graphic artists design menus and stationery for the new hotels for dollars. Cubans who learned skills from their revolutionary education now sell them for dollars. Cuba has become a nascent class society over the last decade, in spite of its revolutionary ideals.

My retired friend cannot live comfortably on his pension and his wife's salary combined, so he got another job. He can buy a few things beyond what the government ensures him on his ration book, but some of his lazy neighbors sate themselves on restaurant food, fresh vegetables, and frozen meat at the dollar market, plus the occasional new VCR. He, like many Havana residents, suffers from an unpredictable water supply, periodic blackouts, and deteriorating housing.

His kids' future, once bright and secure, looks dimmer. Cuba has produced sixty thousand doctors—more than it can use. The state has rented some of them to needy countries for dollars. Others now drive cabs or wait tables.

Scientists, engineers, architects, lawyers, and professors abound in Cuba. But Cuba's economy cannot absorb them. The dream has faded.

Colonizing the Cuban Body

G. Derrick Hodge

Much has been written about the discrimination and hardship experienced by Cuban homosexuals, works emphasizing that the prejudices behind this treatment reflect the tradition — sometimes myth — of both male sexual authority and of armed struggle to achieve political ends, inherited by the Cuban Revolution's largely male leadership. But an exclusive focus on the repression of homosexual behavior ignores the ways in which the meanings of homosexual roles and behaviors have evolved over the course of the Revolution. In this rare example of fieldwork conducted among male sex workers in contemporary Cuba, anthropologist G. Derrick Hodge explores the impact of the Revolution on male-male sexual roles and the ways the emergence of market relations during the Special Period has commodified not only sexual relations but desire itself. Sexuality, he argues, continues to be structured by political, economic, and ideological factors.

"Because My Addiction Is Money, and My Professionalism As Well."

He was twenty-one years old, an Afro-Cuban sex worker in Havana. He started the work when he was thirteen and the Cuban economy was at its worst, two years into the "Special Period during Peacetime" but one year before the state reluctantly legalized the dollar for internal exchange in 1993. The dollar changed everything, he told me. Now, his addiction was money, dollars to be precise, and the Nike shoes they could buy. And his profession was not sex per se, but rather the dollars that sex could bring in the new tourist economy of the neighborhood of El Vedado in central Havana. Of course he could not understand the role that his work — and his body — had for the new Cuban economy nor his role in the struggles over the meaning of Cuban nationalism in an era of foreign capitalist incursion. He did not understand that the collapse of the Soviet Union had brought as well the collapse of the Council of Mutual Economic Assistance (COMECON), the socialist states' trading alliance, and the extremely lucrative trade relations it facilitated. He didn't know about Fidel's Decree Law 50, which had as early as 1982 provided the first "revolutionary

legal base for normalizing and organizing the process of foreign investment,"
nor about the Fourth Party Congress of 1991 that paved the way for the constitutional reform of 1992, codifying capitalism.

What he did know was that in 1992 there were foreigners at the Hotel Deauville who would pay top dollar for a chance to sample the famous Cuban phallus, renowned both in gay travel networks and in literary representations of
cubanidad. And he knew that the dollar had changed everything. What was
in 1992 a tiny number of male sex workers who catered to the few foreign
capitalist investors was by 1999 an industry of perhaps five hundred young
Cubans whose developing identities as Cuban men had been interrupted by
a dramatic change in both economy and nationalist identity. A new class of
male sex workers had been born, the *pinguero*. Now twenty-one years old and
struggling to survive on the streets of Havana, the man quoted above incor-
porates in his very body the contradiction of the Cuban Revolutionary regime
inviting capitalism to do its work on the bodies and souls of its people. Capitalism is hungrily devouring every resource in Cuba, including its male and
female bodies, commodifying them and configuring them according to the
logic of the market. Both the meaning of Cuban masculinity and the gendered
nationalist project are being transformed in the face of economic exigency.

"When Two People Are in Bed, There Is Always Something
Economic That Complements or Impels Sex."

This young man, white, slightly older, and newer to sex work, was not alone
in his rather cynical belief that money is behind all sex and love in Cuba; more
than once a pinguero repeated to me the formula: "Here, there is no love without money." This is not a new development. Havana before the Revolution
was little more than a casino and brothel for wealthy U.S. capitalists in search
of exotic pleasures. And the use of Cuban women was ideologically in keeping with U.S. economic colonialism. As Northern capitalists invaded the island
en masse, backed by the power of the dollar and the U.S. navy, they individually penetrated the bodies of its women. Symbolically and literally, the island
was repeatedly assailed by the laissez-faire capitalism of the Batista dictatorship
and of its primary support ninety miles north. Little wonder that the Revolution viewed prostitution as a blatant representation of foreign domination. The
Revolution had fashioned itself a male affair, a matter of strong, tough, long-
bearded guerrillas expelling the island's invaders. The newspaper *El Mundo*
affirmed in 1965 that "no homosexual represents the Revolution, which is a
matter for men, of fists and not feathers, of courage and not trembling, of certainty and not intrigue, of creative valor and not sweet surprises." As an affair of

macho men, it was the duty of the Revolution to rescue the (feminized) island and its women from what was seen as the corruption of penetration from the North, and a product of capitalist exploitation. And so one of the first projects after 1959 was the retraining of female prostitutes in Havana and Guantánamo as seamstresses. This effort was largely successful, all but eliminating prostitution by 1961.

Some sex work did continue, but it was slowed to a trickle and took on a character consistent with the changing political and cultural economy of the island. One category which did survive the cultural upheaval of the Revolution was the nineteenth-century *bugarrón*, a man who was active-insertive during anal intercourse. His partner was a *maricón*, a man feminized by his receptive role during intercourse. *Bugarronismo* left intact traditional gender roles: Sexual object was less important than sexual act, so that penetration of another man did not irreparably call into question a Cuban's gender identity. That is, a bugarrón was still an *hombre* because he penetrated with his phallus, even though the object was another man. And the maricón was no longer a man because he was penetrated, even though he had a male body. Though in practice it is possible that all manner of sexual activity did occur and that some bugarrones did allow themselves to be penetrated, in representation the gender identity of the bugarrón was stable and protected.

During the Revolution the bugarrón-maricón interaction took on a specifically relational character: it tended away from the transactional and toward the relational. It is true that, as in the United States, there was a fairly brutal oppression of homoerotically inclined Cubans in the 1960s, but this was ended with laws of legalization and tolerance in the mid 1970s, far sooner than such activity was legal in most of the states of the North. But even if some formal oppression did continue with the Law of Dangerousness or the Law of Public Scandal, this does not mean that male-male interactions did not follow the carefully instilled logic of a socialist model. A relationship between a bugarrón and his maricón was often more than a sex-for-money exchange; it may have lasted for years and involved exchange of favors or cohabitation. This is likely the result of three characteristics of Cuba during the Revolution. First, in an economy in which most wealth was socialized, barter reciprocity was more common and efficient than currency exchange. Second, a more relational model of sex exchange, in which naked material interest is often obscured, is common to sex tourism (and romance tourism) all over the Caribbean basin. A currency exchange would have laid bare the sometimes material interest in the bugarrón-maricón sex act. Though it is being rapidly eroded with the onslaught of market relations in sex work, this relational tendency persists to this day. Money or, especially, clothing are accepted from tourists, but this exchange is constructed as "help" from a "friend," not as payment from a trick.

A twenty-year-old medical student described his relationship with a Spanish tourist: "He offered me material incentives. But not as payment, right? More like a gift. I accepted it because I knew that it wasn't in the spirit of payment. He kept insisting. . . . He always helps my mother." Most sex workers refuse to even discuss money, accepting whatever the tourist chooses to give them as a "gift": "I will never ask you for anything, I will not ask for money. If your heart dictates to you that you give me something—like, for example, money—it will come from your heart, you understand? But I will never ask you for anything." And some complain that tourists want only sex and not relationships. But under the influence of a new capitalist cultural economy, the new class of sex workers is abandoning even a pretense of relationality in their work. Some of the younger pingueros admit that "for me, being a pinguero is a business. A business in which I get what I need to dress, eat, help my family, and enjoy myself. I don't do it because I like it, I do it just for the money."

"The Pinguero Killed the Bugarrón."

Pinguerismo killed bugarronismo because it was far better suited for the new capitalist relations. For two reasons, the relational bugarrón was not a category that could withstand the transition to capital market relations. First, because the bugarrón-maricón relationship was not based on a currency exchange and could not function in the now dollar-based neighborhood of El Vedado. The dollar initiated the explosion in sex work not only by encouraging tourism but also by providing a medium of exchange so that the workers could gain more than a gift or a meal from their clients. This in turn allowed the beginning of a standardization of pricing and it irrevocably unmasked an increasingly material interest in the sex relation, despite the continued effort of many of the workers to construct the work as relational. Secondly, to be efficient in a market exchange, the workers had to have a category which was identifiable, marketable, and distinct. The new sex tourist workers in El Vedado needed a gender category which would both reproduce Cuban tradition but also conform to the demands of the clients for an insertive but "gay" worker—an odd configuration for a macho Cuban man.

The new sex workers had to distinguish themselves from the female sex workers, *jineteras*, now reemerging with vigor since the legalization of the dollar. They could not simply masculinize *jinetera*, since that would suggest that they, too, are penetrated by tourists. There is indeed a group of young men in El Vedado who call themselves *jineteros*, but these are sellers of black-market cigars, tour guides, promoters of private restaurants, and small-time con artists. They are a specifically nonsexual category and are adamant about that point, since if they were seen as sex workers, they might be imagined to be passive partners, like their female counterparts. Those young men who are sex workers, then, had to radically distinguish themselves not only from the con-artist jineteros (despised by *habaneros* because they threaten tourism), and from the invaded bodies of the jineteras; they had to announce to the world that their work was precisely the opposite: masculine virility. So, to the slang term for "dick" *(pinga)* was added the suffix *ero*, meaning, a man whose activity, or profession, has to do with his pinga. Thus, soon after the legalization of the dollar, the word *pinguero* was born. With such a name there is absolutely no confusion as to the role that the workers have in a sexual encounter. This saves the men's images as *hombres hombres*, or manly men, but it also is a marketing tool that announces to the sex tourists—who in Havana and elsewhere are usually in search of an insertive partner—who they are and what they are about. And the category "pinguero" is also an accommodation to the Cuban nationalist sensibility. . . .

"Because What They Love Is Money."

Materialism, especially adoration of U.S. brand-name products, has been one consequence of capitalism in Cuba. Many of the pingueros blame either socialism or "Fidel" for their poverty, and they express their anti-"Fidel" sentiments with an adoration of U.S. fashion. Tommy Hilfiger clothing gives the illusion of the kind of prosperity which capitalism is imagined to bring. If socialism has brought poverty, capitalism must mean wealth. Tommy Hilfiger is a symbol of that coming economic prosperity which some believe will accompany the death of Fidel and of the socialist experiment. Of course, these pingueros do not understand that the wealth which Tommy Hilfiger represents—with its advertisements of young men yachting off the coast of Nantucket—is well beyond what will ever be possible for the huge majority of capitalist citizens. Even more adored than Tommy is Nike. New shoes, for young habaneros, are rare and coveted jewels, and the wealthiest tourists don Nikes. The craving for shoes causes honest pingueros to do whatever they have to do, to steal from whomever they can, to get a pair of Nikes. The Nike obsession is beyond what we might call idolatry; one pinguero has a Nike swoosh tattoo on his right outer biceps. Every time he flexes, he promotes the values of consumption and proclaims the pending capital onslaught. Both his gold Nike swoosh and his commodified body proclaim the triumph of capitalism.

A second consequence of the introduction of capitalism to the island has been what we might call the commodification of desire: Pingueros' ability to experience and explore their desires has been interrupted by their need to conform these desires to opportunities to make money, that is, to the needs of the market. A number of pingueros explained to me that they are unable to have sex—even with a young man or woman to whom they are physically attracted—unless there is a financial element. The "Father of the Pingueros" told me: "I like sex with young guys, but as much as I like it or want to fuck, if you don't pay me, I won't go with him, you understand? So if you don't pay me, I would rather jerk off with a magazine alone at home, because having sex for money is my profession. . . . I would like to, but I can't have sex without money. . . . My heart won't let me." Similar sentiments were expressed by others. One pinguero even recently paid a woman to have sex with him, even though he was eighteen years old and very attractive; he could have had sex easily for free with a Cuban woman, but preferred to pay a jinetera ten dollars. Not only the bodies but even the desire of the pingueros has been configured to turn them into sex machines, functionaries of a sex tourist industry, and indirectly, of the foreign capitalists whose investments in hotels are reaping rapidly expropriated and exported profits.

This commodification reaches not only the bodies and desires of the pingueros, but also their sexual and gender identities, and this is a third consequence of capitalist incursion. For sex workers, identity functions like a packaging label on a product: It informs potential consumers of what they can expect if they purchase that product. Sexual identity in the past in Cuba has been fairly flexible, in that youthful experimentation—especially if in the active role—has been permissible without a Cuban man having to call himself "maricón." But a flexible identity, allowing a man to engage in some homoerotic behavior without having to change his gender self-representation, does not well serve the marketing of sex workers, who need to be easily identifiable to consumers. This is one of the functions which the label "pinguero" serves. Already widely disseminated among privileged white capitalist males who can afford to travel, the category of pinguero allows the workers to be marketed externally, letting the traveler know what to ask for, where to get it, and what to expect. Though Cuban men are not accustomed to having to declare themselves members of a category other than *hombre*, despite adolescent homoerotic experimentation, the needs of the market insist that they concretize themselves as sex workers for male tourists. So capitalism, through the logic of market relations, has claimed these young men from a world of (relatively) nebulous and permissive sexual experimentation and forced them into a concrete category which announces to themselves, to each other, and to their clients that their sexual being and their bodies are inextricably linked to their economic function. *Pinguero* is not primarily a category of sexual preference: it is first and foremost an *economic* category. The transformation of sex, body, and desire into a marketable product is precisely what I mean by "commodification of desire," and the construction of an economic category—the pinguero—to contain that product is what I mean by "commodification of identity."

For complete references and notes, consult the work as cited in the acknowledgment of copyrights section.

Pope John Paul II Speaks in Cuba

Pope John Paul II

The Cuban Roman Catholic Church responded without great enthusiasm to the 1991 Cuban Communist Party decision to define the state as "secular" rather than "atheist" and to allow believers to become members of the party, continuing to emphasize the irreconcilable differences between Marxism and Christianity. However, this change set the groundwork for Pope John Paul II's historic visit to Cuba in January 1998. At several public masses, the pope incorporated elements of Liberation Theology into his critique of capitalism (and specifically of the U.S. embargo), even as he criticized aspects of Cuban government and society ranging from the availability of abortion to the lack of religious education.

Sermon in Havana

A modern state cannot make atheism or religion one of its political ordinances. The state, while distancing itself from all extremes of fanaticism or secularism, should encourage a harmonious social climate and a suitable legislation that enables every person and every religious confession to live their faith freely, to express that faith in the context of public life, and to count on adequate resources and opportunities to bring its spiritual, moral, and civil benefits to bear on the life of the nation.

On the other hand, various places are witnessing the resurgence of a certain capitalist neoliberalism that subordinates the human person to blind market forces and conditions the development of peoples on those forces. . . .

In the international community, we thus see a small number of countries growing exceedingly rich at the cost of the increasing impoverishment of a great number of other countries; as a result, the wealthy grow ever wealthier, while the poor grow ever poorer. . . .

For many of the political and economic systems operative today, the greatest challenge is still that of combining freedom and social justice, freedom and solidarity, so that no one is relegated to a position of inferiority. . . .

As everyone knows, Cuba has a Christian soul and this has brought her a universal vocation. Called to overcome isolation, she needs to open herself to the world and the world needs to draw close to Cuba, her people, her sons and daughters, who are surely her greatest wealth. This is the time to start out on the new paths called for in the times of renewal that we are experiencing at the approach of the third millennium of the Christian era.

Sermon in Santa Clara

The family, the fundamental cell of society and the guarantee of its stability, nonetheless experiences the crises which are affecting society itself. This happens when married couples live in economic or cultural systems which, under the guise of freedom and progress, promote or even defend an antibirth mentality and thus induce couples to have recourse to methods of regulating fertility which are incompatible with human dignity.

There is even an acceptance of abortion, which is always, in addition to being an abominable crime, a senseless impoverishment of the person and of society itself. . . .

The social situation experienced in this beloved country has created not a few difficulties for family stability: for example, material scarcities—as when wages are not sufficient or have a very limited buying power—dissatisfaction for ideological reasons, the attraction of the consumer society. These and other measures involving labor and other matters have helped to intensify a problem which has existed in Cuba for years: people being obliged to be away from the family within the country, and emigration, which has torn apart whole families and caused suffering for a large part of the population. . . .

The family, the school, and the Church must form an educational community in which the children of Cuba can "grow in humanity." Do not be afraid; open your families and schools to the values of the Gospel of Jesus Christ. . . .

It is true that in the area of education, public authority has certain rights and duties, since it must serve the common good. Nonetheless, this does not give public authority the right to take the place of parents. Consequently parents, without expecting others to replace them in a matter which is their own responsibility, should be able to choose for their children the pedagogical method, the ethical and civic content, and the religious inspiration which will enable them to receive an integral education. They must not expect everything to be given to them.

TRANSLATED BY THE VATICAN

Emigration in the Special Period

Steve Fainaru and Ray Sánchez

Emigration has been a fact of life for Cuba, as for the rest of the Caribbean, throughout the twentieth century, and the United States has been a major receiving country for these emigrants. In the first years after the revolution, Cuban emigration was distinguished from other Caribbean emigration by a number of factors. Cuban émigrés tended to come from the higher socioeconomic levels of society, and they tended to define their status in explicitly political terms. By the 1980s, the profile of Cuban emigrants had shifted to something closer to that of other people from Latin America and the Caribbean.

Several aspects of the Special Period worked to accelerate emigration. From 1993 to 1995, Cubans experienced a level of material scarcity unknown since the revolution. The social safety network established by the revolution was not only fraying; it was disintegrating. Basics such as food, medicine, and fuel were simply unavailable. The émigré community in the United States continued to beckon, and more and more Cubans began to consider emigration an option.

Starting in 1994 economic reforms began to gradually ease the crisis — but at the price of encroaching capitalism and consumerism. By the late 1990s Cuba was inundated with material goods — there was no more scarcity per se — but these goods were available only with dollars, and dollars were available only through access to the export or tourist sector. For some Cubans, this was impossible; for others, it sharpened the longing for material abundance. The visibility of the new, consuming sectors, whether native Cuban or tourist, only served to increase many Cubans' dissatisfaction with their humble lifestyles.

Although U.S. baseball teams and agents had had their eyes on Cuban players for years, it was not until the Special Period that they succeeded in wooing Cuban talent to join the Major Leagues. The Cuban government's response — an attempt to prevent defections by banning some of the country's best players from the game — proved counterproductive, as this only contributed to players' desire to leave. U.S.-based sportswriters Steve Fainaru and Ray Sánchez followed the celebrated case of pitcher Orlando "El Duque" Hernández.

El Duque came to the affair as a true child of the revolution. He was born on 11 October 1965, fewer than seven years after Fidel took power. Unlike his parents, he had lived his entire life under communism. He was well schooled and extremely bright, a beneficiary of one of the great literacy campaigns of the twentieth century, which transformed a society in which 40 percent of adults could neither read nor write into one whose literacy rate now rivals that of the United States. Although he was black, he never had to experience the segregation of prerevolution Cuban baseball, when players of color — including the greats like Martín Dihigo and Orestes "Minnie" Miñoso, as well as El Duque's own father — were excluded from the popular Amateur League. In his style, his penetrating intelligence, his fearlessness, and optimism, he seemed to represent the best that Castro had to offer. On his uniform he wore number 26, one of the revolution's most powerful symbols, representing the date, 26 July 1953, when Fidel launched his famous attack on the Moncada Barracks in Santiago, effectively launching the Cuban Revolution. El Duque later wore the same number with the Yankees. The number held no political significance to him — he had inherited it from his father — but for a time he was so articulate in defending the principles of the revolution that he became known around international baseball circles as a true believer. The scouts and agents who circled the rare and valuable Cuban ballplayers never really believed he would defect. Gordon Blakeley, the Yankees' director of international scouting, followed El Duque for years, from Barcelona to Buenos Aires, salivating and penning a half-dozen reports that merely disappeared in his files. "I know the prettiest word in the world is *money*," El Duque once said while sitting in the living room of his three-bedroom house near the Havana airport. "But I believe that words like *loyalty* and *patriotism* are very beautiful as well."

El Duque could have been a model had he grown up in the States. He was tall, about six-foot-two, weighed 190 pounds, and had the flexibility of Gumby, a result of early morning yoga exercises he continued even after he was banned. He had the kind of presence that takes over a room and the voice to match, a low roar that seemed to emanate from somewhere around his spikes. He had a slick, bald head, which he shaved not to imitate Michael Jordan or Charles Barkley but because his hair had started falling out in clumps after applying some cheap Soviet hair tonic. El Duque's favorite expression, a kind of signature greeting, was "¡Todo bien!" (All is well), and he employed it constantly as both a question and an answer: "¿Todo bien? Sí, ¡todo bien! ¡Todo bien!" The expression had originated with his charismatic older brother, Arnaldo, a ballplayer and a barber who had died suddenly at thirty. El Duque looked like a major-leaguer long before he ever was one, particularly when he wore his blue Yankee pullover, a gift from a friend in the States. After he was banned, he wore the jersey to the only games in which he was allowed to participate, those in a neighborhood league that convened each weekend in front of several sorry-looking cows at Vladimir Ilyich Lenin Park. El Duque was manager and third baseman; he was forbidden to pitch for the same reason that Roger Clemens would be forbidden to pitch if he came out for the thirty-five-and-over league in the Bronx.

El Duque couldn't stop himself from competing. He argued with the umpires and chewed out his ragtag ball club, but it was obvious to everyone that *todo* was definitely not *bien*. His wife, Norma Manzo, had left him in his disgrace, and he was living with his new girlfriend, Noris Bosch, in a cramped one-room cinder-block extension of her parents' house. He spent most of his time hanging out with his best friend, Osmany Lorenzo, who owned a house that abutted the parking lot of the Havana airport's international terminal. Lorenzo had no real job; he had been fired as an airport bartender for playing cassette tapes of a Miami comedian who made his living cracking jokes about Fidel. But the dismissal had freed up Lorenzo for his true calling: the shadowy life of the black marketeer. He was one of a new breed of Cubans who knew how to exploit the recent legalization of the dollar and, with his contacts at the airport, he was especially well situated. All day people came and went through his back door, hauling cases of Hatuey Beer, toilet paper, even jet fuel that could be used in some of the old Soviet-made Muscovys that chugged around the capital. Lorenzo's primary role in this lucrative enterprise was to advise the couriers—"Hey, *chico*, put it over there!"

In some ways, the harsh punishment against El Duque was odd, because Fidel knew better than anyone the pressures building inside the country, particularly for ballplayers whose skills were worth millions in another world. "If you have to compete against six million dollars versus three thousand Cuban pesos you cannot win," he admitted to a group of visiting American newspaper editors one evening inside the Palace of the Revolution. Because of the cancellation of the Soviet Union's annual six billion dollar subsidy to Cuba—the result, of course, of the cancellation of the Soviet Union—the Cuban economy had contracted by 35 percent between 1989 and 1994. In effect, it had imploded. The ensuing depression corroded every aspect of Cuban life, including, inevitably, the powerhouse sports system of which baseball was king. Soon, bats and balls were scarce. Games were canceled because of power outages. Fans watching the nightly televised games would see relief pitchers exchange spikes [cleats] with the pitchers they had replaced, right there on the mound. One typical night, Sánchez and I bought tickets from a scalper for a weeknight game between Sancti Spíritus and Metropolitanos, the other Havana club. We were taken beneath the stands and were being led to our box seats by way of the home dugout when we were approached suddenly by a player, in uniform, hanging out near the clubhouse.

"Hey!" the player shouted, motioning for us to stop.

We froze, fearing that we had been busted.

"You guys want to buy a ball?" the player asked. "They're two dollars apiece."

While Cuba's economic crisis was deepening, and fewer and fewer people were attending the games—about three hundred turned out at the 55,000-seat stadium the night of the ball-selling incident—Major League Baseball, despite its poverty-pleading owners, was expanding into cities such as Miami and Tampa and Phoenix. The demand for new players accelerated the globalization of the sport. Baseball was no different from Gillette or Nike in this respect; it was the age of free trade, and the game was on the lookout for new, relatively cheap labor. Teams began to send scouts into remote places where the game had been mostly a rumor. They searched for players in such far-flung countries as South Korea and Australia. Cuba, meanwhile, which had been playing baseball since the 1860s, which before the revolution had produced Dolf Luque, Camilo Pascual, Tony Pérez, Luis Tiant, and Bert Campaneris (and José Canseco and Rafael Palmeiro, who left as babies), remained untapped, an island ninety miles from Florida, teeming with impoverished, disgruntled, bored young prospects. Cuba was a forbidden gold mine, the last great frontier. The trade embargo prohibited teams from doing business there. (Theoretically, the Canadian clubs—the Toronto Blue Jays and the Montreal Expos—could have cut their own deals, but the Commissioner's Office sent out directives making the island off-limits to everyone.) So the only way to sign up a Cuban was to get him to leave his country. A few players figured this out for themselves. But for most, a middleman was needed to orchestrate the often harrowing defections, then work through the migratory hassles that inevitably followed.

The entrepreneur who stepped forward to introduce supply to demand happened to be named, implausibly enough, Joe Cubas. And he brought much more than his name to the role. In many ways Cubas was the perfect man for the job. He walked like a Cuban and talked like a Cuban even though he had never set foot on the island. A squat, angry-looking man, he seemed ready to explode with raw ambition and an inbred hatred of Fidel, passed on to him by his mother, Berta, whose family had lost everything to the revolution. Cubas's fervor and political savvy helped him recruit the support of the heavyweights in the Miami exile community: the politicians and the businessmen who for nearly four decades had shaped U.S. policy toward Cuba. When Cubas needed a visa or a plane, he could enlist the help of the Cuban American National Foundation, the powerful lobbying group, or Brothers to the Rescue, the volunteer aviators whose unarmed planes were attacked and shot down by Cuban MIGs in 1996. Cubas was the classic "man of action" out of Joan Didion's Miami. He wasn't afraid to break a law or grease a palm to get things done. But Cubas's singular talent was that he was a bullshit artist without peer. He was able to get people to do extraordinary things for him, often for free. He extracted money and favors from a wide range of relatives and acquaintances who seldom saw either returned.

For years, Cubas trailed Cuba's national baseball team around the world. He wooed the ballplayers in Tennessee hotel rooms, in Tokyo shopping malls, in hundreds of dark corridors, promising the holy trinity of American-style capitalism: baseball, apple pie, and Chevrolet. Technically, Cubas was an agent, but he was like no agent that professional sports had ever seen. He was part Jerry Maguire, part Oliver North. The Cuban players who saw him lurking around every corner began to refer to him as El Gordo (the Fat Man). He was the kind of agent who held conversations over encrypted phone lines, with smugglers who traveled with code names like "Santa Claus." His operatives seemed to have walked straight off the set of *Scarface*. René Guim, who worked as Cubas's publicist, recalled asking one of the agent's burly cousins, a former West Palm Beach bouncer named Iggy Fong, whether it was true that he carried a gun. The two were standing inside Victor's Café, a famous exile haunt, but Fong enthusiastically pulled a nine-millimeter pistol out of his fanny pack. "I want you to meet Cheech," he said to Guim. Then he hiked up a pant leg to reveal a .38-caliber revolver holstered to his ankle. "And this is Chong."

Cubas would have been the logical man to help El Duque defect that winter, but circumstances had gotten in the way. In 1995, Cubas had engineered the escape of El Duque's younger half-brother—another pitcher, named Liván Hernández—while the Cuban national team was training in Monterrey, Mexico. Shortly before midnight, Liván had gathered up his belongings, sneaked out of his dorm room, and stumbled through his tears into Cubas's waiting rental car. With Cubas negotiating, Liván, who had earned the equivalent of five dollars a month in Cuba, signed a $4.5 million contract to pitch for the Florida Marlins. But after taking his commission Cubas disappeared, leaving Liván to fend for himself in his strange new world. Liván, alone, nearly ate himself out of baseball, as they say, having discovered one of the ubiquitous manifestations of American capitalism: the Burger King drive-through window. He defected again—to another agent. And he alleged publicly that Cubas had tried to charge him a 25 percent commission, some 20 percent above the industry norm. The breakup left both men extremely bitter, so much so that Cubas told one of his associates, Ramón Batista, that he wanted nothing to do with El Duque, who was likely "to fuck me the way his brother did."

El Duque pinned most of his hopes on his great-uncle Ocilio Cruz, a private investigator who worked out of an office down the street from the *Miami Herald*. To his family and friends, Cruz was known as Tío (Spanish for *uncle*). He was among the tens of thousands of Cubans who had come to Miami during the 1980 Mariel boatlift. A large, bald man with an easy smile who could be both intimidating and disarming, he had risen to become a bodyguard for Jorge Mas Canosa, the late, much-feared chieftain of the exile community. Tío was especially sensitive to his grandnephew's plight. A former first baseman himself, after the revolution he had spent fifteen years playing baseball in a prison on the Isle of Youth, off Cuba's southern coast. He had been sent there because of his membership in an anti-Castro terrorist cell that had organized itself around the Havana bus terminal, where he had worked as a security guard.

Using his sources in the Miami underworld, a melting pot of smugglers and spies, Tío set out to liberate El Duque from Castro's grip. He used an anonymous courier to deliver four thousand dollars — a small fortune in Cuba — to El Duque, who then entrusted the task of hiring an escape vessel to his best friend, Osmany Lorenzo, shadow master of the Cuban economy. Osmany located the perfect candidate: a fisherman from Caibarién, a small city on Cuba's northern coast that had become a mecca for rafters setting out for the United States. In exchange for a guarantee that he could bring himself and his wife to America, Lorenzo agreed to use his thirty-foot fishing boat to smuggle El Duque and his entourage out of the country.

It was December 1997. The plan was to leave Havana under the cover of Cuba's first legal Christmas since 1969. Because it was a holiday, the streets would be empty. There was less likelihood that El Duque would be followed. The group planned to spend the day in normal activities, doing nothing that would attract attention, then gather after midnight near an on-ramp to the National Highway for the five-hour journey to Caibarién. On Christmas Eve, El Duque went to see his mother. He spent several hours with her but never told her about his plans. On Christmas Day, he and Noris attended the wedding reception of a friend, the Italian photographer Ernesto Bazan. El Duque betrayed nothing. Tom Miller, an American who wrote *Trading with the Enemy*, an account of his travels through Cuba, happened to be at the reception. When he introduced himself to El Duque, the pitcher wrote down his Havana address and invited Miller to visit him some time.

The afternoon wore on. White-coated waiters filtered through the reception, bearing trays filled with *mojitos* and Cuba Libres. By the time night fell over Havana, nearly everyone was drunk. El Duque, a moderate drinker, lingered in the background, sipping juice and talking to friends. He wore a Nike cap, a white vest thrown over an aqua T-shirt, a gold crucifix dangling from his neck. He chain-smoked Marlboros, devoured a plate of pork chops and rice and beans, and then cleaned the plates of everyone around him. Someone turned on some music, and he and Noris got up to dance. Noris was an expert; she belonged to a modern-dance troupe in Havana and had once been on television. Together they made a stunning pair: the finest pitcher in modern Cuban history, the beloved El Duque, and his slender, dark-haired *novia*. The song was by the masters of Cuban *son*, Los Van Van, and the familiar lyrics washed over the crowd:

¡Ay dios, ampárame! [O God, protect me!] ¡Ampárame! ¡Ampárame! ¡Ampárame!

The Old Man and the Boy

John Lee Anderson

After the crisis of the summer of 1994 — when the numbers of Cubans (and Haitians) fleeing to U.S. shores provoked President Clinton to close U.S. doors to incoming Cubans for the first time since the revolution — the United States and Cuba negotiated an emigration agreement that came to be known as the "wet foot, dry foot" policy. Instead of automatically accepting Cubans picked up at sea, the United States would distinguish between those arriving on U.S. soil — who would be granted refugee status and be allowed to stay in the United States — and those found at sea — who would be returned to Cuba. The United States would also work to deter dangerous, illegal migration by expediting the granting of visas through the U.S. Interests Section in Havana.

The agreement did not, however, do much to improve relations between the two countries. Tensions flared in the spring of 1996, when Cuban missiles shot down two unarmed planes piloted by Brothers to the Rescue, an organization that had originally devoted itself to searching for Cubans at sea to bring them to the United States, but had shifted to dropping antigovernment leaflets over the island after the 1995 immigration accords. Clinton responded by signing the punitive Helms-Burton legislation, which he had previously vowed to veto, further restricting economic relations with Cuba.

Then in late 1999, what was to become the best-known case in immigration history began. Young Elián González — taken from Cuba by his mother, without the permission of his father, who shared custody of the boy — was picked up at sea, one of three survivors on a small boat heading from Cuba to the United States. Family members in Miami demanded that he remain with them, while his father and all four grandparents in Cuba demanded his return. The child became a cause célèbre among Cubans on both sides of the Florida Straits, and the world watched as the U.S. government slowly exhausted the option of negotiation, then ended up seizing the child at gunpoint and returning him to his father and the island whose government the United States was still trying to overturn. John Lee Anderson, a U.S. author and journalist, describes the atmosphere in Cuba during the crisis.

Fidel has been obsessed with the Elián González tragicomedy from the beginning. It is as if he were a general overseeing a great battle, moving his troops into position, plotting tactics and strategy, organizing skirmishes, and conducting psychological warfare to undermine the enemy. . . .

Despite Cuba's improved economic situation, and the opening up of cultural possibilities, a huge percentage of Cubans have indicated their desire to leave the island. In 1998, the U.S. Immigration and Naturalization Service sponsored a lottery for six thousand immigrant visas, and during the month they were available more than 540,000 people between the eligible ages of eighteen and fifty-five applied for them. Concomitantly, taking to the seas on rafts and boats is on the increase. A law passed in 1994 permits Cuban immigrants who manage to reach U.S. shores to stay in the country. Those who don't make it to dry land have to go back. Cuban government officials point out that this "wet foot, dry foot" policy has encouraged illegal immigration and is being fuelled by smugglers operating out of Miami, a growing number of whom are being caught and imprisoned in Cuba.

One of the prime spots for setting off for Florida is Cárdenas, a little town eighty miles east of Havana that has become well known in recent weeks because it is the home of Elián González. Cárdenas is an eloquent example of the "unfinished nature" of Fidel's revolution. Separated by only eight miles of narrow road from the tourist-resort peninsula of Varadero, with its stunning beaches and massive, fanciful hotels, Cárdenas is a listless, unkempt place dotted here and there with sun-scorched plazas. It seems to have been bypassed, somehow, by history's advance, like those American towns which disintegrate when a new highway routes traffic away from them. In Cárdenas, sewage flows down the old streets, which are laid out in a colonial grid and fronted by long, irregular lines of weather-beaten one-story homes painted a patchwork of colors. Horse taxis clip-clop briskly past every few minutes, and people lounge lethargically in their doorways. At a brightly painted, grubby little café with plastic tables and chairs under "Cerveza Cristal" umbrellas, with raucous salsa blasting from a boom box, groups of men and women with all the accoutrements of Cuban *gusanos* or would-be gusanos (gold chains, iridescent orange, green, and zebra-striped Lycra bodysuits, fishnet T-shirts, Nikes, and baseball caps) sit nursing beers and smoking. When I was there recently, a mentally ill woman—a rare sight in Havana—wandered in and, talking to herself, began dancing alone to the salsa, her hair twisted into a long little-girl braid. On a nearby street corner, in the late afternoon, a group of freshly dressed young Cubans gathered, waiting for buses to take them to their jobs as waiters, busboys, maids, and cooks in Varadero, which is where Elián's father works, and where his late mother worked as well.

Cárdenas exists because Varadero exists. It slumbers, suspended in its own marginality, more like an emigrants' waiting room than anything else. Which

"Free Elián" poster on a wall in a primary school. Ciudad Libertad, Havana, 2000. Photo by Aviva Chomsky.

is exactly what it is, by all accounts. The ill-fated boat trip that Elián and his mother took last November was only one of many that have been made from Cárdenas's swampy mangrove shores. The point of land on which the town sits is uniquely situated for emigration: Cubans say that all you have to do is row a boat out a little way and the Gulf Stream current, which sweeps up past the Cuban coastline there in a strong northeasterly arc, will do the rest. Most make it, some don't.

A few weeks ago, a friend of Raúl Castro's was gloating to me about the spectacle of Cuban schoolchildren singing revolutionary hymns and marching on behalf of little Elián. "The gringos have given themselves to us on a silver platter, and we are reaping the rewards," he said. "You know, it's not really important if Elián is returned in the end, because we've already won. Fidel has managed to involve not only the Party cadre in protests but ordinary people, too. And he's reached the young people who were up to nothing before this." The struggle over Elián had solved the problem of national identity. "This is like Cuba's own Cultural Revolution," Raúl's friend said.

Last fall, Fidel launched a campaign that was meant to revive lagging nationalist sentiments and also get the United States to take him more seriously, but it didn't work very well. The campaign took the form of a $180 billion lawsuit seeking compensation from the U.S. for suffering inflicted on the Cuban people by the embargo and other "aggressive policies." By the time I arrived in Havana, early in November, billboards all over town were touting the Demanda del Pueblo, the people's demand for justice in this matter. Cuban friends told me that programs on the Demanda had replaced much of the regular television fare for the two previous months. Most of the people I know rolled their eyes wearily when they talked about this latest of Fidel's "fixations." All their children wanted were the afternoon cartoons back.

The lawsuit was formally announced to the international community on 9 November, the day of the annual vote in the United Nations about whether or not the U.S. embargo of Cuba should be lifted. As usual, the UN voted overwhelmingly against the embargo, this time 155 to 2, with eight abstentions. The two votes in favor of the embargo were cast by the United States and Israel. Ricardo Alarcón, the president of the Cuban National Assembly, pointed out to the delegates in the General Assembly that, since the United States had recently lifted bans on the sale of food and medicine to Iran, Libya, Sudan, and North Korea, the only country that was still denied humanitarian assistance was Cuba.

As usual, the United States pretty much ignored the UN vote, and the $180 billion lawsuit went largely unreported, which must have been very frustrating for Fidel, since he had been working on the Demanda for months. Then, a week later, the Ibero-American Summit—the biannual gathering of the heads of state of the Latin American countries, Spain, and Portugal—opened in Havana. This was a proud moment for Fidel, proof that he is a respected statesman. After years of isolation, almost all of Latin America's republics had reopened their embassies in Cuba. New airplane routes had been established and bilateral trade initiated. King Juan Carlos of Spain, the prime ministers of Spain and Portugal, and eighteen Latin American heads of state came. But, despite the fact that more than a thousand journalists from around the world arrived to cover the event, the summit itself seemed of little interest, and the reporters looked around Cuba for other stories, or interviewed Cuban dissidents. "It's as if there weren't even a summit in Cuba," Fidel complained one evening, waving a briefing book of wire-agency bulletins in the air.

The Ibero-American Summit ended on Tuesday, 16 November. The following Sunday, Elián González and his mother left Cárdenas with twelve other people in a rickety boat manned by Elián's mother's boyfriend. On Thanksgiving Day, Elián was plucked from the inner tube he was clinging to, and the next day his father's relatives in Miami took the boy home from the hospital. By that time, a U.S. Border Patrol spokesman had announced that Elián (and two other survivors from the boat) could stay in Florida. On Saturday, Cuba asked for Elián's return, and a complaint signed by his father was filed with the UN.

In Havana, the Demanda placards all over town were replaced by "Return Elián" posters. Fidel had been handed a much more potent vehicle for focusing attention on the injustices inflicted on the Cuban people by a government that remained curiously in thrall to the Miami exile community.

Throughout the Elián saga, Cuban children have been pushed to the front of the protest movement, and the revolutionary Old Guard has been thrilled with their performances, holding them up as proof of the excellence of Cuba's educational system and its superiority to that of the United States. In early December, Fidel visited Elián's school in Cárdenas. He stood at the front of the classroom as Elián's schoolmates, one by one, trooped up to a microphone, where they delivered little speeches asking for their friend's return. A young boy named Yuniel Díaz González said, "Here we have schools, hospitals, we have cinemas, we can go out at night. But there if you go out at night you get attacked. Anything can happen to you. Cuba will always be a socialist and anti-imperialist country, and all of us love our Comandante because he takes care of us! Come back soon, Elián, because here your Fatherland, your people, and your Comandante await you!" Fidel seemed very pleased with this.

A few weeks later, backstage at Havana's Palacio de las Convenciones, I met a chubby ten-year-old girl, Jenny Sotolongo, whose black hair was tied up with ribbons in looping old-fashioned pigtails. Jenny was wearing a tight red dress, knee socks, and clunky black shoes. She had come to the Palacio de las Convenciones as a member of the fifth-grade choral group from the Paulita Concepción primary school. Out in the vast auditorium, a *tribuna de protesta* was under way. This time, doctors and medical students were expressing their concerns for Elián and their own fealty to the revolution that had taught them their trade. Fidel was sitting in the front row of the audience, deep in his seat, watching the proceedings raptly, as if he were at a movie. Above the stage hung a huge painting that was divided into two counterposed scenes. On the right were the brightly colored figures of happy Young Pioneers and the red, white, and blue colors of the Cuban flag; on the left, black-and-white images included the Statue of Liberty with her hands pressed over her eyes, strands of barbed wire, Donald Duck, and a faceless Adolf Hitler, wearing a swastika armband. Above, in bold letters, there was a quotation from the Cuban poet Cintio Vitier—"The innocence of a child can mobilize an entire nation."

In a few minutes, Jenny told me, she was going to sing a solo onstage. I asked her if she was frightened about performing in front of the Comandante. "Frightened, no. Excited, yes!" she said. Then she marched out and was soon belting a throaty ballad with the aplomb of a young Celine Dion. Her song was about "the importance of children," and her performance brought the house down.

Amid thunderous applause and delighted laughter, Jenny bounced down from the stage, where a woman took her by the hand and led her to Fidel. He leaned forward, patted her face, and exchanged some words with her. Eyes shining, she skipped out of the auditorium. A few minutes later, I found Jenny backstage again and asked her what Fidel had said. "He asked me where I had got my voice from!" she replied breathlessly.

Two days later, at a demonstration at the intersection in Vedado where, in 1961, as the Bay of Pigs invasion began, Fidel had declared "the socialist nature of the Cuban Revolution," thus launching Cuba into the Cold War, I watched Jenny perform again. This time, she strode onstage, mike in hand, her little face contorted with anger, and screamed out "Abajo la gusanera imperialista!" ("Down with the imperialist worms!"), and "Devuelvan a Elián!" ("Return Elián to us!") The crowd repeated the slogans, and Jenny made a pirouette. Then, in her strong, sweet voice, she sang her song about children. A star had been born, a child hero of the revolution.

The police closed down a section of the Malecón one night at the end of January, and a contingent of workmen began bulldozing a small triangular park in front of the U.S. Interests Section. They even dismantled a billboard with the cartoonish figure of a bearded Cuban militiaman saying to Uncle Sam, "Mr. Imperialist, we are absolutely unafraid of you." The men have been busy with cement mixers and dump trucks ever since, working around the clock in shifts to build what appears to be a ramplike plaza. For several days, no official explanation for the activity was given. There was half-facetious speculation that Fidel was putting up a huge platform from which to permanently harangue the Americans, and this turned out to be not far off. Early in February, the government announced that it is building something called "The Plaza of Dignity of the Cuban People."

The new Dignity Plaza is one of the rather pathetic "Mouse That Roared" details of the dénouement to Fidel's forty-year struggle with the United States. Fidel knows by now, of course, that, whatever happens to Elián, he has pretty much won the most recent battle. One can only imagine what he acknowledges to himself about who will win the war. As a friend in Havana remarked recently, "It's all over. You want to know who won?" He dug into his pocket and pulled out a dollar bill. "This won. The war is over, and no shots were fired."

Civil Society

Haroldo Dilla

The impact of the Special Period has not been restricted to the economic sphere. The deepening of market relations and the weakening of the ideological and political resources available to the Cuban state have created opportunities for the expansion of spaces that have been filled by a range of cultural, religious, economic, and community actors. The expansion of civil society has been uneven, sometimes almost invisible (in the political sphere), and always contested by sectors of the Cuban political class ever on the alert for evidence of "counterrevolutionary" sabotage and destabilization and U.S. exploitation of civil society "opportunities." In this provocative essay Cuban political sociologist Haroldo Dilla (b. 1952) maps the diverse and internally contradictory currents that make up civil society and asks whether the opening of the Cuban economy and the actions of nervous government "hard-liners" will permit the creation of a civil order which can draw on the rich experiences of social solidarity created by forty years of revolution.

Much of Dilla's most important research on political decentralization, community development, and the challenges of civil society was conducted while he was an investigator attached to the government think tank, the Center for the Study of the Americas (CEA). In the mid-1990s, CEA became the target of hard-line criticism, leading to the dispersion of some of Cuba's most creative intellectuals. Dilla is currently living in the Dominican Republic, where he is Research Coordinator at FLACSO (Latin America Faculty for Social Sciences).

The first time that I heard someone argue about the importance of civil society in Cuba was in 1984, during a talk by the well-known political scientist Rafael Hernández at the then-vigorous Center for the Study of the Americas. Hernández was one of the first to raise the issue, and was thus quite isolated. At the time, Cuban society was still not very differentiated socially and had been shaped by an intense process of social mobility led by a government that had relatively plentiful resources and considerable social autonomy. Thus, ideas like those of Hernández were viewed, at best, as needless intellectual subtleties.

The situation changed in the late 1980s, when Cuban society began to undergo a profound transformation as a result of the acute economic crisis and the gradual dismantling of prevailing forms of social and political control. The economic reforms implemented by the government to address the crisis — although different from the neoliberal reforms that other Latin American countries were implementing — opened considerable space for the market and the circulation of dollars, while undermining the average citizen's purchasing power. One of the most significant signs of this change has been the decline in the state's previously unchallenged capacity to control the distribution of resources, social and political discourse, and ideological production.

The partial withdrawal of the state opened spaces that were filled by associations, communication networks, or simply aggregates of people. Independent spaces for activities and debates that were unthinkable only a few years earlier appeared, either as a result of the opening to the market or simply as a result of the inability of the old ideological apparatuses to control the whims of thought. A civil society demanding its own space began to emerge in Cuba.

In the early 1990s, pronouncements about civil society were very cautious, given the reticence of the people involved to discuss a subject that had been harshly proscribed by Soviet Marxism and that had become the rallying cry of those on the Left and the Right who had struggled against the recently defeated Eastern European regimes. To make matters worse, it was also a topic that appeared in the U.S. agenda aimed at subverting the Cuban Revolution. Fortunately, this reticence vanished in 1992 when Fidel Castro made a positive allusion to the role of civil society in Latin America in a speech at the Rio Summit. Cuban intellectuals and social activists interpreted that speech as a signal that the subject was now safe to talk about.

Although these intellectuals and activists expressed a variety of opinions, they all shared the same set of fundamental concerns. No one was worried about defining what civil society in Cuba was, much less studying it. Everyone simply wanted to know whether the role of civil society would be positive or negative in rebuilding Cuba's political consensus in the midst of a deep crisis.

It was not a coincidence. This new debate about civil society was constrained by hostility from two fronts. On one side, there was the hostile meddling of the U.S. government, which was interested in using Cuban civil society for subversive and counterrevolutionary ends. On the other, there was the Cuban political class, which was not inclined to allow competition in the control of resources and values.

I confess that this debate did not interest me at first, which was a bad miscalculation on my part. But in 1995, I wrote an article that was published in a bulletin put out by a group of nongovernmental organizations. These NGOS published my article even though my perspective was quite different from theirs, a sign of tolerance and pluralism that has not been very common in Cuba. In essence, I argued that the civil society that had emerged in Cuba was not only comprised of local communities and the popular sectors, but also of economic actors originating in the market and conservative institutions such as the Catholic Church. I then suggested that it was a political error to advocate more autonomy for civil society. Instead, I proposed that the only way to deal with this matter from a Left perspective was to call for more autonomy for the popular sectors of civil society and from there, to open spaces for the construction of a pluralist and participatory democracy.

The article turned out to be my last foray into the debate. In late 1995, strong negative opinions against the idea of civil society surfaced within some sectors of the Cuban political class. These opinions were encouraged by a climax in U.S. hostilities most vividly expressed with the passage of the Helms-Burton Law. In this context, it was best to keep a clear head about the meaning of civil society. In January 1996, the newspaper *Granma* published an article with the suggestive title "Civil Society, or a Sleight of Hand Trick," which denounced civil society as a neoliberal excrescence. It likened its institutions to a Trojan Horse that would try to undermine socialism from within—a "fifth column" operating at the behest of U.S. interests. The article would have been quickly forgotten as an unsubstantiated essay had it not been immediately followed by a public declaration of the Central Committee of the Communist Party adopting a hard-line position with respect to several intellectual centers in Cuba. This declaration included an official definition of civil society with the moniker "socialist" that included the official mass organizations as well as those NGOs and associations "that acted within the law, did not attempt to undermine the system and . . . together with the revolutionary state, pursued the common objective of constructing socialism."

There was nothing objectionable about encouraging the development of spaces in civil society that favored a socialist program. The problem was that behind this declaration lay both a mistake and an unspoken intention. The mistake is elemental. Civil society is not a socialist construction simply because officials declare it to be so in a party forum, particularly since the state's own policies have generated segments of civil society that are linked to the market and capitalist accumulation which have nothing to do with socialist goals. The unspoken intention is even clearer. Behind this formulation lurks the desire of the bureaucracy to control civil society, to dictate what belongs and what does not, and therefore to exercise a sort of administrative control over its evolution. This illustrates Umberto Eco's remark that there is a short distance between the excess of virtue and the outbreak of sin.

What caused this clash between the Cuban political authorities and a segment of emerging civil society that was completely aligned with socialist goals and national independence? To answer this question, which I will try to do at the end of this article, we need to first analyze the anatomy of "really existing" Cuban civil society.

To do this, we need a working definition of the subject. Closely following political scientist Philip Oxhorn, I will define civil society as the social fabric formed by associations, communication channels, and ordinary relationships, which are varied in their social composition and aims and coexist in states of conflict, negotiation, and agreement. By definition, civil society is different from both the state and the market, but it is not necessarily opposed to these. Civil society may thus be seen as the interaction — in words or deeds — among groups that form new power relations or affect existing ones, either by consolidating or chipping away at them. At the same time, civil society in each place is a cultural and historical construct and is thus shaped by the national or local community in which it emerges.

This last distinction is vital for understanding the Cuban situation. Above all, civil society in Cuba has emerged from the bosom of a socialist project that generated strong upward mobility and numerous participatory spaces characterized by solidarity and collective action on behalf of the common good. As a result, it created a social subject with high levels of education and training in civic activism. From this perspective, the revolutionary state has been an important builder of civil society. And the emergence of civil society is a sign that speaks well of the revolutionary project.

In addition, there is within this emerging civil society a deep current of popular consensus in support of the political system. This does not mean that the predominant associations and discourses in Cuban civil society are merely appendages of official discourse. They advocate greater autonomy in official political structures, greater democracy, and greater freedom of action and discussion, among other things. But, if we exclude several segments of civil society that oppose the system, it is not hard to see a high level of agreement about crucial questions and activities that complement state actions. Support for socialism, the defense of social equality, and the repudiation of U.S. intervention are not simply camouflages; they are elements of a discourse rooted in the new civility generated by the revolution.

When party officials, association leaders, and academics discuss the vitality of civil society, they routinely refer to one statistic: in Cuba, there are a total of 2,154 civil associations legally inscribed in the register created for this purpose by the Ministry of Justice. A significant number of these associations were created after 1989, indicating a recent surge in interest in these types of activities.

The statistic, however, is a confusing one. On the one hand, not all of these associations have a significant public presence. On the other, many associations that do have a public presence are not legally registered and so do not appear in the official data.

The majority of these legally registered organizations are cultural, sports, or social organizations that do not have public influence beyond their small memberships. Some of these associations may project themselves more actively in the public arena in the future, but for now, the majority are irrelevant for the purposes of our analysis.

The case of the traditional mass organizations — officially recognized as the heart of "socialist civil society" — is more complex. Here we would include the diverse organizations whose common trait is their relationship with the state and the party as "transmission belts" according to the classic top-down scheme. Some of these organizations have millions of members, in particular the Committees in Defense of the Revolution, the Federation of Cuban Women, and the Union of Cuban Workers. Other mass organizations, such as the different student organizations and the organization of small peasants, have smaller memberships. Finally, we would also include professional organizations in this "transmission belt" category.

In reality, these organizations constitute an imprecise threshold between civil society and the state, not because they share similar political aims but because of the negligible autonomy evident in their public stances on a variety of issues. In practice, however, these organizations do adopt their own positions on specific problems that affect their spheres of action. They regularly participate in decision making in arenas in which they have representation, and in some organizations a dynamic autonomy is visible among the rank and file. This is the case, for example, with the labor unions. Leaders are democratically elected, and the adoption of decisions and accords is based on broad participation in the decision-making process. This has made it possible for the rank and file of the trade unions to have a powerful impact on national policy, as occurred in 1994 when they impeded the government from imposing an income tax that was part of an adjustment package scheduled to go into effect that year.

With the crisis, this tendency toward autonomy has been accentuated. This has been most evident in the trade unions and several professional organizations, particularly those connected to artistic and intellectual circles. Undoubtedly, the official policies of economic adjustment and reform will have an impact on the rank and file of these mass organizations. To what extent these organizations will prove capable of effectively representing the interests of their members in these new conditions, particularly if that means opposing certain state policies, will be a definitive test of their capacity for independent action.

The third component of civil society is comprised of a diverse group of churches and religious assemblies, some of which have become involved in social activities that extend beyond mere pastoral functions. This has been particularly the case since 1991, when the Fourth Communist Party Congress adopted a more flexible position concerning religion.

A majority of Cuban believers profess faith in the Afro-Cuban sects, which lack national or regional centers, making them atomized and extremely fluid in organizational terms. These religious sects nevertheless often serve as very effective informal networks for passing along information and for socialization at the community level. Today there is a tendency to involve Afro-Cuban religious authorities in cultural promotion and other aspects of local development in certain neighborhoods. These religious assemblies clearly possess a considerable ability to mobilize people—an ability that is bound to increase in the future.

The Catholic Church has experienced numerous ups and downs in its public activity. Today, it faces favorable conditions both in terms of attracting new followers and exerting greater influence over society, partly because of the government's adoption of a more flexible attitude toward religion, and partly because of the tendency to seek refuge in spiritual questions during moments of intense crisis. In fact, the Church hierarchy has developed the most coherent—and also the most viscerally reactionary—vision of civil society for Cuba. The hierarchy, of course, places the Catholic Church at the center of civil society as the only space of communion and true participation in the country. In economic terms, the Church's vision is based on private property and the free-market economy, where individual initiative can flourish. In political terms, it envisions a multiparty democracy, while in ideological terms, the new civil society would be based on the traditional values of the Church. The result would be a transition from the "structures of sin to more authentic forms of social life."

There are a small number of Protestant churches in Cuba, but their congregations have been growing in recent years. Some of these churches have become actively involved in projects of community development, popular education, and theological reflection that are politically progressive and that have had significant public impact. Two notable examples are the Martin Luther King Center in Havana and the Center of Reflection and Dialogue in the city of Cárdenas. Both engage in such extensive public outreach that they have become virtual development NGOs. The Martin Luther King Center, for example, supports numerous community-development projects in popular neighborhoods, and has trained hundreds of community activists in popular education methods. They also publish a well-known magazine which includes theological essays as well as articles focusing on the environment, gender, and other topics. The Protestant Churches in Cuba have achieved a certain degree of coordination in the Cuban Council of Churches, which has played a progressive role and has directly supported development projects.

Other important actors within civil society are the NGOs, especially those that are engaged in development work. While some observers put the number of developmental NGOs across the country at around fifty, there may in fact be no more than two dozen, and some of them have very narrow roles or are really appendages of state organizations with very little decision-making autonomy. The developmental NGOs, which benefit from financial aid obtained from their Canadian and European counterparts as well as from their contacts and exchanges with other Latin American NGOs, have had a very significant qualitative impact on Cuban society. By 1996, NGOs were involved in over fifty projects in six areas: alternative energy, community development, the environment, popular education, the promotion of women, and institutional development. Habitat Cuba, for example, has been very active in urban planning and housing construction based on the principles of community participation and environmental protection. Its development program in the eastern city of Holguín is a paradigm of integral community development as well as an example of how an institution of civil society can work side by side with the state without sacrificing its autonomy.

Other actors to keep in mind are the community-based social movements that began to emerge in the late 1980s with the goal of improving local neighborhoods within a self-help model. The origin of these movements is diverse, but almost all involved some state initiative, either by technical agencies, municipal governments, or popular councils. One of the most successful is the El Condado movement in the city of Santa Clara, which came into being after neighbors designed a technical plan to remodel the town. The residents and their leaders, in cooperation with municipal authorities, became involved in a dynamic and creative process of participation to improve various aspects of community life, from housing construction and educational facilities to health services and recreation.

Over time, the agendas of such groups have diversified, encompassing not just local development, but also protecting the environment and reclaiming cultural identities. These groups also tend to become more autonomous, which exposes them to frequent run-ins with local authorities.

Artistic and intellectual institutions are also significant. Many of these institutions tend to present themselves as key actors in the articulation of the new civil society and in the establishment of communication networks, whether because of the type of opinions they have, the debates they promote, or the social activism in which they are involved. The theater groups that have injected public opinion with critical appraisals of contemporary society and laudable displays of political valor are good examples here. Social research centers and cultural and academic publishing houses have also had a strong impact beyond the intellectual community. The academic journal *Temas*, for example, which is published out of the Ministry of Culture since its founding in 1994, has had an enormous impact.

The process of economic reform has opened doors to new economic actors, derived from or intimately linked to the market, who are also important if embryonic actors in civil society. First, there are the agricultural cooperatives. Until recently, Cuban agriculture was organized into large unproductive state enterprises, in addition to small cooperative or individual peasant properties. In 1993, there was a profound restructuring of agriculture with the creation of Basic Units of Cooperative Production (UBPCs). Although there are no official statistics, it is estimated that there are close to four hundred thousand people working in the cooperative agriculture sector and that number will likely increase in the future.

Even though the creation of the UBPCs has been a laudable step forward in Cuban socialism, it is important to note that since their inception, the main emphasis of the new cooperatives has been productivity. This has given rise to oligarchic tendencies within their organizational structures, resulting in increasing inequality and predatory relations with other social groups. Economic success alone will not alter this situation; rather, the general political framework in which these cooperatives are inserted must actively promote alternative values and organizational structures. Not a single association of cooperative members exists. Cooperative members have been urged to affiliate with existing labor unions, which is in keeping with bureaucratic goals of political control but incongruent with the goals of both independent unions and cooperatives. This situation has hindered them from developing greater public autonomy, except in the local sphere.

Other potentially influential economic actors in civil society are the close to two hundred thousand legally registered self-employed workers. Most of these workers are individuals who depend for their survival on their own labor or that of family members and have little or no money to invest in their businesses. A small segment, however, is made up of people who run profitable enterprises, such as restaurants and room rentals. These people could become important economic actors when such activities become legal. To date, there are no organizations of self-employed workers. They have been urged instead—with very little success—to join existing labor unions.

The new technocratic business class linked to foreign investment and to national enterprises in dynamic economic areas may yet become more relevant in the new civil society. Individuals in this sector do not yet have a distinctive organizational structure. Even so, their particular social role gives them easy access to the state as well as a great capacity for social influence based simply on the demonstration of their personal success to a population impoverished by the crisis.

Is there a future for civil society? Of course there is. It is the playing field on which all the main actors in Cuban society operate. The question is what its purpose will be.

The Cuban political class has given one answer: creation by decree of a controlled "socialist civil society." This is not completely off base in my estimation. Nobody disputes the right of the state to protect national sovereignty from the attempts of the U.S. government to use civil society as a destabilizing space in order to achieve its old ambition of becoming an internal actor in Cuban politics. Nor can we argue with the government's need to establish filters or restrictive political policies. It could even be argued on grounds of political realism that—in a critical moment such as the present—these restrictions are necessary to prevent dissident groups from taking demagogic advantage of the growing discontent of the population. But it is neither acceptable nor legitimate that such policies fall heavily on organizations that have supported national independence and socialism.

Analysts and those affected by the government crackdown have tended to attribute the reaction of the Cuban political class to the predominance of non-competitive forms of exercising power. This argument has some merit. But if we examine the course of Cuban politics in recent years, there is a notable contrast between the caution the leadership expresses in the political field and its considerable audacity in terms of the very controversial opening of the Cuban economy to the capitalist world market. It is probably this latter point that explains why the government is uneasy with a strong civil society in contemporary Cuba. The insertion of Cuba in the capitalist world economy and the embrace of a new model of accumulation based on the overexploitation of the workforce can only be achieved in a controlled political environment. The expansion of free-trade zones, for example, is incompatible with militant unionism, since such a development model requires low-cost labor and other cost-saving devices which normally result in horrendous working conditions. Similarly, the expansion of mass tourism is incompatible with feminist and environmental commitments, since the way this industry has developed in the Caribbean tends to be based on the mercantilization [commodification] of sexual power—and the consequent commercial use of the image of women—as well as the destruction of the environment. This has led to a tacit understanding between the technocratic-business sectors and the traditional bureaucracy—economic surpluses in exchange for social tranquility.

This is of course just one, if powerful, trend. There are others that are nourished by a civil society based on the social solidarity generated by four decades of socialist revolution, and by leaders and social activists who understand the meaning of the Marxist utopia, which holds that the free development of each one depends on the free development of all. These trends constitute the backbone of a larger story of dramatic events waged in the pursuit of freedom.

Not only is there a future for Cuban civil society, but there can be no future without it. Only in that space can effective barriers be constructed to withstand the market's colonization of daily life and to ensure that utopia is not reduced to eating a hamburger. If, despite everything, the transition to socialism fails in Cuba, it would be from within civil society that anti-capitalist alternative programs would arise. There is no room here for pessimism or fear of the future. In the end, as the Roman poet Lucano said just before committing suicide, fearing a bad future is more dangerous than the bad future itself.

TRANSLATED BY DEIDRE MCFADYEN

Forty Years Later

Senel Paz

Senel Paz (b. 1950) is best known outside of Cuba for authoring the short story on which Tomás Gutiérrez Alea's award-winning film Strawberry and Chocolate *is based.* Strawberry and Chocolate *was released at the height of the Special Period, in 1993, and it criticized, not so gently, the culturally and sexually repressive atmosphere and policies of the revolution in the 1970s. The film is credited with bringing the issue of homosexuality into public discussion by depicting a male homosexual artist as its hero. The artist, Diego, is a freethinker who manages to convince a young communist revolutionary that the revolution should value, rather than repress, difference.*

In his presentation at the conference "Culture and Revolution, Forty Years Later," hosted by the Casa de las Américas in Havana and attended by such international luminaries as Nobel prize winners José Saramago and Gabriel García Márquez, Paz reflected on the paradoxes of the revolution's cultural policies and on his optimism for increasing autonomy for artists and writers. Although he does not explicitly say so here, many Cubans feel that Cuba's subordination to the USSR through the 1980s contributed to cultural repression, and they see the island's forced political and economic independence in the 1990s as bringing the potential for new cultural openness, despite the economic hardships that have necessarily limited cultural production.

For me and my family, for the young people of my age and my origins, what fell on that 1 January 1959 was not the Tyranny. What fell for us, from the sky, was the Revolution. I became a writer, which was what I wanted to be. But if I had to say today what I consider the most important conquest of the Revolution in the cultural sphere, I would not think of the personal opportunity that so many children of peasants and workers had to become writers and artists. Rather, I would point to the fact that culture has become popular, not in the sense of mass participation, although this is also sometimes true, but because it is enjoyed, consumed, so to speak, by the whole people, because the people have become cultured. I am referring to the creation of a public, of a reading public, too, of a public that is experienced and demanding with respect to all of the arts, a public that needs the arts, that is better and better educated, more avid for cultural production, and sometimes desperate for it. A public that needs art, and that is prepared to enjoy it. This, from my perspective, is the greatest accomplishment of the Revolution in the sphere of culture. And this public, to a much greater extent than the writers and artists, has been the victim in these times of the Special Period and the globalization of culture.

Since the triumph of the Revolution we have also committed important errors. They are part of our life, as much as the achievements are. One of the things that I least understand about this Revolution that I belong to is when it avoids recognizing its errors and reflecting on them, as if to err—and to recognize this—would diminish it. We insist on the value of the example; we are more stimulated by the work we have done than by what we need to do. This is the reason that we have fallen victim to rhetoric. . . . I am also confused by the "political or diplomatic" relationship we have with errors, in the past and the present. Even now, we are usually advised to mention conflicts in a low voice, or ignore them, so as not to harm our relations with the politicians, the correlation of forces, the balance, and the moment. If you were to comply, you'd end up with the sensation that you are not being true to yourself, but only saying what the politicians permit you to say. Criticism must be made, we have always heard, at the opportune moment, in the opportune place, and in the opportune way. There are no requirements for making errors. I confess that I am more stimulated in my work by what I have done wrong, by what remains to be done, than by what I've already achieved, no matter how good it is.

It is true what I have heard here, that socialist realism did not take root in Cuba. This does not mean that there were not efforts, sometimes brutal efforts, to sow it. And I don't want to deny that the attempt caused damage. And we, the writers and artists, rather than destroying the initiative, only managed to resist it at the cost of an entire decade of creative inhibition, at least in literature, a fact that inevitably had drastic consequences for the culture of a country, and that needs to be reflected upon. And it was not only the issue of socialist realism; there was also censorship, pure and simple. Not self-censorship, which is another form of censorship. There was also negation, for political and ideological reasons, perhaps specific to the time, of part of our culture, which is like saying of part of our being as a nation. We silenced Celia Cruz, who is so difficult to silence, we silenced religious manifestations, we covered up the works of authors like Lino Novás Calvo, Carlos Montenegro, Labrador Ruiz, Gastón Baquero, and others who remained on the island, like Lezama Lima, without whom we *also* cannot understand our present, nor understand how we came to the point where we are now. We have prohibited films, and it does not matter if it has only been one, we have done it, mobilizing groups of people to criticize and protest it, because we did not know how to discuss it. I am aware that it is in bad taste to bring this up on an occasion like this, but I am not among those who believe that disagreeable things disappear if you can forget about them.

How, I have wondered, could a Revolution that sought to bring freedom, all freedoms, get to this extreme? How could a revolutionary, whose sincerity, abnegation, and dedication to the cause can't be doubted, come to believe that making a Revolution, conquering the future, meant acting this way: censorship, prohibition, limits? Why have other revolutionaries, just like the institutions, lacked the integrity, the courage, but above all the intelligence and the wisdom, to successfully oppose acts like these, to make the reasons that belong to the future prevail?

These are things, I have understood, that come with a Revolution, convulsions of this living organism that is a Revolution, that goes on unknown paths, that explores. What is disconcerting for me has never been the existence of conflicts and the errors, but rather the attempt to ignore them, instead of learning what we should from them, and studying them to understand ourselves. Personally, I have never been ashamed to recognize these gray moments in the Revolution, nor have I been disappointed in the Revolution. They are part of the Revolution, not the essence of the Revolution, as a character [in *Strawberry and Chocolate*] said. But I believe that it is our duty as intellectuals—and here I don't mean just the Cubans, but rather us, I include all of us, since I believe that in no other aspect as much as the cultural the Revolution belongs to all of us— to study our negative experiences in depth, with strength and without shame, without becoming discouraged. Disillusionment would only be appropriate if errors were committed in bad faith, and thus were not really errors at all.

One of my worries, when this meeting was called, was whether we were only going to thank our guests for their loyalty and their affection and ask them to stick with us in the future; or whether we were going to ask them to look at us critically, that they would join their intelligences to ours to help us to also understand our errors. How do you see us? How do you see the good and the bad that have happened in this country? What hopes do you have, what do you need, what do you see in us? What are you disappointed with, and what do you admire? Are we still, as has been said, a lighthouse and a guide, beacon of hope, a land where possibility and hope are nearer?

In other words: do you see Cuba, today, now, as a place where freedom of expression, freedom of creation, access and circulation of information, plurality of ideas, are more possible? These things are very precious needs for us, and we know that they are indispensable not only for our fulfillment, but also, and what is more important, for the fulfillment of our people, for their culture.

We ask this question of you, who have the same ideals as us. We do not ask it of the imperialists, since we already know that they have an arsenal of trick responses, false and illusory. We want to find the truth in a leap forward, not backward, because if not we run the risk of becoming an example of "do as I say, not as I do."

Utopia placed Cuba in the trenches for conquering these eternal aspirations. How do you see the trench, how are you going to help us, now that we know that you still love us, and still have faith in us?

I also leave you these questions.

Perhaps it is important, before finishing, that I tell you my personal opinion in this regard is that at the present time these possibilities are renewed for us, they are certain.

Cuban art and literature have become more and more autonomous. In the recent UNEAC [Cuban Writers' and Artists' Union] Congress, our enthusiasm has been renewed. This was not a renovation that came from a directive or a resolution of a Party Congress, but rather a force, an enthusiasm that has come from us, from our own maturity. I think that we are conquering a greater space and authority than ever before, even perhaps a definitive space, in the consensus of this country, by our own hand.

If art and culture are consolidated in our country, this means that they are no longer subordinate to politics, that their creators have made them more and more independent. And it will also mean that our culture is becoming more Cuban, more revolutionary and it will be more convincingly united with the Revolution. But not, to the surprise of many, because of fear, nor because of fanaticism, nor because of control, nor because of opportunism, nor pressure, nor repression, but rather because of our own vocation, because our hearts and our heads, independently, take us there.

TRANSLATED BY AVIVA CHOMSKY

A Dissident Speaks Out

Elizardo Sánchez Santacruz

Elizardo Sánchez Santacruz is an unusual figure in the Cuban political scene—a social democrat who calls for fundamental changes in the political system but who does so from within Cuba and who denounces right-wing exile activities and the U.S. embargo of Cuba. He is the founder of the Cuban Commission for Human Rights and National Reconciliation, and he is frequently sought out by foreigners as the voice of dissidence inside Cuba. Although he has been jailed in Cuba, he continues to be a vocal spokesperson for a perspective that probably attracts more sympathy from non-Cubans than from Cubans either on the island or in exile.

Like people everywhere, Cubans yearn for peace, prosperity, and freedom. Our challenge is to make our existing totalitarian state, which is obsolete and inefficient, evolve into a more open system that is better attuned to the global economy and the world around us. The Cuban people fervently want that change, but they insist that it occur peacefully.

Peaceful transformation can only be achieved through a process of national reconciliation in which all political voices are included—even those of the leaders of the present government. The transformation, after all, must begin under them. How could it be bloodless if the ouster of the regime is a precondition?

Some will argue that the Castro government will not permit change. To speak of reconciliation, says the Cuban exile leadership in Miami, is treasonous. The pressures against Cuba must be maintained—even though those pressures haven't produced anything in more than thirty-three years.

I have spent more than nine years in Fidel Castro's prisons, yet I am convinced that a hard-line approach against his government is based on false assumptions. True, some top officials do not want to change anything. But they do not have that luxury: Cuba, now without Soviet help, is poverty stricken. To recover, it must change.

Modern economies depend on access to information, on having people think for themselves, on the abilities of tens of thousands of managers to make instant decisions. The centralized economy and strait-jacketed political culture we now have simply cannot be competitive. I believe that the large majority of Cubans understand this fact and want change. I believe that even the overwhelming majority of Cuban officials understand it as well and that the top leadership is sufficiently pragmatic to move with the times.

Unfortunately, American policy impedes the transformation we seek. Efforts to pressure and isolate Cuba simply give the leaders pretext to continue their repression and allow them to divert attention from their failures.

The vast majority of us on the island who oppose the government believe that a dialogue and a relaxation of tensions between the United States and Cuba would better facilitate a transformation. Unfortunately, the Helms-Burton Act, which among other things mandates sanctions against foreign companies that do business in Cuba, makes it very difficult for the United States to take part in such a dialogue.

Still, even with the Helms-Burton Act in place, the United States can play a less obstructive role. At the very least it should allow Europe, Canada, and Latin American countries to encourage economic and political liberalization in Cuba. It should also drop its objections to Cuba's reintegration into hemispheric affairs and its eventual reentry into the Organization of American States.

Washington should also lift all restrictions on travel to Cuba by Americans. Is not the United States committed under the Helsinki agreements to the free flow of people and ideas across borders? And how can one sincerely argue that the cause of a more open Cuba would not be advanced by having as many Americans as possible in the streets of Havana? (Critics will say that Cuba, too, has travel controls. Well of course it does: it is a totalitarian state. That is no reason for the United States to make the same mistake.)

Finally, America should lift its embargo on sales of food and medicine to Cuba, a prohibition that violates international law and hurts the people, not the regime. Denying medicine to innocent citizens is an odd way of demonstrating support for human rights.

The basic responsibility for Cuba's future rests with the Cubans themselves. We must begin reforms that offer hope to all. But less rigidity on the part of the United States would do a lot to help that change begin.

Originally published in *The New York Times*, 22 April 1997.

One More Assassination Plot

Juan Tamayo

Through the 1990s, Cuban exiles in the United States continued military training in the hopes of an armed overthrow of Cuba's government, and the Cuban government continued to accuse the United States of tolerating or promoting exile attacks against the island. United States politicians and analysts continued to predict—and to work for—the fall of the revolutionary government, and the revolution, against all odds, survived. Journalist Juan Tamayo has chronicled many of these events for the Miami Herald. *A 1998 article detailed the involvement of Cuban exile Luis Posada Carriles— also know for his role in the Iran-Contra affair—in recent bombings and yet another assassination attempt against Fidel Castro.*

A Cuban exile implicated in several terror attacks was plotting to assassinate Fidel Castro during the Cuban president's visit to the Dominican Republic next week, three Miami exiles and two U.S. law enforcement officials say.

Luis Posada Carriles, a lifelong anti-Castro militant, and three Miami exiles who met with him at the Holiday Inn in Guatemala City last month discussed how to smuggle guns and explosives into Santo Domingo, the exiles said.

A *Herald* report in November identified Posada as the mastermind of a dozen bombings of Havana tourist centers last summer that killed one Italian visitor. A second *Herald* report in June linked him to other plots in Guatemala, Colombia, and Honduras.

In the most recent conspiracy, Cuban exiles in the Dominican capital had begun gathering information about Castro's movements and stood ready to help house and transport a "hit team that was to arrive at the last minute," exile sources and law enforcement officials said.

The hit was to have occurred between 20 and 25 August, when the Cuban president is scheduled to attend a summit of Caribbean leaders in Santo Domingo.

"The plan was to kill him any way we could—explosives on the road, grenades in a meeting, shots on the street. We would have strangled him if we had to," said an exile involved in the plot.

But Posada's plot was betrayed to U.S. authorities.

FBI agents last month searched a shipping complex owned by Enrique Bassas, identified by three exiles as one of the militants who met with Posada in Guatemala City to discuss the assassination plot. The search was triggered by an informant's tip that guns and explosives for anti-Castro activities were hidden aboard a boat there.

A week earlier, the U.S. embassy in the Dominican Republic had issued an unusually public warning about possible terrorist threats against airliners flying between Santo Domingo and Cuba.

Dominican security officials immediately went on alert and "urged" two Cuban exiles living there, both close friends of Posada, to leave the country during Castro's visit, said two Miami exiles with intimate knowledge of the plot.

"Someone Betrayed Us"

"It's all over," a dejected plotter told the *Herald*. "Someone betrayed us. Now it's a matter of waiting for the FBI to forget about this. But be assured that we or someone else will try again."

Rumors of Posada's gambit began trickling out among Miami's militant exile community almost from the day in April that Santo Domingo announced the Castro visit.

Cuban exiles have dogged Castro's foreign travels for decades in attempts to kill him. Exile hit teams shadowed him in Spain in 1992 and Colombia in 1994, and allegedly planned another approach in the Venezuelan island of Margarita last year.

Posada, 71, portrayed the Dominican plot as the best shot yet at Castro because local security was likely to be porous and he could easily smuggle in explosives and weapons from neighboring Haiti, the exiles said.

But the trickle of rumors turned into a gusher after a *New York Times* article on 12 July quoted Posada as saying that the late exile leader Jorge Mas Canosa had "personally supervised the financing of his terror attacks."

Posada later disavowed his statements. But some Miami militants, angry with Posada, began speaking almost openly about his Dominican plot.

By coincidence, on 12 July, Posada had just finished a string of meetings with three Miami militants in Guatemala City to discuss smuggling weapons into the Dominican Republic, said two exiles with direct knowledge of the talks.

The exiles identified them as Bassas, Ramón Font, and Luis Orlando Rodríguez. Holiday Inn records seen by the *Herald* show that the three were registered there 10–12 July, and that their tabs were all paid by Rod Rodríguez.

Bassas, 50, the wealthy owner of several homes for the elderly, was one of the founders of the Miami Medical Team, a group of exile medical personnel that aided anti-Communist guerrillas in Nicaragua and Angola in the 1980s.

Font, 76, is a CIA-trained explosives expert, lifelong anti-Castro militant and a former military commander of Comando L, a paramilitary group that claimed responsibility for several attacks on Cuba as recently as 1993.

Rodríguez was described as being about 50, a Vietnam veteran, and Miami resident, but he could not be identified because at least three militant exiles have that same name.

Font told the *Herald* he knew nothing about any plot. Bassas said he did not want to make any comment. The *Herald* could not contact Posada or Rodríguez for comment.

FBI agents ran into Bassas when they searched a shipping complex on the Miami River on 24 July.

An affidavit filed in support of the search warrant said an informant had tipped the FBI that guns and explosives for anti-Castro activities were hidden aboard a boat there. But the affidavit made no mention of Bassas.

Bassas turned out to be the owner of part of the docking facilities and of Bassas Cargo International, a firm that handles cargo for the wooden Haitian freighters that dock on the Miami River.

Bomb-sniffing dogs found nothing, and Bassas was not detained. But police seized a wooden boat of the type common among Cuban shrimpers in Miami except for one thing: a new racing motor estimated to cost about twenty thousand dollars.

Law enforcement veterans saw the search as an FBI hint to Bassas to cancel any conspiracies. That's a common practice in South Florida, they said, known as "admonishing" or "demobilizing" an operation.

Just who leaked Posada's plot to U.S. law enforcement agents remains a mystery, although law enforcement and exile veterans of the anti-Castro struggle offer three possibilities:

- One or more of the plotters got cold feet and tipped authorities to raise the alarm — for instance by sending FBI agents to search Bassas's firm or tipping them to threats against Dominican air connections with Cuba.
- One or more of the plotters alerted authorities so that they could filch part of the money raised for the plot.
- Cuban intelligence agents, presumed by most law enforcement and exile experts to have penetrated many exile organizations, tipped the FBI to protect Castro's life during the visit to the Dominican Republic.

Posada's anti-Castro credentials are impeccable, but even some of his closest friends admit that in his passion to get at Castro he may sometimes come dangerously close to Cuban agents.

Posada has repeatedly boasted of having contacts with "dissident military and intelligence officers inside Cuba." They are just as likely to be Castro agents trying to get information from Posada, said veterans of the U.S. war on Castro's agents in Miami.

"To get at Fidel, Posada will go like this," said a Miami exile who has known him for thirty-five years, using his hands to mark a wild zigzag course.

Posada has lived in hiding, mostly in El Salvador, since he escaped from a Venezuelan jail in 1985 while awaiting trial in the bombing of a Cuban airliner that killed seventy-three people.

But he has kept up anti-Castro attacks.

Posada has told Miami friends that he had a plan to blow up a jetliner on the ground in Cuba on 25 April, but that Cuban police captured two of his agents as they tried to smuggle explosives to Havana aboard a TACA airline flight from Costa Rica in late May.

Another lingering mystery is why Posada identified Mas Canosa as his main financial supporter in his interview with the *New York Times*.

Posada claimed in an interview broadcast last week by CBS Telenoticias that he had "disinformed" the *New York Times* to lead its reporters away from the real source of his operational money.

Posada made the same claim in one of three brief telephone calls to the *Herald* on July 15, 16, and 17. He called in response to *Herald* requests to interview him on the *Times*'s stories, but eventually refused the interview.

"In intelligence work, there is an operational axiom that you blame everything on the dead guy," he said.

Posada's explanation got little credibility in Miami, where many who know him say he talks too much, exaggerates too often, and then lies to cover up his mistakes.

"Posada's words cannot be trusted," said Félix Rodríguez, a CIA veteran and Mas Canosa supporter who worked with Posada in El Salvador from 1985 to 1998 helping the CIA-backed Nicaraguan contra guerrillas.

Posada, now hiding in Central America, has told friends in Miami that he now feels intensely hunted.

Cuban intelligence agents might try to kill him and make it appear as a Cuban American National Foundation "hit" in retaliation for his comments on Mas Canosa, he has said.

And Salvadoran leftists may be after him because he paid a Salvadoran mercenary to set off the Havana bombings. The accused mercenary, Raúl Ernesto

Cruz León, was arrested in Havana in September and could face a death sentence.

In his calls to the *Herald*, Posada would not reveal the country where he was staying and said he could not send e-mail because he was far from his desktop computer at home in El Salvador.

"Guess I'm going to have to buy one of those little portable computers," he said with a chuckle before he hung up.

An Errand in Havana

Miguel Barnet

Miguel Barnet's (b. 1940) most recent short story, subtitled "A Cuban Returns Home to Havana on an Errand," is evocative of the Special Period of prolonged crisis in which it was written. The protagonist, like so many Cuban artists and writers, shuttles back and forth between Havana and Europe. Nostalgic for Cuba when in Europe, hauntingly estranged when at home, the narrator embarks on an errand that takes him across Havana, causing him to take stock of the city, his city. The narrative ends with a streetscape, like a snapshot, an image of the time-worn yet still magnificent Malecón. The seawall, usually bustling with Cubans strolling, fishing, or just sitting and talking, is oddly empty and silent, as if caught in a still, a pause, just before the action resumes.

Miosvatis

The Zurich Museum is square. And cold. But it's got the best collection of Giacomettis I've ever seen. They're pretty sad, these sculptures by the Swiss master: old patinated bronze figures—attenuated, contrite, their arms fused to their bodies—recall Baulé or Senufo carvings, I couldn't say which for sure anymore. Restricted, those arms rob the body of freedom, turn the figures into prisoners chained to the artist's fancy. Of all the pieces in that museum, the saddest is a skinny but enormous dog mounted on a base that could be wood or marble, I don't remember that anymore either. It's the famous Giacometti dog reproduced on postcards that have been sent all over the planet. I didn't look at it for long because I like my animals alive, especially dogs. But Wolfgang did. Wolfgang looked at it carefully and then said, "Let's go downstairs and have a drink. I'm going to buy a postcard of Giacometti's dog."

In the cafeteria, I opened a diet Coca-Cola and watched as Wolfgang hurried off to get it. "This postcard," he told me when he returned, "you're going to take it back to Cuba and deliver it to Miosvatis, my black love, who lives on Trocadero Street. She's a very beautiful and tender woman. Do you mind?"

"Of course not, Wolfgang. I know your sweethearts always expect to get something from you."

Zurich is a gray city, an untouched cardboard stage set with a river and bridges like the ones in Leningrad, with ice-cream and peanut venders and violet-breasted pigeons that alight on your shoulder and eat from the palm of your hand, just like in a Vittorio De Sica movie. In the summertime, Zurich opens up like a music box, but in winter it's as sad as a cenotaph.

Wolfgang and I walked over the bridges, through the city, along the narrow medieval streets. We visited cafés where Tristan Tzára, Lenin, and Thomas Mann had sat to contemplate those same steel skies.

In one of the cafés, Wolfgang wrote up the card I was to take to Havana. "I'm called Juanito, over there," he said, "because my real name is so strange." Then, sitting beside me, he wrote:

Dear Miosvatis—This skinny sad dog is what I'm like here in Switzerland without you. Soon we'll meet in Cuba and I'll be a happy dog again.

I'll be your puppy. All my love, Juanito.

I spilled my black-currant ice cream on my trousers, but so what? It was out of keeping with the Heineken Wolfgang was drinking, as we sat on a bench facing the river. An overcast late-summer sky made our conversation more intimate. We talked about Cuba as always, about the future, about the city of Dada; we saw a black barge loaded with Japanese tourists, and we were glad to be together again, my friend Wolfgang—I mean, Juanito—and I . . . setting the world to rights while the tourists photographed the bridge and the pigeons; maybe we even appeared in the photograph.

"We're going to buy some shoes for your mama," Wolfgang said. "Tell her the German sends them. And then we're going to buy some perfume for Miosvatis, and a blue Swatch—blue will go well with her skin."

Zurich is elegant. It's not a city where the crowded rush of consumer culture presses up against you. You shop in peace, and nobody comes along to shove merchandise in your face. We bought the shoes, perfume by Giorgio, and a watch with a blue wristband and a kaleidoscopic face.

Wolfgang and I said our good-byes until we'd meet again in Havana.

The next morning, I took the train to Paris. I crossed the loveliest lakes in Europe with the postcard, the Giorgio perfume, and the Swatch in my leather briefcase. Mother's shoes traveled in my luggage.

Juanito came along to say farewell at the station, but first we had mint tea in one of Zurich's fanciest pastry shops.

During the following month, I trotted all over Paris with these things in my bag for fear that someone would steal them or I'd lose them in one of the houses where I slept. In Paris, the whole story seemed unreal. Paris is not made of cardboard: it's a gray elephant that breathes with exuberance. The watch was a little more expensive in the Paris stores than in Zurich, but not the perfume; that we could have bought cheaper at any counter in the Galeries Lafayette or La Samaritaine. I sent Wolfgang a card—a lovely photo by Man Ray of Marcel Proust on his deathbed—and I assured him that the perfume, like the watch and his postcard, were safely stowed in the leather bag that never left my side.

Miosvatis became an obsession, or, rather, a talisman protected by a demi-urge. Whenever I opened my bag and saw the card, the watch, and the perfume, I got an odd feeling: I wanted to go to Havana immediately and meet the object of Wolfgang's passion. I didn't want to take the things out of my bag. It was as if my city, the barrio Colón where she lived, and the idyllic Miosvatis herself were all very close to me. Sometimes I felt this was the only real thing I possessed, my strongest tie to the world.

Flying back in an Iberia DC-10, I wondered whether the customs officer at José Martí Airport would ask me to account for the blue watch. No! Anything but give up the watch that Juanito had bought for his beloved. But since my suitcase was small and I was carrying all my books and chocolates in my shoulder bag, no one asked me to account for anything, and the little watch entered Cuba duty-free, pretty and glowing with its wristband of translucent turquoise blue shining just as it had in the Swiss showcase—the chimerical faraway dream of Miosvatis.

As I got off the plane, even before I'd set foot on the tarmac, the humidity steamed up my glasses. It's Havana, I said to myself. This humidity will be the death of me someday, but then we all die, after all. And, full of happiness and new stories to tell, I made my way through the airport.

Outside the terminal, groups of relatives and friends of the passengers leaned against the barricades and with a mixture of joy and envy watched us come in from outside.

The first thing I did when I got home was unpack the watch, the perfume, and the postcard. The jet lag, six hours' worth, kept waking me up that night. In this waking dream, Miosvatis appeared in many different guises: as a mill-worker's daughter, a schoolteacher, a taxi driver, or simply a hooker who had opened Wolfgang's eyes to the fact that she was not just an ordinary black streetwalker.

The only thing that took my mind off my friend's sweetheart was my neglected apartment. The towels hung crooked on the towel racks, the plants had dried up, and the dust gave the place an air of faded dereliction that kept me from enjoying my happy return home. When I picked up the telephone, my mother informed me fearfully, "It's been broken ever since you left." I resigned myself "Fine," I said. "Now my stay in Europe will be extended, since without a telephone I'm simply not here, I am no one, one who has not yet arrived."

I waited patiently for the telephone to be repaired, and then I made a few calls to give signs of life. Then, unable to hold off any longer, I headed for the barrio Colón bearing gifts, like one of the Magi.

The barrio Colón isn't really the barrio Colón anymore. Now it's one more barrio of Havana, a hive of people sitting along the sidewalks or playing dominoes in the streets, the men shirtless and the women in plastic sandals and hair curlers. Just another barrio with a few glowing embers of its ancient fame—a celebrated old red-light district come down in the world, where idleness spreads like an oil slick, or something even more viscous. The Revolution rooted out prostitution, but not the Cuban habit of living one's most intimate life, without shame, in the middle of the street.

It wasn't easy to park my car, because a number of chairs had to be moved and a couple of sharply dressed young girls had to be asked to get out of the way so that I could get close to the curb. They laughed and took their time moving onto the sidewalk, convinced that I was insolently robbing them of their space. The barrio reeked of rotten cabbage and cheap cologne, a peculiar stench that one soon gets used to. Neither of the girls was Miosvatis. I knew this without even asking.

Miosvatis was something else again. I didn't inquire after her, because that would have aroused curiosity. I simply knocked on the door of the address I had, and a thickset woman with hair dyed with *bijol* opened the door. To her, I mentioned the name of my friend's darling.

She answered me with an evil smile. "She lives on the top floor," she said, "but she's not there, she went out with a boyfriend. But come in, come in. In this barrio everybody wants to know your business—gossip spreads like weeds here. Look, they're already watching us."

The old woman invited me into her ground-floor apartment—the ceiling peeling and the floor a carpet of silent cats and dogs. "Don't your dogs bark?" I asked.

"No, that's the way they are. I've got them trained." She ignored them, as if they weren't there.

Against the light, I was able to make out a tinted photograph of the old woman in her youth, pretty and with her lips accentuated by an imprudent use of lipstick which dated the image to the mid-fifties—an era of thick features and lurid colors. She said something softly that I couldn't hear because she feared eavesdroppers. She talked a lot, eager to take advantage of a stranger's ear, and of course she wanted to know what I was doing there. I explained that I wasn't sure of Miosvatis's apartment number. And she looked up wide-eyed, but not so much surprised as complicit. "You bringing her something? That little package is for her? You're Spanish?"

"No, Ma'am, I'm Cuban. . . ."

"Ah, Cuban! But you live outside."

"No, Ma'am, I live here, and I've come to bring a present for your neighbor."

"Good enough, but she's not here—I told you, she went out with a friend. But not a guy from here, from this barrio, no. Me, it's the first time I've seen him. He's mulatto, lighter-skinned, a lot lighter-skinned than her."

The woman's opaque eyes searched mine. Staring back at them, I realized that the irises were ringed with a halo of white, and that her eyelashes were white as well. As I did not speak, she told me that Miosvatis lived on the top floor. "But she's not there, you know, she's always going off into the streets and leaving the kids up there with her younger sister. Look, nobody's up there, because the window that faces my courtyard is closed, unless the sister's asleep and the girls are running around in the street. If you want, I'll hold on to something for you. The little package, that's for Miosvatis? Don't worry, you can leave it with me, but they don't deserve it. They throw filth down at me. I'm sorry to have to tell you this, but yes, sir, just to annoy me they throw wads of Miosvatis's daughters' shit out the window, and I've reported them to the police, but nothing, they won't even listen to me. But come on through here—would you like some water? You could suffocate in this heat. Where'd you say you were from? Oh, yes, Cuba, but you live on the outside! Well, however you want, either you leave the little package with me or you come back another day, make up your mind."

A plaque of the Virgin of Charity of Cobre, her robe stained with grease and her sparse hair also colored by the dust of bijol, was hung high on the wall. The floor in this room was uneven and seemed almost like an ancient artifact, made up of filthy tiles, shabby and broken.

The old woman was about to say something when an earsplitting scream came from above. "It's her," she said. "It's her, she was there all the time, but they hide to spy on people—and I only do them favors. It's on account of me that those baby girls drink condensed milk." There was a second scream, this time a little less sharp, as if the screamer knew she'd been heard down in the first-floor apartment, where I was now sitting in a wicker armchair with a broken seat. The old woman pointed at me and said, "Go up, go on up. It's four flights, you'll know which one is theirs."

"I'm Yalaine," said the woman who answered the door. She was a beautiful black woman, compact, a sculpture composed of solid volumes. "It's a pleasure, come in, make yourself at home. Pardon that I haven't dressed the girls — it's the heat, it puts us right to sleep. I heard you talking to that old gossip and I said to myself, 'That's a message for me from Manuel.' Right?"

"No, *compañera*, it's for Miosvatis."

"Ah, for my sister! You can leave it with me — don't worry, that way you won't have to come back. My sister went out on an errand about an hour ago, but she won't be back till late. It's from Gunther?"

"No, no, it's from Juanito."

"Ah, Juanito, yeah, yeah, my sister's fiancé. Thanks!"

Yalaine shut the twins in the other room, and between the girls' screams and my own uneasiness in that slum I don't remember the moment when I handed her the perfume, the postcard, and the watch.

"Miosvatis has been waiting to hear from Juanito for days," she said. "He wants to marry her, but my sister's not sure because of the two kids, and she just got a little job. . . . It's not easy, you know? But you're not German."

"No, no, I'm Cuban and a friend of Juanito's. I saw him over there, and he gave me this for your sister. He talked a lot about her."

Yalaine offered me coffee. "Juanito bought these cups because he likes to drink Cuban coffee in fine cups. He's sure got white hands, and delicate. He's a man who's very. . . ."

Miosvatis and Yalaine's apartment could have been a set for a vernacular piece at the Teatro Martí. Off to one side, near the window that opened onto a tiny balcony, was a pair of vases with wax flowers covered in soot. On the other side, a broken clock that had stopped at ten sat next to a statue of St. Barbara with black ovals embroidered on her cloak and the tip of her nose chipped off.

The smell of rotten cabbage was now mixed with a sweet and penetrating French perfume to which I had an allergic reaction that was impossible to hide. "Excuse me," Yalaine said. "I'm going to put this stuff for my sister under lock and key, because if I don't the girls will ruin it in no time — they grab everything, but everything. And for my sister what comes from Juanito is sacred. Would you like some more coffee?"

"No, thanks."

Yalaine went into the other room and came out again dressed in brilliant blue satin, with earrings she'd got from the diplomats' store brushing against her Baule princess shoulders. She looked at me with suspicion, but also with ap-

preciation. She'd have liked me to stay longer. She apologized for the disorder
and the dust that covered everything.

"With these girls, there's never time for anything. And my sister and I are
alone here. Our mother died and we're all the family we've got." I didn't look at
her in any way indiscreetly. I just wanted to get up and leave. Then she asked,
"Did Juanito say he was going to marry my sister?"

"No, he didn't say."

"I'm asking because I'm not going to get stuck with the girls. Imagine! She's
going to have to take them."

"They're very pretty—they look like you."

"Yeah, but they're not mine. It's on account of my sister and me; we look
alike."

I started to sneeze. I don't know if it was the dust or the cloying super-sweet
perfume. I said goodbye, thinking of Wolfgang in that Zurich pastry shop,
under those orange umbrellas in that dry and elegant autumn in the city of
Giacometti.

As I went down the stairs, the odor of rotting cabbage got stronger, now
mixed with cat piss. Dirty black stains splotched the marble stairs of what might
once have been a bright and flamboyant house of prostitution. The cat woman
had her door open, but she made no move to say goodbye to me. Maybe she
was afraid I'd told Yalaine something of what we'd talked about. In her eyes I
saw only empty indifference.

Coming out into the high afternoon sun, with my shirt sticking to my skin,
I saw a group of men around my car. I shot a quick glance at the tires, the rearview mirror, the windshield wipers, and opened the door, feigning confidence
in this barrio and its people. I didn't start the car right away; I even looked up.
Yalaine was waving goodbye, and I realized from this distance that her front
teeth had an even wider gap than I'd noticed. Who was lovelier, Yalaine or
Miosvatis? Perhaps I'll never know. The engine turned over, and I was about
to step on the accelerator when two girls approached the car window. Curious, and with assumed familiarity, they asked in unison, "You're a friend of
Juanito's?" I smiled and stepped on the gas. At that hour, the Malecón was almost deserted. Only a tourist couple in Bermuda shorts and a sad and sickly
dog, like Giacometti's, were silhouetted against the landscape.

TRANSLATED BY CHRIS BRANDT

No Turning Back for Johnny

David Mitrani

The short story "No Turning Back for Johnny" is structured as a collage of voices and perspectives that, in concert, capture the uncertainty of life in the Special Period. All of the known elements from this period are present: dollar and sex tourism, jineteros, mild scams and hustles, an increased U.S. tourist presence, and the return of racism, as well as remnants of the original revolutionary institutions, such as volunteer agricultural work in the countryside.

Each section of the story is told from the perspective of one, or a pair, of the characters: Johnny, a tall, athletic U.S. visitor who rents a 1957 Chevrolet; his girlfriend Lila—a university dropout who devotes most of her time to dating foreigners—and Lila's mother; Huevi, who used to be Lila's sweetheart, and his buddy, who provides much of the narration, who together hire a truck and driver to transport a mattress Huevi found to his current fiancée's house; the drunken truck driver who hits Johnny's rented '57 Chevrolet; and the chorus of residents of the Old Havana neighborhood where it all takes place.

The monologues intersect and become entangled, forming a brilliant tapestry of the contradictions of the new Cuban economy with its social and cultural malaise—an as-yet unfamiliar world in which everything has become a transaction and everyone seems ill at ease.

The story appears in a Spanish anthology of new Cuban writers, all born after 1959. The author of the story, David Mitrani, born in 1966, is a poet, novelist, and computer engineer who lives in Havana.

A Note on the Translation

Some terms of contemporary Cuban slang that appear without translation have been footnoted. Others, where the meaning is clear from the context, have not. In the Spanish original, Johnny speaks a mix of pidgin Spanish and English. In the translated version, Johnny speaks pidgin English, with a few Spanish words thrown in here and there, meant to approximate his poor grasp of Spanish.

[*Huevi's buddy*] Me here, so what, the giant said, defiantly. Huevi and I looked at each other, surprised, frightened, and skeptical. He's not the same. Close, but not the same. If I really stretch, my shaved *testa* comes up to his chest, and Huevi, who's a bit more corpulent than I am, is the fringe on a tassel compared with that colossal blond from the armies of the north. Before, he seemed to us to be a guy of medium height, medium strength, medium rage, and now he has evolved into a pivot for the NBA, with his thoracic area all dilated, threatening to pop the buttons on his shirt, pointing at us with a finger as thick as a broom handle. He has become a warrior of the Middle Ages, with muscles toughened by countless battles, parsimonious as a veteran gladiator. He's not the same. Two hundred and some odd pounds distributed mostly in the upper area, a frightening melon with legs who had once appeared defeatable by any one of us, but we are now verifying that even if we all attack him at once we won't make a scratch, that one of his punches, on our cheekbones, would cause hematomas, extravasation, visits to the eye doctor, humiliations, and remorse.

You abused one of our friends a little while ago, Huevi stuttered. Ah, a friend of yours, no? he says, making fun; overestimating his strength, he scratches his neck, intentionally contracts his right biceps, and, savoring my friend's vocal quivering, he adds: I don't give a fuck about that. We are impressed that, despite his English accent, he has mastered the semiotics of the slums, the secular slang of the *aseres*; that, standing there, looking out from the cement entryway, he tightens the muscles of his front paws and assumes the posture of an imposing gorilla. We are impressed that not a single one of his features trembles, that only his nostrils and blue eyes are open, and that, displaying contempt for us mere Caribbean mortals, he has made a fish mouth.

[*Johnny*] With Lila I have good time, much pleasure. Sexy, pretty *negrita*. Cuban women not like our women. Our women mix with Saxons, cold, stiff . . . and here *cubanas*, mix with Spanish, Arabs, Africans. You are different, yes. Lila walk, dance, move waist, hands: Celia Cruz, yes, Celia Cruz. You don't know because you inside don't realize. *A Cuba falta* money, a lot of money. If I had . . . eh . . . *si yo tengo* money, build stores, *muchas*, and hotels on beach, *muchos*, and . . . you see pro-spe-ri-ty. It's a beautiful country, beautiful people and hot, I mean . . . *fuego*, yes, *caliente*. I see great things here one day. We, I mean, *mis amigos*, believe this be good country in future. Every time I come Cuba bring clothes for you, for children, there is too much over there. People throw in garbage something you can use here. There they ask me, Can Cubans use this, Johnny? Yes, yes, I say, everything, *todo servir*. I dream always of coming to this island. My grandfather in Havana in 1898, with our army, and. . . . always tell me about here. When I was child, imagine, yes, I imagine playing with soldiers, carriages, that I have come to fight the Spaniards. Today I laugh, before no, it was an ob-ses-sion. Then I grow, study history *de ustedes*, learn who is Maceo, the battles, eh, the women he had, *los hijos*. He the biggest in Cuba. He brave, strong, very strong.

[*Lila*] *Ay, mamá*, of course it's the same as it is with a Cuban. Well, there are some things. For example, he always speaks in English, but sometimes he does it in Spanish, especially with certain words. . . . You know, the ones that just come out when you get carried away? Yes, Ma, don't tell me you didn't say them when you were with Papi. Yeah, those same ones, he screams them, with an accent, of course, but with such force that I begin to like it more than if a Cuban said them. But don't think everything is rosy. Sometimes his armpits are so stinky, Lord have mercy and God help me. At first I would rather have died than say anything, but now, without thinking twice, I say to him: rinse with water, Papi. And he, poor thing, goes straight to the bathroom without a word. But does it go away? Hah! There's always a little odor left, ever so slight, but more annoying than the smell of a public bathroom. The Europeans are worse. Much worse. Jean Pierre had such body odor. It's a good thing our relationship only lasted two weeks. Like a cat and water, that French guy. He'd go into the bathroom, shave, put on deodorant, perfume, and that was it, he thought he was clean. I think he had no sense of smell. When I was with him, yes, even in the middle of screwing, *vieja*, I'd get dizzy and feel like throwing up. And he did such stupid things. If he saw, let's say, a man looking for handouts for San Lázaro, he'd start up a conversation with him as if he were the official historian of the city. Was he stupid, abnormal, or what? Johnny isn't like that. You've seen him. He's like us in his sense of humor and the way he goes about life. He can tell a story about Pepito, or dance *casino*, like the day of the party, remember? But the truth, the real truth, is you never get to feel the same sense of connection as you do with a Cuban. With my first boyfriends I used to talk a lot, talk about any old thing: about the fights that went down in the neighborhood, the dollar stores, the Brazilian soap operas. . . . But ever since I got together with my first *yuma*,[1] I got bored with that, talking so much shit. Finding Johnny has been, in some ways, a stroke of luck. He's not much to look at. If you go by the movies everyone's seen, you come to think a yuma on the make is going to look like the leading men, and you forget that in the real world, Cuban or Yankee, there are piles of bald guys, guys with big ugly teeth, huge ears. You say Johnny looks like wolf-man, that's your opinion. You never had good taste. For me, his only defect are his legs. The other day he was naked, combing his hair in front of the dresser mirror, with his back to me, and I could check him out without his knowing. He has muscles all over his back, right down to his buns, which are hairy, and hard like a ballet dancer's. To there, he was perfect. Then, I checked out his thighs, and they're skinny, and his knee caps are two big fat balls, and his leg bones look like they're about to snap. Yeah, I checked him out and laughed to myself as much as I wanted. Until he turned around and caught me looking at him, and asked me: What, do I look good? I responded, without looking at his legs, looking only at his chest, his abdomen: Delicious, Papi, delicious.

[*Huevi's friend*] The force of the blow, delivered with both hands, is guaranteed. After what he did to the last victim, his left hand looks like a surgeon's glove, full of air, or perhaps even the udder of a Holstein cow. Because he whipped his previous opponent's face until he was satisfied, because, indifferent to his pain, he unleashed all his fury, releasing it from his body like one more fluid, like a river of blood: boiling, timely, flowing, in the form of fists, against the plaintive drunk. Until the neighbors arrived and surrounded him and the yuma ran off because something terrible was about to happen. Afterwards, assisted by the spectators, the one who had taken a beating got to his feet, climbed into this truck, and the trip was over. In the midst of an animated group that gathered to receive it, the mattress descended from the truck and entered the house where Huevi's fiancée lived. Before he was out of our sight, before the vehicle accelerated, the truck driver moved us when, upset by our passivity, he accused us of being cowards, calling us hacks, rats, assholes; he accused us of being renegades, pro–North American, calling us sycophants, ass-kissers. We all went off, then, to capture the fugitive North American. It was difficult to find his hideout. First we returned to the scene of the event, but nobody knew anything. The neighbors, presuming close ties between us and the truck driver, inquired what was going on with sincere concern. Huevi calmed them down and things improved. We tried to track them down through Old Havana and Central Havana, investigating, facing suspicious looks, useless, evasive responses. We almost gave up before we decided to check out Diez de Octubre Avenue, and finally we found the mechanic's shop near the corner of Toyo where we spotted the blue '57 Chevrolet with its dented door, and we knew we had found the yuma. The trip had worn us out. From ten in the morning to five p.m., riding a Chinese bicycle, pedaling hard, desperate for revenge, taking turns on the pedals and the bar, because Huevi isn't what he used to be; before, he never got tired, but now, after a horde of parasites upholstered his intestine, he's weaker, and always afraid that the powerful anal valve will give in to the push of osmotic diarrhea. It was not a good idea; I enrolled in this venture mistakenly, because I was headed for less conflictive territory, to see my grandmother, when Huevi, the old wolf, intercepted me and begged me to help him, because he and his fiancée would enjoy the mattress after their wedding, that I would be the witness, and drink a few beers, free. With such a powerful argument, how could I say no. The mission was to transport it to his in-laws' house, and for that we needed adequate means of transportation. In Virgen del Camino, on the narrow block leading up to Restaurant Terry, that filthy, green truck appeared, parked all by itself, as if it were waiting for us. *I'm not married, my wife is the married one*, I could read on the upper edge of the windshield. The driver was asleep, snoring and drooling. Hey, my friend—I move the pompon hanging from the rearview mirror and tap him on the shoulder—is the truck for rent? The truck driver, in a foul mood, as if he were chewing on an uncooked croquette, informs us that if we don't fork over fifty pesos there's no deal. I don't feel like grabbing the wheel today, he adds, crossing his arms, so if you don't want to pay, you can go to hell. He looked at us through puffy eyes, full of beer, twisted up his mouth and spit out the window, letting fly a heavy gob of spit, right over our heads, moistening our faces with the spray from his alcoholic saliva. Nevertheless, despite our tight economic circumstances, and the sensorial unpleasantness produced by the ensemble of truck driver and cab, we accepted the rate. Huevi convinced himself that it was okay, and asked me if he could borrow twenty to add to what he had on him, I said yes, it wasn't for nothing that I was going to be the witness at this wedding. We decided to load the decrepit matrimonial mattress onto the truck. To hold onto it more firmly, I slipped my hand into one of the holes, grabbed a pair of springs, and heaved it up. Huevi and the truck driver pushed from below. Half of it went up first. I pulled my hand out of the hole, and, without being able to prevent the fabric from ripping, I pulled it by one of the corners, and the other half landed on the truck bed. The three of us got into the cab, and, rounding the first curve, through a lucky spin of the wheel, the drunk managed to avoid running down a slow and squalid Karpaty motorcycle. From then on, the truck driver's drunkenness began to worry us. While I am remembering this, Huevi, without a word, responding to the Yankee's challenge, has grabbed a half-inch galvanized pipe he found nearby, and I, for my part, latch onto a thirty-six millimeter Spanish wrench.

[*Lila's mother*] Johnny's never going to learn Spanish, Lilita. If he keeps hanging out with your cousin Tato and the other guys from the tenement, he's going to end up talking like them. Yesterday I heard him utter his first vulgarities, and today, as soon as he got out of the car, he spit out another one. He kicked the tire, because it was flat, and said: ¡*Pinga!* not giving a damn if anyone around there heard him. Apparently he does it to ingratiate himself with them, because everyone on the sidewalk laughed, and then he laughed too. Anyway, people like him, and ever since he brought presents he's had the whole tenement eating out of his hand. It's not the kind of thing just anyone does, and he didn't forget anyone either: he brought Tato razor blades for his shaver, a pair of underpants for Nesa; he even brought a cap for that idiot Felipe. . . .

And he relates to the neighbors the same way. He doesn't care who he talks to; you know the other day, Tuesday, when he stayed over with you, I got up early to wash the bedspread and hang it out to dry, and found him chatting with Meña. I had to laugh. You know Meña is half nuts. She was complaining as usual, about how there's no milk, about the blackouts, and he—so you understand how things are—began to talk to her about the same things Fidel does, that the hospitals are all free, that *there* operations cost thousands of dollars and here even one of us can have one. He even talked about Martí. Meña was quiet at first, not knowing what to say, but finally broke down and answered: You can explain and explain all you want; all I know is there's a lot of hunger around here . . . then turned around and went into her house, still talking to herself. Johnny's a riot. But if Tato keeps on teaching him all that low-life talk, when we least expect it he's going to get us all into trouble. The day before yesterday I heard your cousin telling him that when you want to buy a girl a drink you were supposed to say: *¿Quieres templar, mi cielo?*² And that instead of saying: I think I'll go to sleep now, he should say: I'm sorry to have to leave you all now, but I . . . and I'm not going to repeat what he said, it's so gross. Can you imagine, Lilita? Don't laugh. It's a good thing you're always with him, and you keep him from saying such filthy things. I hope it never occurs to him to say those things in front of anyone important!

[*Johnny*] This Chevrolet, bring much money over there, whatever I ask. All original parts, no accidents, no dents, worth a lot. When hood open, me see shiny motor, it looks wonderful, then me want rent it, me feel good driving old car, feel like in old times, other times, me play music: Nat King Cole, Frank Sinatra, even Elvis Presley . . . and then, eh dream, amigo, dream. *Así*, life is good. Hotels, pools, *restaurantes son mierda*, shit. Live like you is better, drink rum, eat *chicharrones*, play *dominó*, and Lila always here to give kisses. You not know how to be happy. My country not human, like machine, no love, only think about money. You be so-cia-ble. Not there. People say: heat enter soul just like cold. It's bullshit. Not true. Heat not the same as sun, or breeze, or ocean, or beach, or rum. Is culture, yes, cul-ture, rumba, language, mixed breeds, religions, yes! substances mix, reaction produce heat. Hard for me explain in *español*. *¿Exo-ter-mis-mo, no?* Heat also come from you, from smiles, stories.

[*Huevi's friend*] I don't think he'll do it. The yuma should wait, let us be the ones to attack, although me, I'd rather see Huevi be the one to take the initiative. The mechanic has lit the torch, flaming acetylene leaps from it; an angel complex has overtaken that mulatto who tends his business the way a farmer tends his flowers, and who keeps his distance as a warning. Before, he threatened us that he wasn't going to put up with any problems, placing the flame so close to my face he almost burned me. I know what you're up to but if there's any trouble, I'll intervene, he concluded. Huevi promised there wouldn't be a fight. He just wanted the guy to apologize. He had promised the same thing earlier, a few hours ago, when the drunk insulted him and forced him out of the truck. Don't get into a fight, Huevi—I advised him—grab the mattress and we'll carry it the rest of the way, it's not far, *asere*. My friend was ready to listen when the truck driver got out of his seat, looking for a fight, and came over to us. Alternately he flailed his arms around at the level of Huevi's chin and made as if to wash hands violently, spit on the ground, shouted insults in a vulgar and impassioned prose: I'll unman you, and stomp on your head, you damn mare. Huevi finally hit him. A straight jab to the chin and the offended helmsman fell to his knees. The man got up again, and Huevi prepared a better attack: a left, a straight right, and a swing to the left to finish him off, which broke his nose slightly, and the man fell into a sitting position. At that point I intervened. I soothed their tempers. The drunk offended Huevi with devastating cruelty: *hijueputasingaoporculo* I'm going to cut your ass *maricóndel-coñoetumadre*, and I don't know how I managed to get all three of us back into the vehicle, to continue our trip through the winding streets of Old Havana. The drunk let out a string of curses, that we had dragged him into this hellhole of streets that no one could figure out, that shitheadedness was contagious, and that, therefore, we were a real pair of shit-eaters. Huevi had dry mouth, was containing his anger, and I, afraid that the truck driver might refuse to take us a second time, played peacemaker, winking and smiling at Huevi. Not like now, of course. Now I'm smiling at Huevi so he'll cease the unequal combat. The blond is on his guard, not like an unseasoned pugilist, but rather with all the confidence and elegance displayed by Rocky Marciano in better times. He extends his left hand out, ready to, like a serpentine whip, jab us right between the eyes. His powerful right fist remains in waiting, like a coiled spring, at chin level. So that the yuma appears to be sculpted in bronze, an invincible colossus, against which our weapons are all but powerless. Yes, it would be better to beat a retreat right now and say: We made a mistake, *mister, adiós*.

[*Lila's mother*] Mira, *hija*, there's no reason to get angry. It's true Johnny has been very good to us, to Tato, to the whole family, and everybody in the neighborhood. But you've got to try and understand people. When you left the house, the worst was already over, you didn't see anything. It's true he was drunk as a skunk, but then who doesn't get drunk these days? Your cousin Tato gets drunk every single day, but does he deserve a beating for it? Of course not. Your boyfriend is very impulsive, mi hija. He became an animal, ready to eat the guy alive. I understand his obsession with that car, ever since he saw it he was all over the owner, insisting, and would have no peace until he agreed to rent it to him. He was always washing it, wiping it down with a rag as if it were his; looking for the best music for his ride. I would have liked to have one like that too; it reminds me of the one your grandfather had, although it was an old Ford he sold right before he died. . . . When I saw that truck turning the corner at full speed, I was horrified, closed my eyes, and when I opened them, the damage had been done. I never imagined Johnny would go to blows with the truck driver; there was no reason for such aggression. The best thing you can do is make peace with the neighbors. Call each one of them up and apologize. What did you want them to do? If he had been content to just slam the door into him, but no, he had to drag the miserable guy out of the cab, grab him by the neck, and start punching him. People waited quite a while before they did anything, Lilita. If you had gotten there a little later, I don't know what might have happened. Did you see how the poor man was limping as he headed back to his truck, or did you only see what you wanted to see? And you still maintain that he got out of the truck to fight with Johnny. You've got to be kidding. If you'd blown on the man, he would have fallen over, Lilita; and besides, you could see he was a kind soul, after he hit the car the first thing he did, because he felt so bad, was to rest his head on the steering wheel and moan, like a boy. If Johnny hadn't decided to smash his leg with the door, I'm sure they would have worked it out, because the truck driver looked like an alright sort to me. He was going to climb out of the truck and explain, as is expected. But that animal of a boyfriend of yours — yes, he's an animal! — grabbed the door to the cab and bam, bam, bam, smashed it against the driver's leg. No, *chica*, no, people behaved decently. Why did you have to insult everyone? The smartest thing you did was advise your boyfriend to get lost, because later, as you know, when they took a good look at the bruises on the truck driver, and heard the way he was moaning, a few of them wanted to give Johnny a beating. Two of them, they were on the truck, I think, came back a little while ago, looking for him. I pray to God they don't find him because I'm fond of him and I would hate for anything to happen to him. . . . So, talk to everyone, Lilita, explain things to them. I don't know how many times I told Johnny he shouldn't park his car there, on that block, not just because someone might steal it, but because those streets are very narrow, and accidents don't announce themselves.

[*Lila*] I love him, Mami. Yes, and don't laugh. You think, because I make fun of him, that I don't love him? He's made me a person. Before, in high school, the white girls all used to look down their noses at me and I ended up with a complex. There they were shaking their hair, taking about how this shampoo gave you dandruff, how they were off to the beach to get a tan, about their suntan lotion. . . . They gave me a complex. And in twelfth grade? It was worse. Three of us were black, Nelsa, Katiuska, and me, and there were two mulattas with good hair that wouldn't talk to us. The three of us were the same, unbearably shy. . . . In other classrooms, it was different, the black girls formed a group; they teased the white girls and didn't let them push them around. I would have given anything to be in those classes! When you talked me into starting at the university, I thought things would be better. People will be more cultured, more polished, I thought. Was I wrong! The only black women, the only real black women, I say, were a Congolese student, can't remember her name anymore, and me. To make things worse, that girl stuck to me like a leech. You've seen those stray dogs in the street that start following you around all of sudden, wagging their tails, trying you make you love them whether you want to or not. Well, it was kind of like that. I didn't want to have anything to do with her, but she'd sit next to me in lecture hall and in regular classes too. You can imagine how I felt when people started calling us the two Congolese. A nightmare come true. Then there was the whole tenement distracting me, getting ahead of me. Even Nelsa was into something, some kind of business, showing off her good clothes, and me in that green dress, you remember? And those black sneakers full of labels covering up all the holes; can you imagine how I must have looked when I started classes? No, Mami, it wasn't your fault. I've never blamed you for anything. That's the way life is. You should see how people look at me now when I get out of the car with Johnny. They look at me, and they'll do anything just to say hello. Even Katiuska, the other day when I was going to the store with him, she came up all effusive, the life of the party, talking to him in English and everything. I just laughed to myself. Didn't she want to be a doctor? Well she can go fuck herself. Just when she was really getting into it, I cut the conversation short, and took off with my blond guy, killing her with envy. Before, I wouldn't have behaved like that for anything in the world. When I dropped out of the university, even Katiuska turned her back on me, thinking I was a failure. But when I met Johnny, life changed. It was the beginning of a real relationship. Even I began to see myself differently, to discover my good points, to believe in myself. . . . That's why what happened the other day bothers me, and pisses me off, because Johnny, even with all his defects, is good people. He could come to Cuba and just enjoy himself, spend his money on himself, but he doesn't do that. He's always trying to help, to show he's on our side. You remember the time I got so mad because he didn't give me the money to buy the room Nelsa was selling, instead he went and spent a fortune on the oxygen equipment he had delivered to the polyclinic? I treated him worse than a dog that time, and that was when I discovered how much he loved me. He gave me such a pretty watch, and two little stuffed pigs with a banner that said: Friends forever. He got to my heart that day. And that's why I forgave him, afterwards, for going off to work in the countryside with the commies. You didn't know it then, but he got so carried away he almost dragged me off with him. Thank God I stood my ground, and stayed behind, that's when I got involved with Giacomo and Vittorio. When Johnny came back a month later, he had dirt everywhere; you could have planted a whole field of sweet potatoes in his ears, and his nails looked like pigs' hooves. I gave him a bath and scrubbed him with a loofah until he smelled sweeter than a baby. Thank God he never did that again, and decided to make donations instead.

[*Huevi's friend*] Huevi has proven that his balls are as inordinately large as Maceo's. Not me, as he advances, I've been cautiously retreating, it must be because my balls are normal sized, and because it was Huevi's idea, after all, so he should be the one to do it. Just the same, it pains me that my friend is advancing, all alone, and that the mechanic, neutral until just a second ago, is getting ready to head him off with his blazing weapon, while I, limping, am fatigued by unusual hypertension, a vague reaction, the doctor would say, a bit of fatigue, the neighborhood guys would say, an acute attack of assholitis, my father would say. The people's faces are a blur, and I'm feeling bad that El Huevón, as we used to call him in high school, is so brave he doesn't even want me to imitate him. And I go forward, wrench in hand—a Viking blandishing his mace, biting his tongue, coarsening his features—toward the fearful melon with legs, the bull-headed Chevrolet lover. The Yankee looks me over, opens his eyes, moved, as if I were a smaller version of Frankenstein, raises his open hands in a gesture of surrender and says: *Okay, I give up. What do you want?* The mechanic steps aside. Suddenly the giant grows smaller. *Me, apologize to you*, he says, *me crazy because friend of yours break auto, and auto not mine, me promise take care of it. . . .* As he speaks, he casts a sad glance at the door of the Chevrolet. As he continues to speak, he's almost crying: My life almost happy until today, look at auto, look at door, disaster (his voice is quivering), I sorry for your friend, I. . . . He lowers his head, passes a hand over his forehead. Huevi, a little further back, keeps up his threats, unmoved: We'll unman you if you don't give up the cash, got it, no excuses. Huevi threatens, moves his pipe, arches his eyebrows. The yuma not understand, not know what we want. You have to indemnify us, I say. My comrade in arms moves his lethal cannula, one *touche* with that weapon produces lesions and who knows what else. I bite my tongue again, the Stanislowski method, I am a killer, a gangster, a warrior, I look at him crosswise. In-dem-ni-*what?* The blond him not understand that our friend can't work for a few days, that he needs money, yes, dollars, to buy oil, *malangas*, soap, and with the change, lollipops. Him not understand that our friend father to five little children, that he put him out of commission, that he disfigured his face, broke his nose, knocked out a tooth, and that this is sanctioned by the law everywhere in the world. Money? Yes, at least five hundred, Huevi demands. Not for nothing is he the owner of a pair of macrotesticles. Now the weapon is a sports implement, a light bat, and Huevi is a pitcher anxious to sock it to the NBA pivot, reduced to the status of major league pitcher. *Okay, me give you four hundred.* He sticks his hand in his pocket when he sees us put down our weapons, and the blond is surprised every day by the Cubans, even though the Cubans affectionately forgive him as long as he pays the toll for letting his ignoble fists travel over the truck driver's face; even though the Cubans squeeze his hand as if they were friends forever; even though the Cubans smile and say: *Zenkiu* and he responds: You are welcome.

[*Truck driver*] Maestro, I'm a man who's ready for anything. Didn't you see the *guampara* I've got in my truck? It's got a blade that'll take not the hand, but the head off anybody who messes with me. I keep to myself, but if you mess with me, you get what's coming to you, and God help anybody who tries to, because I never forgive. You remember that mulatto who fucked up my finger so bad they had to put a cast on it? I almost killed him. But later he came by and apologized, that it had been an accident, and I forgave him because he's got a two-year-old boy and I don't like to make a boy an orphan. And anyway, the finger healed and my hand was like new. Still, when I remember it you have to hold me back. Like the other day when I had a few drinks and went to his house looking for him, what saved him was that he wasn't home, other-wise he'd be six feet under today. I'm dangerous, maestro. You see how I'm all covered with bruises, well, that's because I don't let anyone get away with anything. The last time, I got into something with a yuma. The guy, because I hit his Chevrolet, went all hysterical on me, tried to mess me up. You should have seen him. He was a tank, each of his arms was like one of my thighs. He looked just like, you know who? you know that Yankee actor who played Rocky, what's his name? Anyway, I slapped him so hard his head spun around. Since his skin was so white, each of my five fingers left a mark. I was ready to checkmate him when the band of jineteros hanging with him jumped me, and I broke one of their noses, then kicked him in the stomach so hard it knocked the wind out of him. Later the *puta* who was with the yuma came out, one ugly *negra*, and she got involved too. I started a terrible ruckus. My left leg was broken to pieces, and they fractured my jaw, that's the truth, but I swear they got theirs too. I swear to God, it's true, but you don't have to believe me if you don't want to: you either respect me or suck my dick, maestro, skinny as I may be.

[*Lila*] Mami, we've let him down. You can imagine, people he loved so much taking the drunk's side who didn't give a shit, wasn't even grateful. Yesterday he was all sad, he didn't even want to pull into the block, let me out in the park near the bus station and he said: We'll meet here, tomorrow. We had eaten lunch together and he told me he was leaving in a week and didn't think he'd be coming back. He feels betrayed. He hasn't used those exact words but I can tell. If he leaves, he won't ever come back, Mami. The final touch was those two who came looking for him. Johnny was a bag of nerves when he told me the story. Two delinquents, Mami, with steel bars and razors, they almost killed him, fortunately a man came out and defended him, but if he hadn't. . . . The four hundred *fulas* that he was going to leave me to get you a television set are all gone,[3] Mami; he had to give it to the delinquents. But don't you worry, Mami, tomorrow I'll go see the Irish guy, the one Nelsa introduced me to yesterday, and in less than a month you'll be watching the soap operas in color.

[*Huevi's friend*] The mechanic observes the exchange calmly: forgiveness for money. We move away. We look at the yuma for the last time. We walked in silence, not believing what we had just pulled off, went back to Old Havana and talked about it for the first time. Huevi admires my courage. He was scared shitless, he admits. He backed off because of you, he adds. You've got some balls on you, he yells. I don't say anything. I invite him for a beer. Guys like you, who don't say much, they're the real tough guys, he says from his heart. I'm all beat up, he says in self-criticism. We drank the beer and divvied up the money, discreetly seated at a table against the wall. Did they ever do that operation to get the water out of your balls? I ask. He says yes, sure, but it didn't change the size of them. They don't bother you? I ask again, interrogating him. I've never sat down on top of them, he answers seriously. They looked like a couple of mameys when we were at boarding school together, I reminisce. I'm real lucky with the *jevas* because of them, he says, in self-defense.[4] They must think you've got more semen than anyone, I comment. I don't think it's that, don't you like big tits? I laugh and take a long sip of beer. That *jevita*, the one who was chasing the yuma, used to be my girlfriend, Huevi confesses and adds, but it was so long ago that neither she or her crazy mother remembers me anymore.

TRANSLATED BY PAMELA MARIA SMORKALOFF

Notes

1. A slang term referring to people from the United States.
2. "Would you like to screw, my love?"
3. *Fula* is slang for dollars.
4. *Jeva* is slang for "girl."

Suggestions for Further Reading

General

Bethell, Leslie, ed. *Cuba: A Short History*. Cambridge: Cambridge University Press, 1993.

Calvo Ospina, Hernando. *Salsa! Havana Heat, Bronx Beat*. Translated by Nick Caistor. London: Latin America Bureau, 1995.

Castillo Bueno, Maria de los Reyes. *Reyita: The Life of a Black Cuban Woman in the Twentieth Century*. Durham, N.C.: Duke University Press, 2000.

De la Fuente, Alejandro. *A Nation For All: Race, Inequality, and Politics in Twentieth-Century Cuba*. Chapel Hill: University of North Carolina Press, 2001.

Díaz Ayala, Cristóbal. *The Roots of Salsa: A History of Cuban Music*. New York: Excelsior Music Publishing Company, 1995.

Kutzinski, Vera. *Race and the Erotics of Cuban Nationalism*. Charlottesville: University Press of Virginia, 1994.

Leymarie, Isabelle. *Cuban Fire: The Saga of Salsa and Latin Jazz*. London: Continuum, 2002.

Liss, Sheldon. *Roots of Revolution: Radical Thought in Cuba*. Lincoln: University of Nebraska Press, 1987.

Martínez-Fernández, Luis, D. H. Figueredo, Louis A. Pérez Jr., and Luis González, eds. *Encyclopedia of Cuba: People, History, Culture*. Westport, Conn.: Greenwood Press, 2003.

Moreno Fraginals, Manuel. *Cuba/España, España/Cuba: Historia común*. Barcelona: Crítica Grijalbo Mondadori, 1995.

Pérez, Jr., Louis A. *Cuba: Between Reform and Revolution*. 2d ed. New York: Oxford University Press, 1995.

———. *Cuba and the United States: Ties of a Singular Intimacy*. Athens: University of Georgia Press, 1990.

———. *On Becoming Cuban: Identity, Nationality, and Culture*. Chapel Hill: University of North Carolina Press, 1999.

Pichardo, Hortensia. *Documentos para la historia de Cuba*. 4 vols. Havana: Instituto Cubano del Libro / Editorial de Ciencias Sociales, 1973.

Portuondo Zúñiga, Olga. *La virgen de la Caridad del Cobre: Símbolo de la cubanía*. Santiago de Cuba: Editorial Oriente, 1995.

Thomas, Hugh. *Cuba: The Pursuit of Freedom*. New York: Harper and Row, 1971.

West, Alan. *Tropics of History*. Bergin and Garvey, 1997.

Zanetti, Oscar, and Alejandro García. *Sugar and Railroads: A Cuban History, 1837–1959*. Translated by Franklin W. Knight and Mary Todd. Chapel Hill: University of North Carolina Press, 1998.

I. Indigenous Society and Conquest

Barreiro, José. *The Indian Chronicles*. Houston, Tex.: Arte Público Press, 1993.

Cohen, J. M., ed. *The Four Voyages of Christopher Columbus*. Harmondsworth, England: Penguin, 1969.

Dacal Moure, Ramón, and Manuel Rivero de la Calle. *Art and Archeology of Pre-Colombian Cuba*. Translated by Daniel H. Sandweiss. Pittsburgh, Pa.: University of Pittsburgh Press, 1996.

Las Casas, Bartolomé de. *The Devastation of the Indies: A Brief Account*. Translated by Herma Briffault. Baltimore, Md.: Johns Hopkins University Press, 1992.

Flint, Valerie I. J. *The Imaginative Landscape of Christopher Columbus*. Princeton, N.J.: Princeton University Press, 1992.

Hulme, Peter. *Colonial Encounters: Europe and the Native Caribbean, 1492–1797*. London: Routledge, 1986.

Wright, Irene A. *The Early History of Cuba, 1492–1586*. New York: Macmillan, 1916. Reprint, New York: Octagon Books, 1970.

II. Sugar, Slavery, and Colonialism

Barnet, Miguel. *Biography of a Runaway Slave*. Translated by Nick Hill. Willimantic, Conn.: Curbstone Press, 1994.

Bergad, Laird W. *Cuban Rural Society in the Nineteenth Century: The Social and Economic History of Monoculture in Matanzas*. Princeton, N.J.: Princeton University Press, 1990.

Gómez de Avellaneda y Arteaga, Gertrudis. *Sab and Autobiography*. Translated and edited by Nina M. Scott. Austin: University of Texas Press, 1993.

Knight, Franklin W. *Slave Society in Cuba during the Nineteenth Century*. Madison: University of Wisconsin Press, 1970.

Martínez-Alier, Verena. *Marriage, Class, and Colour in Nineteenth-Century Cuba: A Study of Racial Attitudes and Sexual Values in a Slave Society*. 2d ed. Ann Arbor: University of Michigan Press, 1989.

Mintz, Sidney. *Sweetness and Power: The Place of Sugar in Modern History*. New York: Penguin Books, 1985.

Moreno Fraginals, Manuel. *The Sugarmill: The Socio-Economic Complex of Sugar in Cuba*. Translated by Cedric Belfrage. New York: Monthly Review Press, 1976.

Moreno Fraginals, Manuel, Frank Moya Pons, and Stanley L. Engerman, eds. *Between Slavery and Free Labor: The Spanish-Speaking Caribbean in the Nineteenth Century*. Baltimore, Md.: Johns Hopkins University Press, 1985.

Paquette, Robert L. *Sugar Is Made with Blood: The Conspiracy of La Escalera and the Conflict between Empires over Slavery in Cuba*. Middletown, Conn.: Wesleyan University Press, 1988.

Pérez, Louis A., Jr., ed. *Slaves, Sugar, and Colonial Society: Travel Accounts of Cuba, 1801–1899*. Wilmington, Del.: Scholarly Resources, 1992.

———. *Winds of Change: Hurricanes and the Transformation of Nineteenth-Century Cuba*. Chapel Hill: University of North Carolina Press, 2001.

Scott, Rebecca J. *Slave Emancipation in Cuba: The Transition to Free Labor, 1860–1899.*
Princeton, N.J.: Princeton University Press, 1985.

Ullivarri, Saturnino. *Piratas y corsarios en Cuba.* Havana: Maza, Caso y Cia, 1931.

Villaverde, Cirilo. *Cecilia Valdés.* Translated by Sydney Gest. New York: Vantage
Press, 1962.

III. The Struggle for Independence

Abel, Christopher, and Nisa Torrents, eds. *José Martí: Revolutionary Democrat.* Durham,
N.C.: Duke University Press, 1986.

Casanovas, Joan. *Bread, or Bullets! Urban Labor and Spanish Colonialism in Cuba, 1850–1898.*
Pittsburgh, Pa.: University of Pittsburgh Press, 1998.

Ferrer, Ada. *Ambivalent Revolution: Race, Nation, and Revolution, 1868–1898.* Chapel Hill:
University of North Carolina Press, 1999.

Helg, Aline. *Our Rightful Share: The Afro-Cuban Struggle for Equality, 1886–1912.* Chapel Hill:
University of North Carolina Press, 1995.

Kirk, John M. *José Martí: Mentor of the Cuban Nation.* Gainesville: University of Florida
Press, 1983.

Martí, José. *Inside the Monster: Writings on the United States and American Imperialism.*
Translated by Elinor Randall, and ed. Philip S. Foner. New York: Monthly Review
Press, 1975.

———. *Our America: Writings on Latin America and the Struggle for Cuban Independence.*
Translated by Elinor Randall, and edited by Philip S. Foner. New York: Monthly
Review Press, 1977.

Pérez, Louis A., Jr. *Lords of the Mountain: Social Banditry and Peasant Protest in Cuba,
1878–1918.* Pittsburgh, Pa.: University of Pittsburgh Press, 1989.

———. *The War of 1898: The United States and Cuba in History and Historiography.* Chapel
Hill: University of North Carolina Press, 1998.

Poyo, Gerald E. *"With All, and for the Good of All": The Emergence of Popular Nationalism in
the Cuban Communities of the United States, 1848–1898.* Durham, N.C.: Duke University
Press, 1989.

Rickover, Hyman G. *How the Battleship* Maine *Was Destroyed.* Washington, D.C.: Naval
History Division, Department of the Navy, 1976.

Samuels, Peggy, and Harold Samuels. *Remembering the* Maine. Washington, D.C.:
Smithsonian Institution Press, 1995.

Schwartz, Rosalie. *Lawless Liberators: Political Banditry and Cuban Independence.* Durham,
N.C.: Duke University Press, 1989.

Turton, Peter. *José Martí, Architect of Cuba's Freedom.* London: Zed Books, 1986.

IV. Neocolonialism

Aguilar, Luis. *Cuba: 1933. Prologue to Revolution.* Ithaca, N.Y.: Cornell University
Press, 1972.

Alvarez Estévez, Rolando. *Azúcar e inmigración, 1900–1940.* Havana: Editorial de Ciencias
Sociales, 1988.

Ameringer, Charles. *The Cuban Democratic Experience: The Auténtico Years, 1944–1952*. Gainesville: University of Florida Press, 2000.

Ayala, César J. *American Sugar Kingdom: The Plantation Economy of the Spanish Caribbean, 1898–1934*. Chapel Hill: University of North Carolina Press, 1999.

Barnet, Miguel. *Rachel's Song*. Translated by Nick Hill. Willimantic, Conn.: Curbstone Press, 1991.

Benjamin, Jules. *The United States and Cuba: Hegemony and Dependent Development, 1880–1934*. Pittsburgh, Pa.: University of Pennsylvania Press, 1974.

Brock, Lisa, and Digna Castañeda Fuertes. *African-Americans and Cubans before the Cuban Revolution*. Philadelphia, Pa.: Temple University Press, 1998.

Buell, Raymond, Leslie, et al. *Problems of the New Cuba*. New York: Foreign Policy Association, 1935.

De Carrión, Miguel. *Las honradas*. Havana: Editorial Letras Cubanas, 1981.

Dye, Alan. *Cuban Sugar in the Age of Mass Production: Technology and the Economics of the Sugar Central*. Stanford, Calif.: Stanford University Press, 1998.

Eire, Carlos M. N. *Waiting for Snow in Havana: Confessions of a Cuban Boy*. New York: Free Press, 2003.

Farber, Samuel. *Revolution and Reaction in Cuba, 1933–1960: A Political Sociology from Machado to Castro*. Bridgeport, Conn.: Wesleyan University Press, 1976.

Fernández Robaina, Tomás. *El negro en Cuba, 1902–1958: Apuntes para la historia de la lucha contra la discriminación racial en la neocolonia*. Havana: Editorial de Ciencias Sociales, 1990.

———. *Recuerdos secretos de dos mujeres públicas*. Havana: Editorial Letras Cubanas, 1983.

González, Reynaldo. *Llorar es un placer*. Havana: Editorial Letras Cubanas, 1988.

Guerra y Sánchez, Ramiro. *Sugar and Society in the Caribbean: An Economic History of Cuban Agriculture*. New Haven, Conn.: Yale University Press, 1964.

Ibarra, Jorge. *Cuba: 1898–1921. Partidos políticos y clases sociales*. Havana: Editorial de Ciencias Sociales, 1992.

———. *Prologue to Revolution: Cuba, 1898–1958*. Translated by Marjorie Moore. Boulder, Colo.: Lynne Rienner Publishers, 1998.

Jenks, Leland H. *Our Cuban Colony*. New York: Vanguard Press, 1928.

Loveira, Carlos. *Generales y doctores*. Havana: Editorial Letras Cubanas, 1984.

Nelson, Lowry. *Rural Cuba*. Minneapolis: University of Minnesota Press, 1950.

Moore, Robin. *Nationalizing Blackness: Afrocubanismo and the Artistic Revolution in Havana, 1920–1940*. Pittsburgh, Pa.: University of Pittsburgh Press, 1997.

Oltuski, Enrique. *Vida Clandestina: My Life in the Cuban Revolution*. Translated by Thomas Christensen and Carol Christensen. San Francisco: Wiley, 2002.

Ortiz, Fernando. *Cuban Counterpoint: Tobacco and Sugar*. Translated by Harriet de Onís. Reprint ed. Durham, N.C.: Duke University Press, 1995.

Pérez de la Riva, Juan, et al. *La república neocolonial*. 2 vols. Havana: Editorial de Ciencias Sociales, 1975–78.

Primelles, León. *Crónica cubana, 1915–1918*. Havana: Editorial Lex, 1955.

———. *Crónica cubana, 1919–1922*. Havana: Editorial Lex, 1957.

Report on Cuba: Findings and Recommendations of an Economic and Technical Mission Organized by the International Bank for Reconstruction and Development in Collaboration with the Government of Cuba in 1950. Washington, D.C.: International Bank for Reconstruction and Development, 1951.

Schwartz, Rosalie. *Pleasure Island: Tourism and Temptation in Cuba.* Lincoln: University of Nebraska Press, 1999.

Smith, Robert Freeman. *The United States and Cuba: Business and Diplomacy, 1898–1934.* New Haven, Conn.: College and University Press, 1960.

Soto, Lionel. *La revolución de 1933.* 3 vols. Havana: Pueblo y Educación, 1985.

Stoner, K. Lynn. *From the House to the Streets: The Cuban Woman's Movement for Legal Reform, 1898–1940.* Durham, N.C.: Duke University Press, 1991.

Stubbs, Jean. *Tobacco on the Periphery: A Case Study in Cuban Labour History.* Cambridge: Cambridge University Press, 1985.

Sweig, Julia E. *Inside the Revolution: Fidel Castro and the Urban Underground.* Cambridge, Mass.: Harvard University Press, 2002.

Whitney, Robert. *State and Revolution in Cuba: Mass Mobilization and Political Change, 1920–1940.* Chapel Hill: University of North Carolina Press, 2001.

Zanetti, Oscar, and Alejandro García. *United Fruit Company: Un caso del dominio imperialista en Cuba.* Havana: Editorial de Ciencias Sociales, 1976.

THE INSURRECTION AND TRIUMPH
OF THE REVOLUTION, 1953–1960

Bonachea, Ramón L., and Marta San Martín. *The Cuban Insurrection, 1952–1959.* New Brunswick, N.J.: Transaction Books, 1974.

Bonachea, Rolando E., and Nelson P. Valdés, comps. *Cuba in Revolution.* Garden City, N.Y.: Anchor Books, 1972.

Castro, Fidel. *History Will Absolve Me.* Havana: Editorial en Marcha, 1962.

————. *Revolutionary Struggle, 1947–1958.* Edited by Rolando E. Bonachea and Nelson P. Valdés. Cambridge, Mass.: MIT Press, 1972.

Franqui, Carlos. *The Twelve.* Translated by Albert B. Teichner. New York: Lyle Stuart, 1968.

García-Pérez, Gladys. *Insurrection and Revolution: Armed Struggle in Cuba, 1952–1959.* Translated by Juan Ortega. Boulder, Colo.: Lynne Rienner, 1996.

Guevara, Che. *Reminiscences of the Cuban Revolutionary War.* New York: Monthly Review, 1968.

Marel García, Gladys. *Memoria e identitidad: Un estudio específico (1952–1958).* Havana: Editorial de Ciencias Sociales, 1996.

Lionel Martin. *The Early Fidel: Roots of Castro's Communism.* New York: Lyle Stuart, 1978.

Matthews, Herbert L. *The Cuban Story.* New York: George Braziller, 1961.

V. Building a New Society

Bengelsdorf, Carolee. *The Problem of Democracy in Cuba: Between Vision and Reality.* New York: Oxford University Press, 1994.

Benjamin, Medea, Joseph Collins, and Michael Scott. *No Free Lunch: Food and Revolution in Cuba Today.* New York: Grove Press, 1986.

Brundenius, Claes. *Revolutionary Cuba: The Challenge of Economic Growth with Equity.* Boulder, Colo.: Westview Press, 1984.

Domínguez, Jorge. *Cuba: Order and Revolution.* Cambridge, Mass.: Belknap Press of Harvard University Press, 1978.

Eckstein, Susan Eva. *Back from the Future: Cuba under Castro.* Princeton, N.J.: Princeton University Press, 1994.

Evenson, Debra. *Revolution in the Balance: Law and Society in Contemporary Cuba.* Boulder, Colo.: Westview Press, 1994.

Fagen, Richard R. *The Transformation of Political Culture in Cuba.* Stanford, Calif.: Stanford University Press, 1969.

Franqui, Carlos. *Diary of the Cuban Revolution.* New York: Viking Press, 1980.

————. *Family Portrait with Fidel.* New York: Vintage, 1985.

Feinsilver, Julie M. *Healing the Masses: Cuban Health Politics at Home and Abroad.* Berkeley: University of California Press, 1993.

Fuller, Linda. *Work and Democracy in Socialist Cuba.* Philadelphia, Pa.: Temple University Press, 1992.

Guevara, Ernesto Che. *The Speeches and Writings of Che Guevara.* Edited by John Gerassi. Translated by Margarita Zimmerman. New York: Macmillan, 1968.

Karol, K. S. *Guerrillas in Power: The Course of the Cuban Revolution.* Translated by Arnold Pomerans. New York: Hill and Wang, 1970.

Kozol, Jonathan. *Children of the Revolution: A Yankee Teacher in the Cuban Schools.* New York: Delacorte Press, 1978.

Leiner, Marvin. *Sexual Politics in Cuba: Machismo, Homosexuality, and AIDS.* Boulder, Colo.: Westview Press, 1994.

Lewis, Oscar, Ruth M. Lewis, and Susan M. Rigdon. *Four Men: Living the Revolution. An Oral History of Contemporary Cuba.* Urbana: University of Illinois Press, 1977.

————. *Four Women: Living the Revolution. An Oral History of Contemporary Cuba.* Urbana: University of Illinois Press, 1977.

————. *Neighbors: Living the Revolution. An Oral History of Contemporary Cuba.* Urbana: University of Illinois Press, 1978.

Löwy, Michael. *The Marxism of Che Guevara: Philosophy, Economics, and Revolutionary Warfare.* Translated by Brian Pearce. New York: Monthly Review Press, 1973.

Lumsden, Ian. *Machos, Maricones, and Gays: Cuba and Homosexuality.* Philadelphia, Pa.: Temple University Press, 1996.

Medin, Tzvi. *Cuba: The Shaping of Revolutionary Consciousness.* Translated by Martha Grenzback. Boulder, Colo.: Lynne Rienner Publishers, 1990.

Moore, Carlos. *Castro, the Blacks, and Africa.* Los Angeles: Center for Afro-American Studies, UCLA, 1988.

Paz, Senel. *El lobo, el bosque, y el hombre nuevo.* Mexico City: Ediciones Era, 1991.

Pérez-Stable, Marifeli. *The Cuban Revolution: Origins, Course, and Legacy.* New York: Oxford University Press, 1993.

Reckord, Barry. *Does Fidel Eat More than Your Father? Conversations in Cuba.* New York, Praeger Publishers, 1971.

Roman, Peter. *People's Power: Cuba's Experience with Representative Government.* Boulder, Colo.: Westview Press, 1999.

Smith, Lois M., and Alfred Padula. *Sex and Revolution: Women in Socialist Cuba.* New York: Oxford University Press, 1996.

Szulc, Tad. *Fidel: A Critical Portrait.* New York: William Morrow, 1986.

Yglesias, José. *In the Fist of the Revolution: Life in a Cuban Country Town.* New York: Pantheon, 1968.

Zimbalist, Andrew, ed. *Cuban Political Economy: Controversies in Cubanology.* Boulder, Colo.: Westview Press, 1988.

VI. *Culture and Revolution*

Arenas, Reinaldo. *Before Night Falls: A Memoir.* New York: Viking Penguin, 1993.

Blanco, Juan Antonio, and Medea Benjamin. *Cuba: Talking about Revolution.* Melbourne, Australia: Ocean Press, 1994.

Betto, Frei. *Fidel and Religion.* Translated by Cuban Center for Translation and Interpretation. New York: Simon and Schuster, 1987.

Bunck, Julie Marie, ed. *Fidel Castro and the Quest for a Revolutionary Culture in Cuba.* University Park: Pennsylvania State University Press, 1994.

Camnitzer, Luis, *New Art of Cuba.* Rev. ed. Austin: University of Texas Press, 2003.

Cardenal, Ernesto. *In Cuba.* Translated by Donald Walsh. New York: New Directions, 1974.

Chanan, Michael. *The Cuban Image.* London: British Film Institute, 1985.

Daniel, Yvonne. *Rumba: Dance and Social Change in Contemporary Cuba.* Bloomington: University of Indiana Press, 1995.

Jamail, Milton, *Full Count: Inside Cuban Baseball.* Carbondale: Southern Illinois University Press, 2000.

Kirk, John M., and Leonard Padura Fuentes. *Culture and the Cuban Revolution: Conversations in Havana.* Gainesville, Fla.: University Press of Florida, 2001.

Pérez Sarduy, Pedro, ed. *Afro-Cuban Voices: On Race and Identity in Contemporary Cuba.* Gainesville: University of Florida Press, 2000.

Pérez Sarduy, Pedro, and Jean Stubbs. *Afrocuba: An Anthology of Cuban Writing on Race, Politics, and Culture.* Melbourne, Australia: Ocean Press, 1993.

Price, S. L., *Pitching around Fidel: A Journey into the Heart of Cuban Sports.* New York: Ecco Press, 2000.

Salkey, Andrew. *Havana Journal.* London: Penguin Books, 1971.

Scarpaci, Joseph L., Roberto Segre, and Mario Coyula. *Havana: Two Faces of the Antillean Metropolis.* Rev. ed. Chapel Hill: University of North Carolina Press, 2002.

VII. *The Cuban Revolution and the World*

Anderson, Jon Lee. *Che Guevara: A Revolutionary Life.* New York: Bantam Press, 1997.

Blasier, Cole, and Carmelo Mesa-Lago, eds. *Cuba in the World.* Pittsburgh, Pa.: University of Pittsburgh Press, 1979.

Carbonell Cortina, Nestor. *And the Russians Stayed: The Sovietization of Cuba. A Personal Portrait.* New York: Morrow, 1989.

Dosal, Paul J. *Comandante Che: Guerrilla Soldier, Commander, and Strategist, 1956–1967*. University Park: Pennsylvania State University Press, 2003.

Domínguez, Jorge I. *To Make a World Safe for Revolution: Cuba's Foreign Policy*. Cambridge, Mass.: Harvard University Press, 1989.

Erisman, H. Michael. *Cuba's International Relations: The Anatomy of a Nationalistic Foreign Policy*. Boulder, Colo.: Westview Press, 1985.

Falk, Pamela S. *Cuba's Foreign Policy: Caribbean Tempest*. Lexington, Mass.: Lexington Books, 1986.

Gleijeses, Piero. *Conflicting Missions: Havana, Washington, and Africa, 1959–1976*. Chapel Hill: University of North Carolina Press, 2002.

Hodges, Donald C., ed. *The Legacy of Che Guevara: A Documentary Study*. Documents translated by Ernest C. Rehder and Donald C. Hodges. London: Thames and Hudson, 1977.

Kaplowitz, Donna Rich, ed. *Cuba's Ties to a Changing World*. Boulder, Colo.: Lynne Rienner Publishers, 1993.

LeoGrande, William M. *Cuba's Policy in Africa, 1959–1980*. Berkeley, Calif.: Institute of International Studies, 1980.

Moore, Carlos. *Castro, the Blacks, and Africa*. Los Angeles: Center for Afro-American Studies, UCLA, 1988.

Olivares, Carlos, et al. *La revolución cubana ante el mundo: Conferencias*. Havana: Impre. Nacional de Cuba, 1960.

Ritter, Archibald R. M., and John M. Kirk. *Cuba in the International System: Normalization and Integration*. New York: St. Martin's Press, 1995.

Smith, Wayne S., ed. *The Russians Aren't Coming: New Soviet Policy in Latin America*. Boulder, Colo.: Lynne Rienner Publishers, 1992.

Taibo, Paco Ignacio. *Guevara, Also Known as Che*. Translated by Michael Roberts. New York: St. Martin's Press, 1997.

RELATIONS WITH THE UNITED STATES

James G. Blight, and Peter Kornbluh, eds. *Politics of Illusion: The Bay of Pigs Invasion Reexamined*. Boulder, Colo.: Lynne Rienner Publishers, 1997.

Brenner, Philip. *From Confrontation to Negotiation: U.S. Relations with Cuba*. Boulder, Colo.: Westview Press, 1988.

Chang, Lawrence, and Peter Kornbluh, eds. *The Cuban Missile Crisis, 1962*. New York: New Press, 1992.

CIA Targets Fidel: The Secret Assassination Report. Melbourne, Australia: Ocean Press, 1996.

Gosse, Van. *Where the Boys Are: Cuba, Cold War America, and the Making of a New Left*. London: Verso Press, 1993.

Mills, C. Wright. *Listen, Yankee: The Revolution in Cuba*. New York: Ballantine Books, 1960.

Morley, Morris H. *Imperial State and Revolution: The United States and Cuba, 1952–86*. Cambridge: Cambridge University Press, 1987.

Smith, Wayne. *The Closest of Enemies*. New York: Norton, 1987.

Torres, María de los Angeles. *By Heart/De Memoria: Cuban Women's Journeys in and out of Exile*. Philadelphia: Temple University Press, 2003.

————. *The Lost Apple: Operation Pedro Pan, Cuban Children in the U.S., and the Promise of a Better Future.* Boston: Beacon, 2003.

Welch, Richard E. *Response to Revolution: The United States and the Cuban Revolution, 1959–1961.* Chapel Hill: University of North Carolina Press, 1985.

White, Mark. *Missiles in Cuba: Kennedy, Khrushchev, Castro, and the 1962 Crisis.* Chicago: Ivan R. Dee, 1997.

EMIGRATION

Bettinger-López, Caroline, and Ruth Behar. *Cuban-Jewish Journeys: Searching for Identity, Home, and History in Miami.* Knoxville: University of Tennessee Press, 2000.

De la Campa, Román, and Juan Flores. *Cuba on My Mind: Journeys to a Severed Nation.* London: Verso, 2000.

García, Cristina. *Dreaming in Cuban.* New York: Ballantine Books, 1992.

García, María Cristina. *Havana USA: Cuban Exiles and Cuban Americans in South Florida, 1959–1994.* Berkeley: University of California Press, 1997.

Masud-Piloto, Félix Roberto. *From Welcomed Exiles to Illegal Immigrants: Cuban Migration to the U.S., 1959–1995.* Lanham, Md.: Rowman and Littlefield, 1996.

Portes, Alejandro, and Alex Stepick. *City on the Edge: The Transformation of Miami.* Berkeley: University of California Press, 1993.

VIII. The "Periodo Especial" and the Future of the Revolution

Azicri, Max. *Cuba Today and Tomorrow: Reinventing Socialism.* Gainesville: University of Florida Press, 2000.

Blanco, Juan Antonio. *Tercer milenio: Una visión alternativa de la posmodernidad.* Havana: Publicaciones Acuario, 1995.

Carranza, Julio, and Pedro Monreal. *Cuba: La restructuración de la economía.* Havana: Editorial Ciencias Sociales, 1995.

Centro de Estudios sobre América. *Cuba en las Américas: Una perspectiva sobre Cuba y los problemas hemisféricos.* Havana: Ediciones CEA, 1995.

Dilla, Haroldo. *La democracia en Cuba y el diferendo con los Estados Unidos.* Havana: Ediciones CEA, 1995.

Erisman, H. Michael, and John Kirk. *Cuba's Foreign Relations in a Post-Soviet World.* Gainesville: University Press of Florida, 2000.

Fainaru, Steve, and Ray González. *The Duke of Havana: Cuba, Baseball, and the American Dream.* New York: Villard Books, 2001.

Fernández, Damián J. *Cuba and the Politics of Passion.* Austin: University of Texas Press, 2000.

Fitzgerald, Frank T. *The Cuban Revolution in Crisis: From Managing Socialism to Managing Survival.* New York: Monthly Review Press, 1994.

Guillermoprieto, Alma. *Looking for History: Dispatches from Latin America.* New York: Pantheon, 2001.

Halebsky, Sandor, and John Kirk, eds. *Cuba in Transition: Crisis and Transformation.* Boulder, Colo.: Westview Press, 1992.

Jatar-Hausmann, Ana Julia. *The Cuban Way: Capitalism, Communism, and Confrontation.* West Hartford, Conn.: Kumarian Press, 1999.

Martínez, Milagros, et al. *Los balseros cubanos: Un estudio a partir de las salidas ilegales.* Havana: Editorial de Ciencias Sociales, 1996.

McCaughan, Edward J. *Reinventing Revolution: The Renovation of Left Discourse in Cuba and Mexico.* Boulder, Colo.: Westview Press, 1997.

McCoy, Terry, ed. *Cuba on the Verge: An Island in Transition.* Boston: Bullfinch Press, 2003.

Miller, Tom. *Trading with the Enemy: A Yankee Travels through Castro's Cuba.* New York: Basic Books, 1996.

Morley, Morris, and Chris McGillion. *Unfinished Business: America and Cuba after the Cold War, 1989–2001.* Cambridge: Cambridge University Press, 2002.

Moses, Catherine. *Real Life in Castro's Cuba.* Wilmington, Del.: Scholarly Resources, 1999.

Oppenheimer, Andres. *Castro's Final Hour.* New York: Simon and Schuster, 1992.

Purcell, Susan Kaufman, ed. *Cuba: The Contours of Change.* Boulder, Colo.: Lynne Rienner Publishers, 2000.

Ripley, C. Peter, *Conversations with Cuba.* Athens: University of Georgia Press, 1999.

Rosset, Peter, and Medea Benjamin, eds. *The Greening of the Revolution: Cuba's Experiment with Organic Agriculture.* Melbourne, Australia: Ocean Press, 1994.

Sweig, Julia E. *Inside the Revolution: Fidel Castro and the Urban Underground.* Cambridge, Mass.: Harvard University Press, 2002.

The Internet

There are a number of Cuba-oriented Web sites. Many can be accessed through the Cuba page of the University of Texas's Latin America Network Information Service at http://www.lanic.utexas.edu/la/cb/cuba.

Acknowledgment of Copyrights

I. Indigenous Society and Conquest

"Christopher Columbus 'Discovers' Cuba" from *The Four Voyages of Christopher Columbus*, edited and translated by J. M. Cohen (Harmondsworth: Penguin, 1969), 73–76. Reproduced by permission of Penguin Books, Ltd.

"The Devastation of the Indies" from *The Devastation of the Indies: A Brief Account* by Bartolomé de Las Casas, translated by Herma Briffault (Baltimore: Johns Hopkins University Press, 1992), 43–47. Copyright Crossroad Publishing Company 1974.

"Spanish Officials and Indigenous Resistance" from *Documentos para la historia de Cuba*, vol. 1 of 4, edited by Hortensia Pichardo (Havana: Instituto Cubano del Libro / Editorial de Ciencias Sociales, 1973), 87–91.

"A World Destroyed" from "Desaparición de la población indígena cubana" by Juan Pérez de la Riva, *Universidad de la Habana* 196–97 (1972): 68–70, 72–73, 78–79, 80–83.

"'Transculturation' and Cuba" from *Cuban Counterpoint: Tobacco and Sugar* by Fernando Ortiz, translated by Harriet de Onis (New York: Alfred Knopf, 1947; reprint, Durham, N.C.: Duke University Press, 1995), 98, 103. Copyright 1947 by Alfred A. Knopf Inc. Used by permission of Random House, Inc.

"Survival Stories." An earlier version of this essay appeared as José Barreiro, "Indians in Cuba," *Cultural Survival Quarterly* 13, no. 3 (1989): 56–60. Reprinted (revised) by permission of *Cultural Survival Quarterly*.

II. Sugar, Slavery, and Colonialism

"A Physician's Notes on Cuba" from *Notes on Cuba* by John G. F. Wurdemann (1844; reprint ed. New York: Arno Press, 1971), 149–50, 153–57.

"The Death of the Forest" from *The Sugarmill: The Socio-Economic Complex of Sugar in Cuba* by Manuel Moreno Fraginals, translated by Cedric Belfrage (New York: Monthly Review Press, 1976), 73–77. Reprinted by permission.

"Autobiography of a Slave" from *Autobiography of a Slave* by Juan Francisco Manzano, translated by Evelyn Picon Garfield (Detroit: Wayne State University Press, 1996), 69–73, 89–99. Copyright © 1996 by Ivan A. Schulman and Evelyn Picon Garfield. Published by Wayne State University Press, Detroit, Michigan, 48201. All rights

III. The Struggle for Independence

Hortensia Pichardo (Havana: Instituto Cubano del Libro / Editorial de Ciencias Sociales, 1973), 370–73.

"Memories of a Cuban Girl" from *Memorias de una cubanita que nació con el siglo* by Renée Méndez Capote (Havana: Bolsilibros Unión, 1964), 95–99.

"Jose Martí's 'Our America,'" Published in *El Partido Liberal*, Mexico City, 30 January 1891. Translated in *José Martí Reader: Writings on the Americas*, edited by Deborah Shnookal and Mirta Muñiz (Melbourne: Ocean Press, 1999), 111–20. Copyright © Ocean Press, 1999. Reprinted by permission of Ocean Press.

"Guantanamera" from *Versos sencillos* by José Martí (New York: Louis Weiss and Co., 1891).

"The Explosion of the *Maine*," *New York Journal*, 17 February 1898, 12.

"U.S. Cartoonists Portray Cuba" from *Latin America in Caricature* by John J. Johnson (Austin: University of Texas Press, 1993), cartoons no. 61 (163), 45 (127), and 62 (165).

"The Devastation of Counterinsurgency" from "Consular Correspondence Respecting the Condition of the Reconcentrados in Cuba, the State of War in that Island, and the Prospects of the Projected Autonomy," 55th Congress, 2d session, Senate Doc. 230 (1898) (Washington, D.C.: GPO, 1898) (Serial Set 3610).

IV. Neocolonialism

"The Platt Amendment" from *U.S. Statutes at Large*, 21, 897–898; Treaty between the United States and Cuba, signed in Havana 22 May 1903; proclaimed by President Theodore Roosevelt 2 July 1904.

"Imperialism and Sanitation" from "The Interplay between Socio-Economic Factors and Medical Science: Yellow Fever Research, Cuba, and the United States" by Nancy Stepan, *Social Studies of Science* 8 (1978): 397–98, 402, 408–11, 412–13. Reprinted by permission of Sage Publications Ltd. Copyright © Sage Publications Ltd. (1978).

"A Child of the Platt Amendment" from *Memorias de una cubanita que nació con el siglo*, by Renée Méndez Capote (Havana: Bolsilibros Unión, 1964): 9–12.

"Spain in Cuba" from *Cuba/España, España/Cuba* by Manuel Moreno Fraginals (Barcelona: Crítica Grijalbo Mondadori, 1995), "La huella indeleble," 295–300.

"The Independent Party of Color": "Programa político del Partido Independiente de Color" (Political program) and "Acta de la constitución de la Agrupación Independiente de Color" (Constitutional act) from *El Negro en Cuba, 1902–1958: Apuntes para la historia de la lucha contra la discriminación racial en la neocolonia* by Tomás Fernández Robaina (Havana: Editorial de Ciencias Sociales, 1990), 192–95, 195–96. Earlier reprinted in *Previsión* [Havana], 15 October 1908, 3 and 15 September 1908.

"A Survivor" from "The Voice of a Survivor" by Isidoro Santos Carrera, *El combate*, 10 August 1920; and "Cuban Brotherhood" from "Fraternidad cubana" by Isidoro Santos Carrera, *El combate*, 14 August 1920.

V. Building a New Society

VI. Culture and Revolution

VII. The Cuban Revolution and the World

Index

Aviva Chomsky is a professor of history and the coordinator of Latin American studies at Salem State College. She is the author of *West Indian Workers and the United Fruit Company in Costa Rica, 1870–1940* (1996) and coeditor of *Identity and Struggle at the Margins of the Nation-State: The Laboring Peoples of Central America and the Hispanic Caribbean* (published by Duke University Press, 1998).

Barry Carr is the director of the Institute of Latin American Studies at La Trobe University in Melbourne, Australia. He is the author of *Marxism and Communism in Twentieth-Century Mexico* (1993) and coeditor of *The Latin American Left: From the Fall of Allende to Perestroika* (1993).

Pamela Maria Smorkaloff is the director of Latin American and Latino studies and an assistant professor of Spanish at Montclair State University. She is the author of *Cuban Writers on and off the Island: Contemporary Narrative Fiction* (1997) and *Readers and Writers in Cuba: A Social History of Print Culture, 1830s to 1990s* (1997) and editor of *If I Could Write This in Fire: An Anthology of Literature from the Caribbean* (1994).

Library of Congress Cataloging-in-Publication Data
The Cuba reader : history, culture, politics / edited by
Aviva Chomsky, Barry Carr, and Pamela Maria Smorkaloff.
p. cm. — (Latin America readers)
Includes bibliographical references and index.
ISBN 0-8223-3184-5 (cloth : alk. paper)
ISBN 0-8223-3197-7 (pbk. : alk. paper)
1. Cuba—History.   I. Chomsky, Aviva.   II. Carr, Barry.
III. Smorkaloff, Pamela Maria.   IV. Series.
F1776.C85 2003   972.91—dc21   2003013448